W9-CKH-719

MANAGEMENT OF SERVICE OPERATIONS

Text, Cases, and Readings

MANAGEMENT OF SERVICE OPERATIONS

Text, Cases, and Readings

W. EARL SASSER
Graduate School of Business Administration, Harvard University

R. PAUL OLSEN
IMEDE, Switzerland

D. DARYL WYCKOFF
Graduate School of Business Administration, Harvard University

ALLYN AND BACON, INC.
Boston, London, Sydney, Toronto

Case material of the Harvard Graduate School of Business Administration is made possible by the cooperation of business firms who may wish to remain anonymous by having names, quantities, and other identifying details disguised while basic relationships are maintained. Cases are prepared as the basis for class discussion rather than to illustrate either effective or ineffective handling of administrative situations.

ISBN: 0-205-06104-4
ISBN: 0-205-06820-0 (International)

Library of Congress Catalog No.: 78-7137

Printed in the United States of America.

10 9 8 7 6 5 85 84 83 82

To Our Children:

Meredith and Trey Sasser
Heather and Mathew Olsen
Michele and Abby Wyckoff

CONTENTS

PREFACE

In 1972 when the development efforts began for Management of Service Operations, a new course at Harvard Business School, we were operating on the hypothesis that the tasks of managing service firms differ significantly enough from those of manufacturing firms to justify separate (or at least special) treatment. Our work since 1972 has provided us with evidence to support the original hypothesis.

In our opinion, the course, Management of Service Operations, as it has evolved under our joint efforts, has led to new ways of looking at the managerial tasks of the service manager. We contend that formal business training has too frequently focused on management tools, techniques, and concepts that are more applicable to manufacturing firms than to service firms. While the traditional techniques of manufacturing management are invaluable to service managers—and are not utilized enough—service managers must contend with a set of problems that cannot be attacked with the traditional tools.

The characteristics of a service operation place unique demands on the service manager. In the production of a service, the process not only creates the product but delivers it to the consumer. The process is a service delivery system in which the consumer participates. While the production of a manufactured good is typically separated from the consumption, the production and consumption of a service occur nearly simultaneously. This interface of the production and marketing functions in a service delivery system dictates a number of constraints on the management of the system.

This book includes text, cases, and readings that address the critical implications of these constraints on the management of the service delivery system. We have four objectives:

1. To explore the applicability of operations management concepts to the design and management of the service delivery system.
2. To compare and contrast problems of designing, producing, and delivering services and products.
3. To review the special demands for organization and control imposed on the managements of often decentralized service delivery systems.
4. To identify the important elements of success of a service-oriented business.

The major portion of the book describes actual company situations and management decision making in case studies. We stress the fact that they are actual cases, drawn from the experiences of real managers. Only the short caselets in Chapter 3 are fabricated illustrations. We have disguised some names where it was appropriate, but all cases are used with the approval of the companies involved and with their agreement that the cases are a fair portrayal of the full complexity of the situations they faced.

The conceptual framework of the book is as follows, with a small sample of the questions introduced in each chapter:

Chapter 1 SERVICES IN THE U.S. ECONOMY

— What is the service sector?

— How fast is it growing?

— What are the implications of the growth of the service sector for economic policy?

Chapter 2 UNDERSTANDING SERVICE OPERATIONS

— What is the best way to classify a product as a good or a service?

— How does one measure service?

— What are the distinct characteristics of a service delivery system?

— How can production-line approaches be applied to service firms?

Chapter 3 THE SERVICE DELIVERY SYSTEM

— What tools does one use to analyze a service delivery system?

— What are the different types of systems?

— How well is the system balanced?

— How appropriate is the system to meet the objectives of the business?

Chapter 4 ESTABLISHING AND CONTROLLING SERVICE LEVELS

— How does one decide what service level is appropriate to achieve a business objective?

— How well are different service activities integrated?

— To what extent are they mutually reinforcing?

Chapter 5 CAPACITY MANAGEMENT FOR SERVICE FIRMS

— How does one measure capacity?

— How does one measure capacity utilization?

— How can one manage the demand for, as well as the supply of, a resource in a service business?

Chapter 6 DESIGNING THE SERVICE FIRM ORGANIZATION

— How should a service firm be organized?

— What type of organization—functional or geographic—is best?

— What are the problems of control that are of particular importance to a service organization?

— What are the stages of the life cycle through which the multisite service firm passes?

Chapter 7 THE MULTISITE SERVICE FIRM LIFE CYCLE

— What are the stages of the life cycle through which the multisite service firm passes?

— How must the firm's organization, management, controls, and service delivery systems change to meet the requirements of each stage of the service firm life cycle?

In summary, the goal of this book is to demonstrate to existing service managers, aspiring service managers, and educators of service managers that managing service operations requires a special touch, special concepts, special tools, and special techniques. We believe that message is significant; we wrote this book to demonstrate the point.

W.E.S.
R.P.O.
D.D.W.

ACKNOWLEDGMENTS

The approach to the problems and opportunities of managing service firms recorded in this book has been formulated through the efforts of a notably able group of research assistants, doctoral students, and colleagues. This book could not have been produced without the support, hard work, and stimulation of these people.

We wish to extend a special thanks to John R. Klug. He was a student in a developmental seminar on the topic of managing service firms in the spring of 1972. He became the first research assistant for the Management of Service Operations course in the fall of 1972 and its first research associate in the fall of 1973. His pioneering case development efforts resulted in many of the cornerstones of the course, including Benihana of Tokyo, Sea Pines Company (A), and Dobbs House (A). Even more important than his cases were his commitment to the development of the course, the great amount of time and effort he expended in getting the job done, and his conceptual thinking about an appropriate course structure. John is an entrepreneur; and the project needed an entrepreneur in its formative stages. He deserves a great deal of credit for getting the project off the ground.

We were equally fortunate to have Robert L. Banks succeed John Klug as research assistant for the course in the fall of 1974. Bob had been a student in the course in the prior spring and was able to help develop material that filled specific gaps in the course material. Leo's Foodland, Hartford Steam Boiler Inspection and Insurance Company, and Victoria Station, Inc. (B) are three of his cases.

Ivor P. Morgan, as a part-time casewriter while enrolled in the doctoral program at Harvard Business School, wrote several cases for the course in 1975–76. One of these cases, Premier Cinema Company, is included in this book. He also made several conceptual contributions to our understanding of the multisite service firm life cycle.

David Maister, a former doctoral student and now an assistant professor at the University of British Columbia, was the casewriter of Federal Express Corporation (A) and Perlis Truckstop.

Another former doctoral student, William L. Berry, jointly (with D. Daryl Wyckoff) developed the case, Wendy's Old Fashioned Hamburgers, after joining the faculty of the Ohio State University as an assistant professor. He made contributions to other cases, including Braniff International.

During the 1976–77 academic year, John N. Korff, a second-year MBA student, wrote several cases for Management of Service Operations under the supervision of Professor James L. Heskett. One of his cases, World Team Tennis, Inc., appears in this book.

Not only did Professor Heskett help supervise the development of materials for the course, he also has served as a sounding board for our ideas and has used his strong background in Logistics and Marketing to provide new insights about managing service firms.

One other colleague deserves special mention for his impact on this book. Professor Theodore Levitt has written a number of articles about the management process in service firms. His article "Production-Line Approach to Service" is included in this book with the permission of the Editor of the *Harvard Business Review* in which it appeared in the September–October 1972 issue.

Besides Professor Levitt's article, we have included two additional readings at the end of Chapter 4. "Overview of Competitive Situations" was written by John Hammond while an associate professor at Harvard Business School. "Will Innkeeping Repeat Itself with the Budget Motel?", which appeared in the November 1972 issue of *Hotel and Motel Management,* is reprinted in its entirety by permission of Robert C. Freeman, editor and publisher of that magazine.

In addition to the World Team Tennis case mentioned above, we selected for inclusion in this book seven cases that were not written or supervised by one of the three of us. We are indebted to the authors of these cases for allowing us to use their material in our book.

Lex Service Group (A) and (B) were developed by Cliff Baden and Colin Carter as research associates at IMEDE (*Institut pour l'Etude des Méthodes de Direccion de l'Enterprise*).

Max-Able Medical Clinic (A) was adapted by Professor William J. Abernathy of Harvard Business School from a case developed at Stanford University.

Trans World Airlines—The Crêpe Suzette Decision, has been used at Harvard Business School since the late sixties. Professor Karl Ruppenthal of the University of British Columbia developed the case as Director of the Transportation Management Program in the Graduate School of Business at Stanford University.

Leo's Foodland, originally developed by Professor William Applebaum of Harvard Business School, was later revised by Robert L. Banks under the supervision of Associate Professor W. Earl Sasser.

Loma Vista Hospital, which is used with the permission of the Board of Trustees of the Leland Stanford Junior University, is another classic in the Trans World Airlines tradition. It has been used at Harvard Business School for nearly a decade.

Triangle Maintenance Corporation was developed by Associate Professor Benson P. Shapiro of Harvard Business School with the assistance of Robert L. McDowell for use in the required marketing curriculum in our MBA program. However, the case rapidly found a permanent home in Management of Service Operations.

Since some of the cases used in this book are disguised, we cannot publicly express our thanks to managers in each firm. However, we have thanked them all personally because the firms represented in these cases represent a major source of our understanding about the key management tasks of the service manager. And our thanks extend beyond those service firms represented by cases in this book. Because of space limitations and a question of balance, we did not include 50 percent of the service cases that have been developed in the past five years. Each case written, whether included or not, added to our collective knowledge base. In addition to the cooperation of these firms in opening their doors to casewriters and researchers, we are extremely grateful for their encouragement. When embarking upon a project like we were undertaking, such words of encouragement helped us in the tough start-up phases of the project when we were groping for mission.

We also want to thank the more than 1600 students who have taken the course "Management of Service Operations" in the past six years. Their preparation and discussion of these cases have made our teaching experience a rewarding one and their feedback has helped shape our development efforts.

Funds for development of several of the cases on the transportation industries were partially made available by the UPS Foundation (previously known as the 1907 Foundation). This foundation has provided vital support to many researchers throughout the United States and Canada.

The brunt of the typing of the cases and text fell on two able assistants, Adelle Lewis and Rona McCrensky. They have been most helpful in moving the final manuscript toward publication.

The Intercollegiate Case Clearing House (ICCH) staff at Harvard Business School has been most generous in their support of our efforts. To all these people we are indebted.

We wish to thank Dean Lawrence Fouraker of the Harvard Business School for providing the resources and opportunity to write this book. We are particularly grateful to the President and Fellows of Harvard College, by whom the vast majority of the cases included in this book are individually copyrighted. The cases copyrighted by them are published here with their special permission and may not be reproduced in whole or in part without the written permission of the President and Fellows of Harvard College.

CHAPTER 1: SERVICES IN THE UNITED STATES ECONOMY

During the two decades preceding the 1970s the United States was moving toward what Daniel Bell has described as the postindustrial state. The social and political manifestations of these changes were given extensive attention by the nation's journalists, political scientists, historians, sociologists, and economists. All of them were charting the events, analyzing the implications, and predicting the profound effects they would have on the future of the nation's and the world's social, political, and economic structure. While the civil rights demonstrations, peace movements, and growth of international corporations were carefully observed by all the national media, a fundamental change in the U.S. economy was occurring that was having a more profound effect on the economic, social, and political structure of the United States than all of the more visible changes combined. Indeed many of the political and social scholars are beginning to believe that this quiet revolution of the 1950s and 1960s may be the root cause of the more popular social and political movements. These changes were fundamentally economic, stemming from increased productivity in the manufacturing sector. This increased productivity created a higher level of disposable income in the population, which in turn led to increasing purchases of nontangible products known as services. The result has been a fundamental shift of the U.S. economy from an economy geared primarily to the manufacture of goods to an economy geared primarily to the creation of services—a metamorphosis from an industrial to a postindustrial service economy.

The implications of this change are highlighted in a recent policy report of the U.S. Department of Commerce[1]:

> The evolution of the United States into a services economy has significant implications for U.S. economic growth and for economic policy formation. Services are less cyclical than goods—growing less in booms, and falling less in recessions. Services tend to be more labor intensive and to use less capital equipment than manufacturing. Productivity increases have been slower in services, and price increases generally have been more rapid. The average size of service establishments tends to be small, and there has been less concentration of production into large firms than is the case in many manufacturing industries. (These characteristics may, of course, change as technological advance affects the services sector.)

[1] *U.S. Service Industries in World Markets,* December 1976, p. 12.

A major portion of future economic growth and job creation—not just in the United States, but in the entire industrial world—is expected to originate in the services sector. This would seem to suggest major implications for international patterns of economic growth, investment and capital formation, employment, productivity, inflation, and economic relations.

In spite of the social, political, and economic implications of this fundamental shift toward service economies, little has been done to understand its implications and how to deal with them. Although some work has emerged in the 1960s and 1970s on a policy level as an expression of governmental concern, study of the implications of managing service organizations is just getting under way. A major reason for this neglect is because the terms "service," "service firm," "service industry," and "service sector" are not well-defined concepts. In this chapter these concepts are clarified, thus providing a basis for discussing, in the following chapters, the differences between service and nonservice operations.

DEFINING A SERVICE INDUSTRY

The slow recognition of the importance of the service sector is mainly caused by a lack of understanding of what constitutes a service firm or industry. To many people, services connote personal services such as auto repair, dental and legal work, consulting, and hairstyling. Every discussant of service industries defines the boundaries of service industries (as opposed to manufacturing industries) by using one of a number of classification schemes, but there is no generally accepted definition of the service sector.

One classification scheme is the U.S. Government's Standard Industrial Classification (SIC) provided by the Office of Management and Budget (OMB). The SIC is used as a "classification of establishments by type of activity in which they are engaged for the purposes of facilitating the collection, tabulation, presentation and analyses of data." Economists use it as the primary source for the industry definition of the service sector. The SIC defines services as establishments:

> Primarily engaged in providing a wide variety of services for individuals, business and government establishments, and other organizations. Hotels and other lodging places; establishments providing personal, business, repair, and amusement services; health, legal engineering, and other professional services, educational institutions; membership organizations, and other miscellaneous service, are included.

This limited definition, however, leaves out nonmanufacturing sectors such as the financial community, real estate, and wholesale and retail operations.

A more inclusive definition of the service sector would include other divisions of the SIC—transportation and public utilities, wholesale and retail trade, public administration, and finance, insurance, and real estate, which more accurately reflects the service sector because the consumer purchase from the firms in these industries involves substantial intangible benefits. This broad definition is frequently used by the Department of Commerce and the Department of Labor and is used in this text.

ECONOMIC IMPLICATIONS OF THE GROWTH IN THE SERVICE SECTOR

Using this broader definition we can see from Table 1-1 that services have grown from 54.7% of the economy in 1947 to 65.6% in 1975.

Table 1-1

GROSS PRODUCT ORIGINATING IN THE SERVICES SECTOR
1947 and 1975
(percent of current dollar, GNP)

Sector	*Proportion of U.S. GNP*	
	1947	*1975*
Transportation	5.8%	3.7%
Communications	1.3	2.5
Utilities	1.6	2.4
Wholesale trade	6.7	7.9
Retail trade	12.2	10.0
Finance, insurance, real estate	10.0	13.8
Miscellaneous services	8.7	12.0
Government	8.4	13.2
Total	54.7%	65.6%
Total excluding government	46.3%	52.4%

From *U.S. Service Industries in World Markets,* Department of Commerce, December 1976.

These figures do not reflect the variation of inflation between the manufacturing and service sectors. According to the Department of Commerce study this differential is substantial:

> Much of the growing importance of services is attributable to the generally faster rate of price increases that have characterized services as opposed to goods. The prices of services, for example, rose 40 percent more than goods from 1947 to 1972. (Since 1972, however, services prices have been rising less rapidly than goods prices—putting services in the unaccustomed position of moderating the price increases experienced by the economy as a whole.)

Even in real terms, however, the relative growth of services has been significant and continuing—providing the bulk of the U.S. economy's expansion. Figure 1-1, show-

Figure 1-1

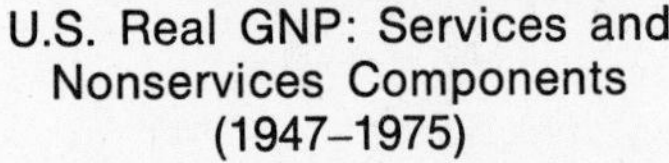

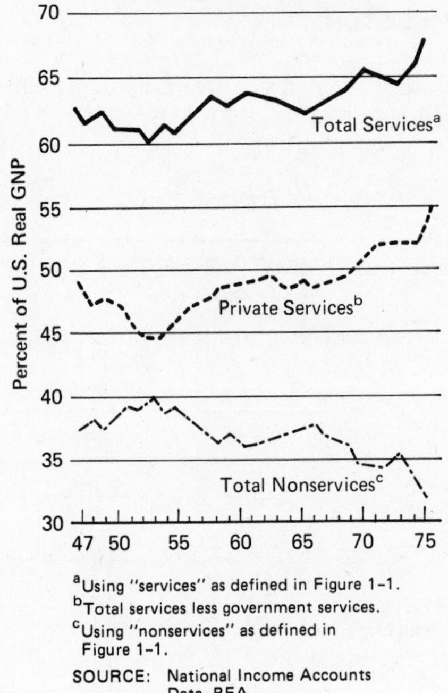

ing the real growth of the services and nonservices components of the U.S. economy in constant dollars since 1947, depicts the more rapid growth of services relative to nonservices and the greater stability of services during times of economic recession. The more rapid relative growth of services is even more clearly illustrated in Figure 1-2, which shows in constant dollar terms the proportion of the economy comprised of services. A gradually rising trend is clearly evident, particularly for private services.

The significance behind the more rapid growth of services in terms of constant dollars as opposed to current dollars lies in the productivity growth of the two sectors, goods and services; that is, the output per worker in the goods sector has increased more rapidly than the output per worker in the service sector. At the same time wages in these two sectors have risen at a commensurate rate. The increased productivity in the goods manufacturing sector and the lack of increase in productivity in the service sector coupled with the rapid growth of demand for services have resulted in a large increase in the employment of human resources in the production of services. This factor is illustrated by Exhibit 1-1, which shows employ-

Figure 1-2

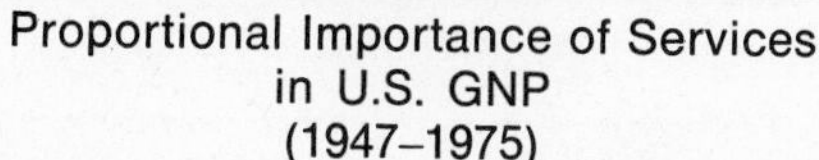

Proportional Importance of Services
in U.S. GNP
(1947–1975)

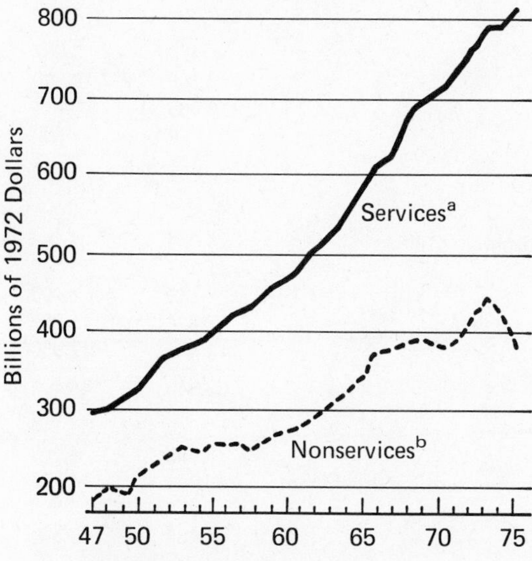

[a]Value added in transportation, communications, utilities, wholesale trade, retail trade, finance, insurance, real estate, miscellaneous services, and government.

[b]Value added in agriculture, forestry, fisheries, mining, construction, manufacturing, and the "rest of world" sectors.

SOURCE: National Income Accounts Data, BEA.

ment by sector for 1960 and 1971. Note that the overall growth of employment in the production of goods grew at less than three-tenths of 1%, while the overall growth of persons employed in the creation of services grew by 42.2%. These figures reflect only those people employed in establishments employing two or more people.

Exhibit 1-1 also shows the relationship of total service employment to the total workforce. The growth in the total civilian workforce grew by 20.8% from 1960 to 1971, or by roughly 15 million people. Almost all of this increase was absorbed by the production of services, which grew from 33.8 million to 48 million employees, a growth of almost 15 million. The impact of services on the U.S. economy is illustrated in Exhibit 1-2. In 1971 the total employment in services as a percentage of the total nonagricultural employment was 68%; more significantly, the total services employment and self-employed (almost all self-employed people are employed

Exhibit 1-1

EMPLOYMENT IN ESTABLISHMENT BY SECTOR 1960–1971
(millions)

	1960	*1971*	*Growth (%)*
Total	$59,701	$74,032	24.0
Agriculture	5,458	3,387	−37.9
Manufacturing	16,796	18,529	10.3
Construction	2,885	3,411	18.2
Mining	712	602	−14.3
Total Goods	$25,851	25,929	0.3
Services			
Transportation and public utilities	4,004	4,442	10.9
Wholesale and retail	11,391	15,142	32.9
Fire	2,669	3,796	42.2
Services (SIC classification)	7,424	11,869	59.9
Government	8,353	12,856	53.9
Total Services	33,840	48,105	42.2
Total civilian workforce	69,628	84,113	20.8
Unemployed	3,852	4,993	29.6
Employed in agriculture and establishment	59,701	74,032	24.0
Proprietorship and self-employed	6,075	5,088	−16.2
Housekeeping	34,464	35,561	3.2

Compiled from *U.S. Statistical Abstract 1973.*

in the production of services, such as doctors, lawyers, store owners, and so on) as a percentage of total workforce was 63.2%.

Even with the broader definition of services the existing data still do not accurately reflect the high growth of services because the in-house service operations of manufacturing firms are not reflected in these figures. When speaking of service output, what is actually referred to is only the output of those industries classified in the services sector—not the total production of all services per se. The two kinds of production are not the same, for many services are produced in the goods sectors and are counted as part of the output of the goods sectors. The distinctions can be arbitrary. The output of a consultant employed by a consulting firm, for example, is counted as part of the services sector. If the same consultant were performing the same functions as part of the internal consulting group of a manufacturing firm, his or her output would be considered part of the manufacturing sector.

A phenomenon that is not reflected in these figures but which may have a profound effect on the U.S. economy is the fact that increasingly more people who previously were employed in the nonpaying role of housekeepers are joining the workforce. Presently housekeepers and the work they perform are not included in either employment or GNP figures. As these people join the workforce, the work that they had previously done as housekeepers must be performed either by other people or a professional worker for pay, by automated equipment, or by the employed individuals in free time. It is believed that the trend will be to replace the housekeepers with (a) more automated equipment and (b) part-time personal services. As a result of these changes, portions of the housekeeping task will be added to the GNP. To show the potential impact of these changes Exhibit 1-2 shows the relationship of the total services, self-employed, and housekeeping to the total potential workforces; this figure for 1971 was over 74%. Most projections show that the service industries will employ almost 80% of the workforce by 1980.

In summary, there are three major economic trends in the service sector.

1. There is a rapid growth of expenditures for services.
2. Almost all of the recent growth as well as potential growth of employment has occurred in services.
3. There is a pronounced lack of productivity growth in the service industries.

These factors have focused the attention of government and economists on the productivity issues of the service sector. The key to productivity in the service sector lies in the effective management of service operations. The remainder of this book will explore the major managerial tasks of service industry executives.

Exhibit 1-2

COMPARISON OF SERVICE SECTOR EMPLOYMENT TO TOTAL EMPLOYMENT 1960–1971

	1960	*1971*	*Growth %*
Total services to total nonagricultural employees	62.4%	68.1%	5.7%
Total services to total workforce	48.6	57.2	8.6
Total services and self-employed to total workforce	57.3	63.2	5.9
Total services, self-employed, and housekeeping to total potential workforce	71.5	74.2	2.7

CHAPTER 2: UNDERSTANDING SERVICE OPERATIONS

GOODS VS. SERVICES

Goods are defined as "articles of trade, merchandise, or wares," while services may be defined as "the organized system of apparatus, appliances, and/or employees for supplying some accommodation and activities required by the public" or "the performance of any duties or work for another." It seems clear that goods are things such as food, clothing, books, television sets, and the like. They are tangible physical objects purchased in a store and carried home. Services are things such as hotel or motel "accommodations," bowling, tennis, skiing, or theater "activities," or someone who is hired to "perform" auto repair, cleaning, nursing, consulting, or other "duties or work." Unlike manufactured goods, services are consumed in the process of their production. The consumer cannot carry home a service from its place of production or purchase; however, the consumer of a service can carry home or continue to possess the "effect" of a service—enjoyment of entertainment or recreation, a clean house of a maintenance service, a haircut of a barber, or clean clothes of a dry cleaning firm.

A precise definition of goods and services should distinguish them on the basis of these attributes. A good is a tangible physical object or product that can be created and transferred; it has an existence over time and thus can be created and used later. A service is intangible and perishable. It is an occurrence or process that is created and used simultaneously or nearly simultaneously. While the consumer cannot retain the actual service after it is produced, the effect of the service can be retained.

SERVICE AS A PRODUCT

With such a clear distinction between goods and services, it would seem easy to classify all purchases as either purchases of goods or as purchases of services. Look at all the purchases you have made in the past month. Try to classify them as either services or goods. The train, bus, or taxi ride was obviously a service. The radio or book was a good. See, it's simple. Or is it?

Let's look further in the purchase process of one of the above items. When you purchased this book, did you purchase a good or a service? You have a physical object that was obviously manufactured. Yet you probably bought it at a bookstore where you paid a higher price for it than the bookstore paid the manufacturer. Therefore, you paid the bookstore for something. What? Several things that should come to mind are convenience of location, information, and other retailing services. Thus you purchased a physical object and some retailing services. Almost all purchases of goods involve the purchase of services.

Conversely, almost all the purchases of services involve the purchase of goods, either directly by the consumer or by the producer of the service. The meal at a restaurant centers around the purchase of food. The taxi driver's business is based upon his purchased automobiles. The barber has to purchase combs, scissors, clippers, hair tonic, and other materials and tools.

One of the most complex packages of goods and services is television. Most consumers would consider television a manufactured good. The television set is clearly a physical object that is purchased, carried home, and used over time. Fine, but how do you consume that good? You don't. You actually consume the services of television broadcasting companies, and this consumption is facilitated by the television set. The situation is even more complex. You purchase the services of an electric utility company; these *services* facilitate the use of the manufactured *good*—the television—which facilitates the consumption of *services* of broadcast companies that pay for production and transmission of programming by selling advertising *services,* which stimulate the purchase of more *goods*—in some cases, more televisions. You perceive your expenditure is for the television set and not for the programming viewed on the television set. Yet Americans spend more for programming (through advertising costs of goods and services purchased) every year than for television sets. In 1970 Americans purchased $2,983 million worth of television sets, and television stations sold $3,035 million worth of advertising. The average American family spends 1,200 hours a year watching television. The annual cost for this entertainment is $26 for the television set, $20 for the utility service to run the television, $15 in advertising, and another $10 for repairs. Thus, 63% of the total consumer expenditure on television entertainment is for services.

In summary, almost all purchases of goods are accompanied by facilitating services, and almost every service purchase is accompanied by a facilitating good.[1] Each purchase involves a bundle of goods and/or services.

One of the first steps in understanding the service product of an organization is to be able to define all the elements of the purchase bundle perceived by both the buyer and seller. A good example would be the purchase of a dinner at an expensive restaurant. What do you buy when you spend $20 to $30 for dinner at a restaurant? First, you purchase physical items, actual food and drink. Second, you purchase a number of characteristics that can be defined by one or more of the five senses: the taste and aroma provided by the chef, the service of the waiters, and the atmosphere created by the structure, furnishings, and fellow diners. Third, you purchase a set of psychological benefits that cannot be clearly defined by any of the senses such as status (I can afford to eat at this restaurant), comfort, and a sense of well-being. Table 2-1 summarizes the elements of the meal purchase.

[1] The term "facilitating good" was suggested by John Rathmell in *Marketing in the Service Sector* (Cambridge, Mass.: Winthrop Publishers, 1974).

Table 2-1

THE BUNDLE OF GOODS AND SERVICES OFFERED AT AN EXPENSIVE RESTAURANT

Food Drinks Other materials (matches, napkins, etc.)	Physical items
Taste and aroma Waiter service Structural atmosphere (the sight and sound of the facility) Social atmosphere (the sound and sight of people)	Sensual benefits
Comfort Status Sense of well-being	Psychological benefits

Note that there are three distinct bundles.

1. The physical items or facilitating goods.
2. The sensual benefits or explicit services.
3. The psychological benefits or implicit services.

One of the key problems in designing a service package and service delivery system is articulating the full range of elements in the purchase bundle. The first two groups of elements are fairly easy to communicate to both the manager and the consumer. The third group is not only difficult to articulate, but since it rests totally in the consumer psyche, it is also difficult to design and control. The tendency of an organization's management (once the need for the elements in the third group is recognized) is to attempt to embody the characteristics in the service facility or service personnel (such as the use of antique fixtures and foreign waiters to create status).

A problem occurs when a service organization begins to view itself as a goods manufacturer and attempts to embody all the elements of the purchase bundle in the facilitating good. Management must understand what the proper service emphasis should be in their product. "Are we a manufacturing organization with ancillary service or a service organization with a facilitating good?"

The best way to approach this question might be to consider it a matter of emphasis. As a first step, we can evaluate the relative importance of the goods and service content of a purchase by determining what percentage of the purchase price is the factory cost of the facilitating goods in our bundle. If we do this we find that our purchases range from high goods content purchases such as self-service discount purchases of goods (groceries and drugs) to high service content purchases such as a stay at a motel in which little (matches, free postcards) or no material goods are received by the consumer. If we do this across the spectrum of purchases we get the comparison represented in Table 2-2. Intuitively interpreting Table 2-2,

Table 2-2

A COMPARISON OF VARIOUS GOODS AND SERVICES PACKAGES

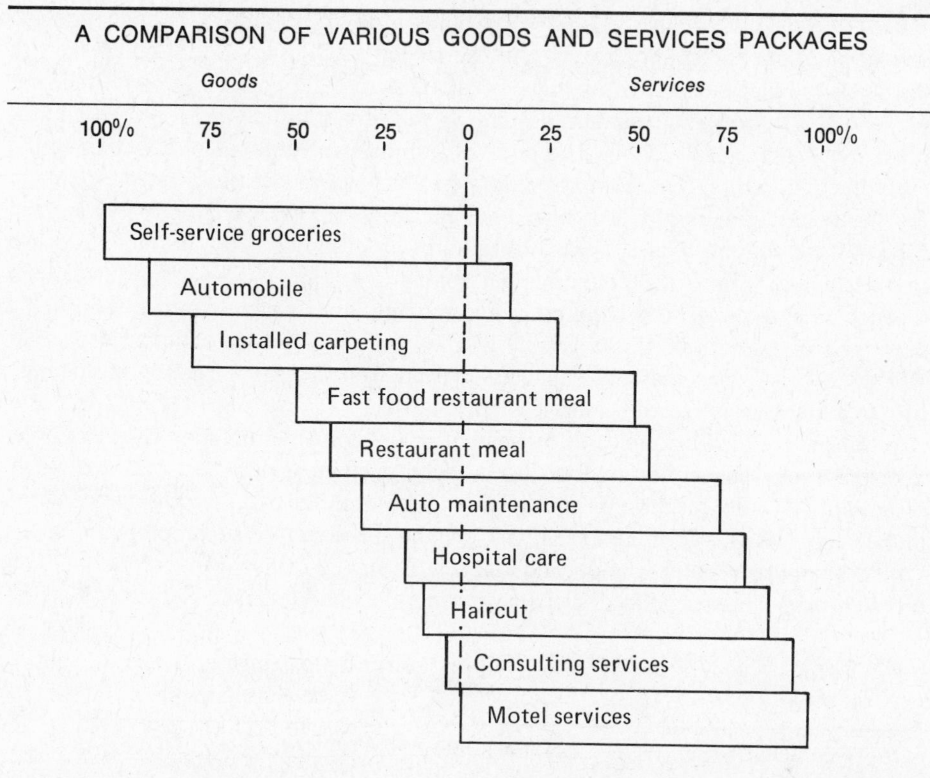

we would probably decide that the top three purchases shown are goods and the rest are services. That is, at the point at which the goods content decreases to about 50% or less of the bundle, a purchase becomes a service in the mind of the consumer. Note that the distinction becomes somewhat hazy at the margin. While an expensive restaurant has a high service content, a fast-food takeout outlet has a high material cost content. The consumer expectations from these two restaurants would obviously be different even if the facilitating good in the purchase bundle, say, a hamburger, were identical in the two cases.

SERVICE FIRMS

Distinguishing what constitutes a service firm is even more difficult than defining services. What's the problem? If a firm sells a service, it is a service firm, which is true for such businesses as a dry cleaning firm, a movie theater, and a consulting firm. However, how are firms that sell a range of products defined? Consider, for example, the development of a chain of retail fish outlets. In order to find an outlet for its daily catches the fishing company opened a chain of retail outlet stores. Because fresh fish is highly perishable, products not sold within 24 hours of being caught were packaged and frozen. But the frozen product could not compete with the fresh product because of its higher cost (freezing and packaging) and its lower perceived value to the consumer. To remedy the situation, the firm followed a natural diversification and added "takeout" fish dinners in its retail outlets during the early evening hours. The complementary product was successful, but the demand for "takeout" dinners was not high enough to absorb the excess supply of fresh fish. Added volume was achieved by adding a "sit-down" restaurant to the fish market. Thus, from a basic commercial fishing operation this company diversified through four steps—processing, retailing, cooking, and serving—into a thoroughly new type of operation. If we graph this on our goods/service comparison chart (Table 2-3), we see that the firm has evolved from a fishing (goods producing) firm to a multiservice retailer (service firm).

There are also examples of movement in the opposite direction. For example, take the evolution of the fast-food firms. Such firms normally start out as a single restaurant. As the restaurants multiply, volume (and profits) requirements often dictate that the fast-food chain embark on the manufacture of preprepared foods (rolls, hamburger patties, and condiments). Even the atmosphere is premanufactured through mass produced fixtures and modular buildings. In the growth stages

Table 2-3

THE GOODS/SERVICE CONTENT OF A NATIONAL SEAFOOD CHAIN

Goods	*Services*
Fishing	Wholesaling
Fishing	Retailing
Fishing and processing	Retailing
Fishing and processing	Retailing and cooking
Fishing and processing	Retailing, cooking, and serving

Table 2-4

TRENDS IN SERVICE CONTENT
Prepackaging of Services
Direct mail order as prepackaged retailing
Preprepared fast foods with specially designed "cooking" equipment
Throw-away medical equipment—thermometers and syringes
Do-it-yourself kits for such things as carpeting, paneling, and plumbing
Self-instruction courses—language, occupational, and self-improvement
Prepackaged insurance policies
Tune-up kits and throw-away parts for automobile servicing
Increasing the Service Content of Goods and Services
"Have-it-your-way" fast foods
Mix-and-match clothing
Service centers and service warranties for autos, electronics, and appliances
Specialty food departments (bakeries and delicatessens) in self-service groceries
Decorator and other consumer "consultants" in department and discount stores
Consumerization of Production
Knock-down products requiring final assembly by the consumer
Use of electronic tellers in banks
Self-service retailers
Self-service gasoline stations

of various fast-food chains, the firms become manufacturers of standardized dining environments with dining atmospheres well known to the consumer.

These are only two examples of how firms move along the spectrum between services and goods. As companies grow, there is a tendency to push in both directions. Cost reduction and the need for centralized control of such things as cost, quality, and standardization tend to foster increasing the "premanufacturing" and "prepackaging" of services.

In contrast, large firms and small firms alike react to competitive pressures in marketing highly standardized goods and premanufactured services by personalizing their products to the consumer. The results have been to increase the service content of the final consumer service.

A third trend that often affects the service content of a firm's product line is the "consumerization" of a service. This trend involves the transfer of part of the production of the good or service to the actual consumer.

Examples of these three trends are given in Table 2-4.

Because of the service content's impact on the requirements of staffing, marketing, inventory, capital formation, process design and control, training, and advertising, it is important for management to understand the position of their product on and its direction of movement along the service-goods spectrum. How a firm views itself will determine how it presents itself to the marketplace. A misunderstanding will hinder management in selling its product and operating effectively.

THE SERVICE CONCEPT

Unfortunately, managers of service firms often think of their products in terms of the facilitating good ("we sell hamburgers") rather than in terms of a total bundle of goods and services that the consumer purchases. Such a simplistic analysis often results in management neglecting the intangibles. A fast-food restaurant that "sells hamburgers" often has slow, surly service personnel, dirty and unattractive facilities, and few return customers.

One of the main reasons for adopting a simplistic approach is the difficulty of defining a single product for a service operation. A manufacturing organization can define its product in terms of specific cost, quality, and performance characteristics, which are embodied and observable in the physical goods. For a service firm the situation is almost reversed; the intangibles are an integral part of the total product bundle. In some cases the facilitating good is ancillary to the intangible benefits a consumer purchases. This issue will be explored in depth in Chapter 4.

For many restaurant patrons the object is to have a "night on the town" with his or her dining companions. The meal itself is simply a vehicle for obtaining a psychological and emotional experience. This fact is even more true for patrons of bars and cocktail lounges. How should the service manager treat these intangibles?

One of the first steps the manager of a service operation must consider is to define the service concept in terms of the bundle of goods and services sold to the consumer and the relative importance of each component to the consumer. This analysis will enable the manager (1) to understand some of the elusive implicit intangibles that affect the consumer decision and (2) to design and operate his organization to deliver a total service package that emphasizes the important elements of that package.

A primary reason for defining the service product in terms of a total service concept is the role the process plays in creating the product. In purchasing a service, the consumer interacts with the workforce, equipment, and physical environment that create the service. The process itself is, therefore, one dimension of the product. In contrast, the manufacturing process is isolated from the consumer and has an impact on the consumer only through what effect it has on the product. The elements of the manufacturing process are designed for the effective production of the physical good that is its output. The labor, equipment, and facilities are functionally designed with the cost and quality of the product being the primary criteria for evaluating how effectively these resources are utilized. In contrast, the service delivery system must be designed with the presence of the consumer in mind.

THE SERVICE DELIVERY SYSTEM

In the production of a service, the process not only creates the product but also simultaneously delivers it to the customer. The *service delivery system* is a process in which the consumer participates. In a restaurant the food, beverages, and atmosphere are produced either just prior to or during consumption; the entertainment of a movie or theater occur simultaneously with consumption; and the consumer is intimately involved in the production of a haircut, a physical examination, a health spa visit, or a ski lesson. This participation by the consumer in the production process of a service requires that the service delivery system be defined in terms of, and as an element of, the total service concept.

The interface of the production and marketing functions in a service delivery system dictates a number of constraints on the management of the system. It is useful to understand the distinct characteristics of services that make the management tasks of service executives different from their counterparts in manufacturing firms. The characteristics may be classified into four areas: intangibility, perishability, heterogeneity of the product, and simultaneity of production and consumption.

Intangibility

Services are intangible or much less tangible than physical goods. As noted by Carman and Uhl,[2] "A buyer of products normally has an opportunity to see, touch, hear, smell, or taste them before he buys." Not so for the buyer of services. Service marketers must emphasize the benefits to be derived from the delivery of the service and not from the service itself. Intangible services are difficult to describe, demonstrate to the buying public, illustrate in promotional material, and demonstrate to potential buyers. Design of the service package and control of the design require a greater understanding of consumer psychology than for a manufactured good because of the intangible and, often, nonexplicit nature of the product.

Steve Unwin clearly understands the implication of the intangibility characteristic for advertising:[3]

> Creative advertising can articulate the abstract benefits of services, and help convince the affluent consumer that such intangible satisfactions as freedom, fulfillment, health, love, and security are more faithfully and fully supplied by services than through the surrogacy of a product.
>
> Further than that, advertising can particularize abstract benefits. The bank's "friendly image" can be spelled out in terms of receptiveness to inquiries for loans, a relaxed atmosphere in which to discuss matters of personal financial security and risk, and the avoidance of banking jargon.

Because of the complex combination of intangible perceptions, service firms may not be particularly successful unless management can effectively attract customers with marketing efforts that identify and solve a particular need or demon-

---

[2] James M. Carman and Kenneth P. Uhl, *Marketing: Principles and Methods* (Homewood, Ill.: Richard D. Irwin, 1973), p. 362.

[3] Steve Unwin, "The Chances Are Advertising of Services, Not Products, Will Be the Wave of the Future," *Advertising Age* (May 27, 1974), p. 40.

strate a competitive advantage.[4] A guard company, for example, sells the time of its employees but markets the sense of a secure plant to its industrial customers. An airline sells a seat from point A to point B but markets getaway vacations.

The intangibility of services also presents another challenge. There are no patents for services. This results in very short life cycles for new service innovations. Note how quickly airlines add lounges, remove lounges, add leg space, remove leg space in response to competitive pressures. No one was surprised that, when Hertz started the Hertz #1 Club to bypass the process of filling out forms for its car rental customers, Avis quickly followed with its version, the Wizard of Avis.

Eugene Johnson pinpoints another implication of the intangibility characteristic:[5]

> Buyers are usually unable to judge quality and value prior to a purchase. Consequently, the service company's reputation and the reputations of its salesmen are far more essential to services marketing than to goods marketing. The importance is further magnified because branding, brand development, and brand acceptance are usually not prominent in the marketing of services.

Perishability

Services are perishable; they cannot be inventoried. Three very perishable commodities are an airline seat, a hotel room, and an hour of a lawyer's day. In a service delivery system, the absence of inventory removes from the service manager an important buffer used by most manufacturing managers to handle fluctuations in demand. In essence, the service manager is without an important "shock absorber" available to most of his counterparts in the manufacturing sector to absorb fluctuations in demand. In manufacturing firms, inventory also serves to decouple the various stages in the production cycle from each other and from the external environment. The act of decoupling simplifies the planning and control functions of each operation, because the existence of inventory between stages makes each stage relatively independent of its antecedent and subsequent stages. Such opportunities are not so readily available to service managers.

If the demand for a service did not fluctuate, the capacity of the service facility could be set at the level of demand and few scheduling and stockout problems would arise. However, the demand for service displays the same gyrations found in the demand schedules for goods. The seasonality of the revenue of ski resorts, the daily variations in meal counts for restaurants, and the hourly fluctuations in transactions for a commercial bank are only a few examples.

The combination of perishability and wide swings in volume place heavy pressure on the marketing executives of service firms to develop and implement plans

---

[4] This problem is not unique to service firms. Perfume manufacturers sell hope; car manufacturers sell a life-style.

[5] Eugene M. Johnson, "The Selling of Services," *Handbook of Modern Marketing,* Victor B. Buell, editor (New York: McGraw-Hill), 1978, p. 112.

to alter the demand schedule for a firm's service to fit more closely to its physical capacity. If the marketing effort fails, the firm either has periods of idle capacity or periods of insufficient capacity or both.

Heterogeneity

The third characteristic of services is the heterogeneity of output produced by firms claiming to produce the same service. In fact, there is a great deal of variability in the output of a single firm and even of a single service employee. The combination of the intangible nature of services and the presence of the consumer at the point of production attributes to this characteristic. The service rendered by the flight attendant varies from flight to flight and from person to person on the same flight. The output of desk clerks at a hotel, the counter personnel for car rental firms, and even tennis instructors varies in the same manner. The heterogeneity characteristic means that it is difficult to establish standards for the output of a service firm and even harder to ensure that standards are met each time the service is delivered.

This characteristic places a great premium on the quality control function of a service firm. Because the provider of the service usually comes in direct contact with the consumer, the education and training of service employees (the firm's sales personnel) are extremely important. In effect, such training is a key lever for quality control, since it is usually impractical to monitor the output of each service provider. Such emphasis on training had led to the establishment of training centers like McDonald's Hamburger University and Holiday Inn's Holiday University. In addition to training service managers and employees, McDonald's has created field inspection teams that visit service facilities unannounced to check on the level of "Quality, Service, and Cleanliness" in each unit.

Simultaneity

Simultaneity of production and consumption compounds the problems created by the three service product characteristics described above. Services do not move through distribution channels. Customers must come to the service facility or the service provider must be brought to the customer. Thus, each service facility has a limited geographic area from which to attract customers. Carman and Uhl note the consequences[6]:

> . . . producers of services generally have smaller size operations than do producers of products, largely because the producer must travel to get the services, or vice versa. When the producer travels to the buyer, time is taken away from the production of services and the cost of those services is increased. It also costs time and money for buyers to travel to the producer of services. These economies of time and travel provide incentives to locate more

[6] Ibid., p. 364.

service centers closer to prospective customers, which results in smaller service centers.

A manufacturing facility can take advantage of economies of scale by producing for multiple geographic markets at one location. However, the close production-marketing interface requires that the service delivery system must be located within the market and therefore sized for the specific market. The fixed costs of many service delivery systems prevent their establishment in low-density population areas.

The producer-seller interface enables greater usage of promotional strategies than is possible by manufacturers. For example, a restaurant is able to use point of sale literature (the menu) and personal selling (waiter's suggestions) to increase the size and yield of the sale.

A manufacturing facility is designed with the product and the workforce in mind. A service facility is designed by focusing on the needs of the consumer, as well as the product and the workforce. Like a manufacturing system, the service delivery system may be standardized (assembly line), flexible (job shop), or an individualized unit. Unlike a manufacturing system, the consumer interacts with parts of the service delivery system, and the type of system observed by the consumer at the points of interaction creates perceptions in the mind of the consumer about the quality of the product.

SERVICE LEVELS

So far we have described the service concept, the service delivery system, and the role of the consumer in each of these factors. Another key concern of service executives is the *service level* delivered by the service delivery system. As noted in the discussion of the intangibility characteristic of services, the level of service is an elusive concept. In addition to the stated service, service firms sell atmosphere, convenience, consistent quality, pleasant interpersonal relations, status, anxiety removal, and so on. In one way or another these intangibles must be delivered. Expected service levels are met by delivering those components of the service that the consumer perceives are important. When the perceived service level is combined with the price the perceived value is created, as we shall demonstrate in Chapter 4.

The service level is a measure of the levels of the explicit and implicit benefits provided to the consumer and is comparable to the quality level of a manufactured good in the sense that it specifies performance characteristics of the product. The difference is that the quality level of the manufactured product can more readily be quantified. For example, a television set can be defined by screen size, enclosure finish, reception range, types of controls, operating life, picture tube power rating, audio speaker power rating, operating audio frequency, receiver signal to noise ratio, and so on. All of these qualities can be quantified on a scale. A screen may be 19 inches or 24 inches, the reception range may be 25 miles or 35 miles, the speaker may be 1 to 10 watts, and so on. All of these characteristics are very specific and may be objectively measured to determine if they meet the quality performance characteristics specified to the consumer.

This quantification is not true for service levels, however. The intangible nature of a service product coupled with the multifaceted nature (bundle of goods and services) of the service product make measurement and, in some cases even specification, of service levels difficult and often impossible. However, the basic facilitating good may be objectively measured; for example, a hamburger may be defined as being made with a 4-ounce pure beef patty with less than 30% fat by weight. Since standards of quality for facilitating goods are definable and quantifiable, they are easier to measure and control than intangibles in the service concept.

Conceptualizing and setting service levels—and understanding implied cost tradeoffs—is an important decision area. What's an adequate service level? It's a level of performance that will satisfy customers' needs or expectations of the service. A service manager must understand what "satisfaction" really means to his or her customers and must translate performance into discernable service levels, whether or not they are easily quantifiable or subjective, for the many phases of the service production process. Some examples of areas that require service level decisions include: staffing, customer throughput, quality of facilitating goods such as food or beverages in a restaurant, and length of wait for the service facility.

Setting initial service levels is a process that should be approached with care. Though service levels can often be altered to some degree once the service is in operation, they often set the tone of the service in a customer's eyes. While a restaurant can switch from a luxury establishment to a restaurant that caters to people of more moderate means, the transition can be traumatic and is not guaranteed to succeed. And certainly there's no turning back to higher prices and more waiters once the image is altered in the customer's mind.

The problem is matching management and consumer perceptions of what the service concept and service level are and should be. This problem can be approached from two directions. The first is to understand what consumer perceptions and expectations are by constantly seeking feedback from the consumer. The second is to shape consumer perceptions and expectations to those which the service concept is expected to appeal. This is often done through advertising. The advertising campaigns, "Have It Your Way" and "We Do It All for You," of two competing fast-food chains were attempts to soften the consumer's image that the chains' products were standardized and bland by promoting an image of a more individualized service level. Advertising is a vehicle to convey a sense of the intangibles associated with various services. The advertising can create a high perceived service level by tickling the customer's conscious and subconscious desires as they relate to his or her perceptions of the service.

The definition of service levels becomes more important as top management gets farther away from the actual service production point. This is a thorny problem in large service organizations and even in smaller service firms that are growing into larger organizations. It is difficult for management to notice that service levels are slipping as the organization becomes a multiunit operation spread over a wide geographic region. Service executives must be sensitive to customer perceptions, and if they cannot be there themselves, they should have personnel in the field monitoring service levels and reporting back to headquarters. Very often service managers are in the unenviable position of not knowing if their firms are satisfying customers until customers are sufficiently dissatisfied to complain. Indeed, the branch manager of a large aviation services organization admits that's the case with him. But he knows his organization well enough that he can usually tell, by the nature and location of the complaints, what or who the problem is, and he can solve it in short order. This is subjective but effective.

INTEGRATING THE SERVICE CONCEPT, SERVICE DELIVERY SYSTEMS, AND SERVICE LEVELS

Managing a service operation requires that the manager understand the *service concept, service delivery system,* and *service levels*. Since the consumer has a key role in the definition and evaluation of all three elements, the service manager must have a clear understanding of consumer expectations and perceptions. A problem arises when management and the consumer have different perceived service levels for the service product or when management does not understand how the three elements of the service delivery system influence the consumer's perception of the service level. Some examples of conflicting images produced by poor management understanding of how the elements of the delivery system fit together are illustrated below.

1. A restaurant stressing an authentic eighteenth-century colonial atmosphere spent a great deal of money developing authentic interior decorations and controlling the dress of service personnel. However, in order to handle overflows during peak demand periods they used steel folding chairs and plastic card tables to augment their seating capacity.

2. A men's grooming salon that desired to create a cultured atmosphere spent a great deal of money decorating the salon with valuable art and antique furniture and installed a stereo system to play classical music. However, because of the hiring, training, and control procedures, the atmosphere of the salon was usually permeated with loud rock music.

3. A producer of a television series designing a science fiction program to appeal to the Star Trek market spent a great deal of money on exotic sets and gadgetry but did not employ researchers or consultants to evaluate the scientific validity of the sets, gadgetry, and story lines. The result was that Star Trek audiences, which consisted of scientists and engineers, were critical of the science content of the science fiction and, as a result, viewed the new series as pure fantasy, not science fiction.

The service manager must understand and deal with the consumer met at the production-marketing interface. As shown in Table 2-5, the service manager is faced with the critical tasks of defining, integrating, evaluating, and redefining the service concept, service delivery system, and the service levels. The service manager, in doing these tasks well, must understand how the elements of the service delivery system fit together and avoid the disasters described above. The next two chapters deal in detail with the service delivery system and service levels.

Table 2-5

OPERATING CHARACTERISTICS IN A SERVICE ENVIRONMENT

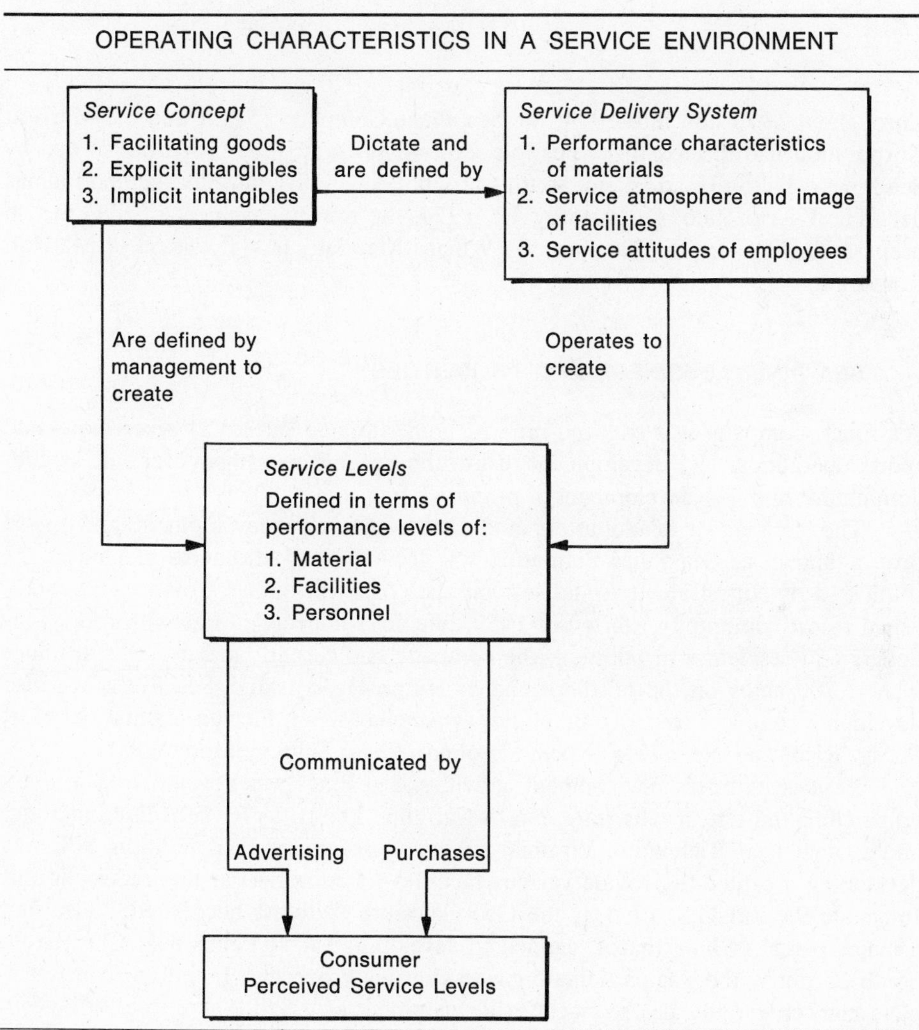

Sea Pines Company (A)

Throughout 1973 and into 1974, the Sea Pines Company (SPC) and the Marriott Corporation had discussed the possible joint ventures at three properties owned by Sea Pines—Hilton Head Island, South Carolina; Amelia Island, Florida; and Palmas del Mar, Puerto Rico. On January 12, 1974, the top management of SPC met in preparation for a trip to Sea Pines by Willard Marriott, Jr.—President of Marriott Corporation.

SEA PINES' BUSINESS AND PROPERTIES

Sea Pines Company was engaged in: (1) homesite land sales; (2) resort hotel and sports operations; (3) development of townhouses and apartments for sale as condominiums; and (4) development of primary home communities.

The company's headquarters and first community development and resort project known as Sea Pines Plantation was located on 5,200 acres of land at the south end of Hilton Head Island just off the coast of South Carolina. This established resort community, started in 1957, offered a full range of activities for vacationers and residents. In addition, the company had recently acquired for development 3,700 acres on the northern end of Hilton Head Island. Sea Pines was also developing complete resort communities at Amelia Island, Florida, Palmas del Mar, Puerto Rico, and Nantahala, North Carolina (Great Smokey Mountains).

Besides its resort development activities, Sea Pines was developing a primary home community near Charlotte, North Carolina, known as River Hills Plantation, and another near Richmond, Virginia, known as Brandermill. In addition, SPC was developing a center to provide various facilities for motorists at the intersection of Interstate 95 and U.S. 17 near the Georgia-South Carolina border. SPC also had a major parcel of land that it planned to develop at Isle of Palms near Charleston, South Carolina, and was participating with Cousins Properties, Inc., to provide complete marketing and sales services for development of a 5,400 acre tract of land in the North Georgia mountains, 60 miles northwest of Atlanta.

SEA PINES PLANTATION AND HILTON HEAD ISLAND

Sea Pines Plantation embodied many concepts of real estate and resort development that SPC was applying to its new resort projects. SPC sold homesites and condominiums and also developed and operated various resort and recreation facilities, including an inn, golf courses and clubhouses, restaurants, tennis courts, swimming pools, marinas, and parks and nature preserves. The condominiums consisted of townhouses, apartments, and groups of cottages.

Although SPC's principal source of revenues at Sea Pines Plantation had been from the sale of land and villas, its real estate activities were, in general, comparable to that of the urban and community development industry, not the retail land sales industry. In contrast to the retail land sales industry, SPC did not sell land through sales offices in market cities; it typically deeded homesites to buyers shortly after the contracts were signed, obtaining mortgage security for the unpaid part of the contract price, if any; improved all homesites sold with paved streets, water, sewers, and other utilities, generally within two years of the contract dates; did not sell under contracts with cancellation provisions; sold only to approved credit risks in a generally upper income market; and had experienced virtually no contract defaults or cancellations since beginning business in 1957.

Hilton Head Island was substantially undeveloped and sparsely populated when SPC began development of Sea Pines Plantation in 1957. In developing Sea Pines Plantation, SPC prepared and periodically updated a comprehensive land use plan; developed residential subdivisions, parks, utilities, golf, tennis and other recreational and resort facilities; and donated land for churches, medical facilities, and other community purposes. SPC maintained strict control through deed covenants over subsequent use of land that it sold, over architectural design and appearance, and over siting of buildings. Exterior materials were controlled, so that buildings blended with their natural forest settings. SPC had its own staff of architects, engineers, and planners and also made extensive use of design, engineering, and planning firms and other outside consultants. The architectural design, master planning, and community development programs of Sea Pines had been recognized for major design awards from professional societies and by national publications.

SOURCE OF REVENUE

Substantially all of Sea Pines' revenues and profits were derived from Sea Pines Plantation. Since nearly all homesites and planned new residential units at Sea Pines Plantation were to be completed and sold by 1977, future revenues and profits would become increasingly dependent on the success of other Hilton Head Island landholdings and projects that were in the early stages of development. Compared with its recently acquired land in Florida and Puerto Rico, both the original costs of land and initial selling prices of homesites at Sea Pines Plantation were relatively low. SPC had also benefited in the recent past from relatively low capitalized costs of land sold at Sea Pines Plantation coupled with relatively high sales prices. To complete development of its many projects Sea Pines would need a substantial amount of external financing for a number of years.

Financial statements from the 1973 annual report are included as Exhibit 1. Summary statistics of Sea Pines' properties are shown as Exhibit 2.

Exhibit 1

SEA PINES COMPANY (A)

Statements of Consolidated Income

For the Years Ended February 28, 1973 and February 29, 1972

	1973	1972
	000's omitted	
Revenues:		
Resort, brokerage and community operations	$10,797	$ 8,459
Current sales		
Homesites	22,147	11,406
Homes and villas	11,380	2,140
Developed and undeveloped parcels	5,502	1,830
	39,029	15,376
Deferred sales		
Sales deferred to future periods—		
Homesites	(4,760)	(1,222)
Homes and villas	(2,179)	(414)
Developed and undeveloped parcels	(1,904)	—
	(8,843)	(1,636)
Sales recognized from prior periods—		
Homesites	496	129
Homes and villas	414	—
	910	129
Net deferred sales	(7,933)	(1,507)
Net sales of homesites, homes, villas and parcels	31,096	13,869
Marketing, development and management fees	1,663	765
Income from joint venture	283	358
Total revenues, net of deferrals	43,839	23,451
Costs and Expenses:		
Resort, brokerage and community operating expenses	10,189	8,238
Cost of current sales		
Homesites	6,636	3,990
Homes and villas	8,455	1,505
Developed and undeveloped parcels	2,086	393
	17,177	5,888
Cost of deferred sales		
Costs deferred to future periods—		
Homesites	(1,850)	(735)
Homes and villas	(1,667)	(304)
Developed and undeveloped parcels	(886)	—
	(4,403)	(1,039)
Costs recognized from prior periods—		
Homesites	216	136
Homes and villas	304	—
	520	136
Net cost of deferred sales	(3,883)	(903)
Net cost of sales of homesites, homes, villas and parcels	13,294	4,985
Selling, general and administrative expenses	11,954	6,469
Interest expense, net of interest income of $949,000 and $355,000 in 1973 and 1972, respectively	1,621	842
Total costs and expenses, net of deferrals	37,058	20,534
Income Before Income Taxes	6,781	2,917
Provision for Deferred Income Taxes	3,452	1,424
Net Income	$ 3,329	$ 1,493
Net Income Per Share of Common Stock		
Primary	$1.45	$.68
Fully diluted	$1.44	$.68

The accompanying notes are an integral part of these statements.

Exhibit 1 (continued)

SEA PINES COMPANY (A)

Consolidated Balance Sheets

February 28, 1973 and February 29, 1972

Assets	1973	1972
	000's omitted	
Properties, at cost		
Investment and development—		
Land held for future development	$ 4,861	$ 9,292
Land in process of development	50,263	30,081
Homes and villas completed or under construction	8,146	1,572
	63,270	40,945
Operating—		
Land and improvements	6,872	1,921
Buildings and leasehold improvements	11,302	4,262
Machinery and equipment	2,157	1,830
Furniture and fixtures	1,690	1,124
Other property and equipment	1,456	907
	23,477	10,044
Less—Accumulated depreciation	(2,896)	(1,936)
	20,581	8,108
Construction in progress	12,809	2,112
	33,390	10,220
Total properties	96,660	51,165
Cash, $1,730,000 restricted and $755,000 used for compensating balances in 1973	4,791	1,824
Receivables		
Homesite and parcel notes	19,092	10,565
Home and villa sales contracts	7,700	1,150
Resort	1,107	353
Miscellaneous	2,011	837
Lease contract receivable	—	826
	29,910	13,731
Less—Allowance for doubtful accounts	(324)	(54)
	29,586	13,677
Investments, at underlying equity in net assets in joint ventures and less than 50%-owned companies	1,956	436
Other Assets:		
Prepayments and other deferred charges	690	1,092
Merchandise inventory, at cost	895	574
	1,585	1,666
	$134,578	$68,768

The accompanying notes are an integral part of these balance sheets.

Exhibit 1 (continued)

SEA PINES COMPANY (A)

Liabilities and Stockholders' Investment	1973	1972
	000's omitted	
Notes Payable, substantially all collateralized by land, buildings, and receivables		
Construction, 7 to 5.5% above prime	$ 10,874	$ 2,146
General use and development less unamortized debt discount of $1,186,000 in 1973 and $944,000 in 1972, 5 to 13%	42,467	30,422
Mortgage, 4 to 10%	20,238	4,369
Equipment, 5 to 13%	1,296	697
Other, 4.5 to 8.25%	697	3,046
	75,572	40,680
Accounts Payable:		
Trade	4,220	2,333
Construction	4,204	1,136
	8,424	3,469
Accrued Liabilities	2,710	2,789
Deposits	1,980	718
Deferred Sales		
Homesite sales	5,798	1,535
Home and villa sales	2,179	414
Developed and undeveloped parcel sales	1,904	—
Other	993	293
	10,874	2,242
Deferred Income Taxes	6,886	3,434
Subordinated Mortgage Notes Payable	8,274	11,143
Subordinated Convertible Debentures Payable	6,000	—
Long-Term Leases, Commitments and Contingent Liabilities		
Stockholders' Investment		
Common stock, $.10 par value; 6,000,000 shares authorized, 2,663,167 shares and 2,218,722 shares issued in 1973 and 1972, respectively	266	222
Paid-in surplus	6,826	634
Retained earnings	6,821	3,492
	13,913	4,348
Less—Treasury stock (31,500 shares), at cost	(55)	(55)
	13,858	4,293
	$134,578	$68,768

Exhibit 1 (continued)

The following table shows the Company's gross volume of business, net revenues, and operating profits for its principal lines of business for the years ended February 28, 1973 and February 29, 1972. Operating profit was computed by deducting all costs (including depreciation) directly associated with the operations. Corporate expenses such as administration, selling and marketing, public relations and finance were not allocated. Amounts for resort and community operations include brokerage resale activities.

		Deferred (1)		Gross	Net Revenues for Period		
(000's omitted)	Gross Volume of Business	To Future Periods	From Prior Periods	Gross Revenues for Account of Others (2)	Amount	Percent of Total	Operating Profit
1973							
Resort and community operations	$27,191	$ –	$ –	$(16,394)	$10,797	24.7%	$ 608
Home and villa sales	11,380	(2,179)	414	–	9,615	21.9	2,523
Homesite and other land sales	27,649	(6,664)	496	–	21,481	49.0	15,279
Other–							
Share of joint venture income, net	283	–	–	–	283	.6	
Marketing, development and management fees	12,285	–	–	(10,622)	1,663	3.8	
	$78,788	$(8,843)	$910	$(27,016)	$43,839	100.0%	
1972							
Resort and community operations	$17,948	$ –	$ –	$ (9,489)	$ 8,459	36.0%	$ 221
Home and villa sales	2,140	(414)	–	–	1,726	7.4	525
Homesite and other land sales	13,236	(1,222)	129	–	12,143	51.8	8,359
Other–							
Share of joint venture income, net	358	–	–	–	358	1.5	
Marketing, development and management fees	5,892	(172)	–	(4,955)	765	3.3	
	$39,574	$(1,808)	$129	$(14,444)	$23,451	100.0%	

(1) In accordance with the Company's accounting policies, sales relating to uncompleted development costs are deferred and recognized as development work is completed.

(2) Represents brokerage sales and collection of home and villa rentals for account of others and sales of villas for joint ventures.

Executive Committee Meeting of January 12, 1974

Present:

Charles E. Fraser	President and Chairman of the Board, founder and major stockholder of Sea Pines Company
James W. Light	Executive Vice-President of Sea Pines Company
E. B. LeMaster, III	President of Sea Pines Resorts
James J. Chafin	Vice-President for Real Estate Sales and Marketing
Glen E. McCaskey	Vice-President for Recreation and Environmental Services

The meeting had been called by Charles Fraser and the subject was the upcoming trip to Hilton Head Island by Willard Marriott, Jr., President of the Marriott Corporation, and his chief assistants. Several of these assistants had spent the latter two weeks viewing the various Sea Pines' projects and learning about SPC operations first hand. The discussion began as follows:

Charles Fraser: As you all know, Bill Marriott flies in with his troops tomorrow night to look us over. We've been courting Marriott off and on for the last year and things are finally coming to a head. I've called this meeting so we can establish our negotiating position.

Late yesterday I distributed to each of you a memorandum (Appendix I) which I asked you to read and prepare notes on for this meeting. The memorandum outlines the evolution of Sea Pines Community Development and Resort Operations and our present bargaining position on many issues. Attached to the memorandum was an exhibit (Exhibit 3) that provided some summary statistics and data on Marriott. I thought you might find it useful. Jim, why don't you lead off by outlining Marriott's objectives and criteria as you view them.

James Light: Marriott has diversified into cruise ships, international hotels, and other major ventures but has refrained from adding a staff to undertake the acquisition and development of a complete resort destination area. In essence, Marriott has elected not to become generally involved in the four- to five-year process required for land selection, acquisition, master planning, zoning approval, and construction of roads, sewers, and the like, to build complete resort regions such as our Palmas del Mar in Puerto Rico.

Marriott's new resort hotel operations have been very profitable, thanks in part to its marketing organization's ability to keep them nearly full with very profitable corporate and association convention type of business.

Marriott has a strong in-house capability in the design/construction area for restaurants, hotels, and conference facilities. Marriott does not intend to develop and build resort condominia in the immediate future.

Marriott is very interested in managing some of our resort operations on Hilton Head, Amelia, and in Palmas del Mar, the latter being subject to the avoidance of any involvement with unions in Palmas. They have discussed the possibility of Marriott's managing all our lodging and food facilities at Sea Pines, Amelia, and possibly Palmas. They stated concern that the two firms not compete for labor.

Marriott has 25,000 employees, primarily in the area of lodging and food services, and has excellent training programs, including Spanish-language training films for hotel and food facilities.

Let me add that Marriott has a tremendous reputation in the food side of the business, which is not true for most hotel chains.

As a fundamental strategy, we intend to strengthen our competence in resort operating management as a fundamental compo-

SEA PINES COMPANY (A)

Summary Statistics of Sea Pines Properties

Community	*Date of initial acquisition*	*Total acreage*	*Portion of acreage in salt marsh conservancy*	*Beach, lake shore, and salt marsh frontage (feet)*	*Type of community*	*Sales started*	*Villas completed or under construction as of 2–73*
Sea Pines Plantation	1957	5,414	745	82,400	Resort Residential Recreation	9–57	1,215
Amelia Island	1970	2,442	830	60,000	Resort Residential Recreation	5–72	223
Palmas del Mar	1969	2,404	None	31,417	Resort Residential Recreation	9–72	144
River Hills Plantation	1970	762	None	16,600	Primary residential Recreation	10–70	94
Hilton Head Plantation	1971	4,056	354	46,400	Resort Residential Recreation	5–73	—
Point South	1965	1,567	None	None	Interstate rest stop	6–71	—
Big Canoe	—	5,462	None	10,300	Recreation Mountain Weekend retreat	11–72	—
Isle of Palms	1973	1,537	581	45,500	Resort Residential Recreation	—	—
Nantahala, N.C.	1973	6,481	None	20,000	Recreation mountain	—	—
Brandermill	1973		None		Primary residential Recreation	—	—

Source: 1973 Annual Report of the Marriott Corporation.

nent of our capacity to finance, build, and sell resort destination regions. In order to protect the values in our existing resorts, we must retain the capability to operate facilities in resorts we now have, and will have, under our ownership and development management.

We do, however, recognize the limits to the rate of our growth and would like to limit our operations to manageable and profitable size. We believe that growth of 25 to 30% per year, from our current base of 1,000 companywide service employees, is as much as we shall schedule for the next four years. In addition, we intend to limit our total property and rental management at any one resort location to 1,000 to 1,500 condominiums.

We are most interested in negotiating with Marriott a relationship that would include immediate or long-term Marriott involvement in each of our existing and new resorts. The relationship would vary by resort.

E. B. LeMaster: You know I'd be the first to admit that some of our operations need to be improved, but I really question the need to go outside and hook up with somebody like Marriott. I think it's simply a question of lack of *emphasis*.

Up until now *development* has been our main thrust, but that doesn't mean we can't shift gears and develop a good operations capability. We've just hired John Curry who formerly ran Disney World and before he even has a chance to make an impact we're chasing after Marriott. I don't think we've really explored all our options.

Also, I would just add that even though our major emphasis in the past has been on development, our long-term potential has to come from operations. We can't be a land sales and development company forever. If we give up the golden goose to Marriott now, just because of some short-term operations problems, we may never recover.

Charles Fraser: Well, I think that's putting it rather strongly, Ebbie. We won't give up *everything* to Marriott. We can negotiate on a property-by-property basis. The place where we need immediate help is in Palmas. You know the situation we face down there. It's one thing to develop in a foreign culture, but it's entirely another to have to work on a day-to-day operating basis with the Puerto Rican gastronomic and hotel unions that are controlled by the Teamsters. We've found it practically impossible, as you know. Marriott has a strong Spanish-language training and operating

Exhibit 3

SEA PINES COMPANY (A)

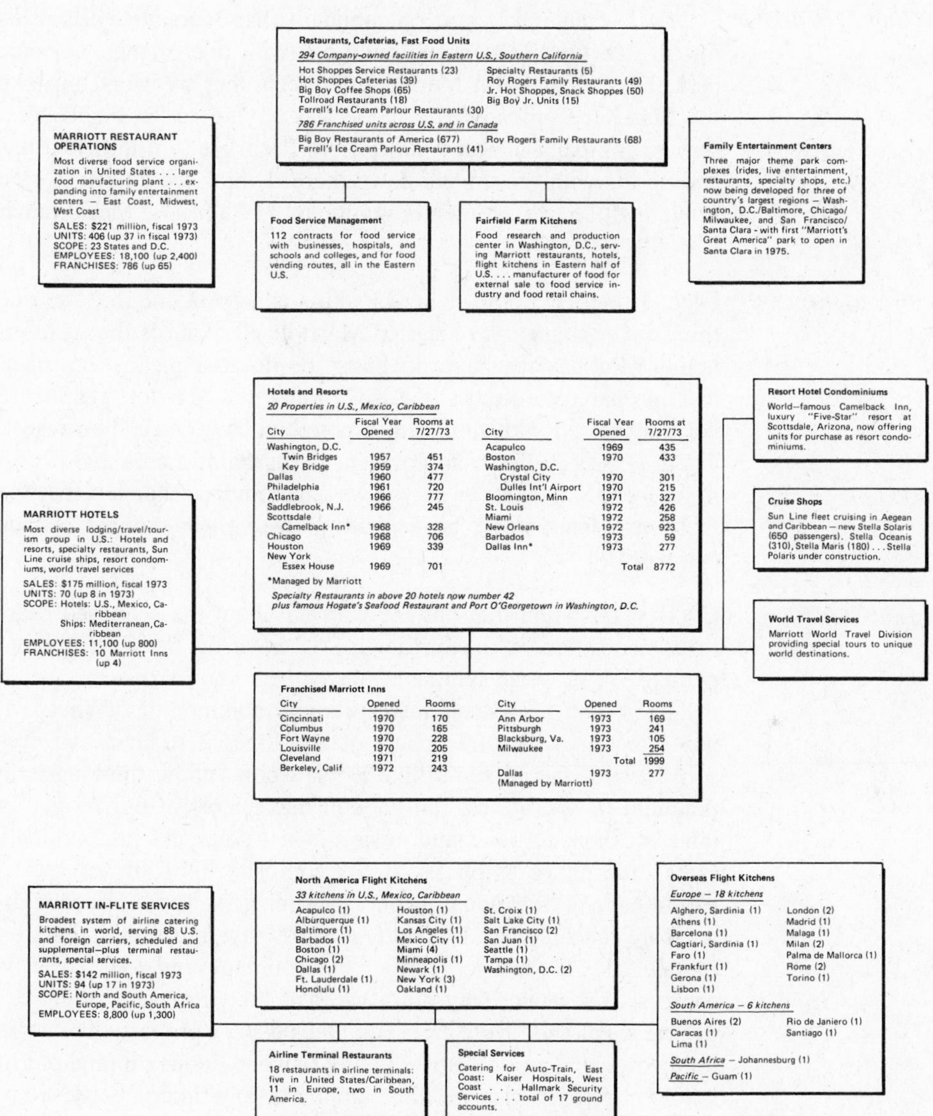

Source: 1973 Annual Report of the Marriott Corporation.

capability and we need their help down there. If we have to give up other parts of Sea Pines Company to get them involved down there, then we'll just have to do it.

Glen McCaskey: Charles, what makes you so confident that Marriott will bail us out in Puerto Rico? In conversations with one of their advance men, he said that Bill Marriott, Jr., feels that the worst mistake the Marriott Company ever made was buying an "in-flight" food service company in San Juan, Puerto Rico. He said they had unending fits with the unions down there. I think we'd have to give up an awful lot to get their commitment at Palmas, if they'd touch it at all!

Jim Light: Glen, I think the point you're making is a good one, but the one thing we've made very clear to Marriott all along is that without help at Palmas we have no basis for discussion. So, they're at least prepared to discuss it. Also, I know the Marriott people are very impressed with the Palmas potential as a destination resort. There is over 30% unemployment in the Palmas area and it's 60 miles from San Juan, so maybe we can convince Marriott that the labor problems won't be as bad as with their in-flight service company.

Jim Chafin: Charles, the thing that has me worried about the proposed Marriott association is the impact it will have on the development people. We're world famous as developers and marketers of only the finest and most tasteful resorts and communities. What is it going to do to the atmosphere at Sea Pines if suddenly all eyes turn toward operations? I take Ebbie's point about the long-term potential in operations, but we still make most of our money in land and housing sales and always have. You can't just suddenly switch the entire emphasis of the company like this. At best it would have to be gradual. I think if we bring in a well-honed high-pressure machine like Marriott, it could have a drastic impact on morale. If we want to redirect the company and look for new sources of revenue, why don't we take the strong marketing expertise we already have and sell *other* people's property like we're doing at Big Canoe? Also, if you're worried about running out of land for resorts, can we shift emphasis to primary house communities? We have a strong capability there as proven by our record at River Hills and the demand is practically guaranteed.

Charles Fraser: Jim, I think we're getting a little far afield. The point is that to sell new land and condominiums and protect the value of those we've already sold, we *have* to operate our properties well—something we're not doing. Now, we can develop our own capability in house—but how long and how many dollars will it take? And what is our *risk* in doing so?

We're growing at a 25% annual rate. Just how many things can we do, and do them well, when we're growing at that rate? To my mind it's an invitation to disaster if we don't get some help in operations. I'm not suggesting we give up everything, but we need *somebody* in here to make sure we don't make some of the terrible mistakes we've made in the past. I don't have to remind you that we built the Old Fort Pub, only to find we failed to put in a kitchen large enough to serve dinner meals. That's just a microcosm of our problems.

Glen McCaskey: Well, I still think a well-tuned profit machine like Marriott will change the whole character of what Sea Pines has worked 15 years to build. I know we're a public company now, but is earnings growth the objective of Sea Pines, or is it to develop a quality product? And who is going to referee the ground rules between ourselves and Marriott? It's one thing to handle conflict within an organization. It's entirely another matter to handle problems between two different ones with possibly conflicting goals and objectives.

Jim Light: But, does running an efficient operation necessarily conflict with what Sea Pines Company *should* be doing? Isn't a well-run operation what people *expect* from us? Maybe the way to maximize profit is to be good at development, but then turn the operation over to Marriott.

E. B. LeMaster: That sounds nice, but I'm not sure Marriott necessarily wants to come in and operate things we've built. I think we need some input from them earlier on.

You know, we keep talking about "operations" as if it encompasses everything. It seems to me that if we break it down into food and lodging operations, food is by far a more difficult operations "technology," if you can call it such. We've actually done a pretty good job on the condominium and hotel management side. Maybe what we need to consider is exactly *what* it is we want Marriott to help us with, both by property *and* by function.

Jim Light: That's a good point Ebbie. But, as we all know, the sales prices we get for our condominiums, which most of the owners have us rent out when they don't occupy them, is directly related to the money we return to the owner as rental. As the number of rental units has grown, our capability to *market* those units has not kept pace. In fact, the one group salesman we had has just left us to join Marriott. That's where Marriott has a tremendous capability.

If they can book conventions and groups into our properties and get our off-season occupancy levels up, it will have a dramatic impact on our property sales. They have a 200-person sales force just booking group business.

Jim Chafin: That sounds very nice, Jim, but who says that the guests Marriott brings in are earning $25,000/year and over—the type people we need to buy our property? If we get a different guest profile, it could have a drastic impact on our sales.

Also, convention business is often booked 3–5 years in advance. It may be a long time before we feel the effects of any Marriott efforts in this area.

Glen McCaskey: That's right! Also, Marriott is used to running high-rise motels with lots of easily serviced room cubicles. We have condominium vacation resorts with widely dispersed villas. It's a totally different operation. It will be quite awhile before they become efficient at running our type business.

Charles Fraser: Ok, ok, I hear your objections and I think they're good ones, but the fact still remains that we're growing at a prodigious rate and there are just so many things we can do at one time. If time and money and personnel are our constraints, we've got to decide how to allocate them. I personally think with Marriott we have a sure thing with the best operator in the business. There's a big question mark based on our past performance as to whether we can do it alone.

Look at the figures. Palmas will be six times the size of our operation here at Hilton Head. Amelia will have 3,000 units. Brandermill is going to be a community of 40,000 to 60,000 people. We only have 12 people there at present. Last year, as a corporation, we hired 40 employees at the master's degree level or higher. We were the largest single employer of Harvard MBA's. How long can we absorb that rate of growth? Can Marriott help us?

We have about $13 million in equity after our stock issue in 1973. But we have over $90 million in debt for which we pay a ridiculously high rate. In the past we haven't been able to get our construction loans switched to permanent financing until we had four to five years' experience operating the property. With Marriott and their reputation we should be able to get a permanent mortgage as soon as they start operating the facility. We *have* to get some help. It's just too risky if we don't.

As far as I'm concerned we're fortunate to have such a quality potential partner as Marriott. The trouble is, in other areas of resort operations such as cable TV we haven't been able to find suitable bedmates. The Marriott deal is just the beginning. It is a model for what we are going to have to do to grow on a sound basis—rely more and more on outside help.

Now, my question to you and the reason I called this meeting—how do we reduce all the things you've brought up to writing so we can propose a nice crisp position to Marriott? What should be our terms?

Appendix I
Nature of the Sea Pines Company

The Sea Pines Company is one of several dozen enterprises that are relatively unique in their *mixture* of characteristics and are not "just like" any other similar enterprises. In many activities, e.g., operation of golf courses, it is "like" other private golf course operators, but only in that particular characteristic. An abbreviated list of characteristics (other than resort operations) is noted below:

Sea Pines is an investor in acquisition of large parcels of waterfront property that are fully developed prior to resale.

Sea Pines is a community planner and developer of roads, water, sewage, and sports, and community facilities in new communities, both resort and urban.

Sea Pines is a developer of townhouses, villas, and cluster homes.

Sea Pines is a developer of homesites on which others build homes, subject to strong design review and plan approval process administered by the company.

Sea Pines is a developer of tracts within its communities for sale to and use by other investor/developers for residential, commercial, and resort facilities, subject to stringent design controls.

Sea Pines is a manager of community services—security, police, maintenance, etc.—both directly and indirectly.

Sea Pines is an operator of sports facilities, tennis clubs, golf courses and is a sponsor of nationally televised tennis events.

Sea Pines is a marketing organization capable of handling recreational planning and direct-to-customer real estate sales programs for high-quality recreational developments of others.

In most of the eight major activities above, the company has acquired an international reputation for excellence and is generally regarded as one of the top two or three leaders in the United States of companies engaged in activities of the type listed, and it steadily receives recognition of this position by national and international societies and major magazines.

AREAS OF EXCELLENCE

Recognized excellence in the eight listed fields takes many forms, including:

Architectural and design harmony of the total community;

Ecological sensitivity from the corporate inception in 1957 that is continuing today in new communities;

High socioeconomic strata of customers—catering to the $25,000 and up group, which has grown tenfold from one-half of 1% to 5% of population since 1955—with growth to 27% projected by the Conference Board by 1990;

Exceptional beauty and desirability of extensive waterfront and beachfront landholdings and ease of access to market areas;

Strong legal controls over all land use and architectural design controls over all buildings;

Leader in pioneering development of accounting systems and budgeting systems for land and community development;

Strong new thrusts in recruiting and training programs for community and resort development managers;

Economically efficient real estate and family vacation marketing and sales programs;

Leader in research on the $25,000 to $75,000 per year leisure and recreation market.

THE SEA PINES COMPANY
GROSS VOLUME OF BUSINESS

*Fiscal Year**	*Total volume of activity*	*% Growth of activity*	*Real estate gross receipts*	*Brokerage and resort** gross receipts*	*Other*
1965	3,256,000	—	1,240,000	1,971,000	45,000
1966	6,046,000	85.7%	2,409,000	3,584,000	53,000
1967	7,708,000	27.5%	3,304,000	4,162,000	242,000
1968	11,618,000	50.7%	4,534,000	7,071,000	13,000
1969	13,317,000	14.6%	5,668,000	7,458,000	191,000
1970	—Fiscal year conversion, data not applicable.				
1971	17,611,000	—	7,607,000	6,772,000	3,232,000
1972	39,574,000	124.7%	15,376,000	17,948,000	6,250,000
1973	78,788,000	99.1%	39,029,000	27,191,000	12,568,000

* Fiscal years ending August 31st, through 1969. Fiscal years ending February 28th, through 1973.

** Resort revenues include all villa rental receipts, including amounts subsequently disbursed to villa owners from the company as rental agent; the column also includes the gross volume of real estate sales made as broker for the account of the owner within the resort.

The resort food, lodging, and sports revenues of the company (included with brokerage real estate sales in the previous table) grew at a healthy rate, as noted below:

FY 1965	$ 1,213,000
FY 1966	2,061,000
FY 1967	2,953,000
FY 1968	3,933,000
FY 1969	5,008,000
FY 1970	Fiscal year conversion
FY 1971	5,972,000
FY 1972	9,008,000
FY 1973	11,334,000

The pretax profit trend for the past three years has been as follows:

Fiscal Year	*Net revenues*	*Pretax profit*	*Pretax profit as % of net revenues*	*After-tax profit* after reserve for taxes*
1971	13,365,000	973,000	7.28%	399,000
1972	23,451,000	2,917,000	12.43%	1,424,000
1973	43,839,000	6,781,000	15.46%	3,452,000

* Because of depreciation and interest charges, few income taxes were actually paid during such years, however.

EXPANSION PROGRAM

With its acquisition of major new properties in Richmond, Virginia, Isle of Palms, Charleston County, and in the mountains of western North Carolina, the company expects to be highly cautious on new land acquisitions and to focus on its *current* landholdings for the next three years. A 20% to 25% annual growth rate is targeted during the next five years to provide an orderly pace of new community and new resort startup. We will undertake during this consolidation period new joint ventures only with extremely capable partners, no matter how financially attractive are the offers that we must reject.

RESORT OPERATIONS

Sea Pines Plantation is one of the major pioneers in a new form of mixed vacation-retirement outdoor sports resorts, where there is both strong emphasis on year-round retirement homes and special villages of privately owned resort rental townhouses, patio homes, and architecturally distinctive vacation cottages used seasonally. Most of the townhouse and villa buildings are sold under the condominium legal form. Seventy-five per cent are subsequently offered to the company for rental management.

The number of villa units—typically two- or three-bedroom townhouses—managed as daily and weekly rental properties by the company, have grown steadily as construction is completed, as illustrated below:

Date	Sea Pines homes	Sea Pines villas	Hilton Head Inn zone villas
July 1972	132	251	
June 1973	147	383	116
July 1973	157	402	127

RESORT REGIONS

The company has been planning and constructing over the past three years new resort *regional areas* at Palmas, Amelia, and the northern end of Hilton Head whose development will collectively add to the stock of oceanfront villas and apartments approximately 1,000 bedrooms a year in 1974 and 1975 and 1,500 to 2,000 bedrooms a year for the following several years. While the company wishes to manage a significant number of these bedrooms, it is desirous of entering into arrangements with Marriott or others to operate the balance, including 100% of the bedrooms at agreed-upon resort regions.

MIXED RECORD OF RESORT OPERATIONS

Unlike the eight major community development, real estate, and sports activities of the company (described earlier), where excellence has been a characteristic, the resort area of the company's business is a paradoxical mixture of outstanding achievements and sloppy performance. Only in the past year have the excellent operations outnumbered the "so-so" performances. But while performance has been mixed, growth in the past three years has been very strong, with resort gross revenues jumping from $5,972,000 to $11,334,000 between February 28, 1971, and February 28, 1973.

While the past 12 months have seen a great strengthening of the resort focus of senior management, this area had not regularly received prior sustained leadership. Historically, chief corporate officers have concentrated attention in the eight major real estate and sports areas, where excellence has been common, and have given only spasmodic attention to Inn, clubs, and the home and villa operations. This has not hampered steady growth of the resort business, but inattention has led to low profits in several areas and little satisfaction in a "job well done."

FAMILY TRADE AND GROUP BUSINESS

The two most serious resort economic problems have been that, as villas within Sea Pines Plantation grew in number to a level equal to the Inn, then twice the Inn, then four times the Inn's size, (a) the revenue sharing with owners in this department has been inequitable to the company, and (b) Group Sales have remained primarily an element of the Inn, and Group Sales attention focused on the 136-room *Inn* group business, not the 300, then 500, then 1,000, then 1,200 bedrooms in the villas.

Marketing to individual families in spring and summer by Sea Pines marketing and public relations programs has been highly successful, with total number of guest units rented (but not always percentage of occupancy) jumping strongly each year, generally matching rapid growth in total supply of new rental units.

Villas have generally been nearly fully occupied in the family seasons of mid-March to mid-April and June, July, and August, but the group and association seasons have been largely untapped except for the Harbour Town Conference Center. In contrast, the group business at the Hilton Head Inn gives that installation a strong profit picture.

The comparative percentages of occupancy for the Inn, with its group business, and the homes and villas, which largely lack this business, for fiscal year 1973 are noted below:

	Mar.	*Apr.*	*May*	*June*	*July*	*Aug.*	*Sept.*	*Oct.*	*Nov.*	*Dec.*	*Jan.*	*Feb.*
Hilton Head Inn	87	96	88	93	96	96	83	92	80	50	73	73
All villas	62	77	63	77	90	91	61	55	42	21	20	38
Homes	43	52	37	73	94	88	25	24	29	15	12	26

The high seasonality of business in villa and villa-serving operations resulting from tardy movement toward villa group sales and group meeting facility construction has not only led to low resort profits but also has limited capital investments in needed amenity facilities, etc., to balance villa construction. We are striving to catch up in this area in 1974.

NEW SEA PINES RESORT THRUSTS IN 1972–1973

The company initiated in late 1971 the design of a modern villa guest reception center with computerized reservations and computerized accounting. This reception center opened for the 1973 season.

The company, 12 months ago, hired E. B. LeMaster, III, President for 12 years of the Ponte Vedra Company of Florida, a leading beach and golf resort for 30 years, as President of Sea Pines Resorts. He has just been joined by John Curry, formerly head of hotels for Disneyworld. They are leading an economic and quality transformation for Sea Pines resort operations.

The company has initiated in 1973 detailed five-year historical studies (to be computerized) to track its experience and make projections for the future correlating the relationship between guest number, type, and season on demand for golf, tennis, and restaurant facilities. Such studies and the Sea Pines Amenity Analysis computer forecasting model will aid in the proper mix of facilities and timing of new construction. Three-year forecasts of demand for selected activities are included in Exhibits 4–6. Present capacity for these amenities is given in Exhibit 4.

The company initiated in January a comprehensive study of the development of strong group meeting sales and marketing program for its new Palmas del Mar (Puerto Rico) and Amelia Island resorts. Marriott's thinking on this business is far in advance of Sea Pines', however, and Marriott's recommendations will be taken into account in Sea Pines planning.

The company has under way a comprehensive study of (a) the income and profits derived by owners of villas under the company's management over the past five years and the (b) appropriate new contractual relationships between the company as rental manager and the individual who buys a villa in a company resort and has it managed for resort rentals by the company.

The company plans extensive enlargement of its profitable sports facilities and plans to make a major thrust into adult teaching centers in tennis, sailing, golf, paddle tennis, and camping, under its emerging Compass Club program.

It is quite clear from the dynamic growth in family season patronage that the "mix" of facilities, recreation, and accommodations in Sea Pines Plantation is highly in tune with the family vacation instincts at the $20,000 (and up) income American family. However, while the two- and three-bedroom villas built in the past in Sea Pines are well suited to owners' needs and the family-vacation rental market, they are not well suited to the needs of many groups whose members do not wish to share accommodations that are, in essence, large suites.

The multi-bedroom typical Sea Pines villa has proven popular with corporation meetings and board of directors meetings, where joint use of a villa by two couples who know each other has proven quite appealing. Thus, quite specific groups, not just "groups" should be sought for the type of accommodation as Sea Pines sharply expands its corporate group marketing efforts.

Exhibit 4

SEA PINES COMPANY (A)

Forecast of guest nights and demand for tennis, golf, and formal dining at Sea Pines Plantation in FISCAL YEAR 1974 (March 1, 1973–February 28, 1974)

		March	April	May	June	July	August	September	October	November	December	January	February
Total Guest Nights	Forecast Actual	35,526 (30,093)	41,576 (47,312)	33,632 (33,578)	59,950 (51,687)	83,887	86,475	34,514	36,221	27,180	18,509	16,293	30,330
Tennis	Demand Forecast (Court Hours) Act.	1,417 (2,014)	2,532 (3,880)	1,540 (2,821)	2,492 (3,359)	4,686	4,830	1,971	2,327	1,701	1,632	753	1,172
	Current Capacity	5,544	5,544	7,018	6,776	7,337	7,337	6,440	6,003	4,968	5,152	5,152	4,600
Golf	Demand Forecast (Rounds) Actual	16,839 (12,946)	20,123 (15,892)	16,446 (13,341)	15,167 (10,868)	17,532	15,652	14,047	18,581	10,383	11,716	7,967	15,226
	Maximum Capacity*	15,568	16,240	18,592	19,440	20,160	19,584	12,940	14,768	13,248	13,728	13,728	13,788
Formal Dining	Demand (Dinners)	15,489	17,794	14,495	16,186	21,307	21,416	11,700	16,191	12,394	9,932	6,632	10,919
	Seats Required ** (Current—420)	250	297	234	270	344	345	195	261	207	160	107	195

* Not Adjusted for "Split-nines."
** Assumes Turnover of 2.0.

Exhibit 5

SEA PINES COMPANY (A)

Forecast of guest nights and demand for tennis, golf, and formal dining at Sea Pines Plantation

FISCAL YEAR 1975 (March 1, 1974–February 28, 1975)

		March	*April*	*May*	*June*	*July*	*August*	*September*	*October*	*November*	*December*	*January*	*February*
Total Guest Nights		57,741	66,462	53,992	95,620	130,696	129,111	53,218	55,197	39,819	24,627	21,717	37,083
Tennis Demand (Court Hours)		2,304	4,047	2,472	4,015	7,301	7,230	3,040	3,532	2,492	2,172	999	1,433
Golf Demand (Rounds)		27,369	32,168	26,402	24,192	27,315	23,369	21,660	28,316	15,211	15,589	10,620	18,616
Formal Dining	Dinners	25,336	28,396	23,271	25,817	33,196	32,019	18,041	24,673	17,911	13,348	8,839	13,350
	Seats Required	409	473	375	430	535	516	887	398	299	215	143	238

Exhibit 6

SEA PINES COMPANY (A)

Forecast of guest nights and demand for tennis, golf, and formal dining at Sea Pines Plantation

FISCAL YEAR 1976 (March 1, 1975–February 29, 1976)

		March	*April*	*May*	*June*	*July*	*August*	*September*	*October*	*November*	*December*	*January*	*February*
Total Guest Nights		73,580	83,773	68,607	120,826	168,797	166,263	66,168	68,883	50,435	31,530	28,550	49,487
Tennis Demand (Court Hours)		2,934	5,110	3,156	5,026	9,453	9,311	3,772	4,408	3,177	2,774	1,313	1,930
Golf Demand (Rounds)		34,877	40,546	33,549	30,569	35,279	30,094	26,930	35,337	19,266	19,958	13,937	24,842
Formal Dining	Dinners	32,080	35,855	92,391	32,623	42,123	41,233	22,431	30,791	22,998	17,089	11,620	17,816
	Seats Required	517	598	474	544	679	665	374	497	383	276	187	318

Benihana of Tokyo

"Some restaurateurs like myself have more fun than others," says Hiroaki (Rocky) Aoki, youthful president of Benihana of Tokyo. Since 1964 he had gone from a deficit net worth to becoming president of a chain of 15 restaurants that grossed over $12 million per year. He sported a $4,000 sapphire ring, maintained a $250,000 home, kept five cars including three Rolls-Royces. One wall of his office was completely covered with photographs of Rocky with famous personalities who had eaten at a Benihana. Rocky firmly believed: "In America money is always available if you work hard."

BACKGROUND

By 1972 Benihana was basically a steakhouse with a difference—the food was cooked in front of the customer by native chefs and the decor was that of an authentically detailed Japanese country inn. From a humble 40-seat unit opened in midtown Manhattan in 1964, Benihana had grown to a chain of 15 units across the country. Nine were company-owned locations: New York (3), San Francisco, Chicago, Encino and Marina del Rey, California, Portland, Oregon, and Honolulu. Five were franchised: Boston, Fort Lauderdale, Beverly Hills, Seattle, and Harrisburg, Pennsylvania. The last unit, Las Vegas, was operated as a joint venture with Hilton Hotels Corporation. Rocky, who was a former Olympic wrestler, described his success as follows:

> In 1959, I came to the United States on a tour with my university wrestling team. I was 20 at the time. When I reached New York, it was love at first sight! I was convinced that there were more opportunities for me in America than Japan. In fact, the minute I was able to forget that I was Japanese, my success began. I decided to enroll in the School of Restaurant Management at City College basically because I knew that in the restaurant business I'd never go hungry. I earned money those early years by washing dishes, driving an ice cream truck and acting as a tour guide. Most importantly, I spent three years making a systematic analysis of the U.S. restaurant market. What I discovered is that Americans enjoy eating in exotic surroundings but are deeply mistrustful of exotic foods. Also I learned that people very much enjoy watching their food being prepared. So I took $10,000 I had saved by 1963 and borrowed

$20,000 more to open my first unit on the West Side and tried to apply all that I had learned.

The origins of the Benihana of Tokyo actually date back to 1935. That was when Yunosuke Aoki (Rocky's father) opened the first of his chain of restaurants in Japan. He called it Benihana, after the small red flower that grew wild near the front door of the restaurant.

The elder Aoki ("Papasan"), like his son who was to follow in the family tradition, was a practical and resourceful restaurateur. In 1958, concerned about rising costs and increased competition, he first incorporated the hibachi table concept into his operations. Rocky borrowed this method of cooking from his father and commented as follows:

> One of the things I learned in my analysis, for example, was that the number one problem of the restaurant industry in the United States is the shortage of skilled labor. By eliminating the need for a conventional kitchen with the hibachi table arrangement, the only "skilled" person I need is the chef. I can give an unusual amount of attentive service and still keep labor cost to 10–12% of gross sales (food and beverage) depending whether a unit is at full volume. In addition, I was able to turn practically the entire restaurant into productive dining space. Only about 22% of the total space of a unit is back of the house, including preparation areas, dry and refrigerated storage, employee dressing rooms, and office space. Normally a restaurant requires 30% of its total space as back of the house. (Operating statistics for a typical service restaurant are included in Exhibit 1.)
>
> The other thing I discovered is that food storage and wastage contribute greatly to the overhead of the typical restaurant. By reducing my menu to only three simple "Middle American" entrees—steak, chicken, and shrimp, I have virtually no waste and can cut food costs to between 30% and 35% of food sales depending on the price of meat.
>
> Finally, I insist on historical authenticity. The walls, ceilings, beams, artifacts, decorative lights of a Benihana are all from Japan. The building materials are gathered from old houses there, carefully disassembled, and shipped in pieces to the United States where they are reassembled by one of my father's two crews of Japanese carpenters.

Rocky's first unit on the West side was such a success that it paid for itself in six months. He then built in 1966 a second unit three blocks away on the East side simply to cater to the overflow of the Benihana West. The Benihana East quickly developed a separate clientele and prospered. In 1967, Barron Hilton, who had eaten at a Benihana approached Rocky concerning the possibility of locating a unit in the Marina Towers in Chicago. Rocky flew to Chicago, rented a car and while driving to meet Mr. Hilton saw a vacant site. He immediately stopped, called the

Exhibit 1

BENIHANA OF TOKYO

OPERATING STATISTICS
FOR A TYPICAL SERVICE RESTAURANT

Sales	Ranges %
Food	70.0 – 80.0
Beverage	20.0 – 30.0
Other income	
Total Sales	100.0
COST OF SALES	
Food cost (% of food sales)	38.0 – 48.0
Beverage cost (% of beverage sales)	25.0 – 30.0
Other cost	
Total Cost of Sales	35.0 – 45.0
GROSS PROFIT	55.0 – 65.0
OPERATING EXPENSES	
CONTROLLABLE EXPENSE	
Payroll	30.0 – 35.0
Employee benefits	3.0 – 5.0
Employee meals	1.0 – 2.0
Laundry, linen, uniforms	1.5 – 2.0
Replacements	0.5 – 1.0
Supplies (guest)	1.0 – 1.5
Menus and printing	0.25 – 0.5
Miscellaneous contract expense (cleaning, garbage, extermination, equip. rental)	1.0 – 2.0
Music and entertainment (where applicable)	0.5 – 1.0
Advertising and promotion	0.75 – 2.0
Utilities	1.0 – 2.0
Management salary	2.0 – 6.0
Administration expense (including legal and accounting)	0.75 – 2.0
Repairs and maintenance	1.0 – 2.0
OCCUPATION EXPENSE	
Rent	4.5 – 9.0
Taxes (real estate and personal property)	0.5 – 1.5
Insurance	0.75 – 1.0
Interest	0.3 – 1.0
Depreciation	2.0 – 4.0
Franchise royalties (where applicable)	3.0 – 6.0
Total Operating Expenses	55.0 – 65.0
NET PROFIT BEFORE INCOME TAX	0.5 – 9.0

Source: Bank of America *Small Business Reporter*, Vol. 8, No. 2, 1968.

owner, and signed a lease the next day. Needless to say, a Benihana didn't go into the Marina Towers.

The number 3 unit in Chicago had proved to be the company's largest money maker. It was an instant success and grossed approximately $1.3 million per year. The food and beverage split was 70/30 and management was able to keep food (30%), labor (10%), advertising (10%), and rent (5%) expense percentages at relatively low levels.

The fourth unit was San Francisco and the fifth was a joint venture in Las Vegas in 1969. By this time literally hundreds of people were clamoring for franchises. Rocky sold a total of six until he decided in 1970 that it would be much more to his advantage to own his units rather than franchise them. Following are the franchises that were granted:

Puerto Rico	(Not successful due to economic turndown)
Harrisburg, Penn.	
Ft. Lauderdale	
Portland	(Company bought unit back)
Seattle	
Beverly Hills	
Boston	

The decision to stop franchising was because of a number of problems. First, all the franchises were bought by investors, none of whom had any restaurant experience. Second, it was difficult for the American investor to relate to a predominately native Japanese staff. Finally, control was considerably more difficult to maintain with a franchisee than a company employee manager. During the period to 1970 several groups attempted to imitate the Benihana success. One even included a group with intimate knowledge of the Benihana operation who set up in very close proximity to one Benihana unit. They, however, folded within the year. Bolstered by the confidence that the Benihana success could not be easily replicated, management felt that one of the classic pressures to franchise was eliminated—i.e., to expand extremely rapidly to preempt competitors.

The amount of space devoted to the bar/lounge/holding area accurately indicates when the unit was built. When Rocky opened his first unit, he saw the business as primarily food-service sales. The Benihana West had a tiny bar that seated about eight and had no lounge area. Rocky quickly learned that this amount of bar space was insufficient, and at the second unit, Benihana East, he doubled the size of the bar/lounge area. But since the whole unit was larger, the ratio of space was not too different. A typical floor plan is included as Exhibit 2.

His third Manhattan operation, called Benihana Palace, opened in 1970. Here, the bar/lounge area was enormous, even in ratio to size. 1972 figures bear out the wisdom of the growth. At West, beverage sales represented about 18% of total sales. At East, they ran 20–22%. And at the Palace, they ran a handsome 30–33% of total sales. The beverage cost averaged 20% of beverage sales.

The heart of the "show biz" was in the dining area. The "teppanyaki" table was comprised of a steel griddle plate, with a 9½″ wooden ledge bordering it to hold the ware. It was gas-fired. Above every table was an exhaust hood to remove cooking steam and odors and much of the heat from the griddle. Service was provided by a chef and waitress; each such team handled two regular tables.

The four food items—steak, filet mignon, chicken, and shrimp—could either be had as single entree items or in combinations. A full dinner had three, with the shrimp as appetizer. The accompaniments were unvaried: bean sprouts, zucchini, fresh mushrooms, onions, and rice.

Normally, a customer could come in, be seated, have dinner, and be on his way out in 45 minutes, if need be. The average turnover was an hour, up to an hour and a half in slow periods.

The average check, including food and beverage, ran about $6 at lunch, about $10 at dinner. These figures included a drink (average price $1.50) at lunch, an average of one-plus at dinner.

The big purchase was meat. Only U.S.D.A. Prime Grade, tightly specified tenderloin and boneless strip loins were used. The steaks were further trimmed in house. Only a bit of fat at the tail was left, which was for effect only. When the chef began cooking the meat, he dramatically trimmed this part off and pushed it aside before cubing the remaining meat.

The hours of operation for the 15 units varied according to local requirements. All were open for lunch and dinner, though not necessarily every day for each. Lunch business was important; overall it accounted for about 30–40% of the total dollar volume despite a significantly lower check average. Essentially the same menu items were served for both meals; the lower menu price average at lunch reflected smaller portions and fewer combinations.

SITE SELECTION

Because of the importance of lunchtime business, Benihana had one basic criterion for site selection—high traffic. Management wanted to be sure that a lot of people were nearby or going by both at lunch and at dinner. Rent normally ran 5–7% of sales for 5,000–6,000 square feet of floor space. Most units were located in a predominately business district, though some had easy access to residential areas. Shopping center locations were considered, but had not been accepted by 1972.

TRAINING

Because the chef was considered by Benihana to be a key to its success, all of them were very highly trained. All were young, single, native Japanese and all were "certified," which meant that they had completed a three-year formal apprenticeship. They were then given a three- to six-month course in Japan in the English language and American manner as well as the Benihana form of cooking, which was mostly showmanship. The chefs were brought to the United States under a "trade treaty" agreement.

Training the chefs within the United States was also a continuous process. In addition to the competition among the chefs to perfect their art in hopes of becoming the chief chef, there was also a traveling chef who inspected each unit periodically as well as being involved in the grand opening of new units.

While Benihana found it relatively difficult to attract chefs and other personnel from Japan due to the general level of prosperity there as well as competition from other restaurants bidding for their talents, once in the United States they were generally not anxious to leave. This was due to several factors. One was the rapidity with which they could rise in the U.S. Benihana operation versus the rather rigid hierarchy based on class, age, and education they would face in Japan. A second and major factor was the paternal attitude that Benihana took toward all its employees. While personnel were well paid in a tangible sense, a large part of the compensation was intangible, based on job security and a total commitment of Benihana to the well-being of its employees. As a result, turnover of personnel within the United States was very low, although most did eventually return to Japan. To fully appreciate the Benihana success, the unique combination of Japanese paternalism in an American setting must be appreciated. Or, as Rocky puts it; "At Benihana we combine Japanese workers with American management techniques."

ORGANIZATION AND CONTROL

Each restaurant carried a simple management structure. It had a manager ($15,000/year), an assistant manager ($12,000/year), and two or three "front men" ($9000/year), who might be likened to maitre d's. These front men were really potential managers in training. All managers reported to the manager of operations Allen Saito who, in turn, reported to Bill Susha, vice-president in charge of operations and business development (see Exhibit 3).

Susha came to Benihana in 1971, following food and beverage experience with Hilton, Loew's, and the Flagship Hotel Division of American Airlines. He described his job as follows:

> I see management growth as a priority objective. My first step was to establish some sort of control system by introducing sales goals and budgets. At the most recent manager workshop meeting in New York, with managers from all over the country, I asked each to project his sales goal on an annual basis, then break it out by month, then by week, then by day. After I reached agreement with a manager on the individual quota figures, I instituted a bonus plan. Any unit that exceeds its quota on any basis—daily, weekly, monthly, yearly—will get a proportionate bonus, which will be prorated across the entire staff of the unit. I've also built up an accounting staff and controller to monitor our costs. It's been a slow but steady process. We have to be very careful to balance our needs for control with the amount of overhead we can stand. We

Exhibit 2

BENIHANA OF TOKYO
A Typical Benihana Floor Plan

2 Towel washer by Hamilton
3 Work table, custom
4 Work table, custom
5 Three-compartment sink, custom
6 Double overshelf, custom
7 Double slant overshelf, custom
8 Rice stocker, custom
9 Rice cooker
10 Range with oven by Vulcan Hart
11 Stock pot stove by Vulcan Hart
12 Swing faucet
13 Exhaust hood, custom
15 Reach-in refrigerator by Traulsen
16 Scale by Howe Richardson
17 Combination walk-in cooler-freezer by Bally
18 Adjustable modular shelving by Market Forge
19 Adjustable modular shelving by Market Forge
20 Shelf, custom
21 Dishwasher with electric booster by Champion
22 Soiled dishtable with prerinse sink, custom
23 Slant overshelf, custom
24 Clean dishtable, custom
25 Exhaust hood, custom
26 Double wallshelf, custom
27 Twin soup urn by Cecilware
28 Single tea urn by Cecilware
29 Towel warmer
30 Water station with sink, custom
31 Rice warmer
32 Utility table, custom
33 Double wallshelf, custom
34 Two-compartment sink, custom
35 Overshelf, custom
36 Work table, custom
37 Open-front cold cast with adjustable shelves by Tyler
38 Double overshelf, custom
39 Precheck register by NCR
40 Utility table with dipperwell, custom
41 Double overshelf, custom
42 Ice cream dipping cabinet by Schaefer
43 Ice cream storage cabinet by Schaefer
44 Double wallshelf, custom
45 Reach-in freezer by Traulsen
46 Ice cube maker by Kold Draft
47 Ice crusher by Scotsman
48 Adjustable modular shelving by Market Forge
49 Pass-through refrigerator by Traulsen
50 Sake warmer
51 Cash register by NCR
52 Underbar workboard by Perlick
54 Back bar refrigerator by Perlick
56 Underbar bottle cooler by Perlick
57 Remote soda system dispensing station by Perlick
58 Remote soda system power pak with stand by Perlick
59 Precheck register by NCR
60 Cash register by NCR
61 Shelving, custom
62 Glasswasher by Dorex
63 Time clock
64 Telephone shelf booth
65 Platform truck by Roll A. Liss
66 Utility table, custom

can justify extra "front men" standing around in the units. At the corporate level, however, we have to be very careful. In fact, at the present the company is essentially being run by three people—Rocky, myself, and Allen Saito.

ADVERTISING POLICY

Rocky considered that a vitally important factor in Benihana's success was a substantial investment in creative advertising and public relations. The company invested 8–10% of its gross sales on reaching the public.

Exhibit 2 (continued)

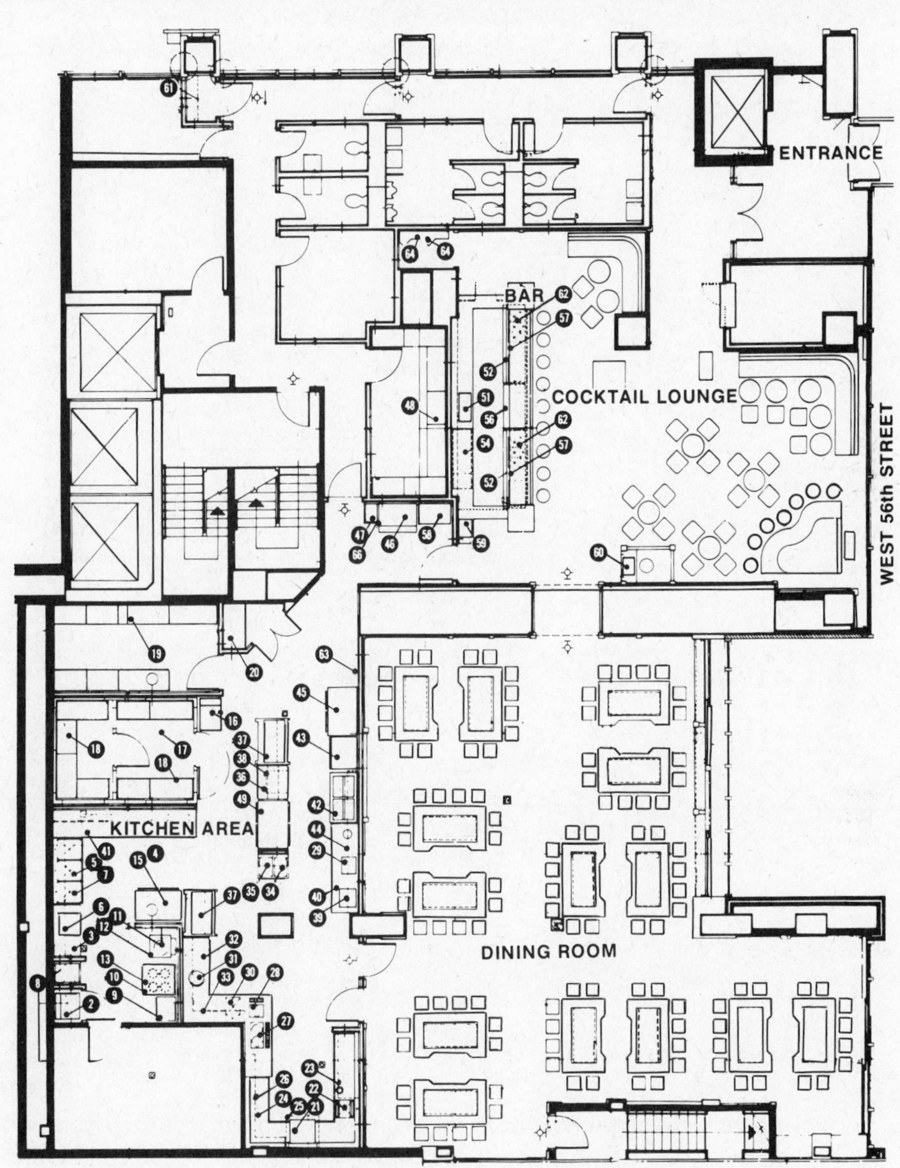

Glen Simoes, the director of advertising and public relations summed it up:

We deliberately try to be different and original in our advertising approach. We never place advertisements on the entertainment pages of newspapers on the theory that they would be lost among the countless other restaurant advertisements.

Exhibit 3

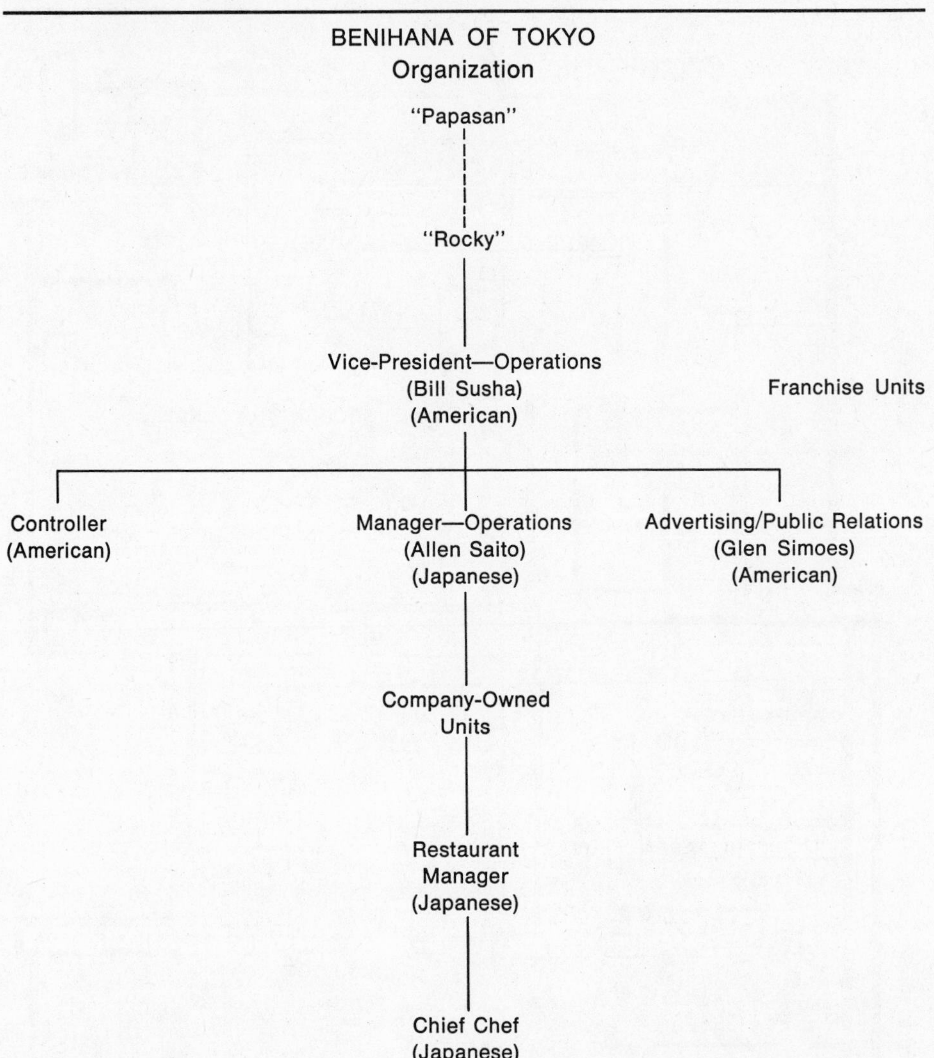

> We have a visual product to sell. Therefore, Benihana utilizes outstanding visuals in its ads. The accompanying copy is contemporary, sometimes offbeat. A recent full-page advertisement which appeared in the *New York Times, Women's Wear Daily,* and *New York Magazine* did not contain the word "restaurant." We also conduct a considerable amount of market research to be sure we know who our customers really are.

Exhibit 4 shows the results of one market research survey. Exhibit 5 is a further discussion of Benihana advertising policy.

Exhibit 4

What the Customers Think

Every foodservice operator thinks he knows why customers come to his operation. Benihana, which has served two-and-a-quarter million customers in eight years, a high percentage of which were repeat business, thought it knew.

But when he joined as v-p of operations a year-and-a-half ago, Bill Susha wanted to be sure the hallowed presumptions were true.

He devised a questionnaire, and arranged that it be handed to departing customers. A remarkable number took the time to fill out and return the form.

The percentage figures shown here are averages of six stores. While there were many variations from unit to unit, the general thrust was constant, so the six-store figures have been averaged to save space.

The six units included the three in New York City, plus Chicago, Encino, Cal., and Portland, Ore. The questions and averages are as follows:

Question / Response	%
Are you from out-of-town?	
Yes	38.6%
No	61.4
Here on:	
Business	38.7%
Pleasure	61.3
Do you live in the area?	
Live	16.0%
Work	35.9
Both	45.1
Have you been to a Benihana in another city?	
Yes	22.9%
No	77.3
How did you learn of us?	
Newspaper	4.0%
Magazine	6.9
Radio	4.6
Recommended	67.0
TV show	1.0
Walk by	5.0
Other	11.5
Is this your first visit?	
Yes	34.3%
No	65.7
What persuaded you to come?	
Good food	46.7%
Service	8.2
Preparation	13.1
Atmosphere	13.3
Recommendation	5.7
Other	13.1
Food was:	
Good	2.0%
Satisfactory	20.1
Excellent	77.9
Portions were:	
Satisfactory	21.8%
Good	33.0
Excellent	45.4
Service was:	
Satisfactory	9.8%
Good	21.6
Excellent	71.3
Atmosphere is:	
Satisfactory	6.3%
Good	29.9
Excellent	63.2
Would you consider yourself a lunch or dinner customer?	
Lunch	17.3%
Dinner	59.0
Both	23.7
Which aspect of our restaurant would you highlight?	
Food	38.2%
Atmosphere	13.0
Preparation	24.6
Service	16.3
Different	2.2
Friendly	2.4
Other	3.3
How frequently do you come to Benihana?	
Once a week or more	12.1%
Once a month or more	32.5
Once a year or more	55.6
Age:	
10–20	4.2%
21–30	28.3
31–40	32.0
41–50	21.4
51–60	10.1
60 and over	4.0
Sex:	
Male	71.4%
Female	28.6
Income:	
$ 7,500–$10,000	16.8%
$10,000–$15,000	14.2
$15,000–$20,000	17.3
$20,000–$25,000	15.0
$25,000–$40,000	17.9
$40,000 and over	18.7
Occupation:	
Managerial	23.0%
Professional	26.6
White Collar	36.9
Student	6.9
Housewife	5.0
Unskilled	1.1

Exhibit 5

SUMMARY OF BENIHANA MARKETING PHILOSOPHY

No icky, sticky, slimy stuff

"Part of what makes Benihana successful," Rocky Aoki believes, "is our advertising and promotion. It's different, and it makes us seem different to people."

Indeed it is, and does. Much of the credit belongs to Glen Simoes, the hip director of advertising and public relations for Benihana of Tokyo. With a background mostly in financial public relations, Simoes joined the chain a little over two years ago to help open the flagship Benihana Palace. Since then, he's created a somewhat novel, all-embracing public relations program that succeeds on many levels.

"My basic job," he explains, "is guardian of the image. The image is that of a dynamic chain of Japanese restaurants with phenomenal growth." Keeping the image bright means exposure. Part of the exposure is a brilliant advertising campaign; part is publicity.

Each has its own function. Advertising is handled by Kracauer and Marvin, an outside agency, under Simoes' supervision and guidance. Its function is to bring in new customers.

"Our ads," Simoes points out, "are characterized by a bold headline statement and an illustration that make you want to read on. The copy itself is fairly clever and cute. If it works properly, it will keep you reading until you get the message—which is to persuade a stranger to come into Benihana.

"The ads are designed to still fears about icky, sticky, slimy stuff," he adds. "We reassure folks that they will get wholesome, familiar food, with unusual, unique and delicious preparation, served in a fun atmosphere. We want to intrigue the people celebrating an anniversary or taking Aunt Sally out to dinner. A Japanese restaurant would normally never cross their minds. We're saying we're a fun place to try, and there's no slithery, fishy stuff.

"We have an impact philosophy. We go for full pages in national publications on a now-and-then basis, rather than a regular schedule of small ads. We want that impact to bring the stranger into Benihana for the first time. After that, the restaurant will bring him back again and again, and he will bring his friends.

"We do a good media mix," Simoes concludes. "We advertise in each of the cities in which we operate. Within each market we aim for two people: the resident, of course, but even more, the tourist-visitor. With them you know you're always talking to new people. We appear in city entertainment guides and work with convention and visitor bureaus to go after groups and conventions."

The second factor is publicity. Here, the intent is not the quantity of mentions or exposure, but the type. As Simoes sees it, "We are building. Each mention is a building block. Some are designed to bring customers into the store. Some are designed to bring us prospective financing, or suppliers, or friends, or whatever. We work many ways against the middle. And the middle is the company, the people, Rocky, the growth and all of it put together that makes the image."

Publicity takes many forms, it's media stories, and TV demonstrations. Simoes cites clipping and viewing services to prove that every day of the year, something about Benihana appears either in print or on radio or TV, a record he believes is unique. Publicity is department store demonstrations, catering to celebrities, hosting youth groups, sending matchboxes to conventions and chopsticks to ladies' clubs, scheduling Rocky for interviews and paying publicists to provide oneliners to columnists.

But no engine runs without fuel. And Rocky believes that advertising and promotion are a good investment. Believes so strongly, in fact, that he puts an almost unprecedented $1 million a year into advertising, and probably half that again into promotion, for a total expenditure of nearly 8% of gross sales in this area.

A few months back, Simoes, wholeheartedly pitching his company to a skeptical magazine writer, said heatedly there are "at least 25 reasons people come to Benihana." Challenged on the spot, he came back a few days later with a list of 31. They are:

1) the quality of the food; 2) the presentation of the food; 3) the preparation of the food; 4) the showmanship of the chef; 5) the taste of the food; 6) authenticity of construction; 7) authenticity of decor; 8) continuity of Japanese flavor throughout; 9) communal dining; 10) service—constant attention.

11) Youthfulness of staff; 12) frequent presence of celebrities; 13) excitement created by frequent promotions; 14) type of cuisine; 15) moderate price; 16) the uniqueness of appeal to the five senses; 17) the recent growth in popularity of things Japanese; 18) quick service; 19) unusual advertising concept; 20) publicity.

21) No stringent dress requirements; 22) recommendations from friends; 23) the basic meal is low-calorie; 24) banquet and party facilities; 25) the presence of Rocky Aoki, himself; 26) chance to meet people of the opposite sex; 27) the presence of many Japanese customers (about 20%); 28) locations in major cities giving a radiation effect; 29) acceptance of all major credit cards; 30) the informality of the dining experience; and 31) the use of the restaurant as a business tool.

FUTURE EXPANSION

Bill Susha summed up the problems of the future as he saw them:

I think the biggest problems facing us now are how to expand. We tried franchising and decided to discontinue the program for several reasons. Most of our franchisees were businessmen looking for investment opportunities and did not really know and understand the restaurant business—this was a problem. The Japanese staff we provided were our people and we have obligations to them that the franchisee could not or would not honor which at the time made us unhappy. The uniqueness of our operation in the hands of novices made control more difficult. Finally, we found it more profitable to own and operate the restaurants ourselves.

Presently, we are limited to opening only five units a year, because that is as fast as the two crews of Japanese carpenters we have can work. We are facing a decision and weighing the advantages and disadvantages of going into hotels with our type of restaurant. We are presently in two Hilton Hotels (Las Vegas and Honolulu) and have recently signed an agreement with Canadian Pacific Hotels. What we have done in these deals is to put "teeth" in the agreements, so that we are not at the mercy of the hotel company's management.

Further, one of our biggest constraints is staff. Each unit requires approximately 30 people who are all Oriental. Six to eight of them are highly trained chefs.

Finally, there is the cost factor. Each new unit costs us a minimum of $300,000. My feeling is that we should confine ourselves to the major cities like Atlanta, Dallas, St. Louis, etc., in the near future. Then we can use all these units to expand into the suburbs.

We've been highly tempted to try to grow too fast without really considering the full implications of the move. One example was the franchise thing, but we found it unsatisfactory. Another example is that a large international banking organization offered to make a major investment in us which would have allowed us to grow at a terrific rate. But when we looked at the amount of control and autonomy we'd have to give up, it just wasn't worth it, at least in my mind.

Another thing I'm considering is whether it's worth it to import every item used in construction from Japan to make a Benihana 100% "authentic." Does an American really appreciate it and is it worth the cost? We could use material available here and achieve substantially the same effect. Also is it worth it to use Japanese carpenters and pay union carpenters to sit and watch? All these things could reduce our costs tremendously and allow us to expand much faster.

Rocky described his perception of where the firm should go:

I see three principal areas for growth, the United States, overseas, and Japan.

In the United States we need to expand into the primary marketing areas Bill talked about that do not have a Benihana. But I think through our franchises we also learned that secondary markets such as Harrisburg, Pennsylvania, and Portland, Oregon, also have potential. While their volume potential obviously will not match that of a primary market, these smaller units offer fewer headaches and generate nice profits. Secondary markets being considered include Cincinnati and Indianapolis.

The third principal area I see for growth is in suburbia. No sites have yet been set, but I think it holds a great potential. A fourth growth area, not given the importance of the others, is further penetration into existing markets. Saturation is not a problem as illustrated by the fact that New York and greater Los Angeles have three units each, all doing well.

We are also considering someday going public. In the meantime, we are moving into joint ventures in Mexico and overseas. Each joint venture is unique in itself. We negotiate each unit on the basis that will be most advantageous to the parties concerned taking into account the contributions of each party in the form of services and cash. Once this is established, we agree on a formula for profits and away we go.

Four deals have now been consummated. Three are joint ventures out of the country. An agreement has already been reached to open a Benihana in the Royal York Hotel, Toronto, Canada. This will provide the vanguard for a march across Canada with units in or outside Canadian Pacific Hotels.

Second is a signed agreement for a new unit in Mexico City. From here, negotiations are under way on a new hotel to be built in Acapulco. Benihana stands ready to build and operate a unit in the hotel or, if possible, to take over management of the entire hotel. These units would form a base for expansion throughout Mexico.

The third extraterritorial arrangement was recently signed with David Paradine, Ltd., a British firm of investors headed by TV personality David Frost. Again, this is a joint venture with the Paradine group to supply technical assistance, public relations, advertising, and financing, and Benihana the management and know-how. This venture hopes ultimately to have Benihana restaurants, not only throughout Great Britain, but across the Continent.

Rocky also had a number of diversification plans:

We have entered into an agreement with a firm that is researching and contacting large food processors in an effort to interest them into producing a line of Japanese food products under the Benihana label for retail sale. There has been a great deal of interest and we are close to concluding a deal.

I worry a lot. Right now we cater to a middle-income audience, not the younger generation. That makes a difference. We charge more, serve better quality, have a better atmosphere, and more service. But we are in the planning stages for operations with appeal to the younger generation.

For instance, there is no Japanese quick service operation in this country. I think we should go into a combination Chinese-Japanese operation like this. The unit would also feature a dynamic cooking show exposed to the customers. Our initial projections show margins comparable to our present margins with Benihana of Tokyo. I see a check of about 99 cents. We are negotiating with an oil company to put small units in gas stations. They could be located anywhere—on turnpikes or in the Bronx. I think we should do this very soon. We might call it the "Orient Express." I think I will get a small store in Manhattan and try it out. This is the best kind of market research in the United States. Market research works in other countries, but I don't believe in it here. We are also negotiating for a site on Guam and to take over a chain of beer halls in Japan.

The restaurant business is not my only business. I went into producing; I had two unsuccessful Broadway shows. The experience was very expensive, but I learned a great deal and learned it very fast. It's all up to the critics there. In the restaurant business, the critics don't write much about you if you're bad; but even if they do they can't kill you. On Broadway they can. They did.

I promoted a heavyweight boxing match in Japan. It was successful. I am going into promoting in the entertainment field in Japan. I am doing a Renoir exhibition in Japan with an auction over television. I am thinking about buying a Japanese movie series and bringing it here. I am also thinking of opening a model agency, probably specializing in Oriental models.

My philosophy of the restaurant business is simply to make people happy. We do it many ways in Benihana. As we start different types of operations, we will try to do it in other ways. I have no real worries about the future. The United States is the greatest country in the world to make money. Anybody can do it who wants to work hard and make people happy.

Russ Carpenter, a consultant and editor for *Institutions/Volume Feeding* magazine summed up his perceptions as follows:

I basically see two main problems.

What is Benihana really selling? Is it food, atmosphere, hospitality, a "watering hole" or what? Is having entertainment in the lounge consistent with the overall image? All the advertising emphasizes the chef and the food, but is that really what the public comes for? I don't know. I'm only raising the questions.

The other thing is how do you hedge your bets? Is Benihana really on the forefront of a trend of the future with their limited menu, cooking in front of you, and Oriental atmosphere or is it just a fad? This relates to whether the firm should emphasize restaurant operations only.

Production-Line Approach to Service

THEODORE LEVITT

Once service "in the field" receives the same attention as products "in the factory," a lot of new opportunities become possible

The service sector of the economy is growing in size but shrinking in quality. So say a lot of people. Purveyors of service, for their part, think that they and their problems are fundamentally different from other businesses and their problems. They feel that service is people-intensive, while the rest of the economy is capital-intensive. But these distinctions are largely spurious. There are no such things as service industries. There are only industries whose service components are greater or less than those of other industries. Everybody is in service.

Often the less there seems, the more there is. The more technologically sophisticated the generic product (e.g., cars and computers), the more dependent are its sales on the quality and availability of its accompanying customer services (e.g., display rooms, delivery, repairs and maintenance, application aids, operator training, installation advice, warranty fulfillment). In this sense, General Motors is probably more service-intensive than manufacturing-intensive. Without its services its sales would shrivel.

Thus the service sector of the economy is not merely comprised of the so-called service industries, such as banking, airlines, and maintenance. It includes the entire abundance of product-related services supplied by manufacturers and the sales-related services supplied by retailers. Yet we confuse things to our detriment by an outdated taxonomy. For example:

The First National City Bank (Citibank) is one of the biggest worldwide banks. It has about 37,000 employees, over half of whom deal directly with the public, either selling them things (mostly money and deposit services) or helping them with things they have already bought (cashing checks, taking additional deposits, writing letters of credit, opening lockboxes, managing corporate cash). Most of the other employees work back in what is called "the factory"—a massive congeries of people, paper, and computers that processes, records, validates, and scrutinizes everything the first group has done. All the corporate taxonomists, including the U.S. Department of the Census, classify Citibank as a service company.

IBM is the biggest worldwide manufacturer of computers. It has about 270,000 employees, over half of whom deal directly with the public, either selling them

Source: Theodore Levitt, "Production-Line Approach to Service," *Harvard Business Review* (September–October 1972), pp. 41–52.

things (mostly machines) or helping them with the things they have already bought (installing and repairing machines, writing computer programs, training customers). Most of the other employees work back in the factory—a massive congeries of wires, microminiature electronic components, engineers, and assemblers. All the corporate taxonomists, including the U.S. Department of the Census, classify IBM as a manufacturing company.

Something is wrong, and not just in the Bureau of the Census. The industrial world has changed more rapidly than our taxonomies. If only taxonomy were involved, the consequences of our contradictory classifications would be trivial. After all, man lives perfectly well with his contradictions: his simultaneous faith, for instance, in both God and science; his attachment to facts and logic when making important business decisions, but reliance on feelings and emotion when making far more important life decisions, like marriage.

I hope to show in this article that our contradictory notions about service may have malignant consequences. Not until we clarify the contradictions will companies begin to solve problems that now seem so intractible. In order to do so, they must think of themselves as performing manufacturing functions when it comes to their so-called "service" activities. Only then will they begin to make some significant progress in improving the quality and efficiency of service in the modern economy.

FIELD VERSUS FACTORY

People think of service as quite different from manufacturing. Service is presumed to be performed by individuals for other individuals, generally on a one-to-one basis. Manufacturing is presumed to be performed by machines, generally tended by large clusters of individuals whose sizes and configurations are themselves dictated by the machines' requirements. Service (whether customer service or the services of service industries) is performed "out there in the field" by distant and loosely supervised people working under highly variable, and often volatile, conditions. Manufacturing occurs "here in the factory" under highly centralized, carefully organized, tightly controlled, and elaborately engineered conditions.

People assume, and rightly so, that these differences largely explain why products produced in the factory are generally more uniform in features and quality than the services produced (e.g., life insurance policies, machine repairs) or delivered (e.g., spare parts, milk) in the field. One cannot as easily control one's agents or their performance out there in the field. Besides, different customers want different things. The result is that service and service industries, in comparison with manufacturing industries, are widely and correctly viewed as being primitive, sluggish, and inefficient.

Yet it is doubtful that things need be all that bad. Once conditions in the field get the same kind of attention that conditions inside the factory generally get, a lot of new opportunities become possible. But first management will have to revise its thinking about what service is and what it implies.

Limits of Servitude

The trouble with thinking of oneself as providing services—either in the service industries or in the customer-service sectors of manufacturing and retailing companies—is that one almost inescapably embraces ancient, pre-industrial modes of thinking. Worse still, one gets caught up in rigid attitudes that can have a profoundly paralyzing effect on even the most resolute of rationalists.

The concept of "service" evokes, from the opaque recesses of the mind, timeworn images of personal ministration and attendance. It refers generally to deeds one individual performs personally for another. It carries historical connotations of charity, gallantry, and selflessness, or of obedience, subordination, and subjugation. In these contexts, people serve because they want to (as in the priestly and political professions) or they serve because they are compelled to (as in slavery and such occupations of attendance as waiter, maid, bellboy, cleaning lady).

In the higher-status service occupations, such as in the church and the army, one customarily behaves ritualistically, not rationally. In the lower-status service occupations, one simply obeys. In neither is independent thinking presumed to be a requisite of holding a job. The most that can therefore be expected from service improvements is that, like Avis, a person will try harder. He will just exert more animal effort to do better what he is already doing.

So it was in ancient times, and so it is today. The only difference is that where ancient masters invoked the will of God or the whip of the foreman to spur performance, modern industry uses training programs and motivation sessions. We have not in all these years come very far in either our methods or our results. In short, service thinks humanistically, and that explains its failures.

Promise of Manufacturing

Now consider manufacturing. Here the orientation is toward the efficient production of results, not toward attendance on others. Relationships are strictly businesslike, devoid of invidious connotations of rank or self.

When we think about how to improve manufacturing, we seldom focus on ways to improve our personal performance of present tasks; rather, it is axiomatic that we try to find entirely new ways of performing present tasks and, better yet, of actually changing the tasks themselves. We do not think of greater exertion of our animal energies (working physically harder, as the slave), of greater expansion of our commitment (being more devout or loyal, as the priest), or of greater assertion of our dependence (being more obsequious, as the butler).

Instead, we apply the greater exertion of our minds to learn how to look at a problem differently. More particularly, we ask what kinds of tools, old or new, and what kinds of skills, processes, organizational rearrangements, incentives, controls, and audits might be enlisted to greatly improve the intended outcomes. In short, manufacturing thinks technocratically, and that explains its successes.

Manufacturing looks for solutions inside the very tasks to be done. The solution to building a low-priced automobile, for example, derives largely from the nature and composition of the automobile itself. (If the automobile were not an assembly of parts, it could not be manufactured on an assembly line.) By contrast, service looks for solutions in the *performer* of the task. This is the paralyzing legacy of our inherited attitudes: the solution to improved service is viewed as being dependent on improvements in the skills and attitudes of the performers of that service.

While it may pain and offend us to say so, thinking in humanistic rather than technocratic terms ensures that the service sector of the modern economy will be forever inefficient and that our satisfactions will be forever marginal. We see service as invariably and undeviatingly personal, as something performed by individuals directly for other individuals.

This humanistic conception of service diverts us from seeking alternatives to the use of people, especially to large, organized groups of people. It does not allow us to reach out for new solutions and new definitions. It obstructs us from redesigning the tasks themselves; from creating new tools, processes, and organizations; and, perhaps, even from eliminating the conditions that created the problems.

In sum, to improve the quality and efficiency of service, companies must apply the kind of technocratic thinking which in other fields has replaced the high-cost and erratic elegance of the artisan with the low-cost, predictable munificence of the manufacturer.

THE TECHNOCRATIC HAMBURGER

Nowhere in the entire service sector are the possibilities of the manufacturing mode of thinking better illustrated than in fast-food franchising. Nowhere have manufacturing methods been employed more effectively to control the operation of distant and independent agents. Nowhere is "service" better.

Few of today's successful new commercial ventures have antecedents that are more humble and less glamorous than the hamburger. Yet the thriving nationwide chain of hamburger stands called "McDonald's" is a supreme example of the application of manufacturing and technological brilliance to problems that must ultimately be viewed as marketing problems. From 1961 to 1970 McDonald's sales rose from approximately $54 million to $587 million. During this remarkable ascent, the White Tower chain, whose name had theretofore been practically synonymous throughout the land with low-priced, quick-service hamburgers, practically vanished.

The explanation of McDonald's thundering success is not a purely fiscal one —i.e., the argument that it is financed by independent local entrepreneurs who bring to their operations a quality of commitment and energy not commonly found among hired workers. Nor is it a purely geographical one—i.e., the argument that each outlet draws its patronage from a relatively small geographic ring of customers, thus enabling the number of outlets easily and quickly to multiply. The relevant explanation must deal with the central question of why each separate McDonald's outlet is so predictably successful, why each is so certain to attract many repeat customers.

Entrepreneurial financing and careful site selection do help. But most important is the carefully controlled execution of each outlet's central function—the rapid delivery of a uniform, high-quality mix of prepared foods in an environment of obvious cleanliness, order, and cheerful courtesy. The systematic substitution of equipment for people, combined with the carefully planned use and positioning of technology, enables McDonald's to attract and hold patronage in proportions no predecessor or imitator has managed to duplicate. Consider the remarkable ingenuity of the system, which is worth examining in some detail:

To start with the obvious, raw hamburger patties are carefully prepacked and premeasured, which leaves neither the franchisee nor his employees any discretion as to size, quality, or raw-material consistency. This kind of attention is given to all McDonald's products. Storage and preparation space and related facilities are expressly designed for, and limited to, the predetermined mix of products. There is no space for any foods, beverages, or services that were not designed into the system at the outset. There is not even a sandwich knife or, in fact, a decent place to keep one. Thus the owner has no discretion regarding what he can sell—not because of any contractual limitations, but because of facilities limitations. And the employees have virtually no discretion regarding how to prepare and serve things.

Discretion is the enemy of order, standardization, and quality. On an automobile assembly line, for example, a worker who has discretion and latitude might possibly produce a more personalized car, but one that is highly unpredictable. The elaborate care with which an automobile is designed and an assembly line is structured and controlled is what produces quality cars at low prices, and with surprising reliability considering the sheer volume of the output. The same is true at McDonald's, which produces food under highly automated and controlled conditions.

French-Fried Automation

While in Detroit the significance of the technological process lies in production, at McDonald's it lies in marketing. A carefully planned design is built into the elaborate technology of the food-service system in such a fashion as to make it a significant marketing device. This fact is impressively illustrated by McDonald's handling of that uniquely plebeian American delicacy, french-fried potatoes.

French fries become quickly soggy and unappetizing; to be good, they must be freshly made just before serving. Like other fast-food establishments, McDonald's provides its outlets with precut, partially cooked frozen potatoes that can be quickly finished in an on-premises, deep-fry facility. The McDonald's fryer is neither so large that it produces too many fresh fries at one time (thus allowing them to become soggy) nor so small that it requires frequent and costly frying.

The fryer is emptied onto a wide, flat tray adjacent to the service counter. This location is crucial. Since the McDonald's practice is to create an impression of abundance and generosity by slightly overfilling each bag of french fries, the tray's location next to the service counter prevents the spillage from an overfilled bag from reaching the floor. Spillage creates not only danger underfoot but also an unattractive appearance that causes the employees to become accustomed to an unclean environment. Once a store is unclean in one particular, standards fall very rapidly and the store becomes unclean and the food unappetizing in general.

While McDonald's aims for an impression of abundance, excessive overfilling can be very costly for a company that annually buys potatoes almost by the trainload. A systematic bias that puts into each bag of french fries a half ounce more than is intended can have visible effects on the company's annual earnings. Further, excessive time spent at the tray by each employee can create a cumulative service bottleneck at the counter.

McDonald's has therefore developed a special wide-mouthed scoop with a narrow funnel in its handle. The counter employee picks up the scoop and inserts the handle end into a wall clip containing the bags. One bag adheres to the handle. In a continuous movement the scoop descends into the potatoes, fills the bag to the exact proportions its designers intended, and is lifted, scoop facing the ceiling, so that the potatoes funnel through the handle into the attached bag, which is automatically disengaged from the handle by the weight of the contents. The bag comes to a steady, nonwobbling rest on its flat bottom.

Nothing can go wrong—the employee never soils his hands, the floor remains clean, dry, and safe, and the quantity is controlled. Best of all, the customer gets a visibly generous portion with great speed, the employee remains efficient and cheerful, and the general impression is one of extravagantly good service.

Mechanized Marketing

Consider the other aspects of McDonald's technological approach to marketing. The tissue paper used to wrap each hamburger is color-coded to denote the mix of condiments. Heated reservoirs hold pre-prepared hamburgers for rush demand. Frying surfaces have spatter guards to prevent soiling of the cooks' uniforms. Nothing is left to chance or the employees' discretion.

The entire system is engineered and executed according to a tight technological discipline that ensures fast, clean, reliable service in an atmosphere that gives the modestly paid employees a sense of pride and dignity. In spite of the crunch of eager customers, no employee looks or acts harassed, and therefore no harassment is communicated to the customers.

But McDonald's goes even further. Customers may be discouraged from entering if the building looks unappealing from the outside; hence considerable care goes into the design and appearance of the structure itself.

Some things, however, the architect cannot control, especially at an establishment where people generally eat in their parked cars and are likely to drop hamburger wrappings and empty beverage cartons on the ground. McDonald's has anticipated the requirement: its blacktop parking facilities are dotted like a checkerboard with numerous large, highly visible trash cans. It is impossible to ignore their purpose. Even the most indifferent customer would be struck with guilt if he simply dropped his refuse on the ground. But, just in case he drops it anyway, the larger McDonald's outlets have motorized sweepers for quick and easy cleanup.

What is important to understand about this remarkably successful organization is not only that it has created a highly sophisticated piece of technology, but also that it has done this by applying a manufacturing style of thinking to a people-intensive service situation. If machinery is to be viewed as a piece of equipment with the capability of producing a predictably standardized, customer-satisfying output while minimizing the operating discretion of its attendant, that is what a McDonald's retail outlet is. It is a machine that produces, with the help of totally unskilled machine tenders, a highly polished product. Through painstaking attention to total design and facilities planning, everything is built integrally into the machine itself, into the technology of the system. The only choice available to the attendant is to operate it exactly as the designers intended.

TOOLING UP FOR SERVICE

Although most people are not aware of it, there are many illustrations of manufacturing solutions to people-intensive service problems. For example:

Mutual funds substitute one sales call for many; one consultation for dozens; one piece of paper for thousands; and one reasonably informed customer choice for numerous, confused, and often poor choices.

Credit cards that are used for making bank loans substitute a single credit decision (issuing the card in the first place) for the many elaborate, costly, people-intensive activities and decisions that bank borrowing generally entails.

Supermarkets substitute fast and efficient self-service for the slow, inefficient, and often erratic clerks of the traditional service store.

In each of these examples a technological device or a manufacturing type of process has replaced what had been resolutely thought of as an irrevocably people-requiring service. Similar devices or processes can be used to modify and alleviate the customer-repelling abrasions of other people-intensive service conditions.

Consider the airlines. This industry is highly unusual. It is exceedingly capital-intensive in the creation of the facilitating product (the airplane), but it is extremely people-intensive in the delivery of the product (travel arrangements and the customer's flight experience). The possibilities for revenue production that a $20-million airplane represents are quickly vitiated by a surly or uncooperative reservations clerk. The potentials of repeat business that the chef so carefully builds into his meals can be destroyed by a dour or sloppy stewardess.

In fact, stewardesses have a particularly difficult job. A hundred passengers, having paid for reasonable service, understandably expect to be treated with some care. While three young ladies are there to serve them, a number of these passengers must inevitably get their drinks and meals later than others. Most experienced travelers are understanding and tolerant of the rushed stewardesses' problems, but a few usually harass them. The pressure and abuse can easily show in the stewardesses' personal appearance and behavior, and are likely to result in nearly all passengers being reciprocally mistreated. This is human. Besides, the ladies may have been on their feet all day, or may have slept only a few hours the night before.

"More and better training" is not likely to help things very much. When the pressure is on, service deteriorates. And so does a stewardess's cheerful manner and appearance, no matter how well schooled she is in personal care and keeping her cool or how attractively her clothes are designed.

But it might help to put mirrors in the airplane galley, so that each time a stewardess goes in she sees herself. There is some reason to expect that she'll look into the mirror each time she passes it, and that she'll straighten her hair, eliminate that lipstick smudge, put on a more cheerful face. Improvement will be instantaneous. No training needed.

Here is another possibility: the stewardess makes a quick trip down the aisle, passing out rum-flavored bonbons and explaining, "For those who can't wait till we get the ice out." This breaks the tension, produces an air of cheerfulness, acknowledges the passengers' eagerness for quick service, and says that the ladies are trying their hurried best. Further, it brings the stewardess into friendly personal contact with the passenger and reduces the likelihood of her being pressured and abused. She, in turn, is less likely to irritate other passengers.

From the manufacturing point of view, these two modest proposals represent the substitution of tools (or, as I prefer, technology) for motivation. Mirrors are a tool for getting self-motivated, automatic results in the stewardesses' appearance and personal behavior. Bonbons are a tool for creating a benign interpersonal ambience that reduces both the likelihood of customer irritation and the reciprocal and contagious stewardess irritation of others. They are small measures, but so is a company president's plant tour.

In each case there is considerable presumption of solid benefits. Yet to get these benefits one must think, as the factory engineer thinks, about what the problems are and what the desired output is; about how to redesign the process and how to install new tools that do the job more automatically; and, whenever people are involved, about how to "control" their personal behavior and channel their choices.

Hard & Soft Technologies

There are numerous examples of strictly "hard" technologies (i.e., pieces of equipment) which are used as substitutes for people—coffee vending machines for waitresses, automatic check-cashing machines for bank tellers, self-operated travel-insurance-policy machines for clerks. Although these devices represent a manufacturing approach to service, and while their principles can be extended to other fields, even greater promise lies in the application of "soft" technologies (i.e., technological systems). McDonald's is an example of a soft technology. So are mutual funds. Other examples are all around us, if we just think of them in the right way. Take the life insurance industry:

A life insurance salesman is said to be in a service industry. Yet what does he really do? He researches the prospect's needs by talking with him, designs several policy models for him, and "consumer-use tests" these models by seeking his reactions. Then he redesigns the final model and delivers it for sale to the customer. This is the ultimate example of manufacturing in the field. The factory is in the customer's living room, and the producer is the insurance agent, whom we incorrectly think of as being largely a salesman. Once we think of him as a manufacturer, however, we begin to think of how best to design and manufacture the product rather than how best to sell it.

The agent, for example, could be provided with a booklet of overlay sheets showing the insurance plans of people who are similar to the customer. This gives the customer a more credible and informed basis for making a choice. In time, the agent could be further supported by similar information stored in telephone-access computers.

In short, we begin to think of building a system that will allow the agent to produce his product efficiently and effectively by serving the customer's needs instead of performing a manipulative selling job.

Manufacturers Outside the Factory

The type of thinking just described applies not only to service industries but also to manufacturing industries. When the computer hardware manufacturer provides installation and maintenance services, debugging dry-runs, software programs, and operator training as part of his hardware sales program, he acknowledges that his "product" consists of considerably more than what he made in the factory. What is done in the field is just as important to the customer as the manufactured equipment itself. Indeed, without these services there would generally be no sale.

The problem in so many cases is that customer service is not viewed by manufacturers as an integral part of what the customer buys, but as something peripheral to landing the sale. However, when it is explicitly accepted as integral to the product itself and, as a consequence, gets the same kind of dedicated attention as the manufacture of the hardware gets, the results can be spectacular. For example:

In the greeting card industry, some manufacturer-provided retail display cases have built-in inventory replenishment and reordering features. In effect, these features replace a company salesman with the willing efforts of department managers or store owners. The motivation of the latter to reorder is created by the visible imminence of stockouts, which is achieved with a special color-coded card that shows up as the stock gets low. Order numbers and envelopes are included for reordering. In earlier days a salesman had to call, take inventory, arrange the stock, and write orders. Stockouts were common.

The old process was called customer service and selling. The new process has no name, and probably has never been viewed as constituting a technological substitute for people. But it is. An efficient, automatic, capital-intensive system, supplemented occasionally by people, has replaced an inefficient and unreliable people-intensive system.

In a more complex situation, the A. O. Smith Company has introduced the same kind of preplanning, routinizing, people-conserving activity. This company makes, among other things, grain storage silos that must be locally sold, installed, serviced, and financed. There are numerous types of silos with a great variety of accessories for loading, withdrawing, and automatically mixing livestock feed. The selling is carried out by local distributor-erectors and is a lengthy, difficult, sophisticated operation.

Instead of depending solely on the effective training of distributors, who are spread widely in isolated places, A. O. Smith has developed a series of sophisticated, colorful, and interchangeable design-module planning books. These can be easily employed by a distributor to help a farmer decide what he may need, its cost, and its financing requirements. Easy-to-read tables, broken down by the size of farm, numbers and types of animals, and purpose of animals (cattle for meat or cows for milk), show recommended combinations of silo sizes and equipment for maximum effectiveness.

The system is so thorough, so easy to use and understand, and so effective in its selling capacity that distributors use it with great eagerness. As a consequence, A. O. Smith, while sitting in Milwaukee, in effect controls every sales presentation made by every one of its far-flung distributors. Instead of constantly sending costly company representatives out to retrain, cajole, wine-and-dine, and possibly antagonize distributors, the supplier sends out a tool that distributors *want* to utilize in their own self-interest.

Product-Line Pragmatics

Thinking of service as an integral part of what is sold can also result in alteration of the product itself—and with dramatic results. In 1961, the Building Controls and Components Group of Honeywell, Inc., the nation's largest producer of heating and air conditioning thermostats and control devices, did a major part of its business in replacement controls (the aftermarket). These were sold through heating and air conditioning distributors, who then supplied plumbers and other installation and repair specialists.

At that time, Honeywell's product line consisted of nearly 18,000 separate catalog parts and pieces. The company had nearly 5,000 distributor accounts, none of which could carry a full line of these items economically, and therefore it maintained nearly 100 fully stocked field warehouses that offered immediate delivery to distributors. The result was that, in a large proportion of cases, distributors sold parts to plumbers that they did not themselves have in stock. They either sent plumbers to nearby Honeywell warehouses for pickup or picked up parts themselves and delivered them directly to the plumbers. The costs to Honeywell of carrying these inventories were enormous, but were considered a normal expense of doing business.

Then Honeywell made a daring move—it announced its new Tradeline Policy. It would close all warehouses. All parts would have to be stocked by the distributors. The original equipment, however, had been redesigned into 300 standard, interchangeable parts. These were interchangeable not only for most Honeywell controls, but also for those of its major competitors. Moreover, each package was clearly imprinted to show exactly what Honeywell and competing products were repairable with the contents.

By closing its own warehouses, Honeywell obviously shifted the inventory-carrying costs to its distributors. But instead of imposing new burdens on them, the new product lines, with their interchangeability features, enabled the distributors to carry substantially lower inventories, particularly by cutting down the need for competitive product lines which the distributors could nonetheless continue to service. Thus they were able to offer faster service at lower costs to their customers than before.

But not all distributors were easily persuaded of this possibility, and some dropped the line. Those who were persuaded ultimately proved their wisdom by the enormous expansion of their sales. Honeywell's replacement market share almost doubled, and its original equipment share rose by nearly 50%. Whereas previously nearly 90% of Honeywell's replacement sales were scattered among 4,000 distributors, within ten years after Tradeline's introduction the same proportion (of a doubled volume) was concentrated among only about 900 distributors. Honeywell's cost of servicing these fewer customers was substantially less, its trade inventory carrying costs were cut to zero, and the quality of its distributor services was so substantially improved that only 900 of its distributors captured a larger national market share than did the nearly 4,000 less efficient and more costly distributors.

Again, we see a people-intensive marketing problem being solved by the careful and scrupulous application of manufacturing attitudes. Motivation, hard work, personalization, training, and merchandising incentives were replaced with systematic programming, comprehensive planning, attention to detail, and particularly with imaginative concern for the problems and needs of customers (in this case, the company's distributors).

STOPGAPS: COMPLEXITY . . .

Exaggeration is not without its merits, especially in love and war. But in business one guards against it with zeal, especially when one tries to persuade oneself. The judicious application of the manufacturing mentality may help the service industries and the customer-service activities of others. Yet this does not necessarily mean the more technology, the better.

Entrepreneurial roadsides are littered with the wrecks of efforts to install Cadillac technologies for people who cannot yet handle the Model T. This point is illustrated by the failure of two exceedingly well-financed joint ventures of highly successful technology companies. These joint ventures attempted to provide computerized medical diagnostic services for doctors and hospitals. The companies developed console hookups to central diagnostic computers, so that everybody could stop sending off samples to pathology laboratories and agonizingly poring through medical texts to diagnose the patients' symptoms.

The ventures failed because of hospital and doctor resistance, not for want of superior or reliable products. The customer was compelled suddenly to make an enormous change in his accustomed way of doing things, and to employ a strange and somewhat formidable piece of equipment that required special training in its use and in the interpretation of its output.

Interactive teaching machines are meeting a similar fate. The learning results they achieve are uniformly spectacular. The need for improved learning is a visible reality. The demand for greater individualization of teaching is widespread. But the equipment has not sold because technologists have created systems employing equipment that is at the cutting edge of technological progress. The teachers and school systems that must use them are far behind, and already feel badly bruised by their failure to comprehend even simple new technologies. For them, the new Cadillac technologies do not solve problems. They create problems.

. . . & Compromise

On the other hand, failure to exploit technological possibilities can be equally destructive. When a major petroleum company with nearly 30,000 retail outlets in the United States was persuaded to pioneer a revolutionary automobile repair and servicing system, compromises of the original plan ensured the system's failure.

The theory was to build a gigantic service and repair system that could handle heavy volumes of continuous activity by using specialized diagnostic and repair equipment. With this equipment (rather than a harried and overworked man at a gas station) pinpointing the exact problems, cars could be shuttled off to specific stations in the repair center. Experts would work only on one kind of problem and section of a car, with newly designed, fast-action tools. Oil changes would be made in assembly-line fashion by low-paid workers, electrical work would be performed by high-paid technicians doing only that, and a post-diagnostic checkup would be made to guarantee success.

Since profitability would require high volume, the center would have to draw on a vast population area. To facilitate this, the original proposal called for a specially constructed building at a center-city, old warehouse location—the land would be cheaper, the building would be equally accessible throughout the entire metropolitan area, the service center's technological elegance and see-through windows for customers would offset any run-down neighborhood disadvantages, and volume business would come from planned customer decisions rather than random off-street traffic.

The original concept also called for overnight pickup and delivery service; thus a car could be repaired at night while its owner slept, rather than during the day when he would need it. And because the required promotion of this service would tend to alienate the company's franchised service station dealers, perhaps driving them into the hands of competitors, it was recommended that the first center be installed in a major city where the company had no stations.

This sounds like an excellent manufacturing approach to a service situation; but the company made three fatal compromises:

1. It decided to place the center in a costly, high-traffic suburban location, on the grounds that "if the experiment fails, at least the building will be in a location that has an alternative use." The results were an awkward location, a land-acquisition

cost five times higher than the original center-city location, and, therefore, a vastly inflated break-even point for the service center.

2. It decided not to offer overnight service, on the grounds that "we'd better crawl before we walk. And besides, we don't think people will leave their cars overnight in a strange and distant garage." The fact that the results would be guaranteed by a reputable, nationally known petroleum company operating an obviously sophisticated new type of consumer service facility was not persuasive to the corporate decision makers.

3. It decided to put the first center in a city occupied by its own franchised dealers, on the grounds that "we know it better." To offset the problem of not being able to advertise aggressively for business, the company offered its dealers a commission to send their repair jobs to the center. The dealers did this, but only with jobs they could not, or did not want to, do themselves. As a result, the traffic at the big, expensive center was miserably low.

Companies that take a manufacturing approach to service problems are likely to fail if (a) they compromise technological possibilities at the conception and design stage, or (b) they allow technological complexity to contaminate the operating stage. The substitution of technology and systems for people and serendipity is complex in its conception and design; only in its *operation,* as at McDonald's, is it simple.

It is the simplicity of mutual funds that, after all, accounts for their success. But the concept is in fact much more complex than that of selling individual stocks through a single customer-man sitting at a desk. Mutual funds are the financial community's equivalent of McDonald's. They are a piece of technology that not only simplifies life for both the seller and the buyer but also creates many more buyers and makes production more profitable.

Mass merchandising is similar. It substitutes a wide selection and fast, efficient self-service for a narrow selection and slow, incompetent salesclerk service. The mass merchandising retail store (e.g., general merchandise supermarket) is a new technology, incorporating into retailing precisely the thinking that goes into the assembly line, except that the customer does his own assembling.

WHY THINGS GO WRONG

The significance of all this is that a "product" is quite different from what it is generally assumed to be. When asked once what he did, Charles Revson, head of Revlon, Inc., made the now well-known reply, "In the factory we make cosmetics, in the store we sell hope." He defined the product in terms of what the consumer wanted, not in terms of what the manufacturer made. McDonald's obviously does the same—not just hamburgers but also speed, cleanliness, reassurance, cheerfulness, and predictable consistency. Honeywell defined it not in terms of replacement parts but, rather, in terms of those needs of its distributors which, if met, would result in substantially larger proportions of patronage for Honeywell. Thus a product is not something people buy, but a tool they use—a tool to solve their problems or to achieve their intentions.

So many things go wrong because companies fail to adequately define what they sell. Companies in so-called service industries generally think of themselves as offering services rather than manufacturing products; hence they fail to think and act as comprehensively as do manufacturing companies concerned with the efficient, low-cost production of customer-satisfying products.

Moreover, manufacturing companies themselves do not generally think of customer service as an integral part of *their* products. It is an afterthought to be handled by the marketing department.

The marketing department, in turn, thinks of itself as providing customer services. There is a hidden and unintentional implication of giving something away for free. One is doing something extra as a favor. When this is the underlying communication to one's own organization, the result is about what one would expect—casual, discretionary attitudes and little attention to detail, and certainly no attention to the possibilities of substituting systems and preplanning for people and pure effort. Hence products are designed that cannot be easily installed, repaired, or modified.

(Motorola's "works in a box" television set, which has been promoted so successfully on the basis of its easy replacement and repairability, is an outstanding example of the sales-getting potential of proper care in design and manufacturing.)

Chill Winds from Ice Cream

An excellent example of the confusion between what a company "makes" and what a customer "buys" is provided by a producer of private-label ice cream products for supermarket chains. Since supermarkets need to create low-price impressions in order to attract and hold customers, selling successfully to them means getting down to rock-bottom prices. The company (call it the Edwards Company) became extraordinarily good at producing a wide line of ice cream products at rock-bottom costs. It grew rapidly while others went bankrupt. It covered ten states with direct deliveries to stores out of its factory and factory warehouse, but continued growth eventually required establishing plant, distribution, and marketing centers elsewhere. The result was disaster, even though the company manufactured just as efficiently in the new locations as it did in the old.

Under the direct and constant supervision of the president in the original Edwards location, an exceedingly efficient telephone ordering and delivery system had been working to meet the supermarkets' rather stringent requirements. Because of limited storage and display space, they required several-times-a-week delivery at specified, uncrowded store hours. To make up for low volume in slow periods, they needed regular specials as well as holiday and summer specials. Over time, these needs had become so automatically but efficiently supplied from the original Edwards factory location that this delivery service became routinized and therefore taken for granted.

In building the new plant, the president and his compact management team focused on getting manufacturing costs down to rock bottom. After all, that is what made the sale—low prices. Not being very conscious of the fact that they had created in the original location an enormously customer-satisfying, efficient, automatic ordering and delivery system, they did not know exactly what to look for in evaluating how well they were working out these "service" details at the new plant, distribution, and marketing centers.

In short, they did not know what their product really was (why Edwards had become so successful) and they failed to expand Edwards' success. Service was not considered an integral part of the company's product. It was viewed merely as "something else" you do in the business. Accordingly, service received inadequate attention, and that became the cause of the Edwards Company's failure.

CONCLUSION

Rarely is customer service discretionary. It is a requisite of getting and holding business, just like the generic product itself. Moreover, if customer service is consciously treated as "manufacturing in the field," it will get the same kind of detailed attention that manufacturing gets. It will be carefully planned, controlled, automated where possible, audited for quality control, and regularly reviewed for performance improvement and customer reaction. More important, the same kinds of technological, labor-saving, and systems approaches that now thrive in manufacturing operations will begin to get a chance to thrive in customer service and service industries.

Once service-industry executives and the creators of customer-service programs begin seriously to think of themselves as actually manufacturing a product, they will begin to think like product manufacturers. They will ask: What technologies and systems are employable here? How can things be designed so we can use machines instead of people, systems instead of serendipity? Instead of thinking about better and more training of their customer-service representatives, insurance agents, branch bank managers, or salesmen "out there," they will think about how to eliminate or supplement them.

If we continue to approach service as something done by individuals rather than by machines or systems, we will continue to suffer from two distortions in thinking:

1. Service will be viewed as something residual to the ultimate reality—to a tangible product, to a specific competence (like evaluating loans, writing insurance policies, giving medical aid, preparing on-premises foods). Hence it will have residual respectability, receive residual attention, and be left, somehow, for residual performers.
2. Service will be treated as purely a human task that must inevitably be diagnosed and performed by a single individual working alone with no help or, at best, with the rudimentary help of training and a variety of human-engineering motivators. It will never get the kind of manufacturing-type thinking that goes into tangible products.

Until we think of service in more positive and encompassing terms, until it is enthusiastically viewed as manufacturing in the field, receptive to the same kinds of technological approaches that are used in the factory, the results are likely to be just as costly and idiosyncratic as the results of the lonely journeyman carving things laboriously by hand at home.

CHAPTER 3: THE SERVICE DELIVERY SYSTEM

The managing director of a multinational service firm commented that most companies in his industry are still in the "cottage-industry phase" of development when compared to the industrial development of firms in the manufacturing sector. He believes that the service industries are on the edge of a late but powerful "industrial revolution." His firm has selected one service business at a time, bringing "industrial" thinking to it to his company's competitive advantage. In each service industry selected his managers have identified what the firm calls the "key elements of the profit formula." A major part of this formula has been reexamination of operations, often using analytical tools and approaches developed in manufacturing.

Why has there been a delay in firms in the service industries adopting this strategy, particularly if they see other companies successfully gaining an advantage from it? In the preceding chapter, Theodore Levitt argues that if companies stop thinking of service as servitude and personal ministration, they will be able to effect drastic improvements in their quality and efficiency.

The traditional attitude that good service is produced by the consumption of labor explains part of the slow acceptance of industrialization in the service industries. However, another part of the explanation may come from the fact that most service industries have had strong entrepreneurial roots, as well as little opportunity for return to scale. In most cases, the entrepreneurs have had little training or inclination for the discipline of industrial engineering or operations research. They have been more typically "promoters" and "developers" of business than "refiners" and "rationalizers." As businesses have grown through the takeoff stages, wasteful practices and operating mismanagement are frequently overlooked or excused in a vigorous market. In manufacturing companies there were rich rewards for engineering as the scale of an enterprise increased. The salary of an engineer or analyst could be easily justified in the investment for a new operation. Services often have many relatively small operating units that individually cannot afford these analysts.

But if these units can be combined, and if the idea is appropriate, the potential payoff can be substantial. Together, these reasons may well describe why the service industries have been slow to adopt these methods. But they also point up competitive opportunities for the service firms and take advantage of the "soft underbelly" of its industry.

The following sections describe an approach to apply operations analysis in designing or refining the service delivery system.

VIEWING THE SYSTEM

Developing a flow chart is one of the first steps to analyze a new operation. The flow chart is an important tool for analyzing the layout of a facility and understanding the physical and informational flows. Graphic representation of the service delivery systems provides a structured way of visualizing what occurs and how each activity relates to other activities. Once a flow chart is drawn, it is generally useful to estimate the capacity of each system component. The capacity calculations pin-

Figure 3-1

Flow Chart of Car Rental Check-In and Check-Out Process

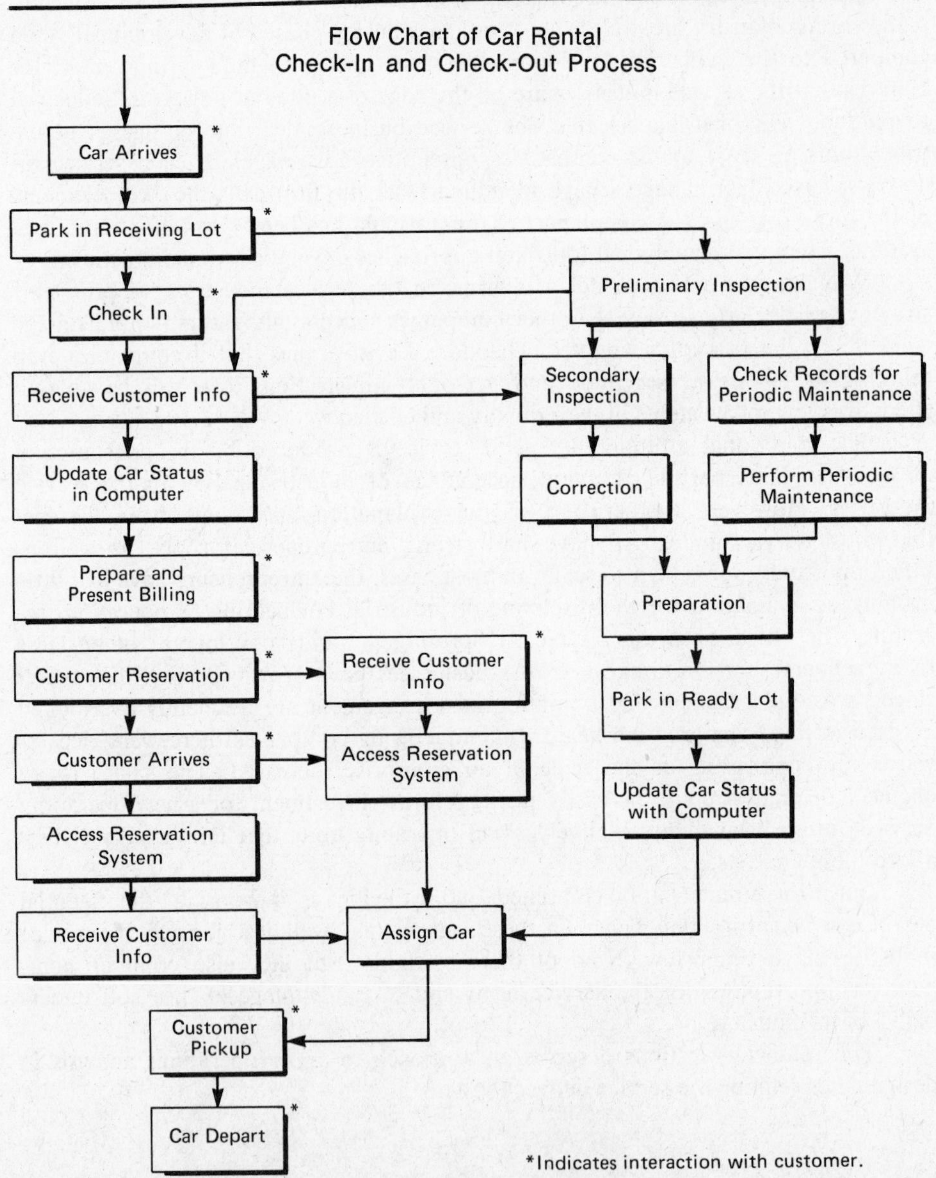

*Indicates interaction with customer.

Figure 3-2

These days you've got enough things to worry about on a business trip.
Your rent-a-car shouldn't be one of them. That's why effective September 1st...

Figure 3-2 (continued)

Hertz intro
standards in the rent-a-car
clean and reliable car. Fast

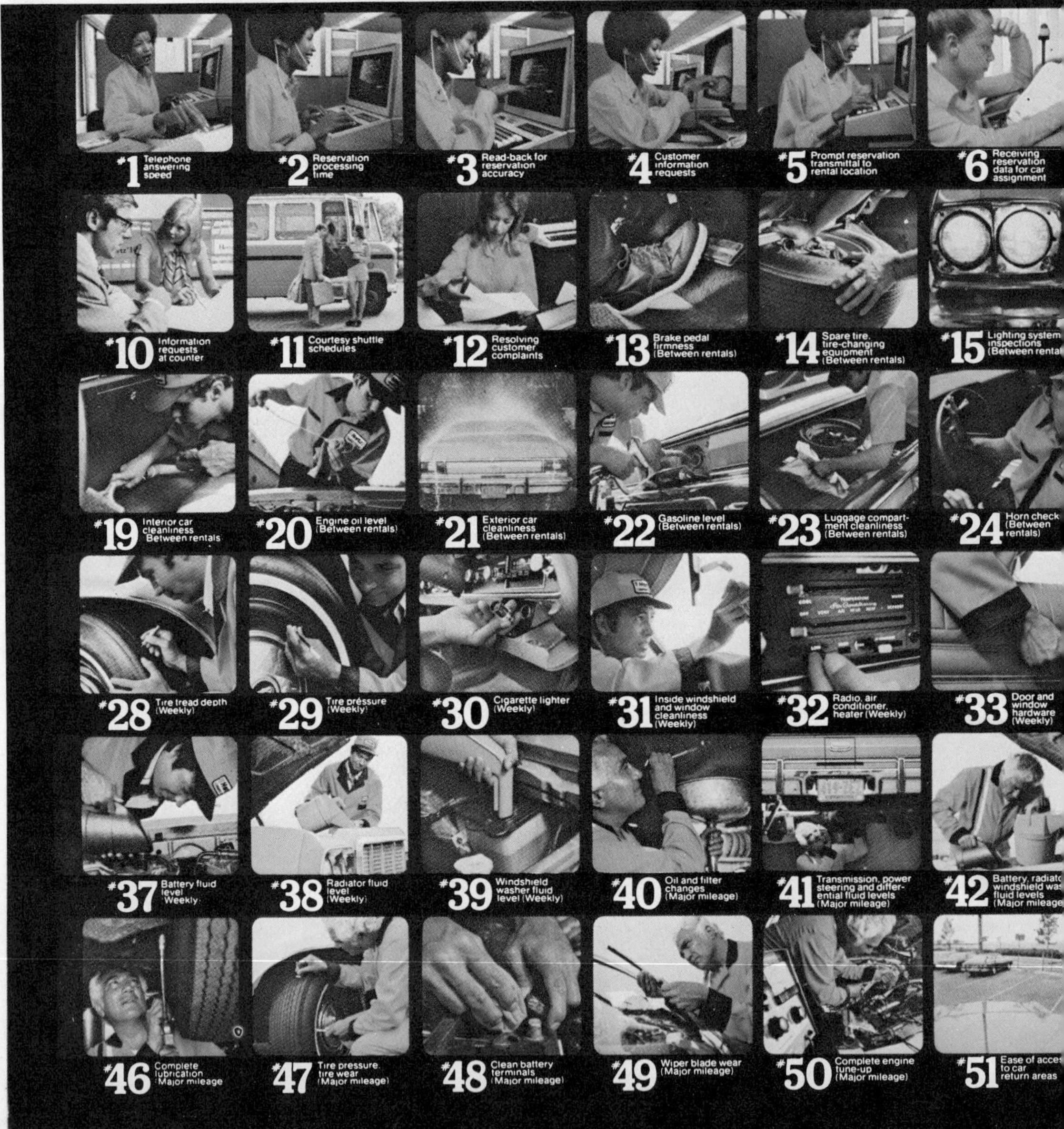

Figure 3-2 (continued)

uced 54 of the toughest new ndustry. So you can expect a very time you rent.

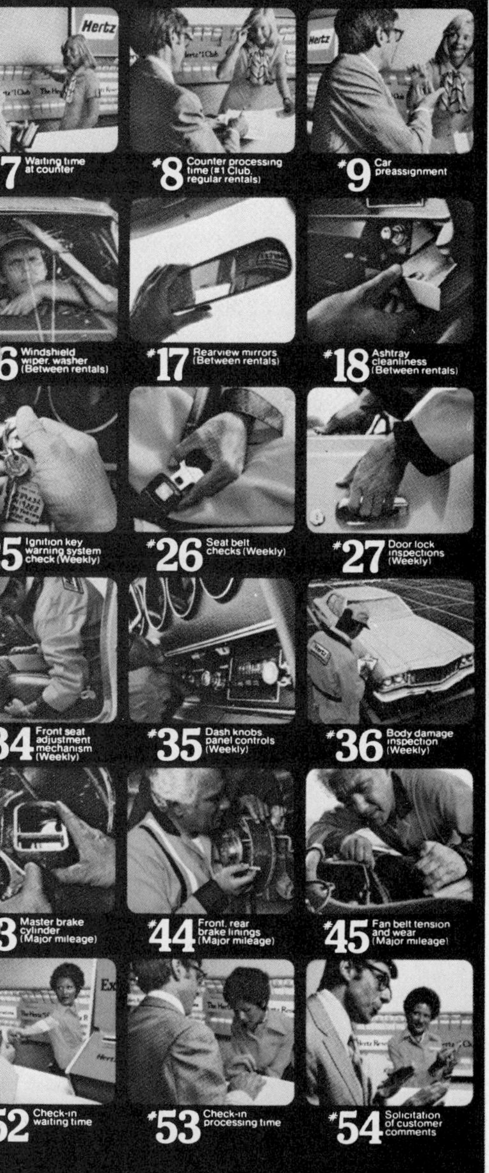

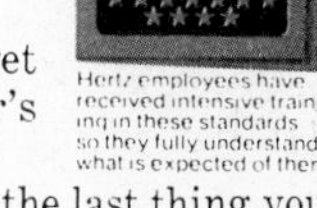

Hertz employees have received intensive training in these standards so they fully understand what is expected of them.

Terrific! Another all-expense-paid business trip. You can start counting the worries now.

Did your secretary check out those last minute figures?

Will the meeting go well this time?

Can you close the deal and get home in time for your daughter's class play?

You know what it's like. So, the last thing you should have to worry about is something that should be relatively simple: getting a clean and reliable car. Fast.

That's why Hertz introduced these 54 tough new standards. Standards to speed up your reservation. Standards for faster counter service. Standards for more intensive car maintenance. Right down to checking those windshield wipers between each rental. Even if it's sunny.

54 tough new standards. You'd expect them from Hertz. The worldwide leader in rent-a-cars. After all, Hertz created rent-it-here/leave-it-there, express check-in. As well as #1 Club service.

54 tough new standards. Because, you've already got enough to worry about.

© HERTZ SYSTEM INC 1974

Your Hertz car. One less thing to worry about.

HERTZ RENTS FORDS AND OTHER FINE CARS

point bottleneck operations and operations with excess capacity. Figure 3-1 is a simplified flow chart of the process of checking in and checking out a rental car. It is particularly illustrative because the flow of the automobile, customer, and information can all be shown in one flow chart.

The flow chart identifies the critical steps in which the service process interacts with the customer. As noted in Chapter 2, one of the most striking features of the service industry firm is the heavy involvement and interaction of the customer in the service delivery system. For this reason, the service industry manager must be aware of this process-customer interaction.

The flow chart in Figure 3-1 shows 11 points where significant process-customer interaction occurs. At these points there are opportunities to make an impact on the customer in either a positive or negative way. For example, what image is presented to the customer upon arrival? Are there adequate directions available to permit easy access to the receiving lot? Is there sufficient room in the receiving lot to park conveniently? Is the lot clean? Is there an attendant on duty? How close is the lot to the check-in station and the customer's final destination? Does the customer have to wait at the counter to check in? How is the customer's information received? Are the counter clerks pleasant and efficient? How quickly can information be typed into the computer and billing be prepared? How accurate is the billing? How is the billing presented? How are complaints and questions handled?

On the check-out side, how are customer reservation calls handled? How long does a customer have to wait for a telephone to be answered or to receive correct information? Is the information received and stored in the computerized reservation system accurately? When the customer arrives, how quickly can he or she be processed? Is the processing accurate? Is the type of car desired by the customer available? Can the counter personnel provide good directions on how to get to one's destination? After the automobile has been assigned, can the customer locate it conveniently? Is the customer's departure convenient? Are exit directions available?

Another group of activities must occur in the receiving inspection and preparation process. Is the inspection made quickly and accurately? Are the corrections made properly? Are preparations such as washing, fueling, and cleaning made thoroughly? Are the data accurately recorded in the computer when the automobile is ready?

The Hertz organization advertises that it maintains 54 standards of performance, as shown in Figure 3-2. Eight of these standards apply to the check-in process, 11 to the check-out process, and 38 to the receiving, inspection, and preparation process. Of course, these applications add up to more than 54 because several of the standards apply to more than one process. The check-in and check-out standards must be achieved in the close proximity of the waiting customer, while the receiving, inspection, and preparation standards are met out of view of the customer. These standards establish the target service levels of the total service package that Hertz produces.

A similar analysis can be performed of Holiday Inn's 152 performance standards discussed in Figure 3-3.

Figure 3-3

HOLIDAY INN ADVERTISEMENT

A good meeting should have a few surprises. A good meeting place shouldn't.

At Holiday Inn,® there are 152 reasons why the best surprise is no surprise.

As you know, a productive meeting usually consists of a proper mixture of the expected and the unexpected. But at over 1,700 Holiday Inn hotels and motels, we've taken steps to make sure the only unexpected happenings at your meeting are the ones you've planned on.

We've developed 152 performance standards to eliminate inadequate meeting rooms, lost reservations, lumpy beds and other surprises that any meeting is better off without.

A meeting room with no surprises.

Perhaps the highest compliment we can pay to our meeting rooms is that they're covered by the same 152 special standards that cover all our other rooms. So even though your meeting room might not have a comfortable bed (Standard #1) with fresh sheets (2) and soft pillows (3), it will be in top condition (4-5), and so will the equipment in it (6).

When you do get back to your private room, you'll find, besides the three standards already mentioned, a comfortable sofa or lounge chair for you to lounge in (7), free TV (8), and 49 other standards (9-57) that cover your bedroom and bath. Things like the thickness of your carpet, the required number of hangers, your individual year-round temperature control, the firmness of your mattress, the soap, the towels and the all-over cleanliness of every square inch of your room.

We don't cook up surprises.

We don't make wild promises about our restaurants. Just that you'll get a tasty, nourishing meal (58), presented appetizingly (59). Our meats, vegetables and desserts are top quality (60) and will be served the way you ordered them. Seven other restaurant regulations (61-67) mean you get good food and prompt service in clean surroundings. We are very finicky about our glasses and silverware and tables, even our kitchen floors. Everything.

Service without surprises.

Is it possible that no one would ever be surprised by anything in a Holiday Inn meeting room, guest room, or restaurant? Our Innkeepers and Food and Beverage Managers are going to try to deliver no surprises. They are required to know our rules inside out (68). Each is a graduate of extensive training at the multi-million-dollar Holiday Inn University (69) and takes refresher courses every year. Holiday Inn employees receive specialized training, too. They've got 12 rules of their own to live up to. (70-81). Including being well-groomed and courteous and offering you at least 14 hours of continuous room service daily, and being able to refer you to a baby sitter or a dentist or a doctor quickly.

Don't look for surprises in our lobby.

Our lobbies are neat and uncluttered (82) with plenty of helpful information from an area map and schedules (83) to brochures on local attractions (84). There's even a church directory (85). Plus six other standards (86-91) that deal

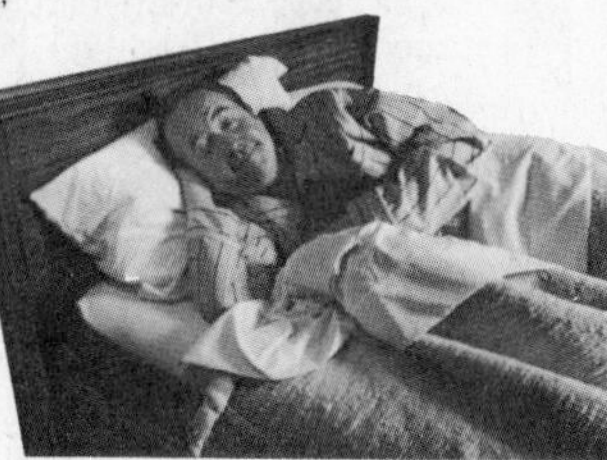

only with keeping the lobby clean, comfortable and safe.

Some other things that won't surprise you.

Free Holiday Inn swimming pools (92) are well-maintained (93-96). And we have standards that cover things like hallways, mechanical rooms, and storage rooms (97-99).

And 13 more standards (100-112) cover miscellaneous items, from housekeeping supplies to parking space to security.

Our unsurprising prices.

We offer reasonable rates and we stick to them. Three regulations (113-115) assure that. You can make reservations at any of our inns, anywhere in the world, 24 hours a day. And children under 12, when they're in the same room as their parents and require no additional beds, are always free.

And besides all these standards, there are six covering our reception desks (116-121), three covering our rest rooms (122-124), five covering our laundry rooms (125-129). Plus twenty-two others covering everything from Holiday Inn Guest Certificates to baby beds (130-151).

Probably the most important rule of all is, that every inn is inspected several times each year to make sure it lives up to the other rules (152).

Meet with us soon. And give us a chance not to surprise you.

Meet at Holiday Inn® where the best surprise is no surprise.

Courtesy: Holiday Inns, Inc., Memphis, Tenn. and Agency: Young and Rubicam, New York, N.Y.

Figure 3-4 illustrates the information, records, and instructions necessary to initiate and complete the movement of a railroad car to the shipper's facility to departure in an outbound train. Each step of the physical process of moving the car and its contents is supported by an important flow of information that allows quick tracing of the location of the shipment and control of the movement.

It is useful to determine what information is required at each step for the process to function smoothly and to identify what decisions are made and who makes them. The flow chart is useful besides simply identifying the sequence of the specific steps of a process. As mentioned above, it can also be very helpful for identifying potential inadequate (or excess) capacity in each step. For example, as shown in Figure 3-4 a railroad yard might have the capability of receiving calls from shippers for a hundred shipments per hour but be limited to no more than 50 cars (shipments) per hour or flat switching no more than 100 cars (shipments) per hour. Such capacity limitations must be recognized and taken into consideration.

In Figure 3-4, the steps in which the customer interfaces with the railroad process are in placing the initial call, receiving the empty car, loading the car, releasing the car to be switched to the yard, and executing the bill of lading. Each of

Figure 3-4

Flow Chart of Outbound Operations of a Railroad Shipment

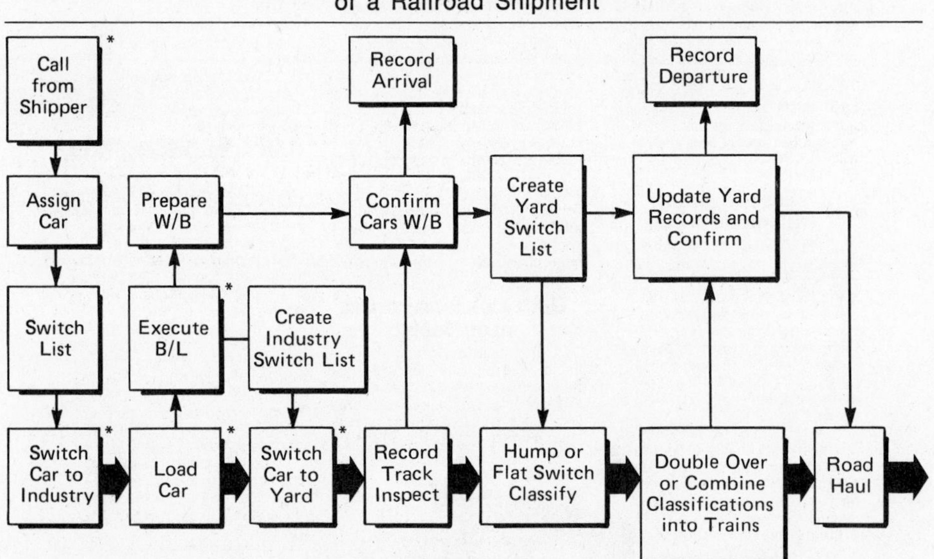

*Indicates interaction with customer.

Note: Heavy lines indicate physical movements of cars and freight.
Light lines indicate information flows.

W/B = Waybill

B/L = Bill of Lading

Adapted from: D. Daryl Wyckoff, *Railroad Management* (Lexington, Mass.: Lexington Books, D.C. Heath, 1976), p. 24.

these steps in the process requires critical inputs from the customer. The accuracy of the information given to the railroad in the initial call is vital. Clearly understanding the flexibility of the shipper's schedule and the exact type of equipment required avoids errors in switching equipment to the shipper's location and may mean that the dispatcher will be able to wait for an expected inbound car rather than deadheading an empty car from another point. The efficiency and courtesy of the railroad employees at each of these steps are part of the overall service mix perceived by the customer. The accuracy of the shipment's description and routing as stated in the bill of lading are vital to the service performance of the railroad. In addition, the overall capital productivity of the railroad is highly influenced by the speed and care with which the shipper loads and releases the cars. In 1976, the typical freight car was moving only 14% of the time.[2] Many railroads could profit greatly by making an analysis of their process and the customer interactions that occur.

When designing or analyzing a service delivery system, a service manager should consider:

1. *Are the steps arranged in a logical sequence?*

2. *Are the capacities of each step balanced?* Bottlenecks that limit flows should be eliminated.

3. *How much flexibility is available at each step?*

4. *Can steps be combined or should parallel steps be considered?* It may be desirable to expand one step to permit elimination of other steps. In addition, it might be desirable to provide parallel flows at some steps, which might include identical redundant steps or alternate steps.

5. *Have customer-process interactions been considered at each step?* It is possible to categorize operations on the basis of similar characteristics. After acquiring this skill, it is relatively easy to anticipate behavior and establish expectations of operations of a particular type.

TYPES OF OPERATIONS

Using the terminology developed in the manufacturing industries, three types of processes of interest to the manager of a service operation are: (1) *line* (or *flow*) *operations,* (2) *job-shop operations,* and (3) *intermittent operations.* The following section describes the general characteristics of these three processes, although seldom is an actual process strictly a pure line operation or job-shop operation. However, being aware of the characteristics typical of each type assists the service manager in avoiding the inappropriate mixing of the concepts.[3]

---

[2] D. Daryl Wyckoff, *Railroad Management* (Lexington, Mass.: Lexington Books, D. C. Heath, 1976), p. 28.

[3] For a further discussion of the concepts of job-shop and line processes, refer to: P. W. Marshall, et al., *Production Management: Text and Cases* (Homewood, Ill.: Richard D. Irwin, 1975), pp. 153–159.

Line (Flow Shop)

In a line shop, the activities are arranged in a sequence of operations to produce a desired service or product. A cafeteria is an example of an assembly line, which is one type of line operation. Army induction physical examinations where the inductee moves from one station to the next is another example. Both examples have the characteristics of following a single, established flow pattern or sequence of progressive steps. In the true line process, no steps are skipped, and usually a substantial amount of attention is devoted to the physical layout of the process to minimize the confusion and movement necessary in passing from activity to activity. It is much easier to visualize a production line operation in a manufacturing context with conveyor belts or other mechanical handling equipment moving the work in progress past work stations. In the service industries the line process has a wide variety of applications. Customers may be served by moving themselves through a series of service locations as in a cafeteria. Or the customers may remain stationary while a series of service people pass them, as in a hospital room. Because of the high degree of interrelation between the individual parts of the line process, the performance of the entire process may be limited by the performance of any part of the process. For example, a slow cashier slows the progress of the cafeteria line, or the people drying cars at the car wash delay the line if they do not keep pace with the cars coming off the line.

Another general feature of a line operation is that it is relatively inflexible to accommodate major changes in volume handled or services performed. However, if the line manager accepts this degree of inflexibility, the activities can be divided into relatively simple tasks to facilitate specialization and training.

Line processes operate most effectively if they do not have to start and stop frequently. For this reason, line processes are usually associated with producing a highly standardized product at a steady pace to a finished goods inventory. Since most service industries do not produce a service or product that can be inventoried, this feature of a line process is not usually considered important. However, some service organizations have found that producing for inventory is more feasible than first imagined. For example, McDonald's discovered that hamburgers could be cooked and held in inventory for a brief time to speed service. Nevertheless, the line process does impose a form of discipline and regularity of the process that make this process appropriate for handling large volumes of customers who desire fairly standardized services.

Job Shop

A job shop is usually characterized by the large variety of goods or services it produces by using different combinations and sequences of activities. In most respects these goods or services are much more likely to be customized to the customer's specifications, which essentially eliminates the opportunities for developing a fixed or regular flow and the use of finished goods inventories. The conventional restaurant providing meals prepared to order is an example of a job shop. General practitioners usually provide medical services and general management consultants provide business services on a job-shop basis.

While job shops are desirably flexible, in terms of variety of services performed and the capacity to cope with changes in volume, there are several negative aspects. There are usually fewer opportunities for substitution of capital for labor. It is often difficult to estimate the capacity of a job shop because of the degree of uncertainty as to what will be required in it. Similarly, the job shop is often very difficult to schedule because it may be difficult to forecast the demand for certain parts of the shop, such as the broiler in a kitchen or the x-ray machine in the hospital.

For a comparison of job-shop and line-shop approaches to the same task, consider the case of alternative approaches to producing a car wash. The conventional hand-wash operation is a job shop. It is highly flexible but usually has little division of labor. On the other hand, the automated or semiautomated car wash system that has substituted technology for labor and divided the task into simple and repetitive jobs is relatively inflexible.

A choice must be made about the training and skills of the workforce in a job shop. Usually there are fewer opportunities to fully employ specialists in a job shop. Often the job-shop employee is cross-trained to handle a greater variety of activities.

Other considerations in choice of continuous process. When making a choice of type of process to produce a service, a manager should consider the following factors:

1. *Potential opportunity for reduction of the cost of the service through introduction of capital equipment.* The line process typically offers more opportunities to become the low-cost producer.

2. *The need for reproducibility or consistency of service.* Line processes usually impose a substantial degree of discipline on output, which *may* have highly desirable effects on the quality.

3. *The need for flexibility for changing volumes of output.* Job shops normally have a better ability to accommodate such changes by the use of more general purpose employees and less capital equipment tied together in a rigid sequence.

4. *The need for flexibility for producing a wide variety of services.* Job shops usually can absorb more "custom order" production because of the use of more general purpose employees.

5. *Workforce management.* Most line processes give little variety to employees and may reduce activities to such simple repetitive tasks that they become boring. The selection, training, and supervision of employees working in a line process may be substantially different from that of a job-shop operation.

Comparison of the features of the line or flow process and job-shop process are summarized in Table 3-1.

Table 3-1

TYPICAL CHARACTERISTICS OF PROCESSES

	Line	*Job Shop*
Suitability to Type of Service:		
Volume	Suited for high-volume standardized service.	Suited for service that has low volumes of identical outputs and considerable variety in characteristics. Service changes are easily accommodated.
Service change	Change is costly since the entire process must be changed or balanced with each service change.	Service changes are easily accommodated.
Demand variation	Best suited to stable demand without heavy cyclicality.	Lumpy or uncertain demand easily accommodated.
Market type	Standardized service.	Custom service to order.
Suitability to Method of Service Delivery:		
Task characteristics	Tasks with high specificity—well defined, divisible, teachable, and of known duration.	Tasks with low specificity are accommodated. Difficult to acquire skills and uncertain or variable completion times.
Capital embodied technology	Permits process automation via specially designed equipment often unique to service or industry and requiring technological development.	Permits capital intensity via general purpose equipment that can be purchased from several suppliers.
Human Inputs:		
Labor skills	Tolerance for repetition.	Broader skills and high degree of flexibility.
Work environment	Highly visible, paced performance, teamwork, repetition, tightly coupled achieving unit.	Unpaced individual work, craft-skill specialization, fixed work-place, and long-term assignments.
Labor characteristics	Workers become highly proficient but only in one type of operation.	Valuable skills.
Production Characteristics:		
Productivity	Typically high when demand is stable due to division of labor, specialization, and learning that	Labor tends to become efficient in a variety of tasks but per unit productivity is lower than line

Source: Adapted from P. W. Marshall, et al., *Production Management: Text and Cases* (Homewood, Ill.: Richard D. Irwin, 1975), pp. 158–159.

	Line	*Job Shop*
	occurs with scale. Little setup cost and, greater opportunity for automation.	operation due to changes and little repetitive learning opportunity.
Control	Control is straightforward under stable conditions.	The variety of different jobs and uncertain completion time make job control complex.
Capacity	Capacity is well defined but expensive to change in even a moderate degree due to pervasive effects of change throughout the system.	Capacity is ill-defined but flexible within broad limits. As demand approaches capacity in-process inventory tends to become very large and out of control.

The type of delivery system selected must be "right" for the task to be performed. As can be seen in this discussion, several types of delivery systems can be considered for a general category of services such as food services, lodging, or automobile repair. The service manager, however, must closely examine the task at hand to decide which delivery system is most appropriate for the situation.

Intermittent Operations

Line and job shops are ongoing processes. However, there are many situations that are "project processes," even if they are infrequently repeated. Service firms are frequently involved in the management of projects of intermittent nature. Restaurants and hotel chains must manage the construction of new units. Other companies find they must manage the task of introducing a new service.

Service firms such as architects and consultants often find that most of their activities are projects being managed for others. For example, motion picture studios are really managing a series of unrelated projects, feature motion pictures. As the scale of projects grows, it becomes increasingly more difficult to manage all the interrelations of parts of the project. Project control and scheduling systems such as PERT (Program Evaluation and Review Technique) and the closely related CPM (Critical Path Method) find excellent applications in the management of service industry projects.

These tools provide a means of identifying and keeping track of the various activities that comprise a project. Perhaps more importantly, they recognize the relationships of individual jobs and how they relate to the completion of the project. CPM and PERT provide a means of determining which jobs or activities are critical in their effect on the total project completion time. From this evaluation, it is possible to test a variety of schedules to meet a target date at a minimum cost or determine the potential cost associated with changing completion target dates.

The main criteria for selecting CPM (or PERT) for project management are the following. First, the project must be complex and large enough to justify this level of control. CPM (or PERT) contributes little to trivial projects with a few very simply monitored activities. Second, the project must consist of clearly defined separable activities that have identifiable "starts" and "finishes," and when all of the activities are completed, the project is completed. Third, the activities must have a defined logical order or sequence. Examples of projects in the service industries that are potential applications of CPM (or PERT) include:

Construction of new service facilities
Introduction of a new service
Installing new computers or management information systems
Production and marketing of feature length motion pictures
Preparation for opening of professional football season

There are several aspects of CPM (or PERT) that may make them less effective in some service applications. The application of these tools depends on the nature of the tasks. There are cases where a substantial amount of creativity is contained in the tasks and the results are not directly measurable. While the task might be forced to completion "on time," the result may only be acceptable rather than inspired, which does not negate the value of these tools but implies that the service manager may have to be more sensitive about their use.

The following section describes applications of several analytical tools that are helpful in designing and managing delivery systems. Most of these tools were originally developed in a manufacturing context but have important applications in service firms.

TOOLS OF ANALYSIS

Balancing a Service Operation

One feature of great importance in the design of a service system is balance. As described in the previous section, many processes are a structured sequence of several clearly identifiable steps. The manager of a service process should be alert to the possibilities for creative arrangement or combination of the steps of the process and the need to balance the capacities at each point in the process. Failure to balance leads to bottlenecks. Not only are bottlenecks wasteful, but they are also annoying to the service customer who perceives that the service is being delivered ineffectively.

Each step or activity in the process requires an identifiable amount of time (activity time). If there are parallel locations that can perform the same activity, that is, several airline checking points at the ticket counter, the time required to process a number of people in parallel (process time) is the activity time divided by the number of parallel stations. The total process is limited by the activity with the longest process time. That activity is the bottleneck. In a balanced process all the activities have the same process time.

The service manager has some interesting opportunities for process balancing that might not be available to an industrial engineer designing a manufacturing assembly line. For example, it may be possible for the person being served to help willingly in the process itself. Salad bars, instant hotel check-out systems, and car rental information identification systems are all examples of involving the service customer in the process to the benefit of the service delivery system and the served.

The service manager who ignores ways of involving the customer in the process, by creatively combining or resequencing tasks or minimizing bottlenecks, is running the risk of delivering service in a wasteful way. This type of service failure arises from the structural design of the delivery system and usually cannot be overcome by the most enthusiastic and dedicated workers.

Allocation

Another way of thinking about balance is to examine the allocation of scarce resources. For the service manager this may mean deciding on the most appropriate mix of services that may be produced by a capacity. In the usual service operation, there are many combinations of outputs or offerings that might be demanded from the capacity.

Linear programming provides one tool to optimize the allocation of a service capacity. The following factors are representative of the use of linear programming in assigning service capacity:

1. *Scheduling.* Allocating activities among several locations is a frequent use of linear programming. Such allocations may be made based on the cost and capacity of each location to accommodate an activity and the travel time between locations. Linear programming can also be used to optimize scheduling of fleets or facilities. Linear programming has been used very successfully to plan the loading of maintenance shops, nurse training schedules, and kitchen staff workload.
2. *Blending.* There are instances in which certain ingredients are combined to produce an output that meets a specification. In some cases it is possible to modify such combinations to take advantage of changes in costs of ingredients of the mix. A classic example is the blending of sausages in which certain cuts of meat may be substituted within prescribed limits without detracting from the quality of the output.
3. *Purchasing.* Choosing between the purchase of various materials that can be substituted for others and are available at different prices, qualities, and quantities is a complex problem that can often be solved for the least-cost solution using linear programming. This choice may also apply to solving make-or-buy decisions.

A unique formulation of linear programming called a transportation model provides a useful tool for analysis of a variety of problems dealing with optimization of movement of goods and services. Simply stated, the transportation model optimizes the allocation of goods or services in a variety of locations to demands in other locations on the basis of cost, time, or other criteria. For example, linear programming has been used to reassign excess capacity as in the case of matching excess empty boxcars at various locations to boxcar requests from other locations on the railroad. Similar assignments of trucks for backhauling or relocating excess rental cars can be made using linear programming. Special formulations of the transportation model have been used in site location of service facilities.

Waiting for Service

How long a wait may be experienced by a service customer? This is a question of great concern to most managers in the service industry because promptness of service is directly involved in the customer's perception of service level.

There are a number of psychological aspects to waiting. First, waiting may imply an unwarranted waste of time. A customer may easily become irritated because he or she feels that the service organization that has caused the wait has planned poorly or is inconsiderate of the customer's time. Either impression may be very annoying. Many customers have become aware of the value of their time. Executives who are delayed reaching meetings may have an explicit idea of the value of time. Now, however, vacationers are becoming increasingly aware of the value of personal leisure time.

It has been found that the attitudes of people waiting depend heavily on the conditions under which they are waiting. Customers must be convinced that what they are waiting for is worth it. An annoying wait may produce a very sensitive and overly critical customer when the service is finally delivered.

There are several ways to minimize the impact of a wait. One is to make the wait comfortable. Another is to distract the customer during the wait. Entertainment may accomplish this. One illustration of reduced impact is the case of the well-known hotel group that received complaints from guests about the excessive waiting time for elevators. After an analysis of how elevator service might be improved, it was suggested that mirrors be installed near where guests waited for elevators. The natural tendency of people to check their personal appearance substantially reduced complaints, although the actual wait for the elevators was unchanged. Some distraction occurs in the waiting process if people are moved from one waiting point to another. This is the army's routine of "hurry up and wait."

The perception that time is being consumed in a useful manner or that the process has already begun can minimize the distress of waiting. The lounge areas in restaurants accomplish this, and they contribute substantially to profits. The British restaurant tradition of presenting diners a menu and taking dinner orders in the lounge is a practical way of giving the impression that something useful is being accomplished.

Many customers agree to a waiting period if they think they are being treated fairly and the situation is under control. For example, the three following irritants are frequently mentioned by guests at restaurants:

1. I made reservations that were not honored because of an error in recording, poor planning, or other failure.
2. A waiting time was specified by an overly optimistic host or hostess but was not honored.
3. Customers who arrived after I did have already been seated.

Each of these remarks indicates a concern over lack of control. Psychologists indicate that a perception of a lack of control often results in irritation and may lead to intense distress, which is hardly the psychological setting for providing service.[4] Some restaurants follow the practice of promising guests a waiting time in excess of the actual "expected time." If people are willing to agree to wait this length of time, they are quite pleased to be seated earlier, thus starting the meal with a more positive feeling.

The feeling that somebody has successfully "cut in front" of you causes even the most patient customer to become furious. Great care to be equitable is vital.

The questions the service manager should ask are:

1. Does the customer perceive that he or she is waiting?
2. How is waiting (or not waiting) seen by the customer as part of the service level?
3. Does the customer resent the wait?
4. Can the wait be made a useful or positive part of the experience?

Forecasting

Service firms have a particular need for making forecasts using probability distributions. These distributions include upper and lower limits as well as assigning probabilities to various levels. While forecasting of this type is useful in manufacturing or retailing, it is vital in the service industry where the service product cannot be inventoried or carried over. Unfortunately, forecasting in service situations is tied to capacity decisions, which are usually particularly costly if incorrect. One of the key decisions the service manager must make is how much service coverage is to be provided.

One problem that many service firms experience stems from the high degree of personalization (or customization) that is often a fundamental feature of the service offering. This may mean that it is relatively easy to predict the number of customers that a service organization might be required to accommodate in a particular time period, but it might be quite difficult to forecast with any confidence what specific mixture of services they will require or how long it may take to provide those services. For example, it is relatively easier to forecast how many individuals might appear at a check-in counter at an airline than to estimate the amount

[4] "The Tyranny of Life Without Options," *Technology Review* (February 1977), p. 21.

of time that will be required to accommodate each person because this depends on whether the person is already ticketed, needs changes to tickets, or has other complications.

Some managers seem to believe that forecasts must be quantitative to have authority. Many excellent and useful qualitative forecasts often have no quantitative support. For example, anticipation of social trends in capturing the concerns or desires of audiences has been the mark of one of the top entertainment companies in Hollywood. Forecasting these trends has contributed directly to the successful development of television and feature films by this firm. Similarly, forecasting changes in travel attitudes and a general shift in business travel led to the successful creation of a major motel group while other hotels continued to operate as they had in the past.

The considerations the service managers should have in mind when designing a forecast are[5]:

1. *The Time Horizon.* What exact time span will be covered? Why is this period relevant? Will the forecast provide information leading to decisions different from decisions that would have been made if the forecast did not exist?

2. *Level of Detail.* Will the forecast deal with specific services or aggregate levels?

3. *Number of Items.* How many individual forecasts are required to produce the total forecast?

4. *Control vs. Planning.* Is the forecast intended for management control? Will it be used to detect exceptions to determine if control is lost? Or will the forecast be used as part of a planning process to test decision alternatives?

5. *Stability.* Is the forecast dealing with situations that are stable or must it cope with highly unstable and dynamic conditions?

6. *Existing Planning Procedures.* The forecasting procedure must fit with the planning procedures. Is the forecasting procedure consistent with the company's organization? How easy will the forecast be to apply?

Service Coverage

An important element of providing service is to be able to deliver it when called for. We measure this as service capacity coverage or the service critical fractile. It is the percentage of potential but uncertain demand that the firm wishes to be prepared to meet economically.

Inventory managers have called this problem the "newsboy's dilemma." This classic problem may be described as follows. A newsstand operator purchases newspapers for five cents and sells them for ten cents. The newsboy may not return unsold newspapers for a refund. How many newspapers should he stock each day to maximize his income?

Carrying excess capacity can be expensive. The prudent manager should be

[5] See Steven C. Wheelwright and Spyros Makridakis, *Quantitative and Technological Methods of Forecasting and Planning* (New York: Wiley-Hamilton, 1976), pp. 6–8.

prepared to make the tradeoff between the costs of stockout and the costs of excess capacity. Managing capacity is the topic of Chapter 5.

Applications of this tradeoff readily come to mind in the restaurant industry, where one has to prepare meals or specific menu items in advance against an uncertain demand or in the lodging and airline business with the question of overbooking to guard against "no-shows."

The critical fractile is calculated as follows:

$$CF = \frac{C_{so}}{C_{so} + C_o} \times 100$$

where CF = Critical fractile or desired coverage, %
C_{so} = Cost of stockout, \$/unit of capacity
C_o = Cost of overage, \$/unit of capacity

The cost of stockout is often difficult to estimate. It is likely to be at least the contribution lost by not being able to provide the service. However, the true under-coverage or stockout cost may include a variety of additional costs that are not as easily estimated. These costs might include lost associated sales or the loss of a customer's business forever. Though it should be noted that a customer might be switched to another service that would be as satisfactory and might even result in a higher contribution.

The key to the successful use of service critical fractile analysis to determine service coverage is forecasting the distribution of anticipated demand and carefully calculating the costs of stocking out and overage correctly.

The critical fractile coverage measure can be applied directly to the probability forecast described in the previous section. For example, if the critical fractile calculation indicates that 75% coverage is desirable, the manager should plan to provide enough service to cover demand up to a level of which he is 75% confident of experiencing. Some managers tend to cover only the most likely level of demand. If they follow this behavior strictly, they tend to stockout half the time. Other managers tend to never stockout. Assuming that there is a cost for overage, the implied cost of stockout in a policy that has a critical fractile of 100% is (an unlikely) infinite.

Every service manager should experience stockouts unless he or she has an infinite stockout cost. However, a stockout can often be managed to mitigate the negative impact. This may require creative solutions, but it also suggests a policy and plan of action that should be communicated to employees before the stockout occurs.

Make-or-Buy Decisions

One of the vital means of expanding capacity available to the service manager is the use of the capacity of others. Service managers often do not address the issue of make-or-buy decisions as explicitly as their manufacturing counterparts. Explicit recognition of make-or-buy decisions is a valuable step in analysis of alternatives. The following questions are typical of the types of make-or-buy decisions a service manager might be required to make.

1. *Should a restaurant buy prepared foods?* The supplier may have economy of scale in producing a specialty item. The outside supplier may also be able to exercise stricter quality control to provide a consistent product with portion control. However, the cost of goods may be higher than if the restaurant made the item itself. In addition, the restaurant may be less distinctive if the identical item is available from competitors who use the same vendor.

2. *Should a hotel train its own managers or proselytize experienced managers from other hotels?* Managers from other hotels may be a proven product. This policy may also mean that it is not necessary to invest in a training program and unproductive management trainees. But every organization has its own character. Will managers trained by other firms be successful in another chain?

3. *Should a professional baseball club operate its own "farm team" organization or depend on trading for experienced and proven players from other clubs?* Some baseball clubs have been very successful in developing their own players through the farm team system. This approach may also provide a number of redundant players who provide the team with "trading stock" to help secure needed talent. However, such a farm program is costly and demands management time. Other club owners have been very successful by trading for proven players.

4. *Should a trucker buy a commercially available and tested data processing and fleet management system?* There are several well-designed and proven management systems available from software firms to truckline managers. But these systems may not include all the specialized features a specific carrier or manager would desire. Several carriers have invested great amounts to design and implement their own systems. This effort has required the investment of developing computer capabilities that are far beyond the typical requirements for a truckline. In some cases such developments have placed excessive demands on management for a one-time situation.

5. *Should a motion picture studio invest in the development of its own stable of stars (generally called the studio system) or use independent talent?* In the period through World War II the studios developed their own "captive" stables of stars. Such a practice was easily supported by the large number of feature films produced by the studios in the pretelevision era. More recently, the studio star system has been eliminated as the typical production company may produce only 12 to 18 feature films per year, requiring a variety of talent. The elimination of the studio system has, however, resulted in "bidding wars" for the limited pool of available stars.

6. *Should a hospital prepare its own intravenous solutions or buy prepared solutions?* Intravenous solutions are simply sterile mixtures of distilled water and sugars or salt. They can easily be prepared by hospital staffs. But several firms offer solutions prepared under carefully controlled conditions. The responsibility for quality control of the ingredients, labeling, and sterilization is entirely shifted to the vendor. In addition, purchased intravenous solutions are a direct cost that is a reimbursable expense under most medical insurance programs.

This list of make-or-buy decisions is not exhaustive. However, it does illustrate several classes of issues that should be considered. Table 3-2 summarizes several considerations that the service manager should examine.

Table 3-2

COMPARISON OF MAKE-OR-BUY STRATEGIES

	Make Strategy	*Buy Strategy*
Flexibility	May provide quick responses and opportunities to trade off priorities among individual needs up to the limit of the captive capacity. Assures availability. Does the capacity become a burden when not needed?	Outside suppliers may provide greater capacity and ability to absorb fluctuations if free. But the capacity may not be available when needed the most. May be more difficult to control schedules. Suppliers may integrate forward.
Costs	Problems of transfer pricing. Is the demand of the company great enough to achieve reasonable levels of operation to achieve returns to scale of outside suppliers? Can eliminate one or more levels of profit taken by outsiders.	Provides competitive pricing and the opportunity for shopping. Opportunity to consolidate orders with others to gain the advantage of economy of scale.
Quality	May be easier to control quality of own operation. More control over product or service design to meet needs of the firm more exactly.	May be unwilling to provide customer product or service to fit the needs of the firm. Standards of quality may not be appropriate for the needs of the firm. May be more difficult to control quality.
Expertise	Is it worth developing expertise to integrate backward? Will this divert management attention from the main focus of the business?	Does the specialist have the opportunity to develop greater expertise? Does the specialist's greater volume provide it with advantages of the experience curve?

The desire to reduce expenses by eliminating one or more levels of profit may be a compelling force for integration if the volume needed is great enough to afford the firm the opportunity to achieve economies of scale. In addition, capabilities to provide specialized services and customer products, and to exercise greater control of the process are all strong arguments for integration. But the outside supplier with larger volumes may have the opportunity to develop greater expertise and reduced cost through specialization and focus. But is one developing a potential competitor?

Costs are an important consideration in a make-or-buy decision. Flexibility and potential for capacity expansion may, however, be even more important considerations to the service manager.

Backward integration can provide greater flexibility to make sudden changes in strategy without depending on others, but the commitment creating a captive supplier may limit flexibility by tying up capital in facilities and making commitments to a group of employees.

It is important that the service manager explicitly recognize that he or she is making a make-or-buy decision. Once this recognition occurs, it is easy to examine the considerations summarized in Table 3-2.

CONCLUSION

This has been a very brief examination of how a service manager might design a new service or examine an existing service from the viewpoint of how the service is produced. Service managers who have been able to successfully apply these simple tools substantially differentiate their performance from their less sophisticated competitors.

It should be remembered that our discussion of service delivery systems is in the context of an overall system. Analytical design of one piece of the system, although ignoring the entire system, may produce poorer results than more intuitive approaches. Balance of all portions of a system is always important. While the specific tools mentioned here provide a useful framework for analysis, the application of good judgment and common sense is also vital. Many of the concepts discussed in this chapter are intended to increase productivity. They may seem to reduce the service delivery system to a mechanism. Productivity and industrialization of service are desirable. But the *perception* of the service by the customer is also vital. The total service is a complex "bundle" of many perceptions that are often very subtle. It may be objectionable if the delivery system is sensed by the customer. Some of the magic of the show can be lost if too much of the stagecraft is observable to the audience. A highly efficient and productive approach may be appropriate for the operations of a theme restaurant. But if the delivery system penetrates the magic of the dining experience, the customer may become very resentful. Unfortunately, once this occurs, the reaction shifts from positive acceptance to active resentment and rejection rather than simply stopping at passive indifference. Be careful of allowing your productivity to show where it should not be seen.

State Automobile License Renewals

Henry Coupe, the manager of a metropolitan branch office of the state department of motor vehicles, attempted to perform an analysis of the driver's license renewal operations. Several steps were to be performed in the process. After examining the license renewal process, he identified the steps and associated times required to perform each step as shown in Exhibit 1.

Coupe found that each step was assigned to a different person. Each application was a separate process in the sequence shown above. Coupe determined that his office should be prepared to accommodate the maximum demand of processing 120 renewal applicants per hour.

He observed that the work was unevenly divided among the clerks, and the clerk who was responsible for checking violations tended to shortcut her task to keep up with the other clerks. Long lines built up during the maximum demand periods.

Exhibit 1

STATE AUTOMOBILE LICENSE RENEWALS
PROCESS TIMES

Step	*Average time to perform, seconds*
1. Review renewal application for correctness	15
2. Process and record payment	30
3. Check file for violations and restrictions	60
4. Conduct eye test	40
5. Photograph applicant	20
6. Issue temporary license	30

Coupe also found that jobs 1, 2, 3, and 4 were handled by general clerks who were each paid \$3.00 per hour. Job 5 was by a photographer paid \$4 per hour. Job 6, the issuing of temporary license, was required by state policy to be handled by a uniformed motor vehicle officer. Officers were paid \$4.50 per hour, but they could be assigned to any jobs except photography.

A review of the jobs indicated that job 1, reviewing the application for correctness, had to be performed before any other step could be taken. Similarly, job 6, issuing the temporary license, could not be performed until all the other steps were completed.

The branch offices were charged $5 per hour for each camera to perform photography.

Henry Coupe was under severe pressure to increase productivity and reduce costs, but he was also told by the regional director of the Department of Motor Vehicles that he had better accommodate the demand for renewals. Otherwise, "heads would roll."

Questions:

1. What is the maximum number of applications per hour that can be handled by the present configuration of the process?
2. How many applications can be processed per hour if a second clerk is added to check for violations?
3. Assuming the addition of one more clerk, what is the maximum number of applications the process can handle?
4. How would you suggest modifying the process in order to accommodate 120 applications per hour?

Bay Community Hospital

The staff of the Bay Community Hospital had committed itself to introduce a new diagnostic procedure in the clinic. This procedure required the acquisition, installation, and introduction of a new medical instrument. Dr. Ed Windsor was assigned the responsibility for assuring that the introduction be performed as quickly and smoothly as possible.

Dr. Windsor created a list of activities that would have to be completed before the new service could begin. Initially, three individual steps had to be taken: (1) write instructions and procedures, (2) select technicians to operate the equipment, and (3) procure the equipment. The instructions and selection of the operators had to be completed before the training could commence. Dr. Windsor also believed it was necessary to choose the operators and evaluate their qualifications before formally announcing the new service to the local medical community. Upon arrival and installation of the equipment and completion of the operator's training, Edward Windsor wanted to spend a period checking out the procedures, operators, and equipment before declaring the project was successfully completed. The activities and times are listed in Exhibit 1.

Exhibit 1

BAY COMMUNITY HOSPITAL
ACTIVITIES REQUIRED TO INTRODUCE A NEW DIAGNOSTIC PROCEDURE

Activity	*Duration (weeks)*	*Immediately preceding activities*	*Immediately following activities*
a. Write instructions	2	Start	c
b. Select operators	4	Start	c, d
c. Train operators	3	a, b	f
d. Announce new service	4	b	End
e. Purchase, ship, and receive equipment	8	Start	f
f. Test new operators on equipment	2	c, e	End

Jack Worth, a member of the Bay Community Hospital staff, reported that it would be possible to save time on the project by paying some premiums to complete certain activities faster than the normal schedule listed in Exhibit 1. Specifically, if the equipment were shipped by express truck, one week could be saved. Air freight would save two weeks. However, a premium of $200 would be paid for the express truck shipment and $750 would be paid for air shipment. The operator training period could also be reduced by one week if the trainees worked overtime. However, this would cost the hospital an additional $600. The time required to complete the instructions could be reduced by one week with the additional expenditure of $400. However, $300 could be saved if this activity was allowed to take three weeks.

Questions:

1. What is the shortest time period in which the project can be completed using the expected times listed in Exhibit 1?
2. What is the shortest time in which the project can be completed?
3. What is the lowest cost schedule for this shortest time?

Carving Board Restaurants

The Carving Board Restaurant specialized in serving sliced New York steak and roast beef. The Boston store of the chain experimented with the introduction of a broiled pork tenderloin.

The experiment was an immediate marketing success but led to unexpected operating problems. Specifically, the manager found that the cook complained that he was "swamped" trying to prepare the loin because of the special attention this entree required.

Discussion with the cook and personal observation indicated to the manager that one cook could prepare 80 broiled pork loin dinners per hour but could slice and service 250 sliced steaks or roast beef meals if he devoted himself exclusively to one of these tasks. The contribution to fixed costs and profit of each broiled loin meal was estimated to be $3.50, while the sliced beef meals contributed $2.50 each.

The manager believed that it was not possible to sell more than 60 broiled loins per hour or 120 sliced beef entrees per hour because of market preference. In addition, the maximum number of meals of any type served per hour was estimated to be no more than 150.

Questions:

1. What mix of broiled loin and sliced beef sales maximize the restaurant's contribution per hour assuming one cook is used?
2. The manager of the restaurant found that the loin entree was priced so that customers were led to select it in preference to the sliced beef dishes. This resulted in 60 loins and 60 sliced beef dishes per evening. What would you suggest the manager do?

Gulf Port Harbor Master

Ahmed Abdel is the harbor master of Ben Pasha, a busy port of a little known princedom in the Arabian Gulf. The heavy level of import activity placed substantial loads on the port's limited capacity.

Harbor master Abdel was attempting to speed the unloading process by matching the unique capabilities and facilities of available berths and the characteristics of specific shops and cargoes. Ships entering the princedom's ports carried freight ranging from grain in sacks to heavy machinery. The harbor master had four berths suitable for unloading conventional cargo ships. Each berth had different facilities, so that the time required to discharge a specific ship's cargo was typically different at each location.

Three ships were to be unloaded. The times required to unload each ship at the four berths are listed in Exhibit 1.

Exhibit 1

GULF PORT HARBOR MASTER
TIMES REQUIRED TO UNLOAD SHIPS AT BEN PASHA

Berth	*Times required to unload, hours per ship*		
	Ship 1	Ship 2	Ship 3
A	6	14	20
B	14	11	16
C	12	16	28
D	16	10	7

Question:

1. How should harbor master Abdel assign the ships to berths to minimize the total time required to discharge the ships?

The Gates Hotel

The Gates Hotel, a very popular business traveler's luxury hotel in San Francisco, found that it frequently turned down the rental of a room that was being held for a "no-show" reservation. Mr. Barnes, the manager, felt that the hotel's policy of overbooking should be examined. He wondered how much extra capacity should be maintained to cover these commitments.

The average lost contribution for a room was $20 per night if a customer reserved the room and the hotel was unable to honor the reservation. About 10% of the guests who showed up with reservations that could not be honored could be placated without cost. Another 30% were satisfied with being "walked" (or transferred) to another hotel at a cost to the Gates of $3.00 per reservation. The remaining guests were so upset by this situation that the Gates could expect a loss of future business with a percentage value of the contribution of approximately $50.

Mr. Barnes reviewed his records and found that, when the hotel was approximately at the full-house level, the Gates had the no-show experience summarized in Exhibit 1.

Exhibit 1

THE GATES HOTEL NO-SHOW EXPERIENCE

No-shows	*% of experiences*	*Cumulative % of experiences*
1	10	10
2	21	31
3	19	50
4	13	63
5	10	73
6	5	78
7	6	84
8	4	88
9	3	91
10	2	93
11	1	94
12	2	96
13	2	98
14	1	99
15	1	100

Questions:

1. Based on the economics stated, what should Mr. Barnes's policy be?
2. What other issues might Mr. Barnes want to consider in making this policy decision?

Sweet Revenge Restaurant

The Sweet Revenge Restaurant was famous for its special cream pastry dessert. The dessert was made of layers of pastry and cream filling flavored with coffee liquor and was topped with a delicate vanilla icing and shaved dark chocolate. Simply called the Sweet Revenge, the dessert was based on the recipe of a Thomas Quinn, a famous Georgia chef who had served in the British Army in Belgium during the Napoleonic Wars.

Unfortunately, because of the delicate fresh dairy ingredients, the Sweet Revenge had to be served on the same day it was made. This presented a problem for the manager, since he had to instruct the chef how many Sweet Revenges should be prepared for dinner each day.

The manager, Martin Quinn, decided that the contribution to fixed costs and profit from each serving of Sweet Revenge was 85 cents. This was based on a menu price of $1.15 minus a cost of $.30 to produce.

Quinn believed that stocking out of Sweet Revenge was very serious to the reputation of the restaurant. While he felt that it might be difficult to prove, he felt that stocking out of the dessert might be acceptable to 80% of the customers. However, he felt that 20% of the people would be seriously upset by the situation. He estimated that half of these persons would be upset enough not to come back to the Sweet Revenge for some period. The percentage of the contribution from the loss of business from this group would be roughly $10 per each disappointed person. The other half of the disappointed group would decide to never come back. The present value of the loss of the contribution for this group was estimated to be $40 per each disappointed person.

Mr. Quinn collected data on how many Sweet Revenges were ordered each day for a representative period shown in Exhibit 1. He felt there was no seasonal or daily trend for the demand.

Exhibit 1

SWEET REVENGE RESTAURANT
SUMMARY OF DEMAND FOR SWEET REVENGE
DESSERTS ON WEEK NIGHTS

250, 275, 260, 300, 290
235, 250, 295, 310, 360
240, 275, 286, 236, 294
289, 315, 340, 256, 311

Questions:

1. Assuming that the cost of stockout is the lost contribution of one dessert, how many portions of Sweet Revenge should the chef prepare each day?
2. Based on Martin Quinn's estimate of other stockout costs, how many servings should the chef prepare?

Lex Service Group (A)

In January 1972, the management of the Lex Service Group was trying to define a policy for the implementation of the "service concept." Lex's growth had been very rapid over the past few years, with much of it due to acquisitions of service-oriented companies: car dealerships, travel bureaux, employment agencies, and hotels. Lex was committing itself increasingly to the service sector of the economy; the company had adopted the motto: "Lex is in the service business. Service means customer satisfaction." After several months of wrestling with the service concept, top management wanted to articulate a policy that would enable them both to measure and to manage the quality of service provided at the operating level of Lex.

COMPANY BACKGROUND

Lex was incorporated as Lex Garages in 1928, to build and operate parking garages and petrol stations in London. In 1945, Norman and Rosser Chinn bought control of the company and continued to expand Lex's activities in the parking, petrol, car repair, and motor distribution businesses.

In 1968, Trevor Chinn, the son of Rosser, became managing director and set about a program to streamline and reorganize the company. Petrol stations and parking garages, which provided only small margins, were gradually discarded. At the same time it was decided to concentrate on a limited number of franchises and therefore the Renault, Ford, and Vauxhall distributorships were disposed of. The new strategy saw a concentration of Lex's resources in high-profit, high-growth areas, where existing management expertise was thought to be most beneficial. Motor distribution and service became the focus of company interests, and existing franchises of British Leyland, Volvo, and Rolls-Royce were consolidated through the acquisition of additional distributorships.

This case was prepared by Cliff Baden and Colin Carter, Research Associates, as a basis for class discussion rather than to illustrate either effective or ineffective handling of an administrative situation.

LEX DISTRIBUTORSHIPS

Most British motor car companies had a two-stage distribution system, with cars passing from the manufacturer through an area distributor to a local dealer.[1]

Each distributor had an exclusive franchise for a geographical area, with the right to supply all cars from a given manufacturer to dealers in his area. The distributor received a 4% commission on all dealers' sales in his area. The distributor could also retail cars to the public; Lex's distributorships tried to retail at least half the cars that they received from the manufacturers.

In 1971 Lex owned distributorships for Morris (9), Austin (8), Rover (6), Triumph (5), Volvo (4), Jaguar (2), and Rolls-Royce (3), as well as 16 dealerships. As one London brokerage house noted, "By following a policy of selective acquisition and using advanced management techniques in a relatively unsophisticated industry, Lex has now become the leading motor distributor in this country."

All the Lex distributors and dealers had service garages attached to their new-car showrooms. A separate Parts Department provided parts to mechanics in the garages and also sold parts wholesale to other dealers; a small proportion of parts were also sold retail to the public. Each of Lex's car companies was thus in three different businesses: sales, service, and parts.

THE SHIFT TO THE SERVICE CONCEPT

In the summer of 1968, Trevor Chinn attended the 6-week British-American Marketing Program. On his return to Lex, he took a fresh look at the company and determined to develop an appropriate corporate strategy as a basis for future planning. Mr. Chinn wanted to run a company of considerable size; he realized that rapid growth could not entirely be internally generated, but much would have to come from diversification. After considering various sectors of the economy, he settled on the service sector as the one that showed the greatest promise of growth into the future. The choice of the service sector also fulfilled one of Mr. Chinn's principal strategic goals, that of not tying up Lex's capital in fixed assets of an inherently obsolescent nature.

The commitment to a service strategy was sufficiently well-formed for Mr. Chinn to explain it to Lex's shareholders in the 1970 Annual Report.

> As the vehicle business is based on manufacturers' franchise arrangements, physical growth is not entirely at the sole discretion of a company such as Lex, and the strategic plans of the manufacturers concerned can impose limitations on our growth.

---

[1] Ford and Volkswagen had both changed to a one-stage system, with cars being sold through a few large dealerships.

While continuing to develop our existing motor vehicle distribution interests, we have, in order to meet our growth aspirations, started to diversify into other service businesses. We first moved into areas closely associated with existing activities such as vehicle leasing and retail distribution of tyres, oil and accessories, and then moved further afield as we sought a broad enough horizon of opportunity to ensure the continuing development of the Company in the years to come.

It is our intention to become a diversified company operating in a number of major service industries. Each target industry will be selected on certain criteria:

a) It must be large enough totally to allow Lex to establish a business entity complete in line and staff management of the highest calibre.
b) It must have a growth potential in the coming decade which will enable us to maintain a rate of profit growth equal to that of our existing business.
c) Lex must be able to establish itself among the market leaders of the industry.
d) Lex must expect that within a reasonable time it will draw an important contribution to Company profits from that service industry.
e) We will select industries that require a high level of service to customers that preferably are fragmented and operate on a decentralised basis and where accordingly profit improvement can be achieved through the exercise of modern management skills in the areas of planning, financial control, marketing, and personnel management.

By January of 1972, Lex owned interests in several service-related industries: passenger car distribution and servicing, commercial vehicle distribution and servicing, freight and transportation, hotels and tourism, and employment agencies. However, 80% of Lex's profits were still derived from vehicle distribution and service. Mr. Chinn and his corporate staff believed that any steps taken to implement the service concept at Lex would first have to be proved effective in the motor side of the business.

ATTEMPTS TO DEFINE AND MEASURE SERVICE

At a corporate-level meeting in May 1971, the top managers of Lex discussed the service concept and the company motto: "Lex is in the service business. Service means customer satisfaction." Those attending the meeting were unable to come up with a definition of service beyond "customer satisfaction," nor were they able to choose any measures that would allow Lex to quantify the service it was providing. Measurements such as the number of complaints received were felt to be negative indices; management hoped to be able to measure positive results.

At this meeting, the following directive was given to all the divisional managers.

Objective: To improve level of customer service satisfaction in every part of our company. Each General Manager is to report back to his Divisional Manager by 1st June outlining methods by which service to the customer is to be improved and causes of complaint eliminated. He is also to report specific steps which are being taken to improve communication between management and staff and management and customer to ensure that management is aware of customer complaints and can take speedy action to remove the cause.

Responses to this directive were received at company headquarters the second week in June. These responses varied in length from two to twelve pages; two of them are reproduced in Exhibit 1.

Exhibit 1

LEX SERVICE GROUP (A)
Sample Responses to Headquarters Request
for Service Programmes

To: Group Headquarters, London 10th June, 1971
Subject: Customer Satisfaction

The Group's standard of Service to its Customers must be of the caliber to ensure that Customers return to the Group each and every time they require Service, and knowing that the Service received is of the highest standard we will acquire through the personal recommendations of our Customers, other Customers.

In order to achieve Customer Satisfaction, the following factors must be met:

1. Premises clean and businesslike and Reception points clearly marked so that the Customer can see exactly where he has to go to enquire for the Service required.
2. The Customer expects to be talking to a knowledgeable, helpful individual who shows complete interest in the Service requested and that at this particular moment the satisfaction of the enquiry is the most important task in the Employee's life.
3. Explain the operations or steps entailed in completing the service. After all the Customer has called upon us to satisfy an immediate need and we should treat this with the importance it warrants.
4. Make sure that completion time is reasonably accurate. If things go wrong, let the Customer know. We have had to amend our plans because something has gone wrong; give the Customer a chance to amend his.
5. If an Estimate of charges is requested and a firm one can be given, then give it, and stick to it. If you cannot say so—make it quite clear that charges you are giving are an estimate because of this or that—Explain why.
6. Make sure that the Service is performed correctly.
7. If a Customer complains and you cannot give him satisfaction, make it easy for him to see your immediate superior. Never leave a complaint unresolved.
8. Telephone answering:
   a. Upon the receipt of each call, state the name of the Company, followed by—Good Morning/Afternoon—can I help you.
   b. Ensure that you know the names and extensions of all Employees.

LEX SERVICE GROUP (A)
Sample Responses to Headquarters Request
for Service Programmes

c. Ensure that you know what type of Service is carried out by each extension.
d. If the line is engaged, say so, and offer to ring caller back.
e. If caller decides to "hold on," keep advising that line is still busy until line is free, or offer to ring back.

9. Invoice presentation of highest order, avoid padding to justify price charged.
10. Correspondence to be concise and businesslike.

I feel that appropriate Notices should be displayed at points of Sale informing Customers that our aim is to give a First Class Service and if the Customer feels that he has reason to be dissatisfied with the Service, he should write to a "Customer Satisfaction" Department at Head Office. This would give Head Office an awareness and measurement of the standard of Service throughout the Group.

I believe that the quality of Service is remembered long after the amount charged is forgotten.

To: Group Headquarters, London — 9th June, 1971
Subject: Service means Customer Satisfaction

To our customer service means friendly and professional attention, good availability of goods and services, completion of a supply or work contract within a specified period and a good appearance of the finished product. The service has to be courteous, prompt, honest, and reliable in all Departments of the business which preferably should be carried out in clean, cheerful and modern premises.

Any complaints should be given immediate attention with a fair and unbiased investigation at the highest company unit level.

WHY IS OUR SERVICE NOT ALWAYS AS GOOD AS IT SHOULD BE?

Service Department

1. Staff make promises which they are unable to keep or forget to take action.
2. They quote prices when they are not sure what the correct price is and without checking whether or not the repair is really necessary.
3. They do not check to see if the part is available.
4. They blame the Parts Department or the factory for problems rather than take a positive approach.
5. They do not always advise the customer in time regarding delays in completion of repairs.
6. They do not advise the customer at inception that we require payment on collection.
7. Telephone enquiries are not always answered as promptly as should be.
8. Cars sometimes handed over dirtier than they came in.
9. Failure to advise Accounts Department of action taken after dealing with a complaint.

Parts Department

1. Area of weakness in supplying special order parts and the customer not always advised when parts are in stock.
2. The telephone service not always as good as it should be with customers being kept waiting too long either (1) before phone answered or (2) whilst parts being located.

LEX SERVICE GROUP (A)
Sample Responses to Headquarters Request for Service Programmes

SUGGESTED REMEDIES

Service Department

1. Re-name Tester by calling him Quality Control Supervisor; otherwise only cars with running faults get tested.
   Have check sheet specifying certain known failures in service in addition to the actual repair,
   a. Cleanliness of car
   b. Greasy steering wheel
   c. Cleanliness of carpets
   d. Use of paper car mats
   e. Use of plastic seat covers (throw away type)
   f. Use of wing covers
   g. Oil and water levels
   h. Tyre checks.
2. The Foreman to constantly supervise all work as it progresses and notify either Reception or Progress chaser of any delays and to notify customer.
3. Attach Customer Satisfaction card to all repaired cars and provide a handy receptacle for these, or send out regular mailing letters asking for comments on our servicing.
4. The retailing aspects of service and sales are complementary to each other and are better handled by one person in the Sales Department as they are stronger at this.
5. Service Managers to random check at least one car per day and report to General Manager on the quality of workmanship.
6. General Manager to check at least two cars per week to satisfy himself on the quality of work.
7. To ensure that all customers' complaints are dealt with promptly and sympathetically and if we are at fault to pass credit note immediately.
8. Notify customer of any work found and advise him or her whilst car in workshop and not when the car is called for; they may have returned a hire car.
9. Display all customer complaints on notice board highlighting to mechanic concerned. He would probably be more careful in future. Red label to be attached to works copy of repair order showing name of original mechanic.
10. Have all cars washed (with exception of very minor repair jobs).
11. Install Dynamometers and brake testing equipment to minimize road testing.
12. Train staff to be clean and tidy in themselves and habits by providing good facilities, i.e.,
    a. Rubbish bins
    b. Clean toilets and washing facilities
    c. Clothes lockers and changing rooms
    d. Mess Room.
13. Advertise and give guarantee of service (we do any way, why not say so).
14. Have a good level of investment in special tools and any labour-saving devices, i.e., power wrenches, diagnostic equipment, etc.
15. Have customer participation suggestion box in reception area.
16. Ensure that mechanics attend specialised factory training courses.

LEX SERVICE GROUP (A)
Sample Responses to Headquarters Request for Service Programmes

17. Offer incentive to fitters who carry out complaint-free repairs on monthly basis.
18. Offer incentive to Quality Control for returning cars with genuine faults in repair. (This way he will look for faults instead of disguising them.)
19. Train Receptionist to remember customers' names and their car.
20. Return displaced parts to customer in plastic bag.

Parts Department

1. Ensure that the customer parts counter is always manned and to ensure that customers know that they have been noticed.
2. Questionnaire mailing to all parts customers.
3. Parts Marketing Manager and marketing representatives to report back all complaints.
4. Give help and advice to all do it yourself customers.
5. General Manager and Parts Manager to make random checks as to the promptness with which incoming telephone calls are dealt.
6. One telephone Salesman to be responsible for provision of all parts required for urgent use which are not at the time in stock.
7. Compilation of non-availability record.
8. Separate counter for orders telephoned in so that customers ordering by phone can have orders made up ready for collection to avoid waiting.
9. Investigate van routes, cut out non-paying, long-distance, time-consuming routes to give a better local service.
10. Ensure vehicles properly maintained to cut down "off the road" time. Consider incentives for well kept vehicles.
11. Employ women drivers, as it has been found that dealers prefer them to men.
12. Always try to reserve the last fast-moving item for workshop use.
13. Install interpretation section to Retail Parts Counter, so that customers who know their part numbers can be dealt with more quickly, and so that those who need specialist help can receive it.
14. Improve the level of skill in the Parts Department and to improve its image as the "cinderella" of the business.

MEASUREMENT OF OUR SERVICE

1. Service complaints as a percentage against retail sold hours or as a percentage of number of repair orders issued monthly.
2. Sales as a percentage against vehicles delivered retail.
3. Parts as a percentage against turnover in retail terms. (These percentage targets to be set after a trial period in the light of experience.)

As examples of the efforts being made toward customer satisfaction, some of the Divisional Managers sent copies of public relations material that had been developed at the divisional or local levels. These included a "Customer Satisfaction Card" (Exhibit 2) and an invitation to a free car inspection for vehicles over 12 months old (Exhibit 3).

Exhibit 2

LEX SERVICE GROUP (A)
Customer Satisfaction Card

CUSTOMER SATISFACTION CARD

Help us to provide the kind of service you want for your vehicle. This is one of the most important aspects of our role as a Morris Distributor, and to assist us in appraising our standard of service and guide us in any improvements we make please put a tick in the appropriate box and return this card to us at your convenience.

Does our reception engineer usually attend to you promptly and courteously?	YES	NO
Are we good at diagnosing what is wrong with your vehicle?	YES	NO
Are you satisfied with the quality of our work?	YES	NO
Do we usually complete the servicing on your vehicle when promised?	YES	NO
Do we leave your vehicle in a clean condition after service?	YES	NO

NAME..

ADDRESS...

LEX

Exhibit 3

LEX SERVICE GROUP (A)
Invitation to Free Car Inspection

Distributors for Triumph Agents for Austin, Rover, Jaguar, Daimler

Dear Customer,

We are sure that you will be interested to know that we are running a Special Show and Service Week at our premises for one week only from 22nd to 27th November, inclusive.

For many years now Standard-Triumph have been organizing Show and Service Weeks, and on the dates quoted, their Service Engineers will be available to carry out a free inspection on all Standard and Triumph cars over 12 months old and which are no longer enjoying the benefit of the Manufacturers Guarantee.

If you would like a detailed report on the exact condition of your car, may we suggest that you telephone our Service Reception Department, so that a convenient time and date may be arranged.

In addition to the Engineer's Services, we shall also have our own Special Show of Triumph cars, both on exhibition and for demonstration. If you would like to wait while your car is being inspected, or come and see us anyway during this special week, our sales staff will be pleased to answer any problems you may have.

We look forward to the pleasure of your company during this special week.

Yours faithfully,

DIRECTOR

At the same meeting in May, it was decided to try simultaneously another approach to gauging the effectiveness of Lex's customer service. Questionnaires were sent to over 1200 customers of two Lex garages asking them to evaluate the quality of service they had received. Responses were collected at the divisional level and sent to company headquarters for evaluation (Exhibit 4).

With the responses to the questionnaires and the directives in hand, Mr. Chinn and his staff hoped to define some measures of service that would provide workable guidelines for people at the operating level of the company.

Exhibit 4

LEX SERVICE GROUP (A)
Report on Customer Service Questionnaire

This report covers the results of a survey carried out during early May amongst customers of Cheltenham Car Mart and Lex T.B.C. Kidderminster.

Background

A questionnaire was sent out, under cover of a personalised letter, to all customers who had used our service facilities during the three months period February–April this year. The covering letter stressed that it was our continued aim to seek complete customer satisfaction and to this end would they please complete the attached questionnaire adding any suggestions which they thought might improve our customer service. A reply-paid envelope was enclosed.

At Cheltenham a total of 390 questionnaires were sent out, whilst at Kidderminster over 850 questionnaires were dispatched.

Findings

Question 1. Did you make a prior booking for your service?

	Cheltenham		*Kidderminster*	
Yes	152	95%	158	88%
No	7	5%	22	12%
Not completed	2		8	
Total	161		188	
Base for %	159		180	

Question 2. When did you last receive a service card or letter from us?

	Cheltenham		*Kidderminster*	
1 month	29	21%	113	66%
2 months	18	13%	24	14%
3 months	9	2%	10	6%
Never	85	60%	23	14%
Not completed	20		18	
Base for %	141		170	

LEX SERVICE GROUP (A)

Report on Customer Service Questionnaire

Question 3. Has anyone from our Company ever contacted you by telephone about servicing your car?

	Cheltenham		*Kidderminster*	
Yes	20	13%	33	19%
No	131	87%	141	81%
Not completed	10		13	

Question 4. Were you satisfied with the reception you received from our staff when you arrived with your car?

	Cheltenham		*Kidderminster*	
Completely	140	89%	153	92%
Reasonably	16	10%	8	5%
Poor	1		4	2%
Bad	1		1	
Not completed	3		22	
Base for %	158		166	

Question 5. Was the work carried out to your satisfaction?

	Cheltenham		*Kidderminster*	
Completely	114	73%	112	63%
Partly	42	26%	55	31%
Not at all	1		10	6%
Not completed	4		11	
Base for %	157		177	

Question 6. Were there any grease marks on the steering wheel or seat when you collected the car?

	Cheltenham		*Kidderminster*	
Yes	4	3%	22	12%
No	156	98%	157	88%
Not completed	1		9	
Base for %	160		179	

Question 7. Was the car ready for collection when promised?

	Cheltenham		*Kidderminster*	
Yes	149	96%	146	84%
30 mins. late	6	4%	17	10%
1 hour late	—		1	
Over 1 hour late	1		11	6%
Not completed	5		13	
Base for %	156		175	

Lex Service Group (B)

In January 1972, Mr. Trevor Chinn, Managing Director of the Lex Service Group, was worried about the implementation of the service concept throughout the company.[1] Given Lex's emphasis on profit performance, there had been some uncertainty at the operating level over the added costs that increased customer service could involve. Mr. Chinn felt that clarification would be needed. He also wanted to give further thought to the type of local branch managers Lex would need to achieve the corporation's long-term growth objectives.

PERFORMANCE TARGETS FOR 1972

Lex had established an enviable growth record since 1966. Profits before tax jumped from £292,000 in 1966 to £4,382,000 in 1971. In the same period, fully diluted earnings per share grew at a compound average of over 50 percent per year. Exhibit 1 gives relevant data from Lex's financial statement.

While 40% of the earnings growth was attributed to acquisitions, 60% was attributed to internal growth at Lex. Rationalisation of existing operations and the introduction of effective management control systems were considered to be major factors in the company's growth. For example, Lex management believed that the car servicing and sales of spare parts offered at least as much profit potential as new car sales. This conviction, which was not shared by the motor trade generally, was supported by the information produced by Lex's accounting systems which carefully separated sales, service, and parts as profit centres. In the mid-60's, Lex's emphasis shifted to active promotion of the car service and spare parts aspects of the business. Furthermore, because management believed that the profits from servicing and sales of parts were less subject than new car sales to cyclical swings induced

This case was prepared by Cliff Baden and Colin Carter, Research Associates, as a basis for class discussion rather than to illustrate either effective or ineffective handling of an administrative situation.

[1] See Lex Service Group (A) for background on the company and the origins of the service concept at Lex.

Exhibit 1

LEX SERVICE GROUP (B)
Lex Service Group Six-Year Record

	1966	*1967*	*1968*	*1969*	*1970*	*1971*
Turnover £	23,756,000	25,539,000	32,614,000	45,179,000	85,016,000	111,325,000
Profit before charging interest on long-term debt £	402,038	843,507	1,169,327	1,478,781	2,922,466	5,120,551
Profit before Taxation £	292,191	727,899	1,037,927	1,250,219	2,455,488	4,382,117
Net Assets £	4,541,380	4,815,205	6,586,633	10,619,626	21,575,401	36,290,540
Shareholders Funds £	2,484,152	2,612,695	3,431,042	5,950,443	10,810,858	25,392,481
Earnings per Ordinary Share						
basic	0.9p	2.4p	3.8p	4.2p	6.7p	9.2p
fully diluted	0.9p	2.4p	3.8p	3.6p	5.7p	7.5p
Profit before interest on long- and medium-term debt as a percentage of Net Assets	8.9%	17.5%	19.7%	13.9%	15.2%	17.6%
Profit before Taxation as a percentage of Shareholders Funds	11.8%	27.9%	30.2%	21.0%	26.5%	28.3%

Source: 1971 Annual Report

by the economy at large, the company adopted a "service absorption" policy. According to this policy, the income from service and parts was expected to produce sufficient profit to cover overhead in all areas of the business.

Managers were expected to report "service absorption" information each month to corporate headquarters, where it was viewed as a key measure of managerial performance. An English security analyst commented on the effects of the system:

> Service absorption obviously ensures that profits from new vehicle sales go straight through to the P & L account, and allow Lex to pass on increased overheads to the public relatively easily.

Rapid growth continued to be a prime objective at Lex. A 20% improvement had been sought each year in both profits and earnings per share. Management also looked for a 35% return each year on current assets.

In October 1971, Mr. Chinn issued the "Corporate Targets of Performance for 1972." The first of these targets called for each division to improve its profits by at least one-third over 1971. Division Managers were further advised that

> particular emphasis should be paid to Net Profit before tax expressed as Return on Sales as a key financial ratio through control of trading margins and detailed control of all expenses. Specific targets for this ratio have been allocated to each Business Group.

For the first time, one of the targets in 1972 was concerned with the quality of service provided by Lex. The Managing Director called for

> a dynamic commitment to the improvement of the level of customer satisfaction in each location through the implementation of the "Customer Satisfaction" programme. The level of Customer Satisfaction is to be improved by 25% in each location as measured by:
>
> a. the number of complaints
> b. repeat business
> c. sample questionnaires on customer satisfaction developed and administered by the Publicity Department.

By including service as one of Lex's targets, and by calling for improvement in this area, Mr. Chinn hoped to impress upon Lex's employees at all levels of the company the seriousness of his commitment to the service concept. Now, as the company moved into 1972, he began to hear, through the Divisional Managers, that some local managers were finding it difficult to reconcile the profit targets with the goal of improved service.

PERSONNEL PLANNING

In his original statement outlining Lex's strategy for becoming a service-oriented firm, Mr. Chinn had spelled out the kinds of businesses where he thought Lex would be most effective.

> We will select industries that require a high level of service to the customer, that preferably are fragmented and operate on a decentralized basis, and where accordingly profit improvement can be achieved through the exercise of modern management skills in the areas of planning, financial control, marketing, and personnel management.

Travel agencies and employment agencies were thought to fit this description, as were Lex's local car dealerships and distributorships. The hope was to turn each operation at the local level into a profit center.

Accordingly, Mr. Chinn and his corporate staff decided that a professional manager should head up each local operation wherever possible. Traditionally in the motor industry the manager of a distributorship had come to that position from a job as car salesman, or as head of the Service or Parts Departments. Some local managers had previously worked as mechanics on the shop floor. While people at Lex's head office acknowledged that these local managers were usually able to deal adequately with day-to-day operating problems, they felt that personnel with graduate-level qualifications and professional managerial experience would be better able to run each distributorship as a profit center and to do the kind of analysis that would make most effective use of Lex's management accounting systems.

One member of the corporate staff explained, "Knowledge of the motor trade is not a prerequisite of motor trade management. A good manager should be able to work with our accounting systems and our budgeting and planning systems. That is what a manager's job is: analyzing, planning, and controlling. He should not be out there pumping gas." People at the corporate level hoped eventually to be able to transfer these professional managers from one Lex business to another (e.g., from managing a car distributorship to managing an employment agency).

In November 1971, Lex was advertising in the London newspapers for general managers for its car distributorships (Exhibit 2).

INTERVIEW WITH A MEMBER OF THE CORPORATE STAFF

In an interview at Lex's head office in London, a member of the corporate staff expressed some of his concerns about implementing the service concept.

> It was relatively easy to shift the company's emphasis to service. The hard part comes afterwards, when you have to define service—what does it mean in operational terms?
>
> We are prepared to give that issue a lot of attention because anybody should be able to run the business from a cost-control viewpoint as well as we are. Therefore, the only way to set ourselves apart is by the quality of our service, by what our people do.
>
> We need to develop better measures of service—and positive rather than negative measures. Criteria for performance should be positive. We also have to recognise that the measures must be implementable by relatively unsophisti-

Exhibit 2

LEX SERVICE GROUP (B)
Advertisement for General Managers

GENERAL
MANAGERS

Motor Vehicle Distributorships
up to £4,000

The planned growth of the Lex Service Group is creating a number of opportunities in various parts of the Country within its car and commercial vehicle distributorships. The appointments to be filled involve complete responsibility for the planning and direction of operations of businesses having annual turnovers of between £1m and £4m.

Applicants should be aged between 28 and 40 with graduate or equivalent professional qualifications and with at least two years' experience in a profit-responsible post in a sales or marketing orientated environment. Such experience need not have been in the motor trade since full training will be given prior to appointment.

Salary will be negotiable up to £4,000 p.a. and, in addition to excellent career prospects in an expanding and progressive company, benefits include non-contributory pension and sickness schemes, a company car and assistance with relocation expenses where appropriate.

Applications in writing, giving brief details of age, qualifications and experience, should be sent to:

S.D.E. Dunford, Management
Development Manager,
Lex Service Group,
18 Great Marlborough Street,
London, W1V 2BL.

Source: Sunday Times, 14 November 1971

cated managers. We want them to help identify positive measures, but how do you get them to think that way without having to come down and flog them all the time?

In any case, we are not certain where in the company structure is the leverage to implement the service concept. Can we do it at the corporate level? Or is it at the divisional or local levels? We can design training programs to try to shift the emphasis to providing service, but will people believe them? There is a traditional sales orientation in the motor trade and this is coming into conflict with the more open-minded service orientation of some of the non-motor people who are now entering the organisation. We are not sure if we should encourage this conflict and thereby speed up a change in orientation, or if we should let change take place slowly, one case at a time.

That raises the question of management. Our greatest problem is going to be finding people to manage our local operations. People tend to think that garage work is low level or that you have to be a travel agent to run a travel agency.

It is not true, of course. We want to be able to find people who can run a unit by themselves and who can shift from one Lex operation to another. On the other hand, it may be more important than we suppose that the manager maintain close customer contacts over time with his customers. Some people argue that we are putting too much faith in corporate systems without recognising the harmful effects that these might have on the operating routine in the front-line. I do not think this is right, but we have still to prove our case conclusively. We are just beginning.

INTERVIEW WITH THE MANAGER OF A LOCAL DISTRIBUTORSHIP

The manager of one of Lex's local distributorships discussed his perceptions of the service concept. His comments seemed typical of those of other branch managers.

You know we have Management by Objectives at Lex. We used to express our objectives in terms of financial objectives, like sales, or turnover per year, or ROI. Now Lex is telling us to express our objectives in terms of the issues that are behind the selling of cars—things like improving the existing customer retention rate, or evaluating the cost effectiveness of better service shop equipment in terms of customer satisfaction. They tell us that the arithmetic on the financial performance of the company is only part of a job description or a profit plan. It's not an objective. I do not know if that is right or wrong.

They have a new corporate objective to increase the level of customer satisfaction by 25 percent, and there are some very positive things about this. First of all, we are defining customer satisfaction as an objective. We always try to provide customer satisfaction, of course, but making it an official company objective gives just that much more weight to it. And it's a common-sense thing to say, anyway. It is not contrary to operational things. So, it should enable us to grow.

On the other hand, we have got some problems with the service concept. We are in a very vague area. Defining customer satisfaction and measuring it is a task which the average man is not going to be capable of achieving. Is any objective good if we cannot measure it? Do we need to measure everything? Management theory is that you should be able to measure something if it is an objective. I cannot help thinking that some things—like loyalty—cannot be measured.

There are basic conflicts, too. There is the obvious one between short-term and long-term profits. We are not measured on profits 3 years from now, but in the car business that is when you reap the benefit of a satisfied customer who returns to buy a car. Maximising our profit on today's dealings with him may lose him next time.

The pressure to raise customer satisfaction as well as current profits gives difficult trade-offs. The temptation, if you worry about the first in the case of a demanding customer, is to squeeze more money out of another customer to make up for any loss.

There are lots of delicate problems that are difficult to resolve, but they are important if you decide that customer satisfaction is a paramount objective. For example, what do you do when a little old lady comes to buy a car and is too timid or does not know enough to ask for the normal discount? Should we tell her? Give her a big discount she did not ask for? If we want to get this year's profits up, we'll charge the full price. But what happens when she goes home and finds out that she could have had a discount? That is one customer we'll never see again. So, the customer satisfaction idea really runs head on against the pressure for profits.

Or take another fairly common example. We have serviced a man's car, and he comes back a week later and claims that the work we have done is not satisfactory, and he wants a refund. Should we give it to him? Even when we know we have done the job properly?

And then, there is a contradiction in the way we price our service and our parts, in taking different profits on the same deals. Or in following service manual suggestions saying it's necessary to replace parts when, in the particular instance, they do not really need to be replaced. Do we have a moral obligation to tell the customer that parts do not need replacing until x-thousand miles?

There is a problem of people, too. You have seen that Lex has placed advertisements in the papers for new managers. Now the Personnel Department is sending around university graduates. These are long-term people; you know, thinkers, cold, intelligent planners. But they do not fit the needs of our existing businesses. Personally I believe that we are engaging, for a majority of our companies, the wrong kind of people.

If I have to choose between the entrepreneur and the planner, I'll take the first. We are engaging thoroughbreds to pull a cart. They are all right for the Derby, but not for pulling a cart.

Only a really mature company can afford to take on a profit planner. Most of our businesses—these car and truck distributorships—are not mature yet. They need entrepreneurs running them: people who have excellent relationships with customers, who enjoy a beer with them after work, and inside the business are prepared to jump in and help sweep the—off the floor. And how many university graduates would want to go to the Road Haulage Dances? Not too many, I would guess, but you have got to do that sort of thing if you want to sell commercial vehicles in a tough market.

I agree, though, that long-term objectives are important even if the management performance measures are biased against it, and I might have to say that you would want a different person in the long run to the present.

Flair, Inc.

On a Friday afternoon in late May of 1975, Matt Laidlaw was explaining a business concept to a group of close friends who were sitting in his room in Mellon Hall at Harvard Business School.

> The Flair System will be a chain of haircutting boutiques which will offer efficient, friendly service. We believe that haircutting can be treated as a production line service business. McDonald's took an inefficient service business and transformed it into a successful, fast, courteous chain of business. Our basic product is beauty or at least the hope of beauty. It is essential that each store deliver a uniform quality of service in an environment of obvious cleanliness, order, and cheerful courtesy. The physical layout of the store, the personnel training, and the management supervision combine to limit the discretion of the serving person. Discretion hinders the delivery of a uniform product.

Matt and George Brimwell, a section mate and close friend, had researched their ideas for a new enterprise during the past several months. Now they were trying to decide whether to go ahead with the raising of capital for their new business idea, Flair, Inc. (which was scheduled for incorporation in late May), or to accept one of the several offers they each had to join the corporate ranks of other firms.

Both Matt and George had explored job possibilities through the placement office at Harvard Business School and had been offered positions with several prestigious Wall Street firms. Matt readily admitted that "it's hard turning your back on some of these offers" (reportedly in the $25K bracket plus bonus options). However, they both had agreed that they would prefer running their own show. Therefore, they felt that the viability of their business idea, Flair, Inc., needed closer examination to ensure that their immediate future would not be tied to a losing proposition. It was for this reason that Matt and George had asked several friends to serve as a sounding board for the concept.

Personal Backgrounds

Matthew Laidlaw was graduated from George Washington University in 1968 with a degree in business administration. An honor graduate, Matt initiated and served as the Chairman of the George Washington Growth Fund. Losing both his mother and father during his freshman and sophomore years, respectively, Matt left school temporarily in 1966 to assume the presidency of a company in which his father held a majority interest—a boat retailer and repair facility. His duties included supervising the management and operations, developing a management information system, and finally assisting in merger and acquisitions activities.

Matt returned to school in early 1967 as a junior. After completing his final year at George Washington, he reassumed the presidency of the firm he had left. Matt was successful after several lean years ("a time," he admits, "that I barely had money to go to a movie") in turning the business around. The company grew from one location and sales of $60,000 to the point where it encompassed five marine locations, one wholesale tree nursery, and two retail outlets with combined sales of over $6 million in 1974. Matt decided in early 1973 to give up the presidency of the company to enter Harvard Business School. He retained a position on the board of directors. Matt was slated to serve as chairman of the board of Flair, Inc.

George Brimwell was graduated from the University of London in 1969 with many academic honors to his credit. While in college, George participated in assorted activities and was awarded the Queens Gold Medal for academics. After graduation, George served as a lieutenant in the Royal Navy where he worked on advanced weapons designs. While in the navy, he managed a crew of men as a site electrical engineer for Associated British Combustion. George later resigned from the navy to enter the Harvard Business School. George was to serve as president of Flair, Inc.

Development of Idea for Starting the Business

Because of his experience in managing a firm, Matt felt that it should be possible to establish criteria for an ideal growth company. George also felt that there were key characteristics of the operations of a business which would affect the possibility of growth. They were able to characterize the "ideal" industry by the following:

1. Potential for high growth in primary demand;
2. Sufficient size, i.e., a billion dollar industry;
3. Limited economic concentration, i.e., no one company or group dominating the marketplace;
4. Opportunities for consolidation of existing businesses;
5. Low barriers to entry, with the promise to shift from low entry cost to high entry cost in the near future;
6. Undergone significant changes due to shifts in the environment;
7. Opportunity for substantial profits.

After screening a number of industries, they discovered that the haircutting industry appeared to satisfy their criteria:

1. *High growth.* The haircutting industry had grown from $1.3 billion in 1938 to $6.1 billion in 1975. If cosmetic revenues were included in order to acknowledge the distributive powers of salons, the growth had been from $3.8 billion in 1933 to $13.7 billion in 1975. Traditionally, this market had been only women. Men repre-

sented a new market for increased sales of services and products because men had become fashion conscious and were willing to allocate increasing amounts of money on personal grooming. The growth in men's cosmetics and fashion clothing was dramatic evidence of this change.

2. *A large market.* Between the ages of 16–40, there were over 100,000,000 persons. If 70% of these people had their hair groomed at professional stores, six times a year at $2.50 per visit, the industry sales would have been greater than $1 billion, even using these conservative estimates of potential user frequency and the low per visit charge. Industry sources estimated the market at $6.1 billion.

3. *Not dominated by any single company or group.* There were several major chains which had approximately 25% of the high fashion/high priced business. From interviews conducted in early 1975, it was disclosed that these chains were not targeted at the largest single market of 16–34-year olds, but aimed for the 34 and older market segment (25% of total market). This older clientele required extensive services such as hair coloring. In the 16–34 market, there were no major competitive threats on the horizon unless the traditional salon chains decided to extend their market appeal. Several mini-chains (3–6 locations) had been formed to service the burgeoning 16–34-year-old market.

4. *A fragmented market.* There were over 200,000 individual stores. A great number of these owner/operators had been unable to make the transition from the traditional salon to the more contemporary store. The typical store seemed to follow a pattern of growth. First, a haircutter severed ties with an established salon. He/she built the business for two to three years until it achieved a size which created problems that were too complex for his/her management skills. The accounting, personnel, and production bottlenecks exceeded his/her grasp. At this stage, many store owners were found to be receptive to someone managing the business side and letting them (the owners) return to practicing their profession.

Another indicator of the opportunities of consolidation was the low intrinsic value of a salon. The owner/operator was locked in, because the business had only limited going concern value. In the traditional style, the customers were loyal to the cutter and not the salon.

5. *Easy to enter.* The physical plant and equipment required to enter the haircutting business was inexpensive. Chairs, dryers, plumbing, and signs were about all that was needed. The cost of purchasing a location which was already equipped ranged from $7,000 to $50,000 with an average of approximately $20,000.

However, the cost of becoming established as a viable business was increasing. Marketing expenses had become significant. Shops with eight to ten cutters and better quality furnishings were increasing their local market share at the expense of the two-person shops and the very large traditional salons. Image had become extremely important. Existing chains were expanding, and new chains were starting. These new groups had begun to create a brand loyalty as opposed to an individual cutter loyalty.

6. *Dramatic shifts in the environment.* There were three significant trends in the industry which had changed the critical factors for success. First, people had become oriented toward the youthful/carefree look. This natural trend had seriously hurt the traditional salon which had relied on the more elaborate hairstyles (the "lacquered bubble" look with exotic colors).

Second, customers, both men and women, wanted efficient quality service. They did not have the time to spend two hours for a haircut or all day at the beauty salon. Also, they wanted to be able to take care of their hair at home. They did not want to be tied to the mandatory weekly visit to the beauty salon or barber shop.

Third, the "unisex" phenomenon had become accepted. Most operations had been geared exclusively to either men or women but not to both. Decor, location and personal skills limited the ability of many operations to change.

7. *A profitable opportunity.* From a reliable industry contact, the financial figures for a leased salon in one of Boston's largest department stores were obtained. The salon grossed $700,000/year. The department store received $100,000 and the salon's sixteen cutters received $280,000, leaving the operator with a gross margin of $320,000. The operator earned before-tax profits of $70,000 and earned an after-tax return on his investment of greater than 25%. There were also reports of several small chains which earned a 25% return on invested capital.

The Friday Afternoon Meeting

After describing the basic concept to his friends Matt Laidlaw passed out a sheet of paper with the following eleven headings: target market, pricing, merchandising, site selection, unit design and staffing, training, organization and management control, accounting and financial control, management roles, finance and ownership, and strategy. He asked the group to bear with him as he described his and George's thoughts about each of those elements of their business plan.

Target market. Our product is targeted at those customers who are:

1. Between 18–40 in age with an average of 27 years.
2. Middle or upper income. Working women, housewives, and professional men who can take time during the day are sought.
3. Living or working within a one-mile radius depending on actual site. In New York, a store located in Manhattan could appeal to people within a radius of 40 blocks, but the appeal would most likely be only to those within a 10-minute walk, except on weekends.

Pricing. The haircutting industry is differentiated by price into three basic groupings. High-priced stores such as Charles of the Ritz, Elizabeth Arden, and Sassoon are price insensitive. They charge $20 and up for a shampoo and haircut. The second group is more numerous and prices the shampoo and cut at $8–15. If the salon owner or head stylist cuts the hair himself, it costs $20. The third group, constituting the low-price segment, seems to be dying out because of rising costs and customer dissatisfaction. Customers want greater expertise, nicer surroundings, and a store which can be trusted to deliver a uniformly good product. Running counter to the trend, however, is a chain of four stores in New York which price a cut and blow dry at $4.50. It is run with no service, but as a "Slam-bang, thank-you ma'm" operation. However, in the last six months even their business has been off due to customer disenchantment and the rising economy. The lower-price group charges from $4.50–$6.00 for shampoo and cut.

Flair will price its service in the mid-to-upper ranges at $10 for a shampoo, cut, and blow dry. This segment has the largest number of people in the major metropolitan regions. It is most sensitive to a new, aggressively merchandised chain. It is least sensitive to the economy. Thus, Flair will be in the middle as far as price, yet be high in quality for the limited service performed.

Merchandising. The merchandising plan of action for Flair is based on the belief that articles written about the concept, the people, and the activities will have more impact than advertising alone. Flair is selling an intangible product: fashion. It is essential that the proper image be ascribed to Flair. This image must:

1. Appeal to the target market which is profiled as being 18–40 in age with an average age of 27, medium income, urban, predominantly female (70/30 split), and women who consider themselves as with-it mod (semi-liberated).

2. Flair connotes contemporary good looks highlighted in a natural, warm, free-spirit fashion.

3. Not become associated exclusively with any particular haircutting trend.

4. Denote efficient, professional service executed in clean, pleasant surroundings. Visiting a Flair facility should be looked forward to as an opportunity to pamper oneself and meet new friends while sipping coffee in the waiting room. Consequently, it is hoped that the customers will feel they can be whisked in and out at their own choosing depending on their time demands, not those of the facility. Nevertheless, Flair will try to graciously serve the client in only 45 minutes. Additional time spent by the customers will be of their own choosing such as having another cup of coffee while talking to a friend. It is essential that the ambiance of the store change with the time of the day in order to reflect the differing clientele. Early mornings might be at a fast, cheerful pace. Afternoons should be somewhat slower, more leisurely; late afternoons and early evenings would be busy and, thus, should quicken the pace.

The Flair name will be brought to the public through advertising, publicity, and promotion. There will be three phases in the advertising program.

The first phase is undertaken in support of new store openings. It will start with teasers in preopening ads, move toward service description and gimmick grand-opening push, and end with a tailoff display of haircut alternatives. The ad style will be clear and crisp with careful use of white or open space. The Flair signature will be standardized to create recognition of it over time. These advertisements will be in local newspapers, regional magazines (i.e., Boston, New York), billboards, and radio. If the initial thrust of Flair is opening three to five stores simultaneously, then spot television will also be used.

The second phase is the continuous advertising back-up for existing stores. These advertisements will feature special cuts, descriptions of the professionals, and price breaks during the summer for urban locations.

The third phase is institutional-type ads in fashion magazines. These will ease efforts in getting news coverage. Magazines such as *Glamour, Ingenue, Mademoi-*

selle, Seventeen, and *Cosmopolitan* will be considered. Women are the primary targets. The third phase would not be implemented until there are two major cities covered by at least six shops.

Publicity, as performed by public relations experts, will be the cornerstone of the Flair merchandising. Articles and news features lend credibility to the Flair concept if favorably written. Flair is new and thus needs as much credibility as possible. Once an article is written, advertising will be used in that magazine or newspaper to reinforce the message of the article. Flair is newsworthy for several reasons:

1. It puts the whole natural concept together, not piecemeal, but as an integrated package.
2. It will have an interesting people story. Two Harvard MBA types set out to make fame and fortune in the haircutting industry. The cutters themselves will be encouraged to cut famous heads of hair and be mentioned in society colums, and/or do models for fashion magazine photograph credits.
3. It will make news. Haircut shows will be given for women's clubs, schools, civic organizations and local TV talk shows.

There will be charity promotions whereby Flair, as a company, and the employees, as a group, will donate the revenues from a Monday morning to a community project or a national charity such as the United Fund.

Promotion serves as the underpinnings to advertising and publicity. The objective of the promotional program will be to create an identifiable logo which will embody the Flair concept, while at the same time describing it. Publicity can be secured in a meaningful manner if it is guided. Flair will engage a public relations firm.

There will be a complete corporate identity program. "A hair-brained scheme, Flair" will appear wherever possible—business cards, price lists, flyers, advertisement signatures, placards, etc. The colors in the logo will be carried into the shops to create continuity and good natural design.

Site selection. Careful site selection will encourage traffic to utilize these concepts, but it is not a surrogate for them. Our sites will be located in areas that have a high pedestrian count, parking nearby if not adjacent to the store, middle-income residents, and an emphasis on fashion. At first, we will open in urban settings which are in the clothing boutique section of the city. The Newbury Street section of Boston has a blend of shoppers, residents, and working people. This is the ideal mix, because it allows the store to serve the different audiences at the most opportune times for the store. Residents and shoppers patronize the store during the morning and midafternoon. Some working people drift in during the day, but the majority use such services in the late afternoon and early evening. Unfortunately, the store traffic becomes more seasonal as the environment becomes more urban. The summer months can be very slow. To combat this drop-off during the summer months, advertising will be directed toward hotels. In addition, there will be special price breaks.

Suburban locations, while less seasonal, have fewer people. The residents are not as sophisticated in their daily attire and thus are not as willing to pay $10–15 for a shampoo, haircut, and blow-dry. We will locate our first two locations in an urban environment with an additional two in the nearby suburbs. The units will always be clustered to permit easier management and to develop economies of scale in advertising and promotion.

On the urban sites, the operation will be on the second floor in order to lower rent expense. However, we would want a large street level sign detailing our services. The suburban locations will be on the ground floor on the main street of the town or in substantial shopping malls.

Owing to promised technical support in training and management's familiarity with the city, Boston has been chosen as the first media area. The first store would be opened in early September. After some consolidation, 1976 would see the downtown Boston store opened in January, and two suburban locations in March and May, respectively. Suburban stores would be situated in the business/shopping mall centers of Greater Boston. Thus, the first cluster would be established within eight months of the first store opening. (A listing of store sites for 1975–1977 is shown in Exhibit 4.)

Unit design and staffing. The physical layout of the store shapes the kind of service which the customer receives. The entrance into the store will face the receptionist who can greet customers, take any packages or coats, point out the coffee bar, and ask them to be seated until their cutter is ready to wash and cut their hair. The receptionist is the first point of contact with the customer and establishes at that moment the type of relationship which will exist. The customers will immediately experience someone helping them with their belongings and offering a cup of coffee.

The working area will be the furthest away from the reception and waiting areas. People with wet hair do not want to be embarassed by those who are either finished or still waiting for service. Such feelings are particularly important to consider when there are both men and women being served. The washing area will have seats for waiting. Having two waiting areas may seem foolish except when things are busy, the shift from the front waiting room to the washing area indicates that the wait is not as lengthy as it might otherwise seem.

The cutting area consists of clusters of four cutters operating off an X-shaped service bar which extends between the customers. Being at waist height the service bar unobtrusively divides customer A from customer B but does not create a feeling of claustrophobia. Stored in it are the cutter's brushes, combs, towels, lotions, and handheld dryer. They are in drawers out of sight. The customer faces a mirror which has been fastened to a tinted lucite panel that is hung from the ceiling to the floor. Customer B cannot easily see the opposite customer except by looking around the mirror and through the tinted panel. Thus, each station creates a nook of semiprivacy. The cutters can see each other which encourages conversation. The drying areas have been split up to avoid the wasteland of nine dryers segregated from everything else. They are grouped in threes and are somewhat screened by large plants.

The overall decor will be contemporary and well lighted by modern fixtures. A centralized vacuum cleaner will isolate the noise of the compressor while permitting simple quick cleaning of the floor at all times. Music will be piped throughout the store. Soft rock and other current music will be selected.

In the typical company-owned unit, we expect to achieve revenues of $417,000 in the second year of operation. To achieve this level of revenues, we will be open from 10:00 A.M. to 8:00 P.M., Monday through Friday and 8:00 A.M. to 6:00 P.M. on Saturdays. We will staff the operation and compensate the employees as follows:

Position	*Number needed*	*Compensation*
Manager	1	$833/month + 2.5% of operating profit
Cutters	14	$300/month + 25%* of service revenues
Receptionist	1 full-time	$600/month
	1 half-time	$300/month
Janitor	1 full-time	$500/month
	1 half-time	$250/month

* Standard industry practice to give cutters a percentage of service revenues.

Training. The hard systems technology of equipment and store layout must be augmented by the soft systems technology of policies, procedures, and personnel training. The cutters will be required to attend a Flair school for a minimum of one month. At school they will learn the Flair accounting system as it impacts on them, how to courteously but efficiently serve customers, and the art of personal hygiene and grooming. Flair will introduce a new methodology to this service business. A customer will have his or her style analyzed and kept on permanent record. Each cutter will be trained to break down each style into the required curls, waves, and length of hair by quadrant of the head. This analysis will be recorded in conjunction with any special remarks (no hairspray, type of conditioners, cowlicks, etc.). These cards will indicate the genuine concern of Flair that each customer gets what he or she wants. Also, it reduces the need for a customer to be continually served by one particular cutter. An alternate cutter need only go to the filed record to get a good guide for the desired style. The receptionist will attend school for one week on accounting and personal grooming. While in school, Flair will pay salaries but expect the employees to cover out-of-pocket expenses. Once a month, the corporate creative director will hold in-store seminars on the latest trends. These seminars will allow the central office to monitor Flair operating techniques and, when necessary, take corrective action.

Organization and management control. Our management structure will centralize some functions and decentralize others. Control of advertising, promotion, and public relations will be centralized, however, the actual placement of advertisments will be a local function. Accounting and payroll will be on central computers. The accounting knowledge, and potential computer awareness would be too costly to maintain within each store. However, remote managers will be trained in the use of accounting statements for management control, since their incentive pay will be calculated on bottom line results. Central personnel are best equipped to insure the stores conform in basic construction and degree of maintenance. The business managers and creative director, through their visiting of many stores in different regions and awareness of sales of particular services in the various stores, can best spot trends. Although, a strength of the Flair System is the grass roots network of managers who can raise issues to central management, it is the overview of the central management which can hopefully distinguish between a local short-lived fad and a major trend. This approach signifies a tradeoff that is conspicuously being made in our concept. Flair will not be the promoter of the latest wayout fashion, but will concentrate on the broader trends. This approach means that local competition will occasionally beat the Flair System to a new style. It is our belief that it is more important to have the operators well trained in the new techniques before any promotion, and that our target clientele would be skeptical of a store which changed capriciously to reflect each new fad.

There will be decentralized control of newly hired personnel, on-site personnel, and community relations. (1) Local management, living in their own region, are best equipped to select personnel who would be attractive to the local clientele. Nevertheless, standards will be centrally established and turnover will be monitored by the forms described hereinafter. (2) The remote manager must continually exercise his supervisory function to insure smooth operations and an acceptable level of service. (3) Each Flair store must be regarded as an asset to the community. Promotions and community projects, as described in the marketing section, will be overseen by the local manager. It is expected that each manager will seek to be a leader in his community. Service is provided on a one-to-one basis in the field, not at headquarters. Headquarters is only the service arm to the field staff.

The essential cost items are selling and wage expense, and secondarily, the cost of advertising and promotion. Labor costs represent the largest expense. They are directly controllable at all levels. Advertising and promotion, as a discretionary expense at the central office level, is important because of its impact on revenue generation.

Accounting and financial control. The *sales invoice* is the basic source document. It reports sales revenues by income category and is used for cash control, commission calculations, and customer documentation. From this source document, punched cards could be generated which would allow computer data processing of all transactions. For the first stores, the system will be run manually in order to establish the actual data needs and methods of collection. The cash disbursement slip records actual cash payments for services received or as customer refunds.

The *daily report* serves four purposes:

First, it aggregates the sales information from specific invoices to generate a daily sales figure for on-site management monitoring.

Second, it controls cash and develops in a mechanical, easy to follow manner, the daily bank deposit. Bank deposits will be made daily no matter how small the amount in order to safeguard against burglary and employee dishonesty.

Third, it creates a record of local cash disbursements. All major items will be paid from the central office and, thus, the remote disbursements should not be large. Explicit recording of cash disbursements should help dramatize their expense nature to the local management who receives an incentive bonus of net profits.

Fourth, the daily report includes a sales adjustment breakdown which, by its inclusion, highlights the negative effects of such adjustments. Moreover, the detail records the use of free work as a promotional tool in order that its effectiveness may be ascertained. Lastly, this breakdown is necessary to adjust the commission part of the salary payments.

The *weekly time sheet* summarizes the hours worked by each employee. Time cards need not be used except in large store locations, since this record collects the same information. Despite the commission salaries, a record of hours worked must be maintained for the state and federal departments of labor. Also, it will permit productivity to be measured which should help to refine the relationship between customer scheduling and available staff.

The weekly report of employee hours and operator sales matches labor expense to gross revenues by day, facilitates calculation of service and merchandise commissions, points out the type of business done (local or transient), and cross checks the daily reports through cross total comparison. If the sales invoices were keypunched for data processing and the commission structures were programmed, this report could be generated by the computer.

Finance and ownership. The estimated capital requirement of the Flair strategy is $100,000 of initial funding. The two founders will immediately invest $25,000. The relative shares are displayed below:

	Dollar investment	*Shares*	*Price/share*	*Equity participation*
Founders	$ 25,000	750,000	$.033	75%
Investor Group	$ 75,000	250,000	$.300	25%
	$100,000	1,000,000		

There would be only one class of stock issued initially, which would be common voting stock. The corporation would have its stock registered under Section 1244 which gives an advantage on the downside to high tax bracket investors (i.e., capital loss may be treated as a deduction from current income). A computer simulated financial planning model was used to project Flair's earnings for three years out. (See Exhibit 1 for consolidated statements. Exhibits 2 and 3 show projected earnings for two salons—a company-owned facility and a franchised operation.)

Exhibit 1

FLAIR, INC.
Projected Financial Statements
(Year End 1st–3rd Yrs.)

Consolidated Income Statement	*Year 1*	*Year 2 ***	*Year 3 ****
Revenue, service	$51,923.13	$1,036,646.40	$2,371,169.31
Revenue, goods	3,846.15	77,800.01	182,561.21
Revenue, franchise cash fees[a]	5,000.00	29,000.00	7,000.00
Revenue, franchise sales[b]	0.00	4,333.65	57,577,82
Total Revenues	60,769.28	1,147,780.06	2,618,308.34
Less Cost of Sales			
Base wages	$15,200.00	$ 234,755.00	$ 505,210.00
Incentive wages	12,229.15	257,657.04	593,819.39
Social security	790.40	12,207.26	26,270.92
Fringe and health	906.00	13,560.60	28,780.20
Total Personnel Costs	29,125.55	518,179.90	1,154,080.51
Rent and taxes	$ 6,228.00	$ 59,993.00	$ 114,718.00
Insurance, utility, phone	990.00	9,325.00	16,450.00
Advertising, store	6,788.46	71,322.31	129,686.51
Cost of service	2,376.00	49,445.00	115,238.00
Cost of goods	1,538.46	31,120.01	73,024.49
Operating Profit	$13,722.81	$ 408,394.84	$1,015,110.83
Depreciation, salon	$ 1,483.52	$ 13,510.99	$ 23,692.31
Corporate administration	1,350.00	14,355.00	38,070.00
Corporate salaries	14,769.23	32,000.00	32,000.00
Add back:			
Franchisee administrative charge	0.00	50,000.00	73,000.00
Franchisee interest	0.00	1,805.86	10,580.31
Income Before Tax	−3,879.94	400,334.71	1,004,928.83
Depreciation for tax	$ 2,832.45	$ 23,391.78	$ 34,900.63
Federal income tax	0.00	183,525.50	470,610.84
Profit After Tax	$−3,879.94	$ 216,809.21	$ 534,317.99
Earnings Per Share	−0.004	0.22	0.53

** Includes addition of two franchised salons, i.e., #4 & #7 (See Exhibit 4)
*** Included remaining franchised facilities, i.e., #8, #10, #11 & #12 (See Exhibit 4)
[a] Franchise fees of $5000 in year 1, $6000 in year 2, and $7000 in year 3. Franchise fees treated as income when unit opens, not when franchise is sold.
[b] Royalty payments of 3% of total revenues of the franchisees.

Exhibit 1 (continued)

FLAIR, INC.
Projected Financial Statements
(Year End 1st–3rd Yrs.)

Consolidated Balance Sheet Items	*Year 1*	*Year 2 ***	*Year 3 ****
Ending cash	$74,435.93	$ 195,420.59	$1,121,708.05
Franchisee notes	0.00	19,903.83	91,165.28
Credit line	0.00	0.00	0.00
Stockholders equity	$96,120.00	$ 312,872.00	$ 847,190.00
Shares outstanding	1,000,000.00	1,000,000.00	1,000,000.00
Book value per share	0.10	0.31	0.85
Return on Investment	−3.88%	225.50%	170.78%

Exhibit 2

FLAIR, INC.
Projected Earnings of One Company-Owned Salon
(Years 1–3)

		Store #1	
Income Statement	*Year 1*	*Year 2*	*Year 3*
Revenue, service	$51,923.13	$417,482.22	$436,363.33
Revenue, goods	5,846.15	30,924.60	32,323.20
Total Revenues	55,769.28	448,406.82	468,686.53
Less Cost of Sales			
Base wages	$15,200.00	$ 80,400.00	$ 82,420.00
Incentive wages	12,229.15	108,214.87	113,616.99
Social security	790.40	4,180.80	4,285.84
Fringe and health	906.00	4,632.00	4,742.40
Total Personnel Costs	29,125.55	197,427.67	205,065.23
Rent and taxes	$ 6,228.00	$ 17,992.00	$ 17,992.00
Insurance, utility, phone	990.00	2,860.00	2,860.00
Advertising	6,788.46	22,420.33	23,434.32
Cost of service	2,376.00	19,104.00	19,968.00
Cost of goods	1,538.46	12,369.84	12,929.28
Operating Profit	$ 8,722.81	$176,232.98	$186,437.70

Exhibit 3
FLAIR, INC.

Projected Earnings of One Franchised Salon
(Years 1–3)

	Store #4		
Income Statement	*Year 1*	*Year 2*	*Year 3*
Revenue, service	$ 0.00	$114,598.14	$284,613.88
Revenue, goods	0.00	9,220.54	22,899.97
Total Revenues	0.00	123,818.68	307,513.85
Less Cost of Sales			
Base wages	$ 0.00	$ 44,500.00	$ 88,920.00
Incentive wages	0.00	23,884.77	63,383.70
Social security	0.00	2,314.00	4,623.84
Fringe and health	0.00	2,433.50	4,872.40
Total Personnel Costs	0.00	73,132.27	161,789.94
Rent and taxes	$ 0.00	8,050.00	$ 11,960.00
Insurance, utility, phone	0.00	1,575.00	2,340.00
Advertising	0.00	8,190.93	15,375.69
Cost of service	0.00	6,700.00	16,640.00
Cost of goods	0.00	3,688.22	9,159.99
Operating Profit	$ 0.00	$ 22,482.26	$ 90,248.23

Exhibit 4

FLAIR, INC.
Store Opening Schedule

Store #	*Fiscal Year*	*Month*	*Company/Fran.*	*Location*
1	1975	September	C	Urban Boston
2	1976	January	C	Urban Boston
3	1976	March	C	Suburban Boston
4	1976	April	F	Suburban Boston
5	1976	August	C	Urban New York City
6	1976	October	C	Urban New York City
7	1977	December	F	Urban New York City
8	1977	January	F	Urban New York City
9	1977	February	C	Suburban, White Plains
10	1977	March	F	Suburban, Long Island
11	1977	April	F	Suburban, Long Island
12	1977	May	F	Suburban, Southampton, L.I.
13	1977	August	C	Urban, Chicago
14	1977	September	F	Suburban, Boston
15	1977	October	C	Urban, Chicago

Proceeds will be used for organizational expense, the opening of the first two stores, and working capital.

Organizational		
Legal and professional		$ 2,500
Printing investment circular		2,500
Plans and graphics		5,000
Traveling expense		1,000
Salary before start-up, principals		5,000
		$16,000
Operational		
Capital cost,. first two stores	$ 64,000	
Advertising	10,000	
Working capital	10,000	
Total	$100,000	

Management roles. Psychological testing at the student counseling center has shown that I am a risk seeker who performs best under stress while George is task-oriented, likes detail, and is motivated toward production and day-to-day management in an uncluttered environment.

George and I will initially organize and open the first two stores. Then within the nucleus concept, the goal will be to make the areas self-sustaining. Boston will be the corporate home base. Thereafter, the founders will concentrate on developing new areas, with a regional manager in each cluster. This decentralized system will be possible, given the comprehensive financial reporting system and formal visits by the central management.

Strategy. The Flair strategy is to move quickly into one media area to establish a critical mass for advertising and management control efficiency. After consolidation, the next selected media area will be entered in the same systematic way. Thus new locations will be planned on a media area, rather than individual basis.

In selecting media areas, the requirements are for a population receptive to new ideas, a sufficiently large market to support four stores within ½ to 1 hour of driving, and an urban business district to provide young, professional, affluent people. Flair is targeting that market. Housewives and college people are important in augmenting the target group but would not be the central factors in selecting locations.

For a media area, the urban stores are more profitable and have higher sales than suburban locations. Thus there will be full-time managers in key urban stores, with satellite operations in the suburbs. In essence, Flair stores will be in clusters around a nucleus of management control, within a single media area for advertising impact.

Franchising will be used as a vehicle to maintain and regulate growth. Interviews indicate willing franchisees within the ranks of both store owners and hairdressers. Franchisees would pay a fixed initial contract fee 18 weeks before store opening, but the leasehold improvements could in many cases be financed through Flair with a note to the franchisee.

* * * * * * * * *

As Matt finished the section on strategy, he passed out another sheet of paper (Exhibit 5) which outlined the schedule of tasks to be done. He closed the presentation with a few comments about the schedule and then asked his friends:

> Can we make this concept work as it has been presented to you? If not, are there some changes we can make to enhance the concept? George and I are excited about going into this business. But we might have tunnel vision because we have been working on the concept for so long.

Exhibit 5

FLAIR, INC.
Flair Task Scheule

Date required	*Task*
6/1/75	*Business Plan Complete* *Complete feasibility and applied research
6/15/75	*Consolidation* *Finalize founder's agreement *Contract any outside participants who might join Flair management
6/15/75	*Funds Search* *Submit investment circular to interested parties –Venture capitalists –Friends –Suppliers
7/1/75	*Site Selection* *Develop micro plans for: –local ordinances –utilities –insurance –cultivation of local contacts –banking relationship
7/1/75	*Company Organization* *Spend funds for: –corporate filing –drafting legal papers

Exhibit 5 (continued)

FLAIR, INC.
Flair Task Schedule

Date required	*Task*
7/1/75	*Have $100,000 Raised* *Secure funds contingent on: –finalize corporate form –establish escrow account –authorize and empower management by board
7/15/75	*Fail/Safe Point* *Spend funds for: –lease commitments –equipment, plumbing, furnishings –security deposits –hiring people –ordering supplies –secure operating license
8/15/75	*Have Additional Money Raised* *Make adjustments as necessary to capital accounts
9/15/75	*Open One Store* *Train hired personnel –4 weeks for cutters, after first two weeks select manager –1 week for receptionist *Install equipment –finalize installation –clean stores *Advertise and promote –teasers two weeks in advance –articles and hard sell an opening –Open store 9/15/75
The Future	*Open More Stores* *Iterate through process *Continue to promote existing locations

Max-Able Medical Clinic (A)

Harry D. Eugene, M.D., felt a growing sense of concern for the Automated Multi-test Laboratory project, as he reread the memorandum from his close associate Dr. George Johnson, a radiologist in the Max-Able radiology department (Exhibit 12). As head of the medical systems technology department he had worked closely during the past year with Drs. George Johnson in radiology, Roy Burns in internal medicine, and members of the executive committee at Max-Able, such as Dr. Long to develop plans for an innovative automated multiphasic testing laboratory at the Max-Able Clinic. He reminded himself that he must take concerns such as those expressed in the memo into account as he prepared the final proposal for the project to the Executive Committee.

The Max-Able Medical Clinic was a private, multispecialty group-practice clinic. It was located in a relatively affluent urban area in the Southeast, where it had spacious modern facilities and laboratories. It was organized as a partnership with more than 130 affiliated physicians.[1] (See Exhibit 1.) Individual salaries and participation in earnings were closely proportional to the revenue each physician generated. Revenue from patient charges at Max-Able was generated from three sources: physician visits, tests and other procedures performed by the attending physician during the visit, and procedures ordered by the attending physician. These categories accounted respectively for 37%, 42%, and 21% of the revenue overall but they varied from 70%, 7%, and 23% for general practice in internal medicine, to 10%, 85%, and 5% for radiologists (X-ray). All major specialties and sub-specialties were represented in the clinic, and almost all the clinic's physicians also held appointments as "clinical" faculty at a nearby well-known university school of

---

This case was prepared as the basis for class discussion rather than to illustrate either effective or ineffective handling of an administrative situation. It is adapted, with permission of the authors, from a case developed at Stanford University and was made possible through the co-operation of Asst. Professor J. C. Hershey, R. J. Harrington, and an organization which prefers to remain anonymous.

[1] In typical usage the term "multispecialty group practice" refers to an affiliated group of physicians who largely practice in the medical specialties. They typically treat patients with acute, difficult to diagnose, or complex health problems, who they attract by referral from a primary care physician or by reputation. In contrast, the primary care physician (including general practitioners, internists in general practice, family practitioners, and pediatricians) typically treat the full range of health problems they encounter and assume much of the responsibility for preventative medicine and education.

Exhibit 1

MAX-ABLE MEDICAL CLINIC (A)
The Max-Able Medical Clinic Staff

Executive Board

6 M.D.s

Internal Medicine

- Cardiology—4 M.D.s
- Chest Diseases—6 M.D.s
- Endocrine and Metabolic Diseases—5 M.D.s
- Gastroenterology—3 M.D.s
- General Medicine—5 M.D.s
- Hematology and Oncology—2 M.D.s
- Infectious Disease and Immunology—1 M.D.
- Nuclear Medicine—1 M.D.
- Peripheral Vascular Diseases—1 M.D.
- Renal Diseases—1 M.D.
- Rheumatology—2 M.D.s

Allergy—2 M.D.s

Neurology—3 M.D.s

Dermatology—2 M.D.s

Pediatrics—7 M.D.s

Pediatric Cardiology—1 M.D.

General Practice—7 M.D.s

Psychiatry and Clinical Psychology—3 M.D.s
2 Ph.D.s

General Surgery—3 M.D.s

Administration

5 Administrators

General and Thoracic Surgery—1 M.D.

General and Vascular Surgery—2 M.D.s

Plastic and Reconstructive—2 M.D.s

Neurosurgery—1 M.D.

Orthopedic Surgery—6 M.D.s

Orthopedic Surgery and Athletic Medicine—1 M.D.

Urology—3 M.D.s

Ophthalmology and Optometry—7 M.D.s

Otolaryngology—3 M.D.s

Obstetrics/Gynecology—6 M.D.s

Anesthesiology—5 M.D.s

Environmental Medicine—2 M.D.s

Environmental Medicine/Industrial Surgery—1 M.D.

University Health Service—9 M.D.s

Radiology—7 M.D.s

Laboratory Medicine—1 M.D.

Pathology—1 M.D.

Medical Electronics—1 M.D.

Medical Systems—1 M.D.

---

medicine. Max was one of the early models of "group practice" and had a national reputation for its innovations in community health care and health program organization.

Consequently, it was not surprising that when a firm in the health services industry—now AML International—had developed an automated health testing service characterized by modular design and a "carousel" configuration of patient flow, it had brought the design to Max for consideration.

Dr. Eugene was currently facing the problem of deciding whether to proceed, what tests to include in the automated laboratory (lab.), how the tests would be scheduled in a process flow, proper design of test sequences, pricing, and how to handle possible resistance among the clinic's physicians.

Background on Automated Laboratories

With the recent focus on the nation's health care delivery system, automated multiphasic laboratories were being heralded as an important breakthrough. The basic idea underlying the automated health testing concept was that a battery of critical medical tests could be administered to patients receiving medical checkups through the use of a special facility employing advanced technology and operated by medical technicians rather than physicians. In this way a comprehensive sequence of carefully designed, standardized tests whose quality was carefully controlled could be effectively administered to a large number of patients at low costs and without the use of scarce and costly physicians' time. Such a facility promised to provide better quality information for diagnosing the health status of patients and the early detection of diseases than was typically available for the traditional health checkup.

In traditional medical practice a checkup involved an initial visit to a physician, typically a general practitioner or internist (practicing general medicine). In the course of the visit the physician would write up a lengthy medical history, examine the patient and perform a number of routine tests depending upon the patient's history, condition, symptoms, the equipment available in the office, and the physician's customary procedures. The patient might then be sent for further tests, laboratory procedures, X-rays, etc., often in other locations, and, following the receipt of results, scheduled for another visit with the physician. If medical difficulties could not be diagnosed by this physician or if special procedures were required, then the patient might be referred to a specialist such as a cardiologist for heart diseases or a surgeon in any one of several specializations.

As planned, the multiphasic testing laboratory would be used at Max-Able, to short cut many of these time-consuming steps and improve the effectiveness with which physician and patient used their time. The patient would visit the multiphasic laboratory at his own convenience before the initial visit to the physician and results would be available before the initial physician visit. In this way the physician would have a strong information base even at the initial visit and could make the best use of his time and knowledge in exploring particulars and making judgments rather than on the mechanics of testing procedures. The patient would be assured of a thorough and comprehensive checkup at a low cost and with a minimum waste of time in making repeat visits. Dr. Eugene thought the new laboratory would prove useful in several ways: in providing important diagnostic data for patients that came for general checkups, as a source of baseline data on patients with specific medical problems that came to the specialists at Max; as a service to nonaffiliated physicians in the community that might wish to have such a good workup on their patients, and it might provide a resource for Max physicians who wished to innovate in establishing new programs, like executive health checkup programs, etc.

Multiphasic health testing laboratories had been introduced several years earlier and successfully used in several major institutions. They were currently being introduced in many others. Pioneering work had been carried out, among other places, at Kaiser Permanente in California and the Mayo Clinic in Minnesota. Kaiser was world famous for the success which it, as a private institution, had achieved in providing a rather complete program of health care to several million persons in California at a reasonable predetermined annual charge. Because it provided complete health services at a fixed annual charge and was highly integrated, Kaiser had the incentives to seek the health improvement as well as labor-saving benefits of a multiphasic testing concept. It would experience the direct economic consequence of any improvement in its patients' health condition (or deterioration) that influenced the rate with which costly acute hospital facilities were utilized. It was therefore not surprising that Kaiser had been an innovator in this type of program. The Mayo Clinic, renowned for specialty care and not heavily involved in prepaid comprehensive care, had strong governance and instituted the multiphasic concept as a matter of policy.

In some of the early applications the multiphasic testing laboratory concept was used to screen patients, i.e., to separate the "worried well" from the sick and thereby determine which should receive the immediate and serious attention of a physician. Critics sometimes compared such facilities with military induction physicals where service is impersonal and patients are denied privacy, being required to dress and undress at several stations during the test sequence. There was also concern with use of multiphasic automated tests to screen patients, since it might lead to the denial of appropriate medical care.

The multiphasic lab, as proposed for Max-Able, differed in important respects from some of the earlier approaches. It would complement rather than replace the initial physician-patient contact. Furthermore, it would emphasize personalized services with many patient amenities.

It was technically feasible to include many tests in the lab, but the mix of tests would largely determine the potential demand. Most tests under consideration were costly. Dr. Eugene realized that the facility would have to offer profitable operations before the directors of the clinic would approve its implementation, yet the price for the battery of tests would greatly affect the usage of the facility. He also knew that gaining the support of the physicians before the lab was implemented was especially important in a group practice. Poor acceptance by physicians and their patients would not only cause problems at Max-Able but would also delay the widespread application of the concept elsewhere. AML International was anxious that the system be accepted at Max, because recovery of its development costs required broad adoption of the AML design in many practices. Failure of the design at Max-Able would mean an almost certain end to potential sales.

Proposed Laboratory Design

The modular "carousel" design proposed by AML International promised to offer all the benefits of previous automated testing labs at Kaiser and Mayo:

—More information for the physician's use in diagnosis
—No need for the physician to perform the tests himself
—Less need for the physician to refer the patient to a laboratory for general tests and for the patient to schedule another visit to the doctor

—A sophisticated base of medical data for comparative analysis of long-term health trends

—Use of paramedical and nonmedical personnel to staff the AML

—Substantial decrease in medical costs and improvement in quality of testing

—Early diagnosis of certain diseases at a stage when they are most responsive to therapy.

The new design offered two additional benefits:

—Convenience: no long waits, travel between test areas, or multiple dressing and undressing

—A personal touch: one technician assigned to a patient for the whole sequence of tests.

The general layout of the laboratory as proposed is presented in Exhibit 2. The entire sequence of patient movement through the facility would consist of five stages of activity: (1) pretest arrangements; (2) medical history and patient preparation; (3) initial stationary tests; (4) carousel tests; and (5) final stationary tests. Tests for all stages except the carousel had been tentatively decided.

Pretest Arrangements

Patient processing at the facility would begin when an appointment was made with the laboratory. Only patients referred by a physician could make an appointment, although for self-initiated patients the facility might suggest the names of several physicians to sponsor the tests. The patient would then be assigned an appointment time and asked to fast for five hours beforehand. Except in the case of rush appointments, the patient would be sent a questionnaire to be completed before the appointment. Upon arrival at the lab, the patient would give the questionnaire to the laboratory appointment secretary, who would assign a number to the patient to be used for test identification. The information from the questionnaire would be fed through an on-line terminal into a computerized patient record.

Medical History and Patient Preparation

The patient would then be instructed in the use of a computerized medical history terminal consisting of a back-projected filmed questionnaire and simple answering device. The patient would be presented a sequence of questions with several logical branches. If, for instance, the patient answered a question indicating a prior known medical condition the terminal would branch to present a special questionnaire section to explore this condition. These answers would also be automatically fed into the patient's stored computer record.

Upon completion of the history portion of the exam, a patient would be given a large amount of glucose and shown to the males' or females' dressing area, where disposable garments would be issued for wearing during the tests. (The patient flow can be visualized from the layout in Exhibit 2 where major testing activity groups are indicated by numbers in circles.)

Exhibit 2

MAX-ABLE MEDICAL CLINIC (A), Facility Design

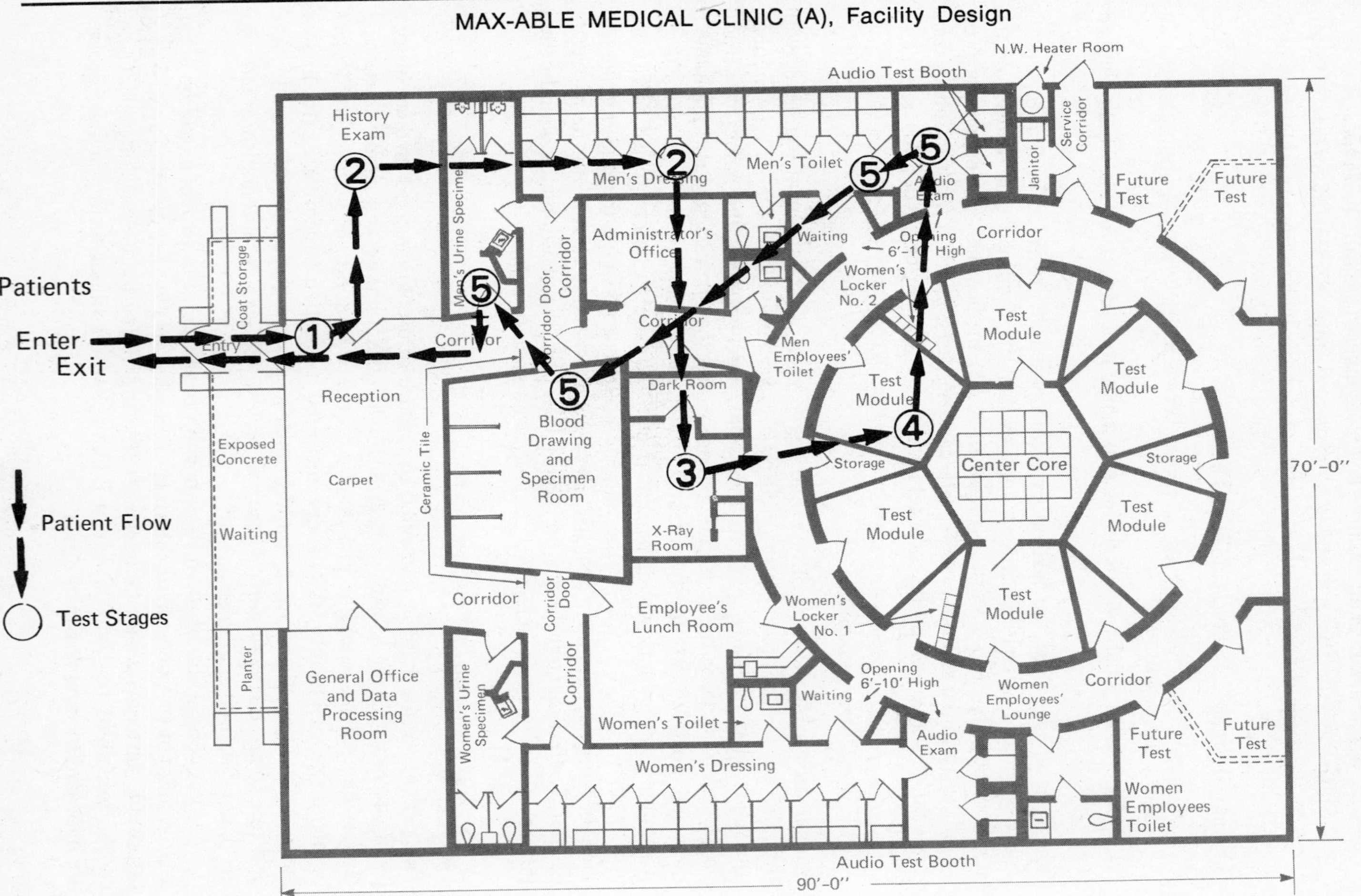

Floor plan for AML international's Automated Multiphasic Health Testing Services Laboratory.

Initial Stationary Tests

The next stage of tests would involve those performed in stationary rooms in the facility before the patient entered the carousel. A technician would be assigned to the patient and stay with the same patient throughout this and the next test stage.

The first test in the initial stationary stage would consist of an X-ray. This would be followed by a digitally displayed measurement of the patient's height and weight. The X-ray test required a shielded X-ray room. After these procedures the patient would be led into one of the modules of the carousel, accompanied by the AML technician for the next stage of testing.

Carousel Tests

The carousel consisted of a "core" room which provided space for a large amount of test equipment, with six patient testing rooms, "modules" in a circle around it (see Exhibit 2). The wall of the core, which was the inner wall of each module, turned to present the connections for various tests to each module. The patient would stay in his assigned module throughout this stage of the testing. Although the carousel could accommodate up to six modules, not every module had to be operable and furnished. Also, the carousel could be operated, if necessary, without having patients in all operable modules. For instance, only three modules might be equipped to handle patients. On any given cycle all three modules might not be full, but each module with a patient would still face, in turn, each side of the central core which paced the test sequence. Large expensive equipment would be located in the core of the carousel (see Exhibit 2), while equipment for other tests would be located in or on the wall of each module. Only the central wall rotates with respect to the modules according to the sequence of test operations.

The technician would perform the appropriate tests or connect electrical leads to the core through input jacks located in the exposed section of the core wall. In fact, if a test were being given which did not require connection to the central core, the rotation of the wall merely served to pace the technician. An interlock device would prevent the carousel wall from rotating until all modules had been disconnected from the core. For instance, failure to get an adequate reading from equipment located in the core would prevent rotation until the core technician signaled that the test had been completed and the patient had been disconnected. Communication on the test's status between the technician in the module and the core technician would be permitted by windows in the core wall facing the module. Testing in other modules would be able to proceed even in the event of one delayed module if connection to the central core were not required at that point in the test sequence. While patients could be loaded into the carousel either sequentially or simultaneously, it was felt that having all the patients that would be tested at one time enter their assigned modules simultaneously provided the easiest organization with only minimal bottlenecks or waiting. Consequently, given morning startup and evening shutdown constraints, about seven hours of operation of the carousel was considered maximum for each of the five days per week the AML would be open.

Final Stationary Tests

After the sequence of tests in the module, the patient would be directed to an audiometer room for a hearing test. Two audiometers each could be located next to the males' and females' dressing areas. After completing the hearing test, the patient would be directed by the AML technician to return to the dressing room and then to proceed to the blood drawing and specimen room. After two hours since the administering of the glucose "load" prior to testing, the blood sample and the urine specimen would be taken and the examination would be over. One-way doors would prevent the patient from returning to the carousel or test areas.

Planning for the Laboratory

The staffing plans for the laboratory were to have it headed by a registered nurse. The number of supporting personnel would largely be a function of the number of active modules per day, i.e., the number of filled modules per cycle around the core, the number of scheduled cycles to fulfill demand, and the general technology of the facility. A computer operator would be required to update the automated records and complete the medical history records in a batch mode using as input the results of the AML tests. The proposed AML staffing requirements, job specifications, and salary requirements are presented in Exhibits 3 and 4.

Proposed Tests

The medical planning committee for the lab had decided that the X-ray, height and weight test, audiometer hearing test, and blood and urine tests should be included in any test sequence. However, the number of duplicate units of each type of test equipment and the complete testing sequence were as yet undetermined. Dr. Eugene realized that each test was expensive and consequently was concerned that the total cost might exceed the level acceptable to a large number of patients. A certain test might also add too much time to the cycle of the carousel, thereby limiting the number of patients that could be handled in a working day.

The committee, including Dr. Eugene and representatives from many departments at Max, had examined a number of technically feasible and medically proven tests and had found that the quality of each testing procedure was acceptable:

—*Spirometry:* a test of lung capacity that required the patient to exhale through a mouthpiece into a device measuring the volume and pressure of the exhalation. Results contribute to the diagnosis of heart disease and lung diseases such as emphysema.

—*Mamography:* a test for cancer of the breasts, an appropriate testing procedure only for females in the mid-forties to early fifties.

—*Electrocardiography:* (EKG) a test for heart disorder or weakness performed with the patient connected electrically to a device measuring the electrical impulses of the heart. Results had to be interpreted by a trained cardiologist.

—*Vision:* a test for corrected vision (reflecting mirrors would provide the standard distance for the test within the confines of the module).

Exhibit 3

MAX-ABLE MEDICAL CLINIC (A)
Staffing Requirements & Costs

Personnel Requirements

Assuming one or two test sequences per half hour:

Supervising nurse	1
Technicians:	
Front desk	1
Test sequence	1 per operative module
Back-up/core	
Equipment operator	1
Computer operator	1/3 part time

Job Descriptions

Supervising nurse: responsible for directing, supervising, and counseling staff members of the AML. Must arrange for EKGs and X-rays to be sent to a cardiologist and radiologists for reading and interpretation and then returned to the AML to be forwarded to the referring physician. Responsible for the purchase of laboratory supplies and the detection and reporting of any malfunction in equipment.

Technician: under the general supervision of the supervising nurse, administers a battery of medical tests to patients and performs clerical duties. Must be able to record test measurements and operate testing equipment.

Computer Operator: must be able to operate a small computer in batchmode to complete the medical records with the results of the AML tests.

Suggested Wage Structure

Supervising nurse	$12,000	average wage
AML technician	6,100	average wage
Computer operator	3,600	part time cost

Exhibit 4

MAX-ABLE MEDICAL CLINIC (A)
General Costs per Annum

1. Office supplies	$ 350
2. Utilities	1,500
3. Maintenance and repair	1,800
4. Telephone	850
5. Insurance and miscellaneous	1,100
6. Taxes	1,850
Total	$ 7,450

—*Ocular Tension:* (Tonometry) a test for the indications of glaucoma (a serious eye disease usually occurring in late middle age or later) performed by placing a rubber probe against the surface of the eye. To facilitate the test, the eye must be anesthetized; consequently, the test must be performed after the general vision test, and the patient must be observed for at least 20 minutes afterwards until adequate vision is regained.

—*Blood Pressure:* a test for blood pressure performed by a device measuring the Doppler effect associated with the changes in pressure.

—*Pap Smear:* a test for cancer of the cervix performed on most adult women.

This menu of tests was developed for possible inclusion in the lab on the basis of medical importance, quality of automated equipment, and the precedents established

Exhibit 5

MAX-ABLE MEDICAL CLINIC (A)
Costs and Test Duration

Capital Costs and Test Duration

Test and necessary equipment	*Cost **	*Duration*
1. History documentation: 5–6 terminals and computer	$80,000	15–45 minutes
2. Chest X-ray: Odelca Camera and darkroom facilities	$22,220	2 minutes
3. Height and weight: load cell, linear potentiometer, and digital read-out	$ 4,200	1 minute
4. Audiometer: Rudmose Model ARJ-4A	$ 1,800/set	5 minutes
5. Blood sample and urine collection	$ 1,200/station	5 minutes
6. Spirometer: Electro-Med Model 780 and Pulmo-digicomp Model 1000	$ 8,180	2–3 minutes
7. Electrocardiograph: Hewlett-Packard 1513A (3 channel recorder)	$ 4,600	15 seconds to 5 minutes
8. Ocular tension: MacKay-Marg Electronic Tonometer	$ 2,000/module	5 minutes
9. Vision: American Optical Project-O-Chart	$275 + $500/module	3–5 minutes
10. Blood pressure: Godart Model 151-CC	$ 3,600	4 minutes
11. Mamography: several types available	$25,000/module	9–11 minutes
12. Pap smear: no capital equipment necessary		2 minutes
13. Miscellaneous (dressing, rotation, instruction)		10 minutes
14. General module equipment	$ 1,000/module	

* Represents total test equipment capital cost for up to six modules except where cost per module is specified.

in earlier automated test labs. The 10-year death risk profiles given in Exhibit 13 show some of the respects in which test applicability varies with conditions in the population segment being served. All tests had been included in existing automated labs previously established for screening. For instance, mamography was included in the Kaiser testing facility. The Pap smear test for cervical cancer (an inexpensive and effective test, especially in particularly susceptible socioeconomic categories including many of Max-Able's patients) was often included, too. This test required professional training, however, because the setup was similar to a general gynecological examination. Several committee members wondered if many physicians would feel that the Pap smear should be an integral part of the doctor-patient relationship. Even though the test might uncover some incidence of the disease, he questioned whether it should be included in the module in the face of such possibly adverse reaction.

As part of the AML International proposal, variable and fixed costs as well as the duration of each test under consideration were provided. The committee had updated these figures and thought they represented the costs he should use in reaching a decision (see Exhibits 5 and 6).

Exhibit 6

MAX-ABLE MEDICAL CLINIC (A)
Variable Costs of the AML

Expendable supplies per patient	*Cost per item, $*	*Sub total, $*
a. Appointment Procedures		
1. Appointment brochure	.06	
2. Confidential medical information form	.02	
3. AML letter size envelope	.02	
4. Stamp (postage)	.08	
5. AML appointment scheduling chart	.02	
	.20	.20
b. Computer Processing		
1. Storage envelope	.05	
2. Labels (identification)	.07	
3. Labels (EKG)	.01	
4. Computer paper	.08	
5. AML medical report folders	.10	
6. Cardboard storage boxes	.01	
7. Computer ribbons	.01	
	.33	.53
c. Main Desk		
1. Glucose drink (100 Gm carbonated cola)	.25	
2. Cups for glucose	.02	
3. Disposable thermometer tip	.04	
4. Exit brochures	.05	
	.36	.89

Exhibit 6 (continued)

Expendable supplies per patient	*Cost per item*	*Sub total, $*
d. Laboratory		
1. Urine specimen cups	.05	
2. Urine specimen cup lids	.05	
3. Bili-Labstix	.12	
4. Testuria	.28	
5. Prepacked	.02	
6. Vacutainers (2 tops, holder, and needle)	.40	
7. Serum tubes	.04	
8. Alcohol wipe	.01	
9. Bandaid	.01	
10. Wood applicators	.01	
11. Glass beads	.02	
12. Dispo pipets	.01	
	1.02	1.91
e. Dressing Booth		
1. Gown	.25	
2. Slippers	.06	
3. Plastic bag	.02	
	.33	$ 2.24
f. X-ray Department		
1. Chest X-ray film	.83	
2. Envelope	.05	
3. Developing chemicals	.02	
4. Radiological interpretation	1.00	(by contract with radiologists)
	1.90	4.14
g. Test Modules		
1. Tonometry		
a. Ophthaine	.02	
b. Tissues	.01	
c. Tonotips	.10	
d. Wetting agent	.01	
e. Recording paper	.05	
	.19	4.33
2. EKG		
a. Electrolyte cream	.02	
b. Alcohol wipes	.02	
c. Tissue	.01	
d. Cardiological interpretation	1.00	(by contract with cardiologists)
e. Interpretation—abnormal EKGs $20 (25% occurrence)	5.00	
	6.05	10.38
3. Blood Pressure no supplies		
4. Vision Visual field pattern card	.01	10.39

Exhibit 6 (continued)

Expendable supplies per patient	*Cost per item*	*Sub total, $*
5. Spirometry		
Spirotubes	.05	10.44
6. Mamography	9.50	19.94
7. Pap smear	4.00	23.94
h. Miscellaneous		
1. Paper head protectors	.04	
2. Paper towels	.02	
3. Tissues	.01	
4. Soap	.01	
5. Technical supplies	.21	
	.29	$24.23

Process Utilization

One of the most difficult problems in designing the lab was determining its potential utilization. Dr. Eugene was able to find little published data that might help him in reaching a conclusion.

The committee approached the problem of obtaining data in several different ways. He believed that ultimate demand would be based on several factors:

1. The number of patients coming to Max-Able for a checkup or for general health care, not for follow-up or "routine" visits.
2. The applicability of the lab for any specialty. Many patients seeing a physician or specialist might not need the sequence since they have a well-defined health problem or because the general tests might not be as thorough or exact as special tests performed in the laboratory.
3. Age and sex of patients.
4. The price of the sequence.

It was felt that demand could be estimated from data on these factors.

Two statistical samples were taken, one that represented all Max-Able patients during a typical "composite week" and the second was a study of new patients only. Fortunately Max-Able used a computer-based billing system; these records contained the patient's name and information about the attending doctor and his services—his name, specialty, charges, and some of the laboratory procedures performed during the visit or subsequently ordered. Using these sources, Dr. Eugene randomly drew a day's history for each day of the week to make up a composite week at Max-Able that was free of seasonal variations. From this composite week he determined the number of eligible patients by types of diagnosis and laboratory procedures. Patients for whom the lab tests were completely inapplicable, such as those returning for follow-up visits, were excluded. Exhibit 7 gives the number of visits to Max-Able by eligible patients during this composite week by selected

Exhibit 7

MAX-ABLE MEDICAL CLINIC (A)
Weekly Composite Study

Visits by specialty	*Total visits*	*Men*	*Women*	*Percentage for whom AML was applicable*
Internists	1357	556	801	75%
General practice	531	232	299	75%
Environmental medicine	118	39	79	10%
Obstetrics/gynecology	487	—	487	5%
Subtotal	2493	827	1666	
Other specialties	4983	2413	2570	1%
Total	7476	3240	4236	

medical specialty and a subjective estimate of the percentage of eligible patients for whose diagnostic and treatment regime the lab tests might be applicable.

The 7,476 visits in the composite week were further examined to determine visits that were equivalent to a comprehensive initial physical examination or regular annual checkup but not necessarily as comprehensive as the lab. Approximately 10% or 781 of the visits fell in this category. Exhibit 8 gives the age and sex distribution of these patients.

Exhibit 8

MAX-ABLE MEDICAL CLINIC (A)
(from the Composite Week Sample)
General Physical Examinations by Sex and Age

Age group	*Males*			*Females*			*Total*	
	Number	*Percent*		*Number*	*Percent*		*Number*	*Percent*
Infants (0–11 months)	35	8.5		24	6.5		59	7.6
Children (1–12 years)	45	10.9		28	7.7		73	9.3
Teens (13–19 years)	22	5.3		25	6.8		47	6.0
Twenties (20–29 years)	35	8.5		39	10.6		74	9.5
Thirties (30–39 years)	55	13.3		44	12.0		99	12.7
Matured (40–49 years)	98	23.7		56	15.2		154	19.8
Middle aged (50–69 years)	100	24.2	53.6	103	28.0	56.5	203	26.0
Elderly (70 years plus)	23	5.7		49	13.3		72	9.2
Total	413	100.1		368	100.1		781	100.1

The best judgment suggested that the highest potential utilization of the lab would come from the groups of patients who were properly most concerned about their health, those over, say, 40 years old. Even though a doctor might prefer that all patients have a comprehensive test sequence like the lab's, the basic good health of young people and the cost of the lab sequence might induce the doctor to omit such a sequence for lower age groups and rely instead on detection during the normal office visit.

To obtain further data, the treatment patterns of new patients at Max-Able were examined. Of the 1,685 new patients seen during a month's time, 14% or 235 were considered candidates for the lab.

Further analysis was performed to obtain the distribution of current total testing fees for these 235 patients at Max-Able. Undoubtedly, the price of the lab facility would be compared by both patients and physicians to fees for similar tests performed by existing laboratory facilities, either at Max-Able or elsewhere. Since Max-Able physicians would not be constrained to refer patients to the lab even if it were built, the price would have a great effect on demand. The present fees for laboratory testing are summarized in Exhibit 9.

Exhibit 9

MAX-ABLE MEDICAL CLINIC (A)
Actual Laboratory Costs for Sample of Initial Patients

Billing $	*Number of patients out of 235*	*Billing* $	*Cumulative frequency* %
$0–9	55	over 0	100%
10–19	12	over $9	77%
20–29	58	over $19	72%
30–34	9	over $29	47%
35–39	10	over $34	43%
40–49	43	over $39	39%
50–59	31	over $49	21%
60 or over	17	over $59	7%

Current Testing Charges
(through existing MAMC laboratories)

EKG (without interpretation)	$17.50
Spirometer	10.00
X-ray	12.00
Blood and urine tests	25.00
History (done by physician)	7.00
Visual Test (done by optometrist or ophthalmologist)	3.00
Audiometer	10.00
Mamography	10.00
Pap smear	5.00
	$99.50

Each test under consideration for the lab would have a different usefulness to a physician depending on his specialty. The committee ranked each test's usefulness for each specialty from "very useful" (an integral part of most diagnoses) to "generally useful" (related only to the physician's concern for the overall health of his patient) (see Exhibit 10).

Exhibit 10

MAX-ABLE MEDICAL CLINIC (A)
Usefulness of Tests by Medical Specialty

	Internists: General Medicine GastroEnteroligy Cardiologists Subspecialties	*General practice*	*Environmental medicine*	*Obstetrical Gynecology*	*Other specialties*	*Radiologists*
History	Very useful	Very useful	Very useful	Very useful		
Chest X-ray	Very useful	Very useful	Very useful	Generally useful	All tests generally useful for diagnosis, but tests often too broad in scope, or doctor has complete medical record when he first sees patient (i.e., patient has been referred, so tests have already been performed)	Only X-rays appropriate; 50% of work done on chest X-rays for routine physicals
Height and weight	Very useful	Very useful	Very useful	Very useful		
Blood and urine	Very useful	Very useful	Very useful	Very useful		
Audiometry	Generally useful	Generally useful	Very useful	Generally useful		
Spirometry	Very useful	Very useful	Very useful	Generally useful		
EKG	Very useful	Very useful	Very useful	Generally useful		
Blood pressure	Very useful	Very useful	Very useful	Generally useful		
Vision	Desirable for patient	Desirable for patient	Generally useful	Generally useful		
Tonometry	Very useful	Very useful	Generally useful	Generally useful		
Pap smear	Very useful	Very useful	Generally useful	Very useful		
Mamography	Very useful	Very useful	Generally useful	Very useful		
Applicability factor (for patients over 40)	75%	75%	10%	5%	1%	—

Dr. Eugene initially felt that the maximum potential demand might be quickly approximated as the 1,068 patients per week that were represented by an adjusted sum of the composite week group plus the new-patient potential. These adjustments involved weighing the composite week demand by patient age percentages and the applicability factor for each specialty. Based on these calculations (presented in Exhibit 11) Dr. Eugene revised his estimate of the maximum potential

Exhibit 11

MAX-ABLE MEDICAL CLINIC (A)
Total Weighted Potential Demand

A. Weighting by patient age percentages over 40.
(Weekly demand from composite study [Exhibit 7] weighted by percent of patients over 40 [Exhibit 8]).

Male = 53.6% over 40 Female = 56.5% over 40

	Male	Female	Total
Internists	556 × 53.6% = 300	801 × 56.5% = 450	750
G.P	232 × " = 124	299 × " = 170	294
Env. Med.	39 × " = 21	79 × " = 44	65
Ob-Gyn	0 × " = 0	487 × " = 275	275
Specialties (other)	2413 × " = 1300	2570 × " = 1460	2760

B. Weighted by Specialty Applicability Factor
(From Specialty Applicability Factor [Exhibit 10])

Internists	750 × 75% = 562
G.P	294 × 75% = 222
Env. Med.	65 × 10% = 7
Ob-Gyn	275 × 5% = 14
Specialties (other)	2760 × 1% = 28
	833

Total Potential Weighted Demand = 833 + 235 new patients = 1068 patients/week or 55,536 per year for a 52-week year.

C. Weighted by Price

	Cumulative %
If AML costs over $29	47% × 55,536 = 26,000
" 34	43% × " = 23,800
" 39	39% × " = 21,600
" 49	21% × " = 11,600
" 59	7% × " = 3,900

demand upward to almost 1,100 patients per week. Finally, this demand was adjusted for each price range that might be charged by multiplying the cumulative percentage of all laboratory procedures that cost more than a given price for the new lab. For instance, only 7% of new patients were currently charged more than $60 for laboratory tests by existing laboratories. Consequently Dr. Eugene assumed that only 7% of the total weighted potential demand would desire the AML tests at a cost of $60 in lieu of Max's regular laboratory tests (even though they may not have been as comprehensive as the new lab sequence).

The Report to the Executive Committee

As he prepared to draw up final recommendations for the automated lab, Dr. Eugene reviewed the basis for his interest in the project and the origin of resistance to the project within Max-Able. The impressive stack of reports on his desk from the Public Health Service and elsewhere, provided convincing evidence that such a lab, if properly implemented and supported, both could and had improved the rate of condition finding in diagnosing patients, helped to reduce morbidity in the population of patients that were processed and reduced the cost of health care.

He felt that it was important to draw up a final plan specifying the exact tests that would be included, the number of units of test equipment that should be purchased, the patient flow through the facility, and a pricing recommendation. The recommendations should be so carefully thought out that potential opponents would find no basis for criticism in these specifics.

At the same time he recognized some very real sources of resistance to aspects of the new project. There was very little doubt but that the tests would be of high quality but in many instances they would present established physicians with new and unfamiliar sources of evidence upon which to base their diagnosis. These would

Exhibit 12

MAX-ABLE MEDICAL CLINIC (A)
Resistance to AML

MEMO

To: Harold D. Eugene, M.D.

From: George P. Johnson, M.D.

Re: Automated Multitest Laboratory

If a vote were held in the X-ray department on the acceptance of an AML, I calculate that it would lose, 4 to 2. Some of the department members are disturbed that there was not more research into the value, patient acceptability, and cost of such an endeavor. Furthermore, there is a genuine desire to practice episodic medicine rather than encourage mass surveys of essentially well patients. There are some reservations against entering into a project with a commercial company (AML International). The Department as a whole would prefer to exclude chest films from the AML and retain the present system of having the individual physician request the films and interpretation from us as indicated.

represent documentary evidence, which the busy, established physician would have to interpret fully if he used the facility at all. Otherwise he would be exposed to the risk of a malpractice suit in the event that a medical problem was overlooked.

There were physicians who claimed that a standardized battery of tests were inappropriate in the first place since patients differed enormously in the conditions that warranted exploration. This line of reasoning led to the argument that the new concept would actually raise health costs since it induced unnecessary testing.[2]

Finally, while results from the lab report would undoubtedly save a great deal of time during the patient's visit, it might also result in a reduction of physician fees for tests that would otherwise have been done in the office. Since each physician's fees were ultimately related to the procedures he performed, the introduction of the lab into the group practice might redistribute fees among physicians and between physicians and the lab. For instance, both the electrocardiograph and X-ray tests would be interpreted by specialists before being sent to the physician who referred the patient. Although Dr. Eugene had negotiated a low $1 interpretation fee, these might run normally from $5 to $25.

Dr. Eugene was sensitive to the large investment that AML International had made for technical, architectural, and system development and realized that if the AML facility were built, Max-Able would have to invest over $250,000 in land and another $500,000 in the building. All the partners of Max-Able would be very concerned with the lab's economic viability, because Max-Able expected to obtain a reasonable net contribution on any investment.

In large part, the executive board of Max-Able would decide the general feasibility of the facility on its merits as a potential investment. Since the project had the strong support of Dr. Long, an eminent national figure in medicine as well as at Max-Able, Dr. Eugene felt confident that a sound proposal would be accepted, provided that affiliated physicians would not be required to use it for their patients. Given the type of resistance that was evident in Dr. Johnson's memo he still wondered if there was other action he should take.

---

[2] It would not be unusual for the results from a particular test to be far outside a normal range for a particular patient when he was otherwise apparently healthy. This anomaly might result from prior diet, emotional conditions, drugs taken, or unexplained reasons, but involve considerable retesting to insure that medical problems were not the source of the test result.

Exhibit 13

MAX-ABLE MEDICAL CLINIC (A)
Death Risk Profiles with Modifyng Condition
(Specifies Probability of Death Within 10 Years
by Four Principal Causes for Each Age Sex Group
in Percentage Terms)

	Male age 20/24	*Female age 20/24*	*Male age 40/44*	*Female age 40/44*
*†@ Motor vehicle accidents	.58%	.12%	.28%	.10%
W/seat belts 75%–100% of time	.46	.09	.23	.08
Heavy social drinking—definite excess	2.90	.60	1.42	.51
@*† Suicide	.13	.04	.26	.09
† Chronic rheumatic heart disease	.02	.03	.17	.13
†# Vascular lesions affecting central nervous system (hemorrhage)	—	.02	.22	.20
* Homicide	.06	.02	—	—
* Accidents, drowning	.04	—	—	—
@# Arteriosclerotic heart disease	.03	—	1.88	.30
1 or more packs cigarettes/day	.04	—	2.81	.62
Cigarettes plus 75% overweight and high cholesterol level	.23	—	10.56	2.34
W/success in prescribed exercise, weight reduction, stopped smoking	.02	—	1.26	.33
@ Cirrhosis of liver	—	—	.22	.13
W/Heavy social drinking—definite excess	—	—	1.11	.66
# Cancer of breast	N.A.	—	N.A.	.35
If mother or sister had C.B.	N.A.	—	N.A.	.70
W/regular self-exam and mammogram	N.A.	—	N.A.	.17
# Cancer of Cervix	N.A.	—	N.A.	.14
Jewish	N.A	—	N.A.	.01
Low socioeconomic status with teenage marriage or sex relations	N.A.	—	N.A.	.60
With three negative Pap smear tests in last five years	N.A.	—	N.A.	.01
Overall probability of death from all causes in %	1.58	.60	5.56	3.02

No entry indicates cause was not included in top 14 causes of death for group in question.

* Four principal causes of death for white males 20/24 years of age.
† Four principal causes of death for white males 40/44 years of age.
@ Four principal causes of death for white females 20/24 years of age.
# Four principal causes of death for white females 40/44 years of age.

All probabilities are approximations.

Source: Based upon data in Robbins and Hall, *How to Practice Prospective Medicine,* Methodist Hospital of Indiana, 1970.

The Office of Senator Ronald R. Kenmore

In May of 1971 Mr. Ted Powell learned of his upcoming promotion to administrative assistant on Senator Ronald Kenmore's personal staff. In his current position as assistant counsel on the staff of the Senate Committee on Banking, Housing and Urban Affairs, Powell's primary responsibilities had been to represent the Senator on the Committee. In his new position he would be responsible for managing the Senator's office operations.

Immediately after learning that he would be changing jobs, Powell called in a team of management consultants to discuss changes which he felt might be called for in the office operations. In an initial discussion with the consultants, Powell expressed his ideas as follows:

> With my background, which is entirely in law, I am no expert on how to set up efficient office operations. But I don't think it takes an expert to see the need for improvement in the way this office runs. We anticipate that in about two months we may be moving to new offices. Before that time comes, I want to have an optimal system developed to handle the work of Senator Kenmore's office. That way we'll be able to make the move and the operational changes all at once. That is why I called you in; I feel we need modern methods.
>
> I have prepared a brief summary of our personnel and their job responsibilities to help you get started (see Exhibit 1). I have briefed all the staff to expect you to be talking with them about their jobs. I'm sure they will be most open with you.

Exhibit 1

THE OFFICE OF SENATOR RONALD R. KENMORE

Mr. Powell's Summary of Operations

5/12/71

INTRODUCTION

In as much as Ted Powell will be assuming responsibilities as Senator Kenmore's Administrative Assistant and Ken Graham will become a member of the Senate Committee staff, some of the information will undoubtedly have to be altered. Our present state of operations are set forth since the functions described must be carried out in each case.

Exhibit 1 (continued)

Personnel Responsibilities

Chandler Arnold—Administrative Assistant to Senator
Responsibilities include patronage, miscellaneous special projects, (e.g., state economy issue). Problems with government agencies. In addition Mr. Arnold will be given administrative responsibilities which relate to meeting important constituents regarding business activities, etc.

Kay Beaver—Legislative Secretary to Ken Graham
General secretarial responsibilities in addition to specific projects relating to environment problems.

Connie Chevalier—ROBO Assistant
Works machines which are located in basement of building for mass mailings on legislative matters and occasionally special projects. Runs mimeograph machine.

Phyllis Coleman—Secretary to Chandler Arnold
General secretarial work. Handles White House political clearances. Answers mail from constituents seeking government jobs.

Fran Collins—Secretary
General secretarial responsibilities which will possibly include work with MTST.

Ken Graham—Legislative Assistant
Responsible for following committees: Commerce, Finance, Interior (national energy). Handles matters regarding home state economy and oversees Commissions of which RRK is member.

Ruth Hagen—Caseworker
Responsible for military cases as well as selective service matters, social security problems and veterans cases.

Lois Hawkins—Mail Assistant
Responsible for counting and sorting all mail. Categorizes mail and marks for form response if applicable. Divides remaining mail according to issue and gives to person handling particular area. Handles all major filing of letters in our master file.

Karen Jenkins—Personal Secretary to Senator Kenmore and Office Manager
Acknowledges Senator's personal mail, handles personal financial matters, miscellaneous mail (e.g., letters of sympathy). In her capacity as Office Manager, she is responsible for all administrative matters including interviewing secretarial staff personnel, possible interns, overseeing office expenditures, office scheduling and supervision of work flow.

Peter Johnston—Press Secretary/political advisor to RRK
Mr. Johnston will be going to the home state in the near future to handle press matters in the state. He will head and coordinate press matters both in the home state and in Washington.

Paul Katz—Paid intern
Legislative responsibilities, including oversight functions with respect to following committees: Aeronautical and Space Sciences, Post Office and Civil Service, Veterans Affairs, Judiciary (assisting Morse) and special work on campaign spending matters. His responsibilities will be shifted to the press operation shortly after a new press secretary is hired. They will include responsibility for operation of press releases, statements and other numerous PR activities.

Arlene Kelly—Secretary to Ted Powell
General secretarial work. Appointments, phone calls, etc.

Exhibit 1 (continued)

Eleanor Kendall—Press Secretary's assistant

Responsible for production of press releases, scheduling Senator's press conferences. Notification to all press in the home state of such press releases. Handles correspondence of PR division. Up-to-date information on all grants, contract awards and makes determination of press value.

Jane Lodge—Head Receptionist

Handles major phone calls and directs to proper person. Greets constituents and sets up White House tours and other government tours. Answers mail on requests for material. A backup for Barbara with phone calls for RRK.

Lynn Middleton—Legislative Assistant

Responsible for oversight of the following committees: Foreign Relations, Armed Services, Atomic Energy, Rules District of Columbia, Government Operations/Government Reorganization, Welfare matters. In addition, Miss Middleton serves as the Senator's primary speech writer.

Susan Miller—Legislative Secretary to Mr. Morse

Responsible for answering constituent mail relating to Mr. Morse's committee assignments as well as handling the flow of legislative mail.

Carl Morse—Legislative Assistant

Responsible for the following committees: Labor and Legal Services, Judiciary, Public Works, Agriculture, Interior Special Committee on Aging (social security), Equal Educational Opportunity. As is true of the other LA, Mr. Morse is responsible for the development of legislation, preparation of speeches, the handling of correspondence in his area. In addition, Mr. Morse is responsible for certain special projects such as a summer camp for underprivileged children in the home state.

Frank Mullen—ROBO Assistant

Responsible for maintenance and addition of names to mailing list. Oversees production of mass mailings.

Ted Powell—Assistant Counsel—Committee on Banking, Housing and Urban Affairs

Responsible for the development of legislation relating to banking, securities, international trade and housing. Oversight function limited to Committee activities, with responsibility for mail relating to these subjects.

Don Russell—Caseworker

Responsible for federal contracts, grants, awards and services which includes communication with "governmental agencies" and follow up on federal assistance programs.

Mary Teeling—Legislative Secretary to Lynn Middleton

Handles correspondence relating to committees which Lynn oversees. Does special work on the Arts and Humanities. General secretarial work for Lynn.

Barbara Thompson—Scheduling Secretary to RRK

Handles all mail regarding invitations, appointments, speaking engagements. Makes daily schedule for Senator. Receives all calls not related to personal financial matters which Karen handles.

Carol Woolten—Caseworker

Responsible for problems relating to immigration, Post Office matters, Civil Service problems, Federal Aviation Administration problems, auto repairs, and miscellaneous casework.

Exhibit 1 (continued)

RICHMOND OFFICE

Jeanette England—Administrative Assistant for Richmond
Personal representative of Senator as well as office manager. Performs casework functions as well as public relations responsibilities.

Irene Orlando—Secretary/Receptionist
Responsible for all incoming calls. Initially opens mail. General secretarial work for Richmond as well as miscellaneous casework.

Mary Sullivan—Caseworker
Handles major casework in Richmond office. Responsible for problems relating to Administration, veterans, Small Business, and federal employment. Immigration matters and military matters which can be handled in Richmond.

FRANKLIN OFFICE

Jean Laplante—Secretary and caseworker
Responsible for local community matters which our office can assist in, i.e. contact local federal agencies. Some casework and general run of office.

Bob Lendzion—Administrative Assistant for Franklin
Part-time office manager and caseworker with public relations responsibilities.

Powell had also outlined the following "obvious problems" which he wished the consultants to consider.

1. The primary problem facing office personnel involved the flow of mail. In this respect, thought should be given to the microfilming of records and the retention of useful information in a computer data base (e.g., for campaigns, statewide surveys). The mailing list should be integrated into office procedures and machine produced letters used to the maximum extent possible.

2. The foregoing primary areas of concern must be accommodated within existing budgetary resources.

To amplify on this list of problem areas, Powell offered, in response to the consultants' questions, the following description of the problems as he saw them:

> Our biggest problem is mail. Our incoming letters in a normal week run from 2,000 to 4,000 pieces. We make a point of replying to every piece individually, though in some cases the reply is a general letter outlining the Senator's views on the issue addressed by the constituent. National emergencies create huge irregularities in this mail count. For instance, after the Cambodian invasion of 1970 we received 150,000 pieces of mail on that subject alone. One of those pieces of mail was a petition containing over 5,000 names and addresses of signers. We sent our reply to every signer. You can imagine the kinds of problems we have. Letters are answered very late, and too much of our staff's time is spent reading and answering mail. I would especially like to free up the legislative assistants' time. These are the people who help the Senator carry on the business of the Senate. They are professionals of very high calibre. By forcing them to spend about 50% of their time answering constituents' letters we are keeping them from more important work.

Exhibit 2

THE OFFICE OF SENATOR RONALD R. KENMORE
Budget and Salaries

	Yearly
Budget [1]	$341,400
Salaries	
Chandler Arnold *	$ 20,400
Kay Beaver	7,900
Connie Chevalier	8,100
Phyllis Coleman	7,600
Fran Collins	8,100
Ken Graham	11,300
Ruth Hagen	10,300
Lois Hawkins	7,300
Karen Jenkins	10,800
Peter Johnston	16,400
Paul Katz	6,100
Arlene Kelly	9,600
Eleanor Kendall	9,100
Jane Lodge	9,800
Lynn Middleton	14,500
Susan Miller	9,800
Carl Morse	12,000
Frank Mullen	4,000
Ted Powell	25,000
Don Russell	10,300
Mary Teeling	8,600
Barbara Thompson	12,500
Carol Woolten	10,300
Jeanette England	13,500
Irene Orlando	7,300
Mary Sullivan	8,300
Jean Laplante	8,400
Bob Lendzion	4,000
Total salaries	$290,300
Available for miscellaneous purchases	$ 51,100

[1] Budget was for salaries and miscellaneous purchases. Office operating costs (such as utilities and maintenance) and much of the supply costs were paid directly by the Senate.

* Powell was replacing Arnold who was going to the Senate Banking Committee.

One of the consultants asked Powell to be specific about his objectives in improving the mail answering problem. Powell replied as follows:

My objectives are, first, to get mail answering work off the backs of the legislative assistants, second, to find a way to get the flow of mail under control (right now no one seems to know what's going on), and third, ideally, to have a *Manual of Operations* detailing systematic methods of handling paper and information.

I'd like you to develop an optimum system. I'll worry about implementation myself.

I guess the only other thing I should mention is our budget. The Senator is allocated exactly $341,000[1] per year to run his offices. This money is available in 12 monthly chunks, and we can't carry over one month's savings to apply the next month. Once unspent budget is gone, it's gone for good.

In reply to a final question regarding equipment alternative, Powell answered:

We can't get any equipment unless it is on the "approved list" issued by the Senate Rules Committee. IBM's Magnetic Tape Selectric Typewriter (MTST) has just been approved, and we would consider using that system in place of our present ROBO[2] machines. Eliminating all these space-consuming desks and file cabinets by installing carrels and a central filing system has also come to mind as a possibility.

If you have any problems or need any more information, see Karen Jenkins. Karen is our office manager, and knows everybody pretty well.

The Present Office Operations

The Senator's office suite was located on the second floor of the Old Senate Office Building. The suite consisted of five rooms, all opening onto the central hallway; however, only the reception room door was kept open to the hallway (see Exhibit 3). In addition to the Senator's Washington office he maintained offices in his home state towns of Richmond (the capital) and Franklin for the purpose of providing contact with his constituency.

The purpose of the office was to aid the Senator in all aspects of his job as an elected representative of the United States Senate. The functions of the Senator's staff were to:

1. Keep the Senator current on information related to issues on the Senate floor and in Committee;
2. Develop legislative issues and programs;
3. Assist in writing speeches; and
4. Handle contacts with a great majority of the public resulting from
   a. Visits to the offices, and
   b. Letters involving case work and answers to legislative problems.

---

[1] See Exhibit 2 for a breakdown of the office budget.

[2] ROBO was the office nickname of the Friden Flexowriter automatic typewriters used to type form letters. Both ROBO and MTST could produce letters which were indistinguishable from hand-typed letters.

Exhibit 3

THE OFFICE OF SENATOR RONALD R. KENMORE
Office Layout (not to scale)

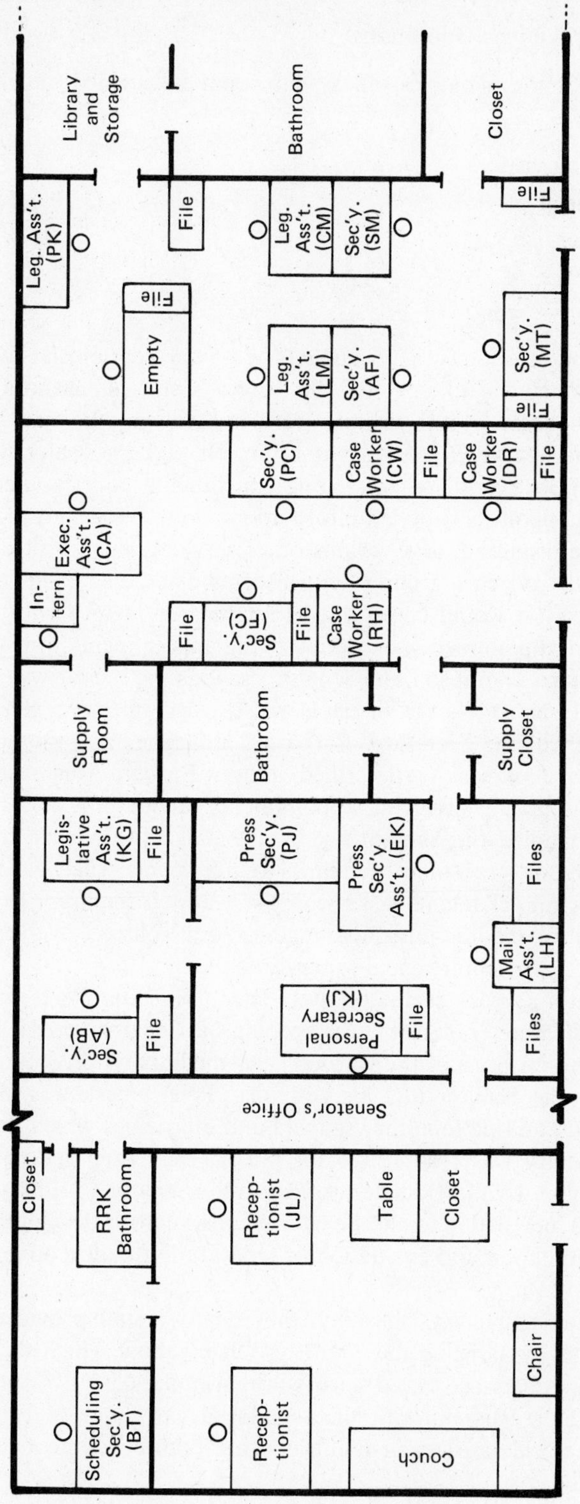

Closet
Scheduling Sec'y. (BT)
RRK Bathroom
Recep- tionist
Recep- tionist (JL)
Couch
Table
Closet
Chair
Senator's Office
Sec'y. (AB)
File
Personal Secretary (KJ)
File
Files
Mail Ass't. (LH)
Files
Legis- lative Ass't. (KG)
File
Press Sec'y. (PJ)
Press Sec'y. Ass't. (EK)
Supply Room
Bathroom
Supply Closet
In- tern
Exec. Ass't. (CA)
File
Sec'y. (FC)
File
Case Worker (RH)
Sec'y. (PC)
Case Worker (CW)
File
Case Worker (DR)
File
Empty
File
Leg. Ass't. (LM)
Sec'y. (AF)
File
Sec'y. (MT)
Leg. Ass't. (PK)
File
Leg. Ass't. (CM)
Sec'y. (SM)
File
Library and Storage
Bathroom
Closet
Hall

The General Office Operation

The operation of the Senator's office staff could be divided into five areas. They were:

1. Handling visitors
2. Secretarial service
3. Press service
4. Case work
5. Legislative work

The reception room was occupied by two receptionists and the Senator's scheduling secretary. Visitors entered the Senator's office suite through the reception room. Although some of the visitors were individuals who had business and/or personal appointments with the Senator himself, a large majority of the visitors (15,000 to 20,000 a year) were visiting constituents, tourists, and even curiosity seekers. The receptionists supplied information about the Senator's activities, Washington tourist information, and various other services which visitors might request.

Occasionally, when a group of constituents made their plans to visit known in advance, the Senator would be on hand to have a few words with the group. Individuals who had appointments, or were seeking appointments with the Senator were referred to Barbara Thompson, the Senator's scheduling secretary.

Secretarial service to the Senator was divided into two general functions—those of the scheduling secretary, Barbara Thompson, and those of the personal secretary Karen Jenkins. As described above, Barbara was responsible for the Senator's daily schedule involving appointments, invitations, and speaking engagements. Karen handled the Senator's personal mail and financial matters and took care of the Senator's personal secretarial requirements, such as dictation, typing, and many other miscellaneous tasks which were often required. In addition, Karen was responsible for the administrative matters of the office—overseeing office secretarial staff, office expenditures, and supervision of work flow.

The Senator's press secretary was Peter Johnston. Peter and his assistant, Eleanor Kendall, were responsible for keeping the Senator abreast of current issues and the editorial positions of the various news media; and providing the media with information on the Senator and his activities. Peter's desk was always piled high with home, state, and national newspapers and magazines which he reviewed daily. The press secretary was responsible for the physical preparation of the Senator's speeches (although Lynn Middleton served as the Senator's primary speech writer), production of a newsletter to the Senator's constituency, development of press releases, and compilation and evaluation of federal information on grants and awards to the Senator's state.

One of the many ways in which the Senator's staff provided services to his constituency was by assisting them with problems about which they had written to the Senator. This service, called case work, was handled by Ruth Hagen, Carol Woolten, and Don Russell, with the secretarial assistance of Fran Collins. Case work involved a wide variety of inquiries from both constituents and nonconstituents. Although inquiries which were not from the home state could be classified as being from nonconstituents, they could often be related to a constituent or constituents who find themselves temporarily displaced for one reason or another. Such was often the case when inquiries came from colleges, military installations, or tourist towns. The volume of mail handled by the case workers was multiplied by the fact that a single case often required the writing of many letters of inquiry and follow-up to the inquirer and government organizations (such as an inquiry to the State Department on a case involving a passport or visa problem).

Exhibit 4 shows the areas of responsibility of the various legislative assistants. The legislative assistants (LA) were responsible for:

1. Being informed on their respective areas;
2. Keeping current with the committees for which they were responsible;
3. Drafting legislation at the request of the Senator or on their own initiative;
4. Answering legislative inquiries from constituents;
5. Drafting speeches related to their area of concern.

Exhibit 4

THE OFFICE OF SENATOR RONALD R. KENMORE
Legislative Committee Assignments
(Assignment covers both authorization and appropriations)

Lynn Middleton

Foreign Relations
Armed Services
Atomic Energy
Rules
District of Columbia
Government Operations/Govt. Reorg.
Welfare—Family Assistance

Ken Graham

Commerce
Finance (Taxes, Trade)
Interior (National Energy)
State Economy
Commissions of which RRK is a member

Paul Katz

Space
Post Office & Civil Service
Veterans Affairs
Judiciary (assisting Carl)
Campaign Spending

Carl Morse

Labor and Legal Services
Judiciary
Public Works
Agriculture
Interior
Domestic Action
Special Committee on Aging (Social Security)
Equal Educational Oppty.

Susan Miller

Education
Drugs

Mary Teeling

Arts and Humanities

Normally the greater part of the legislative assistants' time was spent reading and auditing committee meetings. When assigned to draft a piece of legislation or a speech, almost 100% of the LA's time was spent in researching and writing. These demands left little time for handling legislative inquiries from constituents.

Exhibit 5

THE OFFICE OF SENATOR RONALD R. KENMORE
Legislative Mail Count
For 1970

TOTAL MAIL COUNT			
1968			81,799
1969			98,591
1970			149,591
Total Casework and Miscellaneous		57,490	
Total Legislative		92,101	
Average legislative mail per week		1,771	
Senate legislation	610		
House legislation	370		
Responses to our letters	247		
Thank you's for positions	120		
Other	397		
Total signatories answered			261,739 *
Issues, 1970 †			
Military and the war			182,125
Cambodia		168,566	
Individual communications	56,418		
Petition Signatures	112,148		
Other		13,559	
Imports and trade			3,522
Taxes and tax reform			99
Banking and housing			1,062
Health, education and welfare			3,681
Labor and business			744
Pollution, environment and interior			3,675
SST		2,211	
Other		1,464	
Post Office			1,207
Foreign Affairs			3.818
Arab-Israel conflict		2,865	
Other		953	
Crime, unrest, justice and legal matters			3,528
Carswell nomination		2,031	
Other		1,497	
Transportation			370
General			418

* The legislative mail included a number of petitions with more than one signatory. Since each signatory was answered individually the petitions necessitated 112,148 answers in excess of incoming pieces of mail.

† Number of issues (1970) 165; (1969) 213.

The Mail System

A good part of the office activity centered around the flow of mail—which was generated by the receipt of approximately 400 pieces of casework and 1,600 pieces of legislative mail each week. Exhibit 5 shows the legislative mail count for 1970 and Exhibit 6 shows a typical weekly mail count during 1971. Total mail count in these exhibits include legislative, casework, and miscellaneous mail. There was no mail count available on casework mail.

Mail delivery was made to the Senator's office three times per day. All of the mail (including letters and telegrams) was delivered to Lois Hawkins, who opened and sorted the mail according to a procedure she had developed over the period of time she had worked in the Senator's office.

1. All mail which appeared to be personal in nature was delivered to Karen Jenkins.
2. Requests for assistance from constituents were placed in the mail boxes of the responsible case worker. The individual case workers periodically picked up their mail.
3. Legislative inquiries were placed in the mail boxes of the responsible LA's as specified in Exhibit 4. All legislative mail was picked up periodically by Susan Miller.
4. Particular legislative inquiries (e.g., SST) which were received in volume often had a standard reply letter which was typed by "ROBO" equipment (Friden 2303 Flexowriters). These inquiries were placed in a mail box for Connie Chevalier, the ROBO operator.
5. Outgoing mail was accumulated at Lois' desk for pickup by the mail deliverers.

Case Work Mail

Mail going to the case workers was divided into three groups, with Ruth Hagen handling military, selective service, social security and veterans problems; Carol Woolten being responsible for immigration, civil service, aviation, and miscellaneous problems; and Don Russell responsible for problems related to federal contracts, grants, awards, services, and assistance programs.

Ruth decribed herself as a military case worker:

> My job is to serve the people. All of our cases are initiated by a letter to the Senator. The cases I handle deal mostly with the relationship of an individual to the military. The letter itself usually comes from one of three people: the individual himself, his wife, or his mother. About 50% come from wives and mothers. Whenever we get a request from a wife or mother we must first investigate the desires of the individual involved.
>
> There are two broad types of military cases—those involving people already in the military and those involving people subjected to Selective Service. The first type normally deals with a man's relation to the military structure such as assignment or promotion. The second type is concerned with an individual's rights and obligations under the Selective Service laws. Most of these are requests for aid in acquiring a draft deferment or exemption.

Exhibit 6

THE OFFICE OF SENATOR RONALD R. KENMORE
MAIL COUNT MARCH 20–26, 1971

TOTAL MAIL COUNT 4,394
LEGISLATIVE MAIL 3,207

132 Susan & Paul
- 69 Cigarettes
- 38 Miscellaneous
- 8 Social Security
- 6 FAP/Welfare Reform
- 5 National Health Plan
- 4 Title 29/Apprenticeship Training
- 2 Busing

93 Lynn Middleton
- 35 Draft
- 35 Vietnam; 5 Other
- 5 POW's
- 5 Middle East
- 5 ABM/MIRV/SALT
- 1 Greece
- 2 Africa

2,823 ROBO
- SST
  - 1,126 Con SST
  - 1,207 Pro SST
- 82 Vietnam
- 42 Draft
- 26 Davis/Bacon Con Suspension
- 25 POW's
- 42 HEW Funds
- 16 Abortion
- 14 Nursing—Manpower Training Funds
- 8 Russian Jews
- 7 H.R.5375—Protect Wild Horses
- 6 Pollution
- 5 Animal Protection
- 4 Military Funding
- 3 Social Security
- 3 Vocational Education Funds
- 3 Alaskan Pipeline
- 3 Soil Conservation Service Funds
- 2 Israel
- 2 Deaf-Blind Funds
- 2 Seal Harvest
- 2 Imports
- 2 Jetport Proposal

100 Ken Graham
- 27 SST
- 21 Miscellaneous
- 11 Trade
- 7 Transportation
- 6 Taxes
- 6 National Energy
- 5 Communications
- 3 Airport Noise
- 4 Alaskan Native Land Claims
- 3 Revenue Sharing
- 3 Fisheries
- 2 Railroad
- 2 Defense Conversion

59 Carl Morse
- 8 Law
- 8 Pollution
- 7 Aging
- 7 Agriculture
- 4 White River Valley
- 4 Interior (land, parks)
- 4 Legal Services
- 4 Environment
- 3 Co-sponsorships
- 3 Food Stamps
- 2 Drugs
- 1 Courts
- 1 Public Works
- 1 Indians
- 1 DDT
- 1 Consumer

Exhibit 7 diagrams the legislative mail flow.

Exhibit 7

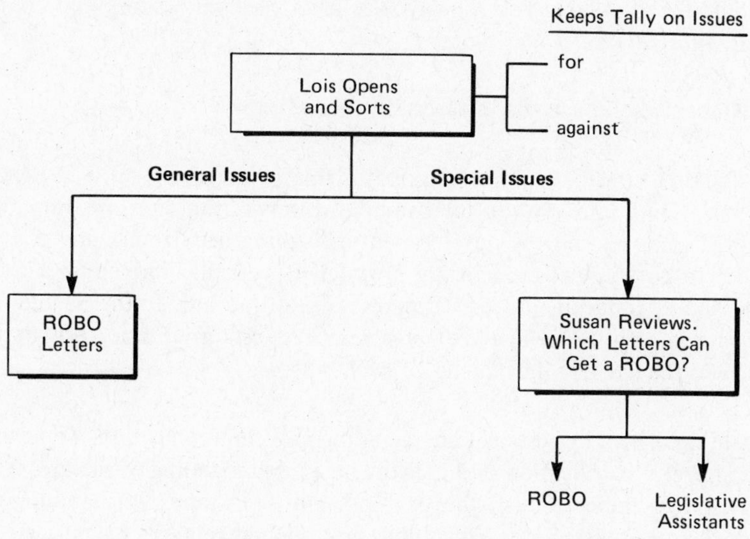

Ruth explained that she received 15–25 letters a day. These included 7–12 new cases and the balance were related to cases she was already working on. The letters relating to old cases were either from the individuals involved or from government departments and were responses to Ruth's inquiries. She kept an alphabetical file of cases pending. This file contained about 200 cases. The number of pending cases tended to hold steady because new incoming cases tended to balance closing cases. The average case went through roughly five steps.

1. A letter was received from the constituent.
2. An acknowledgement was sent.
3. A letter of inquiry was sent to the agency concerned.
4. A reply was received from the agency.
5. A cover letter, with the reply, was sent to the constituent.

Some cases tended to continue because of the need for further investigation of other departments or because of a follow-up inquiry from the constituent, but these cases were rare. Ruth did not use any form letters because she felt that her work required personalized communication.

Ruth expressed enthusiasm for her job:

> The work is very enjoyable. We work on our own. I decide how to handle each case, which ones to refer to the Senator, or which department should handle the problem. The job involves a lot of letter writing and communication with people.

Carol also seemed enthusiastic in describing her work:

> I wouldn't consider any other job. In this job I really get a chance to help people. Take immigration for example. Immigration laws are very restrictive and this has caused the development of waiting lists from many countries. In order to circumvent the existing laws for a particular individual a private bill must be introduced into the Congress. Of all the bills in the Senate 30% are private immigration bills. We get several requests a week for private bills and in 1970 the Senator introduced 11 such bills.

Carol described her job as understanding and communication. Typically a case involved simply a clarification of a constituent's understanding of the law. This often involved guiding them through the governmental "red tape." In handling constituent letters, Carol processed the easy things first, such as requests for information.

Miss Woolten stated that she received 150–200 letters per week. Her file contained approximately 250 cases pending. In order to insure that they were not forgotten she reviewed her file once a month and took follow-up action on those which had been waiting for a reply for longer than a month. Carol's case work often included some unusual problems.

> Many times people are in an emotional state by the time we hear from them. One family was trying to get their son's body back from the Middle East for burial in their home town. For health reasons the State Department was blocking shipment. A member of the foreign government told the parents that unless the body was shipped out soon they would have to stick it in a basket and bury it in an unmarked grave. Well, you can imagine the state the mother was in after that. In another case we received a card from an out of state prison with the single word HELP! written across it. Someone was going to throw it out but I was able to intercept it. Upon inquiry I found that the man needed immediate psychiatric help.

Don Russell's mail ran from 50–75 letters per week; he did not find difficulty handling his mail load. Because of the nature of his area of responsibility Don spent a good deal of his time away from the office dealing with people on a face-to-face basis.

Legislative Mail

Susan Miller picked up all legislative mail from Lois' desk, reviewed and distributed it to the various responsible individuals. Susan explained why she reviewed the mail before distributing it.

> I have a better idea than Lois about the work load of the legislative assistants. Often I can have some mail answered by the secretaries. Also if a particular piece of legislation is getting ten inquiries or more a week we can compose a standard letter and send it down to ROBO. Everything under ten letters per week we have to type individual copies. I also try and flag VIP's for special handling. The VIP's are often sent to Eleanor for Peter's response. The letters going to ROBO I put in a file for Connie. You can see it has gotten pretty thick since she hasn't picked it up for a week or two.

Often a letter was received which had comments about more than one legislative subject. These letters had to be answered individually even though there might have been ROBO letters on the individual subjects. Periodically, a petition was received with thousands of signatures; a ROBO response was written and a typed copy sent to each signatory. Once the legislative inquiries were answered by a legislative assistant, the answers, with the inquiry attached, were filed alphabetically by the addressee. This file was used if another letter was received referring to a previous correspondence. Inquiries answered by ROBO were filed by date answered for a period of about a month and then destroyed. Occasionally a letter was lost for a period of time but all the office staff believed that eventually 100% of the mail was answered by a letter with the Senator's signature.

Each legislative assistant had his or her own way of handling these inquiries. Lynn allowed her mail to stack up, sometimes for two to three weeks before putting aside some time for answering the inquiries. She would then type drafts for all the letters and give them to Arlene to have finished copies typed. Carl spent one or two hours once a week dictating answers to Susan who would then type up and mail the responses. Paul Katz, who was a part-time intern, answered the letters as received. According to Paul:

> I have no trouble answering my mail but then I often have a lot of time. I often have to look for things to do. This will change as I gradually take over more of Peter's responsibility for handiing press information and releases.

Since their main task was to develop and shape new legislation, all of the legislative assistants considered the legislative letter-answering task as something which detracted from their work.

A large part of the legislative mail was not really handled by the legislative assistants but by the secretaries to the legislative assistants—Susan Miller, Arlene Kelly, and Mary Teeling, and the ROBO operator, Connie Chevalier.

The ROBO Operation

Each senator was supplied with certain services for the administration of his office. Utilizing his available budget, a senator could purchase various pieces of office equipment which he might need. This equipment became the property of the Senate but was for the exclusive use of the individual senator. The Senate provided a work area and maintenance for the equipment. When the senator left the Senate his equipment became a part of a pool which could be drawn upon by any senator. Senator Kenmore's office had purchased three Friden 2303 Flexowriters. The Flexowriters, located in the basement of the Old Senate Building, were the responsibility of Connie Chevalier.

A Flexowriter was a typewriter which produced individually typed letters from punched paper tapes. These machines were useful when it was necessary to send a single letter to a large number of individuals. This machine could provide multiple copies of a letter with the same text but different addresses and salutations, by the use of two paper tapes. These tapes were key punched by Connie on the Flexowriter; one tape contained the text of the letter, and the other contained a listing of the individual addresses and salutations. These two tapes were then mounted on the Flexowriter. The Flexowriter sequenced each address tape to type the heading and salutation of the letter. After each salutation the text was typed by the other tape loop. The result was a series of individually addressed standard letters.

The three Flexowriters were used to produce responses to petition letters and large volume inquiries on a particular subject. One Flexowriter was used exclusively for the cutting of letter and address tapes. Using this machine an operator could cut a tape of 45–50 addresses in 30 minutes. The other two were used for the actual typing. The Flexowriters printed at a speed of 100 words per minute (a word averages seven characters). Once the tapes were cut, little time was required to set up the machines; regardless of the number of addresses on the tape it took less than five minutes of down time to introduce new letter and address tapes into the machine.

In explaining the ROBO operation, Connie stated that she had a problem keeping up with the mail flow.

> We don't have much of a backlog now but that is because Fran was down here helping me last week and we pretty much caught up. It's quiet now but it is usually pretty noisy because both machines are going. I guess I send out about 300 letters a day. I have 200 here now ready for the Senator's signature; Karen is sending Fran down to help me sign them so we can mail them.

Connie picked up legislative mail which could get ROBO responses from Lois and Susan whenever she was getting low on work. Each inquiry was put into a folder designated by the ROBO letter number. In all there were about 160 standard letters. These letters averaged about 22 lines of text (a line contained approximately 80–85 characters). Each new standard letter had to have a punch tape cut and occasionally an LA decided to revise an existing ROBO letter. The folders containing inquiry letters were kept in a file on a small table next to the Flexowriter used to cut tapes. The folders were in no particular order and contained letters as much as three weeks old. The folders were entered into the ROBO system in random order. Upon choosing a folder to do, Connie pulled a copy of the designated letter and its tape out of the file or cut a tape if it was a new ROBO letter. She then cut an address tape which contained all of the addresses in the folder. The two tapes were mounted on another Flexowriter which typed the individual letters by automatically processing the complete text tape after each address and salutation. When the address tape was completely run and all the letters typed, the finished letters (typed on a continuous strip of letterhead stationery perforated above each letterhead) was torn off the Flexowriter after the last completed letter. The stationery was then folded on the perforations and Connie carried the pile of letters to a distant office where they were separated and the guide holes cut off the side of the letters. The result was a pile of individually typed letters on 8½″ x 11″ letterhead stationery. Connie then returned to the ROBO office, signed the letters, folded them and inserted the letters in window envelopes. The address tapes were then thrown into a cardboard box which was disposed of when full. At the request of one of the consultants Connie tallied the completed letters for May 13th; that tally came to 209. The Flexowriters were loaded with tapes in the order the address tapes were cut by the operator. If at the end of the day a Flexowriter was working on a tape it was allowed to continue after Connie had left so that the tape would be completed by morning.

One of the steps being considered by Mr. Powell was the replacement of the Flexowriters by MTST equipment. This equipment had the advantage of storing up to 48 individual paragraphs. A letter could be constructed using any combination of these paragraphs. It would then be feasible to construct letters in response to multiple subject inquiries. This would result in a decrease in the mail load of the legislative assistants.

To acquire MTST equipment, Ted would have to either use part of the operating budget ($341,000 per year), or turn in the Flexowriter equipment to the Senate office equipment pool in trade for MTST equipment if it became available. Upon investigation, one of the consultants obtained the following costs for this equipment.

	Purchase Price	*Monthly Rental*
IBM MTST	$11,700	$265
Friden 2303	$ 4,000	$125

Mailing Lists

The Senate also provided each senator with a mailing service. This service could be utilized for bulk mailing such as reports to constituents.

The mailing service incorporated the use of the Senate's IBM 360–40 to provide updated mailing lists and address labels. The tapes from the MTST or Flexowriter could not be used as input without additional coding. The Senator's mailing lists were being developed by the acquisition of existing mailing lists from professional and other organizations. The service of the 360–40 was limited to a mailing system and could not be used for information storage and retrieval. The service was further limited to providing each senator with storage of up to 500,000 addresses on magnetic tape and up to 220,000 mailings per month. These services were administered under the Senate Rules Committee through the Senate Sergeant at Arms and any changes in the services, such as increased storage allowances, had to be approved by the Rules Committee.

At the present time, Senator Kenmore's office had approximately 29,000 addresses on file. It was presently the job of Frank Mullen, a part-time intern, to increase this mailing list.

CHAPTER 4: ESTABLISHING AND CONTROLLING SERVICE LEVELS

The *service level* is the consumer's perception of the quality of a service, which we noted in Chapter 3, and is a complex bundle of *explicit* and *implicit* attributes. The quality or service level is an intuitively integrated value of the appropriateness of the service offerings to the consumer's needs.

Service managers have recently broadened their perspective about what constitutes service. Originally, the focus of the service managers was on the *substantive service,* the essential function of the service. Hotels provide a place to sleep; restaurants serve food; airlines move passengers between points; trucklines move freight; and garages repair automobiles. In most cases customers can readily determine if they had received the substantive service by observing that facilitating goods were received or the location or physical condition was changed. Service customers also buy a variety of other service attributes that go beyond the substantive service. These other attributes of the service are the *peripheral services,* that is, services that surround the substantive service.

CONSUMER MODEL

The service level is established by the consumer's perception of quality or appropriateness of the competitive services. Therefore, it is necessary to examine how the consumer makes this judgment. When we speak of a consumer, we are referring to a market segment of consumers with similar needs and behavior.

The consumer has a set of needs. These needs are summarized in Figure 4-1. The substantive need is the consumer's requirement for the essential service described above; however, the consumer also has a variety of other needs. He or she may need a sense of control, trust, consequence, and self-fulfillment or status. The satisfaction of these needs may raise conflicts when the consumer attempts to translate them into desired service attributes. For example, a consumer may want the sense of control that may be gained by a broad menu but is frustrated by being given too broad a choice, or a customer may desire the exclusivity of a small hotel but find the inconvenience of location or uncertainty of being able to get a reservation annoying.

In Figure 4-1, we have shown the consumer translating needs into a set of desired attributes, which is illustrated in this way for purposes of discussion. Most consumers have only a vague model of the desired attributes and depend on the server to suggest service bundles to satisfy their needs. Over a period of time, how-

Figure 4-1

Consumer Model for Establishing Service Levels

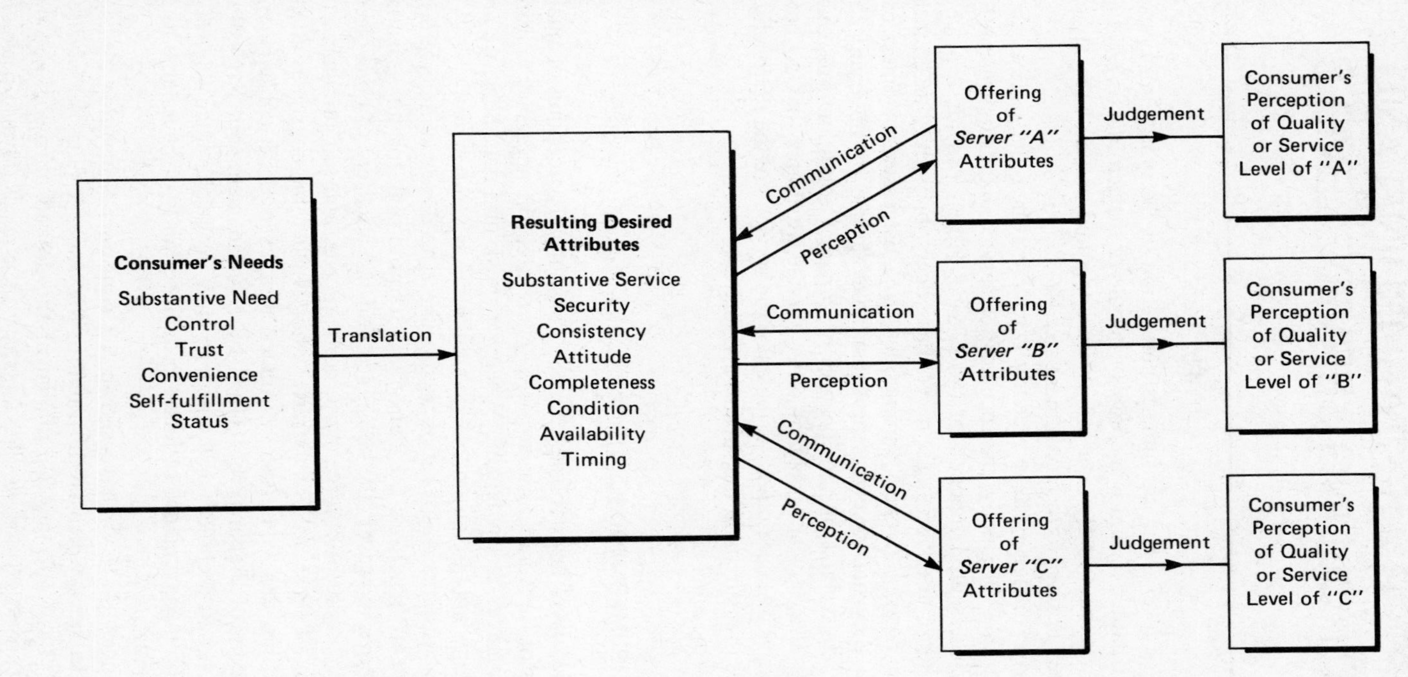

ever, consumers do form a model of what is desired. The terms in Figure 4-1 require explanation. *Security* relates to the safety of the consumer or the consumer's property. Security might be expressed by lighted parking lots at grocery stores, airline safety and crash prevention, or prevention of the loss and damage of shipments. *Consistency* describes standardization and reliability of service; for example, it might mean that the room is always made up the same way in a hotel or that "rare" always means that meat is cooked to the same level of doneness in a restaurant. *Attitude* can be discerned in the interpersonal reactions of the service worker and the customer. It may also be seen in the printed instruction on the pay telephone or implied in the way signs and arrival-departure information are displayed in airports. *Completeness* is connected with the array of services that are provided. Does a travel agent simply provide airline tickets or also arrange other transportation, food, and lodging? Completeness may also be seen in the varieties of services offered. *Condition* is concerned with the environment in which the service is offered and performed. Condition can be found in the "atmosphere" of a restaurant, decor of a hotel room, cleanliness of a restroom, availability of parking, and the level of sound and lighting. *Availability* is the ease of access in time (frequency of schedule or waiting time) or space (locations). Frequent departures of airlines represent availability in one type of service industry, whereas the number of locations of restaurants or easy return to a freeway from a motel are examples of availability in other service industries. *Timing* relates to the length of time required for, and pace of, performance of a service. Examples of service attributes are listed in Table 4-1.

The competitive servers offer services that contain a variety of mixes of these attributes. The service company communicates these attributes to the consumer in a variety of ways, including advertising, performance, manner, or other signals. The consumer perceives the service attributes and judges how appropriate the mix is.

There are three models of how consumers make such judgments. They are:

1. *One Overpowering Attribute*. One attribute basically determines the value. All other attributes receive only nominal or no consideration.
2. *Single Attribute with Threshold Minimums for Other Attributes*. An alternative must achieve at least the threshold condition for certain attributes to be considered. But the final ranking is made among the qualified candidates on the basis of a single attribute.
3. *Weighted Average of Attributes*. The alternatives are ranked on the basis of a weighted average, so that a high score on one attribute may offset a low score on another.

An example is useful to see how such a multiattribute ranking might be made using each model. Assume you were the admissions officer of a school interested in selecting a potential student basketball player. At one school, the candidate's ability to play basketball would be the overpowering attribute. An admissions officer at another school might be looking for basketball ability among candidates who have attained certain minimum high school grade-point averages and Scholastic Aptitude Test scores. The admissions officer at a third school might assign weights to a variety of information and look for the candidate with the highest score. This admissions officer might accept a candidate that was not a top basketball player if

Table 4-1

EXAMPLES OF SERVICE ATTRIBUTES

Security
- Confidence in the airline pilot
- Double locks on hotel room doors
- Confidentiality of records by a tax preparation firm

Consistency
- TWA's on-time airline strategy
- Same flavor or quality of food at each visit to a restaurant

Attitude
- Recognition of regular customers at a restaurant
- Airline V.I.P. rooms
- Restaurant manager asking guests about the quality of their meals

Completeness
- American Airline's introduction of curb-side check-in service
- Acceptance of credit cards at a restaurant
- Holiday Inn's policy of providing a swimming pool at all their hotels
- Airport parking facilities
- Salad bar at a restaurant

Condition
- Clean restrooms at McDonald's
- Decor in theme restaurants
- Nonsmoking seating at Victoria Station restaurants

Availability
- Easy access of race track to public transportation
- Locations of service stations
- Convenient and frequent airline departures

Timing
- Serving of a meal at the "right" psychological moment in the dining experience
- Fast completion of tax reports by tax preparation firms

there were evidence of excellent academic potential. Each model is appropriate for different schools and situations. The service manager must determine the appropriate consumer model in his or her situation.

The resulting rankings or consumer interpretations may be compared on an absolute scale, but more typically the consumer ranks the several offerings relative to each other. For example, compare your impression of the service level of several different types of restaurants with which you are familiar. After you have made this comparison, examine the attributes to which you were particularly sensitive. What model did you use? To what needs were you responding?

SERVICE LEVEL/PRICE COMBINATIONS

The next step is to relate service level and price. Figure 4-2 is a graphical illustration of how a comparison like this might be made. There is a "range of reasonable combinations" of prices and service levels. Combinations above this zone may exceed the upper limit that any reasonable consumer is willing to pay for a particular

Figure 4-2

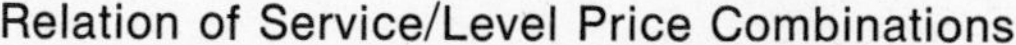

Relation of Service/Level Price Combinations

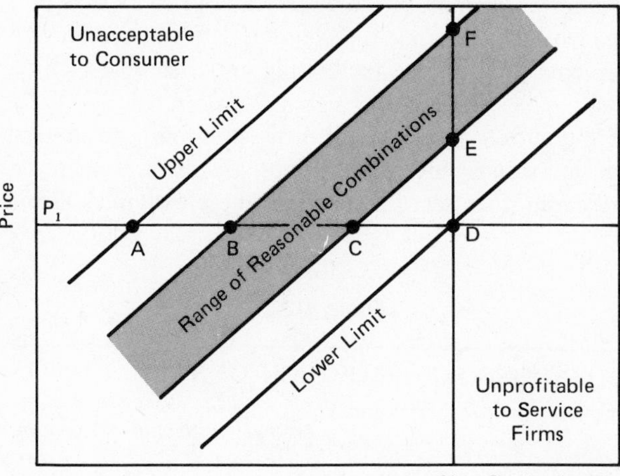

service level. Combinations below the range of reasonable combination may be too expensive for the service firm to produce and sell at a profit. The rational consumer generally attempts to maximize the service level at a given price. Therefore, he or she would seek service offering D in preference to A in Figure 4-2. Conversely, the consumer may decide upon a desired service level and attempt to minimize the price. It is worth noting that the difference in the service level at A and B may not be a difference in the substantive attributes but entirely a difference in peripheral attributes that might have essentially no cost. If offerings E and F are both reasonable combinations, the service firm would presumably want to have the price associated with F. What several service firms have successfully accomplished is to offer the range from B to E by carefully adding peripheral attributes of nominal expense to change the service level. This might be accomplished by washing an automobile before delivering it to a customer after repairs, putting real flowers on a restaurant table, or delivering a morning newspaper to a hotel room.

The market demand is not evenly distributed along the range of reasonable combinations. There are many more restaurant customers in the low-service-level/low-price zone than in the high-service-level/high-price zone. In addition, an individual consumer may find himself or herself very happy eating a quick lunch at a fast-food restaurant and eating dinner at a full-service restaurant with a tablecloth on the table at dinner and be quite pleased with both solutions because each was appropriate for the situation. *Satisfaction* is the ability to find a service level/price combination that the consumer finds appropriate and senses is a good value (that is, in the range of reasonableness or lower).[1]

---

[1] One interesting discussion of "satisfaction" appears in Henry H. Seward, *Measuring User Satisfaction to Evaluate Information Systems,* DBA dissertation, Harvard Business School, 1973. Also see Marvin E. Mandel, *Measuring and Enhancing the Productivity of Service and Government Organization* (Hong Kong: Nordica International, Ltd. 1975).

PROBLEMS OF MEASURING AND COMMUNICATING SERVICE LEVEL

The range and ephemeral nature of service makes it difficult to enumerate, quantify, or even elicit consumer perception of the quality and price aspects of a service. This problem is amplified by the fact that the characteristics of service are embodied in a multitude of elements, that is, the facilitating good, service facility, and the service employee.

Examples of the efforts of individual firms attempting to understand the relative importance of individual service attributes are illustrated in Tables 4-2 and 4-3. While such research does serve a function, these examples illustrate the prob-

Table 4-2

MOTIVATIONS FOR SELECTION OF TRAIN TRAVEL

Motivation	*Positive* %	*Neutral* %	*Negative* %
Cost of trip	36	36	28
Personal comfort	45	24	31
Safety	67	22	11
Interesting sights enroute	63	19	18
Arrive rested and relaxed	50	24	26
Ability to walk around	61	21	18
On-time arrival	42	27	31
Friendly, helpful employees	40	33	27
Speed	35	24	41
Flexible departure	25	33	42
Quality of food available	32	29	39
Modern washroom facilities	33	34	33
Reasonable food prices	23	41	36

Adapted from: "Harris Poll Projects Big Future for Amtrak," *Railway Age* (October 9, 1972), p. 39.

Table 4-3

SUMMARY OF 1975 STUDY OF ATTITUDES OF LESS-THAN-TRUCKLOAD SHIPPERS USING FOR-HIRE MOTOR CARRIERS

Factors Triggering the Need for a Change in Motor Carriers	*Percent*
1. Desire to reduce transit time	25
2. Undesirable performance of present carrier	21
3. Desire to reduce total transportation cost	16
4. Sales effort by salesman	11
5. Desire to cope with rush shipments	8
6. Other	19
	100

Table 4-3 (continued)

Sources of Information	*Percent*
1. Carrier salesmen	23
2. Directories	19
3. Past experience	18
4. Other traffic managers	8
5. Direct mail	8
6. Traffic clubs	6
7. Magazines	6
8. Trade catalogs	4
9. Visiting carrier terminals	3
10. Other	5
	100

Important Criteria for Carrier Selection	*Percent Indicating Most Important*
1. Consistent on-time service	38
2. Reliable pickup	8
3. Shipment tracing	6
4. Ability to handle less-than-truckload distribution in a given area	7
5. Equipment availability, general purpose	7
6. Rates	5
7. Loss and damage experience	5
8. One-carrier service	4
9. Service frequency	4
10. Claims settlement	3
11. Equipment availability, special purpose	3
12. Information services	3
13. Financial status and strength	3
14. Willingness to negotiate rates	2
15. Other	2
	100

	Percent		
Attitudes Toward Carrier Services	*Agree*	*Disagree*	*No Opinion*
1. There is little difference between carriers	13	83	4
2. There are plenty of salesmen calling	29	68	3
3. Carriers usually take little time to learn about our transportation problems	51	42	7
4. Most carrier information on service is inaccurate or misleading	28	60	12
5. Shippers are more likely to use the same carrier for repeat shipments	58	38	4

Source: D. Daryl Wyckoff and David H. Maister, *The Motor-Carrier Industry* (Lexington, Mass.: Lexington Books, D. C. Heath, 1977), pp. 89–90.

lem experienced when the researcher attempts to unbundle and analyze elements of the service package. Table 4-2 appears to tell us a great deal about what potential railroad passengers feel about elements of the service offering of Amtrak. Unfortunately, it is difficult to determine how they weight these elements. Table 4-3 appears to be fairly vague about what constitutes service level. It should be noted that prices are the same for all the motor carriers, so that service competition is of great concern. It is clear that the substantive service of moving goods between points is assumed. Consistency is clearly the important attribute.

The intangible characteristics of the service package also makes it inherently difficult for the consumer to make conscious evaluations and comparisons of the quality of various service offerings. Faced with these inherent uncertainties the consumer often uses price as a surrogate for quality, and thus offering a quality service at a low price may not only reduce margins but also result in a degradation of the product's quality image.

The intangible nature of the product makes it essentially difficult to communicate to the consumer in both advertising and service level/price relationships. The natural tendency is to tie this communication to the facilitating good. For example, a fast-food operation often falls prey to the mistake of focusing its advertising on the quality and price of its hamburgers rather than promoting the total service package of convenience of location, speed of service, cleanliness of facility, attitude of service personnel, and assurance of standards across numerous locations.

When conceptualizing and setting service levels an understanding of the various cost tradeoffs in raising or lowering the various elements of the service is also involved. Management must answer a number of questions. What is an adequate service level? What level of performance will satisfy customers' needs or expectations of the service? What does "satisfaction" really mean to customers and how do you translate that performance into discernable service levels, whether they be easily quantifiable or subjective levels, for the many phases of the service production process? Some examples of areas that require service level decisions include: staffing, customer throughput, quality of facilitating products such as food or decor in a restaurant, and length of wait for the service facility.

One common problem of service level is that of offering too much quality—that is, more quality than is actually needed for customer satisfaction, for example, a consulting firm that sends a senior partner on a small job. The question of too much quality in a service should be examined with the use of paraprofessionals in mind, such as in a law or consulting firm, a medical clinic, or in servicing computers. If personnel with lower skills can accomplish the job being done by highly skilled employees, substantial improvements in productivity may be available without a substantial diminution in the quality of service delivered.

Setting initial service levels is a process that should be approached with care. Though service levels can often be altered to some degree once the service is in operation, they often set the tone of the service in a customer's eyes. While a restaurant can switch from being a luxury establishment to a restaurant that caters to people of more moderate means, the transition can be traumatic and is not guaranteed to succeed. And certainly there is no turning back to higher prices and more waiters once the image is altered in the customer's mind.

The definition of service levels becomes more important as top management gets farther away from the actual service production point. This is a thorny problem in large service organizations and in small service organizations that are growing into bigger organizations. It is difficult for management to notice that service levels are slipping as the organization becomes a multiunit operation spread over a wide geographic region. Service executives must be sensitive to customer perceptions, and if they cannot be there themselves, they should have personnel in the field monitoring service levels and reporting back to headquarters. Very often service managers are in the unenviable position of not knowing if their firms are satisfying customers until customers are sufficiently dissatisfied to complain or stop using the service. Indeed, the branch manager of a large aviation services organization admits that is the case with him. But he knows his organization well enough that he can usually tell by the nature and location of the complaints what or who the problem is, and he can solve it in short order. This is subjective but effective.

SERVICE LEVEL PROBLEMS ARISING FROM SIMULTANEOUS PRODUCTION AND CONSUMPTION

The simultaneity of production and marketing of a service product eliminates the quality filtering mechanisms that exist in manufacturing. First, it is difficult and in many cases impossible to inspect even the explicit characteristics of the product prior to delivery to the customer. Second, the integration of functions of marketing and production hinders the translation of consumer perceptions into more quantifiable production terms, which occurs as a result of negotiations of the two separate functions in a manufacturing organization. Third, operating personnel are required to have a dual set of often conflicting skills, that is, they are the production direct labor or artisans or both and they are also the sales personnel.

The fragmented nature of most service industries coupled with the simultaneity of production and marketing often lead to either unanticipated natural segmentation of markets, on the one hand, or an imposed aggregation of unlike markets by management, on the other. Thus, many multisite service operations find that top management has imposed standardization of materials, procedures, and locations across all operating sites while the sites may be operating in different market segments.

MANAGING SERVICE LEVEL BY SERVICE DELIVERY SYSTEM DESIGN

Because of the problems of introducing inspection or other quality control measures in most service delivery systems, the service level must be designed into the system rather than achieved by inspection.

An illustration of this is a quality hotel that found numerous complaints about small oversights in making up (preparing) rooms. Guests reported oversights: missing water glasses and stationery, televisions not in working order, and burned-out light bulbs. The causes of these problems were debated by management.

Should greater attention be devoted to inspecting rooms? Perhaps the head housekeeper and assistant managers should increase their spot inspections. However, many of the housekeepers resented the continuous inspection of their work, seeing such inspections as mistrust.

Another view was that the housekeepers had to be encouraged to be more careful. It was suggested that the problems were simply symptoms of worker apathy. However, the housekeepers appeared to be generally enthusiastic. In fact, management had received compliments on their attitudes.

The final analysis showed that the housekeepers had no set routine for making up a room. Some began by cleaning the bathroom, while others immediately stripped the bed of all the sheets and covers. It was also found that most of the housekeepers did not necessarily follow the same procedure from room to room.

The solution came from carefully analyzing all the steps necessary to make up a room. There was, in fact, a logical sequence of steps that minimized the effort. This sequence was taught to the housekeepers who enthusiastically accepted it as being a logical way to make their jobs easier. As the standard sequence was memorized, the housekeepers were substantially less likely to miss a detail inadvertently. The result was better and more consistent quality, a happier workforce, and less emphasis on "inspection" to achieve higher quality.

HUMAN INPUT IN SERVICE LEVELS

The service industries are generally labor intensive, and service employees are often difficult to supervise directly. Therefore, quality is a primary concern of the service industry workforce management. Training and incentive programs designed for improving the quality of the service delivery system can have important results. Employees need to know how to achieve quality performance. This is the task of training. A reasonable objective of an incentive program is creating the desire to achieve high quality as well as high productivity.

Substitution of technology may be considered as a substitution for labor inputs in a service delivery system. The amount of human labor has been substantially reduced in some service industries by the substitution of technology and manufacturing solutions. Examples include the methods introduced in the fast-food industry (specifically, McDonald's), mutual funds (individual stock portfolio decisions reduced), credit card loans, and self-service markets. Services such as automatic banking machines, in-room vending devices, and betting machines can be performed wholly without human contact. The question can be asked if these industries are improved because of a reduction of "humanistic performance"?

Hardware or software substitutions are often easier to manage for consistency of service level. Similarly, it is implied that productivity is increased. But there are several examples where technological solutions have proven to be disappointing. Computerized medical diagnostic services and interactive teaching machines both clearly increased consistency and productivity. User resistance prevented their successful introduction. Institutional barriers, lack of user-system fit, and a threat to the users' ego resulted in rejection. There appears to be a set of elements in the human content of certain services that technology has been unable to replace so far. These elements include: (1) human presence (warmth), (2) human assurance (security), (3) human response (idiosyncratic unstructured and infinite variations), (4) human dexterity, and (5) human reasoning.

It is important to identify the functional tasks that are provided by human labor as the starting point for any system of measuring and controlling the level of service.

LOSS OF SERVICE LEVEL THROUGH UNFOCUSING

One of the most frequent causes of service failure is the unconscious unfocusing of the service concept. As discussed earlier in this chapter, the service level is the quality of services perceived by a consumer (or market segment). Failure to maintain the service level in the mind of the target market segment consumer has serious consequences. Many successful service firms begin operations by offering a few highly focused services to a limited and clearly defined market segment, which is shown as Cell 1 in Figure 4-3. As service companies seek growth they frequently move from this highly focused situation to provide the same few services to many more markets (Cell 2) or provide many more services to the same few markets (Cell 3). Examples of the shift from Cell 1 to Cell 2 are the airline that primarily offers services to the business traveler and then attempts to extend its services to the tourist and student traveler markets or the ski resort that attempts to expand from its market of serious skiers to also include recreational skiers on the same facility. The initial market served in each case has very specific needs and a specific concept of the service level. The additional market segment may actually use the

Figure 4-3

Matrix of Services Offered and Markets Served

Markets Served		Services Offered: Few	Services Offered: Many
	Few	1	3
	Many	2	4

same facility (seats in aircraft or slopes and ski lodges), but the service levels required are quite different. Can the same service delivery system control service levels to satisfy both markets simultaneously? Similarly, some service companies move from the highly focused situation (Cell 1) to provide more services to the same market (Cell 3). Examples of the shift from Cell 1 to Cell 3 are Pacific Southwest Airlines, the California intrastate airline, which decided to sell more services (including hotels and car rentals) to its airline passengers, and Hilltop Steakhouse in Saugus, Massachusetts, which opened a butcher shop to sell its high-quality steaks to the large volume of customers who dine at the restaurant. In these examples, Pacific Southwest Airlines' venture into car rental and hotel ownership and operations nearly destroyed the airline's service level and financial structure. Hilltop Steakhouse has carefully managed not to lose its focus on its primary market as one of America's largest revenue single restaurant.

Shifts from the focused situation to either Cell 1 or Cell 2 require careful management. The service manager must be aware of the demands different markets or different services make on his or her company. While there are many cases of successful diversifications, they are far outweighed by the cases where the unfocusing of the company resulted in service levels that were unacceptable in any of their markets. The most common failures of service-level management occurred in instances where a company moved to many markets with many services (Cell 4). Those companies that attempted to be "all things to all people" typically were unable to satisfy any of their markets.

CONCLUSION

The service level is the consumer's perception of the quality of the service. It is a complex bundle of explicit and implicit attributes that attempts to satisfy the needs of a consumer (typical of a market segment). These attributes include the substantive service and a variety of peripheral services.

The consumer explicitly or implicitly ranks service offerings on the basis of service level and price. The same person may choose different service level/price combinations depending on the circumstances. However, the consumer has a range of reasonable combinations at any price or service level. He or she seeks to maximize satisfaction by increased service level at a price or reduced price at a service level. The service firm often can increase the service level beyond the price justified by the substantive service by careful addition of peripheral services at little marginal cost.

The service manager faces several problems in maintaining service levels. First, it is difficult to measure service level because it is determined by the perception of the consumer. Second, the services are usually produced and consumed simultaneously, so that the quality must be designed into the delivery system rather than inspected in. Third, services are labor intensive and are often decentralized multisite operations. While there have been some successful substitutions of technology for the human input, there are several features of the human server that are still very necessary and seen as part of the service level by the consumer.

Finally, the temptation to diversify from a focused service provided to a clearly defined market often leads a service firm to attempt to be "all things to all people" with disastrous loss of ability to manage the company's service level.

Ryder Truck Lines, Inc.

In June 1972, Kinzey Reeves, vice-president of operations of Ryder Truck Lines, was preparing to make his recommendations to the service committee meeting regarding continuation of the program that had been named "Blue Chip Service." This program had been initiated to help Ryder change the lack of revenue growth, a trend that had developed partially because of the company's record of average shipment performance. The question was whether the investment being made by Ryder toward improving service was producing results that would justify continuing the plan.

Company Background

In 1965, International Utilities (I.U.) purchased Ryder Truck Lines, which had been formed the previous year through the merger of several companies in the South, Midwest, Southeast, and East. Since that time, several other motor carriers had been purchased and merged or were being operated as divisions (see Exhibit 1). As summarized by one of the Ryder officials:

> The company had a history of unprofitable operations stemming from three basic factors. First, the operations were concentrated for the most part in the southeastern United States. Traditionally, freight rates in this territory were low. The prevailing levels had been highly influenced by labor costs of non-union carriers. Unionization of Ryder Truck Lines and the successful efforts of the Teamsters to establish uniform national labor rates resulted in a substantial variance between Ryder's labor costs and those incurred by local non-union carriers. Secondly, Ryder had essentially been a group of short-haul, distribution carriers with "local" terminals serving a large number of smaller communities with relatively low daily volume. Although they were under one management, each operated somewhat independently with little coordination. Thirdly, the entire system lacked the organization and controls of responsibility that were to be subsequently implemented by the new management team.

The second point was illustrated by comparison of Ryder's annual LTL[1] tonnage divided by the number of terminals with similar figures for other carriers in Exhibit 2.

[1] LTL = Less than truck load; generally defined as shipments less than 10,000 lbs.

Exhibit 1

RYDER TRUCK LINES, INC.
System Map, 1972

Exhibit 2

RYDER TRUCK LINES, INC.
Average LTL Tonnage/Terminal for Ryder and Other Motor Carriers, 1970

	1000 LTL tons/ terminal—year
1. Gordon's Transport	23.2
2. Georgia Highway Express	15.2
3. Mason and Dixon Lines	14.4
4. Carolina Freight Carriers	12.7
5. Transcon	12.2
6. Yellow Transit	9.8
7. Lee Way	7.9
8. Arkansas-Best	7.5
9. Ryder Truck Lines, Inc.	5.3

Between 1965 and 1969, the basic objectives pursued by Ryder were to:

1. Change the traffic mix to improve the profitability of the freight handled.
2. Expand the territory served, by acquiring carriers with authority to serve key market cities and areas in the highly industrialized Northeast, Midwest, and Central states.
3. Decentralize profit responsibility and establish a management information system that would provide necessary controls and allow results to be measured for evaluation.

By the beginning of 1970, the management of Ryder felt that most of the initial phase of the program had been accomplished. Management made the statement:

> To a large degree, the progress made by Ryder has resulted in a remaking of the company so that it now truly represents a major factor in the transportation scene in the United States. Its growth and profit potential are, we believe, at the threshold phase, and the realization of the full opportunity lies ahead.

The results of this phase of Ryder's development are summarized in Exhibit 3. The main thrust of the period was to clearly identify costs through the use of Ryder-developed engineering standards for terminal operations and providing operating personnel with the controls and incentives to achieve or exceed these standards.

While the cost-control strategy was quite successful, there were unanswered concerns about growth. One comment was:

> Our costs are lower than our competitors, but many of them have better operating ratios. Most of these carriers have had good revenue growth, mostly in LTL traffic. We are actually handling fewer good LTL shipments than before. Why are we not showing sound growth?

Exhibit 3

RYDER TRUCK LINES, INC.
Operating Results, 1966–1969 *

	1966	*1967*	*1968*	*1969*	*1969 Average for southern region carriers*
Revenue ($000)	59,761	57,206	60,726	68,500	N.A.
Maintenance/ revenue (%)	11.4	9.7	9.3	8.15	9.6
Terminal ***/ revenue (%)	26.0	23.7	21.5	20.8	20.5
Transportation/ revenue (%)	38.1	38.5	39.8	42.0	40.6
Operating ratio (%)**	98.3	94.4	93.7	93.7	95.8
Terminals	63	63	103	103	N.A.
LTL tons (000)	813	672	622	570	N.A.
LTL shipments (000)	3197	2458	2156	1830	N.A.
Total tons (000)	1606	1423	1460	1365	N.A.
Average load (tons)	13.2	13.1	13.4	14.4	N.A.
Average length of haul (miles)	581	618	624	797	N.A.
Terminal expense/ LTL ton ($)***	19.11	20.75	20.99	24.99	N.A.
All terminal					

* Results of the Ryder Division of International Utility. Does not include other carriers owned by I.U.

** Operating ratio = operating expenses (not including interest) divided by operating revenue.

*** Terminal expense here is the 4300 account of the I.C.C., which primarily deals with dock operations and does not include pick up and delivery.

The answer to this question was believed by many at Ryder to be related to service.

> The problem was considerably easier to describe than solve. Our company had grown up serving many low-volume markets that could not support regular daily direct schedules, either from or to major terminal points. When this is the situation, there are two basic choices. Freight is held or collected until there is a full load or you use the more expensive break-bulk operations.

"Direct loading" is less expensive and provides significantly better service, since the LTL freight is loaded at origin and moves on the same trailer directly to the destination terminal (see Exhibit 4). "Break-Bulk" operations require LTL freight from a number of smaller terminals to be transported to a central handling point where it is unloaded and consolidated with freight from other smaller terminals for the same destination. Additional rehandling, inherent in break-bulk operations, automatically increases terminal expenses, with additional delays that reflect negatively on service performance and create greater claim exposure.

Exhibit 4

RYDER TRUCK LINES, INC.
Typical Movement of Freight

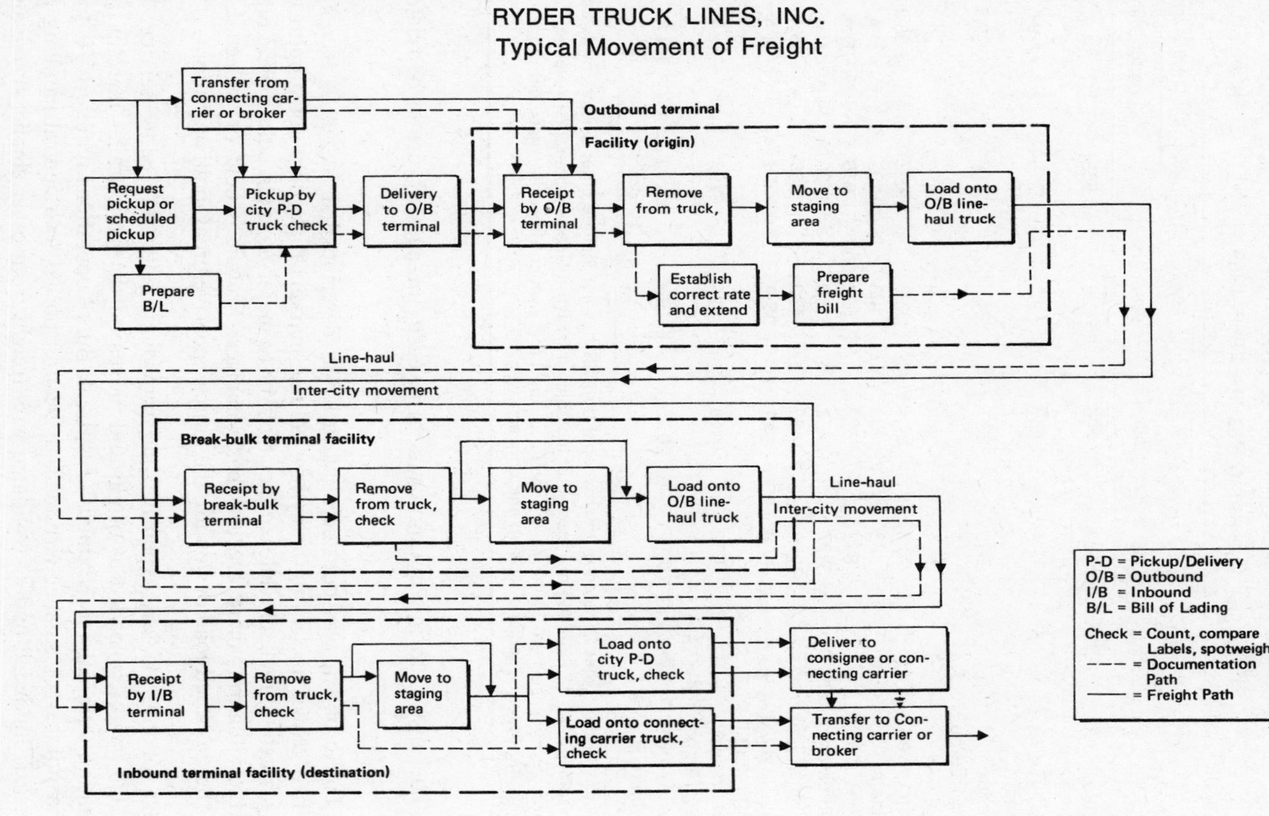

> Our service between major terminal points, where we were making at least a trailer load a day, was good and meeting competition. One of the major problems was that few terminals had existing traffic lanes with that level of volume. On the lanes where there was not sufficient volume to run regular schedules, we were finding problems. The service on those lanes was average but not good enough to attract additional freight, which would automatically make the operation better.

Complaint letters (example shown in Exhibit 5) confirmed these remarks. The trend in "on-time deliveries" (Exhibit 6) was down. Objective evaluation, though several other known and recognized factors had a definite effect on the service's performance, suggested that service was hindering growth. The company had to compete on the basis of service since for-hire trucking rates were regulated by the Interstate Commerce Commission and were the same for all carriers.

By early 1970, service had become a major issue at Ryder.

> We had acquired a reputation as being an "average" service carrier. Our service image predated the acquisition by I.U. Emphasizing cost control programs and increasing operating discipline had aggravated the situation. Few people at Ryder were able to agree on the seriousness of the service problem. Executive management in the past had been insulated from service complaints by strong regional managers and the field organization. With the establishment of more centralized cost controls, a highly accurate management information system, and a restructured organization, complaints began flowing directly to the general offices.

In response to the sensed service problem, a service committee was established. This committee, meeting monthly to discuss and resolve service problems, consisted of the president, executive vice-president, and vice-presidents of sales and

Exhibit 5

RYDER TRUCK LINES, INC.
Excerpts from a Service Complaint Letter

"On March 22, we shipped 8,700 pounds of plastic pellets from Newark to Ft. Lauderdale. After attempting to trace and expedite the shipment, we finally received it on April 6.... Since this is not the first problem we have encountered with Ryder, I want to set up a meeting with you some time during the week of April 12."

NOTE FROM INTERNAL RYDER MEMO DISCUSSING THE CAUSE OF THE SERVICE COMPLAINT

"This is not the first time we have given poor service on this particular movement, which I am sure is highly desirable traffic for the Company. However, it took us a week to get enough freight to make this a decent load to Ft. Lauderdale. Our people followed directions. Any suggestions how we can handle these differently?"

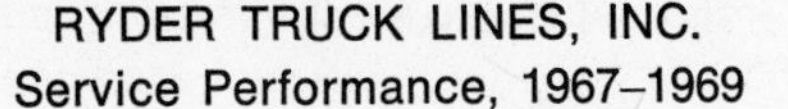
Exhibit 6

RYDER TRUCK LINES, INC.
Service Performance, 1967–1969

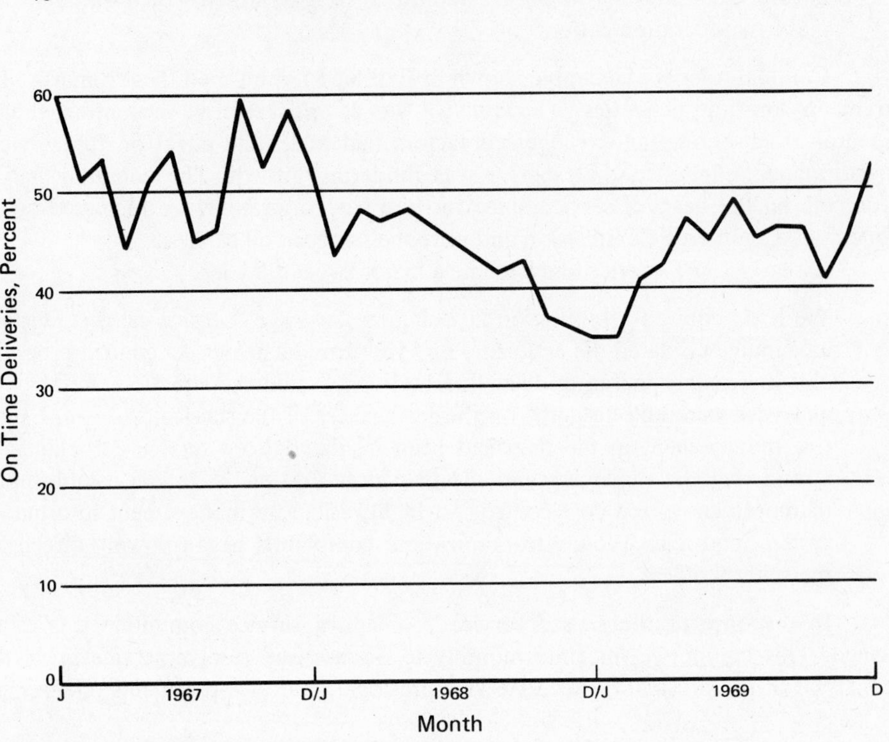

operations. The purpose of the committee was to bring some resolution to the problem of continued service failures.

The 1970 operating results were improved, but not spectacular. Because of the combined results of a 3-month Teamster's strike against the industry in Chicago and the unresolved service situation, growth at Ryder was still lacking. Continued improvement in controls, costs, and operations was being made, as seen in Exhibit 7.

In April of 1971, a program was adopted by the service committee to improve service on several specific traffic lanes. Every lane (city pair) was reviewed and categorized. Loading, dispatching, and allocation of equipment in cases of conflict, in regard to LTL shipments, were to then be handled in accordance to descending priority as follows:

1. *Special Service Lanes* (Scheduled)
   Those lanes in which there is sufficient volume to support direct loading. The objective is to continue to provide excellent service to assure retaining such

Exhibit 7

RYDER TRUCK LINES, INC.
Operating Results, 1970 *

	1970
Revenues ($000)	70,900
Maintenance/revenue (%)	6.8
Terminal/revenue (%)**	19.6
Transportation/revenue (%)	39.7
Operating ratio (%)***	92.3
Terminals	103
LTL tons (000)	540
LTL shipments (000)	1,655
Total tons (000)	1,247
Average load (tons)	15.3
Average length of haul (miles)	850
All terminal labor/revenue (%)	31.9

* Results of the Ryder Division of International Utilities. Does not include other carriers owned by I.U.

** Terminal expense here is the 4300 account of the I.C.C., which primarily deals with dock operations and does not include pickup and delivery.

*** Operating ratio = operating expenses (not including interest) divided by operating revenue.

business. Its on-time target for deliveries was established at 60%. (Ryder measures service against established service standards on *all* shipments, not identifying the reason for delay. Shipments held for shipper or consignee convenience, broker clearance on export shipments, appointment deliveries, consignee vacations or holidays, and all other factors outside Ryder's control were not considered as allowable excuses for delay in their calculations. Ryder's management felt that from their experience in using this service measurement method, a 60% on-time delivery was considered "outstanding.")

2. *Sales Lanes* (Scheduled)
   Those lanes in which there is substantial potential to be realized by Ryder. The objective is to provide excellent service (even if break-bulk operations are required) to develop additional traffic.

3. *Major Market* (Scheduled)
   Those lanes in which there is sufficient marketing potential to justify running at least three scheduled movements per week.

4. *Major Market* (Unscheduled)
   Those lanes in which a strong effort should be made if possible.

5. *Other Lanes*

The results of this program are plotted in Exhibit 8.

Exhibit 8

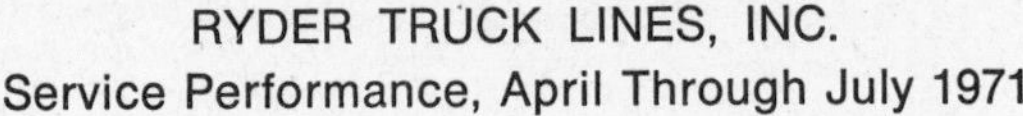
RYDER TRUCK LINES, INC.
Service Performance, April Through July 1971

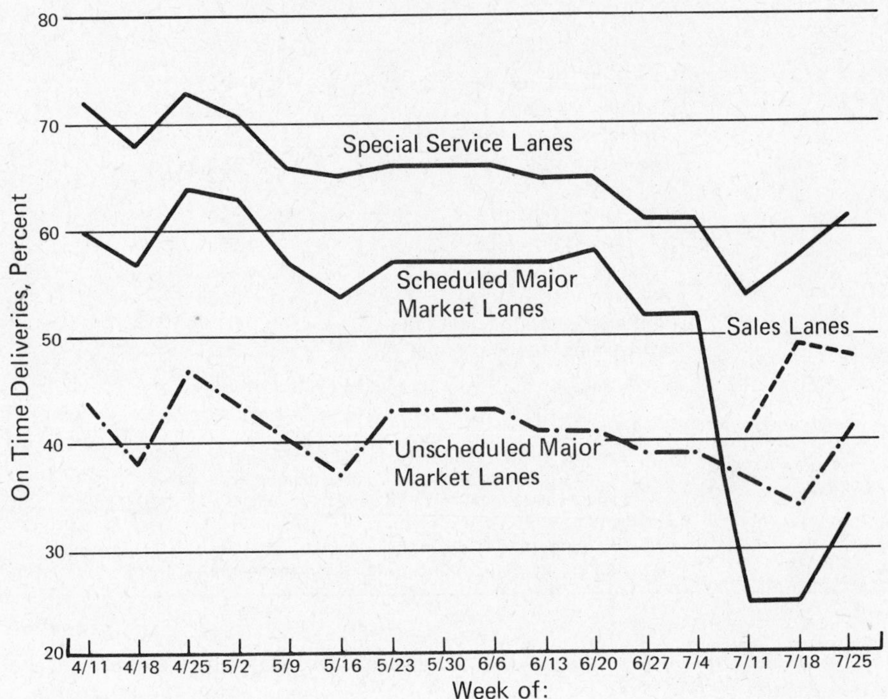

Through the summer months of 1971, Special Service and Major Market Service continued to show declines. While costs continued to respond to controls, service complaints continued and evidence of improved on-time service performances continued to lag.

Two problems had developed with the implementation of the service-lane program. First, an increased number of lanes were being designated for "special service" as the result of customer pressure. By the end of July 1971, the number of Special-Service Lanes had been increased from 45 to 162. Secondly, several shippers became offended at a policy that provided substantially different service quality between different key lanes. It became increasingly necessary to provide priority service on "Other Lanes" to maintain the accounts of good shippers who were familiar with the performance being provided on the Special Service Lanes.

By July 1971, the service situation at Ryder was described by management as "nearly out of hand." Service committee meetings became "muddled" with attempts to place the blame for specific isolated service problems.

Pump-Priming Service Strategy

At the beginning of August, a proposal was made to the service committee to substantially change the company's operations. The argument for the proposal was:

> The major problem in providing service is not a lack of desire but too little volume. We simply cannot direct load enough freight between a sufficient number of points to maintain regular daily schedules. However, by using break-bulk operations through strategic assembly points, we can actually fill at least one trailer a day from every origin to the system. We are already rehandling about 66.3% of our LTL shipments or 74.5% of the LTL tonnage in support of the present program.[1] We must introduce a program to move all

Exhibit 9

RYDER TRUCK LINES, INC.
Criteria for Design of LTL Service Program

TO: Bill Tickle, Vice-President of Sales
FROM: Kinzey Reeves, Vice-President of Operations

The following is a recap of the guidelines we used in constructing the LTL service standards we recommend be adopted by our company. The basic premise is a policy statement to the effect:

To provide a consistent, dependable service that will attract and retain customers in those markets we wish to serve.

I see the key elements in our service plan as being:

1. Establish attainable service standards on our present traffic volume and pattern.
2. Establish operating instructions and controls to assure timely handling of freight.
3. Measure service performance on those lanes that represent our market.
4. Review the operating plan to assure it acknowledges changing traffic volumes, markets, and sales objectives.

Recommended LTL service has been developed for all city pairs using the following criteria.

1. A direct schedule will be established on any lane that our history shows we handled at least 400,000 pounds of LTL freight in a 4-week period.
2. Transfer freight will move through break-bulk operations in not more than 24 hours.
3. Service standards on freight moving through multiple transfer are kept within the following limits:

2 transfers	5 days
3 transfers	6 days

I propose that, concurrent with the adoption of the new program, we eliminate the Special Service, Sales, and Major Market Lanes designation.

I am most enthusiastic about this package. I hope that it provides what you feel we need to get more than our share in 1972.

[1] If a shipment is rehandled once, it is counted as 100%. However, since some shipments might move through several points, it is possible for rehandling to be greater than 100%.

of the freight every day, making provisions for rehandling. While this will impose substantial increases in rehandling and increased costs, it is intended that the improved service will increase the traffic volume in most lanes to the point that rehandling can be eliminated at an early date by a return to direct operations.

The estimated initial increase in cost of operations was $80,000 to $120,000 per month. This was primarily made up of increased rehandling, reduced payload, and increased empty miles on intercity trailers in this program. The duration of the program and the level of expenses each month would depend on how quickly the service improved and how quickly that could be converted into increased freight and the desired direct schedules. In a sense, the program was a pump-priming process. "We have seen other carriers use the technique and it works." The criteria for the plan are outlined in Exhibit 9.

The program was accepted and instituted. At the same time, it was felt that a

Exhibit 10

RYDER TRUCK LINES, INC.
Service Performance, August Through December 1971

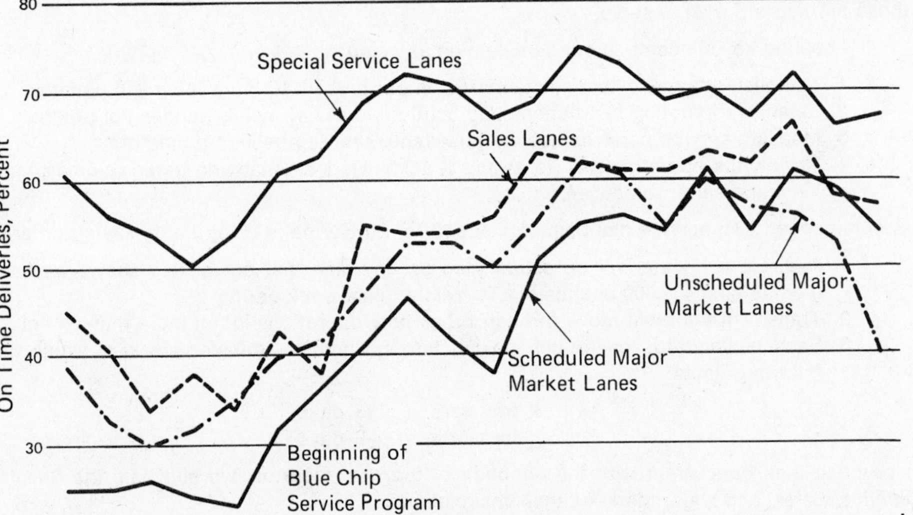

more valid measure of service performance would be reflected in a measurement called "service factor," [1] rather than limiting the service guage to "on-time service" only.

Almost immediately service improved. By the middle of September, service on the Special Service Lanes improved to a 99 point factor (on the basis of 100). Service on major Market and Sales Lanes had reached a level of a 88 point factor by the middle of October.

The service improvement was achieved, as expected, through increased handling of LTL freight, as seen in Exhibit 11. Costs were higher than had been anticipated (Exhibit 12). However, the situation appeared to be under control. While there was revenue growth, the projected increase in LTL traffic did not materialize.

Exhibit 11

RYDER TRUCK LINES, INC.
Less than Truck Load Freight Rehandled 1971

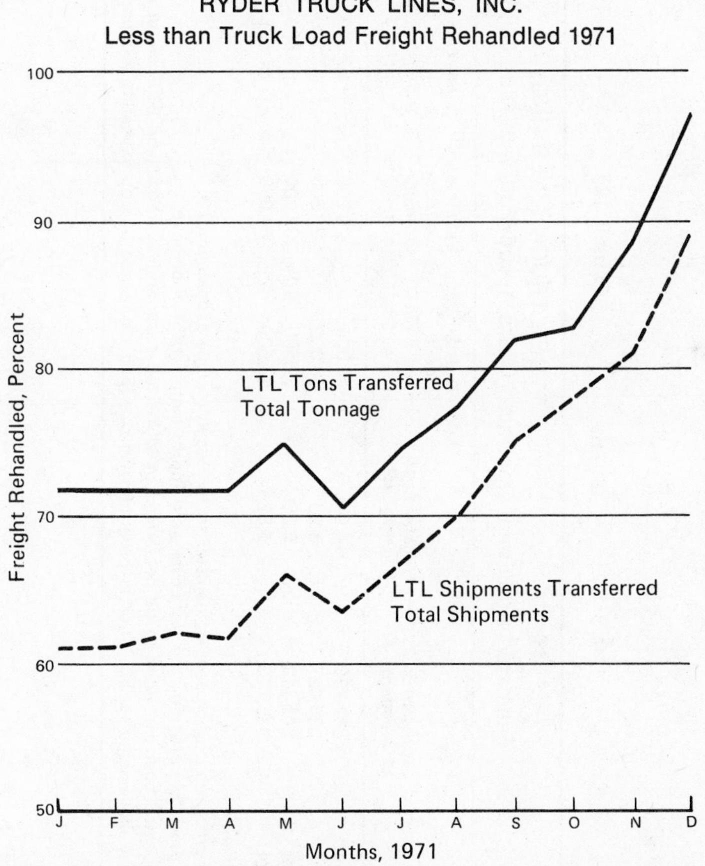

[1] Service factor was defined as the ratio of standard days to actual days for shipments on each lane, and was stated as a percentage. So, the higher the service factor reported, the better the service.

Exhibit 12

RYDER TRUCK LINES, INC.

Estimated Additional Operating Costs Associated with Blue Chip Service Program, 1971

Month	*Transfer costs @ standard, $*[2]	*Transfer cost % revenue*[3]	*Transfer cost above 4.4% of rev., $*[3]	*Estimated direct transfer cost—$*[4]	*Increased line transportation costs, $*[5]	*Increased other terminal labor $*	*Increased maintenance, $*	*Total increased costs $*
September[1]	382,730	4.97	44,000	29,700	67,500	22,500	7,500	127,200
October	334,627	4.93	36,000	24,500	67,500	22,500	7,500	122,000
November	341,112	5.29	57,500	39,100	67,500	22,500	7,500	136,600
December[1]	415,773	5.68	93,500	64,000	67,500	22,500	7,500	161,500

[1] 5-week month.

[2] Transfer costs reflect increases in teamster scale. Based on fully allocated costs.

[3] Prior to Blue Chip program, transfer costs were approximately 4.4% of revenue.

[4] Fully allocated cost estimated to be comprised of 32% fixed costs and overhead and 68% direct out-of-pocket costs.

[5] 7% empty movements vs. 6% prior to program. Average load depressed by approximately 750 pounds.

As shown in Exhibit 13, revenues were not substantially above the level of the previous year, after considering the effect of recent rate increases to offset Teamster wage increases.

In October and November, the service was again reexamined, and movements on specific lanes were reviewed. Through additional transfer, service was further improved. Also in December, the sales department introduced a marketing program called "Blue Chip Service" in support of the operating program. The Blue Chip Service Program was intended to bring the story of Ryder's service improvement to the shippers.

Salesmen were provided with service reports for use with shippers that showed exactly what type service was being provided to points served from their area. The report, a sample page shown in Exhibit 14, indicated the period covered, origin and destination pair, number of shipments, standard days, and service factor.

In addition, promotional material was developed around the theme of Blue Chip Service, and a sales contest was introduced as an inducement to salesmen to promote the Blue Chip Service program in their areas.

The year 1971 closed on a slightly more optimistic note, as seen in Exhibit 15, but the company still had not demonstrated that its growth problems were fully resolved.

Exhibit 13

RYDER TRUCK LINES, INC.
Average Revenue per Day
LTL Weight per Month, and LTL Shipments per Month
January 1970 Through December 1971

	Average revenue per day		*LTL weight CWT per month*		*LTL shipments per month*	
	1970	*1971*	*1970*	*1971*	*1970*	*1971*
January	246,091	286,415	633,829	788,463	95,959	119,408
February	275,854	277,936	851,519	682,356	133,003	122,174
March	276,492	286,426	1,123,677	1,027,906	179,331	160,775
April	235,116	281,000	730,644	761,344	108,502	115,320
May	268,973	289,211	816,957	764,906	116,165	115,907
June	288,982	281,886	1,019,626	907,720	149,600	133,326
July	276,724	290,299	839,794	696,004	124,621	100,914
August	280,710	306,914	859,971	755,879	133,658	114,210
September	306,500	319,715	1,059,932	974,062	162,366	145,312
October	312,023	336,247	947,049	834,767	145,704	124,459
November	296,990	330,526	877,667	797,354	140,338	118,133
December	268,426	302,128	1,013,536	818,066	160,135	129,884

Exhibit 14

RYDER TRUCK LINES, INC.
Salesmen's Service Report

SS050-2 06/30/72 R Y D E R T R U C K L I N E S PAGE 4

SERVICE REPORT

WK OF 06/12 THRU 06/18

TRAFFIC LANE	NUMBER SHIPMENTS	STD DAYS	SERVICE FACTOR	TRAFFIC LANE	NUMBER SHIPMENTS	STD DAYS	SERVICE FACTOR
MIA-KXV	2	5	77	KXV-MIA	6	5	81
MIA-KAN	14	5	137	KAN-MIA	17	5	106
MIA-STL	125	4	112	STL-MIA	83	4	88
MIA-CLE	21	5	112	CLE-MIA	90	5	109
MIA-CBS	14	5	99	CBS-MIA	32	5	102
MIA-DET	30	5	106	DET-MIA	41	5	100
MIA-TEH	3	5	79	TEH-MIA	30	5	109
MIA-MAN	4	5	95	MAN-MIA	12	5	102
MIA-AKR	6	5	111	AKR-MIA	55	5	87
MIA-TOL	9	5	98	TOL-MIA	32	5	118
MIA-YNG	9	5	105	YNG-MIA	20	5	103
				LIM-MIA	7	5	103
MIA-RCK	2	6	86	RCK-MIA	8	5	129
MIA-PEO	6	5	81	PEO-MIA	29	5	106
MIA-ROC	8	5	89	ROC-MIA	35	5	107
MIA-DAT	8	5	93	DAT-MIA	23	5	119
MIA-WHL	1	5	125	WHL-MIA	5	5	109
MIA-PIT	10	5	100	PIT-MIA	16	5	101
MIA-SBN	15	5	84	SBN-MIA	28	5	113
MIA-FWN	2	5	91	FWN-MIA	30	5	115
MIA-LOR	4	6	114	LOR-MIA	8	5	95
MIA-ASB	1	6	150	ASB-MIA	6	5	115
				CBA-MIA	1	5	71
MIA-LEB	2	5	143	LEB-MIA	2	5	91
MIA-NSV	15	4	80	NSV-MIA	7	5	80
MIA-TUL	1	5	167				
TOTAL	1413		91		1988	5	93

NO DEL DTE 39

Exhibit 15

RYDER TRUCK LINES, INC.
Operating Results, 1971 *

	1971
Revenues ($000)	76,300
Maintenance/revenue (%)	8.15
Terminal ***/revenue (%)	21.5
Transportation/revenue (%)	39.6
Operating ratio (%) **	92.39
Terminals	103
LTL tons (000)	499
LTL shipments (000)	1,500
Total tons (000)	1,215
Average load (tons)	14.9
Average length of haul (miles)	849
Total terminal labor/revenue (%)	32.7

* Results of the Ryder Division of International Utilities. Does not include other carriers owned by I.U.

** Operating ratio = operating expenses (not including interest) divided by operating revenue.

*** Terminal expense here is the 4300 account of the I.C.C., which primarily deals with dock operations and does not include pickup and delivery.

Exhibit 16

RYDER TRUCK LINES, INC.
Blue Chip Service Program, 1972

Month	*On-time deliveries, %*	*Estimated net cost of "Blue Chip program," $* [2]	*Average revenue per day, $*
January	54	$183,000	305,947
February	60	181,000	322,450
March[1]	63	229,500	322,434
April	64	200,500	334,001
May	60	203,500	355,160

Month	*LTL shipments rehandled, %*	*LTL tonnage rehandled, %*	*LTL shipments*	*LTL weight CWT*
January	94.6	102.5	109,032	780,223
February	95.7	102.4	120,241	839,251
March[1]	95.0	101.5	154,986	1,096,673
April	92.4	105.7	119,784	859,566
May	93.4	105.5	118,722	871,522

[1] Five week month.

[2] Calculated using same method shown in Exhibit 12.

The 1972 Results

The year 1972 started by showing some positive results from the Blue Chip Service program. Revenue per day was definitely up, and outside of a brief period during January, service was holding at an excellent level. However, to achieve this, it was necessary to further increase the percentage of shipments and tonnage rehandled, as seen in Exhibit 16.

As the month of May closed, Kinzey Reeves was still analyzing results to find additional lanes that could be shifted from transfer to direct schedule operations.

In June, he prepared another monthly review of the program. Again there was no substantial improvement on the low-volume lanes that would permit substitution of direct loading for transfer operations. Regardless of the original intention of the program, it was felt that it had stopped a downtrend in traffic associated with the earlier service difficulties. From that point of view, acknowledging that approximately $1.5 million in additional operating costs had been invested, Ryder management felt that their initial decision had been sound, and that there were measurable indications of success.

Now the question was, did the program merit continued support, or should the decision be postponed, awaiting further indication of progress? How should the new level of service be communicated to customers?

Trans World Airlines

The Crepes Suzette Decision

TWA was one of the major U.S. airlines. It operated extensive routes in the United States and to major cities in Europe, Asia and Africa. Competition was keen on all of these routes. The Company's officials firmly believed in providing service that was in all respects at least as good as that offered by the competition—and a little better if at all possible.

When TWA began jet operations in 1959, it was able to provide a higher degree of schedule reliability than did its competitors. TWA's marketing officials believed that in order to be successful an airline must first have a good product, i.e., excellent equipment, good schedules, on-time performance, and well-run operations. Realistically they knew that competitors could have identical equipment and identical flight schedules. They also knew that, at least in the long run, any competitor could copy a successful innovation and share in some of the traffic that was attracted by such device.

Since TWA flew to Paris and Rome, it seemed quite natural to adopt certain European ideas to its domestic service in the U.S. It began to serve a good French wine with dinner followed by a vintage champagne. Passengers reacted favorably and the competition reacted accordingly: they too began to serve wine and champagne, at least on the competitive runs.

Not content with the status quo, TWA pioneered with freshly brewed coffee, a choice of salad dressing, hot hors d'oeuvres, freshly baked hot rolls and other gourmet touches. While each additional service involved certain costs, TWA management believed that additional expenditures were justified as long as they continued to produce more business. The fact of the matter was that TWA's traffic continued to grow. By 1963 it was outstripping its rivals in terms of percentage growth and in absolute terms in certain markets.

In 1961, TWA pioneered with in-flight movies. The passenger response was good. A few months later it introduced its internationally famous Royal Ambassador menu on its coast to coast domestic flights (see Exhibit 1). It introduced French pastries, attractive parfaits, assorted cheeses, and fresh fruits. Since no service in-

---

This case was prepared by Professor Karl M. Ruppenthal, former director, Transportation Management Program, Graduate School of Business, Stanford University.

Exhibit 1

TRANS WORLD AIRLINES
Royal Ambassador Menu

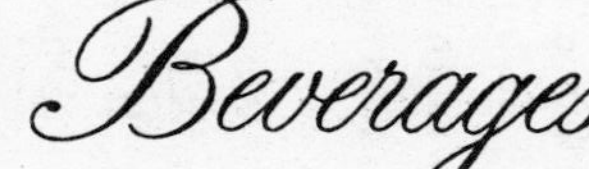

WHISKIES

Scotch Canadian Bourbon

*

COCKTAILS

Gin and Tonic Vodka Gin Martini
Manhattan Vodka Martini Sherry

*

SELECTED AMERICAN WINES AND CHAMPAGNE

Soft Drinks Beer Tomato Juice

*

CORDIALS

Tia Maria Cognac Drambuie Creme de Menthe
Benedictine and Brandy Cointreau

*

A Word about Royal Ambassador Service
If you have occasion to travel overseas may we suggest that you also try the unmatched opulence of our International Royal Ambassador Service, where you will be offered a choice of seven entrees. From appetizers to after dinner liqueurs you will enjoy a menu unsurpassed in the world of travel.

Menu

SHRIMP MARSALA

*

SALAD JOSEPHINE

Choice of Italian, French or Roquefort Dressing

*

for your selection:

N.Y. CUT PRIME SIRLOIN STEAK
Aged to perfection and broiled over charcoal embers

MAINE LOBSTER THERMIDOR
This famous French dish made with the finest New England Lobster

ROAST DUCKLING A L'ORANGE
Served with an imported orange liqueur sauce

EXTRA THICK LAMB CHOPS
Grilled to perfection by TWA's own chefs

Baked Stuffed Potato * Buttered Asparagus Spears
Assorted Dinner Rolls Dairy Fresh Butter
Gateau Glaze Fancy Fresh Fruits
Tea Freshly Brewed Coffee Milk

*

Suggested Low Calorie Combination
(Approximately 750 calories)

BROILED PRIME SIRLOIN STEAK
Asparagus Spears Salad Josephine Fresh Fruit

novation could be protected by patent, there was nothing to keep the competition from following suit. TWA management felt that its future lay in pioneering more new ideas and in staying ahead of the pack.

In April of 1965, TWA was interested in adding another feature that would help to distinguish its service from that of its competitors. After making a detailed canvass for ideas, TWA's Vice President–Customer Service concluded that there would be marketing appeal in serving crepes suzette for dessert. These French delicacies were served on several flights. Passenger reaction was enthusiastic and seemed to indicate that crepes suzette could become another TWA "first."

Before he made final plans for their introduction, the V.P.–Customer Service advanced the idea at the President's staff meeting, inviting comments and suggestions. The reaction there was mixed.

The chief hostess was apprehensive. She took the position that before any additional service features were added, a careful study should be made to determine whether the present cabin force could realistically be expected to provide the service without risking a deterioration in quality. It was her belief that on certain coast to coast flights, when most of the seats were occupied, the hostesses had no "slack" time and that on some flights they did not have adequate time to perform all their tasks in a gracious, leisurely manner.

The Industrial Relations Vice President also expressed some concern over the idea. He pointed out that as the level of service had increased, the demands on the hostess had likewise increased. Because the jets flew much faster than had piston driven aircraft, hostesses made more round trips per month than they had made in the older craft. There were several indications of hostess dissatisfaction, and he was reluctant to have anything done which might lower their morale or disrupt the course of impending contract negotiations.

All of the executives were conscious of the fact that the hostess was a very important employee, generally having more passenger contacts than any other. A good hostess could do much to encourage repeat business—and the contrary likewise was true.

While the executives wanted to institute any innovation that was promising, they did not want to plunge into a program without adequate study. Accordingly they requested a study that would indicate precisely how much work was presently expected from hostesses on the coast to coast flights and how the crepes suzette service would affect that work load. There was general agreement that crepes suzette might well have marketing appeal and that it would be difficult for the competition to copy, because TWA's 707's were equipped with a special type of oven that was not in general use. Should crepes suzette prove to be popular, it would be expensive for the competition to install the ovens, and the installation would take some time.

A staff assistant was assigned to the crepes suzette feasibility study. The following material is drawn from his report:

> This report concerns the possibility of serving crepes suzette for dessert in the first class section of coast to coast Royal Ambassador Flights. At the present

time, these flights have four hostesses on board. Two hostesses are assigned to the first class section and two to the coach section. There presently are 38 seats in the first class section of most of the 707's in this service and 83 coach seats. Coach passengers are provided liquor service on these flights followed by attractive hot meals. The hostesses customarily offer each passenger a hot beverage at least twice during the flight.

Movies are also provided in both sections. This requires a hostess in each section to install the screen and to provide head sets for the passengers. An earlier study indicates that two hostesses can adequately serve the coach section even when it is full. When there are more than 50 passengers in this section both hostesses are very busy and must serve some meals during the movie. (Average movie duration is 90 minutes.) When there are fewer than 40 passengers in the coach section, the hostesses in coach have free time and generally offer to help the hostesses in first class.

Exhibit 2

TRANS WORLD AIRLINES
HOSTESS TIME REQUIREMENTS
First Class Section

	Time (minutes)	
Activity (Not necessarily in order)	*Per passenger*	*Per flight*
Checking, hanging, and returning of coats	0.5	
Taking cocktail orders	0.5	
Serving cocktails	2.0	
Heating hors d'oeuvres		10.0
Serving hors d'oeuvres	2.0	
Preparing salads	1.0	
Serving salads	1.5	
Serving wine	2.0	
Preparing entree		10.0
Serving entree	2.0	
Baking rolls		5.0
Serving rolls	0.5	
Serving coffee	2.0	
Serving dessert	1.0	
Serving cordials	0.5	
Picking up dishes, glasses, etc.	2.5	
Heating (or chilling) towels		5.0
Serving and picking up towels	1.0	
Installing and removing movie screen		5.0
Passing out movie head sets	0.5	
Miscellaneous service	0.5	
Totals	20.0 min/passenger	35.0 min/flight

Time requirements in the first class section are more critical. The result of time studies taken in the first class section on several coast to coast flights are shown in Exhibit 2. (All "per-passenger" times are in terms of the efforts of one hostess; all "per-flight" times require the activity of only one hostess.)

It should be pointed out that these are *average* times. On occasion any item may require more time because of turbulence, the inexperience of hostesses, or for other reasons. On occasion some hostesses adequately perform all these duties in somewhat less time. But the times quoted are normally accurate, considering the nature of the work. Each activity described in Exhibit 2 is considered to be a separate task, and it was intended that they be performed as such. It was known that some hostesses combined some activities to save time.

If crepes suzette service were instituted, preparation will require ten minutes additional preparation time (working) per flight, and one minute serving time per passenger more than were presently required for less fancy desserts. That would effectively mean an increase in hostess work load. Assuming that we wish to maintain our high standards of service, this may mean that an additional hostess will be required on some flights. The work load generally will be more critical on the east bound flights because of westerly winds and consequently faster flights.

This summer we have scheduled daily coast to coast flights as shown in Exhibit 3.

Exhibit 3

TRANS WORLD AIRLINES
DAILY SCHEDULE
Non-Stop Coast to Coast Flights

Origin	*Destination*	*Number of flights*	*Scheduled flying time*
Los Angeles	Boston	1	4:55
Los Angeles	New York	8	4:26
Los Angeles	Philadelphia	1	4:30
Los Angeles	Baltimore	1	4:25
Los Angeles	Washington	2	4:38
Boston	Los Angeles	2	5:25
New York	Los Angeles	6	5:20
Philadelphia	Los Angeles	1	5:00
Baltimore	Los Angeles	1	4:50
Washington	Los Angeles	1	4:58
San Francisco	Boston	1	4:55
San Francisco	New York	5	4:55
San Francisco	Washington	1	4:45
Boston	San Francisco	1	5:40
New York	San Francisco	4	5:35
Washington	San Francisco	1	5:15

Last summer in our heavy traffic months (May, June, July, and August) coast to coast on-time performance was as follows:

>15 minutes over schedule	<1%
15–10 minutes over schedule	3%
10–5 minutes over schedule	5%
5 minutes over—5 minutes under schedule	72+%
5–10 minutes under schedule	10%
10–15 minutes under schedule	5%
15–20 minutes under schedule	3%
>20 minutes under schedule	<1%
	100%

The best meteorological data available would indicate that we can expect about the same type of winds this summer and approximately the same in-flight times.

First class air fare from New York to Los Angeles is $160; coach is $145. The round trip fare is double these one-way fares. We do offer an excursion round trip fare of $217.

At the present time we require a load factor[1] of approximately 39% to cover our full costs on coast to coast jet flights. This means that each additional passenger that we can attract will contribute materially to our profits, since the incremental cost of carrying an additional passenger is small—perhaps ten dollars per first class passenger, and somewhat lower in coach.

Our hostesses are presently paid according to the following schedule:

1st 6 months	$323.87
2nd 6 months	341.22
2nd year	364.35
3rd year	381.70
4th year	393.27
5th year	404.84
6th year	416.40
7th year	427.97
8th year	433.76

These pay schedules are per month, for flying up to 70 hours. The present contract with The Air Line Stewards and Stewardess Association provides that for

[1] Load factor is the ratio of the number of paying passengers to the number of seats available.

every hour of flying per month above 70 hours hostesses will receive additional compensation at the following hourly rates:

1st 6 months	$4.63
2nd 6 months	4.87
2nd year	5.21
3rd year	5.45
4th year	5.62
5th year	5.78
6th year	5.95
7th year	6.11
8th year	6.20

The agreement further provides that cabin attendants may be scheduled for a maximum of 78½ flying hours per month, exclusive of ground time, en route station time, and time spent at lay over stations.

While the composition of the labor force changes from time to time, the following seniority breakdown is fairly accurate at the present time.

6 months seniority	5%
6 months–1 year seniority	10%
1 year–2 years seniority	20%
2 year–3 years seniority	20%
3 year–4 years seniority	15%
4 year–5 years seniority	15%
5 year–6 years seniority	10%
6 year–7 years seniority	2%
7 year–8 years seniority	2%
>8 years seniority	1%

On March 1, we had approximately 1,600 domestic hostesses. Fifty hostesses were on sick leave or otherwise unavailable, making a total of 1,550 domestic hostesses available for flight duty. Hostess turnover was of sufficient magnitude that the company found it necessary to hire some 800 new hostess trainees in 1964. Average monthly hostess utilization in 1964 was approximately 65 flying hours per month. That calculation takes into account vacations, sick leave, and the fact that every domicile must maintain some "reserve" hostesses to be available when regular "bid" hostesses are not available for any reason.

There are definite industrial relations implications in any decision here. For several months many hostesses have been talking about a reduction in flying hours. Others have been requesting that we put a fifth hostess on all coast to coast flights.

Some of these requests have been made via the company suggestion plan. Many of these appear to be thoughtful suggestions to improve our service. Some remarks have been written in the hostesses' regular post-flight reports. There have been many notes and letters to various supervisors and company officials. Recently the union has taken up the cry, and some questionable materials have been distributed in some of our terminals and near some of our sales offices.

Some of these materials have urged passengers to write to the president of the airline asking that a fifth hostess be placed on all flights. Others have asked passengers to write the Federal Aviation Agency to urge that the Civil Air Regulations be amended to require a fifth hostess on all flights. Some of these materials are almost in the nature of the type of materials that would be distributed on a strike picket line. Of course, we have no accurate way of measuring the impact of these materials on our customers; nor do we know whether they have been sanctioned by the officers of the International Union. But it is obvious that the existence of such materials is another factor which we must consider.

Exhibit 4

TRANS WORLD AIRLINES
PASSENGERS CARRIED

		Flight 102 east bound		*Flight 101 west bound*	
Date		*Coach*	*First class*	*Coach*	*First class*
May	1	83	38*	52	19
	6	60	20	83	38
	11	42	19	60	19
	16	51	22	75	21
	21	75	23	76	32
	26	48	16	81	16
	31	35	15	69	14
June	4	62	4	72	25
	9	83	38	83	36
	14	83	34	83	37
	19	82	13	81	19
	24	81	33	83	24
	29	80	14	82	34
July	4	22	4	16	3
	9	65	31	64	31
	14	66	14	68	16
	19	75	18	74	19
	24	76	21	78	19
	29	75	19	72	30
Aug.	3	73	21	69	19
	8	76	14	75	24
	13	78	34	55	18
	18	79	33	53	21
	23	65	29	52	23
	28	62	28	49	16

* All regular seats plus four lounge seats occupied.

It is difficult to determine how much of this activity represents a real concern over work load and how much represents union pressure. We are, of course, approaching contract sessions with the union. It would not be unrealistic to look for a demand for sizeable wage increases coupled with a reduced work load.

Nonetheless, there is a work load problem. If we add crepes suzette, or any other item that requires more time to serve, we will have to add a fifth hostess, at least on some flights.

We analyzed the loads on coast to coast flights in May, June, July, and August of 1964, taking a sample consisting of every fifth day on a representative flight pairing between Los Angeles and New York and return. (See Exhibit 4.) The Los Angeles based crew that flies the east bound trip would normally return home on the west bound flight after a lay over in New York.

As I see the alternatives, we can (a) do nothing in the hostess complement question and hope that the problem does not become serious, (b) add a fifth hostess for all coast to coast flights, (c) calculate the probabilities and carry a fifth hostess on only those flights for which the work load would warrant the additional expense. Should we elect alternative (c) we would inevitably have some stand-by costs for hostesses called out for possible "fifth duty" and not used. Call out pay is at the rate of two (flying) hours pay per call out, but this is a wage cost only. It is not deducted from the hostess' available flying hours.

Flight crews normally return on specific flights in accordance with established turn-around patterns, but it would be possible to hold the fifth hostess awaiting a flight that required her services. Hostesses can be deadheaded, but deadhead rates are the same as flight pay rates; however, deadheading does not count against a hostess's monthly maximum flying time.

Leo's Foodland

At the end of July 1969 the executive committee of Leo's Foodland met to decide whether or not basic changes should be made in the supermarket chain's pricing policies. Leo's was a large regional firm, which for years had charged prices slightly higher than those of the competing markets, but which had prospered by establishing a reputation for clean and modern stores, courteous clerks, and high-quality meat, produce, and groceries. Under this "high-quality–high-price" policy, Leo's had remained the sales leader in its home town of Petropolis and in the nearby areas which it served. Sales rose from $36 million in 1960 to $120 million in 1968 and Leo's consistently earned net profits of more than 4% on sales during those years (see Exhibit 1).

Exhibit 1

LEO'S FOODLAND

Trend of Sales, Gross Profit and Earnings

Fiscal year[1]	*Sales (millions)*	*Gross profit (% of sales)*	*Earnings before tax (% of sales)*
1960	$ 36	21.23%	5.22%
1965	78	22.03	4.13
1966	97	21.93	4.50
1967	109	21.89	4.52
1968	120	21.75	4.04
1969 [2]	62	21.66	3.99

[1] Fiscal Year ends September 1.

[2] 26 weeks.

During the late sixties, however, competition had become more intense in Petropolis. Many new stores had been opened and the concept of "discounting"—cutting prices and margins in hopes of generating increased volume—had caught on. As a result, Mr. Leo Ishtov, Leo's founder and chief executive officer, asked the executive committee to consider alternatives for combatting the inroads being made by competing chains.

There was considerable disagreement within the company ranks about the appropriate competitive response. Some employees felt that Leo's should follow the competitors' example and switch to a low-price policy, either across the board or on a selective basis. Others recommended a well-organized advertising and promotion program similar to Boston-based Stop & Shop's Mini-Pricing[1] concept to make Leo's more competitive without a discount image. Still others maintained that the firm should continue to follow the policies that had proven so successful for so many years, arguing that discounting was merely a fad and that expensive merchandising programs were unnecessary.

Mr. Ishtov knew that whatever course the executive committee chose, it would also have to consider other factors, such as the problems inherent in implementing a low-price program. In addition, Mr. Ishtov was concerned that there might be a better way to make Leo's more competitive, which had not yet been considered.

Company History

In 1930 Leo Ishtov, an immigrant with little capital, settled in Petropolis and had opened a small grocery store. After several trying years, his venture proved successful; in 1940 Mr. Ishtov was able to open a new modern supermarket with 7,500 square feet of selling space and a full basement for product preparation and storage. At this supermarket Mr. Ishtov installed some of the first electric eye doors ever used in a United States supermarket. Mr. Ishtov had opened a second market in Petropolis in 1941, and both stores were highly profitable.

After a World War II moratorium on new store construction was lifted, Leo's embarked on an expansion program. By the end of 1955 there were 10 Leo's Foodland stores in metropolitan Petropolis, all profitable. During the late fifties and early sixties, Leo's centralized buying and warehousing in a modern company-owned distribution facility to decrease buying costs, to achieve better quality control of perishables, and to improve the efficiency of merchandise distribution throughout the chain. In addition to the grocery warehouse space, the distribution center added a meat plant in which carcasses were butchered, a number of frozen food coolers, and ample capacity for fresh fruit and vegetable storage. Adjoining the distribution facility was a bakery and a processing plant which produced a wide variety of prepared foods for the stores. By 1969, Leo's had grown to 47 stores, 37 in Petropolis and 10 in five nearby towns.

Leo's still depended on local suppliers for most of its goods, although deliveries were made to the central warehouse rather than to individual stores. Leo's major supplier in the area was Globus, Inc., a retailer-owned cooperative. Globus produced high-quality private label goods which were considered to be the best-known brand in the state. Retailers generally achieved higher margins on the premium-priced Globus label than on nationally distributed brands.

From the beginning, Mr. Ishtov chose to compete on a basis of quality rather than low prices. When he had opened his first supermarket in 1940, he sought to

[1] Mini-Pricing is a comprehensive merchandising program with emphasis on quality, service, and low prices. When originated by Stop & Shop, Mini-Pricing was the first major discounting program, although the word "discount" was never used in promotion as it connoted poor quality in the view of Stop & Shop management. Stop & Shop franchised the Mini-Pricing merchandising concept to other chains for a fee that varied depending on the number of stores in the chain and other factors. A typical fee was $5,000 per store initially plus $1,000 per store annually. Mini-Pricing is a registered service mark of Stop & Shop.

provide an attractive, clean, comfortable shopping environment, featuring a wide variety of quality merchandise and staffed by friendly and courteous personnel. Great care was always taken in architectural design and interior decor, a tradition evident even in the most recently constructed stores.

Mr. Ishtov felt that Leo's could charge customers more than competing stores because Leo's offered a "better total value" to its patrons. Leo's bakery, delicatessen, produce, meat, and dairy departments were felt to be superior to those of any competitors in the area. Leo's boasted the largest variety of groceries in the area.

Prices on most Leo's items generally ranged two to three cents higher than those on comparable items at other markets. Only on fresh meat products and on well-known branded staples items was Leo's price competitive. Leo's did not offer trading stamps, a customer incentive which generally cost retailers 2% of sales.

Many consumers and even some competitors agreed that Leo's was a leader in a number of areas. Several competitors felt that Leo's architecture, fixturing, lighting, decor, department organization, cleanliness, personnel appearance, and total store atmosphere were among the best in the United States. Consumer surveys conducted by the local newspaper repeatedly rated Leo's number one in Petropolis for cleanliness, neatness, and variety of goods (see Exhibit 2).

Management

Leo's top management consisted of Mr. Ishtov, his two sons, Herman and George, and two sons-in-law, Stanley Lisbon and Warren Oldhome. Herman and George worked at Leo's a number of summers while in high school and college and both joined the firm upon graduation from college, Herman in 1955 and George in 1958. In 1961 Messrs. Lisbon and Oldhome joined Leo's as well. Mr. Ishtov felt that the four men possessed strong educational backgrounds and a great deal of energy, both of which complemented his own seasoned merchandising abilities. The five family members constituted the executive committee, which was the policymaking committee of the firm.

All five family members had the reputation of being "very hard workers." They all spent a large amount of time in the stores each day. It was felt that they set a pace and tone which had helped generate a strong *esprit de corps* throughout the organization. Administrative tasks and paperwork were minimized in favor of maintaining direct personal communication with employees on a frequent basis. EDP and advanced control methods were utilized, but the information produced for use by most employees was carefully sifted to prevent employees concerned with day-to-day operations from being burdened with a flood of quasi-useful reports. Profit figures were known only by members of the executive committee. Leo's executives and key operating personnel avoided "outside activities" if such activities would in any way "interfere with the fullest dedication to their work."

Marketing Trends and Competition

The Petropolis regional market had shown moderate but steady growth over the years. The area had a diversified economic base and suffered no serious unem-

Exhibit 2

LEO'S FOODLAND

What Customers Like and Dislike about Petropolis Food Stores—1969

	Leo's (37 stores)[1]	*Viking (38 stores)*	*Green Circle (34 stores)*	*Prairie (21 stores)*	*Cardinal (14 stores)*	*Red Dot (41 stores)*	*Zenith (4 stores)*	*All other*
Likes								
Prices	3%	12%	13%	54%	55%	33%	76%	15%
Convenient location	8	23	27	20	19	27	6	26
Large selection	27	15	14	9	10	3	14	10
Cleanliness and neatness	40	24	18	8	8	7	4	7
Courteous, friendly service	23	34	28	11	17	27	—	26
Quality of merchandise	19	8	7	7	6	8	2	9
Quality of meats	14	16	9	6	6	3	5	26
Fruits and vegetables	21	7	7	1	2	—	2	5
Other	20	16	12	9	6	6	5	16
Dislikes[2]	25%	25%	31%	49%	47%	37%	51%	30%
Checkout service	14	7	21	27	6	10	25	5
Quality of meat	9	9	12	11	8	12	10	13
Fruits and vegetables	2	21	16	14	14	21	10	7
Limited selection	3	24	12	27	20	29	15	32
Prices	52	16	16	2	3	9	6	27
Too crowded	1	3	—	2	14	—	18	13
Untidy	—	10	5	2	8	16	4	—
Other	9	10	7	1	17	9	6	4

[1] Only stores in metropolitan Petropolis surveyed.

[2] Percentage of customers who reported dislikes. Thus 14% of the 25% of Leo's "complaining" customers disliked Leo's checkout service.

Source: Annual survey conducted by the *Petropolis Tribune*.

ployment problems. Leo's labor relations had always been considered good. The population was in large part of Scandinavian and German ancestry; Leo's delicatessen and bakery departments both thrived.

Beginning in 1966, supermarket competition in Petropolis had become increasingly severe. Cardinal Marts, a strong regional chain, had entered the Petropolis market that year and within three years had opened 14 stores. Also, in 1966, Zenith Corp., a powerful national general merchandise discounter invaded the Petropolis market with four very large general merchandise discount stores, each with a large discount supermarket attached. By mid-1969, Zenith food sales had been averaging $75,000 per store per week. Repeated price checks at Zenith stores by Leo's personnel showed that Zenith maintained the lowest across-the-board food prices in Petropolis. It was felt that Zenith had taken sales from all other supermarkets in Petropolis.

Early in 1969 Cardinal Marts, which had been feeling the pressure from Zenith and other competitors, announced a "price rebellion." Cardinal produced a well-designed, widely distributed low-price advertising campaign that stressed a theme of "high value." The campaign produced immediate and very noticeable increases in sales (as high as 60% in some stores). Leo's Foodland stores located near Cardinal Mart stores experienced sales declines. However, most Leo's executives felt that the sales loss would be a short-lived problem. "Cardinal Marts' 'price rebellion' won't last," said one Leo's vice-president. "It will die."

Prairie Supermarkets, another Petropolis competitor, also lost sales to Cardinal Mart stores and soon began advertising lower prices, too. Prior to Cardinal Marts' price reduction Prairie's advertising theme had been "low prices and trading stamps, too." In spring 1969, however, Prairie dropped trading stamps and emphasized in its advertisements that as a result prices would be even lower. However, this change in merchandising policy did not achieve the desired sales and profit increases, partly because Prairie lowered prices on only about 20% of its items, leaving the other items priced the same as before the change. Prairie's profit position deteriorated.

Through 1969 the five towns outside of Petropolis in which Leo's competed had proven stable markets for Leo's Foodland. However, in May 1969 Red Dot Stores, a national chain, converted its only two units in one of the towns to discount operations under the name Bargain Marts. Red Dot experienced sizeable sales gains, partly at the expense of the three Leo's stores in that area. Prairie stores experienced sales declines believed to be even larger than those of Leo's.

Competition had also become stronger in the nondiscount food arena. Viking Markets, which had for years attempted to emulate Leo's style of operations, had steadily gained in sales. Green Circle Stores, a very strong chain which offered S&H Green stamps, had lost its second place ranking in Petropolis to Viking in 1968 (see Exhibit 3). There had been a rumor in the industry that Leo's and Viking were the only two chains with profitable operations in mid-1969.

The effects of the competition were particularly noticeable at recently opened Leo's stores. Leo's had opened six new stores between January 1967 and June 1969. None of the six achieved the level of sales or profits that were originally

Exhibit 3

LEO'S FOODLAND
Where Last Food Purchase Was Made

Company	*Stores*	*1967*	*1968*	*1969*
Leo's Foodland	37[1]	24.4%	28.4%	28.3%
Viking Markets	38	11.4	14.4	16.3
Green Circle Stores	34	20.4	13.5	13.0
Prairie Supermarkets	21	10.8	9.4	11.8
Cardinal Marts	14	3.9	4.3	8.2
Red Dot Stores	41	7.5	8.2	5.1
Zenith Discounts	4	1.8	2.7	3.1
All other	—	19.8	19.1	14.2
		100.0%	100.0%	100.0%

[1] Only stores in metropolitan Petropolis surveyed.
Source: Annual survey conducted by the *Petropolis Tribune*.

projected for them at the time the store locations had been surveyed. In addition, some of the older Leo's stores showed actual sales declines between 1968 and 1969 despite an increase in the average dollar sales per transaction (see Exhibit 4). Mr. Ishtov had felt that lower-than-projected performance from the six new stores was due in part to "secondary store locations, as the best locations had already been preempted." He continued:

> Still, we must face facts. Leo's stores have lost some of their uniqueness to Viking stores, which have tried hard to copy us and are indeed catching up. Other competitors are also trying to emulate us, with some success. Zenith has gained a strong foothold in Petropolis, and its food discounting program has triggered tougher price competition. Except for Green Circle stores, no store is offering trading stamps. The actions of our competitors and their barrage of price advertising have made the public more price conscious than ever.

Exhibit 4

LEO'S FOODLAND
Trends in Sales, Transactions, and Sales per Transaction

	Sales (millions)	*Transactions (millions)*	*Sales per transaction*
FY 1967	$109	19.9	$5.47
FY 1968	120	21.5	5.59
FY 1969[1]	62	10.7	5.81

[1] 26 weeks

Competition was equally strong in areas outside Leo's established market areas. Leo's for some time had been considering expansion into the largest city in an adjoining state, but all the well-established supermarkets there already had low-price merchandising programs and none offered trading stamps. Any attempt to break into that market without discount prices, Mr. Ishtov knew, would necessitate a strong merchandising program. Partly as a result of Leo's interest in expansion, Herman Ishtov, executive vice president of Leo's, investigated several merchandising plans, of which the most promising for Leo's seemed to be Stop & Shop's Mini-Pricing. The use of Mini-Pricing involved the right to the registered service-mark "Mini-Pricing" and use of standardized newspaper ads, point-of-purchase materials, and other promotional items (see Exhibit 5). For the privilege of using Mini-Pricing, Leo's would pay a license fee. Herman spent two weeks traveling to supermarkets that had implemented discount programs of one form or another and also visited Stop & Shop headquarters to discuss the merits of Mini-Pricing. While Leo's original interest in Mini-Pricing was to facilitate expansion into new areas, some Leo's executives felt that Mini-Pricing might be a good way to ward off competitors' advances at home without resorting to a discount-type image.

Advertising and Promotion

From 1946 to 1956 Leo's advertising was limited to newspapers. The copy emphasized quality rather than specific items and prices. The ads sought to attract customers through a "total appeal." When Leo's in 1956 embarked on its expansion program, the advertising became more aggressive. Newspaper lineage was increased. In addition to newspapers, Leo's began to use radio and, later, television. Some price orientation developed in the ads, and Leo's featured "specials" as attractive as those of any other store.

All of Leo's major competitors similarly utilized newspaper, radio, and television for their advertisements. While Leo's total dollar advertising expenditures exceeded those of all but one of its competitors (Viking), most other chains spent a higher percentage of sales on advertising. Leo's had never employed window signs or any "talking" display material in its stores, since it was felt by management that such devices were not in keeping with Leo's high-quality image.

The July Meeting

At the all-day executive committee meeting, each of the members expressed strongly held views on subjects of image, discounting, Mini-Pricing, and the effects on Leo's that a change in an historically successful formula might entail. There had been few agreements by the end of the day, and Leo Ishtov had decided to call a second meeting the next day to finally resolve the matter. That evening in preparation for the next day's meeting, Mr. Ishtov tried to recall the major areas of discussion and the arguments presented.

Image. One of the key questions raised by the committee was whether or not discounting or Mini-Pricing could really be successfully blended with Leo's long-

Exhibit 5

LEO'S FOODLAND

July 8, 1969

Dear Mr. Ishtov:

In accordance with your request, I restate what we discussed about MINI-PRICING®.

In August 1964, Stop & Shop, Inc., decided to drop stamps, drop prices, and eliminate all prizes and gimmicks in supermarketing. We launched a new concept of food merchandising which we called MINI-PRICING®. Our chief concern at the time was not to injure our quality image and to impress the customer that we would continue to give her the lowest day-in, day-out prices in attractive stores, with good service.

This program has worked out very well for us.

About a year ago, several supermarket chains began to inquire whether or not they could use our MINI-PRICING® concept, the unique advertising materials we had prepared, and some of the point-of-purchase signs we had been using. After due consideration, we came to the conclusion that we might do well to franchise MINI-PRICING® and thereby offset some of the inordinate costs we had in developing MINI-PRICING®.

As of now, we have franchised two firms and we are about to launch MINI-PRICING® in another geographic area.

Our license is for a period of five years and is automatically renewable each year thereafter, or cancellable upon 60 days notice on either party's choice after the five-year period.

In consideration for the license fee you would have in your area the exclusive use of MINI-PRICING®, our registered servicemark, and the use of the following materials:

1. Radio commercials
2. Newspaper ads
3. Direct mail circulars
4. Institutional ads
5. Point-of-purchase materials
6. Library of meat and produce artwork
7. Copies of every piece of advertising and sales promotional material we produce from day to day

We would also give you whatever assistance is possible in launching MINI-PRICING® in your area, by providing you with a campaign strategy and a series of ads and radio and TV commercials that you can adapt to your particular market.

You indicated that you offered quality merchandise, that your stores were attractive, clean, and neat, and that your employees were courteous. All of this fits into the standards of our MINI-PRICING® servicemark and is synonymous with our criteria.

Very truly yours,
Stop & Shop, Inc.

---

established quality image. Most members had agreed that in view of evolving conditions in the supermarket field Leo's future growth rested on its ability to establish a stronger price image. Yet none was willing to let quality slip—or to appear to have slipped—at all. Stanley Lisbon had voiced the concerns of a number of key people in the organization who had grown up with Leo's Foodland and who had become staunch defenders of Leo's philosophy of variety, quality, friendliness, service—and high prices. Stanley felt that customers might not believe that they would receive the same level of service and quality for a lower price.

Leo's merchandisers, Mr. Ishtov knew, were very proud of the unusually high gross margins in their departments. This had been a source of personal pride and satisfaction to them. Frank Yules, who generally had achieved a gross margin of 35% in the delicatessen department (vs. a typical industry gross of 25%), often exclaimed that "any merchandiser can give you 25%. You wouldn't need me if I couldn't produce better than 25%."

Discounting and Mini-Pricing. The executive committee that day had discussed three main topics. First was the advisability of lowering prices across the board to a level competitive with the lowest priced markets. Second was the idea of selective discounting, which would reduce prices on only a number of highly publicized items. Third, the committee considered the Mini-Pricing method of promotion. Herman Ishtov was the strongest proponent of discounting, while the other committee members were less enthusiastic.

Herman: Discounting is clearly the trend of the business. All of our competitors seem to be moving that way, and we are certainly feeling the effects of their efforts in lost sales and lower profits. Undertaking a discounting program seems to me the only way we can continue to grow in Petropolis and in areas outside of our current markets. Certainly discounting isn't as traumatic as some of the old-timers around here seem to think. Since we don't have trading stamps or games, we don't have to worry about adverse reactions to their discontinuance, though we also don't have the 2% stamp cost to automatically pickup by dropping them. All we need to do is drop prices 4%–5% and do a fair amount of heavy advertising. We can even cut back on our stock of 8,000 items to, say, 6,500. And we could shorten hours a bit to save on labor and overhead costs. (Leo's stores were open from 10:00 A.M. until midnight, seven days per week.) Based on the results of Zenith and other chains I observed on my recent trip, each Leo's store can expand its normal two-mile trading area radius to four or five miles. Discounting seems to be a big drawing card. Profits, of course, would decline for six or seven months, since our gross margins would drop to the normal discounters' margins of 15%–17%. But then volume would increase enough to more than offset the lower margins and generate higher profits than before. We've already run a computer simulation of a switch to discounting and the results look pretty encouraging (see Exhibit 6).

Warren: You make it sound pretty rosy, Herman. But I don't think the public wants to know the prices on 8,000 of our items. They couldn't know—even I don't. If you offer high-quality merchandise in a large modern store and maintain a high level of service and reasonable prices, the public is essentially price blind. They know our service costs a lot and are willing to pay for it.

Herman: Come on, Warren. The public can't be price blind if Zenith is as successful as it is. And it's sure hard to miss our prices. Every time I turn

Exhibit 6

LEO'S FOODLAND
Projected 1970 Sales and Profits Versus 1968 Actual Sales and Profits[1]

	FY1968—Actual		*FY1970—Projected*	
Sales	$120,000,000	100.0%	$186,500,000	100.0%
Gross profit	26,100,000	21.75	31,700,000	17.0
Labor expense	11,200,000	9.33	14,332,500	7.7
All other expenses	10,350,000	8.63	12,300,000	6.6
Other income	300,000	.25	582,500	.3
Profit before tax	4,850,000	4.04	5,650,000	3.03

[1] Projection based on computer simulation. Assumptions: 4.5% reduction in prices; 6% inflation rate; 24% annual sales increase FY1969 and FY1970; 17% gross profit margin. Fiscal Year ends September 1. Figures reflect profit lag; profit before tax expected to exceed 4% in FY1971. See Exhibit 7 for labor cost assumptions.

my back Frank Yules has raised his prices in the Deli department, and for years we've had to battle with Andy Pinto to be more competitive in fruits and vegetables.

Stanley: But there's another problem, Herman. You can't sell the idea of discounting or Mini-Pricing to the public if you can't sell it to your employees. They are the people who come in contact with the public and they can make or break any supermarket. They're proud of our image —it is a strong motivating factor with them. We all know that it would be tough to convince many of our 3,400 employees that lower prices would be good for Leo's stores (see Exhibit 7 for labor force data).

Exhibit 7

LEO'S FOODLAND
Labor Force Data for FY1968 and FY1970[1]

	FY1968	*FY1970*
Full-time employees	2256	2345
Half-time employees	1127	1155
Total employees	3383	3500
Average rate of pay per hour		
Full-time	$2.40	$3.00
Half-time	1.75	2.00
Average work week—hours	35	35
Average weeks per year	50	50

[1] Assumptions for projection by computer simulation.

Mr. Ishtov: Well, Stanley, we must be realistic. Leo's cannot be the cheapest market. We couldn't do that to our people. We really couldn't feature price comparisons on all of our items to try to convince the public or the employees that we are the cheapest. Leo's must preserve its image of variety, quality, friendliness, and good service regardless of any changes in pricing policy.

I don't think it would be necessary to lower prices on all of our items. We wouldn't have to lower produce prices, although we do have some room there. We buy superior quality and everyone knows we have to pay for that quality. Besides, we are already close enough on produce prices to other stores. We could make some adjustment on our fresh meats, although we are pretty close to the bone there, too. Meat is an unbranded item and our quality, trimming, and packaging is as good as or better than those of our competitors. I don't think we would have to lower prices in the bakery department. From a quality standpoint our competitors are far behind us. In the perishable departments we probably don't have to go as low as the discount markets. On the identifiable, brand-name grocery items, of course, we would have to drop (see Exhibit 8 for gross profit and labor expense breakdowns by departments).

Herman: Well, I suppose we could adopt a selective discounting program. But there are problems with that approach. The vice-president for sales of a large chain told me that we'd be making a big mistake if we instituted a limited low-price program. He said our initial prices have to be lower than competitors on most all items, particularly on grocery items. If not, he suggested, we're dead. We have to establish credibility with a very cost-conscious consumer. To make a program like that work, we would have to have a strong merchandising program like Stop & Shop's Mini-Pricing. That might be the best approach to any discount mer-

Exhibit 8

DEPARTMENTAL GROSS PROFIT AND LABOR EXPENSE
FY1968

	% of total sales	*Gross profit % of departmental sales*	*Labor expenses[1] % of departmental sales*
Groceries[2]	65.5	19.9	3.6%
Meat[3]	27.3	22.6	9.8%
Produce	7.2	36.0	11.0%

[1] Excludes expense for cashiers and other front-end employees and salaries of bookkeepers and store manager.

[2] Includes bakery.

[3] Includes delicatessen.

chandising, since we are really not experts on promotion. After all, we still don't use in-store displays to any great extent. Still, there is some risk with Mini-Pricing, too. One store manager told me that when he took on Mini-Pricing his sales didn't increase as much as they had expected. He said it took a full year to build up credibility—and profits.

George: I want to know how we can expect to establish credibility with any program with the inflation rate we are experiencing. Inflationary forces are pushing supermarket prices up almost daily, so how are we supposed to establish a low-priced image when, in fact, regardless of any desire to remain low priced we would have to start raising prices almost immediately to cover the increases in our costs of goods?

Warren: That's a good point George, and I can't think of a satisfactory answer other than everybody else will be in the same boat. We'd have to play it by ear.

Herman: True, but when we ran the simulation we factored in inflation and still came out all right. Our calculations show profit dollars coming out in 1970 just about the same as in 1968. We assumed a reduction in gross margin to 17%, a 24% annual sales increase in FY1969 and FY1970, and a 6% inflation rate.

Stanley: Herman, I'm sure glad your machine is confident about us going discount successfully, but I'm not convinced. What if the discounting or Mini-Pricing is a complete bust? What if it's a fad and won't last? What if we say we are a discount supermarket, spend all that money on advertising, and don't get the volume? Then we have to raise prices again to boost margins. And that will make even the remaining customers mad.

Herman: I just don't think we can help but get the volume. I feel that that estimate of 55% sales increase in two years is a conservative one. We have a large share of the metropolitan Petropolis market. With our prices as high as they are now, we are vulnerable to the big chains when they all go discount. I think that A&P and Safeway, for example, are just sleeping giants when it comes to discounting. A&P forfeited price leadership when it took on Plaid Stamps, but I think it may well enter the price arena with a new determination. I think even Safeway will eventually come around to discounting.

Stanley: Okay, Herman, but what about the Mini-Pricing idea? As I see it, that would be a good way for us to merchandise Leo's. I see two benefits from it. First, Leo's would achieve within its trading areas greater public acceptance, increased share of market, and a stronger long-range position. Second, Leo's would be better able to expand into new areas with a combined quality-and-low-price image. We could even join forces with a general merchandise discounter—as some supermarket chains have done—and capitalize on its abilities to enter new markets.

The cost of the program is not too high; especially when you consider the increased volume it should generate.

* * * * * * * * * *

Implementation Considerations

George: One thing that bothers me is that if we do decide to go ahead with some discounting program, we will have to decide how to put it into operation. And that might be tricky. It seems to me that a "new look" would have to be made immediately visible and be quite different from the current image, both in advertising and in the stores. This would be necessary to establish credibility in a hurry. If we go to Mini-Pricing, we will be in effect buying expertise in the promotional end of things, though we could probably handle promotion adequately ourselves if we wanted to. The question is, if we decide to go to any form of low-priced image, should we do it in all the stores or in just one test store? If we do one store for a while and it appears successful, should we add a few stores at a time to the program or go companywide at once? And where, if we do a test, should the test stores be located?

Stanley: If we do a test, George, then we will sure as hell let our competitors know what we are up to—without having all the stores being discount. I think that if we decide to go, it should be storewide from the start. Otherwise, it would give our competitors time to prepare and react.

Warren: Look, who cares if they know—they'll know soon enough anyway. I think a test store is mandatory, as is a careful analysis of the results of the experiment. If we start right off and turn every store discount and the whole gambit fails, then we would be in most serious trouble. Besides, while we may be aware of and concerned with a companywide image, I'll bet most shoppers spent 90% of their time in the same store and would never know that a store across town had gone discount.

Mr. Ishtov: I wonder if one or two stores would really provide dependable results on which to base this decision. Would it really prove anything? If we did a test outside of Petropolis, would it be as important as one done in metropolitan Petropolis? While our quality is known statewide, Leo's quality image in the outlying towns isn't quite as strong as it is in the city. Perhaps a discount operation would work automatically in the outside town and wouldn't work in town. And we wouldn't find out until we went ahead with the program on a companywide basis.

George: That's a good point, Leo. I have another worry also: Viking. It is the company most like us. If we went outside with a discount program, it could preempt us in metropolitan Petropolis with a discount program of its own. Viking is our most important competitor. It competes in every town that we do. And then again, if we go fully discount, Viking might just stay with its high-price, high-quality policies and be the only major store to offer that service. There is clearly a market for our present type of operation, although I don't know if it is large enough to support both of us on a growth basis. Of course, it's possible that Viking won't respond quickly enough to any move we make—after all, it does take a lot of time and effort to put a discounting program together. If we decide now to go low price, we'll just make it after Labor Day.

Herman: Look, George, we can beat Viking any time. As far as I'm concerned, Viking is rowing in our fjord and we can run them out any time. If we go discount, people who know our quality will be so happy to pay a little less for it that they'll flock to us in droves. I've had informal discussions with a lot of our people, and I think this discounting debate is just breaking down along party lines. In a nutshell, the older employees are all against discounting and Mini-Pricing and the younger employees feel that it's the right thing to do. The older people think we would really be putting Leo's future on the line if we went to low-price operations. The young ones don't think we have any choice if we are to grow.

Mr. Ishtov: I think that on that note, Herman, it's time we broke up the meeting. We have covered some very important points, but we haven't gotten close enough to make a decision. Let's meet tomorrow and settle it for sure. This is obviously not an easy decision. I have seen several articles in national magazines (see Exhibit 9) about how some of the larger chains have been wrestling with the same decision and on how those who have tried discounting have been faring. In my mind, a lot of questions remain unanswered.

We own this company. We have been in business for 40 years and can be proud of what we have accomplished. A large segment of the public will always appreciate what we offer. I am approaching the end of my business career. You are taking over. Whatever you decide, I will be with you. If we make no profit for a year or two, we won't be happy, but we'll survive. The same is true for growth and expansion. It will come sooner or later. See you tomorrow.

Exhibit 9

LEO'S FOODLAND

Description of National Supermarket Competition

Beat Them or Join Them?

Safeway has been hurting from the strong trend toward food discounting in its main western bailiwick, but it is still bucking the trend.

The supermarket concept that budded in the Thirties and flowered in the Forties and Fifties involved building chains of self-service stores, paring prices to the bone and making a small unit profit on huge volume. It worked magnificently, though to the near-extinction of the corner grocer. Even as they prospered, the big supermarket chains managed to keep prices low.

But late in 1966 a group of Denver housewives, their household budgets pinched by growing inflation from all directions, took out their ire by picketing local food chains for lower prices. The "housewives' revolt" caught national attention, and the protests soon spread across the U.S. The chains often responded by lowering prices. "A lot of it came through panic," says President Quentin Reynolds of Oakland's Safeway Stores, the nation's second-largest food chain with sales of $3.4 billion. "Members of the industry were afraid they would be singled out as contributing to high food prices, so they began cutting."

Whatever the reason, the price-cutting gave impetus to the growth of a new kind of supermarket, the so-called discount food stores. These in effect merely carry the supermarket concept further by such devices as shortening store hours, curtailing carry-out and other services, limiting product variety and eliminating trading stamps and other promotions. By doing so they are able to cut prices still further.

Worst in the West

Another result was a massive profit squeeze for the supermarket industry in 1967, with Safeway itself one of the outstanding victims. Safeway has been one of the most profitable outfits in the business, netting 1.8% on sales in 1966 while the others averaged less than 1.2%. But in 1967, as sales remained virtually level at around $3.4 billion, Safeway profits skidded 15% to $51 million, or $2 per share. Its net margin fell to 1.5%, a six-year low.

Safeway's own troubles were compounded in 1967 when the housewives' revolt forced it to drop its highly successful "Bonus Bingo" game, a promotion gimmick that a year earlier had sent sales soaring by 14%. Reynolds and Chairman

Source: *Forbes Magazine,* May 1, 1969, p. 36. © *Forbes Magazine.*

Exhibit 9 (continued)

LEO'S FOODLAND

Description of National Supermarket Competition

Robert A. Magowan agree that the absence of Bonus Bingo was a prime reason Safeway's sales failed to grow in 1967, thus worsening the squeeze from price-cutting.

As 1968 began, the outlook was for more price pressure. The discounting idea has caught on, particularly in California and other states in Safeway's western territory. California-based chains like Lucky stores, Alpha Beta (a division of Acme Markets), and Market Basket (a division of Kroger Co.) have gone discount. Estimates are that over half the groceries sold in Los Angeles this year will be sold at discount prices, up to 5% below previous price levels.

With supermarket profit margins low to begin with, the implications are obvious. Those who get into food discounting may experience some quick gains in sales volume. For example, Lucky stores, a discounter for seven years, has more than quadrupled per-share net. But as more chains post discount prices, the gains will be nullified, with lower margins for everyone.

"We Lost Our Shirt"

For such reasons Safeway has been slow to jump on the food discount bandwagon. It has gone into discounting only in a few isolated areas where the competition from other discounters has become intolerable, places like Orange County, near Los Angeles.

Says Bob Magowan, the man who 13 years ago took over and transformed a troubled Safeway into one of the nation's profitable chains: "When Lucky stores started their discount operation in Phoenix, we didn't know how to compete against it. They didn't open their stores until noon and they closed them at 8 p.m. They eliminated carry-out boys and took hundreds of items off their shelves. They began stocking by whole cases rather than bringing out eight or ten cans at a time. Initially our volume there fell by about 25%. What did we do? We took on their prices, but until we got our volume up, we lost our shirt. Now we're making money in Phoenix."

But Magowan and Reynolds refuse to panic and convert entirely to discount operations, though they have been forced to do some selective price-cutting where discount competition has cropped up. Their tack is bred of Magowan's wide retailing experience. Before joining Merrill Lynch, where he was a partner until 1955, he was a buyer at Macy's. "How does Macy's compete with discount operations?" he asks rhetorically. "For one thing, they have better quality and more services."

Thus Safeway, even where it cuts prices and shortens store hours, is still maintaining a wide variety of shelf items and insisting on high-quality meat and produce. These last items make up some 35% of Safeway's volume, or over $1 billion in sales a year, and they also provide the chain's highest gross profit margins (20%–

Exhibit 9 (continued)

LEO'S FOODLAND

Description of National Supermarket Competition

30%). Safeway is counting on quality in meat and produce to keep the housewives filing through its checkout lines. "Anyone carrying less than U.S.D.A. 'Choice' beef in this company will get fired," says Magowan.

To help take up some of the profit slack, Safeway has been bringing in outside consultants and efficiency experts. "We've been doing things the same way for 40 years," Magowan explains. "These people can teach us old dogs some new tricks. For example, when a food clerk carries something to the back room, we try to make sure he carries something the other way."

Survival

Magowan claims the results have been good so far. He says Safeway's sales per man-hour, a key supermarket efficiency measurement, is up to around $39 from about $34 in 1964. The chain's first-quarter results for 1968 seem to bear him out: On 9% higher sales of $803 million, profits jumped 53% to $11 million, or 43 cents a share.

The 8% sales gain measures up to the 5%–7% Magowan looks for each year. "We've got to have regular sales increases to survive," he says. But whether Safeway's reliance on an image of product quality will continue to produce these kinds of gains is a question. The discount food stores have a powerful consumer appeal. Magowan, now 64 years old, is going to find his last years at Safeway's helm the most challenging of his highly successful career.

Volume Is Crucial . . .

California supermarket chain, Lucky Stores, has piled up a dazzling record in the last five years. Will it last?

Price, of course, was the original appeal when the supermarkets got started during the 1930s and 1940s. Chop overhead to the bone, slash prices and make up the difference on volume.

Most supermarket outfits, however, strayed from that concept over the years. They added things like carryout boys, trading stamps, games, and longer operating hours—all of which raised costs and prices. Competition was the apparent reason:

Source: *Forbes Magazine,* March 1, 1969, p. 42, © *Forbes Magazine.*

Exhibit 9 (continued)

LEO'S FOODLAND

Description of National Supermarket Competition

If Kroger started issuing stamps, A&P had to follow or risk losing business. Before long, the price angle began to seem less crucial.

Back in 1962, however, San Leandro, Calif.'s Lucky Stores decided to buck the trend and go back to the real, bare-bones price-cutting that now goes under the name of food discounting. Its reasoning was painfully simple. Lucky's profits hadn't budged for five years and, in the words of Chairman Gerald A. Awes, "We had to do something different."

Redoubtable Record

So Lucky began pruning costs, eventually by as much as $175,000 per year per store in Southern California. It shortened operating hours by seven to 12 hours a week. It concentrated on stocking economy-sized containers. It reduced the number of brands carried, eliminated specials and trading stamps. It closed down smaller stores and opened larger ones, then ran the new ones with the same number of people. It used king-sized shopping carts. It cut prices across the board—by 5% to 15%—and prayed housewives would respond in droves.

Did they? Today, with an average return on equity of 29.5% over the past five years, Lucky Stores is the U.S.' most profitable major supermarket chain, and ranks 15th in profitability among all the companies in the FORBES 500 (*Jan. 1*). This is well ahead of both Winn-Dixie (40th) and Safeway (150th), traditionally the profit leaders among the supermarket chains. Lucky's sales have zoomed ahead from $232 million in 1962 to $627 million in 1967, and, thanks largely to the acquisition of Eagle Supermarkets last year, to around $1 billion in 1969. Profits, meantime, have advanced at an annual rate of 27% over the last five years, which puts Lucky in 31st place in U.S. industry.

"There's just no substitute for volume," says President William H. Dyer Jr. "Your fixed cost of running a store is pretty much the same whether your volume is $1 million or $3 million." And volume Lucky has. Its stores now average around $3 million sales a year *vs.* a $1.5-million industry average.

Lucky's success, plus the "housewives' revolt" of two years ago, prompted other food chains to enter the discount field, especially in California. So far, though, the results are mixed. Food Giant, recently acquired by Vornado (*Forbes, Dec. 15, 1968*), switched to discounting in 1967 but now has backed away. Alpha Beta, another California chain owned by Acme Markets, went discount last year amid a great blare of publicity, but company officials are tight-lipped about the results. The really large national chains have fought fire with fire, but only where Lucky is plainly stealing customers. Other chains have reacted by meeting discount prices selectively on fast-moving items like coffee, eggs and sugar.

Exhibit 9 (continued)

LEO'S FOODLAND

Description of National Supermarket Competition

Does Lucky provide a model for the supermarket industry? Lucky made its move when it was still a relatively small chain with earnings problems. It had less to lose in converting to food discounting than, say, would a Safeway or an A&P, both of whom believe that supermarket customers will in the long run demand a higher level of service just as they have elsewhere in retailing. Moreover, newcomers to food discounting may get no such improvement in volume as Lucky did. And volume itself is not the object of the game, as the story of Stop & Shop (*below*) clearly shows.

Also, there is a curious pattern in this history of food retailing. One hot-shot company after another hot-shot company has emerged from nowhere to set spectacular records, only to lose its luster after it reached a certain size and maturity. Whether Lucky Stores can avoid that pattern is yet to be proved.

. . . Or Is It?

Boston-based Stop & Shop could show a dazzling record only a few years back. It hasn't lasted.

"Today we operate 138 Stop & Shop stores in seven eastern states, each doing an average of over $3.4 million in sales compared with an industry average of $1.5 million," boasts Irving W. Rabb, Stop & Shop, Inc. vice chairman and younger brother of Chairman Sidney R. Rabb.

It's a good line to wake up security analysts at presentations around the country. And it's even better when Stop & Shop can be compared with its most direct competitor, First National Stores. Both are concentrated in southern New England, with outposts in the New Jersey-New York metropolitan area. Their sales are not far apart: First National's were $640 million for the fiscal year ended Mar. 31, 1968 *vs.* $566 million (19% from discount department stores) for Stop & Shop in its year ended some two months earlier. But First National showed an earnings deficit of $6.6 million while Stop & Shop recorded a profit of $6.1 million.

Stop & Shop's swollen volume per store dates back to 1938, the year the Rabbs changed the name of their chain of 425 Economy Grocery Stores, which had average sales of $41,000 each. Then they started replacing these smaller stores with fewer, but newer and larger units, easily accessible along New England's sprouting highway system.

Exhibit 9 (continued)

LEO'S FOODLAND

Description of National Supermarket Competition

"We started research," Chairman Rabb told *Forbes,* "about 1938, using highway routes in determining store location. After the war, we started consumer research. One thing consumers wanted was less-crowded stores, so in 1952 we started building them at 9,000 to 12,000 square feet. By the mid-sixties, consumers obviously wanted more products and service and convenience—but they still didn't want to be bumped from behind. So we built still larger stores."

The Rabbs and President Donald A. Gannon also credit other innovations with helping to ring up more sales per store: Stop & Shop was the first New England supermarket chain, in 1955, to give trading stamps, and in 1965 was the first to drop them. It began to promote discount prices in all Stop & Shop supermarkets in 1965–66, and it learned to alter the product mix in its stores according to the economic and social levels of their trading areas. "What we've done," says Chairman Rabb, "has worked for us, but I don't want you to say that this is what the others should have done. That's like comparing apples and oranges. No two companies are alike."

The Seamy Side

What this happy picture omits is profits, which have been trending downward throughout the Sixties. In fiscal 1960, for example, Stop & Shop had replaced its old, small stores with 117 new ones averaging $2.1 million sales each. With its sales up 23% to $239 million from fiscal 1959's $194 million, earnings rose 27% to $4.1 million, representing a return of 1.7% on sales and 22% on equity. By contrast, in its most recently reported 12-month period the company had sales of some $622 million—but margins of 1% on sales and 13% on equity. Where Stop & Shop was once well up among the supermarket leaders in profitability, it is now well back in the ruck.

Which explains why Stop & Shop has been trying to become much more than a supermarket operation. In 1961 it went into discounting with the acquisition of six Bradlees stores, and since then has increased them to 52, accounting for some $140 million of the company's sales in fiscal 1968. Now it is headed into drug retailing, with three Medi-Mart superdrugstores already opened and more planned. But unfortunately, the relative slide in profitability has occurred despite these moves.

What, then, is the virtue of having over $3 million sales per supermarket? It is worth something only if it results in superior profit performance—as it has, at least so far, for California's Lucky Stores. If it leads only to a period of profit decline, as with Stop & Shop, it is worth very little indeed.

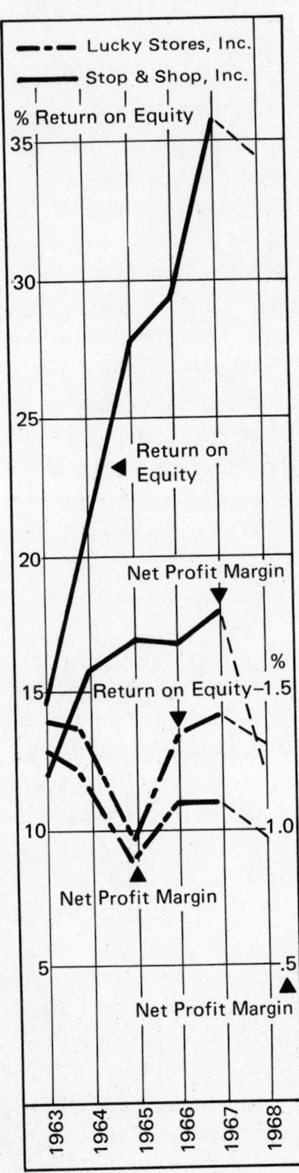

SOURCE: Standard & Poor's

Universal Inns, Inc. (A)

In early October 1973 James Harris, Vice-President of Marketing, was discussing the problems in Universal Inns' southern division with Robert Jameson, Vice-President of Operations, as one step in process of preparing a set of marketing recommendations for the properties of the division. Universal Inns, Inc., a publicly traded firm, operated 28 motels along the eastern seaboard of the United States. All of these motels were operated as franchises of National Inns, Inc., the fourth largest motel chain in the United States. The breakdown of the units by state and number of rooms was as follows:

State	*Division*	*Number of locations*	*Number of rooms*
Connecticut	Northern	3	363
Florida	Southern	5	579
Georgia	Southern	3	368
Maryland	Northern	4	565
New Jersey	Northern	2	496
New York	Northern	1	212
North Carolina	Southern	1	120
Pennsylvania	Northern	2	303
South Carolina	Southern	2	201
Virginia	Northern	5	547
		28	3,754

Total gross revenue for 1972 was $21,500,000. Projected gross revenues for 1973 were $23,200,000. The source of income was as follows:

Room rental	57%
Bar and restaurant	39%
Miscellaneous	4%
	100%

The breakdown of Universal's expenses as a percentage of revenue was as follows for 1972:

Salaries and other operating costs	62%
Advertising	3%
Maintenance	3%
Utilities	4%
Property taxes	3%
Interest	10%
Rents	4%
Depreciation	7%
Net earnings and income tax	4%
	100%

The Harris-Jameson Meeting

Harris: Bob, as you know, the situation in our southern division is getting serious. The budget motels have flooded this area with $10 and under rooms. In some properties occupancy has dropped by 20 percentage points.

Our original response to the budget threat was to maintain our high level of service and keep our prices up. That seemed to stem the tide last year, but we are losing ground. Remember those horror stories we heard about properties on I-75 just south of Atlanta? Well, we've now got a couple of properties which fall into that category.

Hal[1] is so worried that he wants us to halt site work on our Fayetteville, North Carolina, location and cut off our negotiations for any new sites in the southern division. I must convince him that we have to inventory these sites now, before all the choice sites in this area are bought up by our competitors.

We all know that the budget operators are overbuilding. Everyone forecasts there will be a shake-out period just like there was in the fast-food industry. What should be our strategy in light of this condition? The southern division is getting hurt right now, but all indications point to the same situation occurring soon in our northern division.

Jameson: Let's list all the alternatives open to us. First, we can stop our southern division expansion program. In fact, we might elect to sell our losing properties if we can find a buyer.

Second, we can attempt to cut costs. With occupancies down, there is some fat at each location. In addition, we might elect to delay some of our renovation projects. However, we have to be careful because our franchise agreement with National Inns requires us to maintain a certain level of service and accommodations at each property.

Third, we can attempt to improve our local marketing programs. Maybe we should advertise our strengths such as our tie-in with a national reservation system, our children-under-12 free policy, the quality of our

[1] Harold McAdams, Vice-President of Finance.

service, the convenience and good food of our restaurants. This would supplement the national advertising currently being done by National Inns.

Can you think of any other alternatives?

Harris: Yes, there is another alternative, but it is one which has generated opposition from everyone with whom I have discussed it. We could sim-

Exhibit 1

UNIVERSAL INNS, INC. (A)
Lake Park, Georgia
Operating Statistics
September 1973

September		Number of rooms occupied	Room revenue	Food sales	Beer sales	Total revenue
1	S	34	$ 449	$ 446	$ 17	$ 912
2	S	37	548	682	—	1,230
3	M	38	563	599	15	1,177
4	T	41	551	550	10	1,111
5	W	42	579	565	17	1,161
6	T	50	701	595	31	1,327
7	F	46	645	565	19	1,229
8	S	35	503	609	22	1,134
9	S	37	532	696	—	1,228
10	M	34	477	579	16	1,072
11	T	41	599	470	12	1,081
12	W	41	591	561	14	1,166
13	T	48	724	704	32	1,460
14	F	48	702	901	19	1,622
15	S	50	753	683	29	1,465
16	S	42	628	797	—	1,467
17	M	57	720	627	27	1,374
18	T	53	728	670	23	1,421
19	W	55	730	679	20	1,429
20	T	68	1,037	909	24	1,970
21	F	51	804	923	21	1,748
22	S	57	869	792	11	1,672
23	S	39	593	729	—	1,322
24	M	33	501	578	22	1,101
25	T	44	599	564	19	1,182
26	W	47	643	561	23	1,227
27	T	57	801	600	8	1,409
28	F	50	760	737	15	1,512
29	S	51	789	751	17	1,557
30	S	49	702	811	—	1,513
Total		1,375	$19,821	$19,933	$484	$41,613

ply lower our prices and maintain our same level of service. Everybody I talk to is afraid that we will lose even more money if we cut our prices. How do you feel?

Jameson: My first reaction is negative. We are saddled with heavy fixed costs. If we lower our margins, our break-even occupancy levels climb even higher than they are now. What makes you think lowering our prices is a viable alternative? Do you think the National Franchise Association will allow us to promote lower prices? What sorts of pressure will that put on the other franchisees?

Harris: I have been looking at some of our problem properties. For example, I spent a week collecting information on our property at the Lake Park, Georgia (pop. 361), interchange on I-75 near the Georgia-Florida state line. Until last January we shared this interchange with a Quality Inn, although there is an independent motel a mile away on a state road. In January, a new Days Inn opened across the interchange from us.

It appears that we also compete with six motels on the two interchanges 15 and 20 miles north of us at Valdosta (pop. 32,303) and two motels 15 miles south of us at the Jennings, Florida (pop. 582), interchange.

Exhibit 2

UNIVERSAL INNS, INC. (A)
Comparison of 10 P.M. Car Counts
Universal Inn Versus Days Inn[1]
Lake Park, Georgia
(At the Georgia–Florida border on I-75)
9/26/73–10/2/73

Date		*Universal Inn*	*Days Inn*
9/26	Wed	32	60
9/27	Thurs	28	56
9/28	Fri	24	52
9/29	Sat	22	46
9/30	Sun	29	45
10/1	Mon	40	50
10/2	Tues	36	56

[1] Both properties have 120 units. Days Inn offers a single for $8 and charges $3 for each additional occupant in the room. Universal Inn charges $13.50 for a single and $16.00 for a double. There is no charge for children under 12. Both offer a centralized reservation system (800 number).

Days Inn also operates a freestanding Tasty World Restaurant, Gift Shop, and Gas Station on premises. There are also a small swimming pool and play area in front of the motel. Universal Inn has a larger swimming pool and more elaborate play area and operates a restaurant (beer sales only) within the motel unit.

Exhibit 3

UNIVERSAL INNS, INC. (A)
Distribution of
License Plates by State
at Days Inn, Lake Park, Georgia

States	Number of cars	Percent
Alabama	5	1.4
California	2	.5
Canada	7	1.9
Delaware	3	.8
Florida	96	26.3
Georgia	33	9.0
Illinois	14	3.8
Indiana	27	7.4
Iowa	2	.5
Kentucky	5	1.4
Louisiana	3	.8
Maryland	6	1.6
Massachusetts	4	1.1
Michigan	40	11.0
New Jersey	8	2.2
New York	8	2.2
North Carolina	11	3.0
Ohio	54	14.8
Oklahoma	2	.5
Pennsylvania	14	3.8
South Carolina	5	1.4
Tennessee	6	1.6
Virginia	7	1.9
Wisconsin	3	.8
Total	365	99.7[1]

[1] Does not add to 100% because of rounding.

There is a budget motel, Econ-o-Travel, in Jennings and another Days Inn at Valdosta. Most of the other properties are, like us, affiliated with major chains such as Holiday Inns, Ramada Inns, and Howard Johnson's. However, at the I-75 and U.S. 84 interchange at Valdosta, there are three independent motels on U.S. 84 but near enough to the exchange to draw traffic with their budget prices. Road signs are visible 20–30 miles north and south of each property.

Since January our occupancy, compared to the prior year, has slowly dropped. Look at our record last month at this property. (He pulls out Exhibit 1 and shows it to Jameson.) We had 3,600 available room nights and sold only 1,375 for a monthly occupancy of 38.1%. Last

Exhibit 4

UNIVERSAL INNS, INC. (A)
Comments Made to James Harris in Tasty World Restaurant
by Days Inn Guests

—We feel as comfortable in a Days Inn room as we would in a more expensive motel. We have found them to be satisfactory in every way.

—We enjoyed the large room, bathtub, and huge mirror. Retired people and senior citizens need motels with $8.00 rooms. My friends and relatives shall be told.

—I wish there were more Days Inns. It offers everything I need. The price is right. You don't pay for the extra things you don't need. I pay my own expenses, so this is a real savings. Days Inn is as nice as a Holiday Inn.

—I have stayed at this particular inn on numerous occasions. I have also stayed at other Days Inns in other parts of Georgia. My business dictates that I stay in other chains on most occasions, but when the choice is mine, I stay at Days Inn.

—I must admit I am most pleased with these facilities. My wife and I have stayed in motels costing $19 or more per night without comparable efficiency and comfort. We will recommend Days Inn to all our friends.

—I like the facilities, price, and convenience of a Days Inn. I plan to stay in them when there is one along my route.

—It is really great to find a motel with excellent accommodations for a budget price. My husband will be retiring next year and you can rest assured we will be looking for Days Inn.

—I don't owe National Inns anything. They never did anything for me. Why should I want to stay there when I can stay here. Frankly, they could charge less and I wouldn't stay there—about time they got a little competition.

---

year our occupancy was 55.2% for September. Our "no-shows" have increased from 10% to nearly 35% of our reservations. However, reservations still account for 55% of our actual room nights.

To complete my analysis I need some good cost figures for Lake Park. Do you have any?

Jameson: (After thumbing through a thick listing of computer printouts.) Here they are. Our variable room cost (labor, supplies, etc.) as a percentage of room revenue is running 19.8% at Lake Park. Food cost as a percentage of food sales is 48%. In the food side of our business, we treat labor (currently running 30% of revenue) as a semifixed cost. Subtracting other variable costs of 7% gives us a margin of 15% on food sales. Applying some quick rules-of-thumb, it looks as if we can double our food volume without incurring any additional fixed costs or labor. Beer cost is 25% of sales. These percentages are right on our systemwide averages except for the food cost, which is a couple of points higher than average.

Harris: I did some snooping at the Days Inn site. Look at the number of cars at Days Inn compared to the number at ours. (See Exhibit 2.) Both are 120-unit properties. They had 70% more cars than we did for the week I was there. An analysis of the distribution of license plates by states (Exhibit 3) indicates to me that Days Inns are attracting many vacation travelers. Our guests at Lake Park are mainly businessmen from the Georgia-Florida area. The percentage of our guests from those two states is 62%.

I also ate several meals in their Tasty World restaurant. Look at the guests' comments which were made to me or overheard by me. There were very few negative comments (selected comments are contained in Exhibit 4). These reactions lead me to believe that price is the critical variable in Days Inn's success formula at Lake Park.

Jameson: I see your point, but look at the balance sheet (Exhibit 5) for the Lake Park property. The current ratio for September is only .53. Our occupancy for this unit, as you noted, is only 38%, which is below our cur-

Exhibit 5

UNIVERSAL INNS, INC. (A)
Lake Park, Georgia
Balance Sheet
as of September 30, 1972

Assets		*Liabilities and Shareholders' Equity*	
Current assets:		Current liabilities:	
Cash	68	Long-term debt—current portion	75
Accounts receivable—net	15	Notes payable	70
Inventories—cost:		Accounts payable	25
Food	4	Payroll taxes payable	3
Beverages	4	Accrued expenses payable	18
Prepaid expenses	11	Total current liabilities	191
Total current assets	102	Long-term debt	840
Fixed assets—at cost:		Total liabilities	1,031
Land and land improvements	61	Equity and retained earnings	150
Building and improvements	899	Total liabilities and stockholders' equity	1,181
Furniture and equipment	302		
Total	1,262		
Less accumulated depreciation	364		
Total fixed assets	998		
Deferred charges and other assets	81		
Total assets	1,181		

Exhibit 6

UNIVERSAL INNS, INC. (A)

THE PRICE OF RATE CUTTING

Present occupancy	*Occupancy required to make up for reduction if reduction in present rate is*				
	5%	*10%*	*15%*	*20%*	*25%*
76%	81.4%	87.7%	95.0%	103.6%	114.0%
74	79.3	85.4	92.5	100.9	111.0
72	77.1	83.1	90.0	98.2	108.0
70	75.0	80.8	87.5	95.5	105.0
68	72.9	78.5	85.0	92.7	102.0
66	70.7	76.2	82.5	90.0	99.0
64	68.6	73.8	80.0	87.3	96.0
62	66.4	71.5	77.5	84.5	93.0
60	64.3	69.2	75.0	81.8	90.0
58	62.1	66.9	72.5	79.1	87.0
56	60.0	64.6	70.0	76.4	84.0
54	57.9	62.3	67.5	73.6	81.0
52	55.7	60.0	65.0	70.9	78.0
50	53.6	57.7	62.5	68.2	75.0

(Based on cost of operating additional occupied rooms equal to 25% of present rate.)

rent break-even occupancy of 50%.[2] How long can our balance sheet support these losses?

What makes you think the demand for rooms is elastic? Aren't there just a fixed number of cars driving down I-75 every day? We don't want to start a price war in a zero-sum situation. This chart (Exhibit 6) shows

Exhibit 7

UNIVERSAL INNS, INC. (A)

24-HOUR AVERAGE DAILY TRAFFIC ON I-75

AT THE GEORGIA–FLORIDA STATE LINE—BOTH DIRECTIONS

	1972	*1973*
June	24,475	22,881
July	26,644	22,418
August	23,375	23,338
September	16,028	16,228

2 This assumes a 50/50 sales split for room and food sales. Restaurant labor was treated as a variable cost in making this calculation.

Exhibit 8

UNIVERSAL INNS, INC. (A)
COST OF TYPICAL 120-UNIT PROPERTY

120 rooms
15,000 square foot commercial building
  3,600 square foot dining room
  1,160 square foot meeting rooms
  399 square foot lounge
  4,000 square foot rooms support (offices, front desk)
$1,200,000 permanent loan
  $8\frac{1}{2}\%$ interest

Rooms		
Construction	$6,000 per unit	
Furnishings and supplies	2,000 per unit	
Miscellaneous, financing, engineering, architect, franchise, landscaping, signs, pool, etc.	1,000 per unit	
120 units at	$9,000 per unit	$1,080,000
Land for Units		98,000
Land for Commercial Building		27,000
Commercial Building		
Construction	$25.00 per sq. foot	
Miscellaneous, supplies, furnishings and equipment ($5.00 nondepreciable)	16.00 per sq. foot	
Total	$41.00 per sq. foot	
15,000 square feet commercial building		615,000
Total		$1,820,000
Per unit cost	$15,167 for Total Project	
Total Commercial Building Cost—		
Construction, furnishing, and equipment		$ 615,000
Less 4,000 square feet for rooms support		164,000
Net cost for food and beverage facilities (including land $478,000)		$ 451,000
Total Room Facility Cost—		
Construction, furnishing, and equipment *Including land, $1,342,000*		$1,244,000

that if we drop our price by 25%, we will have to increase our occupancy by 50% just to break even.

Harris: The number of cars traveling on I-75 is fixed (see Exhibit 7), but our share of that number is so small that we won't affect our competitors very much.

There is another advantage of lowering our prices now. Our competitors will refrain from building additional properties when they are forced to plug lower prices into their proformas.

Bob, I need your support to experiment with prices in the southern division. If I have your support, I need some advice on how to institute the change, how to promote the price reduction, how to monitor the results, and how to decide if the program is effective.

Jameson: Jim, I wish I could say "yes" right now, but there are still many doubts in my mind. Let me push a few numbers today and I'll give you my answer in the morning. I just completed developing some cost figures for our typical 120-unit property (see Exhibit 8). Perhaps they will be useful to examine.

THE Investment Corporation

We've got to find some way of reaching the multitude of marginal companies which I'm sure exist, and also some way of convincing commercial loan officers that our insurance will virtually eliminate their risks on equipment and inventory loans. In addition, I would like to broaden our capital base and expand geographically, but it is difficult to explain to prospective investors and state insurance commissioners how our business works.

—Ernest Friedlander
January, 1973

Company History

For over 40 years Friedlander's father, Mr. George N. Friedlander, had been turning ailing companies into profitable operations throughout the United States. Bringing to the businesses substantial private capital, contacts in various money markets, and considerable managerial expertise, Friedlander would acquire the companies, turn them around, and sell them. His businesses had ranged in size from $200,000 a year volume to several million and had covered a wide range of industries.

In the mid-sixties, Friedlander teamed up with his two sons, Ernest and Robert. (Robert had only recently graduated from Dartmouth College and Ernest from the Harvard Business School.) Together they bought the nearly bankrupt Whiting Milk Company, turned it into a profitable operation, and early in 1969 sold it to the Dairyman's League of New York. This success in their first joint turnaround venture led the three Friedlanders to formalize their activities. In August 1969 they founded THE Investment Corporation and three subsidiaries in Boston. George Friedlander served as chairman of the board. Ernest Friedlander was president of two subsidiaries—THE Appraisal Corporation and THE Insurance Company. Robert Friedlander was president of the third subsidiary, a management consulting firm called Exeter International.

Exeter offered a wide variety of consulting services aimed almost entirely at ailing companies. The Appraisal Corporation's chief activity was to evaluate the assets of a company that sought a loan. The Insurance Company's principal business was to help marginal companies get bank loans by insuring the company's equipment and inventory against the proposed loans. Each subsidiary often generated clients for the others. Companies that came for management consulting services might be offered appraisals and loan insurance. Companies that sought loan insurance might be advised to seek Exeter's consulting services. The three companies shared the same office and staff (see Exhibit 1).

Exhibit 1

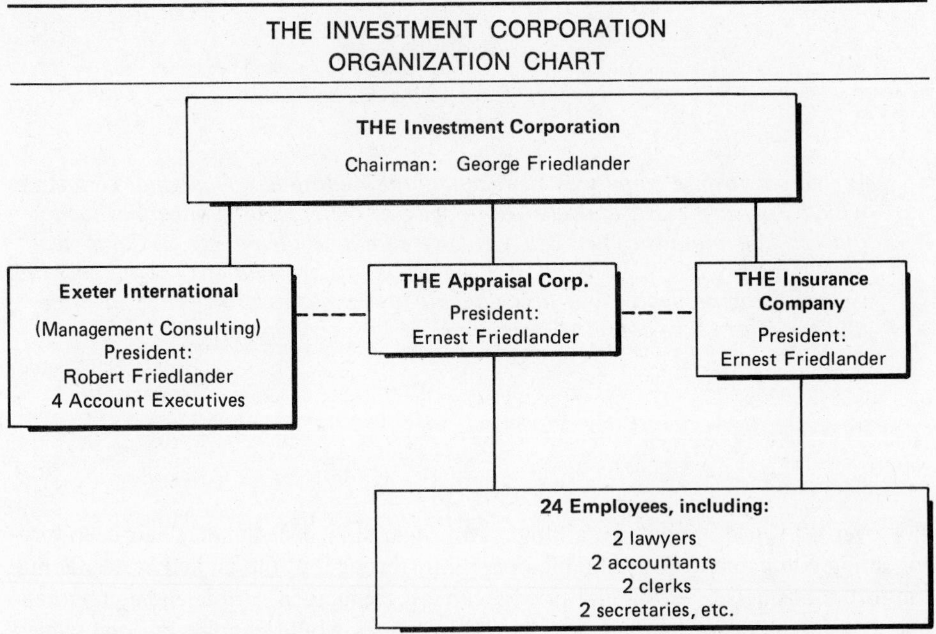

Operations of THE Appraisal Corporation and THE Insurance Company

THE Appraisal Corporation and THE Insurance Company almost always worked hand in hand. Though a company could get an appraisal without getting the insurance, it could not get the insurance without first getting an appraisal. The following is a description of their operations taken from a promotional brochure that Ernest Friedlander used with banks.

* * *

THE NEW, GUARANTEED WAY TO PROTECT YOUR BANK ON EQUIPMENT AND INVENTORY LOANS, REGARDLESS OF RISK. A NEW CONCEPT TO BROADEN YOUR BASE FOR ASSET LOANS FROM THE APPRAISAL CORPORATION AND THE INSURANCE COMPANY.

The Plan: What It's All About

It's a completely new and unique service for banks and lending institutions. In fact, there's nothing even remotely like it available today.

Very simply, to make our new concept possible and practical, we've teamed up an appraisal company and an insurance company.

They cover you completely. And eliminate your risks. On loans secured by equipment or inventory assets which, as you know, are sometimes very difficult to liquidate.

The Guarantee

WE GUARANTEE TO REMOVE YOUR RISK
When we appraise any fixed equipment or inventory, we guarantee the assets will produce the amount of our appraisal. Without question or contingencies.

WE GUARANTEE TO TAKE OVER YOUR PROBLEMS
Upon default and assignment of security documents, we take over the equipment or inventory. Completely eliminating your involvement in foreclosure or disposal of the assets.

WE GUARANTEE BETTER LOAN BUSINESS FOR YOUR BANK
By removing elements of risk and doubt, you can promote "guaranteed" equipment and inventory loans and capture a greater share of this profitable market. Especially when small or medium-sized businesses are concerned.

And, in many instances, you can also offer lower rates. Because depending upon the value and saleability of the collateral, our low charges and total risk removal allow you to realistically adjust your rates and still profit from each loan.

WE GUARANTEE TO HELP BUILD YOUR LOAN BUSINESS
By promoting our service to businessmen in your community. And inviting them to talk to your loan officers about us, whenever they need money.

WE GUARANTEE THE GUARANTEE
We back up our guarantee with an insurance policy from THE Insurance Company, licensed by the Commonwealth of Massachusetts.

IN SHORT, WE GUARANTEE A LOT. FOR JUST A LITTLE.

The Concept: How It Works Step By Step

1. YOU CALL US IN
When a customer requests a loan (whether on equipment or inventory), call us immediately. That's the point where our involvement begins.[1]

2. WE APPRAISE
We make an appraisal in depth.[2] And with this report as your guide, you can determine how large a loan you choose to make on the security of the assets we've appraised.

---

[1] Friedlander said that he first asked a prospective customer if he thought his equipment and inventory were worth $50,000 or more. Anything less would not result in sufficient profitability for Friedlander to be interested.

[2] One of Friedlander's appraisers would visit the company and make an official evaluation. The appraised asset value was based primarily on the estimated market value of the company's in-

3. WE BACK UP OUR APPRAISAL

If your loan falls within our appraisal figure (or if we agree to a greater amount), we guarantee your loan will be without risks or problems. Through an insurance bond from THE Insurance Company. Our appraisal contract and our insurance bond assure you that on default, all your bank has to do is simply notify us and turn over security documents covering the assets. Then you receive payment, according to the terms of THE contract.[3]

4. THAT'S ALL THERE IS TO IT

It's a unique and simple process that permits you to extend greater credit to borrowers in complete confidence. Resulting in better customer relations and increased earnings.

And since we take over full possession of the goods upon default, you are clear of the troublesome, complicated, and costly problems of liquidation.

The Background

As you can see, our concept of guaranteed appraisal backed by an insurance policy is somewhat revolutionary: a totally new idea that can build your Business Loan Department's volume and profit.

WHAT'S BEHIND IT?

THE Insurance Company has an original capital and surplus of $2,500,000. THE Insurance Company and THE Appraisal Corporation are wholly-owned subsidiaries of THE Investment Corporation.

---

ventory and equipment, though its value as a going concern was also considered. This value included factors that related to the expected future profitability of a company, including managerial competence, patents, and soundness of the industry.

[3] Though Friedlander commonly referred to THE Insurance Company's service as "writing insurance policies," technically the "insurance" was a bond on the appraisal contract which THE Appraisal Corporation made. In essence, the bond stated that THE Insurance Company was guaranteeing to the lender that the borrower's fixed assets were worth what THE Appraisal Corporation said they were by promising that, if the borrower were granted a loan equal to or less than his appraised asset value and if he defaulted on that loan, THE Insurance Company would pay the lender the amount of the bonded appraisal (less an agreed upon amortization schedule).

THE Insurance Company was limited by law to insuring on any given loan, up to 10% of its capital and surplus of about $2.5 million in January 1973. Therefore, if an insured company defaulted, the lender was assured that THE Insurance Company had sufficient resources to repay him in full.

In order to participate in larger loans, Friedlander insured whatever amount he could. For example, a bank might grant a loan for $500,000, of which $250,000 would be insured by THE Insurance Company. The $250,000 was 10% of THE Insurance Company's capital and surplus. The bank would be assuming a $250,000 risk. In case of default and liquidation, the bank would have first claim on its $250,000 against the defaulting company's assets. THE Insurance Company would collect whatever it could of the remaining assets and receivables, up to $250,000. Any excess would be used to cover the expenses of the sale, and then the balance would be turned over to the borrower. Since THE Insurance Company's services were actually extended for the full $500,000 loan, even though it had insured only a portion of it, it charged its fee on the total amount of the loan. The insurance fee on a $500,000 loan would be $10,000. In any case, whatever the liquidation collections were, THE Insurance Company was obligated to pay the bank $250,000.

The Board of Directors of THE are: George N. Friedlander, Financial Consultant; Ernest F. Friedlander, Treasurer, Exeter International Corp.; Leo Kahn, President, Purity Supreme, Inc.; Alford Rudnick, Esq., partner Brown, Rudnick, Freed, and Gesmer; Richard A. Smith, President, General Cinema Corp.; S. Sidney Stonemen, Esq., investor; Joe Zel, President, College Seal and Crest Co., Inc.

WHAT ABOUT REGULAR APPRAISALS, PERIOD?
THE Appraisal Corporation is fully qualified to work with you whether or not you require a guaranteed appraisal. If you later decide to make a loan within the limit of THE Appraisal, our performance can be fully covered by THE Insurance Company.

HOW CAN WE GUARANTEE OUR APPRAISALS, AND YOUR SUCCESS?
Because we've proved our ability to be right. For the past 40 years, our staff has handled appraisals and liquidations for some of the leading banks, insurance companies, and business corporations in New England. (Names will be gladly furnished on request.)

Our appraisal group includes many experts with years and years of experience. We stand confidently behind each of them. And their value judgments. All the way.

What Types of Coverage Does Our Plan Include?

Many types.

THE Appraisal Corporation offers three distinct and innovative guarantees. One covers your loans against equipment. Two more cover your loans against inventory. All terms are set forth in our standard contract, and the insurance coverage of THE Insurance Company is set forth in the performance bond form on file with the Insurance Commissioner of the Commonwealth of Massachusetts. We will be pleased to send you copies of both these instruments upon request. Look over the facts. Then simply match our service to your needs.

The Details: Facts About Insuring Equipment Loans

OUR INVOLVEMENT
The appraisal issued by THE Appraisal Corporation is guaranteed, provided your loan is not in excess of our appraisal limit (unless otherwise agreed upon).

POLICY PERIOD
THE Insurance is written for the entire period of the loan. Generally, a minimum of one year and a maximum of five years. But exceptions may be granted on an individual loan basis.

REPAYMENT SCHEDULE
Unless otherwise agreed upon in advance, your loans must set up an amortization schedule calling for equal monthly payments of principal.

APPRAISAL FEE
Our charge for an appraisal is approximately one percent of the appraised valuation, payable whether or not you choose to have our appraisal guaranteed and bonded.[4]

INSURANCE PREMIUM
The premium is payable to THE Insurance Company in advance[5] for the first year of the insurance bond, then on each anniversary date as long as the loan is outstanding.

The first year's premium is based on two percent of the original loan. Subsequent premiums are two percent of the principal balance which would be outstanding on each anniversary date, assuming the borrower had met the repayment schedule or two percent of the actual outstanding loan balance. Whichever is less.[6]

DEFAULT AND CLAIMS PROCEDURES
Upon default by the borrower and acceleration of the balance due you, merely submit a written demand for payment and tender of your security documents covering the equipment.

Within 120 days after we take possession and verify the equipment on hand based on our previous appraisal figures, you receive payment.

The Details: Facts About Insuring Inventory Loans

AMOUNT OF COVERAGE
When you call us in, we analyze the inventory and determine a formula for assigning values. This will serve as our basis for coverage, regardless of fluctuating values or quantities.

At this point, you will be given the choice between making (1) a supervised loan, in which a field warehouse or similar type of protection is set up with a THE Appraisal Corporation representative assigned to oversee the inventory, or (2) a non-supervised loan in which your borrower remains in control of the assets.

Obviously, we will assume broader responsibility on supervised loans. We assume the risks of loss or disappearance of supervised inventory except for fire and extend coverage risks. Our liability will be based on inventory that

[4] Friedlander said that 1% for an appraisal fee was considered high by some companies. THE Appraisal Corporation charged this rate because, once it gave an appraisal, it guaranteed that, for an additional 2% fee (see below), THE Insurance Company would insure the assets up to $250,000.

[5] The fee was actually not charged until the "insured" company received a loan.

[6] THE Insurance Company might bill either the borrower or the lender. Friedlander emphasized, however, that in reality the borrower eventually paid the fees.

should have been on hand at the time we take possession following notice of default, not the inventory that may actually be on hand.

On non-supervised loans, your coverage may be less, and you assume all risks of loss or disappearance of the inventory. In addition, our liability is limited to goods actually on hand which are in good and saleable condition at the time we take possession of the inventory following notice of default.

REPAYMENT SCHEDULE

You may set up any repayment schedule that is mutually agreeable to you and your loan customer.

INSURANCE PREMIUM

Premiums for THE Insurance bond backing up our appraisal and commitment for either a supervised or non-supervised loan will be based on two percent of the maximum coverage you request.

On supervised loans an additional charge will be made by THE Appraisal Corporation for supervision, which we'll agree upon in advance and describe completely in a separate rider.

DEFAULT AND CLAIMS PROCEDURES

On knowledge of default of non-supervised loans, you just submit documents and assignments allowing us to take over the inventory. Within 120 days after taking possession and computing the value of the inventory on hand based on the established formula, THE Appraisal Corporation will make full payment based on THE contract percentage terms. It's a guaranteed loan take over, backed by the insurance bond of THE Insurance Company.

On any default, on supervised loans, we have the right to immediate assignments of the security documents so that we can take over the inventory. Within 120 days after computing the amount of inventory that should have been on hand we will make full payment according to the established formula and the terms of the contract.

* * *

When THE Insurance Company first got started, Friedlander or one of his account executives was frequently involved in actually negotiating a loan. However, as loan officers became more familiar with THE Insurance Company's services, the staff simply told clients that it would insure their loans if they could find someone who would grant them. "If we're going to go out and actually search for the loan," said Friedlander, "we think we ought to be paid extra fees."

Friedlander's financial services had helped a wide variety of companies get loans. These included wholesale distributors of swimming pools, machine tool makers, companies in the aerospace and military electronics industries, a silver plating company, and importers who sought letters of credit from banks. His staff had appraised assets of retailers but had not insured loans for any retailers because, while they often had large inventories, these inventories were difficult to control. "Banks are interested in knowing not only what a company's inventory is worth but also that it will be there to liquidate if that's necessary," Friedlander said. "In retailing you can't tell. They can have a sale tomorrow and sell at basement prices all the inventory you valued yesterday at higher values. The only other companies I shy away from are construction companies. They have expensive equipment, but they tend not to take care of it when they get into trouble, and it often isn't as valuable as you'd think."

Most of the insured companies were located in New England and the Middle Atlantic states, though Friedlander had a few clients in Ohio, Chicago, and Texas. He dealt with about 15 banks, most of which were medium-sized banks in Massachusetts. He preferred to use the bank the client had dealt with previously if possible. THE Insurance Company was licensed to write insurance only in Massachusetts. However, it was Friedlander's interpretation that, if a company or a bank in another state approached THE Insurance Company and requested its services, THE Insurance Company could do business with the company. THE Insurance Company would not, however, solicit business outside of Massachusetts. Once his business was well established in Massachusetts, Friedlander planned to apply for licenses to write insurance in other states. Statistics concerning appraisals and bonds for the years 1969–1972 are given in Exhibit 2.

Mr. Thomas Lee, an assistant vice-president of commercial loans at the First National Bank of Boston, told the casewriter,

> Ernie can be really helpful in some marginal situations. I specialize in technically oriented research companies, and his legal limit is pretty small for these industries. The average loan for them is about $2 million; anything less than

Exhibit 2

THE INVESTMENT CORPORATION

APPRAISALS

	Number	*Fees*
1969	1	$ 850
1970	19	15,105
1971 (January–August)	4	2,476
1971 (September–December)	5	6,771
1972	59	63,458

INSURANCE BONDS

	Number	*Original bond value*	*Premium*
1969	4	$ 760,000	$15,200
1970	10	1,026,064	22,321
1971 (January–August)	2	270,000	5,400
1971 (September–December)	3	550,000	11,000
1972	19	2,028,628	45,297

> $1 million is pretty small. Also, with them, equipment's usually not an important consideration. Of course, I do handle all kinds of other loans of all sizes. I did call Ernie once about a steel fabricating company that wanted a $200,000 loan. It had huge machines and great inventory, but I had no idea how much they were worth, and I certainly didn't want to be bothered with selling them if the company folded. Ernie appraised them and assured me that they would always be worth more than the amount outstanding on the loan, so we made a deal. I don't think many people here have used the insurance, but then the concept is pretty new.

When asked about competition, Friedlander replied,

> So far as I know, we're unique. Government agencies such as the Small Business Administration have loan insurance programs, but ours is better because they place limits on participating banks' lending rates, and to be eligible for government loan insurance, the company must have previously been turned down by a bank. Furthermore, government programs require the bank to cover 10% of the loan guarantee. Consequently, risk-averse banks simply lower the amount of funds provided below what they might otherwise based on the existing collateral. Finally, there's the time factor—we work a hell of a lot faster than the government.

The Commercial Loan Industry

Mr. Donald Miller, executive vice president of commercial loans at the First National Bank of Boston, spoke of the commercial loan industry as follows:

> There's one important thing to remember in this business. Commercial loans are like fingerprints—no two are alike. Customers come to us for a million reasons. For example, in recent years taxes have increased so much that a lot of perfectly healthy companies couldn't hold onto enough money to expand. And since most companies have to offer 60- or 90-day terms, many companies have large accounts receivable but not adequate cash for operations. Then of course there are companies in trouble. We're glad to service them if they can convince us their losses aren't going to continue.

In 1972 when a businessman wanted to borrow money from a bank for his company, he would visit a loan officer in the commercial loan department of a bank. If he were already a client of the bank, the loan officer might check his record and make a "yes" or "no" decision in as little as 15 minutes. This was usually so in the case of loans for working capital or seasonal financing. It generally took substantially longer if the client wanted the loan for some unusual reason such as buying a new company or substantially expanding his capacity.

If the client were new to the bank, he presented to the loan officer any number of financial reports—balance sheets, profit and loss statements, details of his accounts receivable, a summary of inventory, cash flow, and profit-and-loss projections. If the company had been having difficulties, the client had to show in detail how he planned to turn it around. The loan officer always asked for business and character references of the manager and/or owner. Miller said, "We use a bunch of yardsticks here—debt to equity ratio, receivables, past track record, and so forth —and on all these we'll make allowances. But the one thing we won't compromise on is the character of the borrower."

The loan officer directed the verification of the evidence and often did much of it himself. Larger banks usually had a group of credit trainees who did only investigatory work. (First National's "street force" consisted of about ten men.) To do character checks, the investigator talked to the applicant's suppliers, competitors, customers, people in his community, and the bank with which he formerly did business. He called the business references, who were sometimes the applicant's previous employers, to determine the applicant's managerial capabilities.

To check accounts receivable, an examiner from the bank's factoring department reviewed the company's sales journal, general ledger, and receivables ledger. Sometimes he contacted specific customers to verify the amount owed to the client company. The examiner also "took a look at" the company's inventory and equipment. These usually were secondary considerations in a loan decision because banks were reluctant to get involved with selling equipment and inventory if a company were forced to liquidate. Occasionally banks would grant chattel mortgages on machinery. In such cases, they used private appraisers to evaluate the machinery, and about once a month they sent an examiner to verify that the machinery was still there. In the case of a first-time borrower, the total process from his initial visit to the bank until the "yes" or "no" decision was made could take anywhere from 24 hours to 6 months.

In 1972 First National had about 50 loan officers, all of whom had loan-granting power. In larger banks loan officers sometimes specialized—one might handle only construction companies, another oil companies, and so forth. First National had clients all over the world, some among the nation's largest corporations. Most commercial loan officers were college graduates and many had graduate degrees. Most large city banks had a two- to four-year development program for the loan officers. Smaller banks generally tried to hire men who had had some experience elsewhere. According to Miller, smaller Boston banks often looked to larger ones for help. "Sometimes they'll send men to First National for training," he said. "Occasionally one of their men will stay with us, and sometimes they steal one of our guys. It's not a malicious or underhanded business, though. The relationship among commercial loan departments is very good. It has to be because we rely so heavily on each other for credit checks of the thousands of companies we deal with."

Though several persons made inputs to a loan decision, the final decision was the responsibility of the loan officer. "To be a good loan officer, you've got to have imagination," said Miller. "Lots of borrowers don't really know what they need, so a loan officer has to figure out what their needs are now and what they'll be in the future. He's got to be familiar with equity markets too. He really has very broad powers as to what he can recommend to a client and to what he can commit the bank."

Banks were financially restricted by law to lending, on any one loan, no more than 10% of their capital and surplus. (First National's limit was $27 million.) In 1972 there were 154 commercial banks in Massachusetts. Their combined commercial loan portfolios totaled over $3.6 billion. The prime interest rate was about 6%.

One measurement banks used to determine their loan effectiveness was the charge-off rate. This was usually calculated by dividing the total dollar amount that companies failed to pay by the average dollar amount of the loans outstanding. The national average charge-off rate was seldom more than 1%.

Regarding the area covered and the size of the loans which First National made, Miller said:

> We go all over the world. But that's not true of smaller banks—their lending market is far more restricted, just like their dollar lending limit. Also, just because we're a big bank doesn't mean we grant only big loans. We grant a lot of small ones, even though they often take more time than the big ones. The real problem with smaller business loans is that smaller companies simply aren't managed as well as larger ones. They don't have the procedures, the record keeping, the controls, or the market competence that give us a basis for a good evaluation of their prospects. We, like others, want their business, but it's lots more risky and lots harder to appraise their future.

In addition to consulting a bank, a businessman seeking a loan might approach a commercial finance company. Commercial finance companies generally were willing to assume much higher risks than banks, but they also charged considerably higher interest rates. In 1972 the largest independent commercial finance house in the world was Walter E. Heller and Company, Inc. Heller's rates ranged from 12 to 14%. Mr. John D. Rusher, III, President of Walter E. Heller and Company of New England, Inc., said that the loans he granted generally ranged from $200,000 to $400,000. "Most of our client companies are privately owned regional companies, and the predominant characteristic in about 95% of them is managerial weakness. Our Boston operation is pretty small for Heller. We grant only about 30 to 40 loans a year out of about 500 or 600 applications."

Heller's Boston office had five loan officers who gathered information and made approve and decline recommendations to Rusher. Rusher reviewed all applications and could veto the recommendations of the loan officer if he so desired. "Our loan officers are really sharp men," he said. "But that's certainly not true of the industry as a whole. Five years ago there were dozens of small commercial finance houses, but they weren't able to attract high caliber people, and most either went broke or were acquired by larger organizations. The only other firm comparable to us in size is James Talcott, Inc., and it's soon going to be acquired by a large nonfinance corporation."

All the money that Heller lent was borrowed money. Its chief sources were institutional long-term lenders and commercial paper. There were no legal restrictions on the amount that a commercial finance company could lend.

Mechanics of Asset Liquidation

Friedlander described a typical "clean-up" operation when a loan went bad and he was forced to liquidate the assets to make good on his insurance bond:

> Recently there was a company in New Hampshire that had just come out of Chapter XI bankruptcy. Because the bank was nervous loaning them money, they had us appraise and guarantee the assets. Two weeks ago I got a call that the loan was bad. The next day I sent a man to New Hampshire to change the locks on the doors and start the liquidation of the inventory. As it turns out, we're going to do very well on the deal. We will only have to sell a portion of the inventory to get our money out, but because the company liked our approach, they've asked us to liquidate the remaining inventory (outboard motors) and equipment as well as handle their accounting and legal affairs to wind up the company. THE Appraisal Corporation will handle the liquidation and Exeter will do the windup. On all this extra work beyond just getting our own money out we'll get a fee at professional rates. These sorts of liquidations and windups can take anywhere from three weeks to two years.

Advertising and Promotion

Since THE Insurance Company was founded, most of its business had been generated by banks recommending the insurance to their clients. Friedlander thought that this was probably due to the fact that the only promotion he had done was direct solicitation of bank officials. It usually took Friedlander from 30 to 60 minutes to explain the insurance to a loan officer. He gave the loan officer a 12-page brochure that explained how the policy would benefit the bank and a supply of small five-page pamphlets that explained the services to a potential borrower.

In June 1971 Friedlander decided to try to see if he could generate volume outside. He called Mr. Leonard Kanzer, of Marvin and Leonard Advertising Company, Inc., the agency which had done the Friedlanders' brochures and pamphlets. Friedlander's goal was "to reach a level of writing two policies per week (figured at an average of $200,000 face value per policy—or about $400,000/year premium income plus $200,000/year in appraisal fees).

Kanzer recommended that the company undertake a promotional program using the name of THE Financial Services Group. Mr. Steven Kravette, who was assigned to do the creative aspects of the ads, suggested that, since Friedlander wanted to appeal to businessmen who were struggling to make it, he should use a "personal, shirt-sleeve format to create an image of someone who was willing to really get in there and work with them (see Exhibit 3).

Between September 1971 and February 1972 over $35,000 was spent in a multimedia campaign. Advertisements were carried in national general interest magazines (*Time, Newsweek, U.S. News and World Report*), business publications (*Business Week, Forbes, Nation's Business*), newspapers, direct mail, and television. In addition, some $3,000 was spent on public relations.

Exhibit 3

THE INVESTMENT CORPORATION

I just got bank loans for 16 companies that couldn't get bank loans.

"It's a very sad fact of life, but there's only one surefire asset for a guy who wants to get a business loan. Cash on hand. Or it's equivalent. Without it, it can be pretty tough.

"Inventory and equipment assets, even good solid ones, are no guarantee of getting a loan when you need it.

"And a businessman who needs a loan, maybe just to get rolling, or to finance a legitimate new venture, or for any of a hundred worthwhile reasons, can find himself in the lurch.

"That's when my company can help.

"First, we come out to a company's office, warehouse or plant and make an appraisal of its' inventory and equipment assets. Then we agree to pay the amount due if the company defaults on their loan. The businessman brings our agreement to his bank, and submits it along with his loan application.

"What we essentially do is assure repayment of the loan. Which means we assume the risk, instead of the bank. That makes it a whole lot easier for a bank to approve the loan.

"And that's really the whole essence of it. By supporting the small businessman in the form of a guarantee of his loan, we can make it possible for him to get a loan where he would otherwise have been turned down.

"In fact, that's precisely how we got loans for 16 companies that couldn't get loans.

"And you know, a loan at the right time, some ready cash when things get tight can mean a lot. In the long run, it might mean the difference between success and failure.

"Of course we can't help every businessman get a loan. But there are a lot we can help.

"What we can do for sure is sit down and talk it over. Instead of getting discouraged, call 357-5226 and ask for me, Ernest Friedlander, President."

Please contact me about your service that gets bank loans for companies that couldn't get bank loans.

NAME ____________________

COMPANY ____________________

ADDRESS ____________________

CITY __________ STATE ______ ZIP ______

TELEPHONE __________

52D Church Street, Boston, Massachusetts 02116

Friedlander considered the campaign a success. In December 1972 he reported that about 130 companies and two banks had contacted him as a result of the advertising:

> We were able to help 10 to 15% of the contacts. Many were just too small for us to be interested in and we could make those decisions in just a couple of minutes. I don't have figures on the dollar payoff of the campaign, though I'm sure we more than covered our costs since practically all of our business comes either from banks or people we talk to because of the ads. They have been very long lasting because I still get calls from people who say they remember the ads from last February.
>
> Although I think the ad campaign was successful, I came nowhere near the goal I set for increased business. I still consider promotion a problem and overall I've been disappointed with the way our concept has been received. All I can think of is either (1) people don't know we are here; (2) people don't understand what we do; or (3) there isn't the demand for my insurance service that I think exists.
>
> I don't know how to estimate the potential demand for my services. One thing I might do is try and find out how many and what kinds of loans banks refuse and why. If the bank were to come to me, they could get their spread with no risk. Maybe the problem is that the lending offices are evaluated as profit centers and a man is not willing to give up 3% of say an 11% loan to get my bonding and 100% security. Maybe the loan officers feel that they are capable of assessing a firm's ability to pay and don't feel they need any outsider to help them. Also, it's easier for a loan officer to say no to a loan than to call me. I guess I have to educate the loan officers.
>
> Some fairly sophisticated people who saw my ad tell me that they still don't understand what I do. I guess this ties back to the need to educate people to understand our concept. I recently hired a man full-time to be on the road talking to loan officers. Hopefully this will help.

Exeter International

This arm of the company was a management consulting group specializing "in very sick companies." Their fee structure was "very flexible"; it usually covered expenses and included a kicker based on performance; sometimes, a piece of the action. Although the initial contact with clients was made by one of the Friedlanders, the actual implementation of the consulting assignment under the terms of the "management contract" was carried out by one of four account executives with a diverse inventory of skills: one had a degree in chemical engineering plus an MBA from Harvard, another was an attorney and former assistant to the president of ITT-Sheraton, another was an industrial engineer, and the fourth was an experienced labor negotiator.

The size of Exeter's clients varied widely from companies whose sales were less than $200,000 per year to those with sales in the $50 million bracket. Exeter was capable of performing many services for its clients. If the business appeared viable, they would try to help turn the company around. If not, they might negotiate sales of the company's assets (with some part going to THE Investment Corporation as payment for services performed) or try to arrange for a merger. In this respect, Exeter could be seen as a vehicle that performed a slow and systematic liquidation of the client companies' assets. As of January 1973, Exeter held stock investments in about a dozen companies.

Other Operations

THE Investment Corporation also engaged in other business, such as operating two land sales companies in Hawaii and controlled over $24 million in real estate there and in other parts of the United States. In addition, the company was considering taking over the management of a major resort property in Maine. Most of these and other assets were acquired in partial payment for the management consulting services and direct loans from THE Investment Corporation, particularly when the client could not meet his regular contractual obligations for repayment.

Compensation

All employees of THE Investment Corporation were on fixed salary with frequent reviews. Mr. Friedlander (smiling) described their compensation as "generous, considering how much fun the people have working here. We give them all the standard health and welfare things, too."

Problems: Ownership, Control, Growth

The Friedlanders controlled THE Investment Corporation and its subsidiaries, but did not hold 100% ownership. THE Insurance Company, in particular, raised much of its $2.5 million capital through a private placement of THE Investment Corporation stock to those close to the Friedlanders.

Mr. Friedlander was willing to let growth take place slowly and in a controlled manner. He pointed out that the company was profitable enough at present to satisfy the investors, and that "it was a pain to get good people for the consulting company." Nevertheless, there did appear to be some signs of organizational strain at the present level of operations. Because the business was very cyclical, there were periods when the firm was either under- or overstaffed. Both conditions created organizational problems.

He added his thoughts about future directions for growth:

> Some people have suggested to me that I extend our operation. For example, I could do the appraisal for 1%, bond for 2%, and for an additional 1% actually find the money for the borrower. We could probably do that

fairly easily but we decided against it because borrowers might have a tendency to hold off paying us our fee until we got the loan.

Something we are considering very strongly is setting up an accounts receivable department to help smaller banks. We'll guarantee the receivables like a factoring company, except that we won't actually pay out money unless the receivables go bad. In effect, we'd be the factoring department for banks who don't have accounts-receivable expertise. This could be a good business for us as probably fewer than 30% of banks have accounts-receivable departments.

What I am really pushing for is completion of a $10 million private placement so that the insurance company can guarantee larger loans. It's just as easy, if not easier, for us to do a $1 million loan as one for $100,000.

I'd like to go public eventually, but it will be hard. Wall Street will have trouble understanding what we do.

American Home Shield Corporation

When we started out in 1971, we faced many problems. Our market research showed us that we had a good concept for which people were willing to spend several hundred dollars each year. However, people did not respond to our initial marketing approach. The reason was that potential customers had not heard of American Home Shield Corporation. We simply lacked credibility in the marketplace. However, we have bypassed that constraint by dealing with third parties: builders and realtors.

Now, two years later (March 2, 1973), we must decide how fast to expand. At the same time we know there are a host of issues we must consider, including our cash flow requirements, target markets, pricing, selection and training of journeymen, etc.

David Smith, President

History

American Home Shield Corporation (AHS), located in Paramus, New Jersey, provided maintenance and repair services to residences. It was incorporated as Maintenance Corporation of America (MCA) on August 2, 1971, as a Delaware corporation. In the same month the company borrowed $100,000 from Paul Revere Life Insurance Company in order to acquire I. Edward Brown, Inc., a New York corporation engaged in the sale of cleaning and maintenance supplies to commercial users. The parent company assumed the name of Republic Maintenance Corporation in November 1971. In September 1972 the name was changed to American Home Shield Corporation. The balance sheet as of November 30, 1972, is included as Exhibit 1. A profit-and-loss statement for 1972 and projections for 1973 and 1974 are given in Exhibit 2.

The company offered a new service to homeowners in late January of 1972. By March 1973 AHS had closed over 1,000 contracts, had a backlog of approximately 1,900 applications and was receiving applications at the rate of 75 per week. AHS anticipated, primarily based upon the estimates and plans of its major customers, that by the end of the fiscal year on August 31 it would have approximately 2,500 homes under contract. For that year, AHS anticipated total revenues of $1,900,000 with a loss of $474,000. Most of the revenues were projected to come from the Brown subsidiary, because AHS spread the revenues from its maintenance contracts over the life of the contract, thereby delaying revenue recognition. Most

Exhibit 1

AMERICAN HOME SHIELD CORPORATION AND SUBSIDIARY
CONSOLIDATED BALANCE SHEET
AS AT NOVEMBER 30, 1971 AND 1972

Assets	*1971*	*1972*
Current Assets:		
Cash, including $50,000 of Certificates of Deposit (1971)	179,044	66,006
Accounts receivable—trade, less allowance for doubtful accounts of $1,390 (1971) and $8,774 (1972)	174,250	255,105
Merchandise inventory	81,556	132,378
Sundry receivables	3,184	667
Prepaid expenses	11,657	7,002
Total Current Assets	449,691	461,158
Fixed Assets—furniture, fixtures and equipment at cost, less accumulative depreciation of $135 (1971) and $2,489 (1972)	3,012	13,769
Other Assets:		
Goodwill, less accumulated amortization of $450 (1971) and $1,624 (1972)	12,550	11,376
Deferred debt expense, less accumulated amortization of $100 (1971) and $17,979 (1972)	24,400	15,211
Covenants not to compete, less accumulated amortization of $3,624 (1971) and $18,125 (1972)	68,876	54,375
Organization expenses, less accumulated amortization of $50 (1971) and $1,121 (1972)	965	5,955
Preoperating expenses, less accumulated amortization of $25,737 (1972)	24,682	77,553
Security Deposits	600	10,441
	132,073	174,911
	584,776	649,838

Liabilities and shareholders' equity	*1971*	*1972*
Current Liabilities:		
Notes payable—bank	10,000	100,000
10% Senior subordinated promissory note payable—due October 31, 1973 to The Paul Revere Life Insurance Company, net of unamortized discount of $458		299,542
Due to Dinaden, Inc.		
7% Note	40,000	
Other	40,893	25,651
Current portion of long-term debt		10,000
Accounts payable	55,460	146,380
Accrued expenses and sundry liabilities	28,569	34,508
Unearned portion of service contract fee		67,441
Total Current Liabilities	174,922	683,522

Exhibit 1 (continued)

AMERICAN HOME SHIELD CORPORATION AND SUBSIDIARY
CONSOLIDATED BALANCE SHEET
AS AT NOVEMBER 30, 1971 AND 1972

	1971	1972
Long-term Debt:		
10% Senior subordinated promissory note payable—due October 31, 1973 to The Paul Revere Life Insurance Company, net of discount of $1,000	299,000	—
Amounts due to former shareholders	50,000	40,000
	349,000	40,000
Total Liabilities	523,922	723,522
Shareholders' Equity		
Capital stock, par value $.01 per share—authorized 1,000,000 shares; issued and outstanding 560,000 shares (1971) and 729,000 shares (1972)	5,600	7,290
Capital Surplus	93,400	751,004
(Deficit)	(38,146)	(831,978)
	60,854	(73,684)
	584,776	649,838

Exhibit 2

AMERICAN HOME SHIELD CORPORATION
Historical and Anticipated Profit and Loss

	Fiscal year ending August 31		
	(Unaudited)	*(Anticipated)*	
	1972	*1973*	*1974*
Revenues	1,105,353	1,900,329 *	4,568,607 *
Cost of sales	830,922	1,500,526	3,089,056
Gross profit	274,431	349,803	1,479,551
Selling general and administrative	850,067	794,197	1,034,120
Other income	8,277	—	—
Interest expense	26,835	30,000	7,500
Income (loss) before Income taxes	(594,194)	(474,394)	437,931
Income taxes	—	—	210,207
Net income (loss)	(594,194)	(474,394)	227,724

* Assumes $1.3 million in revenues in 1973 and $1.5 million in 1974 with nominal profits from the Brown subsidiary in both years.

of its anticipated loss would come from the costs of expanding its maintenance business.

The Service

Through a Homeowners' Protection Plan the company offered, for a fixed annual fee, repair and maintenance of a home's four major systems: heating, electrical, plumbing, and air conditioning. In addition AHS provided an exterminating service at extra cost. For the four basic services, the homeowner was charged from $150 to $450 per year depending upon the coverage and the age, size, and type of construction of the home (a rate card work sheet is included as Exhibit 3). The average price of the contract was $225. The fee covered all *parts* and *labor* for required repairs of the covered systems. AHS guaranteed service within a 24-hour time period. The plan is outlined in detail in Exhibit 4.

David Smith, President of AHS, explained the appeal of his service as follows:

> Our service sells for two major reasons, convenience and security. A homeowner has the convenience that one call can secure service for any major system in the house, thereby avoiding the necessity of making multiple calls for

Exhibit 3

AMERICAN HOME SHIELD CORPORATION
Rate Card Work Sheet
Age of House

Number of rooms*	1–4 Years	5–10 Years	11–20 Years	21 or more years
1–7	$155.00	$180.00	$220.00	$235.00
8–11	184.00	205.00	235.00	270.00
12 or more	235.00	265.00	280.00	305.00

Basic fee	$ ______
Hot water heater—add $20	______
Radiant heat—add $35	______
For 2 or more family house—add $35	______
Central air conditioning, add $20/ton (12,000 BTU = 1 ton)	______
Sump pump—add $15	______
Humidifier—add $20	______
Sub total	______
Sales tax A.H.S. plan only	______
Chargeable certifications $25 each	______
TOTAL	$ ______

* Excluding bathroom

Exhibit 4

AMERICAN HOME SHIELD CORPORATION
Homeowner Protection Plan

We will provide and perform the services described in this agreement, during the term hereof, subject to the terms and conditions set forth.

MAINTENANCE AND SERVICES

HEATING SYSTEM

a. MAINTENANCE—During the normal heating season, we will inspect the furnace, boiler or other heating unit and provide preventive maintenance service, including cleaning of the entire combustion side of the heating equipment, cleaning and adjustment of all controls and safety devices, decarbonization of boiler, lubrication of all circulator bearings, motors, blowers, blower bearings and burners, analysis of flue gases, adjustment of the unit for greatest efficiency and economy, and cleaning or replacement of the furnace filter.

b. SERVICE—In addition, we will service, repair or, if necessary, replace defective parts and controls, as follows:

Hot Water

GAS FIRED—Circulator motors, expansion tank, aquastat, low water cut-out, pressure reducing valve, relief valve, zone valves, flow control valve, valves, air vents, pressure gauges and pressure controls, gas valve, emergency switches, thermostat (plain, heat-cool), transformer, relays, all electrical wiring to and from the boiler, thermocoupling, burners, gas cocks, flue pipe, radiators, convectors, all heating elements, all small fittings and the hot water boiler.

OIL FIRED—Circulator motors, expansion tank, aquastat, low water cut-out, pressure reducing valve, relief valve, zone valves, flow control valve, valves, air vents, pressure gauges and pressure controls, gas valve, emergency switches, thermostat (plain, heat-cool), transformer, relays, all electrical wiring to and from the boiler, burners, flue pipe, radiators, convectors and all heating elements, fuel pump, nozzle, adapters, nozzle lines, insulators, ignition wires, ignition terminal, drive couplings, circulator couplings, pump strainers, oil valves, impellers, air cone, air-stat, burner head, burner motor, cadmium cell relay, combustion chamber, combustion head, electrodes, end cone, fill cap, filter cartridge, firematic valve, ignition transformer, stabilizer, stack relay, turbulator, vent alarm and vent cap, all small fittings and the hot water boiler.

Steam

GAS FIRED—Gas valve, pressure gauges, pressure controls, relief valve, high and low water cut-out, water gauges and glass tubes, thermostat (plain), emergency switch, relay, transformer, gas cocks, burners, thermocoupling, flue pipe, expansion tank, valves, air vents, radiators and radiator valves, all small fittings and the steam boiler.

OIL FIRED—Expansion tank, high and low water cut-out, relief valve, valves, air vents, pressure gauges and pressure controls, emergency switches, thermostat (plain), transformer, relays, all electrical wiring to and from the boiler, flue pipe, radiators, nozzle, adapters, nozzle lines, insulators, ignition wires, ignition terminal, drive couplings, circulator couplings, pump strainers, oil valves, impellers, air cone, air-stat, burner head, burner motor, cadmium cell relay, combustion chamber, combustion head, electrodes, end cone, fill cap, filter cartridge, firematic valve, ignition transformer, stabilizer, stack relay, turbulator, vent alarm and vent cap; gauges and glass tubes, all small fittings and the steam boiler.

Hot Air

GAS FIRED—Fan belts, variable speed pully, fan and limit controls, gas valves, burners, thermocoupling, heat exchanger, blower fan motor, motor mounts, blower, thermostats (plain, heat-cool), gas cocks, transformer, relay switches, emergency switches, flue pipe and all small fittings and the hot air furnace.

PLUMBING SYSTEM

a. MAINTENANCE—Semi-annually, we will inspect the entire exposed interior plumbing system, including all water pipes, valves, faucets, fixtures, waste and drain pipes, pumps, drains, traps and humidifiers to spot and diagnose malfunctions and trouble areas.

Exhibit 4 (continued)

AMERICAN HOME SHIELD CORPORATION

b. SERVICE—In addition, we will perform the following services relating to the plumbing system within the interior of the home: repair all water line breaks and leaks, remedy all drain and waste line stoppages; repair or, if necessary, replace all defective washers and faucet stems and faucets (plain); clean, repair or replace all traps under sinks and vanities; repair or replace defective assembly parts within water closets; repair or replace all valves leading to sinks and vanities; repair or replace shower body and waste lines on bathtubs; repair or replace pressure reducing valves leading into main water line; repair or replace all main water valves within the house; repair all gas leaks inside house and replace all defective valves and fittings (excluding valves or fittings on appliances, or appliances themselves); repair or replace all hose cocks outside the house; repair or replace all water lines damaged by "freeze-ups"; repair or replace all flexible gas connectors on gas range, oven, dryer or other gas-fired utilities; repair flushometer and replace all defective parts attached to flushometer; and repair or replace all check valves. Optional: service and replacement of sump pumps and humidifiers.

Hot Water Heater

GAS FIRED—Thermocoupling, gas cock, air vent, flue pipe, gas valve, pressure relief valve, all small fittings and the hot water tank.

ELECTRICAL SYSTEM

a. MAINTENANCE—Semi-annually, we will inspect the entire interior electrical system, including all wiring, fuses, fuse boxes, circuit breakers, electrical switches, electrical receptacles, doorbells, door chimes and outside receptacles, to spot and diagnose malfunctions and trouble areas.

b. SERVICE—In addition, we will perform the following services relating to the electrical system within the interior of the house: repair, or if necessary replace all electrical switches, electrical receptacles ("outlets"), electrical circuits (including repair of electrical short circuits), circuit breaker panel, all single and double pole breakers, fuse boxes, doorbells, door chimes and outside receptacles.

CENTRAL AIR CONDITIONING SYSTEM

a. MAINTENANCE—During the normal cooling season, we will inspect the central air conditioning unit and provide preventive maintenance service, including cleaning of condenser coils, lubrication of blower motor and all other moving parts, checking of condensate disposal system for proper operation, adjustment of blower speed (if necessary) and cleaning, or replacement, of the air conditioning filter.

b. SERVICE—In addition, we will service, repair or, if necessary, replace the condenser, compressor, fan motor, all fan belts, thermostats (plain, heat-cool), relays, transformers, filters, magnetic starter, capacitors and high and low pressure controls; check and lubricate all moving parts; clean and service all valves and electrical connections; clean commutators on motors and motor housings; and if necessary, re-charge the air conditioning system.

TERMS AND CONDITIONS

RENDITION OF SERVICES

We will provide a serviceman (or servicemen) to render all service to be rendered by us pursuant to this agreement (items designated "b" above) within 24 hours after telephone request for any such servicing. Repairs will be effected and the services will be rendered by our serviceman within a reasonable time thereafter without charge to the homeowner, provided the homeowner is not in default in the payment of the annual protection plan charge set forth in this agreement. Requests for service will be accepted by us 24 hours a day, 365 days a year.

This agreement only covers repairs, replacement and services made necessary by normal usage. Each servicing will provide labor and parts needed, in our sole opinion, to restore normal operations. We shall have sole option of determining whether a malfunction will be corrected by repair or replacement.

Exhibit 4 (continued)

AMERICAN HOME SHIELD CORPORATION

The homeowner shall give us notice, within a reasonable time after any operating failure of the need for service, and shall endeavor to protect the property from further damage until repairs are made.

All maintenance (items designated "a" above) to be rendered hereunder will be made pursuant to appointment with the homeowner.

TERM OF CONTRACT

This agreement shall be effective and the services to be performed shall be performed for a period of one year from the date of approval of this agreement by us, provided the request for service is made during the contract period. The agreement shall not be in effect until receipt by the homeowner of a written acceptance by us.

ASSIGNABILITY

This agreement may be assigned by the homeowner during its term to any bona fide purchaser or transferee of the property subject to approval by us, which will not be unreasonably withheld. Written notice of any such transfer, and the request for assignment of this agreement, shall be furnished to us within 10 days of such transfer.

REJECTION AND TERMINATION

We reserve the right to reject the Protection Plan requested if, on inspection, we deem any portion of the equipment or utility systems to be covered not in proper working order or unsuitable for servicing.

This agreement shall be void if, whether before or after the request for or rendition of service, the homeowner has wilfully concealed or misrepresented any material fact or circumstance relating to the condition of the home or its utility systems.

This agreement shall, at our option, be void in the event any of the equipment or utilities included hereunder is serviced by anyone other than us.

Our obligation to render services or effect repairs shall terminate in the event that the homeowner alters, modifies or adds to the structure and systems covered by this agreement, unless the homeowner has first advised us of any proposed alteration, modification or addition and we have given our written agreement to extend the coverage under this agreement accordingly.

EXCLUSIONS

This agreement does not cover servicing, maintenance, repair or replacement of any parts or components of utility systems or equipment not specifically enumerated in this agreement. Unless otherwise specified herein, this agreement specifically (but not by way of limitation) excludes household appliances, humidifiers, window or portable air conditioners, lawn sprinklers, pools, electrical fixtures, intercom systems, antennae systems, glass breakage, underground wiring and structural components (including footings, foundations, slab, roof, floor joists and walls). This agreement does not cover service, repairs and replacement required as a result of inadequate power supply, power failure, wars, floods, lightning, earthquake, storms, fire, smoke, electrical failure, riots, vandalism, accidents, acts of God, or other than normal usage of the utility systems and equipment enumerated in the agreement. This agreement does not apply to redecoration necessitated in the opening of walls, floors, or ceilings to repair plumbing, heating, electrical or air conditioning systems or any parts of such systems, and extends only to the repair, replacement or maintenance specifically set forth, and, if necessary, to the restoration to building standard walls, floors or ceilings opened by us in effecting such repairs.

WAIVER OF LIABILITY

We shall not be obligated to correct building code or zoning violations or perform services where permits cannot be obtained because of such violations.

We shall not be liable for any consequential or secondary damages or other conditions resulting from malfunction of the parts, systems, repairs or replacements described in

Exhibit 4 (continued)

AMERICAN HOME SHIELD CORPORATION

this agreement, or from delays or failure to render service due to conditions beyond our control, including labor difficulties. Neither are we responsible for any loss or damage alleged to be caused directly or indirectly by our service or by the timeliness of the rendition of our services.

RIGHT OF RECOVERY

We may request from the homeowner an assignment of all right of recovery against any party for loss to the extent that services with respect to that loss are rendered by us. If any component subject to this agreement is covered by any warranty or guaranty in force at the time of the need for parts or services, we shall be subrogated to the extent of any services performed or materials supplied hereunder to all of the homeowner's rights or recovery therefor. The homeowner shall do everything necessary to secure such rights and shall do nothing to prejudice such rights.

different services. Perhaps more important is the task of security created by the shortage of skilled journeymen. This shortage frequently creates great difficulty for a homeowner in securing a local tradesman and particularly one whose quality is reliable and whose arrival is predictable. We remove the worry of this problem.

To ensure the high quality of our serviceman and prompt, predictable response time, we only use our full-time trained force. We also remove the fear of unexpected major repair expense. Other than our initial fee, there is no charge for parts or labor.

After the receipt of an application, AHS sent one of its skilled inspectors to inspect the house before it accepted coverage on the house. A page from the 10-page inspection form is included as Exhibit 5. Because AHS was at risk for parts and labor

Exhibit 5

AMERICAN HOME SHIELD CORPORATION
Inspection Form

Page ______

EXTERIOR:

Electricity: Overhead ____ Underground ____ No. of Wires ____

Gas: City ____ Tank ____

Water: Well Pump ____ City ____

Sewers: Septic ____ City ____ Other ____________________

Building: Brick ____ Wood ____ Stucco ____ Brick & Wood ____ Masonry ____

Condition: Good ____ Acceptable ____ Poor ____

Exhibit 5 (continued)

AMERICAN HOME SHIELD CORPORATION

Garage: Yes ____ No ____ Number of Cars ____ Attached ____ Detached ____

Doors: Side of house ____ how many ____ Leaders Yes ____ No ____

Rear of house ____ how many ____ Leaders Yes ____ No ____

COMMENTS: ____

____

____

BASEMENT:

Basement Drainage: Sump pump: Yes ____ No ____

Make ____________________ Model ____________________

Serial number ____________________ Date Installed ____________________

Condition: Good ____ Acceptable ____ Poor ____

Walls: Concrete Block ____ Poured Concrete ____ Cinder Block ____

Other ____________________

Condition: Good ____ Acceptable ____ Poor ____

Floor: Concrete ____ Wood ____ Tile ____ Other ____________________

Condition: Good ____ Acceptable ____ Poor ____

Heating System: Gas Fired ____ Oil Fired ____ Coal Fired ____

Elec. ____ Hot Water ____ Hot Air ____ Steam ____

Other ____________________ BTU in ____ BTU out ____

Make ____________________ Model ____________________

Serial number ____________________ Date installed ____________________

Condition: Good ____ Acceptable ____ Poor ____

Circulator Pump: Yes ____ No ____ How many ____

Size of Flanges: 3/4″ ____ 1″ ____ 1 1/4″ ____ Other ____________

Make ____________________ Model ____________________

Serial number ____________________ Date Installed ____________________

Condition: Good ____ Acceptable ____ Poor ____

Zone Valves: Yes ____ No ____ How many ____

Make ____________________ Model ____________________

Serial number ____________________ Date Installed ____________________

Condition: Good ____ Acceptable ____ Poor ____

costs, it attempted to identify potential problems before they occurred. If any of the four systems of the house was not in sufficiently good condition to justify the risk of maintaining it, AHS gave the homeowner these options: (1) AHS makes the needed repairs at a stated cost; (2) the homeowner has the repairs done independently; or (3) AHS omits the system from the contract. In most cases AHS makes such repairs, and this brings additional revenues. Besides the initial inspection, AHS provided semiannual visits for preventive maintenance, checking for incipient problems and thereby protecting the homeowner from the inconvenience of a system breakdown and AHS from added costs.

Marketing

AHS marketed its services through a four-man salesforce primarily to real estate brokers, builders and developers in New Jersey. Charles Smith, Vice-President-Sales, commented on the marketing concept:

> Our success to date is because of the advantages our service offers to both the buyers and sellers of a house. The AHS policy enables a broker to sell a "guaranteed house." This gives a prospective buyer the security that the major systems of the house he buys will have been inspected by an independent party and that if there is trouble we will correct it at no cost. The buyer further receives the convenience and security of buying a house with year-round maintenance and repair service. Both buyer and seller are saved from aggravation after closing. This security expedites sales, maximizes selling price, and consequently increases volume for brokers selling the service. The brokers pass the cost of the AHS service on to the seller and in some cases the buyer. However, for the seller the service represents a small cost in the total selling price of the house. On contracts received from brokers, we receive the entire contract price at the time of closing the house. Since it is the seller who contracts for the service, a broker cannot guarantee us that all its houses will include the guarantee. However, Berg Realty feels that our service is such a valuable marketing tool that it has based a radio and newspaper advertising campaign around it and believes that 80% of its houses will be covered by such contracts.

Because of this emphasis by Berg, the largest realtor in New Jersey, other realtors followed suit where permitted. Berg had an exclusive agreement with AHS in certain counties of New Jersey. In other areas AHS had contracted with other brokers; however, AHS was extremely selective as to which brokers it would allow to offer the service.

For the builder and developer the AHS service offered the same primary advantage it offered to real estate brokers, that of increased marketability of a guaranteed home. A guarantee of no major systems repair costs and the convenience of an ongoing maintenance service expedite sales. Furthermore, AHS removed a major source of buyer aggravation by expediting the initial repairs on a new house. Once a family had selected a new house (prior to moving in), AHS inspected the house to enumerate to the builder all deficiencies of the house, from dripping faucets to cracked foundations. For the builder who subcontracted much of his work, the repair of these deficiencies represented a tremendous problem. He had to contact many different subcontractors and get them back on the job for tiny repairs. Because the subcontractors were busy on new jobs, it might be very difficult and time-consuming to get them back, causing considerable customer aggravation. By hiring AHS, one call by the builder obtained most repairs relatively promptly. AHS, after waiting 10 days to give the subcontractors sufficient opportunity to make the repairs, made the repairs and backcharged the builder who in turn backcharged the subcontractor. Thus, not only did AHS secure ongoing contracts, it received profitable repair business. AHS would not make major repairs such as structural, basement, roof, and driveway work. For the builder, the AHS service represented far more than the convenience of one-call repairs. The decrease in customer aggravation was a very important public relations tool, particularly because a high percentage of a builder's business came from referrals. AHS also gave independent quality control assistance, meeting regularly with builders to discuss recurring problems. These meetings frequently resulted in improved methods and/or different subcontractors. The builder paid for the contract, paying one-half of the contract premium upon closing and one-half six months later.

In 1972 Kaufman and Broad (K&B), a large developer with projects in all parts of the United States, ran an initial test project of the AHS concept of its 196-house "Timber Ridge" development in Lakewood, New Jersey. K&B received such enthusiastic customer response to this test that it subsequently contracted to have AHS maintain a 650-unit condominium complex, a 180-house development, and another 274-house development. K&B had further indicated they expected to use the service on approximately 60% of the nearly 2,500 homes per year they planned to build in New Jersey. AHS was currently negotiating for the maintenance contract for several developments being built by Prel Corporation. It was expected that Prel would deliver 1,500 houses each year. Management anticipated that in the next several months it would provide maintenance services to other major developers as well as other smaller builders.

AHS had also sold its contracts directly to homeowners. Retail contracts had been generated more by referral than from AHS's promotional activities. AHS had utilized both direct mailings and media advertising. It had also used its own salesforce to a small extent for retail selling. In addition, AHS had received considerable media exposure, including articles in local newspapers, an article in the *New York Times,* a feature on WCBS-TV local news, and a nationwide radio feature on WCBS radio. AHS had also commenced marketing its services through mortgage lenders and insurance agents. The results of a casewriter-conducted telephone survey of six randomly selected homeowners with the AHS service are included in Exhibit 6. The results of a survey of an AHS target county in New Jersey is included as Exhibit 7.

Exhibit 6

AMERICAN HOME SHIELD CORPORATION
Telephone Survey of Customers

Question	Customers A	B	C	D	E	F
Like service?	yes	yes	yes	yes	yes	yes
How heard about service?	newspaper	newspaper	friend, newspaper	newspaper	brochure	newspaper
How many times used in 1972? (besides semiannual inspections)	2	3	4–5	4–5	5	6
Was service prompt?	yes	adequate	within 24 hours	yes	within 24 hours	yes
Suggest improvements?	none	none	none	none	none	include appliance repair
How much does it cost?	don't know	$137–140	don't know	$131	don't know	$260–300
Would you pay more?	don't know	up to $20	no	up to $15	up to $50	up to $30
Recommended service to others?	no	yes	yes	no	yes	yes
Age of home?	15	13	35	11	7	5
Length you have lived in it?	15	4	10	11	7	5

Exhibit 7

AMERICAN HOME SHIELD CORPORATION
Survey of 76 Households in Target County

I'd like to ask you how you feel about several parts of the American Home Shield plan.

a. Do you feel the timing (1 to 24 hours) is:

An excellent feature	29	38.2
A good feature	37	48.7
Or unimportant	3	3.9
No answer	7	9.2
	76	100.0%

b. Do you feel the 24 hour a day availability is:

An excellent feature	30	39.5
A good feature	32	42.1
Or unimportant	6	7.9
No answer	8	10.5
	76	100.0%

c. Do you feel the two inspections a year are:

An excellent feature	18	23.7
A good feature	39	51.3
Or unimportant	12	15.8
No answer	7	9.2
	76	100.0%

d. Do you feel the money-back guarantee is:

An excellent feature	27	35.5
A good feature	33	43.4
Or unimportant	7	9.2
No answer	9	11.9
	76	100.0%

e. Do you feel the one telephone number for all repairs is:

An excellent feature	33	43.4
A good feature	27	35.5
Or unimportant	5	6.6
No answer	11	14.5
	76	100.0%

f. Do you feel the price of the plan, $250.00 per year for an average home, is:

Too high	34	44.7
About right	30	39.5
Or too low	1	1.3
No answer	11	14.5
	76	100.0%

Exhibit 7 (continued)

AMERICAN HOME SHIELD CORPORATION
Survey of 76 Households in Target County

g. If this plan were available, would you be:

Very interested in it	9	11.8
Slightly interested	25	32.9
Not at all interested	31	40.8
No answer	11	14.5
	76	100.0%

AHS believed renewals of contracts originally acquired from builders and realtors would provide a source of considerable future business. Although AHS had had little renewal experience to date because few contracts had come up for renewal, it felt it could reasonably expect a 50% renewal rate (see Exhibit 8 for the renewal experience to date). This expectation is based primarily upon customer responses to mailings and is strengthened because its service program, including the semiannual preventive maintenance checks, is particularly aimed at creating customers sufficiently satisfied to renew. This is expected to be a particularly strong force with those customers purchasing new homes where AHS's efforts to ease the early pains of occupying a new home are designed to lay the groundwork for an ongoing customer base.

Economics

In many respects the AHS contract was a form of insurance in that it insured against repair expenses, both parts and labor, on home systems. However, unlike the life or casualty insurance business, there did not exist a substantial body of actuarial statistics based upon historical experience for maintenance costs. The Department

Exhibit 8

AMERICAN HOME SHIELD CORPORATION
Analysis of Renewals
May 1, 1973

Month	*Number of subscribers up for renewal*	*Number rejected by AHS*	*Total eligible renewals*	*Renewals*	*Not yet due*
January	3	0	3	3	0
February	40	5	35	35	0
March	55	1	54	50	0
April	79	1	78	71	0
May	75	0	75	2	73

of Commerce had compiled some statistics on the cost of maintaining homes. This cost information had been further supplemented by the experience of AHS's own tradesmen. These estimated costs had then been factored into a pricing structure. AHS projected the cost of maintaining the average home, for which AHS would receive a $225 per year contract, would run no more than $135. A qualified AHS journeyman could handle a minimum of 150 contracts based on the assumption that on average, an account would require 1.1 hours of service per month.[1] It was felt that 200 contracts/serviceman was not an unreasonable goal, because travel time would be reduced as greater geographic concentration of accounts was achieved. Since the average journeyman received $12,000 annual compensation (including fringe benefits), the average labor cost per contract was $80 allowing $55 per contract for the cost of parts and truck expenses which AHS felt was reasonable. Experience in the first year had verified these assumptions. A monthly cost breakdown is included in Exhibit 9.

AHS closely monitored its cost experience. Each AHS journeyman filled out a complete report after every service call. This information was computerized together with all account information. Thus, on a monthly basis AHS received an analysis of all contracts and their costs to date. AHS was currently operating out of only two service centers, which resulted in considerable inefficiency in journeyman travel time. Parts costs were running approximately $3 per contract per month. AHS believed it had further cause for reassurance because it felt relatively confident in its ability to identify future maintenance requirements at the time of its initial inspection. To test its inspection abilities, AHS chose to take on certain accounts which it had identified as being problems, not only as a test of its abilities but also for their advertising potential. To date, AHS had correctly predicted problems with most of these accounts. In the case of failure of systems in new houses provided by builders, AHS, in most instances, was protected from parts costs by the manufacturers' warranties.

AHS believed that if its cost experience proved unfavorable, it would be able to raise its prices accordingly. To test this belief AHS had recently raised its prices on new contracts 15%. This caused no complaints from any builder or realtor and, in fact, AHS had been led to believe by its major customers that further price increases would be acceptable if required.

Employees

In the spring of 1973 AHS had a maintenance staff of 13 trained and qualified licensed personnel, including two service center supervisors, two inspectors/servicemen, and two full-time exterminators. Jerry Kaufman, Vice-President-Service, supervised all maintenance operations. Mr. Kaufman, prior to joining the company in November 1971, was a sales manager for an educational publishing company. During the mid-sixties, Mr. Kaufman was employed as a journeyman plumber by a New City heating and plumbing company.

---

[1] Includes travel time.

Exhibit 9

AMERICAN HOME SHIELD CORPORATION
Monthly Cost Analysis

		Contracts per man	
		150	*200*
Average contract fee earned per month ($225/yr.)		$18.75	$18.75
Variable expenses:			
Serviceman salary and benefits (10%)	$1,030/mo.		
Uniform rental	18/mo.		
Truck rental, expense, and insurance	460/mo.		
	$1,508/mo.	10.05	7.54
Material cost per contract		3.00	3.00
Total variable cost per contract		13.05	10.54
Contribution margin per contract		$ 5.70	$ 8.21
Monthly fixed expenses:			
Service department—			
Management	3,680		
Office salaries	2,880		
Service supervision	4,529		
Miscellaneous	100		
Selling expense—			
Sales promotion and printing	1,500		
Salaries and commissions	2,000		
Travel and miscellaneous	500		
General expenses—			
Salaries	4,248		
Rent	1,600		
Telephone	2,000		
Accounting and legal	2,500		
Data processing	400		
Miscellaneous	800		
Payroll taxes and employee benefits	2,046		
Interest	1,700		
Amortization	4,500		
Total fixed expense	34,983		

All AHS personnel were uniformed and participated in an in-house orientation program to train them in the AHS method and philosophy of operation and in specific service procedures. AHS servicemen were licensed to operate in any county of New Jersey and Rockland County, New York. The workforce was not represented by a union. In addition to those employees directly involved in the maintenance activities, AHS employed 21 people at I. Edward Brown. The total AHS payroll was 48.

Mr. Kaufman commented on the employee situation:

> We demand high standards of appearance and courtesy of our servicemen. We feel that high-quality service and personnel standards are essential not only to differentiate our service from independent local journeymen but also to expedite renewals. A major determinant in our success will be our ability to attract well-qualified journeymen as we expand both within an area and into new areas. I am confident we can attract journeymen for several reasons. Primarily, AHS offers an independent journeyman a greater degree of security than he knows as an independent with a highly seasonal work cycle. In addition, we offer certain fringe benefits (stock options, life and health insurance, etc.) unknown to the smaller independent contractor.

Property and Equipment

AHS was headquartered in 4,200 square feet of space in Paramus, New Jersey, in a building that housed the executive offices, the communication facilities, and a local service center. Motorola had designed a radio system for AHS with which AHS could not only communicate with all of its trucks, but also identify the trucks' location. The $60,000 system, which was not yet installed, was designed to serve both as an expediency and as a source of management control over servicemen. The service center in Paramus and a second 2,000 square foot service area in Lakewood, New Jersey, served as a storage area for spare parts, a shop, a parking site for AHS trucks, and a coordinating point. AHS anticipated opening enough service centers so that all accounts would be within a 30-mile radius of a service center, thus minimizing servicemen's travel time. AHS had 12 leased service vehicles, two of which were radio equipped. I. E. Brown was located in a 14,000 square foot facility in Hoboken, New Jersey. Rent on all AHS facilities was $40,800 per year.

Competition

AHS knew of no other company which offered guaranteed multiservice maintenance through its own staff. AHS knew of at least two "cooperative" maintenance organizations in the Midwest. These organizations served as middleman between homeowners and local journeymen. AHS felt that in order to reliably control the quality of service and the response time, it must use its own personnel. There were many companies providing service on a contract basis for individual systems, particularly heating and air conditioning; but none of them offered more than the one service. AHS believed that its major competition came from the many local journeymen who provided service on individual systems on a call basis. These journeymen normally charged between $10 and $20 per hour for their services.

The I. Edward Brown division competed with a great number of companies, many much larger than itself and many tied in directly with industrial maintenance contractors. The business was extremely competitive and although service was a major factor, price was an equally important one.

Exhibit 10

AMERICAN HOME SHIELD CORPORATION
Cash Flow Projection:
Last Six Months of
Fiscal Year

	In force	1973 March	April	May	June	July	August
Number of Residences under Contract	1001	157	190	317	341	330	326
Builders	175	40	60	140	140	140	140
Realtors	105	40	40	40	60	60	60
Retail	721	50	50	100	100	100	100
Renewals		27	40	37	41	30	26
Cash Received on Contracts#							
Builders ($215)			4,000	6,000	14,000	14,000	14,000
Realtors ($180 now $225 in June)		7,200	7,200	7,200	13,500	13,500	13,500
Retail ($160)		2,666	5,332	10,665	13,332	15,999	15,999
Renewals			3,808	6,059	6,137	7,027	6,519
Charge-backs ($40/house)			1,600	2,400	5,600	5,600	5,600
Total Inflow		9,866	21,740	32,324	52,569	56,126	55,618
Variable Cost:							
Labor		19,604(13)*	19,604(13)	25,636(17)	27,144(18)	30,160(20)	31,669(21)
Materials ($3/mo./contract)**		2,667	2,817	3,126	3,483	3,873	4,275
Fixed Cash Expense (see Exhibit 9)		30,500	30,500	30,500	30,500	30,500	30,500
Total Outflow		52,771	52,921	59,262	61,127	64,533	66,443
Net Cash Flow (Deficit)		(42,905)	(30,981)	(26,938)	(8,558)	(8,407)	(10,825)

 # Payment terms
Builders—½ immediately, ½ at 6 months
Realtors—Paid at closing, average close 90 days after receipt of application
Retail—Payable within 90 days—1/3 each month

* (Number of men)

** There are no material costs associated with builder contracts since systems in new homes are covered by guarantees.

Exhibit 11

AMERICAN HOME SHIELD CORPORATION
Projected Number of Contracts
Fiscal Year
1974

Month	*Builders*	*Realtors*	*Retail*	*Renewals**
September 1973	140	100	100	48
October	140	100	100	36
November	140	100	100	36
December	140	100	100	70
January 1974	140	100	100	46
February	160	100	100	63
March	180	100	100	78
April	200	100	100	95
May	220	100	100	153
June	220	100	100	170
July	220	100	100	165
August	220	100	100	163

* Assumes a 50% renewal rate.

The Future

David Smith outlined his future plans:

We anticipate entering another major metropolitan market, at the end of approximately one year. At the end of this time, but not before, we will have established a sufficiently large customer base and had sufficient operating experience with this customer base to be in a position to predict the majority of the problems associated with establishing the service in a new area. On this basis we can move into a new area on a "textbook" basis. We should not only be able to predict operating problems, but should experience a fast, profitable buildup of customers. This is for two reasons. First, any new area we move into will be done in coordination with our existing customers. Berg has major operations in Florida, Houston, Tucson, and San Francisco. K&B has major operations on both coasts and in the Midwest. Thus, we would not move into a new area without a minimum number of guaranteed contracts. Second, by the time we expand, we should have established sufficient credibility and reputation to enable us to attract immediately new builders and realtors. At a later date, on a similar basis, we anticipate entering several additional major metropolitan markets.

Cash flow projections for the last six months of FY '73 are included in Exhibit 10. Exhibit 11 contains the projected number of contracts for FY '74.

Overview of Competitive Situations

Competitive situations occur when individuals or institutions are at cross purposes; they represent situations in which there is at least some element of conflict. To cite some business examples, two firms battling for market share are clearly at cross purposes. So are gasoline stations waging a price war, a new car dealer and customer haggling over price and options, a number of companies bidding for a NASA contract, the writer of an insurance contract and the insured, and an IBM salesman and his customer working out the details and price of a multimillion dollar computer installation.

In most of these examples the individuals and/or institutions are not entirely at cross purposes. The car dealer and his customer, for example, while at cross purposes regarding price, share the objective of closing a mutually advantageous deal. Most competitive situations, in fact, contain elements of both mutual interest and cross purpose. This mixture is part of what makes their analysis so challenging.

Competitive situations pervade every sphere of human activity—military strategy, diplomacy, government, politics, business, sports, and our private lives, to mention obvious ones. Because they are so pervasive, competitive situations have been studied from many viewpoints, including those of economics, politics, history, sociology, psychology, military strategy, and the mathematical theory of games. Depending on the administrative situation under consideration, any one or a combination of these various viewpoints may aid decision making.

To facilitate deciding upon which viewpoints to bring to bear on a particular situation—or, indeed, which aspects of a particular viewpoint are relevant—it helps to be aware of the dimensions on which competitive situations differ. For example, two situations may differ in the degree to which the parties have mutual interests. To facilitate thinking about competitive problems in general, it is well to be aware of the elements shared by all such situations.

This note addresses these issues. It explores the common elements of competitive situations and the significant dimensions on which they differ. First, however, a description of a competitive situation is given—the battle for passengers on the New York–California routes by American Airlines, TWA, and United. This will serve as an illustrative backdrop for the discussion of the similarities and differences found in competitive situations.

An Example: The Battle for Transcontinental Air Passengers[1]

Consider the battle for transcontinental air passengers that has been going on since the early 1960s. The long hauls are the routes of greatest profitability and the New York-California runs have been termed the "essence of the essence." Thus, competition has been fierce among the three largest airlines, American, TWA, and United, who collectively control about 90% of the market. In the days of piston aircraft, just before the battle started, TWA was the dominant transcontinental carrier. However, American, then in second place, was more aggressive than the others in introducing jet aircraft. As a result, it surpassed TWA in the early sixties, achieving 38% of the market by 1962. For a while TWA, awaiting delivery of its Convair jets, and United, awaiting DC-8s, used services to counter American's jets. The competitive weapon continued to be used after TWA and United became competitive with aircraft. Since the industry is regulated, price competition was largely ruled out.

About 1963, TWA introduced in-flight motion pictures and it was some two years before American and United followed suit. Later, TWA was to offer a choice of two movies. Shortly thereafter, United introduced stereo entertainment and others soon followed. During the mid sixties, United tried single-class service and after several disastrous years reverted to the traditional coach and first-class service. In a series of moves and counter moves, the three competitors offered increasingly elaborate meal service, including choice of entrees or steak cooked in-flight. By 1967, TWA was touting choice of seven entrees in its first-class service, all cooked in-flight. United increased the number of main course choices from two to four in its coach section. Each carrier, as it introduced a new innovation, featured it in its advertising, which was constantly being used to differentiate the line's service in the eyes of the public. American was the business traveler's line, United the vacation traveler's.

Meanwhile, now that all the carriers had sufficient jets, they began to escalate the frequency of their flights, in part in response to growing passenger demand. More importantly, the escalation stemmed from the widespread belief that the carrier with the greatest number of departures would get a share of market more than proportionate to its share of departures. This was so because many travelers initially contact the carrier offering the most flights to their destinations when they make reservations. Consequently, number of departures became one of the most competitive weapons.

However, by the late sixties, just before the introduction of the wide-body jets, airline capacity became scarce. Nonetheless, the carriers continued their capacity war on the transcontinental routes, at some sacrifice to their less desirable routes. For instance, when American added another flight in 1967, TWA felt it had to delay the introduction of its new Cincinnati-Los Angeles nonstop service to match American's flight. By 1967, flights were so frequent from New York to California that *Aviation Week* (August 14, 1967) called them a "shuttle." American had 16

---

[1] We are grateful to Laurence Doty of *Aviation Week and Space Technology* for providing much of the factual material for this section.

of the 43 flights a day, TWA had 14, and United had 13. Their market shares were ranked in the same order. Further, timing of schedules was important; the lines constantly jockeyed with one another for the more favorable departure times.

The capacity battle intensified with the introduction of the 747s about 1970. The carriers, formerly capacity constrained, suddenly found excess capacity, because the introduction coincided with an economic recession. After load factors (percentage of occupied seats) had fallen under 40%, American finally tried to break the cycle by unilaterally cutting back on capacity. It hoped the others would follow. However, United stood pat and TWA increased capacity. Month by month American watched, waited for the other carriers to reverse themselves, and lost market share and large sums of money. Finally, it relented and again entered the fray.

In the meantime, plane configuration became the chief competitive weapon; the "battle of the coach lounges" took place. Spurred by the empty seats Continental Airlines removed some of the planes used on its Chicago–Los Angeles run and installed a lounge in the coach sections in early 1972. The Big 3 quickly followed suit on the transcontinental routes. Soon one carrier featured two lounges. Then came the piano bars. First American and later the others added pianos to their lounges, where passengers could gather, play the piano, sing songs, and imbibe. The battle of the lounges abated in mid-1973.

In 1972, there was a wave of reoutfitting stewardesses, with first one carrier, then another introducing new uniforms. More moves and counter moves on food took place, with one carrier touting Trader Vic food.

Faced with excess capacity, the carriers then tried fare reductions. TWA filed an application with the Civil Aeronautics Board (CAB) for special look-ahead fares where, if the customer booked 90 days in advance, he paid approximately one-half of the regular fare. In defense, American soon filed an application for an identical plan. Not to be outclassed, United filed for similar fares with seven-day-ahead booking, but a minimum seven, maximum nine-day stay. Defensively, the others matched the United plan. The United plan met with the greatest success and finally was adopted by all carriers. The net effect, of course, was to lower the average fare collected by each carrier.

Up to this point in the battle, the carriers had been making capacity decisions independently, without consulting one another. Load factors had dropped below breakeven to 36–38%; competition was so fierce that running planes through maintenance and scheduling crews was a problem. In 1972, the CAB began to encourage negotiations among the carriers to limit capacity. The negotiations started in the summer under protest from the Justice Department and various consumer groups; by October 1972 the first capacity reductions led to 10% improvement in load factors. Starting in June 1973 fuel shortages provided further incentives to get together; and after protracted negotiations, further capacity reductions followed. As capacity was being cut back, TWA was hit by a six-week strike, thus giving major assistance to the two remaining carriers. In early 1973, the carriers used advertising to vie for market share on the basis of quality of service. This was spurred by American which was trying to recoup market share lost due to a pilot slowdown December 1972–January 1973, causing bad service. Beginning in February 1973 it started touting the improvement in its service and the others countered by praising their own service.

This particular competitive battle well illustrates the richness of competitive situations; the wide variety of weapons used, the constant moves and counter moves both offensive and defensive, the importance of timing, the uncertainty about the opponents' moves, the uncertainty about whether the opponents' moves will succeed, and the great complexity of the total situation. It also serves as a source of examples as we look at the elements common to all competitive situations and significant dimensions of difference.

Elements Shared by all Competitive Situations

The elements common to all competitive situations are:

1. *The Rules of the Game:* Perhaps most important of all, there are specific rules that govern the behavior of the competitors. These are generally agreed-upon competitive practices, general laws, as well as specific industry regulations. For instance, the airline industry is a heavily regulated one; competitors may not change fares without prior approval of the CAB.

2. *Potential Payoffs and Ultimate Outcomes:* There is a range of outcomes or "payoffs" for each competitor that could possibly occur—in the case of the airlines the various market shares, passengers carried, or profits. As a result of the actions of the competitors and possibly events beyond their control, there is an outcome to the situation—one of the potential payoffs. Each competitor considers some outcomes to be more desirable than others—for instance, more market share is better than less. While this seems obvious, each has relative preferences for the various dimensions of the payoff: market share, immediate profits, long-range profits, cash flow, etc.

3. *Outcomes Determined by Competitor Choices and Other Events:* Each competitor has open to it a range of potential strategies it can employ. In the airline example a strategy would consist of a stance regarding number of departures, schedules, plane configurations, in-flight services, advertising, etc. Each competitor has some control over the situation, but it does not have full control. Some of this control is in the hands of the other competitors. American's success, for example, depends in part on its strategy, but is heavily influenced by what TWA and United do. Furthermore, some elements may not be in the control of any competitor, such as the strike closing TWA in 1973, the economic downturn of 1970, and the pilot slowdown that hit American in December 1972.

Significant Differences Among Competitive Situations

We next turn our attention to five dimensions on which competitive situations can differ significantly. As we discuss each dimension, we will try to indicate how it can affect the analysis of the competitive situation.

1. *Number of Competitors:* The number of competitors, or distinct sets of interests, is one of the fundamental ways to categorize competitive situations. We distinguish between those with two competitors and those with more than two. It is

customary to speak of a conflict situation having two competitors as *two-person* and one with more than two competitors as *n-person,* although it may just as well be called a many-person situation. (The word *person* is game-theory shorthand for a party at interest in a competitive situation . . . in short, one of the conflicting "sides." In this sense, a person may be an individual, a group of individuals, a corporation, or a nation, for instance.)

The two-person conflict situation is the common one in which you and your adversary have conflicting interests. Certainly the seller of a house you would like to buy does not share your interest in a lower price. Two contractors have clear conflicting interests in bidding for a construction contract.

When there are more than two interested parties, new analytical considerations enter. First, the situation gets more complex because there is more to keep track of. Second, and more important, there is the possibility that some of the competitors might form coalitions to deal more effectively with the others. For instance, the Arab nations banded together to set a common oil policy with the developed nations in 1973, even though the individual nations had somewhat differing interests. Similarly, companies form trade associations to lobby for common interests, workers form unions, and nations sign mutual aid treaties. Sometimes the coalitions are only implicit and tacit, such as banks following common policies in setting their prime rates. Also, workers sometimes band together in informal groups to socially control "rate busters," and card players will gang up on the leader to keep him from amassing the number of points necessary to win the game.

When one is faced with coalitions, a useful analytical issue is their stability. How likely is it that members of the coalition will break with their original coalitions to join others, form new ones, or strike out on their own? Is it advantageous to encourage or discourage this? Which group is advantageous for you to join?

Another implication of n-person situations is simply the need to recognize the number of different interests. For instance, suppose you are negotiating to purchase a small machine shop from its founder and his son. The founder wants to retire and divorce himself financially from the enterprise. The son would like to continue in its management and if he is successful, share in the rewards. If you fail to recognize these different interests, if you consider "the owners" to be monolithic, you risk missing an appropriately structured deal which will be more in the interests of all parties—including yourself.

2. *The Degree of Mutual vs. Opposing Interest:* There are some situations in which the interests of the competitors are strictly opposed; "one man's gain is another man's loss." At the end of a poker game, for example, there is usually just an exchange of assets. Since winnings are balanced by losses, their net is equal to zero. In game-theory terms this type of competitive situation is called a *zero-sum game.*

The zero-sum game may be thought of as one extreme—that of pure conflict. At the other extreme are situations of pure common interest—situations in which the "competitors" win or lose together, and both prefer the same outcome. For instance, in bridge the two partners do their utmost toward achieving full cooperation. Their fates are inextricably intertwined.

It is difficult to find administrative examples of either pure cooperation or pure conflict, however, since the vast majority of competitive situations lie between these extremes. Here the opponents exhibit varying degrees of common interest and competition. Formally, these situations are designated *non-zero-sum games.*

In a labor negotiation, for instance, labor and management may not agree concerning the division of their joint profit, but both probably want to make the joint profit as large as possible. Thus they have both conflicting and common interests. Similarly, the three airlines competing for transcontinental passengers—while they would each prefer gaining market share at the others' expense—would mutually prefer competitive alternatives that profitably stimulate passenger demand, or permit handling a given number of passengers at lower cost.

The competitive aspects of most business, political and military conflicts can only be analyzed in a realistic way if the elements of common interest as well as conflict are taken into consideration.

3. *Whether Communication or Agreement About Actions Can Take Place Among Competitors:* In the airline example we saw the competing carriers making independent decisions on departures. The eventual result was that departures escalated and load factors dipped below breakeven. Later, when the carriers were permitted to decide jointly on departures, the number of flights was reduced to a profitable level.

This difference in behavior indicates the significance of, perhaps, the most important distinction one can make about competitive situations—whether or not the competitors are allowed to communicate explicitly before making their moves. If so, the situation is said to be *cooperative*. Otherwise, it is designated *noncooperative*.

In general, the more the players' interests coincide, the more significant is their ability (or inability) to communicate. Where there is pure common interest, the problem is entirely one of communication. In competitive situations in which the decision makers have some common interests and some conflicting interests, communication, if permitted, plays a complex role in determining the outcome. In two-person pure conflict situations, communication cannot benefit either competitor.

Sometimes the competitors must take action in the complete absence of communication, as do dealed bidders at an auction. Under such noncooperative circumstances, the analysis of a competitor's potential actions might influence your own actions. Sometimes competitors can communicate to a limited degree, as with public pronouncements, but must stop short of actual agreement on a mutual course of action. For example, the president of TWA might announce that it will match American's departures plane for plane. The purpose of this type of communication —threat, promise, or bluff—is to attempt to influence the opponent's behavior. The effect of these limited communications now enters the competitive analysis.

Finally, there is the cooperative situation where the competitors are in full communication and attempt jointly to reach agreement. Promises, threats, and bluffs continue to play a role in attempting to change each other's preferences and attitudes. But now the adversaries, through dialogue, also attempt to create new alternatives and problem solve—trying to reach a mutually agreeable situation. This is the bargaining situation.

Before leaving the subject of communication, the role of tacit communication bears mentioning. In most market place competition, the law forbids collusion. Nonetheless, although competitors do not communicate directly with each other, "understandings" often develop. Price leadership in the steel industry is a good example. The kinds of understandings that emerge and their stability is an important aspect of such competitive situations. So is the way that competitors "signal" their intent to one another, without explicitly communicating. For example, American was apparently unsuccessful in signalling the other airlines to cut back capacity in 1971.

4. *Whether (and, if so, how often) the Competitive Situation Will Be Repeated:* Another important dimension of difference is whether the same participants will be involved in a similar situation in the future. For instance, the buyer and seller of a house most likely will not, whereas a particular union and company will be back at the bargaining table at the end of the just-negotiated contract. Similarly, the competition between the airlines is an on-going one.

In one-shot situations competitors are usually out for all they can get. In the on-going situation, they often behave much differently. All they can get is tempered by what the impact will be on what they might get in the future. If management negotiates too stringent a contract this time, the union may be more militant the next time.

If an on-going situation is noncooperative in nature, a clear opportunity is provided for tacit communication and understanding to take place.

5. *The Amount of Information Each Competitor Has About the Competitive Situation and About the Other Competitors:* Information is one of the most important commodities in a competitive situation. Were this not so we would not see the tremendous secrecy with which Detroit's automakers treat their new designs. We would not see a petrochemical manufacturer photographing a competitor's outdoor chemical facilities from the air, so that its chemical engineers could infer the production process from the configuration of the facility and thus the competitor's costs. We would not see frogmen from one oil company checking on the offshore drilling rig of another.

Indeed, some feel that much can be gained by analyzing a competitive situation, particularly a bargaining one, in terms of exchange of information. What would you like to know about your competitor? What would you like him to believe about you?

There is a host of things about which you might have relatively abundant or limited information. For instance, you may know specifically who your competitor is or you may not. If you are a building contractor submitting a bid to the city of Hartford for the construction of its proposed civic center, you may not know who your competitors are. In order to make a decision about how much to bid, you may have to hypothesize about the typical competitors facing you.

More frequently you know who your competitors are, but you may still have substantial information gaps. You may not know what competitive options your competitors are considering, much less which ones they will choose. Nor will you have a clear understanding of their objectives, or of their views—sanguine or pessimistic—of future conditions in the markets for which you are competing. You may not have information about the innermost workings of your competitor's organization, such as costs or resource allocation. (In the airline industry cost information is publicly reported, for instance, but in most industries it is not.)

Sometimes there is uncertainty about the value of the item for which you are competing. In competing for oil rights leases, for example, bidders usually do not know for certain the value of the reserves on the property. To make matters worse, some competitors may have a better idea than others about the value of the item. For instance, the seller of a company often has important information unavailable to the buyer.

Sometimes, unfortunately, you fail to have complete information about yourself and your organization. What are your objectives? Do you have the resources necessary for the competitive battle that might ensue if a particular course of action is chosen? (Apparently GE and RCA did not when they announced plans to become greater factors in the computer industry and then withdrew.)[2]

From the discussion and examples cited above it is evident that decision making in competitive situations is a tricky, delicate, difficult business. Hopefully this taxonomy, of similarities and differences in competitive situations, will be a first step toward thinking about these problems more effectively.

---

[2] Fruhan, William, "Pyrrhic Victories for Market Share," *Harvard Business Review,* September–October 1972.

Will Innkeeping History Repeat Itself With the Budget Motel?

> "The budget motel is a good example of how history repeats itself in the domestic lodging industry. The essence of the budget motel concept is to offer clean, modern rooms to the public for $10 or less per night and still make a decent return on investment. Twenty years ago, motel operators were trying to do much the same thing. Their success is well-documented, along with the hard times that befell the hotel industry, chief victim of the motel boom. Now, with the advent of the budget motel, the conventional motels' share of the market must be considered vulnerable to inroads that can be made by this new form of competition. While it is too early to determine how successfully and how rapidly the budget motel will develop, if the budget concept is legitimate (and from all indications it appears to be so), the impact it will have on the industry over the next five years will probably be significant to the top 90 per cent of industry volume."

These words, taken from a recent study of the domestic inkeeping industry, should give operators pause. Still in its infant stage, the budget operation, as presently conceived, seeks the same market as does the conventional motel, and the industry may revert to its practice of garnering market share with a new vehicle rather than developing new business.

Maybe it can be argued that there is a definite new market for the budget room, that it will attract persons quite distinct from those who want the best in accommodations and services and are willing to pay for them. And maybe the budget motel will help prod the 50 per cent or so of the American population who have never stayed overnight in a hotel or motel into trying them. Maybe. But these seem to be the outer parameters of the budget market, and, in the main, the economy operations are out to attract the businessman, young persons, retired persons, and families—just as is the conventional hotel & motel.

We can't extrapolate growth figures, but it looks as if the budget operation will proliferate—and at an above-average return on investment. The attractive profit picture could conceivably entice some of the large existing chains to enter the field.

Source: *Hotel and Motel Management,* November 1972, pp. 40–45. Reprinted by permission.

(Holiday Inns tried it with Holiday Inn, Jr., which proved unfeasible—mostly because of construction costs.) But it isn't expected that the major chains will enter the budget market in a big way because of the negative impact this would have on existing franchises.

It's sometimes hard to believe that the budget operation can be as profitable as it seems—charging such low rates while, on the whole, providing excellent accommodations. Low construction costs, elimination of "frills," keep costs down, of course. Different chains regard different facilities and services as frills, but all seem to have agreed to forego bellhops, valet service, room service, meeting and banquet rooms, suites, etc. Beyond this, efficient operating techniques are essential to the success of the budget operation. Many budget chain corporate philosophies are built around the idea that management and the operational team will be the biggest determinants in whether or not a property will get its share of the market. And if occupancy, long used as a yardstick to measure the industry's progress, is to be taken as an indicator, then the budget chains are doing incredibly well.

But enough theorizing. Let's get down to the practical aspects of the budget motel. Motel 6 was the granddaddy of them all, opening its first property in 1963. The basic rate has gone up from \$6.00 to \$6.60 during the last decade of operation (other rates are \$7.70, \$8.80 and \$9.90), but still is much lower and has increased much less than rates in conventional operations. We don't have profit figures, but it's pretty sure that the chain is making a profit. Motel 6 now has approximately 100 properties in 20 states. Average rate runs about \$7.70, and system-wide occupancy on inns opened two years or more is more than 80 per cent.

Motel 6 was the author of many cost-cutting innovations that have become standard in some of the other budget chains. These include: The hiring of husband and wife teams to manage the properties, in many cases retired persons; the use of one-piece fiberglass shower stalls with rounded corners that reduce bathroom cleaning time; the use of disposable drinking glasses to save on dishwashing; employment of maintenance teams that operate from the headquarters office, visiting each property at intervals and taking care of routine repairs and painting so only emergency work is done by local contractors; an on-premise laundry in which all linen is washed, cutting cost of linen to something like 35¢ per day per room; traveling housekeepers who visit properties to teach maids the latest cleaning techniques and acquaint them with new products; closing the office and shutting off phones at 11 p.m.

Motel 6 rooms are somewhat smaller and more spartan than those of its followers. They have showers but no tubs, are rather plainly furnished. While just about all the other budget chains offer free TV—and many color at that—Motel 6 is still using the coin-operated black and white TV. The properties have no restaurants. The chain's policy is one of cash on the line, and no credit cards are honored. All this economizing keeps average construction and furnishing cost at about \$6,000 per room.

If Motel 6 began the budget trend, others refined it. Let's take a closer look at some of the hot young chains in the field.

Chalet Susse

Based in Nashua, N.H., Chalet Susse International was organized in 1967 by Fred Roedel, president. The inns feature Swiss architecture and decor, are designed for easy add-on unit expansion. All AAA requirements are fully met, and the lodges are approved by the major referral groups. AAA and Mobil reservations systems are used, and credit cards are accepted.

Two types of accommodations are offered: Room with double bed or one with two double beds, and the two prices are permanently posted on electric signs in front of each lodge. Direct-dial phones, coin-operated guest laundry facilities and a swimming pool are among the amenities.

The company does the building itself, using pre-cast, pre-stressed concrete techniques. Operating costs are kept minimal—e.g., laundry is done on premises, furniture and plumbing are designed for minimum maintenance, restaurants and bar facilities are contracted for or provided by other firms and located next door to the Chalet lodges. The chain reaches a breakeven point near 50 per cent occupancy.

Chalet Susse recently stopped issuing franchises, partially because of the tight franchise laws, but also because the company can make more money operating the lodges than by franchising them.

William Johnson, VP of operations, articulated his company's philosophy and in the bargain did a good job of outlining the concepts behind the budget operation:

"In their Operations Breakthrough report, Booz & Allen stated that by 1978 'there'll be a demand for a wider range of rates and accommodations, especially at the economy end of the scale. This demand is attributed to a growing market of young and old travelers and will be required to stimulate the less-affluent non-traveler market.'

"OK, so now we have young and old travelers. But the boys at Booz & Allen missed a few. Those are the ones Chalet Susse is adding on. We work very heavily to attract the businessman or salesman who is operating on his own expense account. He's spending his own money and looking for the best deal. We've also gone after the company auditor who's got maybe 20 or 30 men on the road all the time, and he's singing the blues over the expense sheets lately. We can tell him that if his guys come to Susse Chalet, they'll be spending $9.70 for a room—exactly. Another category we seek is the middle income family—the silent majority. This family is headed by a man who works 50 weeks a year, has big food bills, is paying off a mortgage and a car, has a couple of kids to whom he wants to show the country, two weeks in which to do it and a very tight budget on which to operate. We want to give them what they want.

"Young people are action-oriented. They don't want to hang around a motel. They want to be where things are happening. They're informal, and don't want a fancy place to stay or special services. They've been brought up in the self-service age. I've had young people tell me that they've been embarrassed by the presence of a bellhop.

"As for older travelers—these are often the husband and wife of 50 or more who have plenty of time but a limited amount of money. They're looking for good, clean, inexpensive accommodations. And they all want to be on the first floor—one reason why we build our motor lodges the way we do.

"The businessman who is spending his money is a big, big market. They want a reservations system, a direct-dial phones system, because a lot of them do their work at the hotel. And they want service with a smile.

"We spend a lot of time analyzing location. We take locations with good business or economic bases nearby, fairly close to a large economic concentration. We try to get on an interstate, always in an area with a high incidence of vacationers. We try to add one additional 'gimmick.' If there's a college nearby or a big tourist attraction, we capitalize on this. Our inn in Brattleboro, Vt., has two colleges nearby—Putney and Marlborough. They have functions going on all the time, and they use the rooms just when you've got them available. They go home for holidays, just when other people come for vacations.

"We build our rooms so that they are easily cleaned. We don't have much fancy stuff—which is what takes time to clean. We buy the best beds we can get, have plenty of desk space, a tub and a shower. Women want a bathtub. We have black and white TV. Color isn't necessary. I took a check last year and the average time TVs were in operation was 11 minutes per night. Each motel has a small pool—but it looks big to those who don't see a pool much. We keep them square, so they are easy to cover in winter.

"We have training programs for our husband-wife innkeeping teams. The office is open only from 7 a.m. to 11 p.m. After that it's just trouble for management.

"We buy centrally, and every requisition goes through my office. We have daily occupancy reports, weekly labor reports and monthly profit and loss statements for each property.

"And in advertising, we bang away at price, price, price."

Scottish Inns

The Scottish Inns idea was born with a man in the modular construction industry—Charles E. Scott. In the mid-60s Scott built a prototype 48-room Scottish Inn in Harriman, Tenn., and for two years this operation was studied, motel management procedures developed, construction techniques refined. Scottish Inns of America, headquartered in Kingston, Tenn., builds all its rooms "in the house" on the assembly line. The rooms are standard size— 12 x 20 feet for a single, 12 x 24 feet double, including bathroom and shower. They are built and shipped from either the Tennessee or Florida plant to on-site locations by truck. Rooms are furnished down to the carpeting, drapes, even mirrors on the wall.

Rooms come off the assembly line at the rate of one per hour. Scottish Inns also manufactures much of the furniture used and constructs larger modular units for the restaurant section of the motel complex. Normal time to erect a 100-room Scottish Inn complete with furnishings, restaurant, pool and equipment is 35 to 40 days. Rooms as shipped can be installed, and the operator of the motel can be given the key for something like $6,000 a room, a big factor in setting Scottish Inns rates, among the lowest in the budget realm.

The restaurant, which is included in each motel location, features good food served in a family-style manner. A lazy susan is placed in the center of each table, filled with a large assortment of meats, vegetables, breads and desserts. Costs are modest by industry standards, and the service is fast.

Scottish Inns does not operate the company-owned motels—which constitute a significant portion of all Scottish Inns. (And the trend seems to be toward more company-owned properties.) It leases its hotels to independent operators in return for 50 per cent of the room revenue and 10 per cent of the restaurant revenue. Scottish Inns pays financing costs, taxes, insurance and major repairs, and everyone is happy and gets a nice return on his investment, it seems.

The company has an exclusive franchising agent, Motel Financial Corp., (formerly Scottish Inns International) headed by Doyle Gaw, president. Franchises used to be available to individuals, through Motel Financial, but recently the two companies have encouraged the formation of some 10 corporations to buy and operate multiple franchises. These "chains within chains" operate on a separate basis from the parent company. One of these, publicly-owned Economy Inns, was recently acquired by the parent company. Franchisees pay Scottish Inns a fee of $5,000 for each motel they build, 2½ per cent of room revenues and an $1,800 annual sign fee.

Says Doyle Gaw, "In addition to marketing and selling the budget concept, the method of financing is crucial in building the budget room. Coming from an investment background, one of the ways we approach financing is by putting together equity groups. Right now these groups have raised combined equity money exceeding $21 million. Beyond this equity base, we look for further financing at rates we can deal with. The company has lines of credit for three-year construction financing, based on bank lines. Though the bank lines are for construction, we've been able to place them on into premise loans.

"Locations of the inns are based on careful surveys and are usually near interstate highway access for maximum traveler exposure. To sum it up, the basic concept, construction at the right price, location and financing are prime factors in successful marketing of the budget room."

Regal 8 Inns

Headquartered in Mount Vernon, Ill., Regal 8 Inns is a group of corporate-owned or corporate-controlled motels, based on the premise of "affordable excellence."

The two-story, fire-proof facility, standard in the chain, features block and concrete construction, combination shower baths and tubs, free color TV, swimming pool, free ice, free coffee in the lobby. Regal 8 inns do not operate food facilities, but each property has a suitable restaurant in the immediate vicinity. In those locations where facilities deemed adequate are not available, a restaurant is built and leased to reputable operators.

Regal 8 is big on centralized control which encompasses rigid cost control, group purchasing, simplified accounting, quality control in construction and maintenance, personnel recruitment and training, uniformity of rates, furnishings, cleanliness and service.

The chain considers location of utmost importance, and site selection is determined by a feasibility study, land availabilities and expansion opportunities.

Regal 8 VP Richard Topper, an alumnus of Motel 6, where he served as GM from 1962 through 1967, details the thinking behind his budget chain:

"The budget motel is a discount. It hopes for higher occupancy because of lower rate. But a budget operation shouldn't mean a second-rate operation in a second-rate site. You've got to be seen—to be in the middle of everything. You need to be with other motels. How can you be a discounter unless you have a pattern to discount from? If you go off by yourself somewhere, you might well be considered the highest-priced operation around, as well as the lowest."

Continues Topper: "Different locations qualify for more or less units. When I see a site, I don't judge how many rooms I can fill during the peak period of the week. I'm interested in what my occupancy is going to be on the low night. I judge so that on the low night I have about 50% occupancy. You need high occupancy to make a profit in the budget operation."

The Regal 8 view of the operating team is that the manager needs to be a "working" manager, one who thinks budget.

And says Topper, "Budget units have to hold services to a minimum. No one can put out a Cadillac at a Ford price. We won't attract the salesman who wants a meeting room, but so what? Let him go to a place that has meeting rooms. The conventional operation tries to appeal to a vast spectrum of persons; they want to feel they appeal to 80 or 90 per cent of the entire market. The budget property goes for a specific segment of the market. If you can appeal to 25 per cent of your market area and only have 10 per cent of the rooms in the area, then you've got a good deal."

Days Inns of America

Founded in 1970, Atlanta-based Days Inns of America wasn't heard from much until the last few months. Now its growth is becoming something of a phenomenon. Headed by Cecil B. Day, the chain now has 29 inns open, a 100 per cent growth during the past year. And another 29 inns will be opened during the next five months. Plans call for 100 inns to be in operation by 1974. Of the inns open, about 60 per cent are company-owned, 40 per cent franchised. However, according to Dick Wright, director of advertising and public relations for the chain, future growth should come to a great extent from franchises. The chain expects to be nationwide within eight years or so.

Days Inns offers some services that aren't offered by the other budget chains. One of these is a 24-hour, toll-free, central reservations service. Days Inns also includes a playground and a gasoline service center at each property; none of the other budget chains provide these.

Days Inns' restaurants are operated by Tasty World, owned by Nortico Corp., a Days Inns company. Tasty World also operates the gas stations, along with gift shops.

Construction is on-site, some of it pre-fab. Units are planned so that all rooms open on the outside, meaning no interior corridors to heat. Another saving: There is no lobby, and the registration desk is located between the gift shop and restaurant areas, cutting down on the number of employees necessary to serve these facilities.

The rooms are as luxurious as possible for a budget operation. They are spacious, 12 x 24 feet, air-conditioned, carpeted, equipped with color TV, attractively furnished, have full baths and such extras as in-room coffee pots. Two double beds are in each room.

Bob Dollar, VP of franchising for Days Inns, says: "Our goal is to become the McDonald's of the motor inn field and eventually stretch from coast to coast. The reason we're able to charge such reasonable rates for our accommodations is that we're using our know-how from building apartment units and standardizing construction and operations at all properties."

The Inns generally are constructed in units of 60 rooms, with a 120-room motel and Tasty World representing an investment of around $1 million, depending on land and building costs.

The chain is family-oriented. Says President William Hitson, "Days Inns are designed for the majority of families, factory reps, salesmen and students who need to economize."

And Days Inns seems to have hit its target. A recent three-paragraph menticn in the *Chicago Tribune* Travel Section drew a request from a reader for information on Days Inns. The Trib printed the letter and advised those who were interested to write the company in Atlanta. Some 1,200 of them did—an indication of the interest generated by the budget motels.

There's also the dawning of another new Days. The company is capitalizing on the interest generated by its inns with the creation of Days Lodges, a family-type motel suite that includes a living room, a completely-furnished GE kitchen with all utensils included, a master bedroom with two double beds that opens onto a patio, and a modern bath. The living room has a color TV, two sofas that convert to twin beds, a dinette area, etc. Recreational facilities include swimming pool, tennis court and putting green. The going rates: $14 single, $16 double, $17 for three and $18 for four persons per day! It seems like a sensational value. The lodges cater to those families who plan to stay in one location for several days to a few weeks. Days Inns plan to construct these lodges, where possible, adjacent to Days Inns.

Econo-Travel

And then there is Econo-Travel. The Norfolk, Va., chain opened its first property in 1967, which went in the black within 21 days—an investor's dream. Average time for any Econo-Travel operation to start showing a profit is one month, and the company's projections, based on averages of motels in operation, show that by maintaining a 75 per cent occupancy rate, all investment will be returned in less than seven years. Chainwide occupancy is actually about 90 per cent.

Ralph Malanga, Econo-Travel's president, credits the company's success and rapid growth to its package approach to buildings, furniture, supplies, and its systems of management, bookkeeping, accounting and controls.

The built-in economies in the Econo-Travel method were developed over eight years of planning and testing, before the first property was built. Two years alone were spent surveying persons on what they really wanted in motel accommodations —first by person-to-person interviews, later by direct mail. The chain obtained names and addresses from city directories across the country. The questionnaire was constructed on a rather scientific basis to produce the most candid answer possible.

The surveys covered feelings of the American public on motel restaurants, the quality of food, pricing, what meals were generally eaten there. The same line was followed in regard to swimming pools, large lobbies, recreational facilities, etc.

Says Lloyd Tarbutton, one of Econo-Travel's founders and president of the franchising end of Econo-Travel, "We zeroed in primarily on the feeling of public acceptance for a deluxe room with no extra services outside of the room. The response was overwhelmingly positive. We then started brainstorming specialists, such as engineers, restaurant management, real estate developers, CPAs, commercial contractors, electrical specialists, persons equipped with knowledge in the field of time study and mechanization. The aim was to reduce costs of initial construction and continual operation. We turned up with what we refer to as our electronic building."

The standard design settled on is a two-story motel, with parking but no pool, playground or restaurant. The motels have exactly 48 rooms, require a front footage of only 150 feet and a depth of 250 feet slightly under an acre. This design not only lowers the cost of land acquisition but enables Econo-Travel to place properties on small lots in land scarce areas, such as downtowns.

The motels are all electric (in 1968 Econo-Travel won the first All-Electric Building Award for motel franchises) and are wired into eight blocks of six rooms each. From the control panel the manager can activate lights, heat or air conditioning in multiples of six units when he judges more rooms are needed. Maintenance of the basic structure is economical, and great pains were taken to see that this is so. For example, it was carefully determined that two gallons of latex paint would cover a room, or 15 gallons the entire exterior.

The next package decided on was furnishings. The standard roomsetting consists of a wall-unit head-board and nightstand for the bed, and a combination triplex unit of chest, desk and luggage bench-seat. Econo-Travel's furniture division chose a modern-style contract line produced by American of Martinsville. The 3M finish of durable vinyl looks good, resists scratches and stains, needs only minimal care. The package approach to furnishings includes the black-and-white TV sets, purchased in lots of 500 and leased to the motels, cheaper than any other way to acquire them. Deluxe mattresses are used on the two double beds in each room. The mattresses, plastic glasses, soap and other supplies are furnished by Econo-Travel's own contract division, with mass purchasing producing savings that individual motels could not achieve.

Rugs are non-allergenic, are designed for long life and economy. After they are manufactured, they are run through the mill a second time to laminate a high-density backing to the regular backing. This eliminates the need for binding after cutting, produces a rug that will not curl, slip or slide. It needn't be laid under the baseboard, just fastened at the doorway. This method saves something like $1,200 per motel for rug installation. And, since the rectangular rooms are identical, after five or six years' wear, they can be reversed so the more-traveled section goes under the beds.

The telephone system is transistorized and requires no operator. The system takes up floor space of only two by four feet in a 15-by-15-foot telephone room. This leaves enough space in the room for washers, dryers, extractors and folders for linens, saving a reported $400.00 a month for the individual property.

Since Econo-Travel Motor Hotels are intended primarily for absentee owners, the chain has devised a system of thorough training and continual supervision of management—mostly husbands and wives. The corporation trains managers (at no additional cost to the franchisee) in regional centers. Emphasis is on obtaining retired persons, especially high-ranking military personnel who are married, have no children living at home. The thought behind this is that with a military background, the trainees are accustomed to following and giving instructions and have the ability to carry out the physical task themselves, if necessary. Many of the retirees hired are already covered with some plan of hospitalization and medical-care insurance, precluding the need for another insurance program. Also, most military persons who are retired have a pension income to supplement their salaries. It follows that a considerable cost saving can be effected with lower-than-average salaries.

Managers are furnished quarters independent of but adjacent to the office. From there they can monitor and control the office and any guests—or intruders—by closed-circuit TV and two-way audio. Just off the office is a room, identical to the others and the last to be rented each night, available for guest inspection without the manager having to leave the desk.

Another innovative aspect of the Econo-Travel system is serialized registration forms, which comprise a daily log of business. Once a customer fills out the form, there is no more paper work. Once a week, the originals of these forms are sent to headquarters for checking. "Ratio control" is an important part of this check; for instance, if three per cent more supplies than average are used by one motel, something is wrong. Tarbutton claims that, "with serialized registration forms and our controls, it takes one week to suspect and two weeks to prove."

Another efficient cog in the control system is the "rovers," company inspectors who arrive unscheduled once a month at each motel. They inspect each room and other phases of the operation from accounting to maintenance.

Even colors are used to control. Maids wear blue uniforms one day, white the next, so managers can tell if clean uniforms are being worn.

Maid service is minimized and standardized because of the uniform size and arrangement of the rooms. The linen room is located so that no guest room is more

Exhibit 1

WILL INNKEEPING HISTORY REPEAT ITSELF WITH THE BUDGET MOTEL

Comparison of Budget Motels

	Days Inns Of America	*Econo-Travel Motor Hotels*	*Regal 8 Inns*	*Scottish Inns Of America*	*Susse Chalet International*
Size Range of Existing Properties	60–690 rooms	48 exactly	25–160 rooms	48 rooms–up	60–120 rooms
Average Size of Existing Properties	120 rooms	48 exactly	80 rooms	120 rooms	60 rooms
Construction Costs Per Room (not including land costs)	$8,000–$10,000	N.A.	$5,000–$6,000	$6,500	$7,500–$8,000
Average Annual Occupancy Level	85%	90%	80+%	90%	88%
Rate For Single Room	$8.00	$7.50	$8.00	$6.00	$9.70
Rate For Double Room	$10.00	$10.00	$10.00	$9.00	$11.70
Rate For 3 or 4 Persons	$12.00–$14.00	$12.00	$12.00	$12.00	$11.70
Number of Properties Open	29	15	11	26	9
Number Under Construction	29	60	3	12	2
Number Planned	100+	150+	16	43	20
Franchises Available	Yes	Yes	Yes	No	No
Franchise Costs	$6,000 franchise fee for 60 rooms plus $90 per room up to 200 rooms; plus $60 per room over 200. Tasty World Restaurant License fee of $7,500. Motel royalty 3% of gross room sales. Advertising fee is .06¢ per available room per day.	No initial costs. Fee of 2% of aggregate room rental.	$1,000 for franchise; $1,500 prints; 2% room gross charge; 1% room gross for advertising.		

than 70 feet from it, and four maids are able to handle the cleaning of each property. The beds are on bed boxes, which saves five minutes per room per day in vacuuming time. (And guests can't forget belongings under the bed.) As part of the total control system, maids receive bonuses if they report three persons in a room when only two are registered.

Another form of incentive is used in the method of managing vending machines for soft drinks, ice and snacks. Operation and profits are given to the manager. Self-interest sees to it that the late-arrival never finds a machine empty or broken; the owner is relieved of any worry about theft, and the manager supplements his salary by $75 to $125 a month.

Econo-Travel has spent no money advertising for franchisees but has some 10 representatives traveling around constantly. Word-of-mouth and satisfied motel guests have furnished investors so far. Econo-Travel offers to franchisees the results of its costly eight-year preparation period of planning and testing. It provides aid in selection of a motel site, architectural plans, the furniture package, the bookkeeping system, trained management personnel, all publicity and placement of mortgages.

The company charges no initial franchise fee. Its only fee for services, including a semi-annual profit-and-loss statement, is two per cent of the aggregate room rental rate.

Says Tarbutton, "Progress has been greater than we ever dreamed, although we still have experienced motel owners who tell us we can't do it. At the end of last year, we set our sights at 202 properties in 1972. Since we are now approving between five and ten franchises per week, it is evident we will far exceed this goal before the end of 1972."

The existing licensees give Econo-Travel good basic coverage east of the Mississippi; now the expansion program moves to the west, and the prospects look just as bright there.

A Lesson in Marketing

From all indications, it looks as if the budget chains will keep on growing—and very successfully. And the success won't be accidental. Much of it will stem from the fact that the principals in these chains saw to it that they were in the right place at the right time. They all had master plans to begin with, which guided everything from construction practices, to rate structure, to advertising and public relations methods. This at a time when, too often, hotels & motels are built, decorated, rates set, before the specific markets they will serve have been determined. The budget properties are being built in response to a measurable demand, not in anticipation of a possible demand. They're succeeding very well in doing what all innkeepers should be doing—giving guests value for their money, whether it's $6 or $60.

CHAPTER 5: CAPACITY MANAGEMENT FOR SERVICE FIRMS*

The literature on capacity management focuses on goods and manufacturing, and many writers assume that services are merely goods with a few odd characteristics; these characteristics were discussed on page 15 in Chapter 2. Unfortunately, the researchers never fully explore the implications of these strange traits, namely:

1. Services are direct; they cannot be inventoried. The perishability of services leaves the manager without an important buffer that is available to manufacturing managers.
2. There is a high degree of producer-consumer interaction in the production of service, which is a mixed blessing; on the one hand, consumers are a source of productive capacity, but on the other, the consumer's role creates uncertainty for managers about the process's time, the product's quality, and the facility's accommodation of the consumer's needs.
3. Because a service cannot be transported, the consumer must be brought to the service delivery system or the system to the consumer.
4. Because of the intangible nature of a service's output, establishing and measuring capacity levels for a service operation are often highly subjective and qualitative tasks.

Whereas the consumption of goods can be delayed, as a general rule services are produced and consumed almost simultaneously. Given this distinction, it seems clear that there are characteristics of a service delivery system that do not apply to a manufacturing one and that the service manager has to consider a different set of factors from those that would be considered by his or her counterpart in manufacturing. And if one looks at service industries, it is quite apparent that successful service executives are *managing* the capacity of their operations and that the unsuccessful are not. So, the "odd characteristics" often make all the difference between prosperity and failure.

Consider the following service managers' actions, which resulted in fiasco:

Increasing the wrong kind of capacity—In studying the battle statistics in the war for market share among airlines, competitors observed that an air carrier in a minority position on a particular route would often get a smaller proportion of the total passengers flown on the route than the share of seats flown.[1] Conversely, the

* This chapter was adapted from an article, "Match Supply and Demand in Service Industries," by W. Earl Sasser, *Harvard Business Review,* November–December 1976, pp. 133–140.

[1] See William E. Fruhan, Jr., *The Fight for Competitive Advantage: A Study of the United States Domestic Trunk Air Carrier* (Boston: Division of Research, Harvard Business School, 1972).

dominant airline would carry a disproportionately larger share of the total passengers flown. The conclusion was obvious: Fly the seats, and you get the passengers.

In an effort to fly more seats, the airlines lined up to purchase jumbo jets. However, when competitors began flying smaller planes more frequently on the same routes and reaping a good number of passengers, it became painfully apparent to many airlines that frequency (and, to some extent, timing) of departures is the key to market share. Consequently, the airlines "mothballed" many of the jumbos or sold them if they could.

Not increasing all-around capacity—A resort operator decided to increase the number of rooms in a lodging facility and not to expand the central services required to support the additional guests. The fact that room rentals contribute up to 90% of total revenue and that tennis courts, swimming pools, meeting rooms, parking areas, and so on, contribute next to nothing, or nothing, convinced the operator to create an imbalance in favor of revenue-producing activities. However, the number of guests adjusted itself to the level of occupancy that the central services could support, not to the level of room capacity. The room capacity beyond the level supported by the central services was wasted.

Not considering the competitive reaction—The Orlando, Florida, lodging industry's response to the announcement of Disney World's opening is a classic example of this type of service management fiasco. Disney executives had learned well the lessons of Orange County, California, and Disneyland, where Disney's revenue is limited to on-site entertainment, food, and souvenir dollars. However, businesses besides Disney have made large profits in lodging, restaurant, and recreational facilities. Correctly perceiving that the same thing would happen in Florida, Disney purchased 200,000 acres south of Orlando, eight times the number owned in Anaheim.

When news broke that Disney would build in central Florida, however, everybody with a hotel or motel in his or her portfolio began plans for Orlando units, even though Disney had preempted all the land within two miles of the Magic Kingdom. The subsequent overbuilding has been well documented. While Disney prospered, many others suffered. More than 30,000 rooms were built to service a market estimated to need only 19,000. As an Orlando lender moaned, "We had a great little 200-room property there, the only one at the intersection. In less than a year, there were 5,000 rooms either built, under construction, or planned within a quarter mile of that intersection. We had to foreclose, and our occupancy has been running at only 35%."

Undercutting one's own service—A new entrant in the overnight air-freight transportation industry discovered that attempts to capture market share by adding to the existing number of planes and branch offices increased costs faster than revenues. Still looking for market share, the company then offered lower rates for second- and third-day deliveries. Because it had excess capacity, however, the company always delivered packages on the next day. As consumers discovered this fact, the mix of business shifted dramatically to the lower-priced services. So although there was an increase in volume, the resulting lower margins pushed the break-even volume even higher.

These pitfalls are not inevitable. Successful service executives do avoid them, and there are enough examples of well-managed service businesses from which to glean some wisdom on how to match demand for services with capacity to supply them. There are two basic capacity-management strategies available to most companies and a number of ways open to executives to manage both the demand and the supply sides of their businesses.

TWO BASIC STRATEGIES

Consider the national operations group of the XYZ brokerage firm. The group, housed in an office building located in the Wall Street area, handles the transactions generated by registered representatives in more than 100 branch offices throughout the United States. As with all firms in the brokerage industry, XYZ's transactions must be settled within five trading days. This five-day period allows operations managers to smooth out the daily volume fluctuations.

But fundamental shifts in the stock market's volume and mix can occur overnight, and the operations manager must be prepared to handle extremely wide swings in volume. For example, on the strength of an "international peace" rumor, the number of transactions for XYZ rose from 5,600 one day to 12,200 the next.

However, managers of XYZ, not unlike their counterparts in other firms, have trouble predicting volume. In fact, a random number generator can predict volume a month or even a week into the future almost as well as the managers can.

How do the operations managers in XYZ manage capacity when there are such wide swings? The answer differs according to the tasks and constraints facing each manager. Here's what two managers in the same firm might say:

Manager A—"The capacity in our operation is currently 12,000 transactions per day. Of course, what we should gear up for is always a problem. For example, our volume this year ranged from 4,000 to 15,000 transactions per day. It's a good thing we have a turnover rate, because in periods of low volume it helps us reduce our personnel without the morale problems caused by layoffs." (The labor turnover rate in this department is over 100% per year.)

Manager B—"For any valid budgeting procedure, one needs to estimate volume within 15%. Correlations between actual and expected volume in the brokerage industry have been so poor that I question the value of budgeting at all. I maintain our capacity at a level of 17,000 transactions per day."

Why the big difference in capacity management in the same firm? Manager A is in charge of the cashiering operation—the handling of certificates, checks, and cash. The personnel in cashiering are messengers, clerks, and supervisors. The equipment—file cabinets, vaults, calculators—is uncomplicated.

Manager B, however, is in charge of handling orders, an information-processing function. The personnel are key-punch operators, EDP specialists, and systems analysts. The equipment is complex—cathode ray tubes, key-punch machines, computers, and communication devices that link national operations with the branches.

The employees under B's control had performed their tasks manually until decreased volume and a standardization of the information needs made it worthwhile to install computers.

Because the lead times required to increase the capacity of the information-processing operation are long, however, and the incremental cost of the capacity to handle the last 5,000 transactions is low (only some extra peripheral equipment is needed), Manager B maintains the capacity to handle 17,000 transactions per day. He holds to this level even though the average number of daily transactions for any month has never been higher than 11,000 and the number of transactions for any one day has never been higher than 16,000.

Because a great deal of uncertainty about the future status of the stock certificate exists, the situation is completely different in cashiering. Attempts to automate the cashiering function to the degree reached by the order-processing group have been thwarted because the risk of selecting a system not compatible with the future format of the stock certificate is so high.

In other words, Manager A is tied to the "chase demand" strategy, and his counterpart, Manager B in the adjacent office, is locked into the "level capacity" strategy. However, each desires to incorporate more of the other's strategy into his own. A is developing a computerized system to handle the information-processing requirements of cashiering; B is searching for some variable costs in the order-processing operation that can be deleted in periods of low volume.

The characteristics of these two vastly different strategies are outlined in Exhibit 5-1.

Service managers using the chase strategy are usually responsible for unskilled employees performing jobs with little or no discretion for low pay in a relatively

Exhibit 5-1

COMPARISON OF CHASE-DEMAND AND LEVEL-CAPACITY STRATEGIES FOR THE XYZ BROKERAGE FIRM

	Chase demand	*Level capacity*
Labor-skill level required	Low	High
Job discretion	Low	High
Compensation rate	Low	High
Working conditions	Sweatshop	Pleasant
Training required per employee	Low	High
Labor turnover	High	Low
Hire-fire costs	High	Low
Error rate	High	Low
Amount of supervision required	High	Low
Type of budgeting and forecasting required	Short-run	Long-run

unattractive environment. Managers use the level strategy most often where more highly skilled people perform jobs for high pay, with some or a lot of discretion in a relatively pleasant environment.

Because the skill-level requirement for "chase" is lower than that for "level," the training cost per employee will also be lower for "chase." However, the annual training costs in a department using the chase strategy could be much higher than for one using the level strategy. The chase strategy requires more employees, and those employees exhibit a higher rate of turnover because of the job characteristics just described.

The chase strategy is usually more costly than the level strategy for other reasons as well. The high turnover rate and the use of unskilled employees both contribute to a high error rate, which means that more supervisors are needed to ensure that jobs are performed according to specifications.

For the chase strategy, the lead times required to attract and train new employees in periods of increased volume and to reduce the work force in periods of contraction are so short that forecasting and budgeting is needed only for the short run. However, because managers using a level strategy need a longer lead time to acquire or dispose of equipment and trained personnel, for them, forecasting and budgeting is a long-run process.

Although the chase demand strategy has many negative connotations for enlightened managers, there are some service delivery systems, such as amusement parks and resort hotels with highly seasonal or random fluctuations in demand, that survive only as a result of its successful application.

ALTERING DEMAND

Besides electing to adopt one of the strategies just described, the service executive may select one or another additional way to cope with a fluctuating demand schedule. The manager can attempt to affect demand by developing off-peak pricing schemes, nonpeak promotions, complementary services, and reservation systems. Let's look at each of these demand-leveling options in turn:

Pricing

One method managers use to shift demand from peak periods to nonpeak ones is to employ a differential pricing scheme, which might also increase primary demand for the nonpeak periods. Examples of such schemes are numerous. They include matinee prices for movies, happy hours at bars, family nights at the ball park on week nights, weekend and night rates for long-distance calls, peak-load pricing by utility companies, and two-for-one coupons at restaurants on Tuesday nights.

Developing Nonpeak Demand

Most service managers wrestle constantly with ideas to increase volume during periods of low demand, especially in those facilities with a high-fixed, low-variable cost structure. The impact of those incremental revenue dollars on the profitability of the business is tremendous. Examples of attempts to develop nonpeak demand are not hard to find. Hamburger chains add breakfast items to their menus, and coffee shops add dinners to theirs. Urban hotels, which cater to the business traveler during the week, develop weekend "mini-vacation" packages for the suburban population in their geographic areas, while resort hotels, jammed with pleasure travelers during school vacations, develop special packages for business groups during off-seasons.

However, caution must be used in developing plans to increase demand for the underused periods of the service facility. Many companies have made costly mistakes by introducing such schemes and not seeing the impact they would have on existing operations. As Wickham Skinner has noted, for manufacturing companies, there are some real costs associated with "unfocusing" the service delivery system, which is exactly what market-expanding activities have a tendency to do.[2] New concepts often require equipment and skills not currently found in a service delivery system. The addition of these skills and equipment may require a new type of labor force, a new layout, or more supervision.

Even if the new concept succeeds in creating demand in nonpeak periods, the effects are not always positive. Managers often use slack time productively as a time to train new employees, do maintenance on the equipment, clean the premises, prepare for the next peak, and give the workers some relief from the frantic pace of the peak periods. A new concept, therefore, may have a tendency to reduce the efficiency of the present system at best, or, at worst, to destroy the delicate balance found in most service delivery systems.

Developing Complementary Services

Another method managers use to shift demand away from peak periods is to develop complementary services, which either attracts consumers away from bottleneck operations at peak times or provides them with an alternative service while they are in the queue for the capacity-restricted operations. For example, restaurant owners have discovered that on busy nights most patrons complain less when sitting in a lounge with cocktails than when standing in line as they wait for tables in the dining area. Also, the profitability of restaurants with bars can more than double.

A diversion can also relieve waiting time. A hotel manager installed mirrors on each floor's central lobby so that customers could check their appearance while they waited for the elevator. Banking by mail or by automated tellers are other ways to cut down customer waiting time.

Creating Reservation Systems

Service executives can effectively manage demand by employing a reservation system, which in essence presells the productive capacity of the service delivery system. When certain time periods are booked at a particular service facility, managers

[2] See Wickham Skinner, "The Focused Factory," *Harvard Business Review,* May–June 1974, p. 113.

can often deflect excess demand to other time slots at the same facility or to other facilities at the same company and thereby reduce waiting time substantially and, in some cases, guarantee the customer service.

For instance, if a motel chain has a national reservation system, the clerk can usually find a customer a room in another motel of the chain in a fairly close proximity to his or her desired location if the first-choice motel is full.

In a similar manner, airlines are often able to deflect demand from booked flights to those with excess capacity or from coach demand to first class, especially if their competitors do not have seats available at the consumers' desired flight time.

However, reservation systems are not without their problems, the major one being "no-shows." Consumers often make reservations they do not use, and, in many cases, the consumer is not financially responsible for the failure to honor the reservation. To account for no-shows, some service companies oversell their capacity and run the risk of incurring the wrath of customers like Ralph Nader, who do show. Many service companies have made it a policy to bill for capacity reserved but not used if the reservation is not canceled prior to a designated time.

CONTROLLING SUPPLY

The service manager has more direct influence on the supply aspects of capacity planning than he or she does on the demand side. There are several things a service manager can do to adjust capacity to fluctuating demand.

Using Part-Time Employees

Many service companies have found that it is more efficient to handle demand whenever it occurs than it is to attempt to smooth out the peaks. The peaks vary by type of business—during certain hours of the day (restaurant), during certain days of the week (hair styling), during certain weeks of the month (banking), and during certain months of the year (income tax services). These service businesses usually maintain a base of full-time employees who operate the facility during nonrush periods but who need help during peak periods. One of the best-known resources is part-time labor pools, especially high school and college students, parents who desire work during hours when their children are in school, and moonlighters who desire to supplement their primary source of income.

Maximizing Efficiency

Many service managers analyze their processes to discover ways to get the most out of their service delivery systems during peak demand periods. In effect, such analyses enable the service company to increase its peak capacity for little additional cost. For example, during rush periods employees perform only the tasks that are essential to delivering the service. If possible, managers use slack periods for doing supporting tasks, which in essence they are inventorying for peak periods.

To maximize efficiency, managers examine even peak-time tasks to discover if certain skills are lacking or are inefficiently used. If these skills can be made more productive, the effective capacity of the system can be increased. For example, paramedics and paralegals have significantly increased the productive time of doctors and lawyers. Even rearranging the layout of the service delivery system can have a major impact on the productivity of the providers of the service.

Another way to attack the peak capacity constraint is by cross-training. The service delivery system is composed of various components. When the system is delivering one service at full capacity, some sections of the system are likely to be underused. If the employees in these sections are able to deliver the peak service, they add capacity at the bottleneck. When the demand shifts and creates a bottleneck in other components of the system, the employees can shift back again.

Increasing Consumer Participation

The more the consumer does, the lower the labor requirements of the producer. Bag-'em-yourself groceries, salad bars at restaurants, self-service gas pumps, customer-filled-out insurance information forms, and cook-it-yourself restaurants are all examples of increased consumer participation in the production of services.

There are, of course, some risks to increasing consumer input: consumers might reject the idea of doing the work and paying for it too; the manager's control over delivery of the service is reduced; and such a move can create competition for the service itself. A cook-it-yourself restaurant customer might just stay at home.

Sharing Capacity

The delivery of a service often requires the service business to invest in expensive equipment and labor skills that are necessary to perform the service but that are not used at full capacity. In such cases, the service manager might consider sharing capacity with another business to use required, expensive, but underused resources jointly.

For example, a group of hospitals in a large urban area might agree that it is unnecessary for each to purchase expensive medical equipment for every ailment and that they ought to share capacity. One would buy cardiac equipment, another gynecological and obstetrical equipment, another kidney machines. Participating doctors would have admitting privileges at all hospitals. By sharing equipment, hospitals would not only better use expensive resources, but as groups of trained and experienced specialists developed at each facility, hospitals would also deliver better medical care.

The shared-capacity concept is possible in the airlines industry in several forms. Several airlines with infrequent flights in and out of a particular airport share gates, ramps, baggage-handling equipment, and ground personnel. In fact, some domestic airlines flying different routes with different seasonal demands exchange aircraft when one's dip in demand coincides with another's peak.

Investing in the Expansion Ante

Wise service managers often invest in an "expansion ante." When growth occurs, it sometimes becomes clear that some of the new development could have been done when the facility was originally constructed for much less cost and disruption. A careful analysis before the facility is built will show what these items are. For instance, for a small investment, a restaurateur can build his kitchen with extra space in order to service more diners later on. Contractors can run wiring, plumbing, and air conditioning ducts to the edge of the building where the expansion will take place. The manager can inventory enough land for the expansion and additional parking requirements. These actions will allow the restaurant manager to increase capacity without having to renovate the kitchen, redo the wiring, plumbing, and air conditioning systems, or purchase adjacent land at much higher prices.

SEEKING THE BEST FIT

Managing demand and supply is a key task of the service manager. Although there are two basic strategies for capacity management, the enlightened service manager will, in almost all cases, deviate from these two extremes.

The challenge to the service manager is to find the best fit between demand and capacity. In order to manage the shifting balance that characterizes service industries, managers need to plan rather than react. For example, managers should try to make forecasts of demand for the time periods under question. Then he or she should break the service delivery system down into its component parts, calculate the present capacity of each component, and arrive at a reasonable estimate of what the use of each component will be, given the demand forecast.

Because each system cannot handle infinite demands, the manager needs to question how much of the peak demand the system must handle. Just what is the appropriate level of service for the delivery system to provide? Once the manager can approximate the answer to these questions and has decided which of the basic strategies to employ, he or she is ready to experiment with the different options to alter demand and capacity. Each plan and option a manager arrives at can be costed, and the best fit for the particular service selected.

Ultimately, of course, on the demand side, a manager's true aim is to increase revenues through an existing service delivery system of given capacity. Once the true variable costs are subtracted out, all revenues flow to the bottom line. On the supply side, the manager aims to minimize costs needed to increase or decrease capacity.

When facing increased demand, the business raises its revenues with minimal investment. In times of capital rationing, small investments are often the only ones available to the company. When facing contracting demand, the manager needs to select the best way to adjust the system's capacity to a lower volume.

In following the ideas outlined in this chapter, service managers need to think creatively about new ways to manage demand and supply. The most important thing to recognize is that they both can be managed efficiently and that the key to doing so lies in planning.

The Sea Pines Racquet Club

In June 1973 John Baker, having recently accepted the newly created position as Tennis Director of The Sea Pines Racquet Club, was working on his first assignment for The Sea Pines Company, Hilton Head, South Carolina. His initial project was to formulate a strategy for tennis operations on the Plantation.

A 1970 graduate of the University of Virginia Business School, Baker had accepted the position with The Sea Pines Company in April 1973 after two years as product manager for General Foods and a year as sales manager for a small real estate development firm in Boston. An avid tennis player, Baker had accepted his new position because he had felt that the combination of tennis and The Sea Pines Company represented a tremendous opportunity for him.

Sea Pines Plantation

Hilton Head Island had been substantially undeveloped and sparsely populated when The Sea Pines Company, under the leadership of its president, Charles Fraser, had begun development of the 5200-acre Sea Pines Plantation in 1957. In developing Sea Pines Plantation, The Sea Pines Company had prepared and periodically had updated a comprehensive land use plan; had developed residential subdivisions, park, utilities, golf, tennis, and other recreational and resort facilities; and had donated land for churches, medical facilities, and other community purposes.

In 1973, the company's resort and recreational operations on Sea Pines Plantation consisted of a country club and an 18-hole golf course which it owned (another 18-hole golf course for members only was under construction), two additional 18-hole golf courses operated by it, a 127-unit ocean-front inn leased and operated by it; three marinas; 27 tennis courts, and several food and beverage facilities (see Exhibit 1). While its resort operations had not been profitable to date, the company believed that these activities were an integral part of its overall development plans and that their operation could both produce profits and benefit its real estate activities.

The company's principal business was the sale and resale of homesites, houses, and villas for which it received brokerage fees. The company also acted as agent and received fees for renting privately owned homes and villas (apartments) in Sea Pines Plantation. Substantially, all of the company's sales of homesites and villas were made by its resident sales representatives to vacationers or visitors to its properties, the majority of whom lived either on the eastern seaboard and/or in the mid-

Exhibit 1

SEA PINES RACQUET CLUB

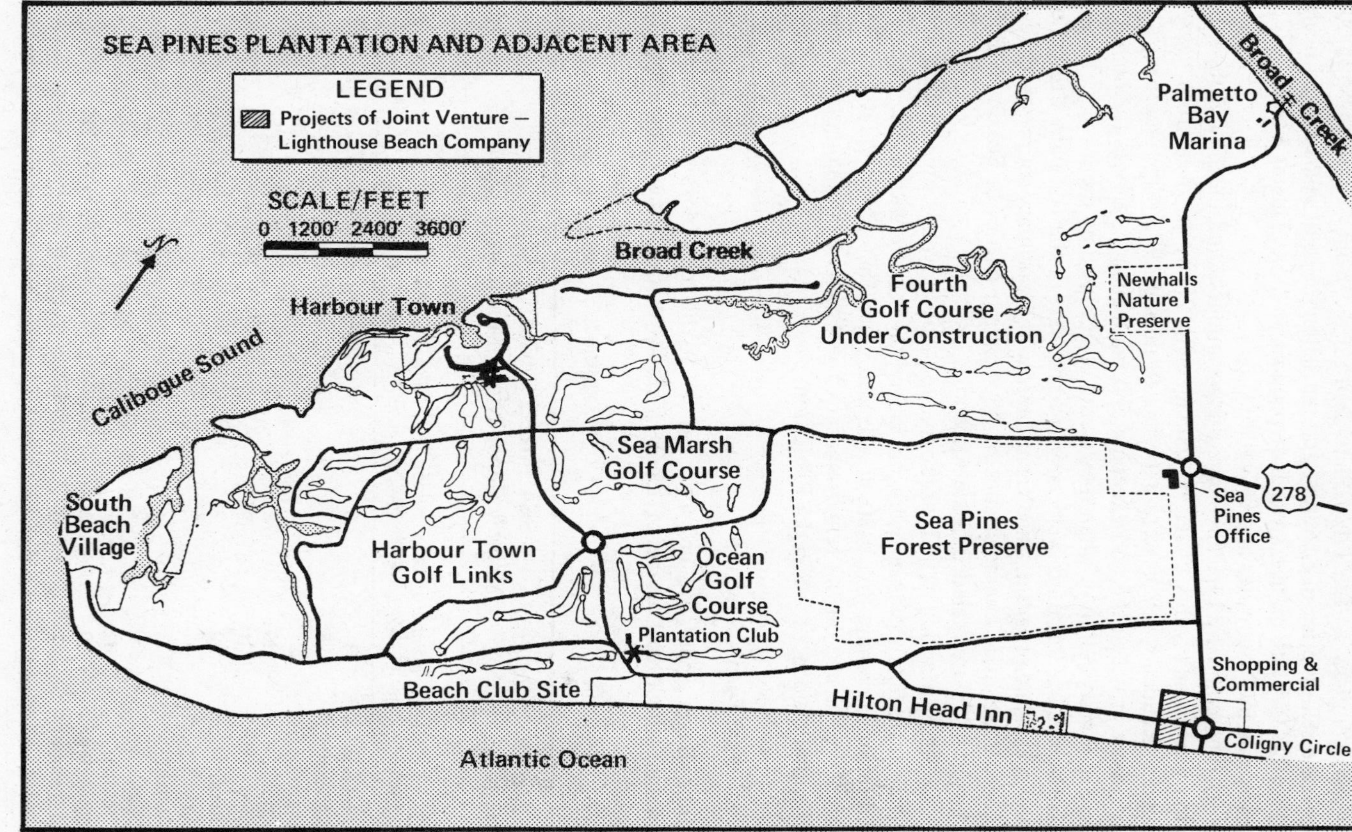

western part of the United States. In Fiscal 1972, the selling price of homesites sold by the company at Sea Pines Plantation ranged from $9,000 to $52,000, with an average selling price of $16,000, and the selling price of villas ranged from $28,500 to $102,000, with an average selling price of $62,000. During Fiscal 1972, the company sold 574 homesites and 93 villas.

The company typically rented to vacationers and meeting groups those vacation homes and villas under its management 20 weeks or more a year, although higher occupancy levels were experienced during 1972.[1] The company's rental department provided the housekeeping and maintenance services for homes and villas in Sea Pines Plantation when they were not occupied by the owners. These noncompany-owned rental units were an important part of the company's resort operations and real estate program, since vacationers were its primary source of real estate sales. The demographic characteristics of 38 vacation parties at Sea Pines Plantation in August 1972 are included in the Appendix.

As of March 1, 1973, approximately 350 privately owned villas and 135 private single-family homes were on the rental market within Sea Pines Plantation. Ultimately, perhaps by 1980, it was estimated that 1,650 villas and 150 or 200 homes would be on the rental market. These units would comprise about 50% of the total residences within the Plantation.

Past Tennis Play

John Baker spent the first two months in his new position accumulating information about past usage of tennis facilities at Sea Pines Plantation. He discov-

Exhibit 2

SEA PINES RACQUET CLUB
Monthly Capacity of a Composition Court

Month	*Number of days*	*Days missed bad weather*	*Daily hours*	*Maintenance hours*	*Total hours available for play*	*Midday temperature*
January	31	3	9–5	0	224	64.9°
February	28	3	9–5	0	200	66.8°
March	31	3	8–6	1	252	73.3°
April	30	2	8–6	1	252	80.0°
May	31	2	8–8	1	319	80.4°
June	30	2	8–8	1	308	89.0°
July	31	2	8–8	1	319	90.4°
August	31	2	8–8	1	319	89.0°
September	30	2	8–7	1	280	86.0°
October	31	2	9–7	1	261	73.3°
November	30	3	9–5	0	216	71.4°
December	31	3	9–5	0	224	64.4°

[1] SEC regulations prohibited Sea Pines and other developers of condominia from promoting condominia by emphasizing the economic benefits of rental income.

Exhibit 3

SEA PINES RACQUET CLUB
Court Hours and Guest Nights
12 Months Ending February 1973

Month	*Total court hours*	*Guest nights*	*Court hours/ Guest nights*
March	889	22,222	.040
April	1,797	29,450	.061
May	938	20,390	.046
June	1,506	35,848	.042
July	2,824	50,434	,056
August	2,885	51,515	.056
September	1,196	20,986	.057
October	1,459	22,798	.064
November	1,090	17,298	.063
December	840	9,551	.088
January	457	9,924	.046
February	629	16,139	.039

Exhibit 4

SEA PINES RACQUET CLUB
12 Months Ending February 1973
Revenues and Expenses

	Shop	*Courts*	*Total*
Revenues	59,400	56,100	115,500
Less cost of sale	35,700		35,700
Gross Margin	23,700	56,100	79,800
Expenses			
Professional and clerical	12,500	11,000	23,500
Labor	1,500	22,000	23,500
Benefits	3,600	2,700	6,700
Supplies	1,800	600	2,400
Repairs and maintenance		2,000	2,000
Utilities	1,400	1,900	3,300
Miscellaneous expenses	4,400	4,000	8,400
Rent	3,000	10,000	13,000
Total Expenses	28,200	54,200*	82,400
CONTRIBUTION	(4,500)	1,900	(−2,600)

* Direct maintenance costs were estimated at $1,950 for each of the 12 composition courts and zero for the 5 hard-surface courts.

ered that recording of tennis play began in June 1970 on the four Plantation Club hard-surface courts and eight composition courts in Harbour Town. Nine additional courts in Harbour Town (five hard-surface[2] and four composition) were completed in the spring of 1972. Construction of an additional six composition courts at Harbour Town was begun in May 1972 and they were completed in March 1973, at a cost of $12,000 per court (excluding land).

Exhibit 5

SEA PINES RACQUET CLUB
12 Months Ending February 1974
Estimated Revenues and Expenses

	Shop	*Courts*	*Total*
Revenues	98,800[1]		
Court fees		109,000	
Annual members		10,000	
Lessons		10,000	
Total Revenue	98,800	129,000	227,800
Less Cost of Sale	58,800	—	58,800
Gross Margin	40,000	129,000	169,000
Expenses			
Supervisory[2]	7,000	38,000	45,000
Clerical	9,000	9,000	18,000
Labor	3,000	10,000	13,000
Benefits	1,900	1,900	3,900
Taxes	2,100	4,000	6,100
Supplies	1,750	750	2,500
Repairs and maintenance	100	3,300	3,400
Utilities	1,500	2,000	3,500
Miscellaneous expenses	3,500	3,600	7,100
Rent	3,000	12,000	15,000
Total Expenses	32,850	84,550*	117,400
Contribution	7,150	44,450	51,600

[1] Includes miscellaneous rentals.

[2] Includes Director of Tennis, Assistant Professional (Base Salary + 50% of Lessons), and Head of Maintenance.

* Direct maintenance costs divided between 18 composition courts estimated at $1,700 in 73–74 (assumes no maintenance for 5 hard courts).

[2] The five hard-surface courts were equipped with lights for night play. The lighting, which had an expected life of five years, was installed at a cost of $4,000 per court. The direct operating cost (electricity and bulbs) was $1.75 per court hour. Tokens ($4 for an hour of night play) for using these courts at night were sold at the pro shop during the day. Statistics on the use of these courts at night had not been collected on a player or court-hour basis.

Mr. Baker learned that monitoring of play at the Plantation Club had been discontinued because of its distance from the Harbour Town facility. The Plantation Club's courts were scheduled to be removed in late 1973 to make way for the planned expansion of the Plantation Club. Statistics on court usage at Harbour Town indicated that usage there had more than doubled each year since 1970 and that the capacity utilization of the courts had increased from 18.4% to 47.3% even though the number of courts had increased from 8 to 23.

Year	Harbour Town Court Usage (by Court Hour)	% Capacity Utilization (Actual ÷ Potential Court Hours)
1970	2,789	18.4
1971	6,101	25.9
1972	16,142	34.8
1973 (estimate)	32,816	47.3

The potential court capacity by month is shown in Exhibit 2. A monthly breakdown of guest nights and court hours for FY 1973 is included as Exhibit 3. Actual revenue and expenses for FY 1973 and projections for FY 1974 are given as Exhibits 4 and 5.

After reviewing the information he had collected, Mr. Baker decided to tackle two related issues in greater detail: pricing structure and overall court capacity.

Court Capacity

Mr. Baker faced a major dilemma with regards to court capacity. Guest night projections revealed that the number of guests on Sea Pines Plantation would double in the next two years (see Exhibit 6). In addition, the number of court hours per guest night for March (.068), April (.082), and May (.084) revealed increases from the prior year. John felt confident that the guest night projections were accurate because many new housing units were scheduled for completion. He also was aware of the rising popularity of tennis and felt that the increase in court hours per guest night reflected a national upward trend.

However, there was only space for four additional courts at the Harbour Town location. Any expansion beyond four courts would require a duplication of facilities and staff at the new location. It was estimated that a new tennis pro shop would cost $100,000 and the annual staffing and maintenance would be similar to those incurred at Harbour Town. There was an area on the master plan near the center of the Plantation with enough space for 40 courts and supporting facilities.

With increased pressure for profitability from top management, John felt that a decision to increase the number of courts had to be carefully balanced against the increased costs of a new facility which might only be needed three or four months each year. On the other hand, Sea Pines Plantation had spent a great deal of effort developing its tennis image and limited court capacity during the summer months would not enhance that image. On recent days, Mr. Baker had overheard some com-

Exhibit 6

SEA PINES RACQUET CLUB
Guest Night Projection
Sea Pines Plantation

Year	*Month*	*Projected guest nights*
1973	March	35,526
	April	41,576
	May	33,632
	June	59,950
	July	83,887
	August	86,475
	September	34,514
	October	36,221
	November	27,180
	December	18,509
1974	January	16,293
	February	30,330
	March	57,741
	April	66,462
	May	53,992
	June	95,620
	July	130,696
	August	129,111
	September	53,218
	October	55,197
	November	38,819
	December	24,627
1975	January	21,717
	February	37,083
	March	73,580
	April	83,773
	May	68,607
	June	120,826
	July	168,797
	August	166,263
	September	66,168
	October	68,883
	November	50,435
	December	31,530

plaints about the unavailability of courts during the prime playing hours of 9–11 A.M. and 4–6 P.M. He was also concerned by comments from visitors from the previous year that the combination of high temperatures and humidity from noon to 4 P.M. created very uncomfortable playing conditions in July and August.

Recommended Rate Structure

After reviewing the available data on pricing (Exhibit 7), John Baker recommended changing the rate structure for use of tennis facilities at The Sea Pines Racquet Club as follows:

1. Charge $5.00 per court hour (singles or doubles) for use of the composition courts in lieu of the present $2.00 per hour per person.
2. Discontinue half rates after 2 hours of play.
3. Charge $3.00 per court hour for the use of the all-weather courts.
4. Discontinue student rates.
5. Discontinue tennis plans.

Exhibit 7

SEA PINES RACQUET CLUB
Present Tennis Pricing Structure

GUESTS:
1 hour $2.00
($2.00 per hour for the first 2 hours of play each day, and $1.00 for each additional hour of play, when courts are available.)

STUDENTS (18 years and under):
1 hour $1.00
($1.00 per hour for the first 2 hours of play each day, and $.50 for each additional hour of play, when courts are available.)

RACQUET RENTAL . . . . $1.00 per hour

BALL MACHINE RENTAL . . . . $7.00 per hour (includes court fee)

LIGHTED COURTS FOR EVENING PLAY . . . . $4.00 per hour per court

TENNIS PLANS (available at all times except July and August)

A. 4-Day Tennis Plan—$13.00
Four days of daily tennis play—one hour in the morning and one hour in the afternoon. Plan to be played within 8 days of purchase (additional hours @ $1.00/hour).

B. 7-Day Tennis Plan—$23.00
Seven days of daily tennis play—one hour in the morning and one hour in the afternoon. Plan to be played within 14 days of purchase (additional hours @ $1.00/hour).

Reasons for Recommendations

A. *Per Court vs. Per Person Charge*

By encouraging and enabling more people to play more tennis, both our court revenues and importantly our merchandising revenues will increase. The present mix of singles and doubles play is 72% and 28% in favor of singles. Those who now play 1 hour of singles for $2.00 may be encouraged to play 2 hours of doubles under the proposed rates for $2.50 or double the amount of playing time for 25% more court fees. They will also take up no more court time by doing so.

Those people who play an hour of doubles vs. an hour of singles will obviously decrease our revenues, but more doubles play will free up court time for others. When more courts are available than can readily be filled, it may not seem so appropriate to charge on a per court basis. However, this is not the case at Harbour Town. We will be extremely close to reaching actual capacity this summer.

B. *Discontinue Half Rates After 2 Hours of Play*

As we reach higher levels of capacity, our present policy becomes more inappropriate. The majority of our guests will be willing to pay regular court fees for all hours of play.

C. *$3.00 Per Court Hour for All-Weather Courts*

From September 1972 to April 1973 the all-weather court capacity utilization was 15% compared to 38% over the same period for the composition courts. Since these courts are less desirable and cost substantially less to maintain, it seems appropriate that we charge less for their use.

D. *Discontinue Half Rates for Students*

With the reduction in rates on the all-weather courts, there is no necessity to charge less for student (under 18) play. The major complaint about all-weather courts centers around leg fatigue and younger players should be less affected by this than our older tennis guests. Students playing doubles with parents (who might insist on playing on composition courts) can still play for less even on these courts —namely $5.00 vs. $6.00 under the present rate structure. Our younger players should be encouraged to use our all-weather courts, thus freeing up the composition courts for more play by our adult clientele who often refuse to play on the all-weather courts.

E. *Discontinue Tennis Plans*

As we reach higher levels of capacity, we are losing rather than gaining revenues by offering plans of this nature.

John Baker's Dilemma

John Baker summarized his feelings on how capacity and pricing fit into the overall tennis strategy for Sea Pines:

> The increase in the popularity and play of tennis at Sea Pines is common knowledge. We expect that July and August of this year will find Sea Pines Racquet Club at capacity. Since potential court hours include all hours except downtime for rain and actual maintenance time, "unbearably" hot hours are *not* excluded. Therefore, it may not be possible to exceed the 80% capacity figure by very much.
>
> Tennis play at Sea Pines has increased at a compounded rate of over 100% a year. While the tennis "boom" must plateau or at least slow down its frantic momentum at some stage, it is generally considered not to have reached its peak.

The argument against building more tennis courts when the tennis operation is making little or no contribution to resort operations is valid. Exhibit 4 illustrates that the *court* operations (as opposed to *merchandising*) barely covered costs last year. The high fixed costs and relatively low percentage capacity utilization have prevented court operations from making a contribution in the past.

My proposed pricing structure in itself will not necessarily bring us much closer to achieving our goal of 25% contribution. Some of the increase will be eaten up by inflation. Our profitability in the next few years depends upon the length of time that we can reasonably hold off building additional courts at another location.

Top Management's Viewpoint

Top management felt that tennis represented a great opportunity for Sea Pines. They had invested a great deal in facilities, promotion, advertising, and management time. They felt tennis operations must not only stand on its own two feet, but also produce a significant contribution to resort operations. Tennis operations were now considered a profit center, not just an inducement for people to buy property.

John Baker's dilemma was not unique among operations managers at Sea Pines. Most managers faced a growing but seasonal demand for their services. For example, Donald O'Quinn, golf director, could foresee a problem with golf course capacity. The members course under construction was the last course scheduled for the Plantation. In resolving the tennis capacity issue, it was hoped that an appropriate methodology could be developed to apply to the capacity planning decisions facing all operations managers.

Appendix
The Sea Pines Racquet Club
Sea Pines Vacationers: Their Demographic Characteristics

Sidney D. Nolan, Jr
Graduate Research Assistant
Department of Recreation and Parks
Texas A&M University

The Sample

Thirty-eight vacation parties at Sea Pines Plantation were interviewed in August 1972. These parties consisted of 36 family groups with both spouses present, one family group with the male head of household only, and one family group with the female head of household only.

Twenty of the respondents were first-time visitors to Sea Pines and 18 were repeat visitors. Two of the repeat visitors owned property at Sea Pines.

Summary of Demographic Characteristics

The summer guest at Sea Pines tends to be middle-aged, well educated, and married with relatively young children. Male heads of household are employed mostly as business executives, or they are in the traditional professions. They earn more than $25,000 per year. Their wives are most likely housewives.

The Sea Pines Trip

Duration of the vacation trip to Sea Pines among respondents ranged from 7 to 30 days with a mean of 12.7 days. Length of stay at Sea Pines ranged from 4 to 26 days with a mean of 9.2 days. First-time visitors averaged 7.1 days stay while repeat visitors averaged 11.7 days.

The average party among respondents consisted of 2.1 adults and 1.7 children. However, among those respondents with children living at home, the average party had 2.3 children.

Of the 33 respondents who gave an estimate of the cost of their trip, 75.8% said they were spending at least $60 per day.

Respondents listed an average of 4.2 activities per party at Sea Pines. These included, in order of frequency of mention:

1. Beach swimming
2. Golf
3. Tennis
4. Dining out
5. Shopping
6. Nature walks and photography
7. Sightseeing in the surrounding area
8. Pool swimming
9. Fishing
10. Relaxing
11. Sailing
12. Real estate shopping
13. Horseback riding
14. Skeet shooting

As a main activity for the vacationing parties, beach swimming led among first-time and repeat visitors. Half of the first-timers named this as their main activity while a third of the repeaters listed it. Larger percentages of repeat visitors listed golf (29.2%) and tennis (16.6%) as their main activities than did first-timers. "Just relaxing" was of primary importance to 16.6% of the repeat visitors and to

10% of the first-time visitors. Two respondents, one from each group, were mainly interested in sailing. Real estate shopping, specifically for a retirement home, was mentioned by one first-time visitor as his main activity.

With the exception of one ardent golfer and a tournament tennis player, respondents emphasized the mix of available activities, along with the esthetics of the setting, as the main reasons for coming to Sea Pines.

Loma Vista Hospital

Loma Vista Hospital was a 435-bed general hospital located in a rapidly growing metropolitan area of northern California. The hospital helped to serve the medical needs of a district which included approximately 170,000 people. Opened in 1961, the hospital's goal was to provide its patients with the entire range of facilities and services required in the treatment of disease and injury of all types. A measure of its success in reaching this goal was the excellent reputation its facilities and services had gained among physicians in the area.

The hospital was a large and complex operation housed in one modern five-story building. In 1966, Loma Vista generated over $9 million in revenues and employed 820 people on a full-time basis—300 of whom were members of the nursing staff. Besides offering both inpatient and outpatient services, the hospital was also associated with a large nearby medical school. A small amount of research was carried on in the hospital's laboratories. Loma Vista's central focus, however, remained that of providing high-quality services and facilities for the medical treatment of its patients, and participating in such community projects as nurses' training programs and area-wide planning aimed at increasing the quality of medical care available throughout the community.

Exhibit 1

LOMA VISTA HOSPITAL
Description of Nursing Units

Nursing Units (Wards)

One South (Psychiatry)—Patients with mild psychiatric disorders receive treatment here. The atmosphere is similar to that found in an individual's home with comfortable home-like furniture, TV, stereo, recreational facilities and individualized rooms. Patients are usually ambulatory and remain an average of 10–12 days vs. a hospital average length of stay of 5-6 days. Nurses working this ward require psychiatric training.

Two East and *Two West* (Surgical)—Preoperative preparations and postoperative convalescence are both done here. Staffing requirements do not include specialized nursing personnel.

Three West, Four West, Five West (Medical)—Patients suffering from illnesses of any type other than those requiring surgery or specialized treatment are admitted here. Internal

Exhibit 1 (continued)

disorders, infections and diseases comprise the majority of cases. No specialized personnel are required.

Three East (Pediatrics)—Ward is for children from the ages of two months to about 14–15 years of age. All child patients, whether surgical or medical, are admitted to Three East. Although general nursing skills are all that are required in this ward, some effort is made to assign nurses who are particularly understanding and fond of children.

A separate part of Three East is the six-bed teenage unit designed to satisfy the particular needs of adolescents. This unit contains refrigerators, stereo, TV, and is intended to solve the problem of adolescents whose needs are different from those of both children and adult patients.

Five East (Orthopedics)—Patients with broken bones, hips and backs are treated here. Patients requiring orthopedic surgery are also admitted to this ward. The length of stay is quite long—usually two weeks or more, and a majority of the patients are elderly persons. Current practice is to include nurses with therapy training on the nursing staff of this unit.

Six East—a small medical ward used to absorb patient overflow when necessary.

Six West—an experimental extended care nursing facility intended to serve chronically ill patients who require the services of a hospital. Patients are normally elderly people who require little nursing care, and then only nursing care of a general nature. It is part of a community experiment to more closely integrate the functions of a general hospital and private nursing homes.

Maternity—for pregnant and postpartum women. The average length of stay is slightly more than two days. The nursing function is divided into two areas—nurses assisting in the delivery room, and nurses attending both the new baby and the mother. The latter function comprises little more than changing diapers and transporting the newborn child from the nursery to its mother for feeding and back again, with only limited nursing assistance given to the mothers.

Gynecology—a 12-bed ward admitting women patients.

Intensive Care and *Cardiac Care*—two units serving critically ill patients. Nurses in these units have specialized training in treatment of cardiac patients or the operation of artificial kidneys, and are usually among the most skilled RNs in the hospital. Patient costs, because of the specialized care given on an individual basis, average $100 per day as compared with $45–$50 per day for the other wards, and the length of stay is about 5–10 days.

In early November 1967 Fred Luthy, the hospital administrator, became extremely concerned over recent operating results: although actual patient loads—and therefore revenues—had been running slightly below forecast levels for the entire planning year (Exhibit 8), he had not felt that the deficits were overly serious until now. This morning he had received the final budgetary summary for October (Exhibit 3); during October the negative variance from projected revenues had grown from $81,000 to $187,000 and the operating loss had grown from $15,000 to $56,000.

Mr. Luthy felt that action had to be taken immediately to bring hospital expenses back into line with revenues but he was concerned as to how this might best be accomplished. He therefore requested Mike Haig, his assistant administrator, to meet him later in the day to discuss possible courses of action.

Exhibit 2

LOMA VISTA HOSPITAL
Organization Chart

Board of Directors
- Medical Staff
- Administrator
  - Assistant Administrator
    - Personnel
    - Purchasing
    - Director of Nursing
      - Operating Room
      - Emergency Room
      - Psychiatry
      - 15 Nursing Stations
      - Central Services
    - Pathology
    - Radiology
    - Psychiatry
    - Physical Med.
    - Med. Records
    - Admitting
    - Business Office
    - Publications
    - Buildings & Grounds
      - Housekeeping
      - Laundry
      - Eng. & Maintenance
    - Food Service
    - Pharmacy
- Auxiliary

Medical Services

Support Departments

Exhibit 3

LOMA VISTA HOSPITAL
Statement of Income and Expenses

	Year to Date					
	August		September		October	
	Actual	Variance	Actual	Variance	Actual	Variance
Net Operating Income	$1,436,948	$(45,868)	$2,139,735	$(81,265)	$2,830,737	$(187,963)
Salaries and Wages	869,264	18,336	1,314,197	22,703	1,773,467	25,633
Overtime Wages	13,873	(3,973)	18,081	(2,881)	22,502	(1,702)
Employee Benefits	89,674	(974)	133,991	(191)	175,538	4,262
Total Labor Expense	972,811	13,389	1,466,269	19,631	1,971,507	28,193
Food	39,255	4,945	54,343	10,957	74,088	14,312
Supplies and Services	193,309	20,391	298,713	24,987	395,500	32,700
Professional Fees	106,628	(5,828)	153,901	(1,301)	203,141	2,659
Utilities	36,094	1,106	54,517	1,283	73,310	1,090
Drugs	15,193	3,607	22,076	6,624	28,910	10,890
Total Nonlabor Expense	390,479	24,221	583,550	42,550	774,949	61,651
Total Departmental Expense	1,363,290	37,610	2,049,819	62,181	2,746,456	89,844
Depreciation	70,526	1,274	105,789	1,911	141,052	2,548
Net Income (Loss)	3,132	(6,968)	(15,873)	(17,173)	(56,771)	(95,571)

Operations

Hospital operations covered a variety of activities including an emergency room, radiology laboratory, pathology laboratory, 12 operating rooms, a pharmacy, two therapy services, an inhouse laundry, a cafeteria, maintenance and housekeeping services, as well as 15 nursing stations or hospital wards.

Mr. Luthy relied heavily on the development and implementation of the Annual Plan for planning and controlling these various functions. In April every year Mr. Luthy, Mr. John Griffin (the hospital systems analyst) and Mr. Haig prepared an Annual Plan for the 12 months beginning July 1.

This plan detailed the general level of hospital operations, capital expenditures, services or facilities to be expanded, and grants or subsidies to be applied for in support of research activities. A key planning input was the forecast of daily patient census. This served as the basis for estimates of patient days for each ward, the level of operation of the cafeteria, laundry and other services, and resources required to support the expected level of demand. These estimates were given to each of the hospital's 32 budgetary units (17 departments and 15 wards) which used them to project their own staffing requirements and operating expenses.

Forecasting

Mr. Luthy and his staff worked out an average census for each ward for each month by analysis of historical data, adjusting where figures were known to be extraordinary. They then estimated the population growth and scaled up their average figures by the percentage of population change. These average figures were further adjusted to reflect any of the various cyclical determinants (see below). Although Mr. Luthy was aware that statistical analyses indicated that demographic factors such as higher income level, percentage of the population possessing health insurance and improved level of education tended to increase the use of hospital services, he had no figures indicating the magnitude of their effect. Therefore, he relied solely on adjustment of the previous year's data by an estimated rate of population growth.

The staff was able to develop increasingly accurate forecasts as the base of operating data grew, and as they became more proficient at identifying cyclical factors and important environmental changes. However, while Mr. Luthy felt that the *aggregate* patient days per month could be forecast within 10% of actual, he still felt that individual units were not being satisfactorily predicted for adequate planning and control. He attributed this to the multiple factors which affected the demand for subunits within the hospital. Although he had not attempted to rigorously differentiate the various factors influencing the timing of demands for various types of hospital services, he felt that there were two major categories of demand factors—those which he referred to as "cyclical" and those which were "totally unpredictable."

"Cyclical" Factors

Many patients entering a hospital were not emergency cases and the timing of their admittance was greatly influenced by personal convenience. For instance, tonsillec-

Exhibit 4

LOMA VISTA HOSPITAL

A Typical Responsibility Statement

Department Cardiac Care Unit — *Date* October 1967

CURRENT MONTH			ACCOUNT DESCRIPTION	YEAR-TO-DATE		
Actual	*Budget*	*Variance*		*Actual*	*Budget*	*Variance*
			— INCOME —			
$10,488	$9,800	$688	Inpatient	$37,892	$39,300	($1,408)
			Outpatient			
−210	−200	−10	Less: Allowance & Bad Debts	−758	−800	42
10,278	9,600	678	Net Operating Income	37,134	38,500	(1,366)
			— EXPENSE —			
			Labor			
7,497	6,700	(797)	Salaries & Wages	25,689	26,000	311
6	—	(6)	Overtime Wages	23	—	(23)
650	600	(50)	Employee Benefits	2,343	2,100	(243)
8,153	7,300	(853)	Total Labor Expense	28,055	28,100	45
			Nonlabor			
266	400	134	Supplies & Services	951	1,600	649
			Total Nonlabor Expense			
8,419	7,700	(719)	Total Departmental Expense	29,006	29,700	694
			— STATISTICS —			
118	109	+9 = +8.3%	Patient Days	446	467	−21 = −4.5%
10.8	9.6	+1.2 = +12.5%	Employee F.T.E.	9.8	9.6	+.2 = +2.1%
			— ALLOCATED OVERHEAD —			
4,207	4,300	93		15,605	17,200	1,595
($2,348)	($2,400)	$ 52	NET INCOME (LOSS)	($7,477)	($8,400)	$ 923

Exhibit 5

LOMA VISTA HOSPITAL

Analysis of Budget Expenditures
October and Year-to-Date

	October	*4 Months*
Supplies and services over (under) budget:		
D.H.S.	($ 2,000)	($ 8,900)
Delivery Room	100	200
Emergency Room	(100)	600
Nursing Administration	200	400
Operating Room	500	(4,700)
Central Service	(3,500)	(6,600)
Inhalation Therapy	500	(300)
Pharmacy	(4,300)	(10,700)
Pathology	(3,800)	(7,900)
Radiology	(2,000)	6,000
Professional Service	1,200	100
Physical Medicine	700	2,700
Buildings & Grounds Departments	(1,800)	(20,000)
Administrative & General Departments	400	2,900
Food Service	(4,300)	(14,700)
Medical Records	(900)	(700)
	($19,100)	($61,600)

Analysis of Budget Income
November and Year-to-Date

	November	*5 Months*
Revenue over (under) budget:		
D.H.S.	($5,300)	($110,000)
Delivery Room	3,700	600
Emergency Room	1,300	3,000
Operating Room	400	(1,300)
Central Service	2,400	200
Inhalation Therapy	—	(400)
Pharmacy	(7,200)	(50,200)
Pathology	(600)	(18,400)
Radiology	1,000	(16,700)
Professional Service	2,200	6,500
Physical Medicine	(1,200)	(4,100)
Cafeteria	300	(100)
Total Revenue (under) Budget	($3,000)	($190,900)

tomies were higher in the summer when school was not in session, and surgery of most other types increases during the winter when summer vacations were not affected. Similarly, patient census dropped dramatically during physicians' conferences; patient census during Christmas vacation and over weekend periods also showed a significant drop from weekday and nonvacation averages as both patients and doctors were reluctant to use the hospital during these periods.

Some aspects of demand were influenced by the weather, for example, pneumonia and skiing accidents. Although cyclical in nature, the exact timing of the cycles often varied significantly from year to year.

"Totally Unpredictable" Factors

Reliable estimates of some of the hospital's most critical functions were most difficult to obtain. Obstetric, cardiac and artificial kidney patients, for instance, tended to be admitted as necessary and frequently on an emergency basis. Such patients could least afford poor service resulting from understaffing, so Mr. Luthy was often willing to tolerate periods of overstaffing in such units as cardiac care, intensive care and the artificial kidney unit.

A further complication was the establishment of such programs as Medi-Care and Medi-Cal. Although Loma Vista had experienced only a slight rise in the number of patients over 65 since Medi-Care went into effect, Mr. Luthy was uncertain whether this would continue to be true. This was a major concern because statistics showed that many older patients required twice as much nursing assistance as younger patients.

Control

The hospital staff produced a number of reports on current operations. Of these, Mr. Luthy regularly used the following to monitor the current state of the system:

—Departmental Responsibility Statements (Exhibit 4) presented monthly by each budgetary unit.

—Analysis of Budget Expenditures (Exhibit 5) produced monthly—shows results of operations for month and year to date, and also provides a summary of the Departmental Responsibility Statements.

Mr. Luthy and Mr. Haig also had available to them the Hospital Full-Time Equivalent Report (Exhibit 6) and the Nursing Full-Time Equivalent Report (Exhibit 7) which were produced bimonthly. These reports were not routinely distributed to either of them; their chief use was as a means of gathering additional statistical data or, in rare instances, as an aid in analyzing operating variances.

Staffing

Because of the wide fluctuations in patient census the Director of Nursing tried to organize the nursing staff with a great deal of flexibility. The nursing labor pool was composed of three different types of staff:

Exhibit 6

LOMA VISTA HOSPITAL
Hospital Full-Time Equivalent

	F.T.E. Actual 9/16/67	*F.T.E. Budget 9/16/67*	*Actual F.T.E. Y.T.D.*	*Budget F.T.E. Y.T.D.*
Nursing Departments	402.8	378.6	405.4	377.8
Operating Room	48.3	49.5	49.1	49.5
Central Service	22.2	23.0	22.1	23.0
Inhalation Therapy	4.1	5.0	3.9	5.0
Pharmacy	11.0	11.5	11.3	11.8
Radiology (excl. students)	17.8	17.7	17.7	17.7
Pathology (excl. students)	47.7	45.5	45.9	45.5
Professional Service	5.0	5.0	4.9	5.0
Physical Medicine	5.6	6.0	6.2	6.0
Buildings & Grounds	2.0	2.0	2.0	2.0
Maintenance & Engineering	25.1	28.8	25.4	28.1
Housekeeping	50.2	48.5	50.3	49.5
Laundry	23.4	23.2	23.6	22.9
Business Service	38.1	41.5	40.0	41.5
Purchasing	6.0	6.0	5.0	6.0
Print Shop & Mail	2.0	2.0	2.0	2.0
Personnel	4.0	3.5	3.6	3.5
Health Service	1.0	1.0	1.0	1.0
Administration	5.0	5.0	5.0	5.0
Admitting	10.7	10.0	10.6	10.0
P.B.X.	10.0	9.5	9.4	9.5
Dietary	59.0	59.1	57.7	60.1
Medical Records	17.2	17.6	17.9	17.6
Total Hospital	818.2	799.5	820.0	800.0
Average Daily Census (incl. Nursery)	288.1	298.2	289.9	290.3
Nursing F.T.E. per Average Daily Census	1.40	1.27	1.40	1.30
Other Departments F.T.E. per Average Daily Census	1.44	1.41	1.43	1.46
Total Hospital F.T.E. per Average Daily Census	2.84	2.68	2.83	2.76

The Permanent Staff worked a 40-hour week. Included in this group were 160 Registered Nurses (RN), 21 Licensed Practical Nurses (LPN), and 94 nurses' aides. RNs were the most highly skilled of the group: after passing formal examinations they were licensed to practice nursing in the State of California. By law an RN was permitted to administer medicine and perform a good many complicated and critical medical procedures with the approval of a medical doctor. At Loma Vista the RNs were not only used in their normal roles as supervisors and head

Exhibit 7

LOMA VISTA HOSPITAL
Nursing Full-Time Equivalent

Department	Shift	F.T.E. Actual 8/5/67 PR	F.T.E. Budget 8/5/67 PR	F.T.E. Variance (%)	Pt. Days Variance (%)
2-West	1	14.7	13.4	+ 9.7	
	2	10.9	7.9	+ 38.0	
	3	5.8	6.1	− 5.0	
Total		31.4	27.4	+ 14.6	−17.0
2-East	1	12.1	12.4	− 2.4	
	2	9.9	9.0	+ 10.0	
	3	6.4	6.0	+ 6.7	
Total		28.4	27.4	+ 3.6	−18.4
3-West	1	13.9	14.0	− .7	
	2	10.6	9.4	+ 12.8	
	3	5.9	5.3	+ 11.3	
Total		30.4	28.7	+ 5.9	−20.8
4-West	1	14.5	13.2	+ 9.8	
	2	11.8	8.0	+ 47.5	
	3	5.4	8.0	− 32.5	
Total		31.7	29.2	+ 8.6	−20.7
4-East (GYN)	1	6.4	5.2	+ 23.1	
	2	8.2	4.0	+105.0	
	3	4.8	2.4	+100.0	
Total		19.4	11.6	+ 67.2	+38.8
5-West	1	12.5	11.4	+ 9.6	
	2	10.6	9.4	+ 12.8	
	3	6.2	5.0	+ 24.0	
Total		29.3	25.8	+ 13.6	+14.4
5-East	1	19.8	15.8	+ 25.3	
	2	11.9	9.8	+ 21.4	
	3	5.7	5.8	− 1.7	
Total		37.4	31.4	+ 19.1	+17.9
6-West	1	3.2	6.0	− 46.7	
	2	2.3	4.0	− 42.5	
	3	1.5	2.0	− 25.0	
Total		7.0	12.0	− 41.7	−38.8
6-East	1	13.0	14.2	− 8.5	
	2	6.6	10.4	− 36.5	
	3	6.1	6.6	− 7.6	
Total		25.7	31.2	− 17.6	+ 1.3
Floats	1	—	—	—	
	2	1.2	—	—	
	3	.1	—	—	
TOTAL		242.0	224.7	+ 7.7	− 6.2

nurses but in some units comprised the entire work force. In most cases RNs claimed distaste for the supervisory role, preferring to devote themselves to "nursing," although they were universally respected and obeyed by other hospital employees on the nursing staff.

LPNs were nurses who had obtained a state license after 12–18 months of formal training followed by an examination. These nurses, although legally empowered to perform many of the same duties as the RNs, were seldom given the same level of authority as an RN and had considerably lower status. This arose not only from tradition but also because legally an RN was responsible for supervising the activities of an LPN. At Loma Vista, LPNs were utilized mainly as aides to the RNs.

Nurses' aides normally received six weeks of training at the hospital; they worked only under supervision of an LPN or an RN and were not empowered to administer medical treatment of any kind. A nurses' aide's duties included the more menial tasks of patient care—making beds, giving bed pans, tidying up rooms, helping with meals, etc. The large wards also employed "ward clerks" to handle administrative details and help with such tasks as charting.

The Float Staff consisted of approximately 42 Registered Nurses. These nurses were hired on a permanent basis by the hospital but were not permanently assigned to any unit. The nursing supervisor assigned these nurses on a daily—or even hourly—basis to meet the needs of the hospital. Besides these "extra" nurses, it was the policy at Loma Vista to shift or "float out" nurses from units whose census was down to those experiencing unexpected demand. Mr. Luthy was uncertain

Exhibit 8

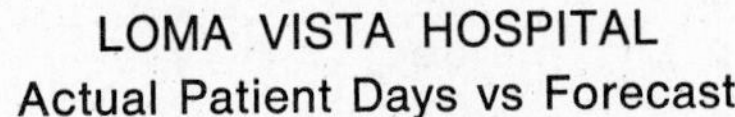

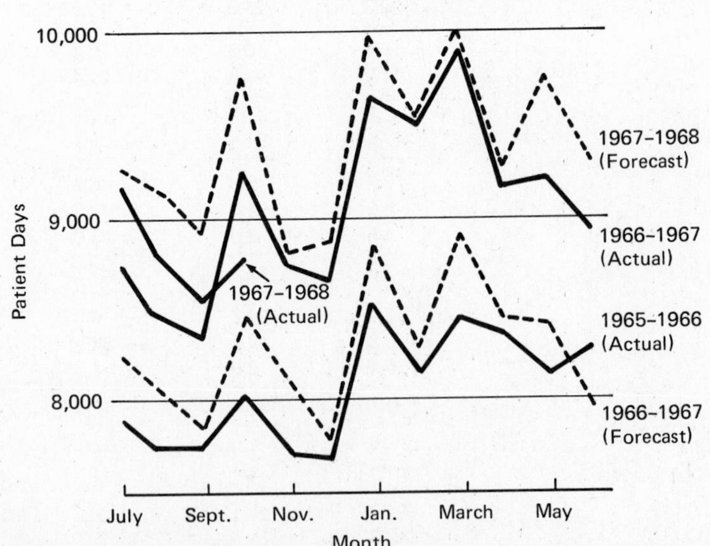

Exhibit 9

LOMA VISTA HOSPITAL
Full-Time Equivalent Employees on the Nursing Staff

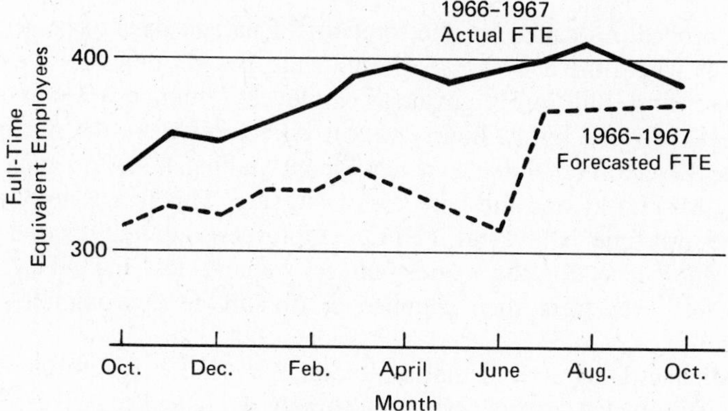

Full-Time Equivalent Employees (FTE) = Total number of hours worked per week divided by 40.

as to the extent or efficiency of shifting nurses: in some situations a good team relationship was crucial to effective performance.

The Part-time Staff was composed of 63 nurses of all types. Typically married women who no longer wished to devote full time to nursing, they arranged to work one to four days a week on a regular schedule. This enabled Loma Vista to hire, in effect, "fractional nurses."

Mr. Luthy felt that, conceptually at least, this method of staffing served to meet the constantly changing requirements of Loma Vista and enabled him to concentrate his efforts on trying to determine what the level of the permanent and float staffs should be. The system worked well in times of rising demand but poorly when demands slackened. He attributed this to several causes:

1. All hospital employees, including the nursing staff, were unionized. Under the union contract the hospital could release any employee at any time during the first 90 days they had been employed at the hospital. After this period, however, the hospital could not release an employee without demonstrating incompetence or lack of work. While the nurses would have little difficulty finding alternative employment, less skilled clerical help and nurses' aides could experience difficulty.

2. Except in such specialized wards as cardiac care or intensive care, the nursing staff generally worked in teams. A typical team was six people: four RNs and two LPNs or aides. A team would be responsible for the patient care for one-half of a ward and would tend to develop some *esprit de corps*. Teams were not shifted between wards when patient census in a ward dropped off. Any "floating" was done strictly on an individual basis.

3. When the patient load dropped, nurses busied themselves with peripheral duties aimed at increasing the comfort of their patients. The nurses tended to feel, therefore, that they were remaining busy. Problems related to reduced census were

compounded by the design and function of the larger wards. Most consisted of private and semi-private rooms, as well as multiple bed rooms; an effort was made to fill all private rooms in the hospital first. Furthermore, patients in the large wards were segregated by disease and by sex. As a result, low patient census in a ward often required nearly a full staff because the patients were widely scattered.

Current procedures called for the forecasts of patient days to be sent to each of the 15 wards where the head nurse of each shift, based on her prior experience, translated these into full-time equivalent employees (number of nursing hours needed per week divided by 40 hours/week). After review by the nursing supervisors and the Director of Nursing, a permanent staffing level for each unit was established by Mr. Luthy and the Director of Nursing. This was generally done by computing the full-time equivalent (FTE) employees required by the unit and setting the staffing level for the nearest integer value below the FTE computed. All fractions left over were then summed to obtain the approximate float staff required.

When Michael Haig arrived that afternoon, Mr. Luthy was poring over some of the statistical data he had requested. He briefly explained to Mike his concern about operating results and added:

Luthy: We've got to do something about the operating loss. Our nursing staff payroll accounts for more than half of our payroll, and this FTE report shows what kind of fluctuations our nursing payroll is experiencing. We could really save some money if we could be more efficient here, so I think we ought to concentrate on the nursing staff.

Haig: It looks straightforward to me. Our forecast of patient days was way off in October—it's been way off since the beginning of the year. We'll just have to lay off some nurses—or keep taking our lumps.

Luthy: Mike, the decision's not that simple. If this is just a temporary thing, we'd have to increase our permanent staff level before recovering from having chopped it. I can't explain this drop in demand, so I'm not sure we ought to do anything yet.

Haig: Well I think we've overstaffed the hospital. Not one of our projections of patient days for the year has been met.

Luthy: Maybe not, but I don't want to antagonize the union *at all.* We've had good relations with them so far, but a layoff could really foul up the bargaining atmosphere next April.

And, you know, we've got a perfect record—we've never had to lay off an employee in six years. This reputation counts when we're trying to attract and retain good nurses. If this situation *is* temporary, we'll be in real trouble when we try to rehire our people. Anyway, we've got a high turnover rate (15%/year), so if our patient census meets next month's forecasts—or at least comes close—we'd probably be better off letting attrition cut our staff.

Haig: That may be, but the Board of Directors is pretty unhappy about rising costs. They're already sensitive about some of those newspaper articles on increased patient charges. This deficit isn't going to make them any happier.

Luthy: That's why I called you in. I want you to draw up some recommendations on these questions. I've got another appointment, Mike, so I'll talk to you again in a few days.

Mr. Luthy handed Mike the following handwritten set of questions and left:

How can we improve staffing and forecasting policies? This flexible staffing is great if it works, but does it work? If we have to lay people off, whom do we let go and why? (I've got those evaluation sheets the head nurses and nursing supervisors filled out, but they're not worth much.) We can't afford *any* accusations of prejudicial treatment.

How did this get so far along before we caught it? I don't want this to happen again.

Mike read this note on the way back to his office. On his desk was a request from the Cardiac Care Unit (CCU) for the assignment of another full-time nurse to the 7:00 a.m.–3:00 p.m. shift. The request stated that ". . . the recent increase in CCU patient census *requires* an additional RN on the day shift in order to provide adequate patient care."

Based on the current annual plan, the CCU staffing level was four RNs on the 7:00–3:00 shift. These four worked 40-hour weeks, rotating their duty to cover all seven days. Recent policy at Loma Vista had been to hire *only* RNs for the CCU.

The supply of qualified RNs in the San Francisco area was not keeping pace with the area's needs. Mike knew of a nearby hospital which had had an opening for an RN unfilled for four months. He was certain that Loma Vista would begin to experience increasing difficulty in finding good RNs.

Exhibit 10

LOMA VISTA HOSPITAL
Nursing Hours per Patient Day
Cardiac Care Unit

Month	*Patient Days*	*Nursing Hours*	*Ratio*
Oct.	112	1820	16.2
Nov.	124	1647	13.2
Dec.	194	1948	10.0
Jan.	151	1808	11.9
Feb.	145	1552	10.7
March	137	1649	12.0
April	169	1578	9.4
May	146	1416	9.7
June	121	1459	12.1
July	130	1382	10.6
Aug.	91	1718	18.9
Sept.	113	1887	15.7
Oct.	118	1913	16.2

Mike asked for and received some historical data on the CCU (Exhibits 10, 11, and 16). He noted that staffing for capacity would insure that peak loads could be handled. However, the data showed that on 51 days out of the last 90 fewer than six of the unit's beds had been filled. Staffing the unit for less than capacity, of course, increased the risk of insufficient qualified staff should a number of simultaneous emergencies arise.

Because of the seriousness of the illnesses being treated and the limited number of specially trained nurses, Mike felt that it was probably desirable to err on

Exhibit 11

LOMA VISTA HOSPITAL
Three-Month History of the Daily Ward Census
Cardiac Care Unit

Date	October	November	December
1	3	1	4
2	2	1	2
3	4	4	4
4	4	5	8
5	5	6	8
6	5	7	7
7	3	7	6
8	3	4	7
9	4	3	7
10	5	4	8
11	6	5	7
12	6	5	7
13	5	4	7
14	2	3	8
15	2	3	8
16	2	3	8
17	2	3	7
18	3	3	5
19	4	3	8
20	3	3	6
21	3	4	6
22	3	1	5
23	6	4	5
24	8	4	4
25	6	4	7
26	5	5	8
27	2	3	8
28	2	3	6
29	2	5	5
30	1	7	4
31	1	—	4
	112	117	194

the side of excess capacity. However, he also knew that specialist RNs like to be busy and that too many in a unit could create serious morale problems.

Looking over past CCU staffing results (Exhibit 10), Mike could see that the unit had experienced wide fluctuations in nursing hours per patient day. He wondered if this meant that insufficient patient care was being provided at times, while at other times the unit was overstaffed.

He decided that a thorough understanding of this unit's staffing needs could help him respond to Mr. Luthy's more general request. Since labor costs were typically 65%–75% of Loma Vista's total operating costs, he realized that proper utilization of RNs, as well as a correct staffing level for each unit, would be central issues in the planning process. Mike decided, therefore, to investigate the CCU's request in some detail, hoping to be able to develop some guidelines or techniques for making these decisions on a hospital-wide basis.

The Cardiac Care Unit

The CCU was on the fourth floor of the hospital, immediately adjacent to the Intensive Care Unit. It was rectangularly shaped, with the patients' rooms located along the outside wall where there was a good view of the surrounding orchards and foothills. The nursing station ran the length of the ward (Exhibit 12).

When Mike arrived, Gale Hummell was the head nurse on duty. She was 26 years old and had been working in the CCU for about two years. Although considered one of the top RNs in cardiac care at Loma Vista, she was planning to leave in about five months because her husband was being transferred to the Midwest.

Exhibit 12

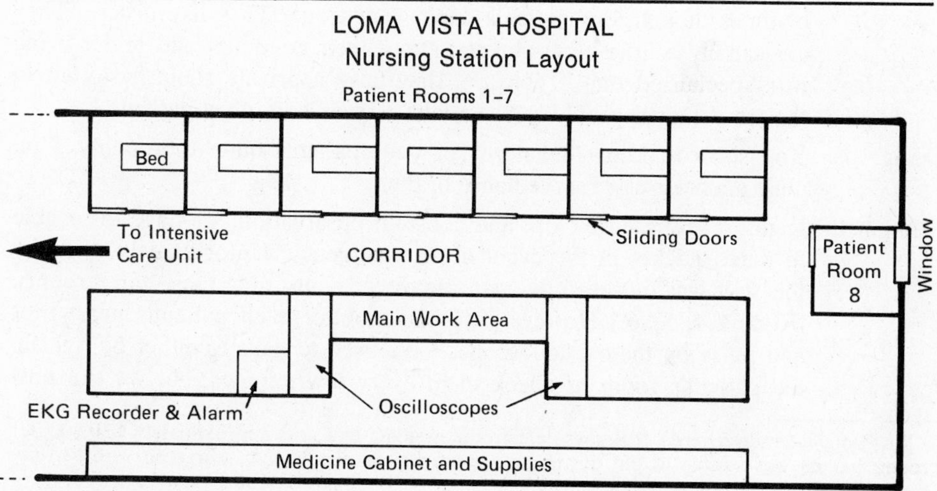

Hummell: What brings you up here, Mike? Don't tell me that the efficiency expert is going to descend on Cardiac Care?

Haig: Not really, Gale. Joan has requested one more RN for the day shift and I really don't know enough about Cardiac Care's requirements to evaluate the request one way or the other. Will you show me around and explain what goes on up here?

Hummell: Sure. We've only got four patients today. The ward has seven rooms along that wall [pointing]. Each of these rooms has a large picture window which helps make the rooms cheerful. The eighth room at the end of the ward isn't nearly so nice; it only has a small window. We try to keep one room free if we can, and it's usually that one. The main working area of the nursing station is right here where we're sitting—between these two banks of oscilloscopes. This is where we do a lot of our work—filling out records, charting, preparing medications, monitoring patients, and so forth.

Haig: What type of treatment is given here in the ward?

Hummell: Well, we get mainly two types of patients: the first is the emergency case where the person admitted has already had a heart attack and is very ill. The second is diagnostic: the patient may be having chest pains or some other danger symptoms and he is placed in here until they find out for sure what is the problem.

We handle only the more acute cases. Normally, we have a patient for five days before he is well enough to transfer out to one of the other wards, although some patients have stayed for a month or more.

Haig: Who makes that decision?

Hummell: The doctors, of course. We sometimes recommend movement—particularly if we are full and the patient is progressing well. We want to make sure we will have room for an emergency case if at all possible. Lots of times though, our patients don't want to go. They like it here. They are usually a little bit frightened about their condition and prefer being in a specialized unit. Then too, they have a private room here, but in the ward they'll probably be in with one or two other patients.

Haig: You seem to know the needs of your patients quite thoroughly. You must maintain close surveillance of them.

Hummell: Right. They require close and constant observation; we have to be able to react quickly in the event of an emergency. Unfortunately, the way this unit was designed, we can see directly into only those three rooms. [Rooms 4, 5, 6.] However, we can monitor each patient's heart beat and pulse on these oscilloscopes.[1] We used to have to either be right in the patient's room or check them every few minutes, but we can now

[1] Mr. Haig later discovered that these electronic systems had cost approximately $30,000 per room; but he was unable to pin down the basis for their justification, nor even who had authorized their acquisition.

do most of the monitoring of all eight rooms from the nursing station. It saves a lot of walking and cuts down our requirement for nurses. Let me show you one of the rooms. As you can see, each room has exactly the same equipment—a commode and wash basin, a night stand, a bed and a chair (Exhibit 13).

We keep a good deal of specialized equipment in each room. We used to keep a lot of these pieces of equipment on a cart and wheeled it in when it was needed, but now we have it already available in each room. It saves valuable time in case of an emergency.

On the wall over the head of the bed there's an "Airway" unit for mouth-to-mouth resusçitation, a suction machine, blood pressure gauge, and two cardiac wires. These wires are connected to small needles which are placed directly beneath the patient's skin and then read directly into an electrocardiogram (EKG) to record the patient's heartbeat.

This thing on the shelf is a continual monitoring device. By taping this small metal sensor to the patient's ear, we obtain a pulse rate. Among other things, we can tell when a patient is moving around too much. Either his pulse rate goes way up, or he dislodges the ear sensor which sets off an alarm. Readings from the EKG and the pulse rate sensor are monitored by this scope and one of the scopes at the nursing station outside. There's one for each patient at the nursing station.

Exhibit 13

LOMA VISTA HOSPITAL
Patient Room Layout

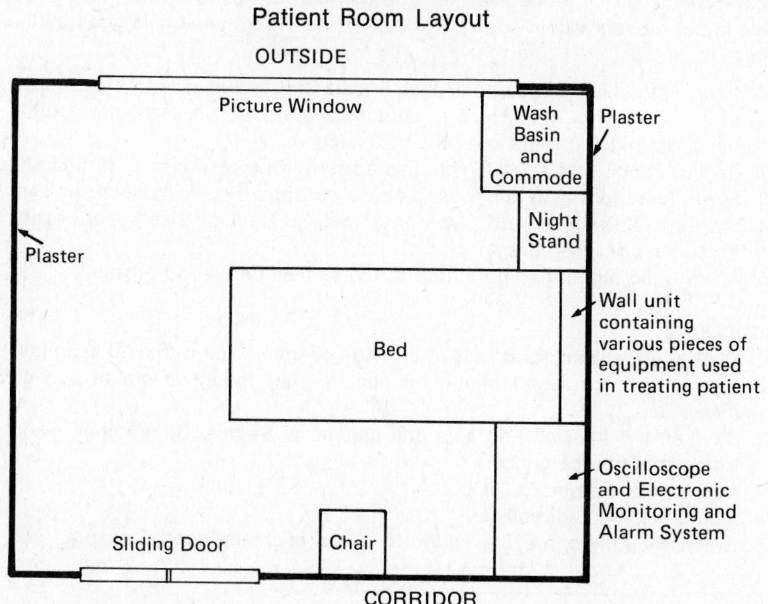

When any of several factors set into the monitoring units are exceeded, an alarm sounds at the nursing station and in the patient's room, and a red light above the patient's door turns on. At the same time, a graph of the patient's heartbeat begins to print on a machine at the nursing station. This graph—plus another produced by a special delayed tape machine which saves the prior two minutes of a patient's cardiogram—provides the attending doctor with valuable information as to what has happened.

Haig: When an alarm goes off, what do you do; I mean, what can you do either professionally or legally?

Hummell: The first thing, of course, is to get to the patient and find out what has happened—usually either cardiac arrest [heart stoppage] or heart fibrillation [uncontrolled heart spasms]. We used to have to wait at least two minutes for a doctor to show up before we could do anything. Now, however, we can begin immediate treatment. We can defibrillate, give mouth-to-mouth resuscitation, heart massage, and/or use electrical pacing to attempt to start the heart beat. I'll give you a sheet listing our emergency procedures before you leave (Exhibit 14). All of the equipment we need to perform any of these emergency procedures is already

Exhibit 14

LOMA VISTA HOSPITAL

Emergency Procedures for the Coronary Care Unit

The following emergency procedures may be carried out by the C.C.U. nurse if the attending physician is not present within one (1) minute. These orders must be signed by the attending physician.

I. *Ventricular Fibrillation*—Ventricular tachycardia and flutter (when patient is unresponsive and there is apparently no effective cardiac output).

1. Defibrillate at 400 watts/sec. within 60 seconds.
2. Repeat shock at 400 watts/sec. immediately if no response from first shock.
3. Start mouth to mouth and closed chest massage if no response from shock 1 and 2.
4. Start an I.V. infusion and give one ampule of Sodium Bicarbonate every 5 minutes from onset of emergency.
5. Aramine 50 mgm. may be added to I.V. to maintain blood pressure.

II. *Cardiac Arrest*

1. Start external pacing at rate of 80 and voltage of 150 within 30 seconds.
2. If no response after 1 minute of pacing, start mouth to mouth and closed chest massage.
3. Start an I.V. infusion and give one ampule of Sodium Bicarbonate every 5 minutes from onset of emergency.
4. Add Isuprel 1 mgm. to I.V. bottle.
5. Isuprel 0.2 mgm. directly I.V.
6. Aramine 50 mgm, may be added to I.V. to maintain blood pressure.

______________________________ M.D.

---

in the room, including these cardiac boards which we place under the patient's back to provide a hard surface against which to push in administering a heart massage. By the way, this board is a big improvement over what we had before. That was about twice as big, a couple of inches thick and must have weighed 10 pounds. This 3′ x 3′ piece of plywood is all we need; not only is it easier to lift, but it's much easier to get under the patient.

Haig: Let me take a bow for the "efficiency expert" who probably did that. You know, that's not the only place around here where a real understanding of the job's requirements might result in some improvements.

Hummell: You're probably right in general, Mike, but the CCU is a special case. In spite of a few improvements, such as the cardiac board and the emergency equipment right in the patient's room, there's not much anyone can do to improve our operations. Things are so unpredictable here. And individual differences between patients and even between the nurses assigned to the unit mean that you just have to play things by ear.

In subsequent visits to the CCU, Mike learned that the nurses assigned to the unit fulfilled three main functions:

1. *Patient care,* which included monitoring or watching the patient and taking care of emergencies as they arose. This was done primarily at the nursing station by observing the oscilloscopes and was supplemented by periodic checks on the rooms. The CCU nurses also carried out the more common nursing functions of administering medications, giving baths, changing bed linens when they became soiled, etc., as well as being present during doctors' examinations in order to receive any orders and relay any observations.
2. *Administrative,* which included preparation of patients' charts, census and staffing reports, preparation of medications, taking phone calls, etc. These duties were normally performed during slow periods when the nurses would otherwise be observing the scopes; i.e., many of these administrative tasks were performed simultaneously with monitoring of the scopes.
3. *Teaching,* that is, explaining to patients what has happened to them, keeping them informed of their progress and, in general, helping promote speedy recovery by reducing a patient's anxiety with as much information as possible. The nurses tried to respond to patients' concerns and fears over both their immediate future and what their illness would mean to their future way of life. The RNs tried to build an optimistic attitude in the patients by helping them to understand their problem and to realize that they could take active measures to help themselves. The nurses felt that this function, while it could be extremely difficult and trying, was the most rewarding they performed.

During one visit to the CCU, Mike questioned Gale Hummell about how much time the nurses needed to perform these functions:

Haig: Gale, could you give me some idea of how much time it takes you to do these jobs? Even better, could you tell me roughly what proportion of your time you spend on each of the three functions? If you could tell me that, I'd have a better idea of what the real requirements are here.

Hummell: Mike, you're missing the whole point. You sound just like my husband—his factory makes lots of plastic parts. Well, I'll tell you just what I tell him. People are *not* just a bunch of plastic parts. They just aren't predictable at all. Now, you take a doctor—we never know when one is going to make his rounds. He'll come when he can, but when he does we have to drop everything and be with him when he sees his patient. And our requirements change from patient to patient, and they also depend on how long the patient has been in the ward. During the first 48 hours or so, we don't spend much time with them beyond keeping them quiet and seeing to it that they rest. When they first come in they're very sick and under heavy sedation. But our job changes a lot as a patient improves and becomes aware of what's happened. Then we go over their cases with them, discuss their future, and all that. When they get even better, our job is about what it would be on one of the wards. We try to encourage patients to increase their activities and get them ready to be transferred out of the CCU.

Mike, the pattern is different for every patient. Right now we've got four: one is ready for transfer and we don't have to give him much care—he can go to the bathroom alone, dress himself, and so forth. But another one who's been here just as long still has low blood pressure and has to have IV [intravenous] medication to keep his pulse and pressure up. So we spend a lot of time with him, checking the IV, taking blood pressures, sponging him, feeding him.

Another patient is 65 and he's doing very well. He's had a heart attack before, so we don't have to spend much teaching time with him.

But the man in Room 5 is 42. We spend a lot of time teaching him what he can and can't do and discussing his fear of what's happened. These younger men are the cases you really want to help, and we usually spend longer with them.

On top of all this is the fact that our patient census just can't be predicted and the fact that we're really an emergency unit. You can see that we have a unique situation here in CCU.

Haig: Yes, but could you at least approximate how much time you spend on patient care, on teaching, and on administrative tasks?

Hummell: Oh, it's really impossible. It all depends on the shift, the nurse, and everything else. If I had to guess, I would say that I spend about 10% of my time teaching and maybe 30% or so monitoring and doing the administrative work. But that's really only a guess.

Haig: How do you go about estimating your staffing requirements now? I mean, what types of people do you use and if you have to, can you get more?

Hummell: We try to have two nurses on the 3:00–11:00 shift, although if the patient load is heavy we go to three. Right now we have three RNs on this shift, all working five days a week. We have another RN who works part-time three days a week. We can usually get along OK—we don't have doctors' visits, and baths and linen changes as much as the morning shift does.

Haig: What happens if all of a sudden you can't? Can you get help? Can anyone work in CCU?

Hummell: We only have RNs in CCU, no aides or even LPNs. It takes a lot of training and orientation before a new RN is really ready to work here. For instance, I have already started working with the RN who will be taking over my job as head nurse when I leave in a few months. It will take her about two months to learn the necessary techniques and then several months of experience to become really well qualified. Luckily, we have three nurses on hospital float who are qualified to work in CCU.

The previous shift supervisor normally determines staffing requirements. The head nurse gives the patient census and general condition of the patients to the nursing supervisor; the supervisor uses this information and her knowledge of the nurses coming on duty during the next shift to decide whether or not extra RNs will be needed. If so, she assigns float nurses to the unit. We usually have no trouble getting the help we need, even in the middle of a shift. Everyone recognizes that a shortage in CCU could be disastrous.

Mike decided that it might be helpful to discuss staffing policies with one of the nursing supervisors. Mrs. Pamela French was in her office when he arrived downstairs. She was a 40-year-old RN who had been working at Loma Vista for six years. After explaining what he was doing, Mike asked Mrs. French about staffing the CCU.

French: Well, we staff the various units of the hospital differently. Most unit staffing is based on the forecast of patient days given to us by Mr. Luthy in the Annual Plan. He forecasts patient days and also sets the float staff level. We use that to shift additional nurses into units with higher than expected loads.

However, we try to staff critical units such as CCU for capacity or near capacity, assuming a sort of normal mix of patients to decide nursing requirements.

Haig: Mrs. French, how can you tell when more nurses will be needed? Conversely, what happens when CCU does not need all of its nurses?

French: This is very hard to say and it all depends on the situation. The nursing supervisor can usually tell by the type and number of patients and by the relative competences of the nurses assigned to the next shift whether the unit is adequately staffed. When the nursing supervisor feels that the unit is *not,* we assign another nurse from the float staff or from another shift. My feeling is that the decision can best be made by a competent nursing supervisor, and it is best to spend the money to hire good people capable of performing the staffing assessments.

Haig: What about periods of overstaffing in CCU—what happens then?

French: Well, these rarely occur. This is a relatively new unit here and we have been gradually stepping up our permanent staff as more and more doctors in the area use our facilities. In cases of overstaffing, CCU nurses—because of their skills and training—would actually be a great asset as they could be floated out to almost any other nursing unit in the hospital. And, you know, if nurses are too idle they can get restless and may search for alternative employment. On the other hand, the girls in the specialized care units take considerable pride in their work and sometimes resist moving to other units on a temporary basis.

Exhibit 15

LOMA VISTA HOSPITAL
Time Standards for Nursing Care

Description				*Per Patient Standard* (Hours)
1. Admit—pick up at admitting office				.050
2. A.M. care				.085
3. Back rub in addition to bed bath				.052
4. Bed change				.067
5. Call lights				.008
6. Census Count				.006
7. Discharge—assist patient to parking area				.150
8. Discharge—strip beds				.023
9. Discharge—make up beds				.144
10. H. S. care				.020
11. Linen—distribute				.030
12. Linen–dispose				.008
13. Medications—administer				.047
14. Menu assistance (selective)				.060
15. Narcotics count and reorder				.008
16. Nourishments				.025
17. Paperwork, including charting				.482
18. Position bed				.007
19. Pre-meal care				.033
20. Report—personnel	Day .026	Even. .012	Night .006	
21. Report—supervisory				.013
22. Rounds, doctors'				.070
23. Rounds, other				.008
24. Temperature sheet				.030
25. Trays, pass and pick up				.042
26. Water				.009

Exhibit 16

LOMA VISTA HOSPITAL
12-Month History of Percentage Occupancy for Each Nursing Station

	No. of	% Occupancy											
	Beds	Nov.	Dec.	Jan.	Feb.	Mar.	Apr.	May	June	July	Aug.	Sept.	Oct.
Ward													
Intensive Care Unit	11	40.9	55.4	38.4	55.2	49.0	41.8	41.6	34.2	33.1	42.8	27.0	35.2
Cardiac Care Unit	8	42.5	49.6	60.9	64.7	55.2	70.4	60.1	50.4	52.4	33.9	47.0	47.6
Obstetrics	39	57.4	60.7	58.6	66.1	62.4	56.7	65.9	54.3	62.0	55.3	71.5	57.6
Teen-Age Ward	6	60.6	60.8	70.4	61.3	75.8	70.6	51.1	69.4	58.6	70.4	63.9	54.8
Pediatrics	42	47.3	55.9	55.1	49.6	46.8	42.1	45.9	51.2	50.0	46.1	38.6	43.0
Psychiatry	29	85.3	68.4	85.9	94.8	85.9	83.3	86.8	75.2	80.1	69.2	87.5	87.1
Medical & Surgical		78.0	74.4	83.9	83.8	80.3	82.2	76.6	70.3	64.5	65.4	64.8	59.0
2 West	34	72	68	85	81	74	82	77	67	63	68	63	62
2 East	34	73	66	82	85	77	77	74	65	57	70	59	58
3 West	34	85	82	88	89	88	89	84	80	72	79	76	66
4 West	34	86	83	93	91	87	90	84	80	76	78	73	66
4 East	20	0	0	30	64	73	80	65	76	76	63	64	75
5 West	34	71	68	82	80	79	75	70	68	69	61	68	63
5 East	42	85	80	87	91	88	90	86	81	83	76	76	79
6 West	26	0	0	0	0	0	0	0	21	26	20	31	15
6 East	34	0	0	62	84	71	74	68	67	51	60	57	44
All Services	427	70	74	71	78	74	74	71	66	63	62	63	58

Haig returned to his office and went over some additional material he had put together. He had checked and found that there were no legal reasons why properly trained LPNs could not perform any of the procedures required in the CCU.

He realized that specialization of the nursing function was a sensitive subject, but also felt that using RNs to watch oscilloscopes, make beds, feed patients and keep records seemed to be a poor utilization of their capabilities. Specialization might result in better utilization of RNs and improve the level of patient care by freeing the RNs for more critical nursing functions.

RNs in particular were reluctant to surrender any portion of the responsibility for the care and welfare of their patients. However, Haig felt that specialization presented an opportunity for reducing costs because of the following differences in pay:

	Salary/Week (average)
Registered Nurse	$115
Licensed Practical Nurse	85
Nurses' Aide	68

Haig was worried about what the nurses had told him concerning the difficulty of specifying adequate levels of patient care, as well as the difficulty of measuring the various activities comprising the nursing function. He was certain that if in fact this could *not* be done, planning and control of the nursing function would be difficult, if not impossible.

Loma Vista had earlier attempted to do just this with a set of standard times for planning staffing levels and trying to control the utilization of nurses (Exhibit 15). It had been abandoned after a short while, however, and Loma Vista had continued to rely on the judgment of the nursing supervisors in allocating nurses on a day-to-day basis and in determining staffing levels in relation to the forecast census.

From his discussions with Mr. Luthy, Mike knew that one of the reasons the system had been abandoned was resistance within the nursing staff. They had felt that the system of standards used was an attempt to rob them of the flexibility and judgment they required to perform their job correctly. Mr. Luthy felt that the system was unworkable because the classifications used were too narrow and rigid and because they failed to take account of differences between units.

The "float" concept which allowed nurses to be assigned to overburdened units as needed, either from the permanent hospital float staff of 12 nurses or from other units whose census was down, *seemed* to work as a basis for allocating nurses. However, Mr. Luthy had commented that nurses permanently assigned to a unit were extremely reluctant to be "floated" out to other units. This plus his figures showing the large fluctuations in nursing hour/patient day in CCU indicated possible underutilization of Registered Nurses and raised the possibility that the "float" system was not as workable as it appeared to be.

Medibus, Inc.

> *Our first two months (January and February 1975) of operations have been much better than projected. Sales have been about double our budgeted figures. We have ordered another ambulette which will be delivered in April. We are well on our way to develop a profitable enterprise and should be a $2 million firm in 2–3 years. My biggest concern is charting the course which will take us there.*
>
> Richard Gabriele, President (age 39)

The Service

MediBus, Inc., a transportation service exclusively for disabled, handicapped, and elderly persons, had begun pilot operations on January 1, 1975. From headquarters

Exhibit 1

MEDIBUS, INC.
MEDIBUS AMBULETTE

in Smithtown, New York, on Long Island, ramp-equipped vehicles were dispatched with uniformed drivers trained in first aid. The air-conditioned vehicles, called "ambulettes," were specifically designed to carry a maximum of four wheelchair and five ambulatory passengers at one time (see Exhibit 1). As Dick Gabriele, MediBus founder and president explained:

> MediBus is not an emergency or ambulance service and does not charge rates required by those services. It will carry anyone in a wheelchair, on crutches, using a walker, or able to walk into the MediBus. Because of its unique approach and equipment, MediBus opens up many possibilities for persons who are unable to use conventional taxi or bus service to visit their doctor, dentist, therapist, or recreational facility.
>
> Modest rates are charged for each trip with special rates for group, Medicare, and Medicaid clients. For those institutions which utilize MediBus for the medical transportation needs of their clients, MediBus will transport their clients on both recreational and social trips. These trips are billed directly to the institution (see Exhibit 2 for a rate schedule). In addition, MediBus, as of March 3, provides health care equipment and sickroom supplies on either a rental or sale basis.

Background

The MediBus concept had been developed by Richard Gabriele during the fall of 1974 while he was serving as a consultant to Ecologic Instrument Corporation, a company which he had founded in 1971 and of which had served as president until October, 1974.[1] Ecologic manufactured analytical instruments and pollution control equipment and had annual sales of approximately $1.5 million. In January 1974, Ecologic had been sold to United States Filter Corporation, and Mr. Gabriele had been retained under management contract as operating head of the subsidiary. However, he had stepped down from this position in October 1974 because of a disagreement with U.S. Filter management over whether Ecologic should concentrate on short- or long-term profits. Mr. Gabriele had explained his view of the situation:

> U.S. Filter wanted Ecologic to reduce all development efforts and concentrate our efforts selling the existing line. I disagreed. We were close to some major development breakthroughs. If our competitors hit the market with the new products, our existing line would be obsolete in a year. Therefore, I thought U.S. Filter's approach was shortsighted although their payout scheme to me placed a heavy weight on short-term profits. As a result of our disagreement,

[1] Prior to founding Ecologic Instrument Corporation, Mr. Gabriele had been a cofounder (1969) of Automated Environmental Systems, Inc., a company engaged in the manufacture of pollution control instrumentation. As vice-president of marketing, he guided AES's marketing efforts for three years until AES was merged with a doubleknit fiber manufacturer. For 11 years prior to the founding of AES, Mr. Gabriele had been involved in sales and sales management in the hospital supply and equipment business including six years with Beckman Instruments, Inc.

Exhibit 2

MEDIBUS, INC.
RATE SCHEDULE

Private—Non Medicaid/Medicare per Client

$15.00 per trip one way with up to 10 FREE miles
$30.00 round trip with up to 20 FREE miles
Additional Mileage: $1.30 per mile
FREE—1 Hour Waiting Time
$15.00 per hour or part thereof after the first hour
(First hour starts at time of pickup.)
These rates apply during the hours of 7 a.m. to 6 p.m.
Monday thru Friday.
Any scheduled service provided, other than during the above hours, including Saturday, ADD $20.00 in addition to the above rates.
For Sunday and Holiday service, please call for rates.

Medicaid/Medicare Client Transportation Service—will be billed at the prevailing rates established by the local Medical Transportation Department.

Recreational and Social Trip Fees

To those accounts where we are providing routine MediBus service for either Medicaid or private transportation, MediBus will provide one of our vehicles, capable of transporting up to 11 passengers, for *$15.00 per hour, per vehicle;* includes 10 FREE miles. Over 10 miles: $.75 per mile. Waiting Time, if required, $10.00 per hour.

In order to qualify for this special rate, scheduling must be made at least one (1) week in advance.

Hours available for this special rate will be from 11 a.m. to 2 p.m. Monday thru Friday.

NOTE: Each 9 passenger MediBus can accommodate four (4) wheelchair passengers and five (5) non-wheelchair passengers. Vehicles for larger groups available.

Prices Subject to Change Without Notice

RATE SUMMARY

	One-Way Trip	*Round Trip*	*Extra Time*[2]	*Extra Mileage Fee*	*Additional Charges*
Medicare/ Medicaid	$10	$20[1]	$10/hour	$.50/mile each mile over first 40	$2.50/ person[3]
Private	$15 (10 free miles)	$30 (20 free miles)	$15/hour	$1.30/mile each additional mile	$20/hour[4]
Recreational/ Social	$15/hour/vehicle (10 free miles) (up to 9 passengers per vehicle)		$10/hour	$.75/mile each mile over first 10	

[1] Minimum fee for round trip.

[2] Over first hour; first hour is included in price of round trip. Extra time is all travel and passenger wait time after first free hour. Additional wait time is subject to this charge, even when the MediBus is utilized for other trips during the wait time.

[3] Nonclient passengers, such as nurses, aides or family members accompanying the client.

[4] Additional charge for nonscheduled hours, such as weekends and holidays.

Exhibit 3

MEDIBUS, INC.
PRO FORMA INCOME STATEMENTS
For Different Numbers of Vehicles
December 1974

	3 Medibuses	4 Medibuses	5 Medibuses	6 Medibuses	7 Medibuses	8 Medibuses
Revenue						
255 average number work days at $100/day/vehicle	$76,500	$102,000	$127,500	$153,000	$178,500	$204,000
Expenses						
Vehicle lease	9,180	12,240	15,300	18,360	21,420	24,480
Insurance	2,400	3,200	4,000	4,800	5,600	6,400
Gas and oil	3,900	5,200	6,500	7,800	9,100	10,400
Maintenance	750	1,000	1,250	1,500	1,750	2,000
Miscellaneous	750	1,000	1,250	1,500	1,750	2,000
*Payroll drivers	21,060	28,080	35,100	42,120	49,140	56,160
Office payroll	7,370	7,370	7,370	7,370	7,370	7,370
**Payroll taxes	2,843	3,545	4,247	4,949	5,651	6,353
Office and furniture rent	3,180	3,180	3,180	3,180	3,180	3,180
***Telephone	1,500	1,500	1,500	1,500	1,500	1,500
Office supplies	240	240	240	240	240	240
Postage	600	600	600	600	600	600
Legal and accounting	1,200	1,200	1,200	1,200	1,200	1,200
Deposits and security	680	680	680	680	680	680
Advertising, promotion	750	750	750	750	750	750
Printing and duplicating	100	100	100	100	100	100
Total Expenses	56,503	69,885	83,267	96,649	110,031	123,413
Income	19,997	32,115	44,233	56,351	68,469	80,587
Income/Revenue × 100%	26%	31%	35%	37%	38%	40%

* Average $135/week/driver.
** 10% Payroll drivers plus office payroll.
*** $125/month average.

U.S. Filter negotiated with me on the remaining term of my management contract. I left officially on December 31, 1974, which gave me time between October and December to plan a new business.

During the month of October, Mr. Gabriele had screened many business opportunities. After a couple of weeks, he had decided to focus on the health care field, which he had gotten to know so well in his 11 years of selling to the health care industry. Promising areas had included medical supplies (especially disposables), clinical laboratories, and rental of health-related equipment. One day he had noticed an ad in the *Wall Street Journal* offering franchises for a medical transportation service. The firm, MediCab, Inc., based in Westchester County, New

York, had been an outgrowth of a taxi company which had begun catering to the transportation needs of nonacutely ill, nonambulatory persons. Mr. Gabriele had explained his encounter with MediCab:

> I visited their headquarters in response to the ad with the thought of acquiring a franchise. They were providing exactly the same kind of transportation service in Westchester County that we are providing today in Suffolk County. We just capitalized on their idea.
>
> A couple of days later, I called together Sam[2] and Julie[3] for a meeting. At that meeting we put together the idea for a total medical service company to provide not only the transportation service of MediCab but to provide, in addition, nursing care, equipment rental, and eventually part-time physician services.

A business plan had been developed during the last two weeks of November 1974. Included as Exhibit 3 is a proforma profit and loss statement for the pilot operations center with three to eight MediBuses. The founders' thinking had been shaped in part by the material contained in a *Long Island Business Review* article. The pertinent sections of that article are included as Exhibit 4.

Marketing Strategy

Because of competitive conditions (discussed below) and the fact that Messrs. Gabriele and Richman were residents, Suffolk County had been selected as the primary market during the start-up phase. In January 1975, the key personnel who had decision-making authority in the choice of medical transportation in each nursing home in Suffolk County had been visited either by Mr. Gabriele or Mr. Richman and given a verbal presentation of the MediBus service. The title of the decision-makers varied from nursing home to nursing home depending upon the size and organization of the institution. In larger institutions, the nursing director was usually the key decision-maker; in smaller ones, it was often an administrator's secretary. The decision-makers had been given promotional literature designed to answer questions for both customers and clients (see Exhibit 5). Several weeks later, a letter which reiterated the earlier delivered "message" had been sent to each key decision-maker. On each sales visit, an effort had been made to stick a MediBus label, which featured the MediBus phone number, on as many phones as possible at locations from which a possible call for the service might be made. Mr. Richman explained the overall strategy:

> We usually call on the recreation director first (each nursing home to qualify for Medicaid was required to have a recreational director). We explain to the director our recreational/social package. He/she usually gets very excited

[2] Samuel Goldstein (age 57) ran a small industrial advertising firm which specialized in advertising and promotion for smaller firms. He often took an equity interest for services rendered. Mr. Goldstein had met Mr. Gabriele when Ecologic Instruments was founded in 1971.

[3] Julius Richman (age 42) was formerly director of marketing and sales of Ecologic Instrument Corporation. He had worked with Mr. Gabriele for over ten years.

Exhibit 4

MEDIBUS, INC.
Facilities, Patients, and Payments

Long Island Facilities[1]

There are at present some 7,040 nursing home beds serving a combined Nassau-Suffolk population estimated at 2,705,172, 8% of whom are over 65. Health-related facilities now provide space for 2,462 patients. In Nassau and Suffolk the number of HRF beds are almost equal—1,418 and 1,044, respectively. In Nassau, however, where the population is somewhat older and larger, there are far more nursing home beds than in Suffolk. For every three beds in Suffolk there are four in Nassau. The actual numbers are 2,901 against 4,139.

The rate of occupancy in both counties is around 98 or 99%. Many facilities have waiting lists. Luckily, expansions of existing homes and the construction of new facilities is presently underway in Nassau and in Suffolk. By the end of the year, nursing home beds in Nassau will expand by at least 100 and in Suffolk by at least 160. Health-related facilities, which are undergoing a more strenuous development, will increase by 432 beds in Nassau and by 612 in Suffolk.

Almost all of the 56 nursing homes and 20 health-related facilities on the Island are proprietary. In each county there is one public institution.

Patient Profile

In 1972, the Suffolk County Department of Health's Division of Hospital Affairs, the bureau responsible for the supervision of local facilities, released its most recent annual report. From its statistical findings, a thumbnail sketch of the typical nursing home patient emerges. The average patient is female and between the ages of 75 and 84. Women, who are known to outlive men generally, outnumbered them in Suffolk nursing homes three to one. Only a small portion of the patients—slightly more than 8%—were less than 64 years old. People 75 to 84 years old were the most prevalent averaging 43.3%. The next largest breakdown was the 85-and-over age group with 28.2%. The remaining 20.1% were between the ages of 65 and 74. It is of tangential interest to learn that according to the Suffolk figures the nursing home population is growing older. In the past three years, the post-75 group has increased noticeably at the expense of the younger people.

The greatest number of patients—over 40%—were bedridden. The rest were almost evenly divided between the ambulant and semiambulant. Few stayed longer than a year—the average being 275 days. Thirty-four percent were discharged and either went home or to other facilities. Twenty-seven percent were transferred to hospitals for more intensive care. Thirty-nine percent died. Predominately, they were county residents, indigent, and on Medicaid.

Paying The Bills

The cost of any kind of medical care is notoriously expensive. A private room in a private Long Island nursing home may run as much as $40 or $60 a day. On top of that flat rate there may be fees for physicians, drugs, and therapy. The same room in a local health-related facility, less expensive because the care is less comprehensive, may still be as high as $25 or $30 a day without considering other costs.

[1] The three sections of this exhibit (Long Island Facilities, Patient Profile, and Paying the Bills) were extracted from a Marine Midland Bank survey of nursing homes published in the October 2–8, 1974, issue of the *Long Island Business Review*.

Exhibit 4 (continued)

Since legislation was passed in 1966, children of an aged parent are no longer responsible for their parents' medical bills. Only the assets of the sick person can be tapped for medical expenses. When these funds are totally exhausted, people over the age of 65 become eligible for Medicaid.

Medicaid will pay for nursing home or health-related facility care. Concomitant costs, such as physicians, dentists, optometrists, podiatrists, and chiropractors fees and drugs and therapy are also covered. Persons with an annual income of less than $2,000 and less than $1,600 in allowable reserves, in which the cash value of any life insurance policy is figured, qualify. Those with assets above these figures must wait until their funds are depleted to these levels to become eligible.

Under Medicaid, all personal income, like social security and pension checks, goes automatically to defray the costs of medical care. Only a $500 burial fund is allowed. Medicaid will pick up whatever part of the total bill the elderly person cannot pay. In addition, it will furnish the indigent person with a $24 a month stipend for his personal needs.

Medicaid is an assistance program enacted under Title 19 of the Social Security Act to furnish medical care to low-income and needy people. It is funded by federal, state, and local taxes. In New York State, 50% comes from federal resources, 25% from the state and 25% from local revenues. Medicare, on the other hand, is an insurance program. All people over the age of 65 are automatically eligible–regardless of their financial assets–if they have paid into Social Security. As with Social Security, Medicare covers dependent husbands and wives.

Medicare can help pay part of the costs of short-term nursing home care. Medicare certification is not extended to health-related facilities. It is less comprehensive than Medicaid and its applicability is more limited. To be covered, an elderly person must be admitted to a skilled nursing facility within two weeks of a hospital discharge. The original hospital stay must have been a minimum of three days. As with Medicaid, admission to the nursing home must be undertaken on the determination of a physician. The patient must require round-the-clock care for recuperation or rehabilitation of the ailment for which he was hospitalized. Unlike Medicaid, Medicare will only pay for the first 100 days of a nursing home stay.

In addition to the cost of the facility, Medicare Medical Insurance will pay for 80% of all doctors' bills, tests, X-rays, medical equipment and devices, injections, and ambulance transportation after the patient pays the first $60.

Many people qualify for both Medicaid and Medicare. And Medicaid can pay what Medicare does not for people who are eligible for both programs. The institutions in which a patient receives nursing care must be certified by Medicaid or Medicare, or both, for the patient to receive benefits. Such certification not only guarantees the facility will accept payment but also that they meet certain minimum standards set by Washington.

Application for Medicare is routine and made through the local Social Security Office. Application for Medicaid requires two investigations to determine financial and medical needs. The latter is usually done through the individual's physician or hospital. The former is lengthy and requires a good deal of documentation.

Because of the high cost of nursing care, Long Island's Department of Health estimate that 70% of Suffolk's nursing home and HRF bills and perhaps 80–85% of those in Nassau are paid by Medicaid. Medicaid pays the homes their costs and, in the case of private facilities, a return on equity now set at 10%. The nursing home reimbursement rates paid by Medicaid now range from $25.53 to $42.35 a day in Nassau and from $25.54 to $46.14 in Suffolk. Some rates include the costs of prescription drugs and therapy.

Medicare, meanwhile, pays an estimated 2% of the total costs in Nassau and about 5% in Suffolk. Privately paid bills amount to 25% of the gross in Suffolk and about 15% in Nassau.

Exhibit 5

MEDIBUS, INC.
Some Questions and Answers About MediBus

What is MediBus?

MediBus is a special transportation service for the disabled, elderly, and handicapped persons including those in wheelchairs.

What service does MediBus offer?

Medibus specializes in transporting wheelchair confined passengers. Specially designed ramp-equipped MediBus vehicles transport handicapped and elderly clients to doctors' and dentists' offices, hospitals, nursing homes, schools, recreational clubs, and any other designated location in Suffolk and Nassau counties.

How do I order MediBus services?

One phone call will bring the MediBus and a trained, courteous driver to the designated pickup location.

Will the MediBus wait for me?

Yes. MediBus rates include provisions for waiting time.

How much does MediBus cost a private individual?

For one person, the rate for a direct point-to-point trip up to 10 miles is $15 one way. Special long-distance rates are available.

What does MediBus charge for transporting Medicaid clients?

Since Medicaid transportation must be authorized by designated County officials, MediBus charges prevailing rates established and approved by the local Medicaid transportation department.

Can MediBus be chartered for special trips?

Yes. Special plans and rates for charter or package trips can be arranged.

Are MediBus costs tax deductible?

Yes. Necessary medical transportation is tax deductible for many individuals. MediBus will gladly furnish receipts on request.

Is MediBus an emergency or ambulance service?

NO. MediBus is not an emergency or ambulance service and does not charge rates required by those services. It will carry anyone in a wheelchair, on crutches, using a walker or able to walk in to the MediBus.

Can arrangements be made for trips at regular intervals such as once a week, every two weeks, monthly, etc.?

Yes. Such arrangements will gladly be worked out with pickup and return trips scheduled as required.

What makes MediBus vehicles special?

MediBus ambulettes are designed to facilitate transportation of wheelchair passengers and persons using walkers or crutches. Special ramps permit easy entry into the MediBus. Wheel wells and unique lock bars hold wheelchairs safely in place. Safety belts offer additional protection. Each MediBus has first-aid apparatus and the latest in safety equipment.

Are MediBus drivers specially trained?

All MediBus drivers are trained in first aid and, more important, are courteous and concerned for the well-being and safety of their passengers.

because many of the nonambulatory residents are restricted to in-house activities because adequate transportation is not available for trips away from the institution.

Next, we locate the person who makes decisions about the medical transportation needs of the institution's residents. We tell him/her we have spoken to the recreational director and that we can not provide the recreational/social transportation service on a regular basis unless we can participate in providing for the institution's normal medical transportation needs. We try, if at all possible, to get the person to inspect our vehicle, which usually impresses him/her and sells itself.

In addition, a direct mail campaign had been targeted to the medical profession in Suffolk County. The promotional pieces explained how the physician's patients could receive medical transportation to and from the physician's office.

Clients and Customers

Only 10% of business came from private sources; the other 90% of MediBus's business came from third parties such as nursing homes, hospitals, outpatient clinics, and charitable organizations. A breakdown of these institutional trips for the period, February 24–28, is given in Exhibit 6. MediBus referred to these third parties as

Exhibit 6

MEDIBUS, INC.
Trips from Institutions
February 24–28, 1975

Name	*Type of Institution*	*Number of Trips*
Broad Lawn Manor	Nursing home	2
Brunswick Hospital	Hospital	1
Huntington Clinic	Outpatient clinic	7
Lakehurst	Nursing home	1
Mather Hospital	Hospital	2
Oak Hollow	Nursing home	15
Saint Charles Hospital	Hospital	1
Saint James Nursing Home	Nursing home	4
Saint James Plaza	Nursing home	6
Sayville	Nursing home	2
Smithtown General Hospital	Hospital	3
Smithtown Nursing Home	Nursing home	1
Smithtown Rehabilitation Center	Outpatient clinic	8
South Country Nursing Home	Nursing home	2
Woodhaven	Nursing home	8
	TOTAL	63*

* There were four private clients during the period, February 24–28.

customers. The persons actually transported were called *clients.* Most clients had a disability, but many did not think of themselves as being sick.

The customers called the MediBus office and made appointments for clients. MediBus appointments were usually made at the same time that appointments were made with doctors, dentists, optometrists, etc. Approximately 90% of the appointments were made at least three days before the day of the trip. Only 2–3% of the appointments were made for travel on the same day.

Payments for over 90% of the transportation services rendered by MediBus were made by Medicare and/or Medicaid. Some clients were regular clients, scheduled for weekly or even daily trips. For example, one client was transported to a methadone clinic six days each week for medication. A random sample of Medicaid invoices for the month of February is included as Exhibit 7.

Exhibit 7

MEDIBUS, INC.
Random Sample of Invoices to
Medicaid of Suffolk County, New York

Job Number	*Round Trip Mileage*	*Trip Time (Hours)*	*Total Fee**
1	6	3	$43.00
2	35	2	32.75
3	20	3	40.00
4	15	2.5	35.00
5	16	3	40.00
6	20	3	50.00
7	45	2	47.75
8	16	3	42.50
9	35	2	32.75
10	8	2	30.00
11	15	3	40.00
12	41	2	37.25
13	35	2	32.75
14	24	4	50.00
15	24	2.5	37.50
16	166	3.5	108.00
17	20	2.5	45.00
18	34	2	34.50
19	19	2.5	37.50
20	69	2	58.25
21	53	2.5	50.00
22	20	2	32.50
23	21	3	50.00
24	12	2	30.00
25	34	2	34.50
Average	32.1	2.5	$42.86

* The actual fees varied from the price list in many cases due to technicalities of the Medicaid system.

A typical client response was provided by a 74-year-old widow who was confined to a wheelchair:

> I have been living in this nursing home for over a year. I must visit my doctor for an examination quarterly. I never did like to ride in an ambulance to the doctor's office. Several weeks ago I rode in a MediBus; the driver was courteous and talked to me all the way there and back. Now, I will request MediBus whenever I go.

A physician explained his first contact with MediBus:

> I received a call late one afternoon from a company for which I serve as company physician that a minor accident had occurred and that a person who was hurt, but not seriously, needed to see me. The quickest an ambulance company could get the patient to me was 2½ hours. They are always slow. Because one of the MediBus stickers was on one of our phones, I asked my nurse to see if they could transport him. They could. In fact, he was in my office in less than 45 minutes. I was so impressed that I introduced the driver to about eight other physicians in this building. We have used them since, and they have not let us down.

A nursing home administrator explained why MediBus was being used by his facility:

> We use MediBus because our residents like MediBus's vehicles and drivers. In the past, we had been indifferent about who transported our clients because, in most cases, the payment was covered by Medicaid. However, our residents have a fear of ambulances and the MediBus has a cheerful, clean appearance.
>
> We plan to use MediBus for a recreational trip or two this summer, but not many because we have to pay for those trips. We can only allocate 50¢ per day per resident for recreational/social purposes.

Competition

In Suffolk County, medical transportation services were provided by three major ambulance companies. In Nassau County the situation was quite different, as Richard Gabriele explained:

> In Nassau, we have a problem. The private ambulance association, consisting of eight ambulance companies, convinced the Nassau County Medicaid office to enter into an exclusive contract for transporting Medicaid clients. As a result, only members of the association can provide our type of transportation service in Nassau County, and we are presently not members of the association.
>
> The association's contract is renewed monthly. We hear rumblings that the Medicaid officials in Nassau County are not pleased with the present level of

> service. We also hear that officers of the association are giving preferential treatment to the officer's firms to the disgust of the other members of the association. We have made overtures to the Commissioner of Health in Nassau County that there has been a restraint of trade because the contract was not awarded on a competitive bid basis.

Mr. Gabriele next explained the competitive advantage of MediBus over ambulances:

> In the past, customers called ambulance companies for their clients. The ambulance companies use this type of business to "fill in" between their emergency calls. They use the same vehicles for both emergency and nonemergency service. Our main advantage is that clients have an intense fear of traveling in an ambulance. Many of their former friends were last seen entering an ambulance. After their first trip with MediBus, clients request our vehicles. Word of mouth has been terrific.
>
> Ambulance companies are not actively seeking our business. They have concentrated on stretcher patients, local emergencies not filled by fire departments, and transportation of patients to major medical centers. In fact, we are not hurting the ambulance companies. Nursing homes are sending out more clients as they use our service and their confidence factor increases—not only more, but more frequently! We are generating a market that really wasn't there before. This fact is confirmed by Medicaid officials.

MediBus claimed another competitive advantage with regards to private clients. Their rates were about 50% less than ambulance charges for private clients. Ambulance companies charged more because their operating costs were higher. Ambulances were required by New York State to have two trained medical attendants in the vehicles at all times. Such emergency medical technicians were paid substantially more than MediBus drivers.

According to Richard Gabriele:

> The response to MediBus by our ambulance competitors has been limited. One competitor circulated a rumor that we are not licensed by New York State, but we are. Other competitors have pointed out that we are not licensed to handle emergency cases (which is true) and that we are not open 7 days a week, 24 hours a day.

Pricing

Each county Medicaid office in New York had a department of transportation which monitored the rates and funds for health-related trips. Each county set its rates independently of other counties. In Suffolk the rate for nonemergency trips was \$10 one-way, \$10 for each hour of waiting time over the first hour, and \$.50 per mile for all over 40. Medicaid permitted MediBus to deposit its clients with doctors, return for pickup when notified by the doctor's office. Dick Gabriele explained, "Medicaid allows us to keep our vehicles moving during wait time because they have not increased their allowable transportation charges since 1970." If more than one person, such as an aide, spouse, or child was carried at the same time in the same vehicle, there was an additional charge of $2.50 per person. The minimum charge for a Medicaid paid round trip was $20.00.

Each new client of MediBus required certification from the Medicaid office that he or she was eligible for transportation benefits. Each month, MediBus submitted its list of clients to the local Medicaid office for recertification. There was no limit to the number of medically related trips a client might take (a price schedule is given in Exhibit 2).

Equipment Rentals

In early March 1975, MediBus began offering a rental service for health-related equipment and supplies such as wheelchairs, hospital beds, walkers, crutches, etc. To minimize investment in equipment, MediBus structured an arrangement with a local surgical supply company to serve as one of the supply company's marketing arms for which MediBus received a 30% commission on all rental income it generated. Mr. Richman commented, "Every transportation client is a potential renter! Every driver is a potential salesman of health-related equipment!" These rentals were covered by Medicaid in most instances.

Operations

In March of 1975, Medibus' facilities consisted of one small office in a professional building, which housed all the officers of the company. With only three vehicles, MediBus management felt that the operations function of the MediBus concept was rather uncomplicated. The ambulettes were operated by three drivers all of whom were members of volunteer fire departments. In addition, there was a part-time driver on call and, if necessary, both Mr. Gabriele and Mr. Richman served as drivers. According to Mr. Gabriele:

> The drivers make or break the business. They are up front. How they treat the passengers and how they maintain the appearance of their vehicles determines whether or not the passenger is satisfied enough with our service to request us on their next trip.

The activity of the MediBus office centered around Ms. Marilyn Hartmann,[4] who was responsible for receiving requests for services, scheduling the drivers, keeping records of trips, billing, and general administrative requirements. A trip was normally initiated by a phone call to Ms. Hartmann from one of the nursing homes or a private individual. These requests were usually made from two days to one week in advance. Upon receiving a request, Ms. Hartmann checked her log book to see if the requested time was available. If time was available, the order was recorded with the particulars as to destinations, point of origin, and expected time of wait. If

[4] Ms. Hartmann, who had been employed by Mr. Gabriele for the past seven years, was a stockholder in MediBus, Inc.

time was not available, Ms. Hartmann first tried to get the customer to reschedule the appointment to a time when a MediBus was available. If this could not be done, then she explained that MediBus could not provide the service at that time. Ms. Hartmann noted that the hours from 10 A.M. to 12 noon and from 2 to 4 P.M. were popular times because these hours coincided with most doctors' office hours. Approximately 70% of all pickups were scheduled in these two time periods for the month of February. Ms. Hartmann explained, "During the last two weeks, I have been forced, on occasion, to decline additional trips during these periods. I try to switch the requests to less hectic times, but often the appointment for medical services cannot be changed."

Ms. Hartmann emphasized the importance of on-time pickups and getting the clients to the physician's office on schedule. However, she did note that the timing of the client's return to the nursing home was not as critical:

> Most of our elderly clients have nothing to rush back to. They don't object to waiting a few extra minutes in the doctor's office or taking a long way back to the nursing home if we want to take two clients in the same vehicle. If we can transport two clients who are headed for the same area at the same time, we can still bill for two trips. However, this only happens a couple of times a week.

At the end of each business day, Ms. Hartmann calculated the charge for each trip made during the day and entered the total on the bottom of the day's page in the log book (February daily statistics, compiled from the log book, are included as Exhibit 8). She then turned the page to the next day's schedule and assigned the requests to the three vehicles to ascertain if there were any potential problems. A definite schedule was impossible to develop because it was difficult to forecast with any accuracy, client delays, traffic delays, and/or physician delays.

The next morning, Ms. Hartmann distributed a schedule to each driver and went over each assignment to ensure the daily schedule was clear. During the day the drivers checked in with Ms. Hartmann by phone[5] when they arrived at their destinations. If a long wait was anticipated, an additional trip was normally scheduled during the wait time. If no additional trip was scheduled, the driver remained available at the destination for unscheduled requests. If the driver did not wait with the client at the destination, Ms. Hartmann periodically checked with the doctor's office (or wherever the destination might be) to ensure that the client would be ready for return at the specified time or to find out if the client was finished early and waiting for the return of the MediBus. This, according to Ms. Hartmann, was her biggest problem:

> Nurses and receptionists underestimate how long a patient will be there. They usually say it will be 15 to 30 minutes and it normally turns out to be longer than an hour and a half. Since the driver remains with the client when a short

[5] Two-way radios for the vehicles were on order and were expected to be operational in late March.

Exhibit 8

MEDIBUS, INC.
Daily Statistics
February 1975

Day	Date	Round Trips Taken	Trips Canceled*	Total Revenue
M	3	13	0	$ 424
T	4	10	1	338
W	5	11	1	663
TH	6	12	0	536
F	7	20	2	672
S	8	1	0	65
		67	4	$2,698
M	10	13	2	$ 482
T	11	10	1	450
W	12 (snow)	3	7	147
TH	13	13	0	527
F	14	8	0	273
S	15	1	0	35
		48	10	$1,914
M	17	16	2	$ 583
T	18	11	2	462
W	19	7	2	232
TH	20	15	0	603
F	21	13	1	484
S	22	2	0	90
		64	7	$2,454
M	24	10	1	$ 412
T	25	21	5	890
W	26	12	3	514
TH	27	16	1	634
F	28	8	2	311
		67	12	$2,761

* Canceled by customers and clients.

wait is expected, this deception often ties up a vehicle for an extended period of time.

In order to minimize driving time, and to utilize ambulettes during wait times for unscheduled requests, Ms. Hartmann tried to assign the vehicles to particular areas. It was often possible to assign vehicles to certain areas such as the "South Shore" because most "South Shore" clients went to "South Shore" destinations. This had a beneficial side effect in that drivers got to know both their passengers and the personnel in physicians' offices and nursing homes very well; it was felt that this personal relationship facilitated the drivers' ability to provide good service.

Mr. Gabriele recognized the key role which Ms. Hartmann played in the company's operations:

> Marilyn is excellent in dealing with people. She is friendly with all the drivers and has developed a rapport with a number of the administrators in the nursing homes who call to schedule trips.

Financial Strategy

The basic financial strategy of MediBus had been to keep capital outlays at a minimum level. Most equipment had been leased: vehicles, office furniture, two-way radios. Even initial promotion expenses had required little capital outlay; the fees[6] for these services had been paid by Sam Goldstein as the contribution for his share of the equity. In the first two months of operation, Gabriele and Richman had received no salaries.[7] Regarding the future sources of financing, Gabriele said, "We have the personal resources to back the company so we don't have to worry about bankers or venture capitalists."

MediBus closely watched the inflow of funds. Because of Medicaid's reputation for slow payment (New York City Medicaid was reputed to take over six months to pay its bills), MediBus billed Medicaid weekly. Although it had been expected to be on a 75-day collection cycle, the first payment was received 45 days after the date of billing; the second took only 40 days. Gabriele or Richman visited the county Medicaid office weekly to ensure requirements for submitting good invoices were being met. According to Dick Gabriele, "MediBus has quickly obtained a reputation for submitting good invoices." Billings to private clients were due upon presentation and were being collected within 10 days.

Franchising

During 1976, MediBus planned to embark upon a national franchising program throughout the United States and Canada utilizing the Suffolk/Nassau County pilot operation as a model for franchise success. Under this franchise program, MediBus planned to lease to franchisees all equipment and vehicles[8] plus supply a training program for new operations managers. In addition, the company planned, on an on-going basis, to guide and assist each franchisee in marketing, promotion, financial controls, scheduling, and training. In return, MediBus would receive from qualified franchisees an initial franchise fee of from $10,000 to $15,000 plus 6% of revenues on a continuing basis.

Gabriele explained his rationale for franchising:

---

6 These fees totaled $1,650 for January and February combined.

7 Beginning in April, Messrs. Gabriele and Richman would draw annual salaries of $25,000 and $20,000, respectively.

8 It was estimated that, annually, the company would earn $250 per vehicle leased.

We have an edge. Our operation will be different than one such as MediCab. We plan on working more with the franchisee. We will handle all their billing, most of their initial selling, factoring of their receivables, and most of their administrative functions. We will be providing a total package of several health-related businesses to the franchisee. Our initial plans are to franchise outside the New York, New Jersey, and Connecticut area. We will definitely operate Suffolk and Nassau counties as company-owned operations because we have a competitive advantage since we know the area so well.

We are not naive. We know it will be harder to penetrate markets further away from here. We hope to overcome this problem by selecting franchisees who are local personalities with good connections.

The Future

Dick Gabriele summed up his feelings about the future:

I am very optimistic about our present position. The profit and loss statement (Exhibit 9) for our first two months of operation must be a rarity for a start-up situation. Our balance sheet (Exhibit 10) is solid. We are beating our quarterly projections (Exhibit 11) by a wide margin.

However, he expressed concerns about several areas:

Operations—As we add vehicles to increase our capacity, it will be easier to schedule and provide better services. But will we get enough business to support the overhead of the vehicles?

And as we expand the number of vehicles, I am not sure our present methods of operation will be adequate. What should I be planning for later this year when I have seven vans in operation?

Marketing—I believe that third-party endorsements of our services are key to the generation of volume because they give us the credibility which is so desperately needed by a small firm. How can we get that third-party support?

Exhibit 9

MEDIBUS, INC.
Profit and Loss Statement
28 February, 1975

	February	*YTD Jan./Feb.*
Total Net Sales	$9,174.30	$15,597.30
Cost of Sales	$3,520.72	$ 6,574.72
Gross Profit	$5,653.58	$ 9,022.58
G&A	$1,606.32	$ 3,107.32
Operating Profit	$4,047.26	$ 5,915.26

Exhibit 10

MEDIBUS, INC.
Balance Sheet
February, 1975

ASSETS		
Current Assets		
Cash	$ 865.94	
Accounts Receivable	$14,863.80	
Prepaid Income Taxes	$ 183.54	
Other	$ 4,088.14	
Total Current Assets		$20,001.42
Property & Equipment		
Vehicles		
Furniture & Fixtures	$ 167.43	
Leasehold Improvements	$ 109.10	
Less Accum. Depreciation		
Total Property & Equipment		$ 276.53
Other		
Deposits & Miscellaneous		$ 2,328.00
Total Assets		$22,605.95
LIABILITIES		
Current Liabilities		
Accounts Payable	$ 3,359.99	
Income Tax (N.Y. State)	$ 33.50	
Notes Payable (Stockholder)	$ 322.00	
Total Current Liabilities		$ 3,715.49
Net Worth		$18,890.46
Common Stock-200 Shares, No Par		
Total Liabilities and Net Worth		$22,605.95

We haven't made a dent in the private market for our services. Marketing in this segment will have to be done by newspaper and yellow page advertising. We cannot afford to sell on a personal basis to individual private clients.

We have only made a couple recreational trips in our first two months of operation. How can we better market our off-peak capacity?

Compensation—How should we compensate our drivers? We need to stimulate them, not only to provide courteous, on-time service, but to sell our rental service as well.

Franchising—I am confident that in 12 months we will have a good handle on the operations here on Long Island. We want to expand quickly to pre-

Exhibit 11

MEDIBUS, INC.
First Quarter Projections

NUMBER OF VEHICLES	2		3		3	
	January		*February*		*March*	*Quarter*
	Budget	*Actual*	*Budget*	*Actual*	*Budget*	*Budget*
SALES	$3,450	$6,423	$4,000	$9,174	$8,000	$15,450
CASH RECEIPTS		469		1,231		
CASH DISBURSEMENTS						
Vehicle leases	780	812	780	987	780	2,340
Communication leases	—	—	—	—	275	275
Insurance	—	61	—	—	1,100	1,100
Gas and oil	220	114	200	381	200	620
Maintenance	—	42	—	411	75	75
Miscellaneous fees	200	100	—	—	100	300
*Payroll-drivers	1,400	368	1,400	831	1,400	4,200
Payroll-administration	1,500	1,610	1,300	1,288	1,306	4,100
Payroll taxes	168	75	168	184	168	504
Rent	265	265	265	265	265	795
Office equipment	—	29	35	167	35	70
Telephone	200	197	200	266	200	600
Postage	110	71	100	96	100	310
Office supplies	50	153	50	42	50	150
Advertising	100	—	50	—	25	175
Legal and accounting	175	360	75	—	75	325
Printing	30	30	20	140	25	75
Interest and loans	—	—	—	35	75	75
Other	50	777	300	—	—	350
TOTAL	$5,248	$5,064	$4,943	$5,093	$6,248	$16,439

* Drivers were paid $2.75 an hour. Messrs. Gabriele and Richman drove a great deal in January and February. Only one driver was hired in January, one more was added in February, and a third in early March.

vent competition from getting a foothold in other areas. MediCab already has several franchise operations including MediCab of Mass Bay which services the metropolitan Boston area.

We cannot get the name MediBus registered as a federal trademark because it too closely resembles other registered names. We need to have this problem resolved by the time we begin offering franchises.

Unknowns—What really bothers me is that there must be some things that I haven't even thought about. Those are the things that can destroy the fragile existence of a firm such as MediBus.

Braniff International

In early 1969, Harding Lawrence, chief executive officer and chairman of the board of Braniff International Airways (BI), in a meeting with his corporate staff stated:

> There is no question that the wide-body look is the airline look of the '70s. Every trunk airline will have to determine its own approach to securing the wide-body look while maintaining and improving service to every city it serves, primarily in terms of frequent and convenient flight schedules.

BI had recently finished an examination of its equipment strategy in the Latin American Division, and was now considering the strategy to be used for domestic operations during the next several years. The company planned to purchase an average of 1,400 seats of aircraft capacity each year for the next six years.

Since coming to Braniff, Mr. Lawrence had stressed the policy of aircraft "communality." That is, the minimization of the number of types of aircraft operated to promote increased economies in maintenance, crew training, and space-parts inventories. At the time, BI operated a number of aircraft types, but it had been suggested that the company might take the opportunity of the recent introduction of wide-bodied aircraft[1] to take steps toward creating a more uniform fleet for domestic operations.

The questions Lawrence asked of his corporate staff were:

a. Are wide-bodies inherently more economic than our present aircraft types?
b. Can they be deployed on our domestic route structure profitably?
c. How will they affect our competitive situation in terms of market share and frequency of service?

Company Background

BI was one of 11 major U.S. domestic trunkline carriers[2] providing passenger and cargo services to points throughout the continental United States. BI also served Hawaii, Mexico, and South America, operating from gateways on the East, Gulf, and West Coasts.

---

[1] Wide-bodied aircraft include the Douglas DC-10 and Lockheed L-1011 trijets and the Boeing B-747.

[2] The U.S. trunkline industry in 1969 included American, Braniff, Continental, Delta, Eastern, National, Northwest-Orient, Trans-World, Western, United, and Northeast Airlines.

The airline, founded in 1928 by T. E. Braniff, had grown to a route structure of 30,000 miles in the United States and Latin America, and was carrying over 6 million passengers annually in 1968.

BI grew through internal development, but major portions of the expansion occurred in 1952 with the merger with Mid-Continental Airlines incorporating 6,241 additional route miles from the Dakotas to Louisiana, and in 1967, with the purchase of Pan American Grace Airways and its routes throughout Latin America (see Exhibit 1).

Braniff had a reputation for innovation in the industry, particularly under Harding Lawrence, who took over direction of the airline in 1965. For example, in 1967 Braniff was the first airline to retire its piston-engine aircraft. This left the Lockheed Electra as the only remaining nonjet aircraft type in service (see Exhibit 2). BI was the first airline to utilize jet assist takeoff systems at high-altitude airports, and was a pioneer in airborne weather radar. On August 1, 1966, Braniff inaugurated the world's first Boeing B-727 "Quick Change" convertible tri-jet. The B-727 QC could be converted from a "passenger" to an all-cargo or combination passenger/cargo configuration in 30 minutes. This greatly improved aircraft utilization, allow-

Exhibit 1

BRANIFF INTERNATIONAL
Domestic Route Structure

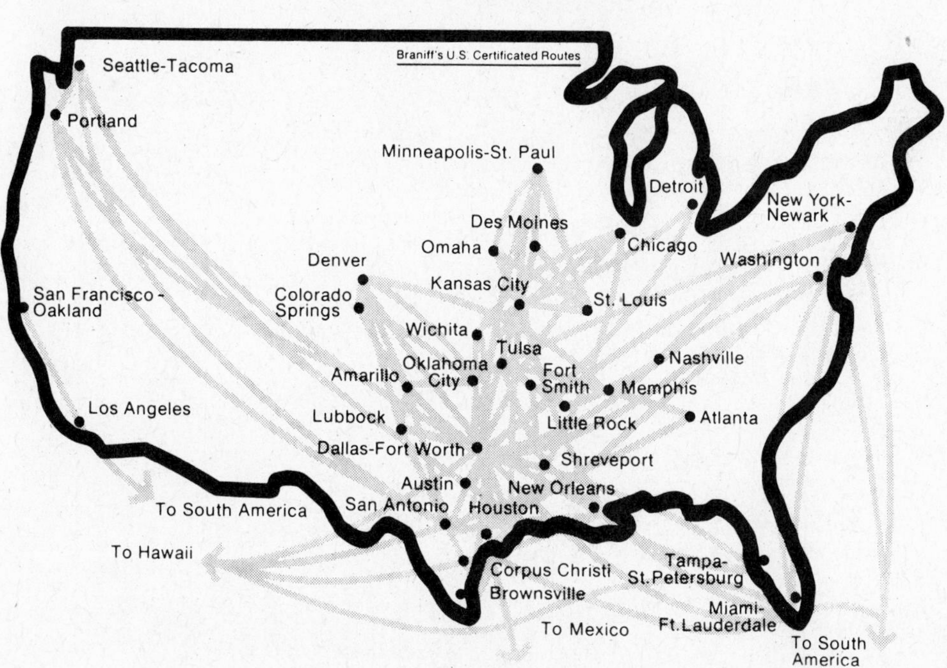

Exhibit 2

BRANIFF INTERNATIONAL
Comparative Fleet Mix and Braniff Domestic Capacity 1968

				Domestic Operations		
Aircraft Type	*Industry Fleet Mix (Per cent)*	*Braniff Fleet Mix (Per cent)*	*Braniff Fleet Mix (No. of Aircraft)*	*Braniff ASM Production Per Aircraft Type (000,000)*	*Braniff ASM Production Per Unit—Aircraft Type (000,000)*	*Braniff Average Domestic Stage Length Per Type*
Electra 188	1.4	11.4	8	595	74.4	210
BAC—111	1.6	18.6	13	757	58.0	236
B—707	17.4	18.6	13*	752	188.0	661
B—720	11.8	7.1	5	820	164.0	441
B—727	33.8	34.3	24**	2,972	124.0	479
B—737	1.8	—	—	—	—	—
CV—880	3.9	—	—	—	—	—
CV—990	.1	—	—	—	—	—
DC—8	15.7	10.0	7***	—	—	—
DC—9	9.2	—	—	—	—	—
Caravelle	.5	—	—	—	—	—
Fairchild 227	.1	—	—	—	—	—
Viscount 700	.2	—	—	—	—	—
TOTAL	100.	100.	70	5,896	N/A	364.3

* Two flown in Latin American Division, seven flown under Military Air Command Operations.

** All B-727-100's, the Annual ASM capacity of the B-727-200 is estimated at potentially 160 million ASM's/year per aircraft.

*** All used in Latin American Division Operations.

ing use of the plane to transport passengers by day and cargo by night. Other innovations included the substitution of Pucci fashions for more conventional hostess uniforms and brightly colored aircraft rather than the conservative "plain planes."

BI was considered to be a financially healthy member of the airline industry, with an above average return on investment during a period of substantial growth. See Exhibit 3 for 1964 to 1968 financial statements and Exhibit 4 for BI operating performance over the same period.

Exhibit 3

BRANIFF INTERNATIONAL
Financial Statements—1964 to 1968
Dollar Figures in Thousands

PROFIT AND LOSS STATEMENT	*1968*	*1967*	*1966*	*1965*	*1964*
OPERATING REVENUES					
Passenger	$211,208	$188,487	$156,771	$114,730	$ 96,857
Military contract services	48,207	38,851	14,041	—	—
Express and freight	17,998	16,707	9,973	8,297	7,090
Mail	8,548	6,661	4,492	3,563	2,942
Other	6,688	5,671	2,550	2,675	2,808
	$292,649	$256,377	$187,827	$129,265	$109,697
OPERATING EXPENSES					
Flying and ground operations	$155,603	$133,751	$ 89,175	$ 63,124	$ 55,325
Maintenance	41,855	39,459	28,502	21,760	18,377
Sales and advertising	32,157	30,759	23,383	15,545	12,022
Depreciation and amortization, less amounts charged to other accounts	24,992	26,393	15,079	10,014	8,376
General and administrative	12,673	11,553	7,265	5,059	4,300
	$267,280	$241,915	$163,404	$115,502	$ 98,400
Operating income	$ 25,369	$ 14,462	$ 24,423	$ 13,763	$ 11,297
Nonoperating expenses—net	11,971	9,711	3,538	718	938
Income (loss) before provision for income taxes	$ 13,398	$ 4,751	$ 20,885	$ 13,045	$ 10,359
PROVISION (CREDITS) FOR INCOME TAXES					
Federal					
Current—before investment tax credit	$ 7,317	$ 1,245	$ 4,816	$ 5,424	$ 4,182
Current—investment tax credit	(3,697)	—	(207)	(1,470)	(731)
Deferred	(806)	—	2,305	—	876
Other	168	—	217	148	61
	$ 2,982	$ 1,245	$ 7,131	$ 4,102	$ 4,388
Income (loss) before extraordinary items	$ 10,416	$ 3,506	$ 13,754	$ 8,943	$ 5,971
Extraordinary items	—	1,245	4,062	505	—
Net income (loss)	$ 10,416	$ 4,751	$ 17,816	$ 9,448	$ 5,971

Exhibit 3 (continued)

	1968	1967	1966	1965	1964
SELECTED BALANCE SHEET ITEMS					
Cash dividends paid	$ 1,155	$ 1,474	$ 1,474	$ 295	$ 295
Stock dividends paid	5,441	—	—	—	—
Current assets	$ 78,292	$ 68,658	$ 60,441	$ 29,406	$ 24,131
Current liabilities	56,594	86,411	20,972	13,971	13,164
Net working capital	$ 21,698	$(17,753)	$ 39,469	$ 15,435	$ 10,967
Property and equipment—net	$270,724	$287,655	$190,844	$ 95,795	$ 65,072
Total assets	372,526	378,082	309,678	130,336	$ 98,806
Long-term debt	213,927	199,000	204,753	51,105	29,600
Shareholders' equity					
Special stock, Class A	$ 7,428	$ —	$ —	$ —	$ —
Common stock	1,561	7,370	7,370	7,370	7,370
Capital surplus	22,208	18,355	18,355	18,355	18,355
Retained earnings	52,607	48,787	45,494	29,151	19,997
Total shareholders' equity	$ 83,804	$ 74,512	$ 71,219	$ 54,876	$ 45,722

The Airline Industry

The U.S. domestic trunk airline group carried approximately 72% of all revenue passenger miles flown in the United States during 1968. Since 1938, which is considered by many to be the beginning of the trunkline portion of the industry, several trends were discernable. There had been a trend toward concentration through mergers with a general lengthening of route structures and increased number of cities served. Also, there had been increased levels of competition as the overlapping of routes and points had intensified.

To maintain productive competition, the Civil Aeronautics Board (CAB) had been created by the Federal Government to regulate the industry to foster its development. The CAB had final approval on fares, routes, mergers, and some aspects of the level of the service. The CAB had set a target of 10.5% as a reasonable return on investment (ROI). This ROI was based on a seat-load factor (ratio of revenue passenger miles to available seat miles) of 55%. In fact, the industry had achieved the target ROI in only two of the ten years prior to 1968. This below-target performance of the industry was due to intense competition between the airlines and the tendency of airline managers to provide excess capacity to gain market share. While the CAB was concerned with this, in a public statement, the board recognized that:

> Schedules constitute the major competitive device of carriers in their efforts to preserve and enhance their participation in the traffic markets which they serve. In any given market, the carrier with the greatest number of schedules will normally carry the largest number of passengers. Thus, the desire to maximize market participation creates powerful incentives to add capacity. The contravailing incentive is supplied only by the imperative of economics: schedules cannot be added indefinitely if the load factor achieved is insufficient, at the prevailing fare levels, to permit the carriers to cover costs and return a profit.

Exhibit 4

BRANIFF INTERNATIONAL
Operating Performance, 1964–1968

	1968	*1967*	*1966*	*1965*	*1964*
REVENUE PASSENGER MILES (000)					
Mainland	2,846,595	2,499,004	2,236,434	1,580,988	1,342,394
Hawaii	—	—	—	—	—
Mexico	121,075	95,163	91,874	44,282	36,461
South America	633,223	562,916	249,705	179,092	136,732
Total scheduled	3,600,893	3,157,083	2,578,013	1,804,362	1,515,587
Charter	1,996,954	1,608,628	481,561	14,339	28,338
Total	5,597,847	4,765,711	3,059,574	1,818,701	1,543,925
AVAILABLE SEAT MILES (000)					
Mainland	5,325,356	4,878,538	3,835,376	2,891,069	2,455,523
Hawaii	—	—	—	—	—
Mexico	240,407	193,979	184,466	68,041	58,412
South America	1,474,634	1,147,201	575,745	385,181	328,048
Total scheduled	7,040,397	6,219,718	4,595,587	3,344,291	2,841,983
Charter	2,269,668	1,773,510	554,485	20,176	40,331
Total	9,310,065	7,993,228	5,150,072	3,364,467	2,882,314
REVENUE PASSENGERS CARRIED (000)					
Scheduled	5,749	5,283	4,585	3,372	2,854
Charter	386	312	105	13	22
Total	6,135	5,595	4,690	3,385	2,876
SYSTEM SCHEDULED PASSENGER LOAD FACTOR (%)	51.1	50.8	56.1	54.0	53.3
BREAKEVEN PASSENGER LOAD FACTOR ON BEFORE TAX EXPENSE (%)	47.6	49.2	48.5	47.5	47.6
REVENUE PLANE MILES (000)					
Scheduled	72,908	67,862	53,331	40,303	35,847
Charter	17,233	13,428	4,846	280	568
Total	89,141	81,290	58,177	40,583	36,415
REVENUE BLOCK HOURS FLOWN	242,329	231,822	191,628	154,903	146,558
AVERAGE SEGMENT LENGTH IN SCHEDULED SERVICE (MILES)	409	376	317	289	282

Airline Economics

The airlines used "available seat mile" (ASM), one passenger seat flown one mile, rather than a "passenger mile" flown, as the unit of production since air carriers *costs* were directly related to the number of *seats* rather than the number of *passengers* flown over a given distance. Once an airplane was scheduled on a particular flight, the total cost of that flight varied only slightly with the number of passengers that the plane was carrying. This characteristic of individual flight operation gave rise to the industry view of itself as having an extremely high percentage of fixed costs.

An industry rule of thumb stated that the variable cost of adding an extra passenger to a flight amounted to only 10% of the fare paid by that passenger and that the remaining 90% passed directly through as a contribution to operating profit. The cost per unit of production was influenced by a variety of factors, including aircraft type and average length of flights. Given this cost per available seat mile, however, an airline's total operating costs were easily found by multiplying total ASM's by cost per ASM and adding to this "fixed" or ASM-related cost the "variable" cost of 10% passenger fares.

Airline costs were, perhaps, less fixed than the industry believed, except in the very short run. Over time spans of a year or more, the industry's growth rate and inflation tended in effort to make other "fixed" ASM-related costs, such as depreciation and salaries, variable.

While costs were tied most closely to available seat miles, the revenue generated on a flight was directly related to (1) the number of passengers carried, (2) how far they were flown, and (3) how much these passengers paid per mile of flight. The product of the first two factors was revenue passenger miles (RPM's). The third term was commonly called yield per RPM.

Given the high proportion of costs that were fixed, profits were very sensitive to the load factor experienced by an airline.

Load Factors and the Equipment Cycle

Since profitability was so sensitive to the load factor, it would seem that the industry would be very concerned with maintaining profitable load factor levels through a policy of restraint in adding capacity.

With the great advances in technology and improved economic performance of aircraft in the 1960s, the airlines undertook massive reequipment programs. Pressure to keep up with other airlines had resulted in the entire industry going through cycles of buying more capacity than the growth of the market justified.

Route Structure

Because of the large percentage of fixed costs of a flight associated with takeoff and landing operations, the average cost per ASM of longer flights was substantially lower. It was generally believed that the rate structure did not reflect this variation of costs with length of flight, and longer flights were thought to subsidize shorter flights.

Route Density

Another factor in profitability is route density. That is the actual "head count" number of passengers flying between any given city-pair. Over a "monopoly route" this would directly affect the actual load factor for the carrier serving the route. That is, depending on the number of departures flown by that airline and the capacity of the aircraft type utilized. Here, the CAB was most vigorous in awarding competitive service in monopoly markets where one carrier has over 80% of the traffic. This was most probably due to the fact that the "monopolist" would not be under pressure to expand capacity as traffic grew, i.e., accruing the benefits of high seat-load factors. But since seasonal, monthly, weekly, and even daily peaks were experienced in air travel, the "public convenience and necessity" demands moderate average load factors testifying to the carriers' ability to accommodate these peaks in demand.

The "S" Curve

The close correlation between an airline's share of passengers flown over a route and the number of seats which the airline flew over the route had long been recognized by the industry. Characteristically, however, on a competitive route served by two carriers, the dominant carrier in terms of seats flown would attract slightly more than its proportionate share of passengers over that route. This relationship may be graphically represented as an S-shaped curve (Exhibit 5). The effect of this curve on industry thinking had been so pervasive that it had become known as the S-curve and had been the basis for airline capacity decisions.

Exhibit 5

BRANIFF INTERNATIONAL

Market Share Versus ASM Share on a Two Carrier Route

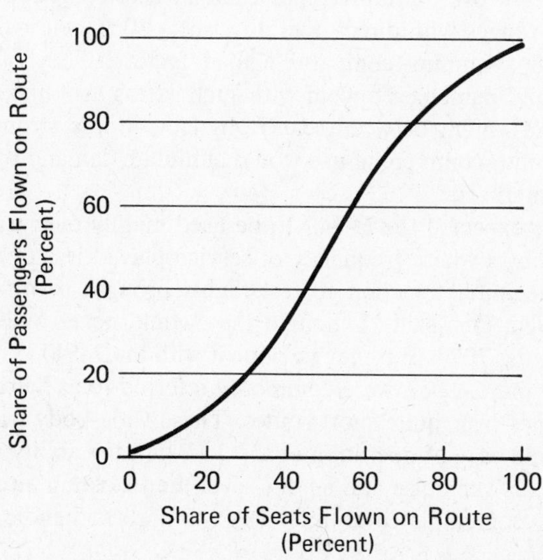

Historically, there had been a marked tendency for competing airlines to fly similar aircraft over the same routes. This was due to the fact that all carriers were facing similar economics, and that the analyses carried out by planners for different airlines lead them to select similar aircraft. One form of competition over these routes had taken the form of addition of more frequent flights, increasing the share of seats flown, and, following the S-curve, the share of passengers flown. This form of competition, with similar competitive responses, was thought to have contributed materially to dramatic overcapacity situations on many routes.

Aircraft Selection

A prominent industry trend had been toward faster and larger aircraft. For example, the average terminal-to-terminal speed in domestic service increased from 314 MPH in 1962 to 413 MPH in 1968. Each aircraft type had its own particular optimization in terms of cost per ASM over a specific range limitation. Generally speaking, total cost per ASM included fixed and variable elements, and decreased on a per unit basis as distance increased. The terminology used in the industry to describe these inherent aircraft costs/ASM were couched in terms of "assignability." This was a delicate transition, since Direct Operating Cost (DOC) should not be confused with "variable costs" because they are not all variable with the amount of ASM's flown. For example, some vary with flight hours, others per departure, and some are arbitrarily assigned, e.g., overhead was estimated to be 40% of DOC. Similarly, indirect operating costs (IOC) were not considered "fixed" since the industry's estimate of them was simply 100% of the DOC.

In early 1969, the advent of the "era of wide-bodies" was imminent. The Boeing B-747 was to be available by the end of 1969. McDonnell-Douglas and Lockheed were taking orders for the DC-10 and L-1101 to be introduced in 1970 and 1971, respectively. Taken as a group, wide-bodies were expected to have decided economic advantages over aircraft types then in service. They were designed to have longer flight ranges with direct operating costs 20% below the B-727-200 and 14% below DC-8, assuming comparable load factors. They offered unsurpassed luxury, comfort, and passenger appeal with such extras as lounges, piano bars, and increased leg room (pitch between seats). In fact, it was strongly suspected that their introduction into commercial use would stimulate demand by as much as 30% in some city-pair markets.

The industry expected the B-747 to be used mainly over transcontinental and intercontinental routes where frequency of service played less of a role in capturing market share. The initial reaction to test flights brought many excited comments from pilots involved. One said "I thought they would never build a better airplane after having flown the 707—But they've done it with the 747!"

The DC-10 and L-1011 were commonly referred to as "airbuses" due to their favorable economics over quite short routes. These wide-body tri-jets combined the maneuverability and ease of operation of the 747 with the ability to fly in and out of small airports at a lower noise and smoke level than existing aircraft. Terminal expansion was being contemplated at many large airports to handle the increased concentration of passengers although flight congestion was expected to decline as the number of flights decreased.

American and United Airlines presently had over 50 DC-10s on order and were expected to purchase at least 150 more DC-10s in the next few years. They were planning to utilize these aircraft on stage lengths primarily ranging from 1,000 to 2,000 miles.

Because of the resulting back order situation at Douglas, other trunks were opting for priority delivery position in the essentially similar Lockheed L-1011. Delta and Eastern thought the L-1011 to be more suited to medium- and short-range hauls. However L-1011 deliveries were still somewhat uncertain due to the tenuous financial position of Rolls-Royce, the maker of the aircraft's RB-211 jet engines.

The DC-10 and L-1011 compared to the Boeing B-727-200, as follows:

	B-727-200	*L-1011/DC-10*
Investment (including spare parts)	$7,969,000	$17,503,000
Seats (low-density seating configuration)	125	300
Effective maximum economic range (miles)	1,700	2,800
Direct cost per takeoff and landing	$ 90	$ 300

Arguments for Wide Bodies

An engineering-staff member suggested that the "airbus" glamour was an important consideration. Also, the wide-bodies were not only likely to stimulate primary demand due to greater flying comfort, they also operated at lower cost per ASM (even on shorter routes) and therefore, they had greater profit potential. He admitted that they used more fuel, but fuel consumed per ASM was actually slightly lower than that experienced with smaller aircraft. "All in all, they are technologically a better aircraft."

This last point was agreed to by the BI pilots who had had occasion to test fly the wide-body aircraft. They felt that for their size, they had as much maneuverability as any aircraft in the market, and they were very impressed by the consumer benefits of more space and comfort.

The scheduling and operations group noted that fewer aircraft would be needed to fill the ASM gap, and fewer operations would facilitate computerized scheduling. However, they felt that large aircraft would be less flexibile to meet short-term fluctuations in specific city-pair markets. At the same time, these aircraft would help to reduce airport congestion.

Finally, it was mentioned that wide-body aircraft could best provide for BI's faster-than-industry growth. BI was experiencing growth in primary demand and market share in most of the markets it served. This would favor the operation of larger aircraft that were most profitable in dense route operations.

Exhibit 6

BRANIFF INTERNATIONAL
Return On Investment (ROI) as a Function
of Passengers Carried and Stage Length[a]
(Figures in Percent)

WIDE-BODY TRI-JET[b]—300 SEATS
Total Operating Cost = 200% of Direct Operating Cost
Number of Passengers

Stage Length (miles)	*50*	*75*	*125*	*200*	*300*
500	—31.7	—22.8	—4.9	21.7	57.3
1000	—28.7	—16.8	6.9	42.5	89.9
1500	—26.9	—13.6	13.1	53.1	106.5
2000	—26.4	—12.3	17.7	62.7	122.6

WIDE-BODY TRI-JET[b]—300 SEATS
Total Operating Cost = 150% of Direct Operating Cost
Number of Passengers

Stage Length (miles)	*50*	*75*	*125*	*200*	*300*
500	—19.3	—10.4	7.4	34.1	69.7
1000	—15.6	—3.7	20.0	55.6	103.0
1500	—13.4	—0.2	26.6	66.5	119.9
2000	—13.0	2.0	32.0	77.0	136.9

BOEING 727-200—125 SEATS
Total Operating Cost = 200% of Direct Operating Cost
Number of Passengers

Stage Length (miles)	*50*	*75*	*125*	*200[c]*	*300[c]*
500	—19.8	6.9	45.6	26.2	26.2
1000	1.1	24.7	76.2	50.5	50.5
1500	4.8	33.8	91.8	62.8	62.8
2000	Maximum Range—1700 miles—				

a. Assumptions:
- Revenue = $0.06 per passenger mile.
- Utilization = 3285 block hours per year.
- Block Speed is approximately equal for 727's and wide bodies and:
  - 500 mile stage length consumes 1.6 block hours
  - 1000 mile stage length consumes 2.4 block hours
  - 1500 mile stage length consumes 3.2 block hours
  - 2000 mile stage length consumes 3.8 block hours.

b. DC-10 or L-1011.

c. Multiple flights.

Source: Casewriter's estimate based on engineering data.

Argument Against Wide-Bodies

The marketing department was not entirely anti-wide-body. They were, however, against its application to the Braniff route structure at this time. Russ Thayer noted that "in terms of density and length of haul, Braniff cannot economically apply a wide-body." He pointed out that BI's most dense route was ranked 28th on the list of the most dense routes served by the domestic airline industry.

Also, Thayer continued, "In my opinion, people don't ask what aircraft you're flying. When they call reservations, they ask for departure times. A transportation company serves the consumer by proper scheduling. That's what I've stressed in my advertising program."

Jack Regan, vice-president of marketing planning, favored the greater flexibility of scheduling the smaller-capacity B-727-200 provided.

A Need for Hard Numbers

Harding Lawrence felt that the Dallas-Chicago market typified the BI situation. Demand over this 811 mile route amounted to approximately 350,000 passengers per year (one way) of which BI carried 144,000. Mr. Lawrence expected demand in this market to grow by about 20 to 30% per year over the coming five years. BI and American Airlines each provided roughly half of the ASM's in this market. On weekdays, when the bulk of this demand occurred, BI served this route with five flights in each direction while American operated eight flights in each direction.

Exhibit 7

BRANIFF INTERNATIONAL

Analysis of Markets—65 Top BI City-Pair Markets

City-Pairs with BI 1969 Estimated Market Share <50%

Stage Length Miles	Average Number Passengers Carried By BI/Day 0–100	101–200	201–400	401–800	>800
<750	7	4	1	0	0
750–1249	3	0	2	0	0
1250–1750	1	0	1	0	0
>1750	0	0	0	0	0

City-Pairs with BI 1969 Estimated Market Share <50%

Stage Length Miles	Average Number Passengers Carried By BI/Day 0–100	101–200	201–400	401–800	>800
<750	14	17	4	1	1
750–1249	2	2	2	0	0
1250–1750	0	1	1	1	0
>1750	0	0	1*	0	0

* Dallas–Honolulu.

Mr. Lawrence believed that it would be possible to finance the necessary investment in new equipment. His staff was asked to calculate the approximate return on investment that might be expected for the B-727-200 and DC-10 or L-1011 for a variety of passenger levels and stage lengths. The conventional practice in the industry was to estimate total cost as 200% of the direct operating costs (which include crew, fuel maintenance, depreciation, and insurance).

There was some argument that this rule of thumb had been developed based on smaller aircraft. Since a significant portion of the indirect costs were related to the number of flights rather than passengers, it might be more appropriate to estimate total costs for wide-bodied aircraft as 150% of estimated direct costs. A return on investment calculation based on average fare yield of 6¢ per revenue passenger mile is summarized in Exhibit 6. Exhibit 7 summarizes the city-pair markets being served by BI in 1969.

Federal Express Corporation (A)

In November 1973, Federal Express Corporation (FEC) was attempting to raise over $50 million in long-term financing in order to continue operations of the small package jet delivery service it had commenced seven months previously. Under the direction of its founder, Frederick W. Smith, Jr., a 29-year-old ex-Marine pilot, the company had engaged New Court Securities, a New York City merchant bank, to raise $26 million of privately placed equity financing. $26 million of long-term debt financing was also being sought.

Company History

Fred Smith traced the origin of his idea for Federal Express to an academic assignment while a student of political science and economics at Yale. He had examined the air freight industry and had concluded that the many needs of the air shipper were not being served.

Smith, who had worked his way through college by flying aircraft, came from a family with close ties with the transportation industry. His father had founded Dixie Greyhound, a bus company later sold to the Greyhound Corp.; his grandfather had been a riverboat captain.

From Yale, Fred Smith joined the Marines as an aviator and, after more than 200 combat missions, emerged with the Silver Star, Bronze Star, Navy Commendation Medal, Vietnamese Cross of Gallantry, Purple Heart, and Combat Action Medal. After his tour of duty with the Marines, he bought controlling interest of Arkansas Aviation Sales. He changed the nature of its business from a "fixed base operator," servicing general aviation aircraft, into the business of buying and selling used jet aircraft. Under his direction, sales increased in two years from $1 million to $9 million and earnings increased from a loss of $40,000 to a profit of $250,000.

By 1971 Smith had formulated his plans for a small package air service and incorporated Federal Express in Delaware. He commissioned two studies at a total cost of $150,000 to examine the market potential for his ideas. The consultants selected were A. T. Kearney, a well-known and respected consulting group, and Advanced Aerospace Planning Group (AAPG), a company with which he had personal connections. Both studies were optimistic about the concept. Several members of the consulting teams later joined FEC as officers.

Upon receiving confirmation that his plans were feasible, Smith and his officers began searching for a small jet aircraft that could be adapted for use as a cargo aircraft. A prime criterion used in the selection of aircraft was the maximum loaded weight. The Civil Aeronautics Board had, in September 1972, ruled that operators flying aircraft with an "all-up" weight of less than 75,000 pounds could be classified as "air-taxi" operators. This meant that the operator could fly to any city in the United States without having to file for a certificate of "public convenience and necessity." Larger transportation companies had to obtain such a certificate for each "city-pair" (i.e., route between two cities) they wished to serve. To obtain the certificate, the applicant had to prove, over the objections of existing carriers, that there was a need for a new carrier. No new scheduled cargo carrier had received a certificate in over 20 years. Since FEC wished to provide a nationwide service, the exemption from this certificate avoided the prohibitive cost, legal contests, and time that such a process involves.

The aircraft finally selected was the Dassault Fanjet Falcon, which was marketed in the United States by Pan American Airways as a 30-seat executive jet (see Exhibit 1). Federal Express assisted in the funding and design of a prototype cargo version of this aircraft. The main alteration, the installation of a large cargo door, necessitated many other minor but intricate structural charges. Modification costs ran to $400,000 per aircraft. The Falcon, with a speed of 520 miles per hour, had a range of 1,400 to 2,000 miles. Its payload, after the installation of the 74-inch door and a roller bed floor, was 6,000 pounds and its capacity, 500 cubic feet.[1] Addition of "single point refueling" as part of Federal's modification of the design meant that the aircraft could be refueled and loaded simultaneously. Due to the sizable order of 33 planes that Federal had placed, the price per aircraft was set at $1,297,-345, some $350,000 less than the market price for a single plane.

Little Rock Airmotive, a company engaged in modification of aircraft, was purchased in January 1973 and, as a subsidiary of FEC, performed all the conversions of the Fanjet Falcons received from Dassault. F.A.A. approval of the modifications was received in 1972, as was the C.A.B. certificate as an air-taxi operator.

The Federal Express Concept

The central principle under which FEC operated was the use of a single "hub" facility, located in Memphis, Tennessee. Aircraft stationed throughout the United States left their base cities at night, loaded with parcels, and all flew into Memphis, with one or two stops along the way for some aircraft. At the Memphis facility packages were unloaded, sorted, and reloaded; whereupon, the aircraft returned to their destinations. The service was offered five days per week. Friday afternoon shipments were delivered Monday morning.

The "single-hub" concept had many advantages. First, it allowed the maximum number of cities to be served with the minimum number of aircraft. Second, the fact that all sorting was done at one location allowed tight control and efficiency of ground handling and provided the basis for an effective tracing service. However, the fact that no aircraft could depart Memphis until the last inbound flight had arrived and its load sorted meant that the margin for error was not great.

[1] The average density of all air cargo shipped during 1972 was 8.5 lbs./cu. ft.

Exhibit 1

FEDERAL EXPRESS CORPORATION (A)

Dassault Fanjet Falcons

The hub concept was used by many motor carriers and United Parcel Service. The area served by the hub usually had a radius of approximately four hours of driving time. FEC applied the same principle, except they drew their radius as four hours of flight time at an average speed in excess of 500 miles per hour. In this way, the whole of the contiguous 48 states of the United States was within the Memphis hub area.

The choice of Memphis as the site of the hub facility was the result of the following factors. First, it was considered relatively close to the "center of gravity" of the United States with respect to package movements. Second, its record of only 24 hours per year of closure due to weather conditions made it a reliable base point. Finally, the Memphis airport authority was prepared to lease on favorable terms considerable space to Federal Express. A $2.9 million bond was issued by the authority for restoration of three large hangars and construction of a sorting facility. The subsequent 20-year lease issued to Federal required them to pay 1.25 times the annual principal and interest on the bond. The sort facility, completed in March 1973, had facilities for docking 30 aircraft simultaneously.

The second principle of the Federal Express concept was that, from shipper's dock to consignee's door, the package was handled entirely by Federal Express. At each of the cities served, Federal used leased vans, painted in Federal's purple, orange and white colors, to perform pickup and delivery (see Exhibit 2).

Through this system Federal offered a premium package service, with a guaranteed next-day delivery. In other words, Federal would undertake to deliver a package to any of the cities it served by noon of the day following pickup. A reduced rate second-day service was also offered. A third service offered was "Courier Pak," by which the company would transport anything that could fit into a manila envelope for a flat fee of $5.

The third principle of the Federal Express concept was the limitation of parcels to 50 pounds and under, with an additional dimensional limit of no more than 108 inches total for the three dimensions. By standardizing the product, FEC hoped to gain the same efficiency of operating procedures as United Parcel Service gained from instituting a similar set of restrictions. Included as part of the A. T. Kearney feasibility study was an estimate of costs of operation. These are included as Exhibit 3.

Competition

The domestic air freight market had grown between 1961 and 1971 at a compound growth rate of 17% to reach a total of 3 billion ton miles. AAPG had estimated that 300,000 tons fell into the category of priority air freight (shipments less than 100 pounds, picked up by 5:00 P.M. and delivered by 9:00 A.M. the following day). A. T. Kearney had further estimated that in 1970 there had been 20.4 million air shipments of 50 pounds or less, with an average of 11¼ pounds per shipment. The latter report went on to establish that 37,000 manufacturing plants in the United States accounted for 86.4% of all air shipments.

Both of the consulting studies had independently discovered, through field interviews and mail questionnaires, that considerable dissatisfaction existed with

Exhibit 2

FEDERAL EXPRESS CORPORATION (A)
Typical Promotion Piece Showing Equipment

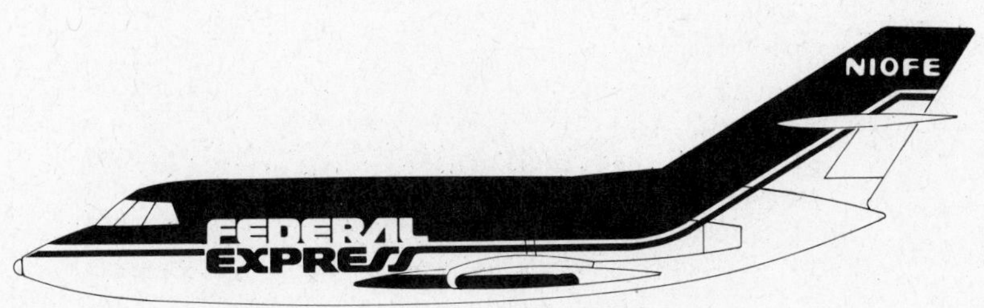

FEDERAL
EXPRESS
The World's Only Small Package Airline

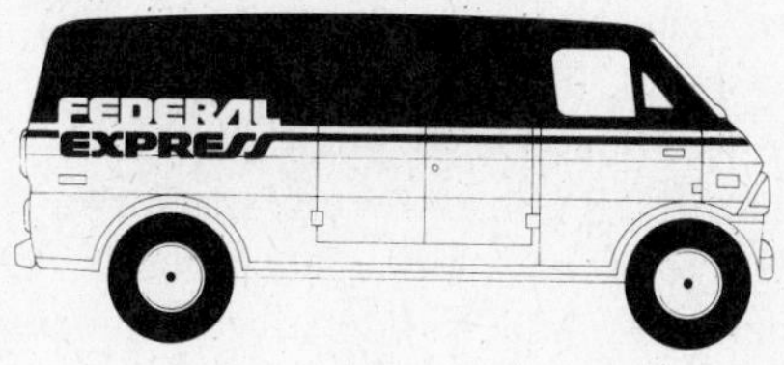

Exhibit 3

FEDERAL EXPRESS CORPORATION (A)
Operating Expenses for Package Service

1. *Flying Operations*			
Aircraft	Fixed[1]	8,367,000	
	Variable[2]	7,222,000	15,589,000
Maintenance			247,000
Operations			2,249,000
			18,085,000
2. *Cargo Operation*			
23 Terminal cities	@ 36,720		844,560
87 On-route cities	@ 17,930		1,559,910
1 Hub city	@ 1,009,000		1,005,000
			3,409,470
3. *General and Administration*			
Salaries			828,000
Systems			291,000
Advertising			300,000
Legal Fees			300,000
All Other			284,000
			2,003,000
Total			23,497,470

[1] Based on 26 aircraft.
[2] Based on 36,200 flying hours/year.
Source: A. T. Kearney Report.

existing services, and there was evidence of a strong degree of support for the type of system Federal was operating.

Many organizations served the existing small package air market. First, the scheduled airlines carried all forms of freight although their rate structures were such as to discourage small shipments. Many of the trunk airlines did offer a small package service, such as Delta's "Dash" system, but these provided no pickup and delivery service and were generally high priced ($20–$60 per shipment).

The air-freight forwarders, the single fastest growing segment in the air-cargo market, aimed themselves particularly at small shipments which they consolidated and tendered to the airlines for line haul. While the forwarders did perform pickup and delivery, they tended to delay shipments in order to achieve consolidation economies. The forwarders also had to hand the shipment on to the airlines and could thus not provide a full tracing service. For this reason, Federal felt that it had a competitive edge. However, one forwarder, Emery, had an excellent reputation for reliability and speed, and in 1972 earned $8.3 million on $142 million of revenues. Federal also recognized that the airlines favored and encouraged the growth of the forwarders, who accounted for 40% of the air-freight market, since by providing pickup and delivery services, the forwarder complemented the service of the airlines. The forwarders had a large number of salesmen in the top markets.

A third group of competitors for Federal were the air taxis and commuter airlines flying small aircraft. In 1970 these lines had accounted for 21,000 tons of cargo and increasing use of them was being made by the forwarders. Unique among the air taxis was Priority Air Dispatch, which had put together a network of 90 operators to provide a service for high value and critical freight. However, Priority's rates, such as $700 for a 20-pound shipment between New York and Chicago, were such that it addressed a very different market to that of Federal.

REA Air Express had been the forerunner of air-cargo operations, handling *all* air-cargo shipments prior to 1944. However, with the development of the airlines and freight forwarders, REA lost its dominant role, although it remained unique in that its shipments had prior claim on available aircraft space, second only to the U.S. mail. With a reputation for unreliability, REA suffered a continuous decline in market share, although some shippers were attracted because it did not delay shipments for consolidation and it would deliver to any point in the United States.

American Courier Corporation, a division of Purolator, which concentrated on very high value priority shipments requiring guard service, experienced a dramatic growth of revenues (surface and air) in 1970 and 1971 of $48 million and $72 million, respectively. The company maintained 16 aircraft, of which five were used to serve 13 cities in the Northeast on a regular basis.

A major competitor was United Parcel Service (UPS) which, apart from its ground operations, offered a "Blue Label" air package service. Of the more than 500 million shipments handled by UPS in 1970, some eight million were air shipments making UPS one of the dominant air-freight forwarders. With a good reputation for reliability, UPS provided a two-three-day service to the 41 states that it served. Although this service was extremely competitive with respect to cost, some customers complained about a lack of tracing services. In addition, unless the customer subscribed to the ground UPS services, no pickup was provided and the package had to be handed in at the UPS terminal.

One of the largest rivals (in terms of volume) for Federal was the U.S. Postal Service, which derived approximately 16% of its revenues from parcels, although only a small portion of this was "air parcel post." The Postal Service reported 158 million ton miles of air parcel post in 1970, with an average haul of 894 miles. The main users of this service were the mail-order houses, since the reputation of the Postal Service for speed was exceedingly low.

A comparison of rates between Federal and its competitors at the start of the small-package service is provided in Exhibit 4, and market shares in the small-package industry are given in Exhibit 5.

City Selection

As seen above, most of FEC's competitors used the scheduled airlines for the line haul between cities. It was here that FEC felt it held the competitive advantage. Art Bass, senior vice president for planning, explained:

> There is a wide gap between the needs of the shipper and the service offered by the airlines. Packages are slaves to when and where the carriers want to move people, which just happens not to be when and where most parcels have to be sent.

Fred Smith pointed out that with the introduction of wide-body aircraft such as the Boeing 747 and the McDonnell-Douglas DC-10, the airlines now had a great deal of "belly" capacity available for cargo on their passenger flights and thus the relative importance of cargo aircraft to the airlines would diminish.

Exhibit 4

FEDERAL EXPRESS CORPORATION (A)
Rate Schedule as of April 1, 1973
Comparison of Representative Air Transportation Rates for Small Packages

(Includes pickup and delivery charges where applicable)

	700 MILES				
Weight (pounds)	*1*	*5*	*10*	*25*	*50*
Federal Express—Overnight	$ 8.10	$10.50	$13.50	$22.50	$37.50
—Two-day	6.40	8.00	10.00	16.00	26.00
—Courier-Pak	5.00	—	—	—	—
Emery Air Freight	14.61	14.61	18.55	23.71	30.41
Airlines	17.75	17.75	17.75	17.75	17.75
REA Air Express	9.50	9.50	9.50	11.00	15.15
UPS (Blue Label)	1.54	2.44	3.64	7.30	13.30
American Courier (Sky Courier)	27.00	27.00	27.00	27.00	27.00
Express Mail (USPS)	25.00	25.00	25.00	28.00	32.00
Air Mail—Special Delivery	1.60	3.77	6.72	15.12	29.12
Air Parcel Post	1.00	3.02	5.82	14.22	28.22

	1,800 MILES				
Weight (pounds)	*1*	*5*	*10*	*25*	*50*
Federal Express—Overnight	$ 8.50	$12.50	$17.50	$32.50	$57.50
—Two-day	6.60	9.00	12.00	21.00	36.00
—Courier-Pak	5.00	—	—	—	—
Emery Air Freight	11.97	11.97	17.58	24.21	32.00
Airlines	20.85	20.85	20.85	20.85	20.85
REA Air Express	9.50	9.50	11.25	15.65	22.26
UPS (Blue Label)	1.69	3.25	5.20	11.05	20.80
American Courier (Sky Courier)	27.00	27.00	27.00	27.00	27.00
Express Mail (USPS)	25.00	25.00	25.00	28.00	32.00
Air Mail—Special Delivery	1.60	4.83	8.98	20.98	40.98
Air Parcel Post	1.00	4.08	8.08	20.08	40.98

Note: Not all competitive services are available between all city-pairs and certain services take up to seven days to effect delivery. The Federal Express "Overnight" and "Two-day" rates include $1.00 for the daily pickup call based on a $5.00 per week "subscription fee." *Federal adjusted its rate schedule in May 1973. The "Overnight Service" rates for heavier packages closely approximated those of Emery Air Freight; the "Two-day Service" rates were patterned after UPS's "Blue Label Service."*

Exhibit 5

FEDERAL EXPRESS CORPORATION (A)
Market Shares of Competitors

Priority (Next Day) Shipments Under 50 lbs.

	Projected 1974 Volume (millions of packages)	%
REA	22.0	47
Forwarders	16.9	37
Airlines	7.2	16

Second Day Shipments Under 50 lbs.

	Projected 1974 volume (millions of packages)	%
U.P.S.	750.00	80.8
Parcel Post	160.2	17.2
U.P.S. (Blue Label)	16.9	2.0

Source: FEC projections.

Fred Smith stated:

Our consulting reports showed that over ¾ of all the cargo moved in the United States has an origin or destination outside of the 25 top markets. Yet airlines schedule 25% of all their flights into four cities. Over 25% of the cities served by the airlines have only one or two flights per day. We therefore intend to aim our service at the neglected markets. We anticipate that we could get only 5% of the total small shipment air freight through Chicago, but 30% in cities like Rochester, and maybe 50% in Des Moines.

A selection of cities currently served by FEC is shown in Exhibit 6.

Exhibit 6

FEDERAL EXPRESS CORPORATION (A)
Cities Served

ABQ	ALBUQUERQUE
ATL	ATLANTA
BAL	BALTIMORE/WASHINGTON D.C.
BED	BOSTON
BUF	BUFFALO
CAK	CANTON/AKRON
ORD	CHICAGO

Exhibit 6 (continued)

CVG	CINCINNATI
CLE	CLEVELAND
CMH	COLUMBUS
DAL	DALLAS
DAY	DAYTON
DEN	DENVER
DSM	DES MOINES
YIP	DETROIT
GRR	GRAND RAPIDS
GSO	GREENSBORO
BDL	HARTFORD
HOU	HOUSTON
IND	INDIANAPOLIS
JAX	JACKSONVILLE
MKC	KANSAS CITY
LEX	LEXINGTON
LIT	LITTLE ROCK
LAX	LOS ANGELES
SDF	LOUISVILLE
MEM	MEMPHIS
MIA	MIAMI
MKE	MILWAUKEE
MSP	MINNEAPOLIS/ST. PAUL
MLI	MOLINE
BNA	NASHVILLE
MSY	NEW ORLEANS
LGA	NEW YORK CITY
EWR	NEWARK
OAK	OAKLAND/SAN FRANCISCO
OKC	OKLAHOMA CITY
PHL	PHILADELPHIA
PIT	PITTSBURGH
ROC	ROCHESTER
STL	ST. LOUIS
ICT	WICHITA

Operations

Prior to commencement of the small-package business, Federal Express used nine aircraft that it had already converted in order to service seven air mail contracts and to perform charter work for such customers as Ford, NASA, GM, Emery, and IBM. It was planned, however, that both air mail and charter service would be phased out relatively quickly as small-package business increased. Other forms of revenue to the company came from the aircraft modification performed for outside customers by Little Rock Airmotive, and from pilot training for the Dassault Fanjet Falcon in the VA approved school set up in November 1972. For the fiscal year ended June 3, 1973, the following revenues were generated: charter operations, $1,361,000; air mail contracts, $2,981,000; aircraft services, $796,000; training, $1,519,000; and small parcels, $113,000. These revenues totaled $6,770,000, but, unfortunately, operating expenses totaled $9,841,000, leading to over $3 million in operating losses.

In the six to seven months that it had been operating the small-package service, FEC considered that it had proved itself in the marketplace. Beginning its operations in April, with two aircraft serving 23 cities, the first night had seen a volume of four packages. However, by October the average nightly volume had risen to over 2,500 packages, utilizing 19 aircraft and serving 42 cities (see Exhibit 7). The October flight schedule is shown in Exhibit 8.

Exhibit 7

FEDERAL EXPRESS CORPORATION (A)
Monthly Package Volumes

	No. of Cities	*No. of Days*	*$Volume*	*Package Volume/ Month*	*Average No. of Subscribers**
May	28	20	*NA*	9,453	N/A
June	28	24	166,000	16,517	N/A
July	33	19	194,000	17,304	214
August	34	20	299,000	28,388	284
September	34	24	640,000	48,316	367
October (estimate)	42	20	693,000	50,330	429

* For $5 fee, Federal would call on subscribers every week day. Nonsubscribers were required to pay $1 per package for pickup.

Mike Fitzgerald, Senior Vice President for Sales and Customer Service, reported that the company had met some market resistance:

> There was a "show me" attitude prevalent. Traffic managers have had their fill of extravagant promises from carriers. But we stressed the totality of our system, which seemed to work, and in addition the traffic managers really seemed to be impressed with our Fanjet Falcon.

Some customer confusion had arisen over the use of Memphis as a hub city. Commented one customer:

Exhibit 8

FEDERAL EXPRESS CORPORATION (A)
Flight Schedule—October 1973

Scheduled Arrivals at Memphis		*Scheduled Departures from Memphis*	
6 P.M.– 7 P.M.	1	3:00 A.M.–3:30 A.M.	5
7 P.M.– 8 P.M.	0	3:30 A.M.–4:00 A.M.	7
8 P.M.– 9 P.M.	2	4:00 A.M.–4:30 A.M.	2
9 P.M.–10 P.M.	2	4:30 A.M.–5:00 A.M.	1
10 P.M.–11 P.M.	4	5:00 A.M.–5:30 A.M.	1
11 P.M.–12 P.M.	2	5:30 A.M.–6:00 A.M.	1
12 P.M.– 1 A.M.	3	6:00 A.M.–6:30 A.M.	2
1 A.M.– 2 A.M.	9	6:30 A.M.–7:00 A.M.	0
TOTAL	23	7:00 A.M.–7:30 A.M.	1
		7:30 A.M.–8:00 A.M.	1
		TOTAL	21*

* Total not equal to 23 since 2 departures take place in the night only to arrive back at Memphis after a short journey. In October Federal had 19 Fanjets dedicated to the small package service.

A customer shipping from Boston to Albany is going to be very mad if a package gets fogged in at Memphis.

In general, however, customer reaction to Federal Express' service was very encouraging. A survey performed in October yielded the comments shown in Exhibit 9. The expected customer resistance to separating parcels of 50 pounds and under from their other shipments had not proven to be too much of a problem.

The company did, however, have to change its pricing policy. In the first month of operation, it was discovered that the rate structure was excessively biased to favor packages under 15 pounds. While this had in part been intentional in order to discourage the harder-to-handle larger packages, the effect had been to deter them entirely. Overnight rates for heavier packages were made competitive with those of air freight forwarders; second-day rates were made competitive with UPS's Blue Label Service for all-weight classes.

FEC aimed at obtaining a core of regular shippers by offering to call on the customer every day for a flat fee of $5 per week. Nonsubscribers were required to pay $1 per package for pickup.

Operations at the Hub

The ability of the company to sort packages at a single location was considered a key element by FEC in optimizing the capital and manpower resources employed in the small package system. As of November 1973, FEC had installed a $36,000 three-belt conveyor belt system in its 12,000 square feet sort facility in Memphis. This unit had a capacity of 5,000–7,000 packages per hour. Approximately 35

Exhibit 9

FEDERAL EXPRESS CORPORATION (A)
Selected Comments from FEC Customer Survey, October 1973

1. What is your knowledge of FEC's concept?
   (a) "High Flying UPS"
2. Price
   (a) "Can't beat it under 50 lbs"
3. Trace Capability
   (a) "traced twice—worked well both times"
   (b) "could not have been better"
4. Local Service
   (a) "Beautiful"
   (b) "very good—nice white shirt, bow tie"
5. How can FEC improve?
   (a) "Memphis is not good base"
   (b) "Keep on doing what they're presently doing"
   (c) "Only problem is that everything goes to Memphis . . . think it's idiotic."
6. How quickly do you get a bill from FEC?
   (a) "Quickly, but it goes to the wrong place"
7. What is your general evaluation of FEC?
   (a) "Will they be able . . . to make a profit?"
   (b) "I think it will go"
   (c) "A godsend"
   (d) "Yeah!"
   (e) "Often get overnight delivery when using 'second-day service' "
8. What else can you say about FEC?
   (a) "Personnel locally are great. Very enthusiastic . . . drivers are polite and courteous."
   (b) "Local guy is great. Fire under his feet."
   (c) "The others are waiting for FEC to fall on its face, but I don't think it will."
   (d) "If I had the money, I'd invest."
   (e) "Payroll checks . . . Courier Pak . . . U.S. Mail stinks . . . this is the need that FEC fills."

men were employed in the facility as unloaders, sorters, and checkers, of whom 12 were full-time employees and the rest part-time, hired for \$3 per hour for a minimum of four hours.

It had been arranged that early in 1974 two more conveyor belts would be added at a cost of \$40,000. The capacity of the new system would be between 8,000–12,000 packages per hour. Replacement of the belts with an automatic tilt-tray sorting system would take place when volume was sufficient to support such a system. The proposed \$1.3 million system which had a capacity of 11,000–22,000 packages per hour, would cut manpower requirements by 60%.

Because there was a little more than an hour between the arrival of the last plane and the departure of the first, efficient operations at the facility were essential.

Fortunately, some aircraft arrived much earlier, allowing the bulk of the sorting to fall outside the critical one-hour period. The proposed schedule for the full 82-city system would imply that 33 aircraft would be on the ground at Memphis at midnight each day (see Exhibit 10). Note that this schedule requires many planes to make two round trips a day compared to the October schedule of just over one trip per day per plane.

Staffing

Among the executives of the company were Roger J. Frock (age 37), General Manager, who had been a principal of A. T. Kearney, one of the groups that had performed the feasibility study for FEC. The president of AAPG, the other consulting group, Art Bass (41), also joined FEC as a senior vice-president. Mike Basch (35) and Mike Fitzgerald (37), both with executive experience at UPS, were also recruited to the management team. The organizational structure of the company was based around the particular talents and experience of each of these men. As may be seen in Exhibit 11, there were two major operational groups in the structure: Flying Operations (reporting to Art Bass) and Sales and Customer Service (reporting to Mike Fitzgerald).

Financing

In March of 1973, FEC had attempted to raise $20 million in long-term financing by means of a private placement of $16 million equity and $4 million second mort-

Exhibit 10

FEDERAL EXPRESS CORPORATION (A)
Proposed 82-City Schedule
Net Aircraft at Memphis Between Hours Shown

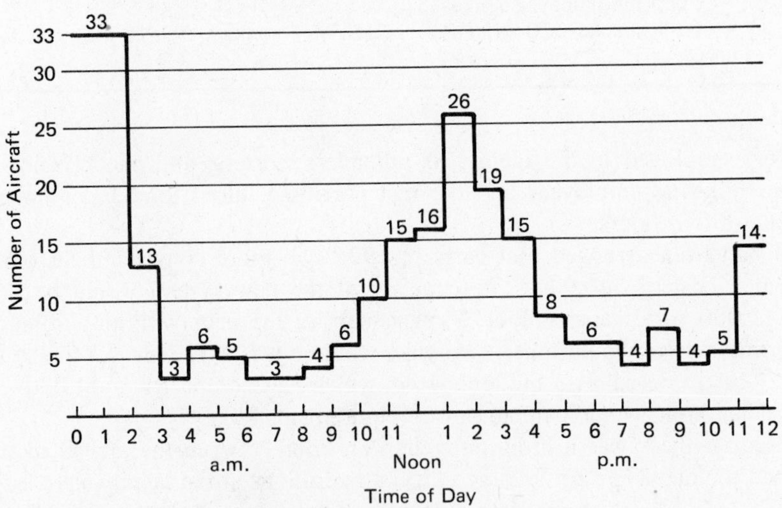

Exhibit 11

FEDERAL EXPRESS CORPORATION (A)
Organization, October 1973

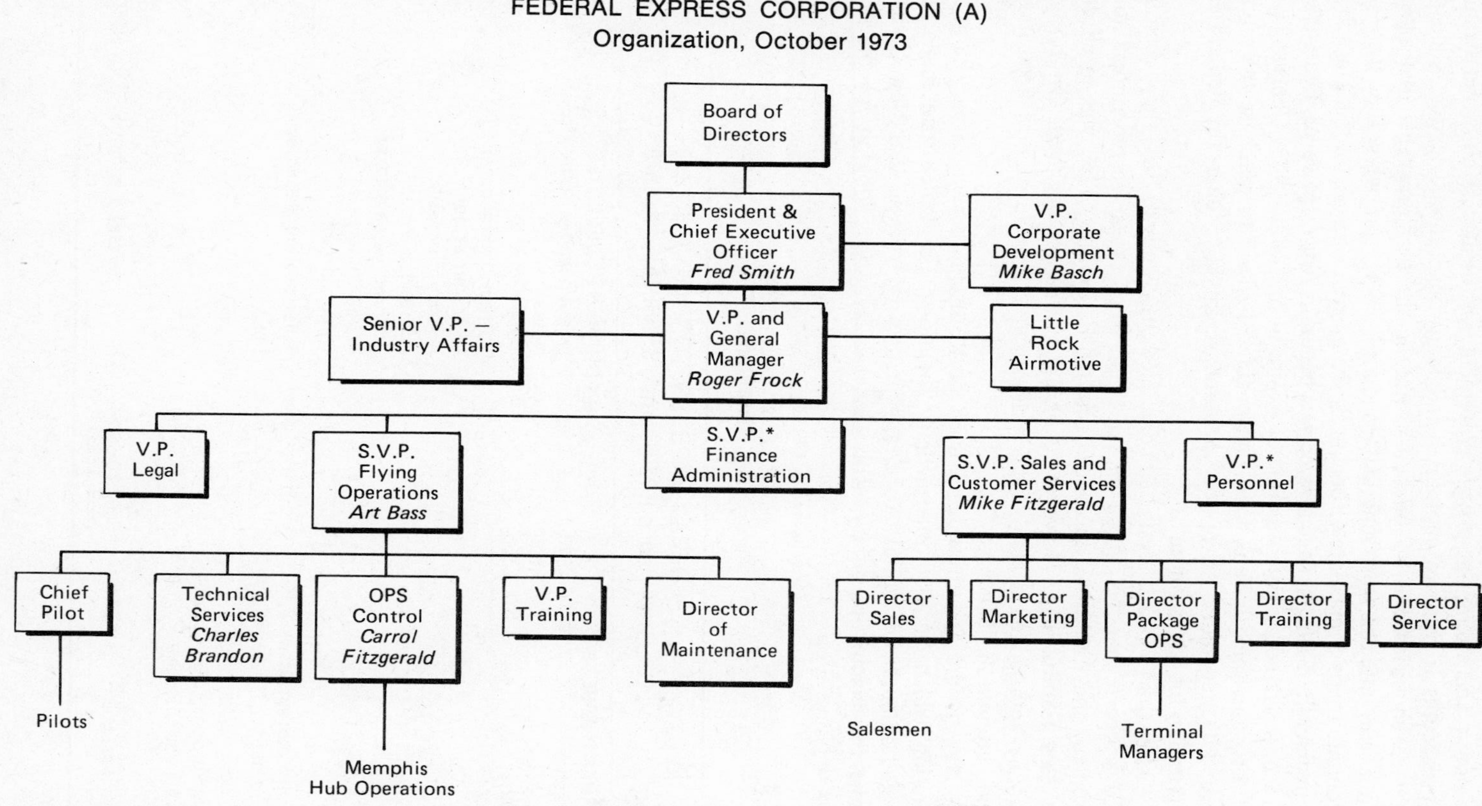

*Position unfilled.

gage notes. The attempt at private placement was unsuccessful. A mass mailing of the prospectus to venture capitalists and many institutional lenders yielded some interested enquiries, but no financing. Among the best prospects that arose from the financing attempt was General Dynamics (GD), who, while they were hesitant to commit funds immediately, began an exhaustive analysis of Federal's business. Meanwhile, the FEC package service was begun in April. However, Federal's option on 18 undelivered aircraft was due to expire in mid-May 1973. General Dynamics agreed to guarantee a bank loan that enabled Federal to purchase the aircraft. In return, GD negotiated an option to purchase an 80% share in Federal Express Corporation for $16 million.

After the 15 GD analysts had completed their study of FEC they recommended to GD's board that the option be exercised. Four times the recommendation was presented, and four times the board rejected it. By now, FEC was in effect bankrupt (see Exhibit 12). However, bankruptcy was *not* declared. On July 19, the company approached a New York venture capitalist, New Court Securities, for a second attempt at financing.

New Court Securities, a division of Rothschild's, was a merchant banking operation which handled intermediary functions, but which also managed some massive amounts of capital. An arrangement was made so that New Court would handle the placing of equity, with General Dynamics looking for placement of bank debt.

Exhibit 12

FEDERAL EXPRESS CORPORATION (A)
Consolidated Balance Sheet, June 3, 1973

CURRENT ASSETS			CURRENT LIABILITIES	
Cash	$ 11,678		Notes payable to banks	$35,933,543
Receivables	1,405,800		Notes payable to stockholders	175,000
Other	2,084,155		Notes payable to vendors	1,015,193
			Current maturities of LTD	1,406,874
			Overdraft at bank	406,525
			Accounts payable	4,579,154
			Accrued interest	434,551
			Accrued income taxes	245,000
			Taxes (other)	464,275
			Other current	288,538
			Total current liabilities	$44,948,653
Total current assets	$3,501,633			
Net property & equip.		$51,085,208	LTD	$11,532,810
Deferred charges & other		2,183,726	Common stock	4,750,000
			Acc. deficit	(4,460,896)
Total assets		$56,770,567	Total liabilities	$56,770,567

Of the $52 million to be raised in the placement, over $37 million was required to service and refinance existing debt commitments, $7 million was to be used to complete the purchase and modification of aircraft, and $5 million was needed to increase working capital. The remainder was to be used to purchase engines, a training "simulator," and sundry other items. The pro-forma change in capitalization as a result of the placement is shown in Exhibit 13. Traffic forecasts are given in Exhibit 14, together with a pro-forma income statement in Exhibit 15.

Exhibit 13

FEDERAL EXPRESS CORPORATION (A)
Capitalization

	Outstanding 9/30/73	*To Be Outstanding After Securities Are Issued*
Notes payable to banks	$36,033,543	$ 0
Notes payable to stockholder, vendor, and others	1,847,386	0
Current maturities of LTD	1,986,360	1,574,880
Long-term Debt		
3-year note, secured by LRA* stock		$ 2,286,395
Note, secured by aircraft	$10,863,750	$11,238,750
Monthly Installment Note	$ 82,855	$ 80,615
Subordinated notes due October 1981		$12,250,000
Subordinated note, payable in 24 quarters beginning August 1975		2,250,000
Revolving loan agreements with banks		19,149,000
Total LTD	$10,946,605	$47,504,760
Capital Stock		
Class A preferred		$ 8,750,000
Class B preferred		3,500,000
Common	$ 4,750	6,620
Additional paid-in capital	4,750,000	4,745,250
Total capital stock	$ 4,754,750	$17,001,870

* Little Rock Airmotive, a subsidiary of FEC.

Exhibit 14

FEDERAL EXPRESS CORPORATION (A)
Small Package Revenue Projection Assumptions
Fiscal Year 1974

		Flight Hours					Small Packages			
	No. Calendar Weeks	Small Package	Other	Total	No. of Aircraft In Service	Airports Served	Quantity[1]	1,000 lbs Estimated Weight[2]	Total Lift (Weight) Available[3]	Load Factor
1973—June	5	1,083	1,043	2,126	13	29	14,521	203.3	1,440.0	14.1%
July	4	862	783	1,645	14	34	17,336	242.7	1,254.7	19.3
August	4	968	970	1,938	14	34	28,590	502.6	1,320.0	38.1
September	5	1,198	955	2,153	14	35	47,645	667.0	1,584.0	42.1
October	4	1,922	615	2,537	19	41	63,000	882.0	2,100.0	42.0
November	4	2,816	630	3,446	19	41	110,545	1,547.6	3,150.0	49.1
December	5	4,134	870	5,004	20	41	200,273	2,803.8	5,820.0	48.1
1974—January	4	3,840	590	4,430	22	48	177,025	2,478.4	4,992.6	49.6
February	4	4,700	680	5,380	24	55	269,273	3,755.8	6,180.7	60.8
March	5	7,439	805	8,244	29	70	388,091	5,433.3	10,060.6	54.0
April	4	6,593	787	7,380	32	79	328,700	4,601.8	8,849.6	52.0
May	4	7,286	679	7,965	33	82	340,550	4,767.7	9,730.0	49.0

[1] Assumed Average Revenue per Package is $11.00.
[2] Assumed Average Weight per Package is fourteen pounds.
[3] Assumed Weight Available per Cycle is 6,000 pounds.

Exhibit 15

FEDERAL EXPRESS CORPORATION (A)
Actual and Projected Statement of Operations
Fiscal Year 1974
($000)

	Actual					Projected							
	June	July	Aug.	Sept.	Oct.	Nov.	Dec.	Jan.	Feb.	Mar.	April	May	Total Year
No. Calendar Weeks	5	4	4	5	4	4	5	4	4	5	4	4	
Revenues													
Sm. Package	$166	$194	$299	$640	$693	1216	$2203	$2142	$2962	$4269	$3616	$3746	$22146
Postal	354	262	268	305	260	260	320	260	260	320	260	260	3389
Charter	31	66	105	68	41	41	51	41	41	51	41	41	618
Training	209	155	196	180	210	210	110	150	180	200	215	225	2240
Service Center	3	34	99	9	115	125	75	100	100	125	125	125	1035
Subscription Charges					12	14	24	23	28	43	41	50	235
Insurance	2	4	6	10	5	9	13	16	27	38	34	37	201
Total	765	715	973	1212	1336	1875	2796	2732	3598	5046	4332	4484	29864
Operating Expenses													
Flt. Operations	551	545	502	560	716	821	1075	1056	1181	1588	1473	1502	11670
Training	84	77	63	59	78	86	57	70	79	80	82	80	905
Line Maint. & Eng.	196	266	321	324	295	370	390	383	401	429	462	481	4318
Sales & Cust. Serv.	332	388	397	495	477	515	585	605	751	835	920	970	7270
Marketing & Traffic	26	15	21	20	77	105	95	85	75	65	55	55	694
Corp. Development	11	11	11	9	17	16	19	22	22	22	22	22	204
Finance	23	27	31	29	37	41	46	48	57	68	64	67	538
Administrative	55	52	40	48	70	62	68	75	79	76	77	76	778
Data Processing	22	23	39	38	47	54	57	60	64	65	66	68	603
Executive	25	22	12	12	25	24	24	25	25	27	25	23	269
Total Oper. Expenses	1325	1426	1437	1694	1839	2094	2426	2429	2734	3255	3246	3344	27249
Oper. Income (Loss)	(560)	(711)	(464)	(482)	(503)	(219)	370	303	864	1791	1086	1140	2615
Other Expenses (Income)													
Interest	195	257	242	296	287	333	363	411	458	501	532	532	4407
Other	(15)	172	28	(140)	64	63	62	121	60	59	59	58	591
Net Income Before Taxes	(740)	(1140)	(734)	(638)	(854)	(615)	(55)	(229)	346	1231	495	550	(2383)

CHAPTER 6: DESIGNING THE SERVICE FIRM ORGANIZATION

In the preceding chapters, we have examined how service industry executives determine the appropriate service levels for their firms by simultaneously evaluating market needs and the service offerings of competitors. The desired service level then dictates the type of service delivery system needed to provide the service. The design of the service delivery system establishes the physical attributes of the facility (for example, a certain size, decor, and equipment configuration) and the mix of employee skills required to operate the facilities. This sequence is depicted in Figure 6-1. However, the sequence is not complete until the activities shown in the two boxes at the bottom of the figure have been accomplished. These activities of establishing appropriate organizational structures and motivational mechanisms are the subject of this chapter. The key questions are as follows. How should a service firm be organized? What type of organization (that is, functional or geographic) is best? What are the important factors to consider in motivating service employees of various skill levels? What are the best methods to motivate and compensate service employees and managers?

Many books, monographs, and articles have been written on the subjects covered in this chapter. For example, much of the published research in the fields of human behavior and organizational design has direct applicability to the topics covered in this chapter. However, it is not our intent to summarize the major conceptual developments in these fields. Our goal for this chapter is extremely modest: to stimulate present and potential service industry executives to devote more time to the important tasks of designing the organizational structures they manage and assessing the needs of the employees slated in these structures. It has been our observation that many service executives have made short shrift of these tasks and this neglect, either intentional or not, has led to disastrous results. Thus, our focus is diagnostic, not prescriptive. For those readers who discover symptoms of organizational malaise, we strongly recommend that they seek assistance from our colleagues who specialize in organizational design.

DETERMINANTS OF ORGANIZATIONAL STRUCTURE

The importance of the organizational structure and the motivational mechanisms in influencing the behavior of both managers and employees is particularly evident in service organizations. Representing the primary sources of quality control for the service firm, these administrative systems should be designed to communicate the goals of top management to the operating personnel, to motivate them to act in a

Figure 6-1

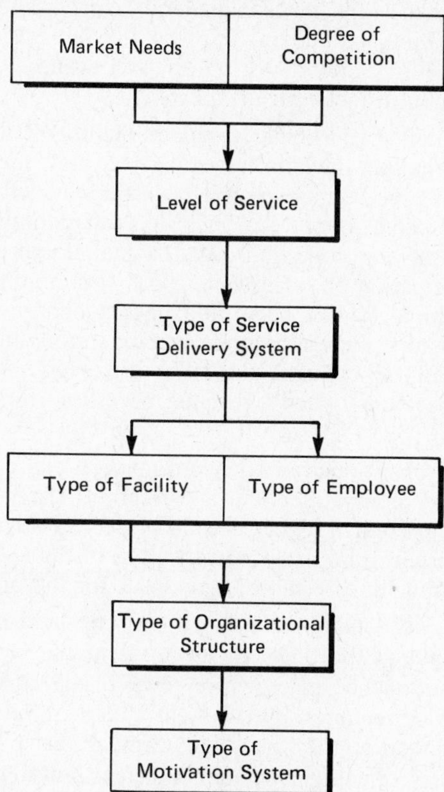

manner consistent with the service concept, and to monitor the performance of the individual employees and the business overall. Several unique characteristics of service operations make the administrative systems particularly important:

1. Employee behavior is often an integral part of the service product. This is not true in a manufacturing operation where employee behavior may affect product quality but is not a part of the product. Two service examples may serve to illustrate the point. In a consulting firm the product is not only the ideas that the staff present orally and in writing to the client, but also the interpersonal interactions between the staff and the client. In a restaurant, diners evaluate the quality of the product as much on the interpersonal behavior of the serving personnel as on the quality of the food and the facilities.

Even if the behavior of the service operation's personnel is only a peripheral component of the service, it is almost always an important determinant of the customer's perception of good service. The more intangible the service, the more weight the buyer's perception carries. In Federal Express, for instance, smiling, courteous, bow-tied drivers were secondary in priority to the planes, pilots, and sorting terminals for the delivery of the service. Federal Express could have carried on business with grumpy and grubby drivers or no drivers at all by subcontracting the ground delivery portion of the service. However, the drivers were the visible representatives of the company and supplied the link between Federal Express and the customers. They demonstrated the reliability of Federal Express and increased the customer's confidence in the service. Flight attendants, tellers, and agents serve the same function for airlines, banks, and insurance firms, respectively.

2. A service operation is particularly vulnerable to disruptions caused by the workforce, since anticipatory inventories cannot be built up as protection against such disruptions. Airline personnel select a peak period such as Christmas to walk off their jobs and basketball referees pick the playoff period as the time to go out on strike for better working conditions. In the manufacturing sector, firms build up inventories in anticipation of such events. The 4½ month long strike by rubber company employees in 1976 had very little impact on tire sales because the tire producers, tire distributors, and automobile manufacturers had stockpiled tires during the preceding period. In contrast, the 1976 strike of United Airlines' personnel had a significant impact on United's revenue because airline flights could not be inventoried.

3. The simultaneity of production and consumption characteristic that gives rise to the multisite nature of most service firms, creates the need for managers and management systems to control highly decentralized operations to meet a single set of standards. The presence and often participation of the consumer at the point of production makes it difficult to establish standards for the output of a service firm.

Among firms claiming to deliver a consistent service, there may be a great deal of variability in the output at the different locations of the firm and a great deal of variability in the output of the same location, even of the same employee, over time. For example, the service rendered by the flight attendant varies from flight to flight and from person to person on the same flight. Similar variations occur in the output of desk clerks at a hotel, of counter personnel for car rental firms, and of instructors at tennis camps.

It is even harder to ensure that standards, if they are developed, are met each time the service is delivered. In a service operation, unlike in a manufacturing operation, an inferior product can seldom be caught by a quality control check. Quality control must be embodied in the organizational structure.

Given these characteristics, how does a service manager design an appropriate organizational structure and establish an effective motivational system? The answer is that it depends on the special requirements dictated by the service delivery system. For the purposes of illustration, we shall describe two extreme cases. At one end of the spectrum is the firm comprised of few nonstandardized branches, offering a broad range of services individualized for each customer and delivered by a relatively high-skill workforce. These characteristics typify *professional service organizations* (PSOs) such as consulting and advertising firms. At the other extreme is the firm comprised of a network of many standardized facilities offering a limited range of services delivered by a relatively low-skill workforce to a large aggregate market. Such characteristics are typical of the *consumer service organizations* (CSOs) such as restaurants and retail stores.

The majority of service organizations cannot be classified unambiguously into these two extremes. However, a useful way of evaluating relevant organizational characteristics is to describe these two theoretical extremes and use them to evaluate the variant service organizations.

PROFESSIONAL SERVICE ORGANIZATIONS

The expression "professional service organization" usually projects an image of a group of lawyers, doctors, management or engineering consultants, advertising executives, or another group of highly skilled, highly paid individuals. And although it might appear at first glance a simple task for a well-educated manager to manage peers, the characteristics of professional service organizations can make the manager's task extremely difficult.

Professional service organizations differ from other service organizations in a number of ways. First, the level of education required of a PSO member is generally quite high—most often one or more advanced academic degrees are expected. Secondly, there is a high level of perceived status connected to membership in many PSOs. Thirdly, while many service operations may be characterized by low-skill, low-pay "undesirable" jobs, PSOs often provide highly desirable positions with high potential earning capacity for a member.

An important characteristic of a PSO is that each member of the PSO can have a significant impact on the firm in many areas, including profits, reputation, and skills "inventory." In a very real sense, the individuals providing the service of the PSO define the organization, and while employees may be replaceable, every replacement alters the nature of the organization (this is true to a lesser degree in very large PSOs with extensive staffs) and the nature of its product. As a result, it is difficult if not impossible to standardize the characteristics and the quality of the PSO product. Clients of PSOs are intuitively (or in some cases, explicitly) aware of this fact because they rarely award business on an impersonal or purely quantitative basis; instead they usually base a service purchase decision on more subjective contact with and knowledge of the individuals providing the service. Very often when a PSO develops problems, the problems are either due to the illusion that the firm, rather than the individual members, is the marketable product, or because of a failure to capitalize on the logic that the individual staff members *are* the firm.

There are certain incentives for a practicing professional to join a PSO. For many young professionals, membership is almost a prerequisite to success, for example, a doctor must become a "member" of a PSO, that is, a hospital, for internship, and a recent law school graduate is hard pressed to develop a personal practice without having first worked for an established firm. Membership in the "right" PSO can provide psychologically important status achievement, and the jobs themselves usually provide substantial responsibility and authority to members. Even newer employess of a PSO might advise giant corporations on multimillion dollar decisions, help launch important new products, or save lives. In addition, salaries in PSOs usually begin above median income levels with opportunities for considerably higher earning levels in later years.

The manager's task in a PSO is complicated by the fact that PSO members can often exert considerable leverage on the organization because of their relative importance to the PSO. There is inevitably more dollar revenue riding on a single employee/customer contact in a consulting or law firm than there is in a restaurant. Additionally, a PSO member who is valuable to the PSO is most likely valuable to other firms as well; as a result, PSO employees generally have a high degree of job mobility. In certain PSO industries, in fact, proselytizing talent from other firms is a common and accepted practice. Motivation and compensation plans can be critical elements in retaining key professionals.

Most PSOs are privately owned by the principal members (usually as partnerships). The absence of fixed assets reduces the need for conventional equity, that is, external ownership. The financing of accounts receivable is the largest use of funds. Incorporation, if done, is usually for tax or liability reasons.

PSO characteristics argue that an autocratic management style might be less likely to succeed in a PSO than in another kind of enterprise. A PSO manager is usually dealing with individuals with strong ego gratification needs (responsibility, power, success) and high material needs, both of which can be satisfied by a PSO. However, it can be extremely difficult to discern what means should be utilized to motivate a specific employee. Many PSO employees are self-motivating; that is, they come to the firm with a high degree of initiative and drive and may only require an adequate salary and a congenial group with which to work for motivation. For others, whose needs are more subtle, effective managers must discover what these needs are and ensure that the job environment provides an opportunity to satisfy them.

In a consumer service organization the management objective is often to remove initiative and autonomy from the front line staff and thereby standardize and better control service delivery. This approach is not widely utilized in a PSO since the work itself cannot be well defined in advance but is usually developed during the course of its execution. The PSO has many of the job shop characteristics described on pages 82–83. Additionally, the nature of the work is often such that it does not pay to have it checked in detail by someone at a higher level of responsibility; furthermore, such supervision might be a demotivating factor.

Compensation schemes vary widely in PSOs, although professionals are often satisfied with a salary level tied to responsibility and performance with bonuses offered for exceptional performance. If a professional is at a responsibility/authority level where he or she can directly influence the firm's overall profitability, his or her compensation might also be tied to the firm's performance. Partnership arrangements usually provide for this situation and offer additional incentive to younger firm members, as the salary and profit-sharing aspects of the partnership can be quite attractive. Many PSOs have attempted to "lock" employees into the firms through contracts and lucrative compensation schemes, but neither scheme automatically provides the desired guarantee of staff continuity.

Measurement of the success of an individual is often done on a basis of billings or net revenues per professional (revenue minus office rental, travel expenses, support staff, and other overhead items). This method is often used to measure the performance of the entire firm as well.

Since each professional contributes certain revenues and incurs certain expenses, some managers feel that compensation should be tied to firm earnings on a share basis. This can be accomplished by dividends per share or by automatic appreciation of the value of the shares caused by an increase in retained earnings. (In ownership situations, a professional is often required to sell his or her shares back to the company upon retirement either for book value or another predetermined value.) This scheme provides two major problems for a PSO manager, however. The first is that it is difficult to place a value on a share of the firm; book value is a common though not fully satisfactory method. The second is that of determining who deserves to participate in ownership of the PSO and how much participation should be meted out to each individual.

Despite the drawbacks, however, there is one strong argument for ownership; that is, if what's best for the company corresponds directly with what's best for the individual, the company usually benefits. Intracompany rivalries for power and prestige exist in nearly all PSOs. Providing employees with ownership of the firm is often an excellent prescription for good intergroup and interpersonal collaboration.

CONSUMER SERVICE ORGANIZATIONS

At the other extreme of the spectrum and demanding a different organizational structure is the consumer service organization. CSOs are the numerous service organizations that provide relatively standardized services to the public. These services are grocery, clothing, and other retail stores; restaurants; delivery services; and the like. We have observed in prior chapters that all service organizations supply a complex product bundle, parts of which are explicit and understood and parts of which are more abstract and difficult to understand. Most service firms with which the public comes in contact on a regular basis fall into a group that can be characterized as having fairly explicit product bundles compared to the products of the PSOs described in the previous section.

In a sense CSOs resemble the high volume manufacturing units described as line operations on pages 82–83. Like the operations in their high volume manufacturing counterparts, operations in consumer service firms are usually explicit and easy to replicate. As such they are subject to standardization and detailed job descriptions. The standard operating procedures (SOPs) that can emerge from such a detailed description facilitate the staffing of the organization units of CSOs at both the service employee and the management level.

CSO employees may be low skilled in both mechanical skills and education, but highly skilled in the specific tasks for which they are responsible. Training for these tasks can often be accomplished in hours or days rather than weeks or months. Because of these characteristics a large labor pool is usually available to the CSO for wages at or just slightly above the minimum wage. CSOs tolerate a reasonably high turnover (50% per year is common) of personnel because the training costs are so low.

The need for employees who can interact with the public reduces the size of the available labor pool and this personality attribute is the key trait which unit managers must seek in evaluating, training, and controlling service employees. Since almost all service employees, unlike their manufacturing counterparts, must deal directly with the consumer, CSO employees require some degree of interpersonal skills. Unlike the PSO employee's interpersonal skills, which are more intellectually based, the interpersonal skills of the CSO employee are personality based. That is, CSO employees are required to be pleasant, to be reasonably attractive in appearance, to be able to communicate clearly, and to be able to control conversations with their peers and their customers. Prospective CSO employees must be screened carefully for evidence of these personality traits. The organization must also encourage the use of these traits by providing the employees opportunities to achieve job satisfaction with a hassle-free environment, a steady income, and an occasional opportunity to earn extra income wtih overtime.

As with CSO employees, CSO first-line managers require less education and intellectual skills than their PSO counterparts. They also require a different set of human behavior skills to motivate the CSO service employee. The CSO first-line manager often participates in the actual delivery of the service for two purposes. The first is to perform the activities of the service employees occasionally to demonstrate that he or she understands the jobs of these employees. The second is to intercede when a service employee is faced with a nonstandard problem or when a volatile situation exists between the employee and a customer.

The CSO first-line manager's job can be divided into two functions. One function is the administration of SOPs. The manager is left with little discretion in decision making. Questions that cannot be resolved by the SOP are referred to the highest managerial level. Eliminating discretion is necessary if standardization across units and across time is to be accomplished. As a result, most minor and routine decisions, such as the size and wording of signs, are made at a very high organizational level.

It is in the second function, people management, that the CSO manager exercises managerial skills. The CSO manager must implement the set of standardized operating procedures to achieve predetermined goals, employing a low-skilled, low-paid, transitory workforce motivated primarily by a paycheck. The nature of the service delivery system and its workforce dictates a multitiered organizational structure with a narrow span of control containing "people managers" at all but the highest level. The primary task of all but the highest organization level of management is to constantly evaluate their subordinates; in essence the CSO organization consists of tiers of checkers checking up on lower level checkers. Motivation for such managers is geared to monetary incentives for meeting or exceeding predetermined goals and standards. Standardization is fostered at the expense of innovation. Job satisfaction for such individuals is obtained through increasing economic status (income) and increasing organizational status (rising in the organizational hierarchy).

The central organization of a CSO differs markedly from the rest of the organization. Central management skills are not people skills but financial and technical skills. Standardization of products and operating units across the organization allows almost all of the functions outside of the people management function to be centralized. Thus such functions as planning, budgeting, product design, facilities design, cost control, procurement, and advertising are centralized when economies of scale can be realized.

These managerial characteristics create a clear conflict at the highest levels of management. To accomplish their individual goals of rising in the managerial hierarchy CSO managers must develop a personality and thinking process that is geared to implementing preset goals and standards. This lack of real decision-making responsibility stifles the innovative and decision-making skills necessary to operate effectively at the very top levels of the organization. Thus, while developing the personality and skills that allows them to move rapidly through the lower and middle management levels of a CSO, the individual managers fail to develop the skills needed to survive at the top levels of the organization.

This conflict can be seen symptomatically in CSO companies in one of two ways. An organization may not perceive the problem and allow middle managers to rise to the top organization, resulting in a growing atrophy of company innovativeness and policy making. Or an organization may perceive the problem and simply hire top level managers from outside the organization, thus frustrating middle managers who desire to rise within the organization.

Two characteristics of the CSO organization structure are useful in dealing with this problem. First, as an organization grows, an increasing number of sites are added to exploit untapped markets. Such growth requires the organization to add managerial levels and provides opportunity for upward mobility of managers so long as the growth occurs at a steady or increasing pace.[1]

Second, each individual unit is normally treated as a profit center. Since the operation (and thus the cost structure of operation) is standardized across units, two elements determine profitability—the available market and the unit manager's ability to meet or exceed standards. As the head of a profit center, unit managers assume the status of owner operators; a status that may be enhanced by actually franchising or licensing the units. Owner operator status provides unit managers with top level organizational status within their individual communities.

DESIGNING THE ORGANIZATION

The characteristics of the two polar types of service organizations, professional service and consumer service, are summarized in Table 6-1. Understanding the characteristics of these two extremes assists the service manager in designing an organizational structure and a motivation system that match the requirements of the service delivery system he or she manages. A mismatch almost surely leads to

[1] See D. Daryl Wyckoff, *Organizational Formality and Performance in the Motor-Carrier Industry* (Lexington, Mass.: Lexington Books, D. C. Heath and Co., 1974).

disaster. Table 6-1 is a useful framework for testing the consistency of the organizational elements with the characteristics of the service delivery system. By describing each of the characteristics listed in Table 6-1 for his or her service firm and analyzing the resulting profile for inconsistencies, the service manager should be able to pinpoint potential problem areas.

Table 6-1

A COMPARISON OF PROFESSIONAL AND CONSUMER SERVICE ORGANIZATIONS

	Professional Service Organization (PSO)	*Consumer Service Organization (CSO)*
Type of Product	Nonstandard with high knowledge and/or manual skill content	Standardized with low knowledge and/or skill content
Type of organizational structure	Flat unstructured hierarchy with loose subordinate-superior relationships with broad discretion at all levels	Rigid pyramidal hierarchy with standard operating procedures and close top-down control
Geographical dispersion	Single centralized office or few major offices serving local regional or national markets	Multisite operations each serving local markets
Transaction volume per time period	Low	High
Value of individual transaction	Large	Small
Locus of profit control	Individual contract	Operating unit
Type of middle management	Professionally trained, self-motivated individuals who also participate in delivering the service	Operating skills geared to managing people and meeting predetermined goals
Type of operating personnel	Professionally trained, self-motivated individuals	Low and unskilled operators
Type of customer contacts	Medium to long-term contact with professional individuals	Short-term contact with a variety of service employees
Initial sale	Personal selling by professionals or marketing team	By advertising and promotion
Repeat sales	By professionals delivering service	By service employees delivering service
Customer loyalty	To service provider	To concept

Table 6-1 (continued)

Motivational characteristics of:		
1. Management	1. Long-term professional and income growth	1. Medium- and long-term monetary growth and long-term growth of status with organizations
2. Operating personnel	2. Opportunity to advance in status, long-term professional growth end. Short- and long-term income	2. Near term marketing reward; pleasant hassle-free work environment
Orientation of facilities	Nonstandard, pleasant, unstructured environment for employees	Multiple standardized facilities and structured environment for employees with atmosphere geared to customer requirements
Quality control	Peer and client evaluation	Built-in training programs and random inspections
Centralized functions	Planning and state of the art knowledge	Planning Procurement Advertising Budgeting Cost control Facilities design Product design Pricing

When using the topology in Table 6-1 it should be kept in mind that services evolve over time. They tend to develop as a nonstandard concept fulfilling market needs that are vaguely defined. As the market needs become more defined, the opportunity for specializing the process increase. Such standardization and specialization often lead to the service becoming a manufactured good. Many of our traditional manufactured goods grew out of service type operations; the cobbler produced shoes to customer specification using customer supplied materials and the seamstress and tailor produced clothing to customer specification using customer supplied materials. Thus a service may move from a nonstandard service operation to a standardized service operation and eventually evolve into a manufactured good.

However, movement is not limited to a single direction. Recall our example of the fish wholesaler of Chapter 2. His organization changed from producing goods to producing service over a period of time. The direction of movement along the standardized/nonstandardized scale should be a function of market needs and competitive pressures. Haute cuisine restaurants and fast-food establishments can both be viable concepts; the same holds true for luxury hotels and budget motels. Once the choice of where on the spectrum to operate has been made, the question is to design the correct organizational structure.

The first step in designing the organization is to determine the one or two most important elements of the service concept. One way to control these elements is to leave the decisions in the hands of the top management at corporate headquarters. A second way is to remove all the other responsibilities from the "decision-making" personnel in the field to allow them to concentrate on the desired behavior. For this approach to work, the employees must understand clearly what the desired behavior is and be rewarded for it, or at least not have their rewards run counter to it.

The manager must also determine what role the people at each level in the organization play in carrying out the service concept. Many service managers make the blanket assumption that the behavior of all their employees is equally important. Again, a careful definition of the service concept and how the business uniquely competes is vital in pinpointing the roles of various personnel. An example may illustrate this point. A major function of some airline personnel may be merely informational. If so, clear and adequate posting of schedules (like those so successfully used in European train stations, not like the feeble television screens favored by domestic U.S. airlines) could reduce the need for clerks or allow the same number to devote more time to their other functions. On the other hand, if airline managers believe that the informational role of the clerks serves other purposes such as giving the passengers confidence, trading them up to the first class from coach, or encouraging use of their airline instead of a competitor, they should hire more information clerks and train them to deal with passengers in a pleasant and confident manner and to develop the skills of personal selling.

An important factor in organizational design is matching the right people to the right job. However, finding the right people for the job is often difficult. The logical alternative is to design the system for the people available. However, this plan puts a constraint on the kind of system that can be established. Not only must the organizational design define the roles and desired behavior, but it must also match the abilities and needs of the actual people available to the organization.

On examination of a variety of service industry jobs, we find that many are dull and routine, hardly the types of positions that would be thought of as inspiring or rewarding to the available workforce. In fact, some authors contend that the secret to success for service firms is to follow a manufacturing approach and make these jobs even more standardized. Because of the need to maintain a consistency of its service offerings over time and space, many service managers agree with this position and seek to eliminate as many opportunities for employee discretion as possible. As Levitt phrases it, on page 64, technology is substituted for motivation. "The only choice available . . . is to operate it exactly as the designers intended."

In assessing what tradeoffs are implicit in the choice of a manufacturing approach to service, it is important to note that service operations vary considerably and generalizations obviously do not apply to all firms. For example, the costs of high turnover of cooks and counter personnel in a fast-food unit where little skill is required and where training is short and easy are much different from the costs of high turnover of chefs and waiters in a French restaurant where the tasks are more complex and take much longer to teach.

Changing the content of jobs can be ticklish in a service firm. If the firm has a well-defined service concept and a service delivery system that effectively limits the workers' discretion in providing the service, the company runs a great risk in changing the jobs. A service concept often consists of a very delicate balance of intangibles. Turning more control over to an employee increases the chances of the balance being tipped in the wrong direction. One possible answer is to make sure that the employees understand what the service concept is and why it works. When confronted with decisions, they will then, hopefully, make them consistent with the concept.

A dilemma arises for the service manager who decides not to risk giving his or her employees more discretion. What does he or she do then? Is there any way to minimize the dehumanizing effect of the system? For example, consider the policy of an area supervisor making frequent unannounced checks on the cleanliness of the washrooms. The employee may understand the reason behind the check and the importance of cleanliness to the firm's image, but the fact of unannounced checks still rankles because of the apparent assumption on the part of the supervisor or the company that the employee is at fault if the washrooms are not clean. Such a system could be modified to require the employee to make a periodic check, duly recording the time and the conditions. The function of monitoring the cleanliness would still be performed, but some of the overt distrust of the employee's judgment would be eliminated. However, most managers of low discretion service operations successfully follow the maxim, "People do what you *inspect* not what you *expect*."

If the job content cannot be changed, the manager has to look at the job environment. Improving working conditions may not improve "job satisfaction," but it can serve as evidence to the employee that the company cares. An effective technique is to develop a sense of team spirit. Although the employee's own work may not be inherently satisfying, the sense of participating in the delivery of a larger product may provide a sense of achievement. This principle is similar to telling a worker tightening 10,000 nuts a day on an assembly line that he is helping to build a Chevrolet. Compensation programs that involve the employee in the larger goals and accomplishments of the organization (for example, pooling tips or profit sharing) can contribute to this larger sense of belonging. Competition among units, regions, and areas also helps foster this team concept.

CONCLUSION

In most service organizations, the organizational structure and motivational systems should be designed to generate a service attitude on the part of service managers and employees. This concept is an overriding consideration because the service employee is the firm's contact with the customer and well-motivated service employees at the point of contact have a tremendous impact on the customer's perceived level of service. And, one of the most, if not most, important levels of management is the lowest level—the branch or unit manager. These managers are the sergeants and petty officers who implement the directives from above. Their performance can significantly influence the profitability of their units. Highly motivated managers at this level are critical to motivated service employees and from their ranks the captains of the future will be selected.

Waffle House, Inc. (J)

In the summer of 1972 Joe Rogers, Jr., openly discussed his concerns about the future of Waffle House.

> It has been over a year since I left Harvard Business School. Although I am supposed to be the company's financial officer, I have had little time to spend on my major function of raising funds to finance our expansion plans for the coming year.
>
> Pop has been spending most of this time out at the river supervising the construction of his home and developing a subdivision with Tom (Tom Forkner was an officer of Waffle House). As a result I have had to get involved in the operations phase of the business. There's a new office waiting for me at La Vista Road. I told them to save it for me because I will be staying at Columbia Drive for a few more months. (Most of the Waffle House, Inc., officers were located at the La Vista Road headquarters; the Waffle House operations group was located on Columbia Drive in an office building directly behind the company's training unit.)
>
> Both Pop and I feel strongly that good customer service has been the key to our success. We want to make sure everything is finely tuned as we take off on our next stage of growth. In the past, most of our units were located in the metro-Atlanta area and we could give them a lot of personal attention. However, as we have grown, control has become more difficult.
>
> There are several specific questions that need our attention if we are to continue to give better service to the customer. First, is our organizational structure adequate to absorb our anticipated growth? Not only is the structure adequate, but do we also have the people to fill the slots? If we don't, where can we get them? Second, is our present management information system an adequate monitoring system to control the operations of a number of widely dispersed units? Third, can we do a better job of controlling our food costs? Should we consider a central commissary in certain areas? Fourth, what should we do with the group of auxiliary services that we have developed to service the Waffle House units? Fifth, what should we do to market our product?

As Waffle House expanded its operations in the late sixties and early seventies, the organization shown in Exhibit 1 developed. The structure that evolved placed major responsibility on Joe Rogers, Sr., to manage the operations of the company units and the auxiliary services. Tom Forkner took responsibility for real estate,

Exhibit 1

WAFFLE HOUSE, INC.
Company Organization Chart, February 1972

Customer

Board of Directors — Rogers, Forkner, Chavers

Joe W. Rogers
Age 52, 1955 (1961 Active)
President and Chairman of the Board

Hugh G. Fly

- Tom Forkner **Age 52, 1955**
  - Real estate — Charles Preston **Age 33, 1968**
  - Franchise sales — Lib Julian **Age 36, 1970**
  - Finance — Joe W. Rogers, Jr. **Age 25, 1971**
    - Gene Petway **Age 28, 1970**
      - General office
      - Louise Wright **Age 35, 1964**
      - Earl Hardy **Age 26, 1970**
  - Pest control — Jim Watson **Age 34, 1971**
- Randolph Chavers **Age 54, 1957**
  - Franchised/leased units — Perry Klee **Age 38, 1971**
  - Food quality control — Sheena Harrington **Age 22, 1971**
  - Franchise supplies — W. A. Love **Age 73, 1963**
- Billy Morrison **Age 34, 1962**
  - North Area — Ronald C. Davis **Age 30, 1965**
  - South Area — Bill Ingram **Age 30, 1966**
  - #17/Training — Mike Thames **Age 28, 1970**
  - Florida — Gene Ingram **Age 25, 1969**
- R. L. Hickman **Age 40, 1967**
  - Hickman Co.
  - Maintenance
  - Trim Shop
- L. Mulford **Age 60, 1964**
  - Richard Hollingsworth **Age 31, 1969**
  - Arthur Grant **Age 50, 1970**
- Ed Tucker **Age 35, 1971**
  - Insurance
  - Taxes

In bold print: Age
Year of employment
Year venture was begun

finance, and franchise sales, and Randolph Chavers maintained control over the noncompany-operated units and food quality control. Until January 1972 Hugh Fly had concentrated his efforts on company operations (the running of company-owned units). At that time, he switched his emphasis to managing the auxiliary services.

Company Operations

The management team which had responsibility for the company-operated units felt that their organization was the lead horse pulling the rest of the company. As one manager put it, "Where would the real estate group, the construction crews, the equipment installer, the franchise group and all the other services be if we don't do a good job?" A detailed diagram of the company operations structure is shown in Exhibit 2.

General Manager

Billy Ray Morrison, age 34, the general manager, reported directly to Rogers, Sr. With responsibility for 39 company units, Morrison visited each of them on a periodic basis, making suggestions about how to improve a unit's operations and assisting managers to locate good grill operators and waitresses, often suggesting a friend or relative for the job. Morrison's major function was to supervise directly the efforts of the area sales managers. In the past he acted as a referee as the two area managers battled for additional units, personnel, and other resources.

Morrison, with only a high school education, had worked himself up through the organization into this $40,000+ position from his early days as a grill operator. According to his subordinates, his main asset was his ability to walk into a unit and, within five minutes, pinpoint all the operational problems. Morrison, who had been working for Rogers, Sr., since he was 19, was extremely dedicated to him and to the Waffle House organization and readily admitted, "I love Mr. Rogers a lot. I'd do almost anything he requests."

Area Manager

The three area managers were Ronnie Davis, Bill Ingram, and Gene Ingram. Davis, a graduate of the University of Alabama, was the son of Curtis Davis, a vice-president of Waffle House until his death in 1969. Bill Ingram, a graduate of Auburn University, was the son-in-law of Mr. Rogers, Sr. Gene Ingram, Bill's cousin, graduated from Jacksonville State University in 1969. Davis and Bill Ingram, both 30, joined Waffle House as grill operators in 1965.

Davis supervised the 19 units of the northern area which included parts of Atlanta, north Georgia, and northwest South Carolina. Bill Ingram's 17-unit area covered south Atlanta and south Georgia. Gene Ingram's newly created Florida area consisted of only two units in north Florida. The area manager's main responsibility was the area organization. He hired and fired district managers who worked directly under him. There were six district managers and one trainee in Davis' area;

Exhibit 2

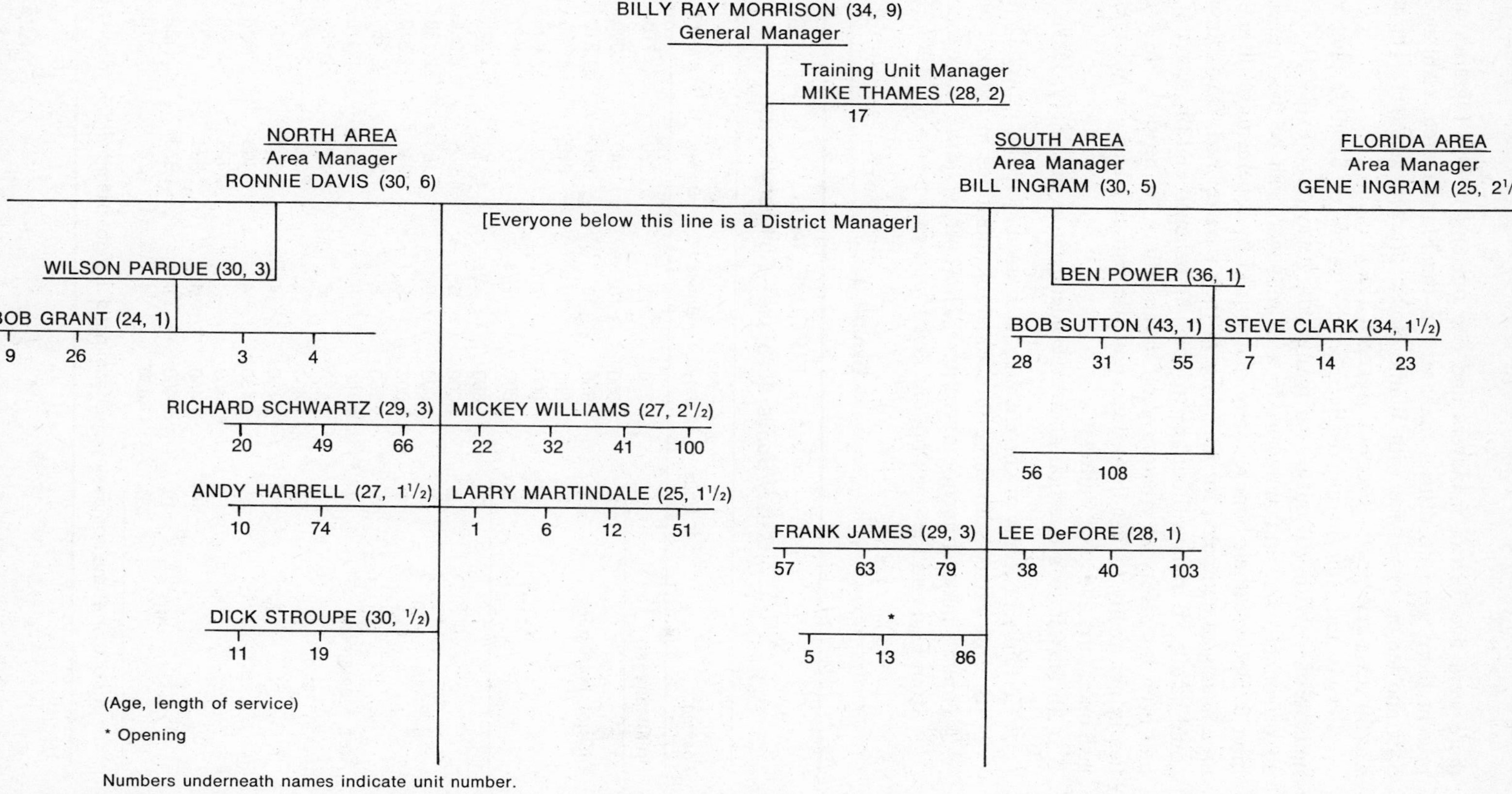
WAFFLE HOUSE, INC.
Company Organization Chart, January 1972
BILLY RAY MORRISON (34, 9)
General Manager
Training Unit Manager
MIKE THAMES (28, 2)
17
NORTH AREA
Area Manager
RONNIE DAVIS (30, 6)
SOUTH AREA
Area Manager
BILL INGRAM (30, 5)
FLORIDA AREA
Area Manager
GENE INGRAM (25, 2 1/2)
[Everyone below this line is a District Manager]
WILSON PARDUE (30, 3)
BOB GRANT (24, 1)
9 26 3 4
BEN POWER (36, 1)
BOB SUTTON (43, 1)
28 31 55
STEVE CLARK (34, 1 1/2)
7 14 23
RICHARD SCHWARTZ (29, 3)
20 49 66
MICKEY WILLIAMS (27, 2 1/2)
22 32 41 100
56 108
ANDY HARRELL (27, 1 1/2)
10 74
LARRY MARTINDALE (25, 1 1/2)
1 6 12 51
FRANK JAMES (29, 3)
57 63 79
LEE DeFORE (28, 1)
38 40 103
DICK STROUPE (30, 1/2)
11 19
*
5 13 86
(Age, length of service)
* Opening
Numbers underneath names indicate unit number.

there were five district managers and one opening in Bill Ingram's area; and at present there were no district managers in the Florida area. Exhibit 2 notes the ages and length of service with Waffle House of each manager. The average age was 30 years and length of service averaged 2½ years.

Davis and Bill Ingram received a base salary of $20,000 plus 5% of their units' profits. With 20 units, each man's salary was close to $40,000. Salaries for all personnel from unit managers to area managers can be determined from Exhibit 3. Because their bonuses were determined by a percentage of net profits, the area managers competed for new units as they were opened. Davis thought that he could handle 50 units without any trouble. He believed that the secret of his success had been his ability to create a good organization. As he said, "My real strength lies in my ability to handle people, not just district managers but unit managers, grill operators, and even waitresses."

In answer to a question about the adequacy of his salary, Davis responded:

> Certainly in terms of current income I am underpaid, especially if you compare my salary with those in comparable positions in Quick Foods (Waffle House's major franchise operation). However, with the stock that I inherited from Dad and the stock options that I have exercised since 1965, I am willing

Exhibit 3

WAFFLE HOUSE, INC.
Salary/Bonus Schedule—Company Units

Position	*# Units*	*Monthly Salary*	*% Bonus*	*Monthly Bonus*	*Total per Month*	*Total per Year*
Unit Manager	1	$ 550	10	$ 220	$ 770	$ 9,240
	2	650	10	440	1,090	13,080
District Managers	3	650	10	660	1,310	15,720
	4	650	10	880	1,530	18,360
	5	800	7½	825	1,625	19,500
	6	800	7½	990	1,790	21,480
	7	800	7½	1,155	1,955	23,960
	8	1,000	6	1,056	2,056	24,672
	9	1,000	6	1,188	2,188	26,256
	10	1,000	6	1,320	2,320	27,840
	11	1,150	5	1,210	2,360	28,320
Area Managers	12	1,150	5	1,320	2,470	29,640
	13	1,150	5	1,430	2,580	30,960
	14	1,450	4	1,232	2,682	32,184
	15	1,450	4	1,320	2,770	33,240
	16	1,450	4	1,408	2,858	34,296
	17	1,450	4	1,496	2,946	35,352
	18	1,450	4	1,584	3,034	36,408
	19	1,450	4	1,672	3,122	37,464
	20	1,450	4	1,760	3,210	38,520

An officer of the company would command a slight premium plus fringe benefits.

to forego short-run income to help establish my long-run financial security. If we went public today, I estimate my holdings would be worth in excess of $500,000.

District Manager

The district managers supervised two, three, or four individual units. In accordance with Wafflle House operating procedures, each new manager went through a "hands on" training program that began on the grill learning to cook waffles and other items on the menu. At the conclusion of such a training effort, the trainee had, hopefully, acquired the common sense approach to customer service and would assume the position of a unit manager. After 6 to 8 months of successful performance at this post, the unit manager was ready to move into the supervisory role of district manager.

Among the district manager's duties were:

1. Maintaining good operating equipment;
2. Checking weekly staffing schedule to make sure that the units would be properly manned;
3. Aiding unit managers in hiring, training, and firing personnel;
4. Ensuring that proper supplies were used (*The Waffle House Food Quality and Preparation Manual* had been developed for this purpose).
5. Accounting for all money. (Cash audits were made on an unscheduled basis. The bookkeeping of the unit manager was doublechecked daily.);
6. Maintaining the cleanliness of the restaurant;
7. Providing, when needed, transportation for unit employees.

Over the sun visor of each district manager's car was found the daily check list shown in Exhibit 4.

Richard Schwartz was a district manager who had been with the firm for three years. Schwartz, a friend of Ronnie Davis at the University of Alabama, hoped that in the immediate future a new area manager position would open up for him with some six or seven units to manage with the help of a couple of district managers. Schwartz had three units and earned over $17,000 in salary and bonuses. According to Schwartz, his main job was handling people. He worked seven days a week and always was available between 9 P.M. and 7 A.M. (third shift) because he felt that this was the unit manager's time off and the unit manager should not be directly responsible for this shift. Schwartz anticipated that he would be making over $30,000 in two years. "I still must be prepared to step behind the counter and handle the shifts on the grill. I haven't had to handle a shift for three months, but it looks as if I will get another opportunity next Friday night."

Unit Manager

The unit manager's daily schedule was outlined in Exhibit 5. The schedule of his daily and weekly cleaning duties is outlined in Exhibit 6. The unit manager was

Exhibit 4

WAFFLE HOUSE, INC.
Daily Check List for District Managers

1. Must be in uniform before entering unit—white pants or dark pants; white shirt and bow tie.
2. Always use front entrance in order to check parking lot and front door.
3. Blinds and awning—cleanliness and repairs.
4. Employees—proper uniform.
5. Restrooms—cleanliness, toilet tissue, soap, towels, deodorizers, and damaged equipment.
6. Build-up sheet and rotation of food.
7. A. Black book—posting. B. Payroll—correct hours.
8. Equipment—condition and cleanliness.
9. Fire extinguisher—three in unit–dry behind the counter, CO_2 in back room; water in the commissary.
10. Before leaving, check sales envelope with the manager to be sure it balances with last register reading. The register tape must be in envelope each day.

REMEMBER—EMPLOYEES ARE ONLY GOING TO DO WHAT THEY HAVE BEEN INSTRUCTED TO DO!

directly responsible for the operations of his individual unit. As indicated by his duties in Exhibit 5, the manager was responsible for the appearance and profitability of the individual unit. He must have certain skills in motivating and managing people, handling money, working with the public, and controlling costs. His main function was selling food and further efforts were being made to relieve the unit manager of some of the administrative tasks which occupied about two hours of his time each day.

Unit managers fell into two categories, according to Rogers, Jr. "One type is moving up the company ladder towards district manager, the other does not have the administrative talent to advance further. The former presents few problems; the latter does require us to deal with a person who is very competent at his job but who cannot advance."

Unit Personnel

Each unit was open 24 hours a day. There were three shifts. The first shift from 7 in the morning to 5 in the evening normally had one grill operator and two waitresses. The second shift from 5 in the evening until 9 at night normally had the same staff as the first shift. The late shift from 9 at night until 7 in the morning was usually staffed by one waitress and a grill operator. As shown in Exhibit 5, the unit manager helped during the busy periods from 7–2 and 5–9. Company policy required that at least one waitress and a grill operator be on duty each shift. On the weekends and during busy shifts a dishwasher was added. A waitress earned

Exhibit 5

WAFFLE HOUSE, INC.
Manager Schedule

6:30 A.M.	Arrive at unit. Check around building, for paper, trash, beer cans, before entering.
6:35 A.M.	Use front entrance. Check front door glass for cleanliness. Check floor, sweep if necessary. Check booths and stools for dirt, crumbs, etc. Check restrooms for cleanliness, towels and soap. Clean and service if needed. Check floor behind counter. See if breakfast menus are out.
6:45 A.M.	Make out commissary order. See that 1st shift employees are in proper uniform before going on duty.
6:50 A.M.	Check cash register; take out night sales. Put in change as needed.
7:00 A.M.	Lower venetian blinds if needed. Take over grill or station to be worked.
10:30 A.M.	Have floor swept.
11:00 A.M.	Take cash register reading. Raise blinds if no longer needed. See that menus are changed. See that unit is set up for lunch; charbroiler, sandwich board, pies cut and displayed.
2:00 P.M.	Take cash register reading, replenish change in register; remove 1st shift sales from register; see that 2nd shift employees are in correct uniform. Raise or lower venetian blinds as needed. Sweep and mop floors, check restrooms. Leave instructions with employees for cleaning stainless steel, formica, booths, stools, etc. Take afternoon break, if possible.
4:50 P.M.	Check unit for cleanliness, floor, restrooms, grill area, etc.
5:00 P.M.	Take cash register reading. Take over grill or station to be worked.
8:30 P.M.	See that grill and waitresses stations are clean and set up for 3rd shift.
8:50 P.M.	See if 3rd shift is available for duty and in correct uniform.
9:00 P.M.	Check cash register, remove sales; replenish change. Check unit food and supplies. If short on food or supplies, restock if a commissary unit. If not a commissary unit, call your supervisor. Leave instructions with 3rd shift for cleaning.

Exhibit 6

WAFFLE HOUSE, INC.
Schedule of Manager's Cleaning Duties

Daily Requirements:
1. Sweep—11:00 A.M.—2:00 P.M.—9:00 P.M.—2:00 A.M. or as needed.
2. Mop—2:00 A.M.—2:00 P.M. or as needed.
3. Clean front door at least 4 times daily.
   Pick up debris on parking lot.
4. Clean cash register twice daily.
   Clean booths, chairs, and stools—frequently.
5. Clean bathrooms—6:30—11:00—3:00—1:00.
6. Sweep off outside walk.
7. Clean pie display case.

Sunday—Additional cleaning items:
1. Clean back-bar.
2. Sweep off front walk.
3. Clean office window.
4. Pick up parking lot.

Monday—Additional cleaning items:
1. Clean return grills.
2. Clean and mop (*good*) under back-bar.
3. Clean around dumpster pad.
4. Wash light globes.

Tuesday—Additional cleaning items:
1. Hose down front and back walkways.
2. Clean blinds.
3. Clean front of counter and stools.
4. Clean waiting chairs.

Wednesday—Additional cleaning items:
1. Have windows washed and clean store front.
2. Wash booths and legs with Lux Liquid.
3. Clean grills and burners.

Thursday—Additional cleaning items:
1. Clean back-bar and shelves and drawers.
2. Clean refrigerators and drawers.
3. Clean ceiling.
4. Clean under dishwashing machine.

Friday—Additional cleaning items:
1. Clean return grills.
2. Pick up parking lot.
3. Clean pie display case good.
4. Clean cigarette and music machines.

Saturday—Additional cleaning items:
1. Parking lot.
2. Clean blinds.
3. Clean office window.
4. Check menus for cleanliness and condition.

$1.00 to $1.25 an hour plus tips; the grill operator earned $1.50 to $2.50 an hour depending upon experience; and a dishwasher was paid $1.25 an hour. Although no formal training program existed for waitresses and grill operators, Waffle House had prepared an employee service manual for these employees. Sections of this manual have been reproduced as Appendix A.

Management Information System

Until January 1972, Hugh Fly, a retired Air Force colonel and boyhood friend of Joe Rogers, Sr., was directly in charge of the operations of the company units. One of his major tasks since joining the company in August 1968 was to administer the management information system that had evolved over time. The system was designed "to compensate for the often limited management ability and educational level of the people on the firing line." The system is described below in detail.

At the end of each operating day the unit manager filled out a daily report which was mailed to the home office. (Prior day sales figures for the metro-Atlanta units were also telephoned to the home office.) The daily report reached the home office the next day and its information was entered in the unit's "black book." The figures so entered corresponded to the unit manager's entries in the "black book" kept in the unit office.

When these reports were received at the home office, they were checked for alterations, duplications, or old dates. All invoices were paid in cash when goods were accepted; the original was retained by the unit manager and enclosed in the

Exhibit 7

WAFFLE HOUSE, INC.
Thirty Day Franchise Shift Sales Report
November 30, 1971

Unit	*First shift*	*Second shift*	*Third shift*	*D/A*	*F/C*	*OPE*	*Sales per man hour*
16 SMYRNA	260	74	188	506	33.7	3.9	7.17
LAST MO	237	71	192	500	33.0	2.6	6.40
LAST YR	234	81	172	471	33.4	4.8	7.39
24 MARIETTA	240	56	141	427	33.3	3.4	6.96
LAST MO	247	55	146	421	33.1	3.2	7.86
LAST YR	230	52	122	391	34.8	3.9	6.39
37 SANDTOWN ROAD	206	56	107	357	33.8	4.1	6.00
LAST MO	199	62	118	367	33.6	3.3	5.91
LAST YR	213	50	110	361	34.3	5.8	5.91
18 MABLETON	268	73	189	481	32.3	3.7	7.41
LAST MO	262	72	162	479	33.8	2.4	7.40
LAST YR	220	68	143	417	32.4	1.7	6.32
39 FULTON IND. BLVD.	329	97	221	627	30.4	2.7	7.97
LAST MO	341	95	237	652	29.8	2.2	8.11
LAST YR	292	93	194	545	32.1	2.4	7.71
21 HAPEVILLE	182	54	147	375	32.4	5.5	7.36
LAST MO	178	45	158	372	32.0	5.6	4.18
LAST YR	208	54	140	395	34.7	3.2	5.79
25 COLLEGE PARK	194	46	154	377	31.5	3.4	6.36
LAST MO	187	49	161	384	32.7	5.5	6.25
LAST YR	202	43	137	364	34.8	3.5	6.01

D/A = Daily Average Sales
F/C = Food Costs
OPE = Operating Cost (%)

daily report. Bank deposits were also monitored; daily deposits were encouraged and note was taken of exceptions. Because Waffle Houses were open 365 days a year, there were 365 daily reports each year from each unit. The "black book" information combined with the weekly compensation information formed the basic inputs to the management information system. One of the outputs from the system was an efficiency report which monitored both food and labor costs by comparing actual costs for a specific sales volume with a standard developed from past experience. Waffle House had discovered that a stable relationship existed between costs and sales if more than one or two days' figures were used to average out extraordinary purchases or sales. For example, food costs averaged 31% of sales revenue. The information from the "black books" was used to compile a 7-day, 14-day, 21-day, and end-of-month report for the company-operated units. Franchise units, which were not required to report daily sales to the home office, were required to submit weekly reports. A sample page from an end-of-month report is included as Exhibit 7. For the company-operated units the information was also arranged by sales areas and districts to form a comparison report.

At the end of each month, all previous end-of-month reports were cumulated and combined with an allocation of overhead costs to provide a year-to-date report for each company unit. Exhibit 8 is such a report for Unit No. 17, the company's training unit. All the company unit reports were combined to yield the year-to-date Waffle House company report (Exhibit 9). The results from the franchise units and subsidiary operations were added to the company figures to yield the Waffle House, Inc. report (Exhibit 10).

Waffle House management believed that this series of reports served not only as good accounting statements, but also as good control statements. All bonuses were calculated from the profits shown on the reports and the bonus amounts were included on the reports. Certain conventions were adopted to enhance the bonus scheme. For example, rent for each unit was calculated as 15% of sales because there was a wide variation in actual rents paid for each location. Waffle House management believed that the unit manager, who was being rewarded on an incentive compensation system, should not be penalized for such inconsistencies in rent. Another such convention was used for maintenance expenses. The manager had, in effect, a $100 deductible insurance policy on each piece of his equipment. That is, if the maintenance charge for a certain project was greater than $100, the manager's charge for that expenditure was only $100. Rogers, Jr. explained the rationale for this convention.

> We feel that the unit manager's timely attention paid to the restaurant will prevent a lot of the maintenance problems. But we try not to penalize a manager for a major expenditure such as an air conditioner compressor, because this expense will wipe out his bonus for the month. We believe that, if the manager is not going to make money during a month, he's not going to be able to give his best effort in Waffle House's behalf.

Several other summary reports were compiled. Exhibit 11 analyzes the profitability by unit for the six-months ending November 30, 1971. Another report, shown in Exhibit 12, is the comparative man hour production figures for both company and franchise units.

After describing the system, Hugh Fly reiterated the motivation for the system:

> Sales first; control second. To accomplish this the system had been designed to assist the district manager in removing some of the administrative responsibility from the unit manager's job, freeing up more time for the unit manager to sell.

Food Control

Obviously, food comprised the bulk of Waffle House's inventory. Several different food distribution systems were in use. One model was that of a central commissary. In the northern sales area, a central commissary served 13 of the 19 units. Ten of these units were served on a daily basis. Experiments were being conducted with the other three units by varying the delivery cycle from 2 to 10 days. Three employees handled the work at this commissary.

Every morning each of the 10 unit managers on the daily delivery schedule called in their commissary order between 6:45 and 7:30. The trucks were loaded according to these orders and deliveries were made from 9 until 2 each day. The commissary operated 7 days a week. The buyer selected only items approved in the *Food Quality and Preparation Manual.* In the southern area a central commissary serviced six units. All other company units operated their own commissaries. Each individual unit maintained its own supplier relationships and was responsible for controlling the unit's inventory. As food moved from the commissaries into the units it was marked up by a certain percentage (usually 10%) to reflect anticipated shortages.

Twice a month, on the 15th and 28th, a physical inventory of the commissary was taken. The actual inventory level was compared to the book inventory and overages and shortages were recorded. If the shortage was less than the mark-up percentage, the unit received credit for the difference in its commissary fund. If it was greater than the anticipated shortage, the commissary fund was reduced.

If shortages were suspected, close monitoring of shift operations was accomplished using the "shift inventory of food" report. A record was made of the opening and ending inventory of the shift. From this report the physical amount used of each item on the menu was determined and multiplied by its unit price. The food costs for the individual items were totaled and compared with the cash register reading for that shift.

Preliminary plans were being drafted to establish a central commissary for the metro-Atlanta area. In addition, some consideration was being given to backward integration into the food wholesaling business. A possible venture would be the purchase of Eastern Foods, the present supplier of waffle batter.

Exhibit 8

WAFFLE HOUSE, INC.
Operating Statement (Year to Date)

Unit # 17 Columbia Drive—Ga.	*November 30, 1971*				*Last Year*			
Account Name	*Curr. Mo.*	%	*Year to Date*	%	*Month*	%	*Year to Date*	%
Food Sales	19093.57	100.00	115245.88	100.00	11858.97	100.00	117339.88	100.00
Less Food Cost	6072.57	31.80	36287.97	31.48	5733.16	30.40	35824.85	30.53
Gross Profits	13021.00	68.19	78967.91	68.51	13125.81	69.59	81515.03	69.46
Controllable Expenses:								
Payroll—Unit	2971.71	15.56	21977.83	19.07	3937.80	20.88	24935.75	21.25
Payroll—Commissary	325.00	1.70	1892.00	0.94	0.00	0.00	0.00	0.00
Payroll—Taxes	282.04	1.47	1932.58	1.67	260.11	1.37	1780.97	1.51
Utilities	526.97	2.75	3092.69	2.68	459.98	2.43	2802.09	2.33
Telephone	21.66	0.11	195.49	0.16	14.19	0.07	142.59	0.12
Maintenance Support	0.00	0.00	0.00	0.00	0.00	0.00	0.00	0.00
Maintenance & Repairs	420.68	2.20	1360.14	1.18	441.13	2.33	2240.75	1.90
Support Services	26.60	0.13	480.55	0.41	0.00	0.00	0.00	0.00
Dishes	43.86	0.22	451.31	0.39	146.52	0.77	424.07	0.36
Laundry	104.18	0.54	680.03	0.59	0.00	0.00	0.00	0.00
Miscellaneous Supplies	387.79	2.03	2495.01	2.16	364.90	1.93	2788.91	2.37
Commissary Expenses	0.00	0.00	0.00	0.00	0.00	0.00	0.00	0.00
Auto, Truck Expense	17.40	0.09	105.67	0.09	0.00	0.00	110.42	0.09
Advertising	16.37	0.08	100.13	0.08	0.00	0.00	76.76	0.06
Total—Controllable Expenses	5144.28	26.94	33964.43	29.47	5624.63	29.82	35302.31	30.08
Indirect Expenses:								
Depreciation	171.84	0.89	817.56	0.70	166.89	0.88	1012.70	0.86
Rent	2889.03	15.13	17530.87	15.21	2705.21	14.34	17714.55	15.09
Taxes and License	165.26	0.86	678.61	0.58	111.67	0.59	535.26	0.45
Insurance	109-62	0.57	572.56	0.49	150.78	0.79	693.50	0.89
Area Manager Expenses	0.00	0.00	0.00	0.00	0.00	0.00	0.00	0.00
General Manager Expenses	10.34	0.05	110.11	0.09	163.68	0.86	1043.99	0.88
Bookkeeping	49.56	0.25	351.40	0.30	78.31	0.41	480.35	0.40

Exhibit 8 (continued)

Unit # 17 Columbia Drive—Ga.	November 30, 1971				Last Year			
Indirect Expenses:	Curr. Mo.	%	Year to Date	%	Month	%	Year to Date	%
Opening Expenses	0.00	0.00	0.00	0.00	0.00	0.00	0.00	0.00
Contest Awards	26.71	0.13	132.65	0.11	0.00	0.00	0.00	0.00
Miscellaneous Expenses	79.17	0.41	510.12	0.44	119.78	0.63	386.83	0.32
Total—Indirect Expenses	3501.53	18.33	20783.88	17.96	3496.12	18.53	21867.18	18.63
Combined Total	8645.81	45.28	54668.31	47.43	9120.75	48.36	57169.49	48.72
Profits before Management	4375.19	22.91	24289.60	21.07	4005.06	21.23	24345.54	20.74
Management Expenses:								
Salary, Unit Manager	575.00	3.01	3450.00	2.99	550.00	2.91	2238.87	1.90
Salary, Asst. Unit Manager	0.00	0.00	0.00	0.00	0.00	0.00	0.00	0.00
Salary, District Manager	0.00	0.00	0.00	0.00	0.00	0.00	0.00	0.00
Salary, Area/Division Mgr.	325.00	1.70	1625.00	1.41	325.00	1.72	1250.00	1.06
Salary, General Manager	56.83	0.29	374.16	0.32	49.02	0.25	318.16	0.27
Salary, Other	0.00	0.00	0.00	0.00	0.00	0.00	0.00	0.00
Salary, Manager Trainee	0.00	0.00	0.00	0.00	0.00	0.00	0.00	0.00
Total—Management Expenses	956.83	5.01	5449.16	4.72	924.02	4.89	3807.03	3.24
Profits After Management	3418.36	17.90	18840.44	16.34	3081.04	16.33	20538.51	17.50
Bonus:								
Bonus, Unit Manager	369.03	1.93	1928.66	1.67	250.00	1.32	902.85	0.76
Bonus, Asst. Unit Manager	0.00	0.00	0.00	0.00	0.00	0.00	0.00	0.00
Bonus, District Manager	0.00	0.00	0.00	0.00	0.00	0.00	0.00	0.00
Bonus, Area/Division Mgr.	553.53	2.89	3076.38	2.66	484.10	2.56	3309.31	2.82
Bonus, General Manager	92.25	0.48	512.71	0.44	81.52	0.43	542.38	0.46
Bonus, Asst. General Mgr.	36.90	0.19	205.07	0.17	32.61	0.17	215.95	0.18
Bonus, Commissary Manager	0.00	0.00	0.00	0.00	0.00	0.00	0.00	0.00
Bonus, Other	0.00	0.00	0.00	0.00	0.00	0.00	0.00	0.00
Total—Bonus Expenses	1051.70	5.50	5722.83	4.96	848.23	4.49	4970.49	4.23
Operating Profit	2366.66	12.39	13117.62	11.38	2232.81	11.83	15568.02	13.26
Casualty Loss	0.00	0.00	0.00	0.00	0.00	0.00	0.00	0.00
Net Profit	2366.66	12.39	13117.62	11.38	15568.02	11.83	15568.02	13.26

Exhibit 9

WAFFLE HOUSE, INC.
Operating Statement (Year to Date)

Unit # Company	November 30, 1971				Last Year			
Account Name	*Curr. Mo.*	%	*Year to Date*	%	*Month*	%	*Year to Date*	%
Food Sales	530647.66	100.00	3124218.05	100.00	410047.68	100.00	2441135.99	100.00
Less Food Cost	158718.15	29.91	955435.30	30.58	131087.17	31.96	778962.83	31.90
Gross Profits	371929.51	70.08	2168782.75	69.41	278960.51	68.03	1662173.16	68.09
Controllable Expenses:								
Payroll—Unit	88730.72	16.72	528224.90	16.90	70448.38	17.18	423146.85	17.33
Payroll—Commissary	4293.89	0.80	22243.14	0.71	4329.68	1.05	32677.58	1.34
Payroll—Taxes	8271.01	1.55	51750.70	1.65	5813.64	1.41	37138.75	1.52
Utilities	15126.54	2.85	94024.38	3.00	9439.73	2.30	66315.05	2.71
Telephone	1529.98	0.28	8836.93	0.28	606.90	0.14	4182.74	0.17
Maintenance Support	2169.21	0.40	14602.25	0.46	0.00	0.00	0.00	0.00
Maintenance & Repairs	10756.38	2.02	51609.47	1.65	7767.76	1.89	42874.65	1.75
Support Services	1708.84	0.32	12149.34	0.38	0.00	0.00	0.00	0.00
Dishes	2157.36	0.40	11204.34	0.35	1709.16	0.41	8721.56	0.35
Laundry	2920.95	0.55	17787.14	0.56	2156.47	0.52	13015.33	0.53
Miscellaneous Supplies	11114.66	2.09	63577.10	2.03	9296.23	2.26	62213.22	2.54
Commissary Expenses	673.63	0.12	3963.55	0.12	671.66	0.16	4809.84	0.19
Auto, Truck Expense	5391.11	1.01	30307.82	0.97	8.70	0.00	1946.06	0.07
Advertising	1274.00	0.24	4627.35	0.14	0.00	0.00	1508.88	0.06
Total—Controllable Expenses	156118.28	29.42	914908.41	29.28	112248.31	27.37	698750.51	28.62
Indirect Expenses:								
Depreciation	4775.71	0.89	21661.19	0.09	3503.21	0.87	20760.66	0.85
Rent	80021.98	15.08	464698.70	14.87	59265.36	14.45	368925.14	15.11
Taxes and License	4846.25	0.91	18567.21	0.50	2628.27	0.64	11728.46	0.48
Insurance	3304.75	0.62	15670.44	0.50	3336.47	0.81	14291.73	0.58
Area Manager Expenses	1713.72	0.32	9085.08	0.29	2984.83	0.72	15846.53	0.64
General Manager Expenses	303.18	0.05	2892.03	0.09	3267.76	0.79	19844.97	0.81
Bookkeeping	1453.28	0.27	9341.07	0.29	1565.86	0.38	9568.45	0.39

Exhibit 9 (continued)

Unit # Company	November 30, 1971				Last Year			
	Curr. Mo.	%	Year to Date	%	Month	%	Year to Date	%
Indirect Expenses:								
Opening Expenses	70.04	0.01	5874.86	0.18	1005.07	0.24	2706.34	0.11
Contest Awards	325.45	0.06	2449.50	0.07	0.00	0.00	0.00	0.00
Miscellaneous Expenses	3141.44	0.59	13857.33	0.44	2516.22	0.61	16127.03	0.66
Total—Indirect Expenses	99955.80	18.83	564089.41	18.05	80153.05	19.54	479799.31	19.65
Combined Total	256074.08	48.25	1478997.82	47.33	192401.36	46.92	1178549.82	48.27
Profits before Management	115855.43	21.83	689784.93	22.07	86559.15	21.10	483623.34	19.81
Management Expenses:								
Salary, Unit Manager	20332.14	3.83	115280.29	3.68	16684.62	4.06	93784.72	3.84
Salary, Asst. Unit Manager	0.00	0.00	250.00	0.00	0.00	0.00	752.90	0.03
Salary, District Manager	8325.00	1.56	46045.20	1.47	5650.06	1.37	34345.32	1.40
Salary, Area/Division Mgr.	3658.36	0.68	21625.14	0.69	4508.33	1.09	26350.07	1.07
Salary, General Manager	1666.68	0.31	10000.08	0.32	1666.66	0.40	10000.04	0.40
Salary, Other	1475.00	0.27	5646.27	0.18	0.00	0.00	0.00	0.00
Salary, Manager Trainee	1202.89	0.22	11297.21	0.36	1114.00	0.27	9073.66	0.37
Total—Management Expenses	36660.07	6.90	210144.25	6.72	29623.67	7.22	174306.71	7.14
Profits After Management	79195.36	14.92	479640.68	15.35	56935.48	13.88	309316.63	12.67
Bonus:								
Bonus, Unit Manager	8593.72	1.61	50486.99	1.61	5635.50	1.37	29292.55	1.19
Bonus, Asst. Unit Manager	0.00	0.00	1262.50	0.04	70.37	0.01	2184.65	0.08
Bonus, District Manager	7082.85	1.33	46910.24	1.50	4565.08	1.11	25628.43	1.04
Bonus, Area/Division Mgr.	4575.91	0.86	27578.08	0.88	3611.94	0.88	20306.82	0.83
Bonus, General Manager	2103.34	0.39	12763.06	0.40	1550.33	0.37	8382.63	0.34
Bonus, Asst. General Mgr.	841.20	0.15	5104.62	0.16	620.05	0.15	3351.84	0.13
Bonus, Commissary Manager	1942.41	0.36	6403.27	0.20	101.12	0.02	1620.34	0.06
Bonus, Other	450.00	0.08	3448.80	0.11	1040.00	0.25	1258.21	0.05
Total—Bonus Expenses	25589.43	4.82	153877.56	4.92	17051.65	4.15	92025.47	3.76
Operating Profit	53605.93	10.10	325763.12	10.42	39883.83	9.72	217291.16	8.90
Casualty Loss	39.63	0.00	602.54	0.01	0.00	0.00	2640.87	0.10
Net Profit	53566.30	10.09	325160.58	10.40	39883.83	9.72	214650.29	8.79

Exhibit 10

WAFFLE HOUSE, INC.
Operating Statement (Year to Date)

Unit # Waffle House, Inc.	November 30, 1971				November 30, 1970			
	Curr. Mo.	%	*Year to Date*	%	*Month*	%	*Year to Date*	%
Income:								
Rent Income	80021.98	41.32	464013.38	40.38	78103.62	54.29	494352.01	60.10
Lessee Income	21944.03	11.33	138421.97	12.04	5000.00	3.47	15000.00	1.82
Commission Income	6904.70	3.56	31320.45	2.72	9382.42	6.52	28231.88	3.43
Interest and Misc. Income	1860.08	0.96	13387.34	1.15	20.02	0.01	3513.79	0.42
Income from Operations	82911.65	42.81	502053.61	43.69	51336.10	35.68	281381.22	34.21
Total Income	193642.44	100.00	1149116.75	100.00	143842.16	100.00	322478.90	100.00
Expenses:								
Payroll Taxes	584.73	0.30	4222.20	0.36	502.00	0.34	3247.40	0.39
Utilities	0.00	0.00	0.00	0.00	0.00	0.00	0.00	0.00
Telephone	379.17	0.19	3070.34	0.26	0.00	0.00	1396.51	0.16
Maintenance & Repairs	221.71	0.11	3386.93	0.28	1134.13	0.78	4911.31	0.59
Support Services	468.83	0.24	1720.29	0.14	0.00	0.00	0.00	0.00
Auto and Truck Expense	1664.89	0.85	9466.85	0.82	731.04	0.50	6540.36	0.79
Advertising	187.85	0.09	1930.26	0.16	500.00	0.34	3103.28	0.37
Depreciation	3538.15	9.57	76904.92	6.69	15309.37	10.64	86760.83	10.54
Rent	22286.93	11.50	132927.66	11.56	18856.93	13.10	102357.68	12.44
Interest	2539.58	1.31	14742.61	1.28	1991.34	1.38	15128.76	1.83
Equipment Rental	1941.91	1.00	10273.67	0.89	0.00	0.00	0.00	0.00
Taxes and License	10.00	0.00	310.97	0.02	512.90	0.35	3198.17	0.38
Insurance	3269.60	1.68	9081.35	0.79	0.00	0.00	2767.31	0.33
Legal and Audit	1000.00	0.51	7050.00	0.61	3875.07	2.69	26250.84	3.19
Research and Development	1296.31	0.66	4433.52	0.38	430.08	0.29	943.69	0.11
Travel and Entertainment	1248.72	0.64	3767.76	0.32	379.88	0.26	3179.93	0.37
Dues and Subscriptions	13.23	0.00	1669.29	0.14	0.00	0.00	0.00	0.00
Postage	479.43	0.24	2214.11	0.19	0.00	0.00	0.00	0.00
Office Supplies	1189.42	0.61	4832.98	0.42	2698.22	1.87	11456.26	1.39

Exhibit 10 (continued)

Unit # Waffle House, Inc.	November 30, 1971				November 30, 1970			
	Curr. Mo.	*%*	*Year to Date*	*%*	*Month*	*%*	*Year to Date*	*%*
Expenses:								
EDP Supplies	139.21	0.07	642.46	0.05	0.00	0.00	0.00	0.00
Freight	372.30	0.19	1776.84	0.15	0.00	0.00	707.59	0.00
Donations	62.50	0.03	112.50	0.00	45.00	0.03	63.35	0.00
Misc. Expenses	1584.97	0.81	9524.50	0.82	0.00	0.00	0.00	0.00
Total—Expenses	59479.44	30.71	303982.01	26.45	46965.96	32.65	272013.27	33.07
Profits before Management	134163.00	69.28	845134.74	73.54	96876.20	67.34	550465.63	66.92
Management Expense:								
Salary, Officers	14110.00	7.28	80910.00	7.04	11800.00	8.20	66000.00	8.02
Salary, Office	9781.20	5.00	54052.72	4.70	6091.55	4.23	44607.12	5.42
Salary, Construction	2640.00	1.36	16313.48	1.41	2288.20	1.59	11102.73	1.34
Salary, Real Estate	1191.67	0.61	5908.33	0.51	0.00	0.00	0.00	0.00
Salary, Training	0.00	0.00	2228.89	0.19	0.00	0.00	0.00	0.00
Salary, Mgr., Trainee	1358.00	0.69	4225.03	0.36	0.00	0.00	0.00	0.00
Salary, Other	0.00	0.00	2742.50	0.23	825.00	0.57	3609.00	0.43
Bonuses	0.00	0.00	566.00	0.04	1366.40	0.94	6235.73	0.75
Total—Management Expense	28992.87	14.97	166946.95	14.52	22371.15	15.55	131554.58	15.99
Net Profit	105170.13	54.31	678187.79	59.01	74505.05	51.79	418911.05	50.93

Exhibit 11

WAFFLE HOUSE, INC.

Dollar Cost Per Unit Per Day—6 Months Ending November 30, 1971 (Company Units)

Unit	Daily Average	Payroll	Utilities	Telephone	Maintenance Support & Repairs	Support Services	Dishes	Laundry	Misc.	Net Profit
1	271.51	57.57	11.60	.19	9.38	3.32	.84	2.40	8.63	(1.34)
3	484.90	89.96	20.21	3.05	5.61	.01	2.24	1.87	9.95	33.25
4	433.20	81.10	17.38	3.10	6.83	.01	1.67	1.72	11.09	32.19
5	381.63	54.51	14.36	.49	7.58	.36	1.45	1.89	7.44	43.77
6	420.60	73.28	11.91	.31	16.13	2.50	1.91	2.91	10.53	33.22
7	366.91	64.74	15.67	1.25	11.63	2.68	.87	2.18	7.73	26.10
9	371.34	74.04	14.12	2.81	4.16	.00	1.16	2.23	7.68	16.58
10	424.10	79.86	10.75	.31	12.50	2.55	1.19	2.23	9.29	41.71
11	343.92	62.10	12.89	.42	11.78	1.95	1.24	2.07	7.78	18.78
12	410.32	66.49	9.56	.28	7.67	2.65	1.91	2.08	9.32	51.30
13	441.84	65.14	16.27	1.62	6.37	.28	.86	1.88	11.05	56.64
14	436.00	68.90	11.37	.21	12.59	2.36	.98	2.01	8.85	52.18
17	629.75	120.09	16.89	1.06	7.43	2.62	2.46	3.71	13.63	71.57
19	337.58	62.70	10.13	.28	11.67	1.99	1.80	2.80	8.37	14.99
20	391.75	68.20	11.80	1.16	11.38	1.02	1.06	2.34	7.32	37.60
22	469.30	80.84	11.74	.25	11.38	2.56	1.68	2.47	9.62	54.63
23	433.03	72.17	12.36	.18	13.77	2.60	1.02	2.01	9.08	41.87
26	395.68	77.18	12.08	3.37	6.61	.41	.44	2.78	11.50	29.67
28	623.31	94.54	15.45	1.34	17.52	2.54	2.92	3.23	10.73	83.57
31	365.64	67.76	14.40	1.68	14.32	2.08	.88	2.00	6.15	29.70
32	697.69	105.87	14.84	1.33	16.33	1.02	3.28	3.92	13.11	101.38
38	270.86	52.02	11.58	2.10	7.21	4.64	2.16	1.89	5.24	8.01
40	421.41	69.73	15.89	1.55	8.80	3.98	3.05	2.85	8.34	24.36
41	495.75	78.02	13.54	1.14	12.65	1.83	2.90	3.30	9.79	63.34
49	638.15	101.65	13.25	1.18	14.23	2.65	2.27	2.79	9.98	95.88
51	578.98	98.66	20.21	1.18	17.23	1.23	1.66	2.89	10.73	65.37

Exhibit 11 (continued)

Unit	*Daily Average*	*Payroll*	*Utilities*	*Telephone*	*Maintenance Support & Repairs*	*Support Services*	*Dishes*	*Laundry*	*Misc.*	*Net Profit*
55	649.68	100.33	13.59	1.44	17.99	4.09	3.45	3.38	9.16	77.96
56	534.87	85.07	6.98	.81	18.18	1.89	.56	3.47	16.40	48.09
57	263.86	50.65	11.65	.86	5.00	.00	.44	1.61	6.20	6.53
63	498.92	78.27	13.79	1.76	6.59	.00	1.62	1.93	8.56	68.34
66	704.91	112.84	15.19	1.03	15.82	2.77	1.14	4.72	4.89	92.07
68	541.92	85.63	20.46	1.84	3.56	.00	1.26	2.83	9.02	73.21
74	481.91	86.57	17.46	1.42	8.33	2.56	2.01	3.38	9.65	44.90
79	322.99	56.40	16.57	.95	2.72	.38	1.04	1.95	6.62	18.89
86	584.64	84.73	16.01	1.98	1.55	.00	.94	3.11	10.61	82.78
91	657.62	89.54	15.78	2.42	3.47	.05	.82	3.94	11.49	108.98
100	571.46	107.21	11.94	1.21	8.34	2.78	1.69	4.12	14.77	55.95
103	491.76	90.39	10.01	2.49	2.86	5.10	2.01	3.10	7.78	80.51
108	576.20	90.42	.15	1.40	9.50	2.30	.00	3.90	15.25	89.65
Average	466.30	78.83	14.03	1.31	9.87	1.81	1.67	2.65	9.45	48.53

Exhibit 12

WAFFLE HOUSE, INC.
Comparative Man Hour Production Figures (Sales Per Unit/Man Hours Per Unit)
Fiscal 71 and 72

	NORTH		SOUTH		SOUTH CAROLINA		COMPANY		FRANCHISE	
	F.Y. 71	F.Y. 72	F.Y. 71	F.Y. 72	F.Y. 71	F.Y. 72	F.Y. 71	F.Y. 72	F.Y. 71	F.Y. 72
June	8.16	8.34	6.89	7.40	7.20	6.43	7.57	7.68	7.03	7.07
July	7.66	8.29	7.04	8.46	6.63	7.04	7.31	8.17	6.84	7.51
August	8.27	8.41	7.80	7.74	6.90	7.07	7.66	7.94	7.16	8.00
September	7.86	8.39	6.97	7.07	6.65	5.16	7.24	7.57	7.46	7.08
October	7.90	8.67	7.48	8.23	7.03	7.23	7.59	8.28	6.49	7.44
November	7.78	8.90	8.27	7.37	7.36	7.40	7.84	7.97	6.69	7.34
December	7.89		7.59		7.85		7.77		6.78	
January	7.77		7.20		6.92		7.43		6.75	
February	7.66		7.35		7.14		7.44		6.83	
March	8.48		7.45		6.90		7.82		6.94	
April	7.90		7.25		7.29		7.60		6.84	
May	8.20		7.43		6.90		7.73		6.95	

Auxiliary Services

Real Estate

The real estate group, which had evolved under the direction of Tom Forkner, had four men including Forkner. Charles Preston, working directly beneath Forkner, was responsible for the real estate operations. Two men, both with experience in real estate departments of oil companies, had been hired in the last six months. Both men earned \$10,000 a year and were given a car and an expense account. Preston, who earned \$20,000 a year including bonuses felt that his work in site selection deserved a higher compensation. His bonus was equal to the daily sales average after two months of operation by a new company unit on a site selected by him.

Waffle House concentrated on interstate highway sites. Sixty sites were under observation by the real estate department. All sites, both company and franchise, had to be approved by the real estate department. In the next year there were plans for 18 new company units and 49 new franchise units. According to Preston, "one real estate man can acquire 8 to 12 sites a year." Preston had some worries about the real estate operation: "In the past, our operation was handled quite informally. Now the operation is growing and a control system must be instituted."

In assessing Waffle House's success to date, Charles Preston enumerated four significant factors:

1. Joe Rogers, Sr., knows the operations of the restaurant business better than any other person alive.
2. Tom Forkner can make the right site location decisions.

3. The organization that has been created to run the firm is outstanding.
4. The menu offered by Waffle House has created a unique market that others have failed to emulate.

The Hickman Company

In its early operations, Waffle House bought substantial amounts of equipment and fixtures and repair and maintenance services from an Atlanta restaurant equipment supplier. The supplier at that time formulated a new business plan to concentrate its efforts on the large single unit restaurants. This plan was unsuccessfully opposed by Robert Hickman who handled the Waffle House account for this firm. Discussions with Hickman and officers of Waffle House led to the organization of an auxiliary business, the Hickman Co. The Hickman Company, wholly owned by Waffle House, was an equipment wholesaler and warehouser which also provided maintenance services to Waffle House units. Hickman charged the various Waffle House divisions (including franchise units) for repair and maintenance through a service contract. In addition to designing, ordering, and maintaining equipment for new Waffle House units, the Hickman Company assisted Waffle House management in creating and implementing new ideas and innovations with food preparation equipment.

The Hickman Company generated sales of $700,000 a year with eight employees besides Robert Hickman. The eight employees included two installers, two maintenance men, one engineer, one secretary, one painter, and one helper. Sales of Hickman and Co. were distributed among three groups. First, Waffle House company units accounted for 40% of sales; franchise units accounted for 40%; and outside restaurant chains accounted for the last 20%. Hickman projected sales revenue of over $5 million and expected to have twice as many employees on the payroll by 1977.

One of Hickman's major goals was to design equipment that minimized the movements of the grill operators and sales girls. He gained ideas for new equipment by observing these personnel at work and by watching equipment developments of competing restaurant chains. The standard unit had 9 stools and 6 booths for a total of 33 seats. Most changes were in the placement of equipment in the unit, rather than in installing new technologies. However, Hickman realized that the company must not be complacent about its past successes. "We must always be looking for new designs and avoid staying in the same old rut."

Installing equipment in a new restaurant took four days. Eighty per cent of the items were drop-shipped from the equipment manufacturers. The other 20% of the items were brought to the site by the installation crew. The scheduling of work during these four days was fairly routine since this equipment with minor modifications had been installed in more than 100 units. Two types of delays were common. First, the building was not completed on schedule; second, the equipment was not promptly delivered. Additional effort was being expended to coordinate this effort. Hickman had felt some additional organizational pressure as a result of Waffle House's recent expansion into new geographical territories. Coordinating the installation of equipment and units in the metro-Atlanta area caused very little difficulty;

coordinating the installation of equipment and units in Florida, Virginia, and Texas introduced complex scheduling, logistics, and control problems.

Other Services

The actual construction of the units was exclusively subcontracted until 1967. At that time Waffle House created its own in-house construction crews. The company had three construction crews, each of which could construct a unit in 90 days for a cost of $42,000. Outside contractors were still used to supplement the construction crews. The average cost of a unit constructed by an outside contractor was $49,000. The typical unit is illustrated in Exhibit 13.

The increased number of units also provided the opportunity for several Waffle House executives to form the Metro-Vending Company. Metro-Vending owned, stocked, and maintained the cigarette machines and music machines in Waffle Houses and other service establishments in the metro-Atlanta area.

Just recently Waffle House had created a pest control division by hiring one man and outfitting him with equipment and a truck. The number of Waffle Houses in the metro-Atlanta area immediately provided some business for the new venture. As contracts with new clients grew, the division planned to expand its operations.

Other services which were being considered for internal operations included janitorial services and air conditioning and heating repair. As with their other new ventures, the buying power of the Waffle House chain was expected to provide a breakeven volume for these services in a short time.

Exhibit 13

Pricing Auxiliary Services

Services rendered to Waffle House by the construction division and Hickman Co. were priced to the company units at cost. For franchise units the charges included a normal profit. These services were formerly priced at a profit to the company units, but an accounting problem arose because plant and equipment was a capitalized asset. Waffle House was prevented from capitalizing intercompany profits. All other services were treated as current expenses and current profits with no accounting repercussions. Joe Rogers, Jr., noted that the company had problems adjusting to the principles of consolidation. "At first it represented some headaches for both our accountant and our management."

Marketing

Waffle House spent very little money on advertising and promotion. The majority of this amount was spent on quasi-charitable items such as programs for high school football games. Media campaigns had not proven successful. Rogers, Jr. described a radio advertising campaign that was run one summer in the northern area.

> Ronnie Davis wanted to test a radio advertising campaign and pay for it out of his area funds. The sales manager from the radio station assured me that the campaign would be an investment for establishing a Waffle House image. The radio ads were placed during the late night hours to attract people driving around into the units. The statistics from the campaign were not conclusive. People are not going to drive out of their way to go to a Waffle House. Our policy in the past has been to invest our money in people and not in ad campaigns. It is not very likely that we shall discontinue such a policy in the future.

An example of Waffle House's investment in their people was the monthly promotional contest.

> We do run monthly promotional contests in each area; $200 in prizes or cash are up for grabs each contest. Although such contests were effective in the beginning, they have now lost some of their impact. We have also observed some "contest behavior" occurring.

Waffle House management believed that they were providing impulse and convenience items.

> Our customers are somewhat price conscious. Compare our 1961 menu with that of 1971 (Exhibit 14). Our food prices have risen very little in the last 10 years, although food costs have skyrocketed during that period. We cannot raise our prices much higher because the customer who pays more for his meal wants a more luxurious setting and a more relaxed atmosphere. We offer a quick, cooked-to-order meal of high quality but with no fancy stuff. If we carpet our floor or use linen napkins, the customer is going to pay for it. However, we attract a broad spectrum of the population. It is not uncommon to have a banker sitting next to someone coming off a three-day drunk.

Exhibit 14

WAFFLE HOUSE, INC.
1961 Menu

GOOD FOOD FAST

WAFFLES

Served with special "WAFFLE HOUSE" Syrup

- Waffle, Cream .45
- Waffle, Pecan .55
- Waffle with Bacon .80
- Waffle with Sausage .80
- Waffle with Ham .80
- Waffle with Two Eggs .80

AROUND THE CLOCK SUGGESTIONS

- Char-Burger .50
- Hamburger .35
- Cheeseburger .40
  Lettuce & Tomato 5¢ extra
- Potatoes .25
  Waffle House style
- Double Cheeseburger .60
- Cereal, Dry-with milk .35
- Ham-Tenderized .35
  Portion
- Sausage (2 patties) .35
- Bacon (3 strips) .35

FARM FRESH EGGS

- Raisin Toast—Jelly .20
- Toast—Jelly .15
- Two Eggs .50
  Toast and Jelly
- Waffle House Eggs .55
  Two Eggs Omelet style, Toast and Jelly
- Omelet, Cheese .75
  Toast and Jelly
- Omelet, Ham .85
  Toast and Jelly
- One Egg .35
  Toast and Jelly

DESSERTS

- Fruit Pie .30
- Ice Box Pie .30

CHAR-BROILED STEAKS

- Filet Mignon 1.50
- Sirloin Chopped 1.25
- T-Bone 1.50

Served with Salad, Waffle House Potatoes and Toasted Bun

SOUPS

- Cream of Tomato .30
- Vegetable .30
- Chicken Noodle .30
- Chili .45

SALADS

- Pineapple—with cheese .35
- Tossed Green .30
- Lettuce & Tomato .30
- Sliced Tomatoes .30

Served with Crisp Saltines

SANDWICHES

- Waffle .55
  Baked Ham, Cheese, Wheat Bread
- Combination — Ham-Cheese .60
- Ham & Egg .65
- Bacon & Egg .65
- Bacon, Lettuce, Tomato .60
- Ham, Baked or Fried .55
- Cheese, American .30
  Grilled or Toasted
- Fried Egg .30

BEVERAGES

- Coffee .10
- Decaffeinated Coffee .15
- Tea, Hot or Iced .10
- Hot Chocolate .15
- Buttermilk .15
- Chocolate Milk .15
- Orange Juice .15-.25
- Tomato Juice .15-.25
- Milk .15-.25

Complete the Treat — Carry an Order Home

GOOD FOOD FAST

WAFFLES

Served with special "WAFFLE HOUSE" Syrup

- Waffle, Cream .60
- Waffle, Pecan .80
- Waffle with Bacon 1.05
- Waffle with Sausage 1.10
- Waffle with Ham 1.10
- Waffle with Two Eggs 1.05

AROUND THE CLOCK SUGGESTIONS

- Char-Burger .50
- Hamburger .40
- Cheeseburger .45
- Double Burger .60
- Double Cheeseburber .65
  Lettuce & Tomato 5¢ extra
- Potatoes .30
  Waffle House style
- Cereal, Dry-with milk .35
- Ham-Tenderized .50
  Portion
- Sausage (2 patties) .50
- Bacon (3 strips) .45

FARM FRESH EGGS

- Raisin Toast—Jelly .25
- Toast—Jelly .20
- Two Eggs .60
  Toast and Jelly
- Waffle House Eggs .75
  Two Eggs Omelet style Toast and Jelly
- Omelet, Cheese .95
  Toast and Jelly
- Omelet, Ham 1.15
  Toast and Jelly
- One Egg .40
  Toast and Jelly

DESSERTS

- Fruit Pie .35
- Ice Box Pie .35

Complete the Treat — Carry an Order Home

CHAR-BROILED STEAKS

- Filet Mignon 2.25
- T-Bone 2.25
- Sirloin Chopped 1.10
- Ribeye .185

Served with Salad, Waffle House Potatoes and Toasted Bun

SOUPS

- Cream of Tomato .35
- Vegetable .35
- Chicken Noodle .35
- Chili .45

SALADS

- Pineapple—with cheese .35
- Tossed Green .35
- Lettuce / Tomato .35
- Sliced Tomatoes .35

Served with Crisp Saltines

SANDWICHES

- The Waffle .75
- Combination — Ham-Cheese .75
- Ham & Egg .85
- Bacon & Egg .80
- Bacon, Lettuce, Tomato .65
- Ham, Baked or Fried .65
- Cheese, American .35
  Grilled or Toasted
- Fried Egg .40

BEVERAGES

- Coffee .10
- Decaffeinated Coffee .15
- Tea, Hot or Iced .10
- Hot Chocolate .15
- Milk .20-.30
- Buttermilk .20
- Chocolate Milk .20
- Orange Juice .20-.30
- Tomato Juice .20-.30
- Cola Drinks .15

Exhibit 15

WAFFLE HOUSE, INC.
Summary of Consolidated Earnings of Waffle House and Subsidiaries
Ten Years Ending May 31st

	1972	*1971*	*1970*	*1969*	*1968*	*1967*	*1966*	*1965*	*1964*	*1963*
Sales Exclusive of Franchise Units	$7,106,042	$5,376,224	$4,699,048	$3,916,065	$2,787,365	$2,009,975	$1,627,200	$1,242,630	$926,375	$647,557
Cost of Sales	2,482,030	1,927,461	1,753,573	1,584,657	1,110,707	712,249	572,002	432,820	329,314	231,597
Gross Profit	$4,624,012	$3,448,763	$2,945,475	$2,331,408	$1,676,658	$1,297,725	$1,055,198	$ 809,810	$597,061	$415,960
Variable Expense	2,920,031	2,241,374	1,662,469	1,346,111	947,752	728,960	623,721	477,900	346,171	252,343
Operating Profit	$1,703,981	$1,207,389	$1,283,006	$ 985,297	$ 728,906	$ 568,766	$ 431,477	$ 331,910	$250,890	$163,617
Other Income (Franchise)	918,063	607,632	491,278	271,806	249,051	137,989	21,662	3,298	4,630	4,513
Earnings Before Overhead	$2,622,044	$1,815,021	$1,774,284	$1,257,103	$ 977,957	$ 705,755	$ 453,139	$ 335,208	$255,520	$168,130
Overhead	1,224,245	1,022,921	1,057,268	838,439	737,831	531,057	340,130	273,003	182,862	118,213
Income Before Income Taxes	$1,397,799	$ 792,100	$ 717,016	$ 418,664	$ 240,126	$ 175,698	$ 113,009	$ 62,205	$ 72,658	$ 49,917
Income Taxes	718,250	406,913	382,907	186,980	78,290	59,239	28,822	12,526	20,390	17,550
NET EARNINGS	$ 679,549	$ 385,187	$ 334,109	$ 231,684	$ 161,836	$ 116,459	$ 84,187	$ 49,679	$ 52,268	$ 32,767

Growth Objectives

Waffle House was expanding on two major fronts, company-operated units and franchised units. Historically, successful growth had been limited by the development of capable, well-trained management personnel. However, the Rogers, both Jr. and Sr., felt that Waffle House was ready to expand. A financial history of Waffle House is contained in Exhibits 15 and 16.

Growth plans of adding 20, 25, and 30 units over the next three years were initially developed by stimulating the growth and development of the operational

Exhibit 16

WAFFLE HOUSE, INC., Ratios from Waffle House Audited Statements

	Year Ending 5-31-72	*Year Ending 5-31-71*	*Year Ending 5-31-70*	*Year Ending 5-31-69*	*Year Ending 5-31-68*
(1) Current Assets	1,452,376	779,691	994,944	608,735	519,809
Current Liabitities	391,392	155,517	489,597	288,078	511,909
Working Capital	1,060,984	624,174	505,347	320,657	7,900
Current Ratio	3.71/1	5.01/1	2.03/1	2.11/1	1.0/1
(2) Total Capital	2,254,728	1,552,451	1,147,880	827,046	588,689
Total Liabilities	854,589	568,054	827,891	585,898	815,085
Capital to Liabilities	2.64/1	2.73/1	1.39/1	1.41/1	.72/1
(3) Total Capital	2,254,728	1,552,451	1,147,880	827,046	588,689
Long Term Debt	400,518	362,037	327,695	297,820	299,390
Capital to Long Term Debt	5.63/1	4.29/1	3.50/1	2.78/1	1.97/1
(4) Net Income After Taxes	679,549	385,187	334,109	231,684	161,836
Total Assets:					
Beginning of Year	2,049,657	1,975,771	1,412,944	1,403,774	811,578
End of Year	3,109,317	2,049,657	1,975,771	1,412,944	1,403,774
Average Assets	2,579,487	2,012,714	1,694,358	1,408,359	1,107,676
Rate Earned on Average Assets	26.3%	19.1%	19.7%	16.4%	14.6%
(5) Net Income After Taxes	679,549	385,187	334,109	231,684	161,836
Capital:					
Beginning of Year	1,552,451	1,147,880	827,046	588,689	440,850
End of Year	2,254,728	1,552,451	1,147,880	827,046	588,689
Average Capital	1,903,590	1,350,166	987,463	707,868	514,770
Rate Earned on Average Capital	35.7%	28.5%	33.9%	32.7%	31.4%
(6) Net Income Before Taxes	1,397,799	792,100	717,016	418,664	240,126
Add Rent	315,413	228,830	182,358	155,911	122,657
Interest	32,249	42,016	35,001	38,632	40,765
	347,662	270,846	217,359	194,543	163,422
Income Before Fixed Charges	1,745,461	1,062,946	934,375	613,207	403,548
Coverages of Fixed Charges	5.02/1	3.92/1	4.30/1	3.15/1	2.47/1

management team along with the growth and development in the staffs of the support functions and then discounting this by a certain factor for the sake of conservatism (see Exhibit 17 for company and franchise unit projections).

Waffle House had franchised to parties with the capacity for a multiunit operation similar to its own and had found these franchisees very willing to emulate the Waffle House philosophy of management and growth. For this reason the number of new franchise units were forecasted to exceed the number of new company stores. It was expected that an eventual balance in the system would be reached at 30% company stores and 70% franchise stores.

Although Waffle House had limited its development to the Southeast, the short order restaurant concept had been used nationally and Waffle House management felt quite confident of continued success as it slowly extended its geographical coverage. The company had set aside the Greater Southwest along with its present territory in the Southeast for the expansion of its own operations (shaded area in Exhibit 17). Company units were under development in South Carolina, Metropolitan Atlanta, Georgia, Eastern Alabama, Northwest Florida, and Metropolitan Dallas, Texas.

Exhibit 17

WAFFLE HOUSE, INC., Projected Unit Openings

FISCAL YEAR	*1973*	*1974*	*1975*	*1976*
Company Units				
Begin	44	64	89	119
Add	20	25	30	40
End	64	89	119	159
Franchise and Leased Units				
Begin	72	116	176	256
Add	44	60	80	100
End	116	176	256	356
Total Units				
Begin	116	180	265	375
Add	64	85	100	140
End	180	265	365	515

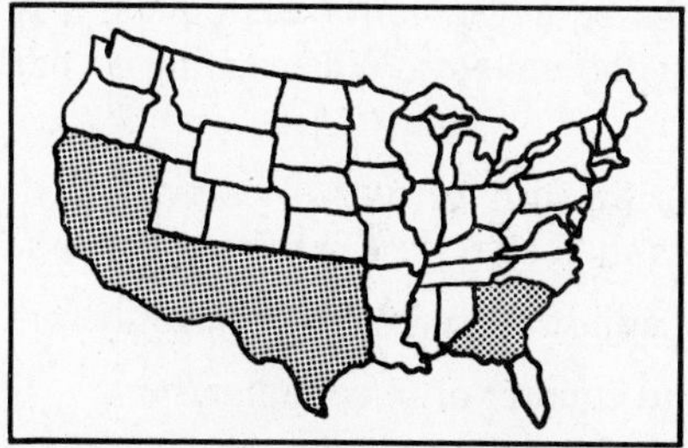

SHADED AREA—RESERVED FOR COMPANY STORES.
UNSHADED AREA—FRANCHISED OR AVAILABLE FOR FRANCHISING.

Appendix A
Waffle House, Inc.

Welcome to Waffle House

We have a dedicated group of employees that are striving for the highest degree of efficiency ever obtained in the fast food field.

Our goal is to bring the utmost in food enjoyment to every potential customer in the areas served by a Waffle House. This can only be accomplished through the coooperation of all personnel.

This manual will serve as a guide or "Blue Print" of our overall operation. Use it consistently—commit as much to memory as possible, and make "Waffle House Way" a by-word in your vocabulary.

Let's everyone strive to reach our goal at an early date and create an image of service and friendliness that the public cannot resist.

Stand erect, dress neatly, smile, be courteous, be proud of your company.

"THE WAFFLE HOUSE"

Personal Appearance, Conduct and Customer Relations

Employees Shall:

1. Report early enough to eat and check register before going on duty.
2. Eat three meals per day, when working. The first before going on duty. The second while on duty, but not during a rush period. The third immediately after checking off.
3. Sign a Meal Check and deposit it in cash register.
4. Never sign a Meal Check during off hours or off days. All meals to be paid for in cash, except when working.
5. In order that booths be available for customers, it is required that employees take their meals at the counter. When eating at the counter, do not sit in a haphazard manner.
6. Always, except during rush periods, be served at the counter by fellow employees. Employees shall be served in the same manner as a guest.
7. Check register and adjust overages or shortages before going on duty.
8. Never smoke behind counter or in commissary.
9. Never carry on conversation with guest. Excuse yourself and find something to do—never be discourteous in doing so.

Customer Is Always Right:

10. Remember the guest is always right. Should any misunderstanding arise, it MUST BE ADJUSTED TO THE ENTIRE SATISFACTION OF THE GUEST.

Never Argue with a Customer:

11. The Waffle House employees never argue among themselves while on duty. In case a misunderstanding arises between employees, it must be corrected by employees in charge and then dropped immediately. Never discuss anything of this nature in front of guests or draw attention to the fact that you are undecided about the price.
12. Never carry on unnecessary conversation while behind the counter. This is strictly prohibited.
13. Greet guest as he enters and give him a glass of water and menu as soon as he is seated.

Personal Conduct Toward Guests:

14. On taking an order, stand erect with arms at side.
15. Never fold your arms in front of yourself and stare at guest.
16. During breakfast hour, always suggest fruit juices and side orders of sausage, ham, or bacon. At dinner suggest various items listed on menu, with emphasis on the steaks.
17. Never take a menu from a guest until he or she has finished with it.
18. Always pass menu to waiting guest and on taking a standing guest's order, be accurate in timing so as to have his food ready when he is seated. Do not bring food out before he is seated and allow it to get cold.
19. Always place set up in easy reach of guest. Place silverware on napkin.
20. In serving coffee see that handle is in correct position to the guest—exactly at 3 o'clock. In case coffee is spilled in saucer, replace with a clean one. REMOVE COFFEE CUP FROM SHELF WITH HANDLE.
21. Keep dirty dishes removed from counter. See that counter is free from dishes and wiped clean before guest is seated.
22. Write out each individual item and price at the *time order is taken before calling it in to grill.* It takes far less time to write the order than it does to hold a conversation with the guest to find out what the correct charge should be.
23. Remember no guest has been properly served until he or she has been issued a correct check. Only the man who serves them should say "Thank you, call again, please."
24. In case a check is to be voided, do so at once and place in cash register immediately. Never leave checks lying around.

25. In case of a guest over paying his check and a refund is necessary, be sure to make a note of all details, such as time, amount of check, etc.
26. Employees must be prompt in collecting for checks. Do not keep the guest waiting. Ring up each individual sale. Do not add several checks and ring them up on the cash register as one sale.
27. Checks should not be removed from the pad until such time as the guest is ready to pay the check (except in booths where no check pads are attached).
28. COURTESY COSTS YOU NOTHING, BUT PAYS BIG DIVIDENDS AND MAKES THE OUTLOOK ON LIFE BRIGHTER. PRACTICE IT WITH A SMILE—MORNING, NOON AND NIGHT.
29. Never whistle or sing either in shop or service room.
30. Never congregate in service room or carry on unnecessary conversation when you must go into service room.
31. Never carry a towel in belt or on shoulder.
32. Never wipe sandwich board with hands or wipe crumbs off onto floor.
33. See that delivery men, who come behind counter or in service room remove their hats and be sure all deliveries are made at the side door.
34. At least one person must always remain behind counter. Never leave the shop unattended.
35. Never go into commissary unless so instructed.
36. Never loaf in shop either during working or off hours.

2. Personal Appearance:

The prescribed uniform must be worn by both male and female employees—and must be spotless at all times.

Male:

1. All employees must wear a clean white dress shirt, broadcloth or other close-woven material—sport shirts or sheer nylon not permissible. Also wear black cloth bow tie, clean white pants, clean cap and apron. Shirt sleeves should be rolled to just above elbow. Change as often as necessary to be presentable.
2. Wear cap with a slight tilt to the right. Cap should never be removed while on duty.
3. Employees shall at all times be properly groomed—hair trimmed and combed, clean shaven, hands and finger nails immaculate, and uniform spotless.

Female:

1. All female employees must wear white uniforms spotlessly clean, without rips or holes, with tea apron and head band.
2. Hair must be pinned up off neck and covered with hair net.

3. Excessive jewelry is not to be worn.
4. Apron bands must be tied properly.
5. Shoes must be shined and heels kept in repair.
6. Hands and nails must always be clean. The use of highly-colored nail polish must be avoided.
7. Pencil must not be put in hair or behind ear or in emblem on apron.

All employees must not eat, drink, or chew anything behind the counter.

Leave excess wearing apparel or street clothes in the dressing room.

Always remove cap, head band, and apron before going out in the street.

A CLEAN OPERATION REQUIRES CLEAN EMPLOYEES FIRST. SEE UNIT EMPLOYEES SERVICE MANUAL FOR OTHER DETAILED INSTRUCTIONS.

Triangle Maintenance Corporation

In June 1971, Mr. Ralph Fine, president of Triangle Maintenance Corporation, was considering how to expand operations beyond the New York City area. Mr. Fine had just returned from a safari in Africa and was attempting to take a fresh look at the situation. During his vacation the company had run smoothly and he was now concentrating on the long-term growth of the firm.

Company Background

Mr. Fine had founded Triangle in November 1960 as a spin-off of a company owned by members of his family. As part of the arrangement, Mr. Fine took a $250,000-per-year customer of the predecessor firm as his first customer. He had originally gained the customer for the predecessor firm and had continued to have a close relationship with the management of the customer. The contract with the customer called for the daily interior cleaning of a building and included services such as emptying ash trays and waste baskets, dusting furniture, cleaning hallways, etc. The work was performed during the night when the occupants of the building were not present.

The company grew through the hard work of Mr. Fine and a small devoted organization. As the number of customers increased and opportunities for providing related services appeared, Triangle began to offer a full line of building services including interior and exterior window cleaning, snow removal, painting, elevator operation, gardening, and security. Triangle also began, with time, to offer specialized mechanical maintenance services including maintenance of heating and air conditioning systems and elevators.

In 1965 the firm substantially broadened its service offering. At the time, Triangle was providing passenger terminal cleaning and terminal building maintenance service to an airline which asked it to bid on a contract for "ramp" services. Aircraft ramp services included the interior cleaning of aircraft, handling of baggage, and the provision of other labor intensive nonmechanical services. The proposed contract

---

This case was prepared by Assistant Professor Benson P. Shapiro, with the assistance of Robert L. McDowell, Research Assistant, as a basis for class discussion rather than to illustrate either effective or ineffective handling of an administrative situation.

also called for the winning bidder to lease equipment to the airline, including motorized passenger loading ramps and baggage handling equipment. Triangle won the contract.

In 1971 the aircraft ramp business (which did *not* include terminal cleaning) accounted for approximately half of Triangle's sales and for about 60% of its profits (see Exhibit 1). The higher margins on the ramp business were due, according to Mr. Fine, to the fact that there were fewer competitors, a higher capital investment, and greater risk. In particular, there were no small independent operators with little capitalization such as characterized the building cleaning industry.

Although the Triangle aircraft ramp business had grown rapidly and shown exceptional profitability, Mr. Fine suspected that the true long-term growth potential of the firm lay in the building cleaning and maintenance field. He was concerned that top management's attention to the aircraft ramp business had led to the company's decline in building cleaning sales in 1969 and 1970. "We have got to learn how to increase sales in the building cleaning business while maintaining growth and profitability in the ramp business," he stated.

The Building Cleaning Business

The competitors in the building cleaning and maintenance business in New York City could be divided into three groups. First, there were many small, independent "mom and pop" type operations. Mr. Jerry Gilbert, a Triangle vice president and manager of the Building Cleaning and Maintenance Division, stated that "Any off duty fireman or moonlighting machine operator can get into the business with

Exhibit 1

TRIANGLE MAINTENANCE CORPORATION
Consolidated Sales

Year	*Aircraft Ramp Services*	*Building Maintenance*	*Total*
1962		$ 856,000	$ 856,000
1963		1,604,000	1,604,000
1964		1,954,000	1,954,000
1965	$ 553,000	2,596,000	3,149,000
1966	1,057,000	2,679,000	3,736,000
1967	1,183,000	2,780,000	3,963,000
1968	1,763,000	3,596,000	5,359,000
1969	1,779,000	3,052,000	4,831,000
1970	3,248,000	3,166,000	6,414,000
1971 (Estimated)	4,500,000	4,100,000	8,600,000

a broom and a bucket." These small operations were typically family concerns and operated with almost no overhead. Their quality, according to Mr. Fine, was inconsistent but usually low. They tended to sell their services on the basis of price. Since they competed almost solely for the small jobs, that segment of the business was highly price competitive.

At the other competitive extreme were the "big four." Mr. Fine believed that the largest building maintenance company in the New York metropolitan area was Kinney National Service, Inc., part of the Kinney conglomerate. It did not engage in the aircraft ramp business but supplied a wide range of other services including pest control and industrial cleaning and maintenance. According to a *Business Week* article, Kinney employed 15,000 persons in its building cleaning and maintenance operation and had offices in 15 cities.

Mr. Fine suspected that Allied Maintenance Corporation, the largest building maintenance company in the United States, was the second largest operator in the New York metropolitan area. In addition, Allied was certainly the most important competitor in the aviation ramp services business. That firm also offered refueling services to the commercial airlines and had the total fuel handling contract for the John F. Kennedy International Airport.

Triangle management thought that Prudential Building Maintenance Corporation had a slightly smaller share of the New York market than Allied. Prudential was not in the aviation ramp service business. It operated branches coast to coast, including Los Angeles, Miami, Atlanta, Chicago, Detroit, Jersey City, and Allentown and Jenkintown, Pennsylvania.

The smallest of the "big four" was Temco Service Industries, Inc., which had recently been awarded a $6.1 million per year contract to clean the new World Trade Center in New York City. This was expected to be a $10 million per year cleaning and maintenance job by the time the various buildings in the Center were completed. Only companies with established competence in skyscraper cleaning and maintenance had been allowed to bid for that contract. According to industry gossip some competitors believed that Temco could make little or no profit on the job because of the lowness of its bid price.

There were a variety of firms between the "big four" and the "mom and pop" operations in size. Mr. Fine estimated that Triangle was one of the ten largest building maintenance and cleaning firms operating in the New York City area. It employed over 800 people, and Triangle management believed it had somewhat less than 3% of the New York metropolitan area building cleaning and maintenance business.

Customers could also be segmented by size. The largest segment of the business consisted of huge skyscrapers. The annual cleaning and maintenance bill for such a building could range from about a half million dollars to several million. Contracts for such buildings were usually granted through bids and typically ran for two years. The owner or manager of the building allowed only "qualified" firms to bid on the work. According to Messrs. Fine and Gilbert, in the New York City area this meant that a firm had to be experienced in cleaning and maintaining skyscrapers before it would be invited to bid on other skyscrapers. Triangle had found it impossible to break into this market in the New York area. Company management believed that its experience was typical of that of other medium sized firms. "We've cut the price to the break-even point and sold as hard as we could, but all to no avail. The big firms have that market tied up."

The skyscraper business usually came in two parts. First, the cleaning firm obtained a contract from the owner or manager of the building to provide routine basic cleaning and maintenance for both the building and its tenants. These services typically included sweeping, dusting, vacuuming, and other cleaning functions as well as window washing, security, and elevator maintenance and operation. This was, according to Mr. Fine, typically a very low profit part of the business because competition for such large contracts was intense.

Once the basic contract was obtained by a cleaning operator, he attempted to sell additional maintenance services to individual tenants under separate contracts. Exhibit 2 provides a list of "extras" offered to the tenants. Almost all skyscraper tenants desired and purchased these services, especially in the newer buildings. It was very unusual for one firm to provide the basic services in a building and a competitor to provide "extras." Both tenant and building manager wanted to minimize the number of people moving through the building at night and desired to have a single organization responsible for all cleaning and maintenance. In addition, because the firm with the basic contract controlled the security function and elevator operation, it could make it most difficult for a competitor to provide "extras" efficiently. Most operators also shied away from attempting to obtain a few contracts for extras in a variety of buildings because the expense and difficulty of moving people and machinery usually made it unprofitable. To the operator with the basic

Exhibit 2

TRIANGLE MAINTENANCE CORPORATION
Extra Services Offered Skyscraper Tenants

Rug shampoo
Private lavatory cleaning
Supplying of hand towels and hand soap
Furniture polishing
Special porter and/or maid service
Furniture cleaning
Floor waxing
Exterminating service
Spray buffing
Carpet care—spot monthly, shampoo yearly
Desk washing and polishing
Chair washing and polishing
Table washing and polishing
Light bulb replacement
Fluorescent fixture washing and bulb maintenance

contract, however, the provision of "extras" to all tenants was an efficient operation. Often more than 40% of the revenue and more than 80% of the profits of skyscraper cleaning and maintenance came from "extras."

Other segments of the market consisted of medium-sized and small buildings which often housed only one tenant. Triangle had been successful in this part of the business and had a variety of contracts for a minimum of $15,000 per year. Mr. Fine felt that contracts below that size were not profitable because the "mom and pop" operations could more efficiently and cheaply service them, and because selling and administrative costs on such jobs were disproportionately high. Although Triangle had many small accounts, most of its sales volume was accounted for by contracts in the $50,000 per year and up range, and included a prestigious museum and several prestigious nonprofit organizations. Mr. Fine believed that the smaller building owners were more price conscious than the larger ones.

Government facilities represented another market segment. Some government agencies were more quality conscious than others, but all tended to stress price. Mr. Fine stated that "Government operations don't care about quality. That's strictly a price business." Government contracts tended to be large and to be awarded by bid. Typically about six cleaning and maintenance firms would bid on a contract with little restriction to so-called qualified bidders.

Some government agencies were quite quality conscious and required bid specifications which were long and detailed. Mr. Fine considered the Port of New York Authority to be an agency which was meticulous. One Port of New York Authority contract, for example, contained 4,000 pages of bid specifications. That was a million-dollar-per-year, two-year contract which Triangle had won for cleaning and maintaining terminal facilities at John F. Kennedy International Airport in New York.

The matter of quality in the cleaning and maintenance business was elusive, according to Triangle management. "Different people mean different things by 'clean'," stated Mr. Gilbert. "It is economically impossible to clean an office perfectly. If I want to demonstrate to a prospective client that his office is not now being cleaned adequately, I merely have to run my finger over the top of picture frames or the inside of lamp shades. Cleanliness is to a great extent in the eyes of the beholder, in spite of all the specifications which might be written. To us, it is the eyes of our customers who are important." Mr. Gilbert believed that an important part of quality was effective response to complaints. "When an executive finds his favorite pen missing or the wastebaskets in the board room weren't emptied, it's awfully important for the client to get an immediate personal response. I often deal with such complaints myself, and when I don't they're handled personally, swiftly, and graciously by a competent Triangle executive. We believe that we compete with larger operators by providing a more personalized service. Some of our larger competitors answer complaints over the telephone. We don't. This is a psychological business where the client wants to see you!"

During its early years, Triangle had attempted to gain both quality and price sensitive business. Over the years, however, Mr. Fine found that Triangle could not "run in two directions at once." He thought it was impossible for one cleaning firm to provide quality on some jobs while cutting corners on others. "It became impossible for first line management to know what to do when." Several years earlier, therefore, Mr. Fine said he had instituted a policy of concentrating on quality-conscious customers.

Selling the Services

The selling process was a rather complex one, according to Mr. Gilbert and a newly hired salesman, Mr. Forrestal. Sales were of three categories: new buildings, existing buildings in which a competitor held the cleaning and maintenance contract, and existing buildings in which the prospect's own personnel did the cleaning and maintenance. Triangle management believed that it was important to begin to sell the owner or manager of a large new building before the building construction had progressed very far. Mr. Forrestal spent a good deal of time attempting to learn of new buildings to be built. Once that information was available the salesman had to find out who in the prospective client firm decided on the cleaning and maintenance services. This was felt to be a difficult task. Because the contracts were large and tenant relations important, the decision was often made at the vice presidential level of the prospective client. Once the appropriate contact was found, the salesman concentrated on selling Triangle's capabilities. Mr. Forrestal believed that an effective brochure describing the firm was a critical part of creating the appropriate image. The salesman's objective was to be asked to bid on the job.

Mr. Gilbert did much of the bid preparation himself. Blueprints of the building were obtained, and the cleaning and maintenance job was "broken down into minute detail." Because Mr. Gilbert knew from experience how much time it took his employees to wash a floor, dust a desk, and make the rounds, he could calculate the cost of performing the desired service. Preparing the bid was a crucial function since details as minor as the nature of the flooring surfaces substantially affected costs. After the costs were determined, allowance for overhead and profit was added. This too took great judgment. Mr. Fine believed that because it often took several hundred man hours to prepare a bid, Triangle should bid only on work where it had the potential of winning the contract. Many customers, he believed, were too cavalier in their requests for bids, asking many contractors to bid and not considering the contractor's expense in bidding.

After the bid was submitted, it was up to the prospective client. Government agencies typically were required to accept the bid of the lowest qualified bidder. Private firms often weighed the expected quality of a bidder against his price. It was suspected by some trade sources that sometimes the management of a prospective customer would invite a favored bidder to resubmit a bid which seemed too high relative to the competition.

The process for obtaining the contract in an existing building was quite similar. If the contract were won, Triangle often retained the employees and direct supervisors of the competitor or the customer.

Another form of selling was the reselling of existing clients. Because the contracts typically lasted for only two years, reselling was a continuous process. Because of the elusive nature of quality in the business, it was often easy for a competitor to find fault with the existing contractor. On the other hand, in many private corporations the past experience of the firm with an operator carried great weight, so much so in fact that in some cases the existing contractor was rehired if his price was "reasonable." It did not have to be the lowest, or even low. Mr. Gilbert believed that personal relationships were especially important in the smaller buildings. Mr. Fine stated that he had a close working and personal relationship with several clients who had been with the firm since "the early days." Because the ownership and especially the management of large New York buildings was somewhat concentrated among a few firms (i.e., firms which either owned and managed large office buildings, or firms which simply managed them), this "experience" factor also became important in obtaining contracts for new buildings. If a real estate firm which managed several buildings had good experience with a particular cleaning operator, that operator was assumed to have an "inside track" to new buildings managed by that firm.

There were typically three reasons why one cleaning operator lost an account to another: quality, price, and "politics." Because the contracts typically carried a 30-day cancellation clause, the client could discontinue the use of an operator if his quality was below expectations. Quality considerations could also make an existing operator unqualified when a contract came up for regular rebidding.

If an existing contractor lost a client as the result of a higher price in the rebidding process and the new contractor proved unsatisfactory it was still almost impossible for the first firm to regain the business. The client manager who had hired the second firm would be in the unpleasant position of admitting his error if he were to rehire the first firm. Thus, according to Mr. Fine, if an operator lost a contract because of either price or quality, he was unlikely to regain it in the near future. Mr. Fine estimated that Triangle kept a customer for approximately four years. He suspected that was about average for the industry.

"Politics" was the generic term used in the industry to refer to situations where strong personal relationships overwhelmed cost and quality considerations. In such a situation, a manager who was promoted to the position of choosing the cleaning contractor might have a brother-in-law in the business. Mr. Fine conceded that in a fragmented industry there was little chance of preventing or overcoming such situations.

Costs

The costs connected with building cleaning and maintenance were largely variable and principally direct labor. Mr. Fine said he held administrative costs to a minimum since these greatly affected his ability to price his firm's services competitively. Triangle employees, like those of its larger competitors, were unionized. In fact, the firm had contracts with twelve different unions. "Moonlighters" and so-called "one-man shops" (they usually had more) had little or no overhead and no union contracts. Some capital equipment was typically needed at each location but this was limited to such machinery as powered floor cleaning machines, special ladders, and snow removal equipment which could easily be transferred between job sites.

Geographic Expansion

In 1962, Triangle undertook its first job outside of the New York City area when it successfully bid for a large building maintenance contract ($350,000 per year) for IBM in Endicott, New York, about 150 miles northwest of New York City. According to Mr. Fine, IBM had had quality problems with the previous contractor and carefully investigated Triangle's quality and capabilities (including financial stability) before allowing it to bid on the work. Although Triangle at that time had no plans for geographic expansion, management decided to bid on the IBM job because it was large, seemed relatively easily available, and offered substantial prestige. After winning the contract Triangle sent one of its experienced New York employees to manage an Endicott branch. It was hoped that the branch manager would provide continuing on-the-spot attention to the IBM contract as well as obtain other building maintenance contracts in the area. The branch manager hired an assistant who impressed Mr. Fine with his sincerity and hard work.

The branch had difficulties from the start. New business seemed hard to obtain, and local unions hard to deal with. After about four months, the labor difficulties subsided although new business was not being obtained. After six months the assistant branch manager resigned. Because Mr. Fine had been impressed with the hard work of the man, he went to Endicott to discuss his reasons for leaving. He learned that the branch manager had quietly opened his own maintenance business, charging some of the labor costs to Triangle, and pocketing the revenues. Mr. Fine dismissed the branch manager and hired the newly resigned assistant to replace him. In 1971, Triangle still retained the IBM contract and the branch was still run by the same man. He earned about $13,000 annually. While some additional business had been obtained by the branch, it was disappointing in size. Triangle was one of three sizable cleaning and maintenance contractors in the area.

The next opportunity for geographical expansion came in 1965 when Eastern Airlines asked Triangle to bid on the cleaning and maintenance of its Miami airport terminal. It had been pleased with Triangle's work at its Kennedy and Laguardia airport terminals in New York. Triangle purposefully sacrificed profits and bid low in an attempt to obtain a sizable contract which would provide a basis for a Miami operation. After winning the contract, a New York Triangle manager was sent to Miami to run the branch. As with Endicott, he was instructed to expand operations. Some additional business was obtained over the next three years, but again results were disappointing. In 1968 Eastern doubled the size of its Miami terminal and reopened the contract. A competitor bid about 1% less than Triangle and won the job. Upon receiving the news, the Miami branch manager resigned. Because the other Triangle business in the area was insufficient to support a branch office, Triangle sold the remaining Miami business and closed shop.

In 1967 American Airlines invited Triangle to bid on the cleaning and maintenance of its Dallas terminal, a contract previously held by Allied Maintenance Corporation. Triangle won the $200,000 per year contract. After looking at the difficulty Triangle had had in obtaining additional business in Endicott and Miami, management decided to hire the Dallas manager locally. "We wanted a salesman who knew his way around the city." A local manager with some cleaning experience was recruited in Dallas. But within six months Mr. Fine had fired and hired several successive branch managers. "The expense and time of traveling from New York to Dallas was becoming prohibitive. We couldn't find a guy who could both manage the existing business and obtain new business. This is a tough business to control and a tough business to sell." Mr. Fine reflected. "We tried several incentive systems and nothing seemed to work." After about a year, the airline expanded the area to be cleaned and asked for bids. Triangle was not the successful bidder and a short time later closed its Dallas office.

While the Dallas branch was still in operation, Mr. Fine was contacted by the friend of a friend of his. The man applied for a job with Triangle on the condition that he be sent to Omaha (a city with which he was familiar), and be paid a commission only on the sales he could generate and manage. Mr. Fine was somewhat impressed with the man, and could see no way that Triangle could lose much on the proposition. He accepted. The man obtained two small contracts in the first three months and within two years had built the branch to modest profitability. He was earning about 12,000 dollars in commissions per year. He then resigned to become an insurance salesman. Mr. Fine decided that it might be easier to acquire a local cleaning operation to merge with the Omaha branch than to hire a manager. But a suitable firm was not found so a local manager was hired. Two of the larger accounts were soon lost, and no substantial additional business was forthcoming. The Omaha business was finally sold in 1970.

Two other smaller abortive attempts to develop branches also occurred during the late 1960s. In 1965 Triangle obtained a contract to clean and maintain an IBM operation in Lexington, Kentucky. This proved to be a "financial fiasco" because confusion about the ambiguous specifications in the contract forced the contract to be reoffered six months after its initial offering. Triangle lost the rebid and was forced to bring several people back to New York who had been moved to Lexington from the Triangle operations in New York six months earlier. In 1967, Triangle secured the cleaning and maintenance contracts for three Indianapolis buildings owned by a real estate firm active in Dallas, where it had learned of Triangle. Although a few other small contracts were obtained, the branch proved unprofitable because of the large amount of New York executive time required, and the difficulty of obtaining a local manager.

In 1969, Triangle management reviewed its unsuccessful branch operations and decided that a major factor contributing to the failure was the long distance between the branches and New York. It was decided to restrict branch operations to within 300 miles of New York City. That area included the populous East Coast from Norfolk, Virginia, to Portland, Maine, and extended as far west as Buffalo. In October 1970, Triangle bid on a Boston airport terminal contract of the Massachusetts Port Authority. That agency had heard of Triangle from the New York Port Authority and had asked Triangle to bid. Triangle won the contract which amounted to about $250,000 per year.

In early 1971 Triangle won the cleaning and maintenance contract at a Boston skyscraper which was then under construction. The contract reward climaxed 90 days of intensive negotiation and selling conducted primarily by Mr. Gilbert. He estimated that the contract would eventually amount to $550,000 per year including "extras" sold to tenants. It had been necessary for Triangle to come in at a low price to obtain the contract, but Mr. Gilbert was sure that the firm would make money indirectly on the contract because of the "extras." He hoped that the two Boston contracts would provide a sturdy base for an expanding Boston branch.

By June 1971, however, Triangle had already hired its third successive Boston manager. One had been fired because Mr. Gilbert, after noticing that the costs for the terminal cleaning operation were above his estimates, found that the manager was "padding" the payroll with his relatives who were in fact doing no work. The other manager who had been fired had not been able to provide Mr. Gilbert with the operating reports he found necessary to control the branch's operations.

In March 1971, Triangle bid on a $750,000 per year contract with the Tampa, Florida Port Authority. Again, Triangle had been suggested by the New York Port Authority. Triangle was the third lowest bidder and did not win the contract. In May 1971, while Mr. Fine was on vacation, Triangle bid on a large contract of the Miami Port Authority who had learned of Triangle from the New York Port Authority. It was not the low bidder and did not win the contract.

The Selling Problem

Mr. Fine and Mr. Gilbert were perplexed by the problem of selling Triangle's services, especially in other geographical areas. Mr. Gilbert stated that, "It's almost impossible to find a branch manager who can (1) manage the operation, (2) provide administration reports such as budgets, and (3) obtain new business." Mr. Fine suspected that the problem lay in the salary and status of the job. "We can't get the right man for $10,000 but we can't afford to pay more. And furthermore, most people don't like the low status of our work. Who wants to be a janitor today?"

In March 1971, Triangle hired a salesman who it was hoped could provide new customers in both New York and Boston. Mr. Forrestal, the new salesman, had previously owned his own business—a franchise of Success Motivation Institute. Three years earlier, before going into business for himself, he had been a district manager with the Readers' Digest circulation sales force, and before that he had sold building materials. Triangle management felt that Mr. Forrestal's drive and youth (he was in his early 30s) would enable him to quickly learn the cleaning and maintenance business.

Mr. Gilbert believed that another solution would be the acquisition of cleaning and maintenance firms outside of New York City. In such a situation he felt that Triangle would gain both experienced and motivated management, and existing contracts. But Mr. Fine felt that such an approach was not financially feasible. "If a firm is doing $1,000,000 worth of business, they're probably making about $50,000 after taxes. They'll want a price earnings ratio of at least ten to one, which means a price of $500,000. Since we can't give stock [Mr. Fine was the sole owner of the firm], we'll probably have to give $150,000 in cash and $350,000 in notes. We can make a lot more money investing in our own business even if it takes us $40,000 to $50,000 to open a new branch."

Wendy's Old-Fashioned Hamburgers

"Why does America need another hamburger chain?" was the question being asked as R. David Thomas and his management team of franchise veterans established Wendy's Old-Fashioned Hamburgers in Columbus, Ohio. Described as "David after the hamburger Goliaths," the 43-year-old Thomas appeared to be attempting to carve out a niche in the highly competitive hamburger and fast-food "jungle" with a frontal attack on McDonald's and Burger King, the industry's highly successful giant and little giant, respectively.

Wendy's was established in 1969, when it appeared to some that America could not absorb another hamburger store, much less a chain. Some skeptical observers were saying, "The fast-food growth curve has already peaked. The rapid expansion is behind us. The chains are going to have to come up with some very innovative methods, which they don't have in their current plans." [1] Hamburger specialists like McDonald's were adding breakfast items and were experimenting with fried chicken to build volume to offset slumping unit sales growth.

Thomas, who described himself as "a person who always liked good hamburgers," believed he had found a distinctive market of people who wanted a better product. Wendy's corporate goal was to become "bigger than McDonald's" without being "another McDonald's."

Background

Thomas' childhood goal was to operate a really good hamburger stand. He took his first job at the age of 11 as a delivery boy in Knoxville, Tennessee. However, when his supervisor discovered his true age, Thomas was quickly fired. A stint as a drug store fountain boy was cut short for the same reason. Following that, Frank and George Regas hired Thomas to work behind the counter of their restaurant, a position he held for over two years. That job was followed by another and another, and, when he joined the Army at the age of 17, Thomas had five years of solid food service experience in a variety of settings. The military trained Thomas as a cook and sent him to Europe. He quickly established himself as his outfit's "outside-of-channels-procurement specialist." Thomas commented:

> In plain language, I was the company scrounge. This was an nonofficial position, of course, but one with great power and prestige. Without exception, every unit had one. We were traders in the most basic sense of the word. The "position" always went to the greatest wheeler-dealer in the unit. To keep that job I learned the meaning of resourcefulness.

---

[1] "Broader Menu for Fast Foods," *Business Week* (July 14, 1975), p. 118.

Thomas' next assignment was working in an enlisted men's club:

> Actually, I ran the place. There's no way any 18-year-old is going to get a cushy job like that unless he's got a lot going for him. I used to hang around the club in my scrounge-job and pretty soon I was making menu recommendations, changing the layout, telling how to prepare the food. Those boys didn't want a fancy *rest-au-rant*—they wanted a hamburger carryout. Fast service—limited menu. I suggested it, and when it took off, I had a permanent job making it work. That's when I knew I'd found my vocation.

After completing his military tour, Thomas returned to Indiana and a series of moderately successful entrepreneurial restaurant activities. In 1954 he met Colonel Sanders:

> In those days the Colonel was like a traveling salesman. But he was selling pots to cook chicken in and herbs for seasoning. He made most of his money from the herbs. His franchises were all established storefront-type restaurants that "featured" Kentucky Fried Chicken (KFC). I hooked up with the Colonel—traveled with him for a while and got the hang of his business. Eventually, some of the things he was doing—or I should say some of the things he wasn't doing—struck me as being just plain wrong. For one thing, his franchisees weren't pushing his product. To them, chicken was just another menu item. KFC needed to be *promoted!* Also, his symbol at the time was a couple of little chicks hatching out of an egg. Awful! Chickens are hateful creatures! I can't stand the things myself. Anyway, I convinced the Colonel to try opening a store that would serve nothing else but chicken. That was in 1958 in Fort Wayne, Indiana. The place was a carryout. Also, we put the Colonel's face where those chicks and eggshells were. Finally, we packaged the product. We sold buckets and barrels instead of wings and drumsticks and aimed at the take-home market. We advertised over radio and TV, gave away Colonel neckties, and made money like we'd invented it.
>
> In 1962 I was looking to settle down. My wife and I took over four KFC restaurants in Columbus, Ohio. At the time, these stores weren't doing too well. In fact, the Colonel's company had put them on C.O.D. which indicates that something pretty serious is going on. We were so short on cash that I actually swapped barrels of fried chicken for local radio and TV time that I could use to promote KFC. To make a long story short, I reformulated these stores after the Fort Wayne model—cut down the menu and used lots of promotion—and turned them around right quickly. You see, in a business like this, the name of the game is, first, establish an identity, second, maintain the image, and third, deliver. It's as simple as that. In 1968 the Colonel's company was going around buying up franchises and we sold out. I've never liked the chicken business anyway. I've always been a hamburger man.

Concept Development

After a brief experience as vice-president for operations in the Arthur Treacher's Fish and Chips organization, Thomas opened the first Wendy's store in downtown

Columbus, Ohio, on November 15, 1969. Thomas talked about the development of Wendy's:

> Our aim was to provide the customer with a "Cadillac hamburger" that could be "custom made" to the individual consumer's taste. The name "Wendy's" was chosen because of its identification potential and because it was easy to pronounce. Also, it was my daughter's nickname. The store's theme, "Old-Fashioned Hamburgers," was selected because it conveyed a sort of natural, back-home feeling and also exploited a trend favoring nostalgic themes that was emerging in many areas besides restaurants in the late '60s.
>
> We had a whole series of menu decisions to make and ideas to try out in that first store. First, we established the one-fourth pound hamburger ($.69) as the basic menu item.[1] This meant that we weren't really in head-to-head competition with McDonald's or Burger King's one-tenth pound burger. Also, we wanted to use only fresh (not frozen) 100% beef hamburger meat converted into patties daily. If people want a bigger hamburger they can order a "double" (two patties on a bun—$1.25) or a "triple" (three patties on a bun —$1.75). I've never actually had a triple myself and only about 2% of the sandwiches we sell are triples, but the idea is that it *is* available if the customer wants it. Also, some of my people think that having the triple on the menu helps the sales of doubles (about 34% of sandwiches) in some way. One other wrinkle to our hamburger design is that the pattie is square and sized so that the edges stick out over the edge of the round bun. This is to show the customer that he's not getting a "breadburger," which is a frequent complaint about our competition.
>
> Our second major menu decision was to offer lots of different condiments to our customers. Cheese and tomato are each $.10 extra while catsup, onion, lettuce, mustard, mayonnaise, and relish are complimentary. Someone figured out that all the permutations of these condiments offer the possibility of having a basic hamburger prepared 256 different ways. We promote that 256 figure as often as we can. It gives the idea of a custom product and shows that you *can* have variety even with our limited menu. The idea of a custom-built hamburger fits well with our goal of freshness. No Wendy's Old-Fashioned Hamburger ever sees the light of a heat lamp! They go straight from the grill to the bun to the customer. On the other hand, tailoring and freshness make quick delivery more difficult. We teach the cooks to plan ahead. Cooks watch customers walking in the door and cars driving onto the lot and they learn to put a few patties on the grill ahead of time. This way they can minimize the customer wait time between order placing and delivery. Most folks think that we are able to score pretty well on this one, too.
>
> A third major menu decision was the Frosty, a 100% dairy product—a cross between chocolate and vanilla flavors—right at the borderline between

[1] Prices quoted were those in most markets, mid-1976.

soft ice cream and a really thick milkshake. You eat it with a spoon. We promote Frosty, and because it makes us different, it brings people into the store. Our customers really like it. Like all fast-food stores, Wendy's has coffee and a variety of soft drinks.

Another menu decision was chili. Wendy's chili is particularly mild, but if you like it "hot," you can add hot sauces and pepper to your taste. Unlimited crackers are complimentary, of course. Chili is cooked today and served tomorrow. It needs to cook at least that long to bring out the flavor. Each serving, selling for $.69, has about a quarter pound of precooked ground beef in it and our experience with chili makes us feel all warm inside. Again, Wendy's chili is unique in the fast-food or hamburger market, and we really promote it. And about one person in 10 or 12 that walks in the door buys chili.

We serve the final menu item, french fries, because we have to. People expect a hamburger store to sell french fries. Here is our one compromise with the freshness theme: we use frozen french fries. That's because fresh potatoes are awful to store and work with. You get a more uniform product using the frozen presliced potatoes anyway.

So there you have it: Wendy's limited menu. That's really the main key to our success. It's so simple that our competitors think that it's complex. But I'll tell you from long experience in full menu restaurants—there's a real limit to how much you can do well in this business. We concentrate on doing only a few things but we do them better than anyone else. I know all the arguments about enlarging menus and the only plausible one just won't hold water. But it's the reason that McDonald's is experimenting with fried chicken and Kentucky Fried is trying spareribs. Those guys believe in the minority veto. They believe that if four people are going out to eat together and if one wants chicken, the group won't go to a place that serves hamburgers only. I just plain don't think that people behave that way. For one thing, people eat together because they want to eat together, not because they want a particular menu item. Even if they *did* vote, the majority would want hamburgers anyway. Besides, everybody likes hamburgers. Someone might want to veto going to a fish place but not a hamburger restaurant. So, what I'm saying is that we're not going to confuse our image by putting these things on our menu. If we did it would only have a bad effect on the few things we can do well. That's not to say that Wendy's menu is forever fixed. There may come a time to change it. But I'll need good reason before Wendy's starts frying fish or chicken.

Building

All Wendy's restaurants were built to company specifications as to exterior style and interior decor. Most were freestanding one-story brick buildings in design constructed on 25,000 square foot sites with parking for 35 to 40 cars (see Exhibits 1 and 2). Some downtown restaurants were of a storefront type which were varied according to available locations but generally retained the standard red, yellow, and white decor

Exhibit 1

WENDY'S OLD-FASHIONED HAMBURGERS
Typical Freestanding Building Design

and sign. The typical freestanding restaurant contained 2,100 square feet, had a cooking area (see Exhibit 3), dining room capacity for 92 persons, and a pickup window for drive-through service. As of the end of 1976 approximately 504 of Wendy's restaurants were freestanding "image" buildings and 15 were of the store-front type. The standardized interior decor featured Tiffany-styled lamps, bentwood chairs, colorful beads, carpeting, and tabletops printed with reproductions of nineteenth-century advertising.

Thomas remarked about the Wendy's building:

> We put a lot of effort into designing a building that reflected the "Old-Fashioned" theme while retaining modern functionality. As we've gained experience we have been able to improve the design considerably. The large plate glass windows let diners look out at the landscaped front lot, and it lets prospective customers get a taste of the interior decor. Another aspect of this design is its flexibility. With some minor changes we could sell almost any kind of food in these buildings. Also, we could change from a Gay-90s theme to space-age theme almost overnight. This desire for flexibility is one reason we don't have any booths—just tables with four not particularly comfortable chairs around them. I'm really proud of this building design. Not that I designed it all—that was done by experts—but I've had my finger in the major part of it. In 1970 no national fast-food restaurant had pickup windows. But I knew that there were more cars out there than ever before and I got to

Exhibit 2

WENDY'S OLD-FASHIONED HAMBURGERS

Typical Lot Layout For Freestanding Unit

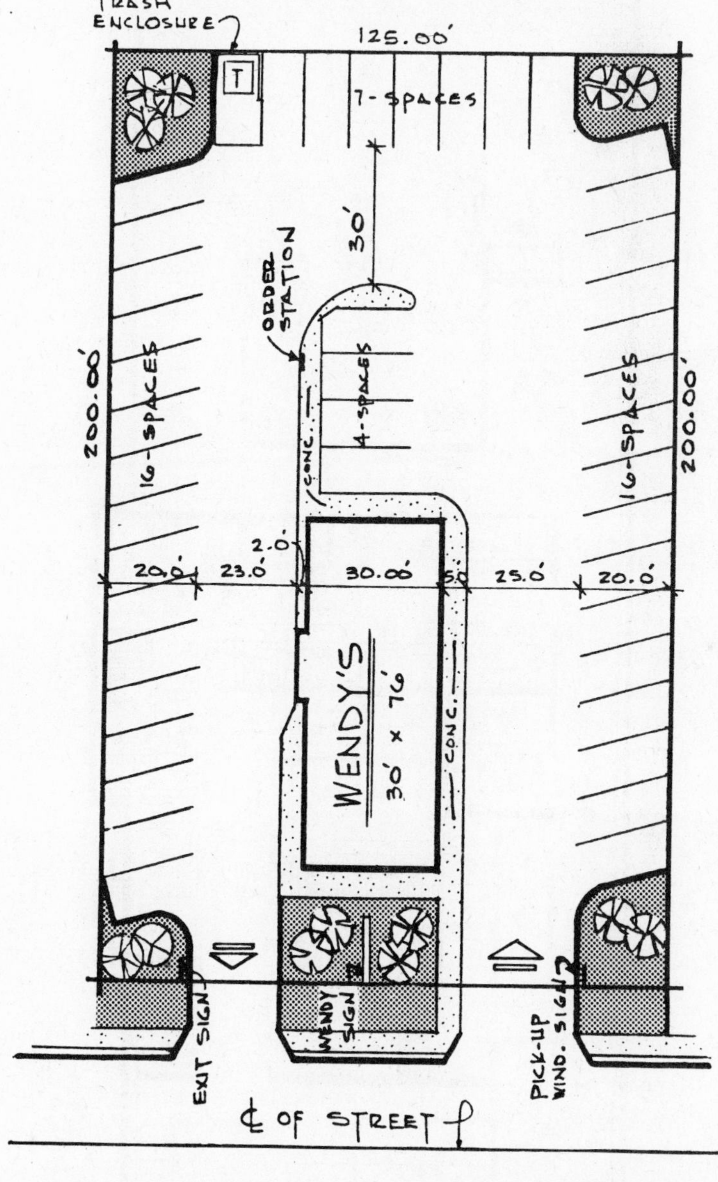

LOT AREA - 25,000 ☐'

BLD'G. AREA - 2,310 ☐'

PARKING SPACES - 43

Exhibit 3

WENDY'S OLD-FASHIONED HAMBURGERS

Restaurant Interior Layout

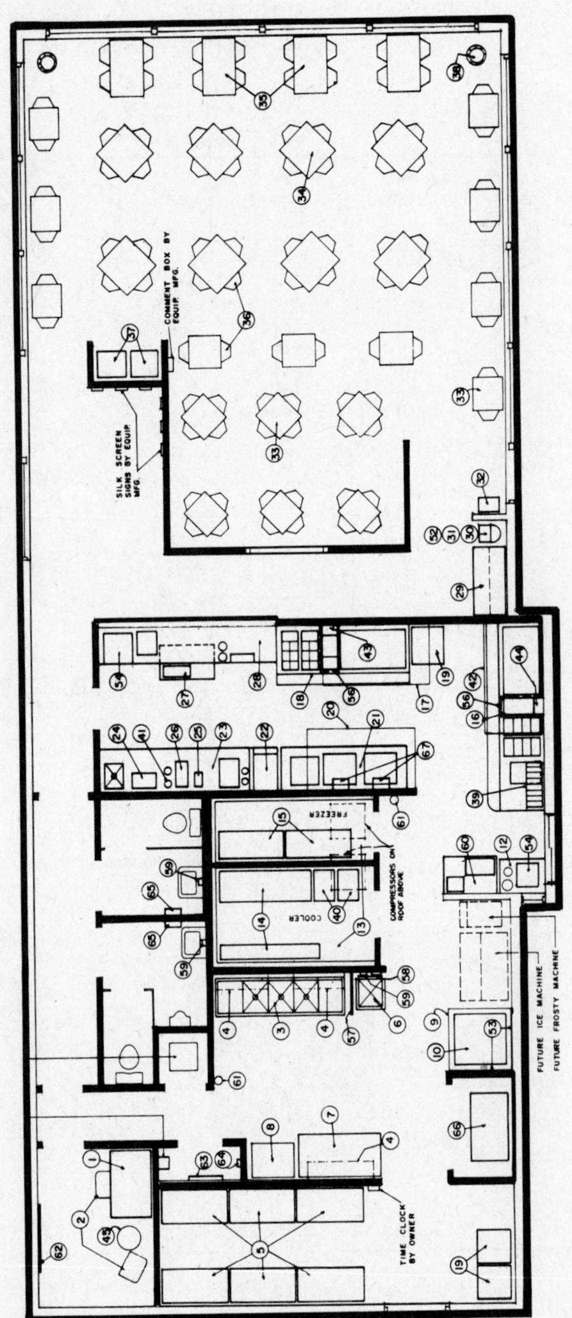

KEY:

(1) desk
(2) chair
(3) sink unit
(4) wall shelving
(5) wall shelving
(6) sink unit
(7) work table
(8) hamburger patty making machine
(9) exhaust canopy system
(10) range top
(11) open number
(12) cashier counter assembly
(13) walk-in cooler/freezer
(14) wire shelving
(15) frozen french fry storage platform
(16) custom cooks counter assembly
(17) exhaust canopy system
(18) custom cook
(19) bun rack
(20) exhaust canopy system
(21) custom fry station assembly
(22) frosty machine
(23) rear counter assembly
(24) coffeemaker
(25) tea machine
(26) hot chocolate machine
(27) ice and drink machine
(28) front counter assembly
(29) condiment station
(30) high chair
(31) booster chairs
(32) water fountain
(33) pedestal tables
(34) pedestal tables
(35) pedestal tables
(36) side chairs
(37) waste containers
(38) costumers
(39) condiment holder
(40) meat racks
(41) marshmallow holder
(42) exhaust canopy system (fire protection)
(43) custom paper holder
(44) custom paper holder
(45) floor safe
(46) litter receptacle
(47) Tiffany style light fixtures
(48) carpet
(49) wall covering
(50) beads
(51) installation package
(52) booster chair hanger
(53) stainless wall panel
(54) cash registers
(55) open number
(56) bun cabinet
(57) stainless partition
(58) towel dispenser
(59) soap dispenser
(60) ice and drink machine
(61) fire extinguishers
(62) coat hook bar
(63) broom holder
(64) hose holder
(65) hand dryers
(66) syrup tank rack
(67) french fry computers

didn't seem to eat in their cars anymore. Why? So, in our second unit I decided to try a pickup window. Once the customers discovered it we really did a lot of business through the pickup window. That may not seem like a big deal to you but those people in their cars don't fill up a table, they don't take up a parking space, and Wendy's units do more business than any other chain on a square foot basis (see Exhibit 4). It must have been a good idea—Burger King and McDonald's are knocking holes in their walls now. That doesn't bother me at all. Our real competition is the supermarket.

The supermarkets knew before we did who the competition was. They were selling self-serve frozen dinners 20 years ago. And we in the restaurant industry weren't even speaking to each other. That's really a bunch of garbage because if we can work together and keep our industry on the upswing, improve things, we'll all be better off.

Order Processing

When a customer arrived at the inside counter he/she was greeted by the order taker-cashier. As the order was placed by the customer, the cashier rang it up and called out the items over the loudspeaker. When the customer finished ordering he/she paid, and a receipt from the cash register was placed on an empty tray. A second employee placed the drinks and Frostys on the tray. A third employee placed fries and chili on the tray and received the completed hamburgers from the fry cook. This third employee, at a point approximately the distance from the cash register required for six people standing in line, checked the tray for completeness,

Exhibit 4

WENDY'S OLD-FASHIONED HAMBURGERS
Industry Comparisons of Unit Economics, 1976

	Sales/Unit	*Capital Cost Per Store*	*Food and Paper Cost % Sales*	*Labor Cost % Sales*
Burger King	$ 463,000	$347,000	40%	21%
Chart House	665,000	750,000	43	18
Cork 'n Cleaver	517,000	550,000	44	17
Denny's	594,000	600,000	33	34
Friendly	312,000	290,500	47	20
Jerrico (LJS)	299,000	200,000	38	14
McDonald's	727,000	502,000	40	22
Pizza Hut	179,000	240,000	30	24
Sambo's	505,000	450,000	35	23
Victoria Station	1,560,000	925,000	43	19
Wendy's	463,000	280,000	42	15
Winchell's	125,000	145,000	45	33

then he/she handed it to the customer. During slack periods this entire process could be handled by two people. This was done by shifting part of the assembly task to the cook, while the cashier prepared and placed the drinks.

As described earlier, the cook was responsible for keeping an appropriate number of patties cooking to accommodate orders with freshly fried hamburgers. As he/she heard the order being placed, the patties would be finished up and the hamburger would be assembled in one of the famous 256 combinations.

The window operation was similar to the interior operations in several respects. The customer would pull his/her automobile to the order phone, about three car lengths from the window. The order would be placed by the customer and rung up and called out by the window employee. Most of the time the hamburgers were prepared by the same cook who prepared the interior orders. However, a separate cooking station was provided for peak periods. The window employee assembled the entire order and received the hamburgers from the cook. After being paid, the order was handed to the driver.

A unit might expect 50% of its business between 12 noon and 1:30 P.M. Another 30% occurred between 5:00 and 7:00 P.M. The remainder was evenly distributed through the day. A typical bill for a customer might be approximately $2.00.

There were three full-time employees per unit: manager, assistant manager, and trainee. All others were part-time, on-call employees. The size of the staff of a Wendy's unit could be expanded or contracted to meet demand. It was estimated that the level of business on a Sunday was only half what might be expected on the other days of the week.

Positioning Strategy

The Wendy's strategy was described by one analyst as "selling better hamburgers than McDonald's or Burger King at a cheaper price per ounce." As he commented, it takes no more labor to prepare a larger hamburger at a higher price. "McDonald's labor cost is about 22% of sales; Wendy's is only 15% because of its larger sandwiches."

In support of the higher-priced hamburger strategy, Thomas stressed the freshness and quality of the Wendy's product. According to him, the words "quality is our recipe" were more than the Wendy's slogan. "This is the way we think about every part of our operation. We do this by quality of raw materials, people, and delivery system" (see Exhibit 5).

By 1976 Wendy's strategy had achieved a remarkable success. Sales in company-owned stores in 1975 exceeded $31 million. Revenues from franchises were at the $1 million level (see Exhibits 6 and 7).

Thomas said:

> There were two major decisions we had to make at Wendy's. First, once our first units were successful, we had to decide if we wanted to be something

Exhibit 5

WENDY'S OLD-FASHIONED HAMBURGERS
Typical 30-Second TV Commercial

TV
30 SECOND COMMERCIAL

This is an example of a Wendy's television commercial in story board form.

(JINGLE MUSIC)
Eat 'em up, eat 'em up good today.
We've got beef and it's pure all the way.

And we start fresh each and every day
At Wendy's Old-Fashioned Hamburgers.

Catsup and mustard or mayonnaise.
Onions and pickles or plain it stays.

256 different ways
At Wendy's Old-Fashioned Hamburgers.

Chili and Frostys and French Fries too.
Making a meal time a treat for you.

It's never pre-cooked and never pre-wrapped
At Wendy's Old-Fashioned Hamburgers.

Eat 'em up, eat 'em up good today.
Eat 'em up, eat 'em up any way.

And we start fresh each and every day
At Wendy's Old-Fashioned Hamburgers.

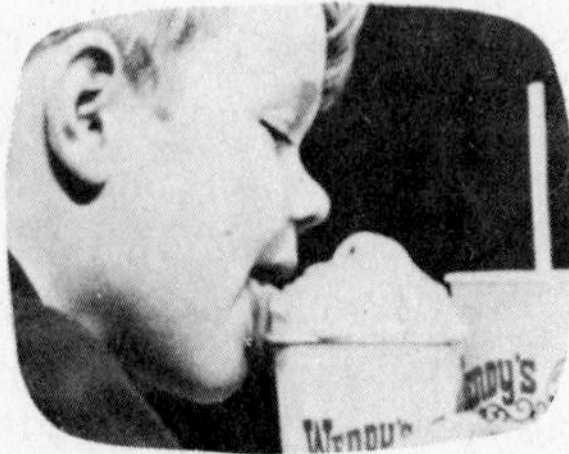

Wendy's Old-Fashioned Hamburgers.
Eat 'em up!

Exhibit 6

WENDY'S OLD-FASHIONED HAMBURGERS
Summary Income Statement, 1971–1975
($ millions)

						Restated[1]	Jan–June Six Months		Jan–June Six Months Restated[1]	
	1971	*1972*	*1973*	*1974*	*1975*	*1975*	*1975*	*1976*	*1975*	*1976*
Company-owned sales	$.682	$1,807	$4.315	$12.742	$31.599	$44.923	$12.966	$23.242	$18.607	$32.080
Cost of sales	.391	.980	2.373	6.983	17.501	25.045	7.365	13.346	10.577	18.442
% Sales	57.3%	54.2%	55.0%	54.8%	55.4%	55.8%	56.8%	57.4%	56.8%	57.5%
Operating costs	.179	.469	1.139	2.808	6.893	9.537	2.376	4.790	3.629	6.815
$ Sales	26.2%	26.0%	26.4%	22.0%	21.8%	21.2%	18.3%	20.6%	19.5%	21.2%
Contribution	$.111	$.358	$.803	$2.951	$7.205	$10.341	$3.225	$5.106	$4.401	$6.823
% Sales	16.3%	19.8%	18.6%	23.2%	22.8%	23.0%	23.9%	22.0%	23.7%	21.3%
Franchise sales	—	.208	1.949	11.491	42.863	29.539	13.591	51.963	8.003	43.125
Royalties	—	.008	.078	.466	1.716	1.189	.544	2.072	.320	1.725
Initial franchise fees	—	.010	.070	.220	.675	.600	.208	.658	.168	.643
Other income	.002	.009	.078	.128	.243	.347	.075	.254	.114	.319
Total contribution	$.113	$.385	$1.029	$3.765	$9.839	$12.477	$4.052	$8.090	$5.003	$9.510
G and A Expense	.030	.140	.214	.909	2.635	3.439	1.073	2.162	1.250	2.440
Depreciation	.018	.040	.096	.287	.733	1.277	.288	.568	.549	.891
Interest	.010	.023	.135	.394	.893	1.320	.392	.563	.570	.811
Pretax income	$.056	$.182	$.583	$2.175	$5.578	$6.441	$2.298	$4.798	$2.634	$5.368
Taxes	.010	.074	.256	1.015	2.659	3.111	1.047	2.235	1.235	2.547
Tax rate	17.9%	40.7%	43.9%	46.7%	47.7%	48.3%	45.6%	46.6%	46.9%	47.4%
Net income	$.046	$.108	$.327	$1.160	$2.919	$3.330	$1.251	$2.563	$1.399	$2.821

[1] Consolidates sales and expenses of 40 franchise units acquired by Wendy's on July 31, 1976.

Exhibit 7

WENDY'S OLD-FASHIONED HAMBURGERS
Balance Sheet, December 31, 1975

ASSETS	
Current assets:	
Cash, including certificates of deposit of $4,030,000	$5,099,049
Receivables	612,627
Inventories	275,172
Deferred income taxes	651,050
Other	64,264
Total current assets	$6,702,162
Other assets:	830,954
Property and equipment at cost:	
Buildings	5,354,528
Leasehold improvements	1,808,880
Restaurant equipment	5,450,976
Motor vehicles	416,859
Office equipment	214,445
Lease and land rights	300,709
	13,546,397
Less accumulated depreciation and amortization	1,159,179
	12,387,218
Land	4,828,623
Construction in progress	225,500
	17,441,341
	$24,974,457

LIABILITIES AND SHAREHOLDERS' EQUITY	
Current liabilities:	
Notes payable to banks	$1,200,000
Accounts payable, trade	2,036,850
Federal, state and local income taxes	2,287,497
Accrued liabilities:	
Salaries	379,553
Interest	97,981
Taxes	201,346
Royalties	—
Other	233,617
	912,497
Current portion, term debt	403,684
Total current liabilities	6,840,528
Term debt, net of current portion	8,905,276
Deferred:	
Income taxes	405,524
Franchise fees	1,660,000
	2,065,524
Shareholders' equity:	
Common shares	336,821
Capital in excess of stated value	2,296,412
Retained earnings	4,529,896
	7,163,129
	$24,974,457

more than just a small Columbus operation. Second, once we decided to grow, we had to decide how much of the company we would give up to be able to expand. With that behind us now, our decision is how to manage our growth.

Wendy's president Bob Barney, who had been associated with Thomas at Arthur Treacher's, stressed that he felt that the company must be careful to maintain its entrepreneurial spirit while carefully formalizing the organization and control as necessary. As Thomas put it, "we are successful enough now that potential franchisees are coming to us. The trick is to pick and choose the right ones. We are franchisors who have been successful franchisees in the past. We know the pitfalls and problems as well as the opportunities."

Exhibit 8

WENDY'S OLD-FASHIONED HAMBURGERS
Units Opened at Year End

Date	*Company-Owned*	*Franchised*	*Total*
1970	2	0	2
1971	4	0	4
1972	7	2	9
1973	17	15	32
1974	44	49	93
1975	83	169	252
1976	150	369	519
12/31/77*	194	709	903
Under Construction			
12/31/76	10	110	120

* Forecast by Oppenheimer and Co., Inc.

Franchise Operations

The Wendy's expansion strategy was based on a "balanced" development of company-owned and franchised stores. As of November 5, 1976, franchise sales and openings had moved ahead aggressively, with 145 company-owned and 315 franchise units opened (see Exhibit 8). An example of the desire to balance the growth of company-owned and franchise stores was the situation where Wendy's obtained a block of 40 franchise units in exchange for Wendy's common stock on July 31, 1976.

While growth in the number of units was a major concern of Wendy's management and the financial community, the chain had exhibited a pattern of increased revenue at individual stores, as seen in Exhibit 9. However, one observer

Exhibit 9

WENDY'S OLD-FASHIONED HAMBURGERS
Unit Revenue Growth

Year	*Average annual revenues of company-owned units open 12 months or more*	*Average annual revenues of all company-owned units*	*Systemwide average annual sales per store*	*Price of 1/4 pound Wendy's hamburger*	*Price index for food away from home (1967 = 100)*
1971	$265,644	$255,600	$255,600	$0.55	126
1972	345,165	361,300	335,700	0.55	131
1973	390,012	392,200	368,400	0.69	149
1974	438,879	490,000	429,900	0.69	161
1975	463,419	518,000	489,800	0.69	174

from the financial community was calling for 350 franchised unit openings in 1977 based on plans for 277 in 1976. He noted that the current rate of openings "while obviously rapid, is not meeting the company's objectives. This seems to mean more pressure on franchise sales." [1]

Wendy's awarded franchises on an area basis rather than single store franchises. The franchise agreement provided for opening of Wendy's restaurants within the franchised area in accordance with a performance schedule. Wendy's and the prospective franchisee agreed upon the number of restaurants which the franchisee should be able to construct in the franchised area after considering, among other things, the size and population of the area and the experience of the Company's franchisees in similar areas.[2] An option fee, equal to the unit opening (initial) fee of $10,000 per unit times the number of units agreed on, was payable when the franchise agreement was signed. As units were opened, the franchise fee was applied toward the unit fee. The option fee was nonrefundable and the company was not required to return it if restaurants were not opened on schedule. As of March 31, 1976, delinquent franchisees had failed to open 102 Wendy's restaurants in accordance with franchise agreements. At that same time, however, some 30 units had been opened ahead of schedule. Wendy's had usually agreed to extend the performance schedules of delinquent franchisees but on November 1, 1975, the company, for the first time, terminated a franchise agreement (for the construction of 15 restaurants in the Phoenix area) for failure to meet the performance schedule.

Wendy's did not sell or lease real estate or equipment to its franchisees. The company provided advice and approval as to site selection, specifications for the restaurant building, training programs and promotional and advertising material. Wendy's did not finance the real estate or equipment. Nor did it sell fixtures, food or supplies to its franchisees. To enable Wendy's and its franchisees to obtain advantageous prices, however, Wendy's had arranged a number of national contracts with major suppliers which are available to franchisees. About 80% of Wendy's franchisees purchased from these national suppliers. As Thomas commented:

> For example, a TV commercial might run us $12,000 but we provide a tape of it to a franchisee for a one-time charge of $11. Even the initial fee is no real income to us. That money simply covers our costs associated with engineering, site approval, legal fees, etc. Our franchise operation income is limited to the 4% of sales. We don't sell them goods or services. If our franchisees do well, so do we. (See Exhibit 10.) Our motivation, then, is the same as theirs. We help these guys any way we can.

Of course, not all of the Wendy's units were steady successes. One store was an example of the type of problems that could occur. The single-store franchise had been operated by the franchisee for two years. A lack of attention from the franchisee resulted in a drop of revenues of $4,400 in the first week to an average of

---

[1] Robert Emerson, "Wendy's International, Inc.; Why Is It So Much More Profitable Than McDonald's?", Oppenheimer and Company, Inc., New York, October 4, 1976.

[2] Whenever possible Wendy's tried to get buy-back options at the time franchise agreements were signed.

Exhibit 10

WENDY'S OLD-FASHIONED HAMBURGERS
Franchise Pro Forma Statement of Operations for One Year

Sales	*$300,000*	*100.00%*	*$400,000*	*100.00%*	*$500,000*	*100.00%*
Cost of Goods Sold:						
Manager or owner	$ 13,000	4.33%	$ 13,000	3.25%	$ 13,000	2.60%
Comanager	10,500	3.50	10,500	2.62	10,500	2.10
Crew	27,750	9.25	37,000	9.25	42,500	8.50
Total labor	$ 51,250	17.08	60,500	15.12	66,000	13.20
Food[1]	111,000	37.00	148,000	37.00	185,000	37.00
Paper	12,000	4.00	16,000	4.00	20,000	4.00
Laundry	1,050	.35	1,400	.35	1,750	.35
Total cost of goods sold	$175,300	58.43%	$225,900	56.47%	$272,750	54.55%
Gross profit	124,700	41.57	174,100	43.53%	227,250	45.45%
Operating Expenses:						
Rent[2]	$ 25,800	8.60%	$ 25,800	6.45%	$ 25,800	5.16%
Royalty	12,000	4.00	16,000	4.00	20,000	4.00
Insurance	2,100	.70	2,100	.53	2,100	.42
Taxes-payroll	3,450	1.15	4,200	1.05	5,000	1.00
Taxes-real estate	2,000	.67	2,000	.50	2,000	.40
Taxes-other	1,000	.33	1,000	.25	1,000	.20
Supplies	3,750	1.25	5,000	1.25	6,250	1.25
Utilities	10,250	3.42	10,750	2.69	11,250	2.25
Repair and maintenance	4,500	1.50	5,000	1.25	5,000	1.00
Telephone	500	.17	500	.13	500	.10
Trash removal	1,500	.50	1,500	.37	1,500	.30
Advertising and promotion	12,000	4.00	16,000	4.00	20,000	4.00
Office expenses	1,200	.40	1,200	.30	1,200	.24
Miscellaneous	250	.08	250	.06	250	.05
Total operating expenses	$ 80,300	26.77	$ 91,300	22.83	$101,850	20.37
Cash flow	$ 44,400	14.80	$ 82,800	20.70	$125,400	25.08
Depreciation[3]	$ 6,000	2.00	$ 6,000	1.50	6,000	1.20
Pretax profit	$ 38,400	12.80	$ 76,800	19.20	$119,400	23.88

NOTES TO PRO FORMA STATEMENT OF OPERATING INCOME

These pro forma statements are based on the composite experience in company-owned stores during the January 1, 1975–June 30, 1975 period. They are intended to reflect an independent or owner-operated unit and as such do not reflect any corporate allocation. Although it is impossible to apply the above costs and percentages to a specific location, management believes that they are representative of an "average" store.

1. Meat—the largest food item represents 40–45% of total food costs dependent on fluctuations in its prices.
2. Rent is based on $2,150 per month for land and building.
3. Depreciation—expense has been computed on a straight-line basis for equipment only. It has been estimated that store equipment will cost approximately $60,000 and that it will be depreciated over a useful life of 10 years.
4. Based on the above costs and percentages, the volume necessary to break even is approximately $225,000 per year or $4,300 per week.

$1,800 to $2,000 per week, well below the breakeven level for this store of roughly $3,200 per week. Wendy's bought back the franchise and immediately changed local management. For a period of approximately four months the store was operated with a new crew to establish a new level of service and product. Once these had been established, sales and promotion under the personal direction of Jay Schloemer, vice-president of marketing, began. Coupons for free meals and 2-for-1 and price-off deals were distributed in the trading area within a one and one-half mile radius of the store. The theme of the program was "give Wendy's another chance." Within approximately one year sales were up to $5,000 per week. As of late 1976, only one Wendy's restaurant had ever gone out of business. To help keep this record intact, the daily results of the "bottom 10%" of the company's stores received Jay Schloemer's special attention. Promotional campaigns could be triggered on a day-to-day basis for those stores to help increase store traffic and unit volume.

In addition to the fees, franchisees were required to spend at least 3% of sales on local advertising and promotion. Also, franchisees were to be required to contribute 1% of sales to a national advertising program that was to be adopted in 1977.

Barney stated that his own experience as a franchisee in other systems had helped him better understand what the potential problems were. Having been on both sides of the "franchise fence" he was committed to providing more and better services to his franchisees. "There is a moral obligation to a franchisee." He felt that Wendy's had to be just as concerned about building the profits of a franchisee's store as a company-owned unit, though Wendy's rewards were tied to the sales of a franchisee rather than his profits.

Wendy's provided the following services to the franchisee:

1. Site approval procedures for evaluating restaurant locations;
2. On-site inspection and evaluation by a staff representative, when available, if requested;
3. Counseling in business planning;
4. Drawings and specifications for a standard Wendy's building;
5. Training for franchisee at Wendy's headquarters or other designated location;
6. Advice on supplies from suppliers selected by Wendy's and assistance in establishing quality control standards and procedures for supplies;
7. Staff representative to assist in the opening of *each* restaurant;
8. Assistance in planning opening promotion and continuing advertising, public relations, and promotion;
9. Operations manual containing all information necessary to operate a Wendy's restaurant.

In addition to these ongoing services, Wendy's agreed to provide:

1. Research and development in production and methods of operation;
2. Information on policies, developments, and activities by means of bulletins, brochures, reports, and visits of Wendy's representatives;

3. Managerial advice;
4. Paper goods standards;
5. National and regional meetings.

Additionally, Wendy's maintained a staff of franchise supervisors who worked directly with franchisees to maintain the company's quality standards and image. As part of the national advertising program, Wendy's provided promotional, merchandising, advertising, and training materials at cost. This included newspaper mats, radio scripts, decals, television and radio tapes, and a variety of other materials. Wendy's also protected all franchisees against infringement of trademarks or service marks.

Training Program

Each franchisee and many store managers attended a training program at Wendy's Management Institute in a Columbus suburb. Bob Barney commented:

> In 1974 we graduated 200 trainees. In 1975, 680. In 1976 we are up to 1,200. Classroom training with slides, workbooks, video-tapes and lectures is coupled with on-the-job training at 17 of the company restaurants in Columbus. In fact, the capacity of the Institute is now limited by the number of people we can place in these training stores. But the demand for training is so great that we plan to open additional training centers in other company markets in the near future. In addition to the two-week "basic training" course where our franchisee principals and their staffs learn precisely how to make a Wendy's hamburger, we are now offering a one-week advanced management course for the franchisee and his store manager.

Franchisee Selection

Graydon Webb, vice president of franchise sales, stressed that Wendy's avoided over-representing the company. "We want the applicant to know the obligation and possible pitfalls."

Wendy's was in a position where the company felt it could be highly selective in choosing among franchise applicants. Publicity of the success of Wendy's had brought an overwhelming number of applicants with a variety of backgrounds and resources. With the large number of applicants, Wendy's could design and develop just about any type of franchise organization management desired. With this in mind, the Wendy's management established the following informal criteria for franchisee selection.

> We are looking for good proven business ability. The applicant must demonstrate intelligence and business sense. This translates into an interest in making profits. We are interested in people who have already demonstrated this ability in other ventures. Many of our franchisees were self-made millionaires before they joined us. While this is not a requirement, successful operators from other franchises are attractive because they understand what it takes to do well.

> We are not interested in investor groups who plan to be absentee owners. The franchisee should have solid net worth and liquidity. We like to see something like $200,000, but we will accept less if the situation is right. We want people who will be involved. Doctors and lawyers who want to invest money do not have the attitude and desire to do well. We don't make our profits from selling our franchisees goods and services. Our income comes from their sales volume. So we are interested in franchisees who can build sales. We will supply them with support to do this, but we must select people who will dig in and do it. We are interested in signing a whole area with one experienced and proven individual who has the ability to build an organization.

As the case writers were walking down the hall of the Wendy's executive offices they met a new Wendy's franchisee. The conservatively clad Mike Scharff was a 1967 MBA graduate of the Harvard Business School. His first experience after graduation had included a series of successful real estate ventures. In 1971 he formed a group of investors that purchased a metals distributor for $100,000. In 1975 the group sold its interest for $14 million. Scharff was looking for a new venture and was interested in fast food. After examining several ventures he decided to acquire an area franchise from Wendy's. He commented that it took him a little longer to put the deal together than he thought it would. "Wendy's really looked me over, but I really studied Wendy's too." As Scharff departed the case writers wished him good luck. He responded: "Thanks, but I don't think I will need luck in this deal. It is solid." Then he turned to Dave Thomas and said, "I'll see you at school (Wendy's Management Institute) in a couple of weeks." Dave Thomas commented, "He will do well because he will get in and be involved. That is what it is all about."

William Fontano Hotel Manager Imperial Hotel, Albany, New York

"The best way for you to understand the tasks that I perform as hotel manager is to watch me in action."

In response to Mr. William Fontano's offer, the casewriter visited him at his hotel, a 300-room high-rise in Albany, New York, on several occasions. The results of those visits have been developed into a four-part case. The interview transcribed below as Part I conveys the perspective of a manager in a downtown motor hotel operation. Part II, a series of interviews with staff members, provides some insight into the personalities and motivations of Mr. Fontano's staff. The next section, Part III, is a description of a series of events that involved Mr. Fontano during a nine-hour period, 8:30 A.M.–5:30 P.M., July 18, 1972. (The hours reflect the work schedule of the casewriter, not of Mr. Fontano.) The final section is a summary of the casewriter's observations on Mr. Fontano's managerial style.

Part I—Interview with Mr. William Fontano

Financial

Q. WHAT IS THE TOTAL ANNUAL REVENUE FROM YOUR OPERATION?

A. $4–6 million.

Q. COULD YOU BREAK DOWN THE REVENUE BY SOURCE AS AN AVERAGE PERCENTAGE OF ANNUAL REVENUE? COULD YOU GIVE US A SIMILAR BREAKDOWN OF MAJOR EXPENSES?

A.

Categories	*Percent of Total Revenue*	*Percent of Revenue for This Category*	
		Materials Cost	*Labor Cost*
Rooms and room revenue	68.0%	10%	13%
Food	17.0%	35–37%	36%
Beverage	12.0%	22–24%	14%
Telephone	2.7%	100%	30%
Other (laundry, rentals)	.3%	50%	10%

Overhead and Profits	*% Total Revenue*
Administrative and general (salaries)	2%
Administrative and general (nonsalaries)	8%
Advertising and sales personnel	.2%
Advertising and promotion	2.5%
Maintenance and repairs (salaries)	3.5%
Maintenance and repairs (nonsalaries)	1.5%
Heat, lights, power	3.5%
Rent, interest, depreciation	15%
Gross operating profit	35%

Our revenue from rooms is very high, 68%. In general, Imperial aims for a higher percentage of revenue from food and beverage. However, our hotel is built somewhat out of proportion. Although we have 300 guest rooms, we have a relatively small banquet facility with a maximum seating capacity of only 120 for a dinner and a classroom of 150. I think that the ideal banquet seating capacity for a 300-room property would be a 400-seat guest dining room which could be divided into smaller rooms. Such an arrangement would yield an equal amount of revenue from rooms and food and beverage. However, there are no plans for expanding this facility. We cannot go up and we are hemmed in on all sides.

You might think that a roadside motel would also have a high proportion of traveling guests as opposed to convention guests. This is not necessarily true because many of the roadside locations, particularly in outlying communities, are now the meeting places of the civic clubs instead of the old downtown hotels. Another factor is their lower room rates. Although their restaurant charges about the same for a meal as we do in the Coffee Shop, their average room rate is $12–13, while my average rate is $22.50.

In regards to expenses for this operation, we are very fortunate to have the No. 1 housekeeper in the Imperial system and an experienced food and beverage man. The figures for our hotel are either standard or better than standard. Systemwide, we have certain goals, but different locations have special advantages and disadvantages that are taken into consideration. For example, we aim for a 13% of revenue payroll figure for rooms. The target for the system is 16%, but ours is 13% because we do such a heavy room business and we are tremendously organized. We run a full house with the exception of a couple of weeks in December and January. This makes it easy to schedule work. In some hotels with wide fluctuations in occupancy rates, a maid may clean five rooms on one day and 15 on the next day. Even our slack time in December and January is put to good use by performing major housekeeping and by allowing our employees to take a long holiday vacation.

We aim for a gross operating profit before taxes of 35%. Our projection for the coming year is 40.8%.

Q. DO YOU PARTICIPATE IN THE DEVELOPMENT OF YOUR ANNUAL BUDGET OR PROFIT PLAN?

A. We prepare the annual budget and submit it to the district supervisor who is my immediate superior. After reviewing and analyzing the budget with him, he submits it to the regional director who compiles all budgets for his region. After close scrutiny by the company accountants all budgets from the region are reviewed by the executive committee at company headquarters, which approves, alters, or disapproves them.

After the budget is approved and we begin the new operating year, we receive monthly reports which compare performance with goals set for all company hotels. Last year, we hit our profit goal within .2%. The company rewards good forecasting by giving bonuses to those units that come close to their goals.

In drawing up the budget, the first thing I did was to sit down with last year's figures and review our occupancy figures for trends or opportunities.

In examining the types of occupants, for example, I realized that we had contracted with an airline for 20+ rooms a night at a guaranteed rate of $16/room. However, we were turning away business at $22.50. I quickly eliminated the airline contract. I may be on my knees begging for the airline to come back, but why give it away when you can sell it? I knew we would feel the impact of this move on the weekends when we do not always have a full house, but I would still be getting paid more for the five days I would fill the rooms. With these sorts of considerations, I estimated room revenue.

Similarly for food, I looked at the banquet book to see if the historical data revealed any patterns, any strong points, or any weak points. On this basis, I made a projection for banquets. We do the same for the regular dining room, the coffee shop, and the lounges. The food and beverage director, the sales department, and I try to formulate all these factors and come up with "guesstimated figures," based on hard facts and projections which we consider reasonable. When you complete a year with the volume of business we do and miss the budget by only .2%, you've done something. Our district supervisor wants a realistic budget not a "rosy picture."

I have a particular worry for this coming year. Because Imperial is a large corporation, we are affected by the price freeze. This has particular impact on our food and beverage operations. I just got a release on our food figures, up 1.3% in November and up 1.0% in December.

Normally, we must forecast an increase in revenues and profitability each year unless we can substantiate that our hotel is located in a depressed area. However, it would be very difficult to submit the same budget year after year. The company will not allow us to become complacent. This year, as a result of the freeze, our budget will be close to the one of last year. If we can achieve that goal in light of rising costs, we will be quite satisfied.

Q. DO YOU REQUEST FUNDS FOR CAPITAL EXPENDITURES?

A. We have a request form for the approval of capital expenditures. This past year we requested more color TV's, new decor in meeting rooms, and new carpeting in 25–50 rooms. We estimate the costs and then fill in the requests. The requests are presented to a committee which distributes the funds available for capital improvements. The requests are made during October and November. By the first of the year, we are informed if our requests have been approved or worthy of further considerations. As the year progresses, the fortunes of business determine whether or not we get the funds. Last year we got all we asked for. We did not request much this year.

We are in the process of constructing two executive VIP suites with sunken bathtubs, gold-plated fixtures, and the like. These funds were approved at the end of last year after we had established that VIP suites and five new dual-purpose suites (rent as meeting rooms with beds up during the day and rent as guest rooms with beds down at night) would pay for themselves as a package even though the VIP suites will only be occupied by paying customers 50% of the time. The other 50% of the time, we will give them away to visiting dignitaries, conference chairmen, and other VIP types. For example, we will extend an invitation to Governor Rockefeller and his wife to be our guests shortly after they are completed, as a token of our appreciation for what state government means to us. We receive a great deal of business from the county, state, and federal governments.

Characteristics of Facilities

Q. WHAT ARE THE TOTAL NUMBER OF GUEST ROOMS YOU HAVE? OCCUPANCY RATE, I.E., ANNUALLY, BY MONTH, BY DAY OF WEEK?

A. We have 300 guest rooms and maintain an average occupancy rate of 93.5%. We begin in January at 87% and increase to 94% level in April and May, June–October, 98+%, November 92–94%, and dip to a low of 80% in December. Except for the last two weeks of December and the first week of January, we are full from Sunday to Thursday. From mid-May to the end of October we are at full occupancy on the weekends. At other times, Friday and Saturday nights, occupancy rate is 85–87%.

One of the lowest occupancy rates occurs during the nine three-day weekends. These weekends help the resort hotels but play havoc with our business because all the banks and government offices are closed.

Q. WHAT FOOD, BANQUET, AND CONVENTION FACILITIES DO YOU HAVE?

A. We have the coffee shop in the lobby. It is a plain food operation offering quick service. At present, we are open from 6:00 A.M.–2:30 P.M. However, beginning on February 14, we will remain open until 9:00 P.M. because of the demands of our guests. Our food and beverage man, who has only been with us a short time, convinced me that with only a little additional revenue, we could cover the costs of remaining open until 9:00 P.M. We have a fine restaurant on the 15th floor with fine china and cutlery, but many of our guests are here on an extended stay and they cannot afford the $5.00–$6.00 cover for supper each night. They are eating elsewhere. In the gourmet dining room, we serve lunch and dinner, Monday–Friday and dinner only on Saturday and Sunday.

Q. IS PARKING A SPECIAL PROBLEM AT YOUR DOWNTOWN LOCATION?

A. Imperial advertises free parking, but we don't have a garage and don't lease space. We have a contract with a parking lot that gives our guests special rates. This clears us of liability and we pay them a flat rate per 24-hour period for our guests.

Purchasing

Q. I ASSUME A SIGNIFICANT PORTION OF YOUR SUPPLIES ARE OBTAINED FROM IMPERIAL. COULD YOU ESTIMATE WHAT PERCENTAGE OF YOUR TOTAL REQUIREMENTS ARE PROCURED LOCALLY?

A. We get our silverware and china from Imperial. Food and other such items are bought locally. However, on some items such as coffee and bread, there is a national contract with a supplier who gives rebates to Imperial. On major renovations, everything is purchased through Imperial. The majority of other items are bought on the local market because of time and freight considerations.

Q. MUST LARGE PURCHASES BE APPROVED BY COMPANY HEADQUARTERS?

A. Large purchases must be approved by the district director. We have a purchase order system for all items in excess of $500 that are not classified as normal supplies.

Sales and Promotion

Q. WHAT IS THE PRICE RANGE OF YOUR ROOMS? HOW MUCH SEASONAL VARIATION DO YOU HAVE IN YOUR PRICE STRUCTURE? AS MANAGER, DO YOU RECOMMEND RATE CHANGES BASED ON THE LOCAL COMPETITIVE SITUATION?

A. We have only two prices for our rooms: $20 single and $26 double with $3 for each extra person in the room and $2 for a cot. There is no extra charge for children under 12 sharing facilities with their parents (extra charge for cot).

All rooms are identical with two double beds. It is foolish economy to build a room with just one bed. The extra bed on the wholesale market costs less than $75. You can always take the room with two beds and put either one person or a couple in it; it is difficult to put two people in a room with just one bed.

Some hotels advertise "singles, for $20." In some of the old hotels, those rooms are so small that you must "open a window to change your mind." The same is true in some hotels in which they build a minimum number of these low-priced rooms as an attractive gimmick for advertising.

Q. DO YOU HAVE ANY SPECIAL RATES FOR WEEKENDS OR OTHER PERIODS FOR GUEST ROOMS?

A. All of our rates are posted in the Imperial directory. We cannot charge more than the posted rate. We must list the entire rate structure from the bottom to the top. The directory normally comes out three times a year. Rates are in effect for four months. Each hotel must present proposed price changes to headquarters along with the reasons for the changes. Reasons might range from competitive pressures to rising costs. There is also an established company policy that no commercial rates are allowed. The parent company insists that when we set a rate, it's a fair rate for a fair return on our investment. Any kind of special rate is to be avoided. Everyone is a valued customer. When reservations come in requesting a commercial rate, we must refuse them. We did offer the airlines a special rate and some Federal organizations get special rates. I do not even have a discounted tour rate because I'm full during the tour season. There is no seasonal variation in our rates.

We will have those new suites ready next month. The smaller suites will rent for \$35/day and the two VIP suites will be priced at \$75–\$100/day. We cannot list those rooms in the directory because there is a company policy that we can only list a type of room if it comprises at least 5% of the hotel's total number of rooms.

Q. DO YOU KNOW APPROXIMATELY WHAT THE PERCENTAGE BREAKDOWN IS FOR DIFFERENT TYPES OF CUSTOMERS, I.E., BUSINESSMEN, CONVENTION, VACATION TRAVELERS? BY SEASON?

A. From Sunday–Thursday better than 90% of our business is single occupancy rooms for businessmen. The other 10% of our business is due to guests associated with the government or local hospitals. In the summer and fall, the percentage of occupancy due to businessmen declines to 80% since 10–15% of the rooms are occupied by tourists who have made early reservations. On the weekends throughout the year, tourist business is basically a family and couples occupancy. With air travel so convenient, most businessmen return home for the weekends.

Workforce Management

Q. HOW MANY EMPLOYEES DO YOU HAVE? BY CATEGORY, I.E., MAIDS, CHEFS, ROOM CLERKS, SUPERVISORY, NONSUPERVISORY?

A. We have 230 employees. The executive staff consists of 10 people, there are 20 subdepartment heads and 20 middle managers (i.e., head cooks, dining room hostesses, assistant housekeepers, etc.). At the lower level of the organization 60% of the workforce is in housekeeping; 30% in food and beverage, and 10% room clerks and others.

Q. SINCE YOUR BUSINESS IS A 24-HOUR-DAY OPERATION COULD YOU GIVE US A ROUGH IDEA WHAT HOURS EACH CATEGORY OF EMPLOYEE TYPICALLY WORKS?

A. All workers are on eight-hour shifts. Because we have a high occupancy rate, we are able to schedule our workforce very easily. Some hotels with heavy peaks during the day use split shifts. Some other hotels have "call maids" to help in high occupancy periods. They work only a half-day or they are paid on a per room basis.

Q. DO YOU RELY PRIMARILY ON OVERTIME OR TEMPORARY EMPLOYEES TO PROVIDE SUFFICIENT FLEXIBILITY IN YOUR OPERATIONS?

A. We don't have much overtime work since our occupancy rate is relatively stable. We also encourage as many people as possible to take their vacations during the slack period of Christmas and New Year's.

Q. COULD YOU GIVE US A ROUGH IDEA OF THE BASE PAY FOR SEVERAL OF THE MAJOR EMPLOYEE CATEGORIES? HOW IMPORTANT ARE TIPS TO EMPLOYEES SUCH AS WAITRESSES AND BARTENDERS? APPROXIMATELY WHAT PERCENTAGE OF THEIR TOTAL COMPENSATION IS COMPRISED OF TIPS?

A. We are a nonunion house, the only major nonunion house in town. We give many employee benefits: hospital insurance, credit union, profit sharing, etc. We have minimal turnover. We pay above average wages because the market for good people is so competitive, e.g., our night auditor earns $3.00/hour compared to the $2.15/hour that he earned at the same position in a competitive hotel. Our lowest wage is $2.10/hour. We pay our tipped employees $1.27–$1.37/hour. Our waitresses, bartenders, and cocktail waitresses are our highest paid employees other than supervisory personnel although we do not know exactly how much they make in tips. They must only report (on a federal form) each week whether their hourly compensation including tips averages more than the minimum wage of $1.75. The official policy is that tips must not be demanded but received in acknowledgment for good service. A flat 16% is added on all banquet contracts.

Q. WHAT NUMBER OF YOUR EMPLOYEES LIVE ON THE PREMISES?

A. Only one, me.

Q. WHAT AMOUNT OF SCREENING IS PERFORMED IN THE SELECTION OF EMPLOYEES? DIFFERENT FOR VARIOUS EMPLOYEE CATEGORIES?

A. We do a very thorough background screening on all cash handlers and supervisors, even to the extent of doing a police background check, since personal integrity and honesty are so important in these positions. For other employees we check with former employers. We are interested in personality, ability, and dependability.

Q. DO YOU EMPLOY A SIZEABLE NUMBER OF MEMBERS OF MINORITY OR ETHNIC GROUPS? DO YOU HAVE ANY SPECIAL PROBLEMS SUPERVISING THESE EMPLOYEES, I.E., LANGUAGE, CUSTOMS, ETC.?

A. We have a sizeable number of minority group employees. We submit a regular report to the Federal Government about our minority hiring practices and report not only the total number of minority employees but also the number of minority employees in supervisory positions. We have no special problems; but in New York City and Miami, I did have problems with the number of Spanish-speaking employees.

Q. DO YOU HAVE ANY FORMAL TRAINING PROGRAMS WITHIN YOUR OPERATION?

A. We have an ongoing training program that includes training films and literature. All new employees in responsible positions undergo a one-week program in which they are paired with our best employees to learn our way of doing things. There is a 90-day training/probation period.

Q. HOW MANY UNIONS ARE REPRESENTED IN YOUR OPERATION?

A. We deal with no unions in Albany, although I had six unions in New York City: bartenders, bellmen and drivers, front-desk clerks, waitresses and kitchen employees, housekeeping and engineering.

Q. WHAT SOURCES DO YOU USE FOR RECRUITING?

A. We use the employment bureau very often. We cannot pay any fees to commercial employment agencies. The most beneficial source for this location is newspaper ads. With this medium, we get people who are working; the other sources tend to attract those who are presently out of work.

Q. WHAT IS THE APPROXIMATE RATE OF EMPLOYEE TURNOVER FOR EACH EMPLOYEE CATEGORY AND FOR THE OPERATION AS A WHOLE? WHAT IS YOUR ESTIMATE OF THE AVERAGE LENGTH OF SERVICE?

A. Turnover is highest in the kitchen (dishwashers, etc.). Most employees stay with us more than a year.

Q. WHAT NUMBER OF EMPLOYEE AWARDS, MONETARY AND NON-MONETARY, DO YOU AWARD LOCALLY? WHAT OTHER EMPLOYEE INCENTIVE PLANS ARE IN EFFECT?

A. We have employee awards. All of our people get certificates for one year's service and for each additional year, they receive pins which indicate the years of service. Some hotels, but not here, have the "maid of the month," "employee of the month," etc., awards which are often monetary. These awards are at the option of the local manager.

We have a top-notch profit-sharing plan. It is a contributory program. The employees can put up to 6% of their salaries into the program; the company matches this amount on a dollar-for-dollar basis. Anybody can join. Tipped employees get double the percentage because their hourly rates are approximately one-half those of other employees. 93% of our employees participate in the profit-sharing plan.

Controls

Q. DO YOU HAVE A CONTROLLER?

A. High-rise facilities in our chain have a controller on the premises. Such controllers are employed by the company and serve to control the manager. It is a system of checks and balances.

Q. DO YOU FIND THAT EMPLOYEE AND GUEST THEFT ARE MAJOR PROBLEMS? DO YOU USE CONTROL SYSTEMS SUCH AS AUTOBAR?

A. Employee theft is a nuisance problem. Guest theft comes in spurts. Last March we got hit hard by a ring of professionals. Occasionally, a maid will take something but this occurs very infrequently.

Control is the name of the game—control over keys, cash, and clerks. Control is the backbone of successful operations and cannot be underestimated in its value to the total operation. All personnel need to understand the reason for controls, not to feel as if they are being spied upon. Control is present in everything we do. For example, we control liquor with a par stock concept. There are a specific number of bottles of each brand of liquor. Each day the bartender turns in his empties and gets full bottles in return.

The audit control system is designed by company headquarters. This is only a paper control system of goals and standards. Exercise of control and the refinement of controls must be suited to the local situation.

Q. TO WHAT EXTENT ARE EMPLOYEES MADE FINANCIALLY RESPONSIBLE FOR THEIR ACTIONS?

A. Imperial has a policy of not holding employees responsible for their financial losses. Waitresses are not held responsible for missing checks and "walk outs." We have controls to know if these incidents occur. Every day I get an analysis of shortages and overages for each handler of cash. I chart these results and look for patterns. For the first 20 days of January we were $.67 out of balance.

We also have a reset reading on our registers. I keep a pattern of readings. This prevents a bartender from working two hours, clearing the machines, pocketing the receipts, and starting over.

If we find a pattern of shortage, we first issue a verbal warning (we note this warning in the employee's folder). If the behavior continues we issue a written warning which usually carries a three-day suspension. The final action is termination. We have no formal appeal procedures. The employee can write to the personnel department or the industrial relations department if he has a complaint.

Q. ARE STANDARDS OF COST EFFECTIVENESS DETERMINED AT COMPANY HEADQUARTERS OR ARE MEASURES SUCH AS COST OF GOODS SOLD PERCENTAGES PECULIAR TO YOUR LOCATION AND NATURE OF OPERATIONS?

A. Standards are set at headquarters, but they are flexible for different locations. Everything is related to the bottom line. If you are making money, standards are not as critical as when you are losing money.

Management

Q. AS MANAGER, I ASSUME YOU WEAR MANY "HATS." COULD YOU GIVE US A ROUGH IDEA OF WHAT PERCENTAGE OF YOUR TIME IS SPENT IN KEY AREAS; I.E., CUSTOMER RELATIONS, PERSONNEL ADMINISTRATION, COMPANY REPORTS, AND CORRESPONDENCE, ETC.?

A. In the smaller properties (less than 200 rooms), the manager wears many hats. He must be a "doer" as well as an administrator. In high-rise properties such as ours the manager spends 95% of his time administering, supervising, coordinating, analyzing, and conferring and 5% of his time as a "doer." I love the front desk and spend a good bit of time behind it. I enjoy checking people in and meeting people. I spend a lot of time out of the office, seeing and being seen. On my rounds, I make notations of things to be corrected. Glaring errors are corrected immediately; others are noted in executive meetings. We try to give as much responsibility as possible down the executive pyramid.

We have an open door policy, but my first question to an employee will be, "Have you talked to your immediate superior?" If he answers yes, I will bring in the superior and let him hear our conversation. My staff member may be completely in the wrong, but I won't admit this to the employee. After the employee leaves, I'll give the supervisor hell. I do this in order to maintain respect for management. You cannot undermine your management. All reports to headquarters cross my desk for perusal and approval although they are all prepared by my staff. The controller and I must sign all checks.

Q. WHAT QUESTIONS AND DECISIONS MUST YOU DEAL WITH MOST FREQUENTLY?

A. This is a difficult question. I don't think that you can say that I deal mainly with thus and so. Very seldom do I have any idea in the morning what I am going to be doing during the day. No two days are alike. Most of my decisions concern cost control and the handling of personnel.

I look at the "summary sheet" every day. I know where every penny of revenue came from and I know my costs for each department. I know my daily averages and my record to date for this accounting period. This sheet gives me the opportunity to review daily the performance of each of my managers. This information is fed to the computer at headquarters and we get summary reports periodically.

We also receive feedback about letters written by our guests. Every week a newsletter is issued from headquarters listing the 25 hotels receiving the most complaints.

Q. WHAT CRITERIA ARE USED BY THE COMPANY TO EVALUATE YOU AS A MANAGER?

A. Every manager is evaluated by his district supervisor quarterly. One evaluation each year is used to recommend salary levels. We are periodically visited by the district supervisor.

The annual audit checks most everything. We passed our most recent for the first time since the hotel has been in operation. We were just inspected on cleanliness and appearance standards and got a 961 out of 1,000 on the room side and a 950 out of 1,000 on the food and beverage side. These numbers fall in the excellent range. We have achieved this rating on four consecutive inspections. Another thing that is used a great deal in the evaluations is the reactions of the workforce toward management. Employee morale is an important factor in the satisfactory operation of any venture in which the public is involved. All of my employees with the exception of a few behind-the-scenes personnel, come into contact with the public. Even my accounting personnel are constantly being called about accounts; the kitchen helpers are about the only employees that don't see the public. Employee morale sets the tone of a hotel.

The quantitative measures for all hotels within a district are reported every two weeks. This forms a very competitive environment. I watch what the other hotels are doing, especially if I personally know the manager.

Q. TO WHAT DEGREE DO YOU FEEL YOU CONTROL REVENUE? EXPENSES?

A. We have almost complete control over our revenues. We have a centralized reservation service which accounts for about 25% of our occupants. We do promote to bring in the revenue. I have a sales representative who calls on major corporations, legal firms, insurance firms, etc. We encourage these firms to place their reservations through their service representative directly with us. We visit them; we have secretarial luncheons; we talk with administrators of hospitals. We have to sell. We control the amount of food and beverage sales by the quality of food and service we offer. The customers who come in through the reservation system will only be one-time customers if we louse things up. You cannot exist on one-time customers.

The reception that a customer receives upon arrival is very important. If we cannot find the reservation or give the wrong type of room, we make an impression that the cleanest room or finest steak will have trouble overcoming. By the same token, if the person receives a good friendly reception and is made to feel welcome, the steak can be a little tough and the customer may not notice it. It's a psychological game.

We have total control over expenses.

We are graded on progress more than performance. This hotel was an ungodly mess when we got here a year ago. If you were to use an absolute standard on our last audit, we were certainly below standard. However, the company recognizes handicaps. If they didn't, they would have tremendous problems with morale when a crew was working itself to death, making improvements, but getting no recognition.

Q. ARE THERE ANY RECENT DEVELOPMENTS IN THE LODGING INDUSTRY OR THE LOCAL COMMUNITY WHICH YOU FEEL WILL HAVE SIGNIFICANT IMPACT ON YOUR OPERATION?

A. Phase II will have an effect on our operation because our prices are frozen but those of our suppliers are not. This will require us to be better managers.

There are several new properties that will open shortly. It forces us to operate at top performance. A good, well-managed business does not have to suffer unduly from competition. However, if too many well-run operations inundate an area, all properties will suffer. This has happened in San Francisco. Usually, the "weak sisters" fall by the wayside.

Part II—Interviews with Staff Members

Marge Anderson (waitress): I have been at this location for three years and four months. I began working shortly before the opening of this hotel. Many of the original employees attended classes and watched movies during a two-week training period. I had previous experience. I worked for the downtown Albany Club and also did a lot of banquet work for the local union. I have been in the union for 25 years. I am a member of the union although this is a nonunion hotel. I pay $5.00 a month to stay in the union for insurance. I have worked at union hotels, but this place is really great. I love it here.

The work here at the Coffee Shop is different for me. I never had worked mornings before. When I started working here, I was upstairs in the restaurant. When they opened the Coffee Shop, they asked me to come down for two weeks. It was a challenge to get accustomed to these hours, but I like the work down here. I help train new waitresses. I like to help new girls learn their jobs, but I do not want a title of supervisor. I am very satisfied to be a waitress.

Our waitress turnover in the coffee shop is much lower than in the restaurant upstairs. The Coffee Shop does a better business during the day than the formal dining room. We offer a nice luncheon. Judges, members of the House of Representatives, and jurors eat here.

I love people. When I worked at the Albany Club, I met the Rockefellers, was Senator Javits's personal waitress, and was interviewed on a local television show, Dateline Albany.

The money is excellent; I never have any complaints. There is not a waitress or cab driver in the world who reports his full income. I could tell you the exact amount but the girls would be on the spot because of the IRS. If a Howard Hughes had a $10.00 ticket, he would leave a $1.50 tip. However, a traveler on vacation with his family for two weeks is uncertain about how much to tip and might leave a $3.00 tip on a $10.00, especially if you have been good with his children. I cater to the children first and to the parents second. Your tip is for services rendered. I prize it. In comparison to the Albany Club, the Coffee Shop has a much faster customer turnover. It means that I have to run a little more (they call me Fleetfoot), especially since my station is the furthest from the kitchen.

At the Albany Club, the chef was number one and the club manager was number two. That was all the management. We all felt a part of the business. We all helped when there was a crunch. It is a different situation here. There are many bosses—the grill chef, the food and beverage man, and the hotel manager. If I have a complaint, I must go up the line of authority.

Every supervisor tries to do a better job than the last one. They have to be careful and do a good job with controls. If a worker takes only three rolls, three pats of butter, or three teabags a day, the supervisor has to get rid of him because this behavior is going to show up eventually in the percentages. Controls are used to pinpoint items that are going out illegally.

We are a happy group. People often come in early because they like their jobs. We often have coffee together. Our managers are just great. Mr. Fontano, our manager, is the man we go to when we think that we are not getting a square deal from the others.

We have meetings each week. Sometimes they show movies on how to dress, what color slip to wear, how to wear your hair and makeup. They also show you how to approach a customer. When a guest comes in, you don't get overfriendly, just friendly enough to make the guest feel at ease.

We are required to have a physical by a state doctor. Anybody who handles food needs an examination. We had a couple of waitresses last summer—college girls—who probably should not have been serving food. This type of girl is out on the town half the night and talks about it. They don't care who they are with. After a couple of weeks, they were coming in late every day. Mr. Fontano realized this and fired them. This is why I like Mr. Fontano. He knows the way things should be done. He's the best manager we've had.

Shirley Thompson (Executive Housekeeper): In regards to my success as a housekeeper, I have to give credit to my people. I did not make it on my own. It's a case of having a strong leader and having the people automatically following one boss and only one boss. My help will do all kinds of extras because they know that I will never ask them to do something I would not do myself. The rules are plain and simple, but everything is aboveboard. If I have something to say, I am woman enough to go to them and tell them exactly how I feel. I also find time to tell them thank you for a job well done. I try to make them feel very important and very much needed but not indispensable.

The maids are trained by other experienced maids. I found that, when I train them myself, they are very uncomfortable with me because I am a perfectionist. The first time around they are very nervous. I try to pair them with people who have compatible personalities.

We cooperate with each other on our language problem. Twenty-five percent of our maids are from non-English-speaking countries, but they all understand some English, because they must be able to communicate with guests. Most of my people are high school graduates. Some have college degrees. Many employees are from the islands, especially Barbados and Jamaica. They are very enjoyable, very pleasant, and take to maid work with little difficulty.

I came here as the assistant housekeeper. After seven months, I took over as housekeeper. I did not have any previous experience as a housekeeper. I am self-taught and use a lot of common sense. I have to think about five steps ahead. I have been in the Marines and the military training teaches you to give and take orders. You learn to think ahead and be a good organizer. My courses in psychology were very helpful. I recognize the importance of every employee. I talk to each as an individual. I do not believe in mass meetings. As a result, they give me more than 100% cooperation.

I try to get my help to feel as if they are running

the whole hotel. They see the housekeeping department as the heart of the hotel. You can have the best desk clerk, the best manager, etc., but unless you have a nice clean place with rooms that are available when the guests want them, they are not going to return to this hotel. This is not a resort so you don't have glamorous things. You have plain simple things, but cleanliness is important.

I have 45 people on my payroll: 15 housemen, 3 inspectresses, 2 laundry girls, and 2 housewomen. I don't work with an assistant. I work a 10-hour day for six days a week although I'm only paid for 40. I care about my job and my people. I want to be fair to the company and myself. I know where my weaker girls are. I spot check more on those floors. I check 30–35 rooms a day. I look at more occupied rooms than check-outs. I want the guest who is paying $20/day to have just as clean a room on his second day as he did on his first. I also check by phone with a room that refuses service. This prevents a maid from skipping a room and saying that the room did not want service. I take a special interest in those guests who stay for an extended period. I get them a refrigerator, extra glasses, etc.

The housekeeper report is completed each morning in duplicate. One copy goes to headquarters; the other stays here. Every room in the hotel is included on the report.

James Roi (night chef): I do not have a title although it is probably night chef. I have been here for four months. I prepare food in the afternoon and cook at night. We produce everything to order. The most important thing is being prepared. When things get busy, you have to be prepared to handle things. A little dirt on the grill won't keep you from feeding customers.

Kitchen work is easy to learn. It doesn't require much thinking or hard work. Most of the people are not serious about the job. This leads to a large turnover. Training is on the job. The same basics are used in all kitchens. You need to gain working experience. If you come out of a school, you've just got theory. It is much different to get on the line and fall behind with the orders. You must be organized.

I came here from New York City. I'm going back to school next fall. I needed a job to support myself and to save some money. I have traveled a lot and have worked in kitchens most of the time. When I start school, I will continue to work on a limited schedule.

Because I have a lot of experience, the preparation chef leaves me a list and I get it done. If he tells me the nature of what he wants, I can do it. But I'm learning all the time by working with different chefs. I have a supervisory role when the chef is not here. The younger boys have to be supervised. The supervisor makes sure that the work is coming out all right. Some people have to be watched all the time if you want to get things done. I always try to do something extra each night, like cleaning the range. I try to minimize customer complaints by making sure that the food looks good going out and of adequate portions. Not much of the food is preportioned like at a Howard Johnson. We portion it ourselves rather than have it come prepackaged.

This is a nice place to work. I have gotten a raise just recently. I never have had a complaint.

Part III—A Day in the Life of a Hotel Manager (July 18, 1972)

Meeting of Executive Staff

In the morning, Mr. Fontano called a meeting of his executive staff, which included:

Roger Filmore—Sales Representative
Joseph Pink—Engineer
Ivan Galik—Assistant Manager
Larry Siegal—Director of Food and Beverages
Grant Leigh—Auditor/Controller
Shirley Thompson—Executive Housekeeper

During the meeting he went over directives from headquarters. He discussed the "austerity program" recently put into effect. According to this new policy, no personnel can be hired, fired, or replaced, and no major purchases can be made without the approval of the manager. He informed the staff that the deadlines on requests for capital expenditures had been pushed up and asked each department head to examine his needs for the coming year so that he could prepare and submit a statement of his expenditure requirements to Mr. Fontano. Mr. Fontano reminded them of the high ratings they received on the most recent inspection (960 for the restaurant, 965 for the hotel) and while congratulating them on their good scores reminded them that "every effort should be made to bring them up for the next inspection."

Several staff members suggested possible improvements (the engineer suggested putting in new carpeting on the pool porch). The group discussed possible changes that would make their work easier. Mr. Fontano called their attention to various details (such as the overly bright light bulbs in the lounge) which should be attended to. He encouraged them by notifying them of expenditure requests that had been granted. He warned them that two of the governor's aides would be coming to inspect the VIP suites. His approach was firm and direct, but always with a sense of humor. He used casual (sometimes corny) terms with them and made them feel at ease. He finished by saying "Hang in there tight and finish out the year as you have so far."

Meeting with Inspectresses

He called a meeting of his four inspectresses (one of whom is the daughter of his executive housekeeper) because his spot check of two rooms showed a dissatisfactory level of cleanliness, which the inspectresses should have reported. Although he knew which of the girls was responsible (because he knew under whose jurisdiction each room fell) he did not isolate the offender; he let them know it didn't matter whose room it was because they were all responsible for keeping up standards of quality. He warned them to be stricter and sterner with the maids they supervise and not just remember when they were maids themselves and be easy going and sympathetic. "You must let the girls know when something is wrong," he said, "and be more disciplined." He was firm with them but not sharp and made them feel that while their job was very important no individual was indispensable. "If you're going to be door openers," he said, "then we will pay you to be door openers." (That is, he warned them that he would pay a salary in accordance with their level of performance.) "If you have duties that interfere with performing your job well, let us know and we'll take care of it. We depend on you; support Mrs. Thompson, support the house." When they left he criticized the grooming of the girl whose room had failed inspection, and suggested that someone who was not neat in appearance couldn't be expected to take an interest in cleanliness. He also criticized the sulky attitude of the housekeeper's daughter. But he said: "They are much more important to me than I am to them. If I go away I have a competent staff to take over for me, but without them I couldn't function."

Hiring a New Chef

(Mr. Fontano's meeting with prospective chef, Jose Ortiz, and Food and Beverage Director, Larry Siegal.)

Having analyzed the market for low-cost food, family meals, and gourmet dining, Mr. Fontano was in the process of rearranging his facilities to better meet current local demand. The lower priced family-meal items were being moved to the coffee shop and the dining room fare was being upgraded. Headquarters sent a team of restaurant specialists to analyze the menu. They visited local restaurants and picked out successful items to incorporate in the new gourmet menu for the dining room. Before the prospective chef was called for an interview, a team from Imperial was sent to observe him at his current job. They analyzed exactly what duties he performed, how well he performed them, his strong points and overall effectiveness. Mr. Fontano was then in the process of deciding whether to lure him away from a competing chain.

Mr. Fontano explained that the outgoing chef had been irresponsible in supervising his staff and unable to cope with on-the-spot problems. He lacked leadership, left early (before preparation was completed), and left employees unsupervised. Moreover, 20 pounds of shrimp had been lost because he had failed to lock a refrigerator. He was the fourth chef Mr. Fontano had fired in a year (all of whom held the rank "sous-chef"). Mr. Fontano's experience told him that it was time to look for a higher level chef to act as executive chef. Mr. Fontano and his food and beverage man discussed the possibility of cutting back to one cook to save payroll costs, but decided that weekend business couldn't be handled by one man. Siegal proposed hiring a chef one rung lower and backing him up with a steward/supervisor to handle organization. But Mr. Fontano was convinced that they needed a chef with flair and creativity to build up the restaurant's reputation. Mr. Fontano emphasized the value of creating an attractive appearance "out front"; he hoped that flair and creativity would improve the restaurant's atmosphere. He was willing, therefore, to pay for presentation time in the kitchen—time to make things look good. Roast beef looks worth its price when surrounded by a bouquetier of vegetables. He told the chef that he was willing to support him on expenditures that would improve quality or atmosphere. "We want to look good," he said. "Increased efficiency and sales, improved employee morale and performance are worth expenditure. We don't want to be penny-wise and pound-foolish."

In considering Ortiz as a prospective executive chef, Mr. Fontano analyzed carefully his capacity for leadership, organization, responsibility, and active participation in getting things done, as well as his purchasing experience. He then made his expectations clear to Ortiz. He told Ortiz that the executive chef position was one of "total responsibility" and required a *working* chef who would be active in preparation. He made it clear that the chef must be responsible for every scrap of food from the moment it was ordered to the moment it was served and/or became garbage. He underlined the supervisory and control capacity of the executive chef and the chef's function of creating a *working* team through proper supervision. He pointed out that he didn't want a theoretical chef, but someone who could prepare every menu—not just give instructions and assume they would be carried out. He reasserted the need for cost control—in purchasing, security, and utilization of wastes (such as converting leftovers into hors-d'oeuvres). He told the chef that the fat had been trimmed from the kitchen staff and he wanted the staff filled out again with careful consideration of where extra help was needed. Ortiz was encouraged to analyze the work schedule and each individual's productivity, and discouraged from adding employees where he could do something himself. Mr. Fontano continually stressed the importance of keeping payroll down.

Mr. Fontano was worried about impressing upon the chef the importance of the Coffee Shop and his responsibility for its operation. He explained to Ortiz that the Coffee Shop was the "bread and butter" which would support the gourmet operation for awhile. Earnings must take priority over glamour. Mr. Fontano recognized the need for a strong person to pull together both operations (the Coffee Shop and the restaurant).

Because Mr. Fontano was concerned about whether the kitchen would pass inspection (by Imperial standards), he was particularly impressed with the chef's clean-cut appearance and his insistence on cleanliness. The chef complained that he could not work in a dirty kitchen and that Mr. Fontano couldn't expect good work if the facilities were inadequate. Siegal and Mr. Fontano planned to prepare a clean kitchen for the chef's arrival so he would see what standards they wanted him to keep up. Siegal said to the chef: "They all hate the person who gives the orders, so before you come in I'll take care of giving the orders to clean things up." Mr. Fontano was also impressed with the chef's belief that investment in people counts. The chef said he didn't like to fire when he could teach or train. Mr. Fontano agreed that employees of some duration are an investment that should be realized and believed that Ortiz was worth more money because he recognized the cost of turnover. Mr. Fontano was also pleased by Ortiz's emphasis on fast service and his plans for rearranging facilities like waitress pick-up stations to expedite service. Mr. Fontano assured him that a door could be moved in two hours if necessary to make the restaurant function more efficiently.

In persuading Ortiz to join the hotel staff, Mr. Fontano emphasized the company benefits. Mr. Fontano's competitive bargaining for the chef was hampered because both the price freeze and company policy prevented him from meeting the chef's salary request. However, he succeeded in hiring the chef at five-sixths of the competitor's offer by promising two 90-day reviews based on productivity with the possibility of salary increases at each and by stressing the advantages of profit sharing increasing the value of his salary.

"We'd like to have you," Mr. Fontano told the chef. "We're enthusiastic about your joining us. It's nice to know you're wanted. You can do the job. I know you would be happy working here. You will have total support of management. We want our chef to be happy and satisfied. You can be sure of 100% support from me."

"I will do my best to stay with this chain," said Ortiz.

The fact that Ortiz is Puerto Rican increased Mr. Fontano's interest in hiring him, because Mr. Fontano had faced two discriminatory employment cases in the previous year. As Mr. Fontano pointed out, recent legislation against discrimination has made management a more difficult task.

Meeting with District Director

Mr. Fontano discussed with W. E. LaPerch, district director, issues they wanted to cover in the upcoming district meeting. LaPerch asked Mr. Fontano to explain some innovative aspects of his room-selling policy at the meeting. As LaPerch pointed out, "If you don't sell a room today, you can't store it and sell it tomorrow—if a room lies vacant for a night its revenue is lost." Like a highly perishable commodity, room space must be sold within 24 hours. To make sure that no room lies vacant because of carelessness, Mr. Fontano insists on a careful housekeeping check every day. To make sure that every room that a guest has checked out of is registered as vacant, a vacancy list is made up and each room is rechecked for occupancy; more important, every room recorded as "occupied" is double-checked for the possibility of an unknown vacancy. The hectic pace behind the desk often leads to errors and this double-check on room status avoids wasted revenue. Because Mr. Fontano has found that so-called "guaranteed" reservations are very rarely paid for when the guest does not show, he finds it far more profitable to sell off the reserved rooms starting about 10:00 o'clock at night. If the guest does arrive and finds his room rented there is often loud and obnoxious complaint, some of which is passed on to headquarters. However, given the odds of collecting on unoccupied guaranteed reservations, holding them indefinitely would seem unwise. A long hard day of traveling often brings out the worst in the guest's temperament and Mr. Fontano makes efforts to train his desk staff to deal with such complaints. However, they have reciprocal arrangements with local operations of other chains to take in overflow patrons when room is available. The Hilton, for example, takes Imperial patrons who are turned away.

Although you can't sell today's space tomorrow, you can sometimes sell it twice today. Rooms rented for day-time activities and vacated in the evening are cleaned by the housekeeping staff—which stays on duty until 9:00 P.M.—and resold that night. Double-selling helps cover complimentary rooms and sometimes brings the occupancy rate up over 100%. The hotel is also equipped with a number of specialized dual-purpose rooms which can act as meeting rooms during the day and bedrooms at night. The "Bennett" bed (which looks like an attractive standard double bed) can be raised or lowered in seconds and the furniture rolled in and out of the closet by a single maid. This system also increases the per-room revenue.

Just filling every room is not sufficient. Every room should be filled with a *paying* customer. Before Mr. Fontano took over there had been a rash of 75 walk-outs. Even a vacant room is preferable to a walk-out. So Mr. Fontano tightened screening techniques at the desk. He personally trains desk clerks to spot "walk-out" types when they check in; using the tactful phrase "And how will you be settling your account?" They require prepayment from prospective walk-outs. A list of suspected walk-outs is posted behind the desk so that all transactions can be watched and all services (even in the bar) paid for in cash. Using what he calls the "eyeball" screening technique, Mr. Fontano has cut walk-outs to a negligible level.

Ideally, Mr. Fontano strives for not only the highest possible occupancy rate for the whole operation, but the maximum occupancy per room, because the room rates increase according to number of occupants. The fact that all rooms are equipped with double beds enables them to put four in one room (five with a cot) which significantly increases the revenue per room without any extra output on their part. Desk clerks are trained to look out for "stowaway" occupants who don't register and don't pay. Moreover, the "up-selling" technique, which Mr. Fontano has utilized with great success, entails giving precedence to families over couples and couples over singles. This often requires discretion and care on the part of the desk staff—especially in the case of simultaneous walk-ins. When a vacancy exists a couple may be turned away in hopes that a family will turn up. Obviously, turning away a patron means running the risk of a vacancy. When family business is running high it is a safe gamble; at other times it requires quick thinking on the part of desk clerks. Fortunately, there is rarely opportunity for guests accepted and guests turned away to compare notes. Mr. Fontano maintains, however, a policy of not turning away the old and the sick, even if they are traveling alone. The company policy against selling blocks of rooms at a discount has proved successful in hotels like Mr. Fontano's where careful management keeps room occupancy high. A group of 100 called to ask if they could have rooms over Labor Day weekend. Mr. Fontano consulted the statistics on Labor Day from last year, discovered that he had a full house, and turned down the request by saying, "No way." Presumably he would do so even if they did not request a discount because it would interefer with returning patrons and turn away the flow of everyday business. Mr. Fontano's constant awareness of weekly and seasonal patterns of guest flow enables him to make successful on-the-spot decisions. He carefully follows and analyzes the statistics computerized and sent back from headquarters. He is always looking for ways to make a room more desirable. For instance, he has invited the governor of New York to inaugurate the VIP suites with a complimentary visit. Afterwards, the door to the suite will bear the New York State seal. Mr. Fontano's recognition of the uniqueness of the guest-host relationship enables him to strike a good balance between courtesy and profitability.

Daily Inspection

Mr. Fontano is very strict on cleanliness and maintains a rigid policy of never allowing a guest to enter a room until it has been completely cleaned and passed inspection. Guests are not even permitted to drop their suitcases off in rooms or wash up unless the housekeeper is satisfied that the room has been thoroughly cleaned. This policy causes complaint from guests, but enables Mr. Fontano to maintain high standards of cleanliness. He is also very strict on maintenance of the facilities and insists that everything be in good repair at all times. He personally inspects 2 to 4 rooms per day. His inspection includes testing the inside of the toilet bowl with a Kleenex, making sure the television works properly and is turned toward the beds, checking vents to see that sufficient air is coming in, running his finger across hanger rack to check for dust (as well as inside lampshade, behind curtains, etc.). In one room he pointed out that the drapes were opened a few inches too much. "Don't we have any standards on this?" he asked the housekeeper, who replied that there was, in fact, an exact point to which the drapes were supposed to be opened, based on letting in the right amount of light and maintaining a symmetrical appearance from the outside. Mr. Fontano personally picks up scraps of paper and bits of lint off the carpets. He rarely enters an elevator without passing his hand over the air conditioner on the way in to make sure it is operating well. He criticized, in particular, the way maids opened the doors to maintenance closets because their carts were causing scratches in the paint which not only detracted from the hotel's appearance but raised painting costs.

Routine Incidents with Employees

—A staff member came in to ask his opinion on some detail of the operation and he said, "Do whatever you want, I'm not that dogmatic about it."

—Housekeeper: "All the girls in the coffee shop are taking off those heavy uniforms and using the rented ones."

Mr. Fontano: "It's all right, I don't blame them."

—He called in the recently dismissed chef and started out by informing him of a new opening that had become available in another hotel chain. He encouraged the chef to apply for the open position and checked into his progress in finding a new job. He informed the chef of his termination date by saying "The new chef will be coming in about August 1 so let's look ahead to that as the turnover time." (He seems to make a special effort to balance the positive and negative content of his dealings with employees.)

—He took the time to explain personally driving instructions to the incoming chef and drew him a map of the area. He also discussed with the new chef personal problems such as the chef's wife's relationship with her parents, the problems of separating with them, and her problems in finding a new job.

—Restaurant employees are supposed to sign their full name on a list to collect their tips. When a busboy named Ed persisted in signing only his first name, Mr. Fontano went in and signed "Ed" and collected Ed's tips himself.

—Mr. Fontano created a job for a seniority (3½ year) employee who could not continue her shift as waitress in the coffee shop because of a sick mother.

—He stopped to speak with a young Oriental employee who works as a busboy in the dining room.

"Hello, Billy. You've been sick the last couple of days, haven't you?"

"Yes, sir, three days I was sick."

"You were out last night again, weren't you?"

(He spoke to him in a gentle voice but conveyed the fact that he was well aware of the absences and displeased. He seems to know the exact absentee situation on an individual day-to-day basis.)

—When a secretary answered the phone in a routine way he reminded her that she was "getting like a broken record." (He is always looking for ways to weed out apathy and complacency).

—Mr. Fontano called in an employee from Jamaica who had, a few days earlier, called in and said he couldn't come to work because he had something else to do. Mr. Fontano told him that while that might be sufficient reason to stay home in his own country it wasn't acceptable in a large American outfit like Imperial. (He takes the employees' background into consideration when dealing with them.)

—When routine payroll forms were brought in for signature, he discussed personal problems of employees and inquired about how they were doing.

—When he called in the engineer he started out by saying, "Hi, Joe, just two or three little items right quick," then proceeded to give him a detailed list of minor problems—number of hangers in each room must be surveyed (some rooms found to have fewer than the set standard of eight); air conditioner "Hotter 'n' a depot stove"; air vents not operating, etc.

—The housekeeper reported that she had discovered a drapery cleaning firm which was willing to clean the drapes at 50% less than the current service. Mr. Fontano praised her discovery and said, "I'm always interested in saving 50%."

Part IV—The Management Style of William Fontano

Mr. Fontano knows the first and last name and personal background of every employee, and takes time in his everyday rounds to stop and speak with a few of them, no matter how obscure the corner in which they work. He eats most of his meals in the restaurants on the premises and speaks on a friendly basis with the waitresses. He seems able to talk on the same level with any employee, and uses many casual and slang expressions to make them feel at ease. He appears to encourage discussion rather than automatic acceptance of his orders. With his food and beverage man, the discussion is a lively give and take. They play devil's advocate with each other and try to poke holes in each other's arguments. (The 23-year old food and beverage man actually trained Mr. Fontano in that line of business, though Mr. Fontano is now his supervisor.) Mr. Fontano seems to have consciously toned down the sterility of his office by decorating it with personal effects and covering the walls with certificates of merit, employee and hotel awards, and pictures of ceremonial occasions. From hiring to firing, he carefully considers the personality of each employee and believes a positive attitude is an essential attribute of a good employee. He seems quite willing to listen to suggestions offered by his staff. He makes a point of showing willingness to do every job himself and of making his on-the-job familiarity with every aspect of the operation known to his staff. On his rounds, he frequently steps into the task he is observing—answering room service, working as a desk clerk, etc. Aside from his work as business manager for the Presbyterian church and as a missionary, he has worked in every aspect of the business—as a desk clerk, accountant, pot and pan scrubber, grillman, bartender, broiler man, waiter and maitre d'. During his training he worked two shifts in two different jobs with a nap in between. The staff never knows when he will be coming around to supervise their work. His main tactic in keeping up quality is to set a good example.

While Mr. Fontano praises excellence in performance he does not accept complacency. Mr. Fontano referred to his staff as his "high-salaried employees"—presumably to remind them to maintain compatibility between payroll and productivity. Although he refers to them as his "executive" staff he makes sure that they view their role as actively participating in getting things done rather than just giving orders. He encourages employees to think for themselves. When consulted about something he often says, "Does that sound reasonable?"

Mr. Fontano believes that the attitude of the manager extends down through the entire staff. He operates on the principle "You don't demand respect, you command it." He stresses the point that employees must have confidence in their supervisor to perform well. He is highly conscious of the "service" capacity of his operation and believes there is no room for temperamental personalities in hotel work. (He carefully schedules a team of even-tempered personalities for high-abuse periods such as the night shift at the desk.) He tolerates no rudeness or flippancy with guests. He tries to straighten out interpersonal conflicts right away before they build up out of proportion. He maintains an "open door" policy, but encourages employees to express their grievances directly to the person concerned. The complaint process is structured as a hierarchy and employees are discouraged from going over their immediate supervisor's head before they have settled conflicts directly between themselves. Even after the problem has been brought to him he tries to persuade employees to call in the person they are complaining about and talk it over together. He believes that he has a great advantage in employee relations because he is so visible and well known (accessible) to his whole staff—a fringe benefit of being in a "people" business. He has a dual "people" role—towards both guests and staff and has the opportunity to talk to and participate with both. He tries to maintain flat policies, rather than an inconsistent mixture of yes's and no's, to minimize confusion and ambiguity. He uses many different tactics to instill incentive, from personal praise to salary increases. He tries to make his staff self-reliant; when he's off duty, even though he's available and on the premises, he leaves even emergencies (such as suicide attempts) to the staff on duty—thereby showing trust in their competence. He wants maximum productivity out of all of his people and lets them know it.

In hiring a new chef he stressed the importance of becoming a member of the corporation. "It's a tremendous corporation," he said, after he had outlined employee benefits. The secret to realizing benefits he says is "the longer you stay, the more they become." He emphasized the fact that employees retain all rights of seniority in transferring to other Imperial properties. He offered to pay for the chef's moving expenses (because the competitor had) although it is not routinely done for chefs. Similarly, he offered to put the chef up at the hotel for two or three weeks until he got settled. "When we have a good employee and we know he's going to stay with us we can make exceptions from company policy on benefits." He covered himself, however, by arranging that moving expenses be reimbursed only after the chef had been employed for six months. He encourages loyalty to the company but the nature of the business itself entails transient status for employees. It has been remarked that Imperial changes managers "faster than it changes sheets." For this reason, he provided the chef with a letter of agreement so that Mr. Fontano's successor would follow through should Mr. Fontano be called elsewhere. He makes sure he is geared up for changeover, however sudden. He is proud of the fact that most of his staff worked their way up through the company—the executive housekeeper gained her experience in the operation before she took over; the food and beverage man started out as a busboy in the bar and moved up quickly, etc. He takes an amusing view of "Cornell graduates" and the like who lack valuable on-the-job experience and the ability to apply their knowledge practically.

World Team Tennis, Inc.[1]

At the July 1976 World Team Tennis (WTT) directors meeting, Mr. John Prince, president of the three-year-old professional tennis league, announced the league's intention to expand from ten to twelve teams for the 1977 playing season. The league had begun operations in 1974 with 16 teams, but through a series of conservative financial requirements had eliminated six of the weaker franchises prior to the 1975 season.

Mr. Gerald Lennox, president and owner of the Phoenix Racquets, a World Team Tennis franchise, was designated chairman of the expansion committee. With the completion of the 1976 season and the receipt of several applications from groups interested in purchasing franchises for the 1977 and 1978 seasons, issues regarding the proposed expansion became more immediate. First, Mr. Lennox felt that the expansion committee should establish a price of $1 million for an expansion team. Second, he wanted to insure that new teams were capable of running a franchise in a way that would enhance the league. This meant signing big name players and capably promoting ticket sales. His Racquets had sold 3,250 season tickets and averaged 6,800 in attendance per match during 1976 with Chris Evert as their female singles star. Lennox realized also that a successful franchise needed capitalization and a willingness on the part of its management to work. A third concern was to expand in a city (or cities) which provided prime national television markets. In this regard a Chicago franchise was considered critical. Fourth, Lennox was concerned with the negative financial and public relations repercussions if the league did not expand after making the announcement. He personally realized the need for star players and wondered if two expansion teams could possible acquire these players without diluting other clubs. Finally, Lennox wondered if the short-term benefits from the two new teams might not preclude long-term gains from selling franchises for $3 million in 1978 and 1979.

In making his recommendation, Lennox considered suggesting that one of the expansion groups consolidate with an existing team. While no specific financial information other than published attendance reports was generally available, it was common knowledge that at least two if not three of the current clubs were having financial difficulty (see Exhibit 1 for attendance reports). Lennox wondered what

---

[1] Names of persons and certain data have been disguised.

This case was prepared by John N. Korff, under the supervision of Professor James L. Heskett, as the basis for class discussion rather than to illustrate either effective or ineffective handling of an administrative situation.

Exhibit 1

WORLD TEAM TENNIS, INC.
Attendance Records 1974 through 1976[1]

Team	*1976 Home Total*	*1976 Away Total*	*1975 Home Total*	*1974 Home Total*
Phoenix	148,539	140,447	80,140	—
Los Angeles	103,376	75,417	28,970	38,807
Pittsburgh	102,617	85,145	82,270	66,270
Golden Gaters	87,212	67,857	47,345	54,080
New York	74,843	90,224	65,894	63,121
San Diego	74,620	80,439	22,274	—
Cleveland	71,425	77,307	55,924	48,887
Hawaii	67,450	105,976	56,470	32,191
Boston	72,170	71,146	35,789	56,404
Indiana	48,639	62,186	33,782	—
Teams not in League After 1974				
Baltimore	—	—	—	40,472
Chicago	—	—	—	30,840
Denver	—	—	—	44,286
Detroit	—	—	—	·48,978
Houston	—	—	—	38,366
Florida	—	—	—	44,227
Minnesota	—	—	—	62,165
Philadelphia	—	—	—	92,364
Toronto-Buffalo	—	—	—	72,508
Yearly Total	856,144	856,144	508,858	833,966
Per Game Total	3,909	3,909	3,083	2,369

[1] The attendance figures were submitted by the individual teams with box office certification. It is doubtful if the first year reports are all paid. Records show, however, that 3rd-year reports are paid sales. Selected figures in this exhibit have been disguised.

the league's obligation was to provide additional support for its current ten teams before expanding. He considered the option of the league not expanding until the ten teams were all on solid ground. He knew that the young league was only as strong as its weakest franchise and that expansion without a solid base had destroyed other sports leagues in the past. He realized, however, that the positive "press" resulting from the sale of an expansion club would help all teams.

World Team Tennis

In 1976, World Team Tennis was a ten-team professional sports league with five teams in the western division and five teams in the eastern division. Each team played 22 matches in its home city and 22 matches on the road during the May through August season. The champions of each division met at the end of the season with the first team winning three games in the series declared the league champion.

World Team Tennis was a revolutionary concept in pro sports. It provided the first real opportunity for men and women to participate equally on a professional team. Each match consisted of five sets: men's and ladies' singles, men's and ladies' doubles, and mixed doubles. Scoring was cumulative, with the team winning the most games in all five sets winning the match.

The league, WTT, Inc., was a nonprofit organization established only to administer interteam playing affairs. World Team Tennis Properties (WTTP) was established to handle the league's sales, marketing and promotional efforts. Each team held an equal share in the profits of properties. This income included television and endorsements (at the league level) and was the cornerstone of financial success in professional football, basketball and baseball franchises. It was generally agreed, however, that only through successful franchise operations could WTTP be successful.

A major source of properties income came from the sale of expansion franchises. This income (net of expenses and finders fees) was included in the general properties pool distributed equally among the existing franchises at the close of the fiscal year. Expansion income could equal all other properties money in a given year.

WTT was formed in 1973 by four men active in pro sports. The league got off to a shaky start during a time when new leagues were in fashion. New basketball, football, and hockey leagues began to play in the late 1960s, but soon showed signs of impending failure due to the tremendous cash flow burdens typical of these sports. Promoting and selling a new league even in an established sport was not as easy as the founders had thought.

The original 16 owners operated franchises during the 1974 season. While WTT was the first professional sports league to have all original franchises start and finish the season in the same cities, several of the clubs closed operations in August 1974 and left outstanding debts to players and suppliers. Specific financial information was not available to Lennox, because most owners refused to share either the details of their personal finances or the specifics of their team losses. In order to prune out weak franchises, the league required that each franchise post a $100,000 letter of credit prior to the 1975 season which could be activated if a team was in default on a player salary, failed to appear for a match, or failed to pay a league assessment. The requirement was enough to force six teams to cease operations and two teams to change ownership (see Exhibit 1).

By 1976, 15 of the top 16 women and 8 of the top 16 men players in the world played WTT, as shown in Exhibit 2. Newspapers in cities in which franchises were located provided coverage of each match. In addition many other newspapers carried reports of scores and league standings on a daily basis (see Exhibit 3).

Players. The major competition for WTT players came from the European and American summer tournament tours. The earnings accruing to players from those tournaments gave WTT owners a basis from which to establish contract offers. In addition, by providing another viable means of income, the tournaments precluded antitrust action against WTT as was occurring in other sports leagues. Players gener-

Exhibit 2

WORLD TEAM TENNIS, INC.
World Rankings of Tennis Players and WTT Team Affiliations, Inc.

	Ladies' Singles			*Men's Singles*	
Ranking	*Name*	*WTT Team*	*Ranking*	*Name*	*WTT Team*
1	Evert	Phoenix	1	Ashe	None
2	Goolagong	Pittsburgh	2	Conners	None
3	King	New York	3	Vilas	None
4	Navratilova	Cleveland	4	Nastase	Hawaii
5	Wade	New York	5	Borg	None
6	Casals	Los Angeles	6	Orantes	None
7	Court	Hawaii	7	Ramirez	None
8	Reid	Boston	8	Okker	San Francisco
9	Gunter	Hawaii	9	Solomon	None
10	Stove	San Francisco	10	Laver	San Diego
11	Fromholtz	Los Angeles	11	Tanner	None
12	Morozova	None	12	Alexander	Boston
13	Durr	San Francisco	13	Reissen	Cleveland
14	Barker	None	14	Dibbs	None
15	Holliday	San Diego	15	Lutz	Los Angeles
16	Overton	Cleveland	16	Gottfried	None
17	Anthony	None	17	V. Amritraj	Los Angeles
18	Meyer	Indiana	18	Cox	Pittsburgh
19	Teeguarden	Boston	19	Smith	None
20	Stevens	Boston	20	Stockton	None
	Ladies' Doubles			*Men's Doubles*	
1	Casals	Los Angeles	1	Lutz	Los Angeles
1	King	New York	1	Smith	None
2	Kiyomura	Indiana	2	McMillan	San Francisco
2	Schallau	Indiana	2	Hewitt	None[1]
3	Goolagong	Pittsburgh	3	Okker	San Francisco
3	Michel	Pittsburgh	3	Reissen	Cleveland
4	Stove	San Francisco	4	Roche	Phoenix
4	Durr	San Francisco	4	Newcombe	None
5	Wade	New York	5	Case	San Diego
5	Navratilova	Cleveland	5	Masters	None
6	Teeguarden	Boston	6	Alexander	Boston
6	Newbury	None	6	Dent	New York
			7	Drysdale	San Diego
			7	Laver	San Diego
			8	V. Amritraj	Los Angeles
			8	A. Amritraj	None
			9	Cox	Pittsburgh
			9	Taylor	None

[1] Signed with Boston.

Exhibit 2 (continued)

ACTIVE PLAYER ROSTER
(World Ranking in Parenthesis)

EASTERN DIVISION

Boston LOBSTERS

Kerry Melville Reid—Aus. (8–LS)
Greer "Cat" Stevens—S.A. (20–LS, 2–U21)
Pam Teeguarden—USA (19–LS, 5–LD)
John Alexander—Aus. (11–MS, 6–MD)
*Ion Tiriac—Rum.
Mike Estep—USA (11–MD)

New York SETS

Billie Jean King—USA (3–LS, 1–LD)
Virginia Wade—GB (5–LS, 6–LD)
Lindsy Bevan—GB
Sandy Mayer—USA (22–MS)
Phil Dent—Aus. (24–MS, 6–MD)
*Fred Stolle—Aus.

Cleveland NETS

Martina Navratilova—USA (4–LS, 6–LD)
Wendy Overton—USA (16–LS)
Rayni Fox—USA
*Marty Reissen—USA (12–MS, 3–MD)
Haroon Rahim—Pakistan (32–MS)
Bob Giltinan—Aus. (36–MS)

Pittsburgh TRIANGLES

Evonne Goolagong—Aus. (2–LS, 3–LD)
Peggy Michel—USA (3–LD)
Jo Ann Russel—USA
*Marc Cox—GB (17–MS, 10–MD)
Vitas Gerulaitis—USA (15–MS)
Bernie Mitton—Aus.

Indiana LOVES

Carrie Meyer—USA (18–LS)
Ann Kiyomura—USA (2–LD)
Mona Schallau—USA (2–LD)
*Allan Stone—Aus. (38–MS)
Ray Ruffels—Aus. (42–MS)
Syd Ball—Rus. (32–MS)

WESTERN DIVISION

Phoenix RACQUETS

Chris Evert—USA (1–LS)
Kristin Kemmer Shaw—USA (32–LS)
Stephanie Tolleson—USA (4–U21)
*Tony Roche—Aus. (14–MS, 4–MD)
Andrew Pattison—Rhodesia (24–MS)
Butch Waltz—USA (6–U21)

Los Angeles STRINGS

Rosie Casals—USA (6–LS, 1–LD)
Dianne Fromholtz—Aus. (11–LS)
Ann Hayden Jones—GB
Bob Lutz—USA (14–MS, 1–MD)
VJ Amritraj—India (16–MS, 9–MD)
*Dennis Ralston—USA

Golden GATERS

Betty Stove—Neth. (10–LS, 4–LD)
Francoise Durr—Fr. (12–LS, 4–LD)
Racquel Giscafre—Argentina
Tom Okker—Neth. (7–MS, 3–MD)
*Frew McMillan—S.A. (36–MS, 2–MD)
John Lucas—USA (1st pick in NBA, tennis All-American)

Hawaii LEIS

Margaret Court—Aus. (7–LS)
Nancy Gunter—USA
Helen Gourlay—Aus. (26–LS)
Ilie Nastase—Rumania (4–MS)
Owen Davidson—Aus.
*Butch Buchholz—USA

San Diego FRIARS

Terry Holliday—USA (15–LS)
Betty Ann Stuart—USA
Janet Young—Aus.
Rod Laver—Aus. (9–MS)
*Cliff Drysdale—S.A. (17–MS, 8–MD)
Ross Case—Aus. (26–MS, 5–MD)

KEY: U–21—under 21 years old
LS—ladies' singles
MS—men's singles
LD—ladies' doubles
MD—men's doubles (mixed doubles not included due to insufficient data)
* —player-coach

Exhibit 3

WORLD TEAM TENNIS, INC.
Example of Daily Newspaper Listing of World Team Tennis Standings[1]

SCOREBOARD

WTT Standings

East	*W*	*L*	*Pct.*	*GB*
New York	31	10	.756	—
Pittsburgh	22	20	.524	9½
Cleveland	19	22	.463	12
Indiana	18	24	.429	13½
BOSTON	17	24	.415	14
WEST				
Phoenix	30	11	.732	—
Golden Gaters	27	15	.643	3½
Los Angeles	19	22	.463	11
San Diego	12	29	.293	18
Hawaii	12	30	.286	18½

LAST NIGHT'S RESULTS

Phoenix 29	BOSTON 20
Los Angeles 22	San Diego 21

TONIGHT'S GAMES

BOSTON at Indiana
San Diego at Golden Gate
Cleveland at Pittsburgh
Phoenix at New York
Hawaii at Los Angeles

LOBSTERS LOSE, 29–20

At Brown Arena, B.U.

MIXED DOUBLES: Mike Estep and Pam Teeguarden, Boston, def. Butch Waltz and Kristin Shaw, Phoenix, 6–3

WOMEN'S SINGLES: Chris Evert, Phoenix, def. Kerry Reid, Boston, 6–0

WOMEN'S DOUBLES: Chris Evert and Kristin Shaw, Phoenix, def. Kerry Reid and Pam Teeguarden, Boston, 6–0

MEN'S SINGLES: Andrew Pattison, Phoenix, def. John Alexander, Boston, 6–4

MEN'S DOUBLES: Andrew Pattison and Butch Waltz, Phoenix, def. Ion Tiriac and John Alexander, Boston, 7–5

Attendance: 3,624

[1] *The Boston Globe,* August 13, 1976.

ally favored WTT to tournaments because of the guaranteed salary, team play, coaching, and identification with a city. Unlike hockey, football, and basketball, WTT was not in competition with existing sports leagues. It did not appear that another tennis league would be formed in the near future. It was essential to the success of the league that the quality of players be maintained. Because most sports fans had only heard of tennis' top men and women, the league made every effort to involve these players in league play. It was equally important that each team be competitive and that no individual franchise have a disproportionate number of star players.

Unsigned players were drafted by teams in the fall prior to the season. No team was permitted to negotiate with a player not on its draft list unless it received specific permission from the team that held that players' draft rights. A team could protect a player from the draft by signing the player to a team contract or by including that player as one of two unsigned players protected from the league draft. Unlike professional football and basketball, however, the draft was of nominal significance after the first two years, because there were few new players of the quality to play WTT each season.

Players were contracted by individual franchises to play for respective clubs for one or more seasons. A season included all regular season matches plus playoffs. As in pro baseball, football and hockey, players were paid a flat salary for the season. The league offered playoff bonuses to participating teams but did not single out individual players. Bonuses based on individual performances were prohibited by league rules based on experience from the 1974 season. It was found that such bonuses served to undermine the team concept by encouraging players to attempt to avoid playing the best players on the opposing team and jeopardizing their games-won averages.

Players could negotiate such extras as a no-cut provision (under which a player could not be cut from the team for any reason other than an injury sustained while not in the service of the team); a no-trade provision (under which a player's contract could not be traded, sold or assigned to another team without the player's written permission); a rent-free apartment and automobile; and a salary payment schedule. The actual dollars received by a player depended on his or her tournament record, ability to play singles and doubles (from the forehand and backhand court on fast surfaces), public relations ability, and perceived fit with teammates and management. A major concern of management was the inflated salaries of individual players. It was reported that many players received several times from WTT what they could make in a comparable period of time playing tournaments. The following schedule was generally considered an accurate reflection of current salary ranges:

A level player—(someone who could "make" a franchise, such as, King, Evert, Newcombe, Nastase, or Laver): \$75,000 to \$150,000 per season

B level player—(a doubles standout who could fill in at singles, such as Stove, Cox, Fromholtz, or Ruffels): \$30,000 to \$60,000 per season

C level player—(a young player, such as Estep, Lucas, Tollason, or Gourlay): $7,500 to $30,000 per season

Player coaches were usually paid $15,000 to $30,000 more than they could earn as a player.

Franchise operations. As in other sports leagues, WTT had experienced problems in maintaining control over the operations of its franchises. Teams were required to participate in scheduled matches, field a competitive team, and conform to certain league rules regarding playing conditions and national promotions (see Exhibit 4 for excerpts from WTT league rules). The league office could impose nominal fines for violations of playing rules. But if a team wanted to operate with a low player salary schedule and risk playing before small crowds, the league had no recourse. In 1975, the owners had held lengthy discussions regarding a rule requiring each franchise to hire a "star" player. The idea failed, however, when neither a generally agreed-upon definition of "star" nor a list of such players could be developed.

The Los Angeles Strings illustrated the essential qualities of a successful franchise. In 1974, their first year of operation, the Strings were owned by several people, the operation was undercapitalized, and it suffered from lack of operational direction. Dr. Gary Guest, one of the major partners in the Strings, secured a majority interest during the team's second year. Guest added a full-time staff on a twelve-month basis, secured a local TV contract, and signed Rosie Casals as player-coach and Bob Lutz as a male singles player. The Strings promoted heavily but did not achieve the expected success because of what management believed to be a poor arena location. In 1976, Guest and General Manager Larry Star put together a more competitive team and moved the matches to the more stylish Los Angeles Forum. As Star explained:

> I think the Forum made the difference. People associated quality events with the Forum and not with the Arena, the former playing site. The Forum is in a better neighborhood and provides easier access to our market. We also signed a better team, which gave us good fan appeal. Next year we hope to get Connors (Jimmy Connors, the top-rated men's singles player), which should really round out the package. We found out that there is no substitution for hard work. You have to constantly keep yourself in the public eye. That might be easy for the RAMS (NFL) or the Lakers (NBA) but in WTT you've got to hustle. Hustle cannot be bought, either. In our market we've got dozens of radio and television stations and hundreds of tennis clubs. Paid advertising does no good since it will get lost. That's where time, energy and creativity come into play. Gary has the commitment and he wants to make it work. He's well capitalized and understands the team's potential for success.

In contrast, a female player on a less successful franchise commented:

> We play out in the sticks before a private audience. It looks like we are going to make the playoffs. I think we deserve to but it'll be a very well-kept secret.

Exhibit 4

WORLD TEAM TENNIS, INC.
WTT Operating Rules

1. LEAGUE STRUCTURE

1.1 The League shall consist of 10 teams.

1.2 The League shall be divided into two divisions. Each division shall consist of five teams.

2. REGULAR SEASON PLAY

2.1 Each team shall play 44 matches during the regular season.

2.2 Twenty-two matches shall be played at home; twenty-two shall be played away from home.

2.3 Each team will play three home and three away matches with each team in the same division, and two home and two away matches with each team in the other division.

2.4 Each team's position in the final division standings shall be determined on the basis of match win-loss record. In case two teams in the same division have identical match win-loss records, the tie shall be broken on the following basis:

2.4.1 That team having the best match win-loss record against the team involved in the tie.

2.4.2 That team which won the most net games during the season. (Games won minus games lost equals net games.)

2.4.3 If a tie still exists, that team having the best match win-loss record against other teams in the same division.

3. DIVISION STANDINGS DURING REGULAR SEASON

3.1 Division standings will be on the basis of win-loss percentage.

3.2 Division standings will list each team's win-loss record, the percentage of wins, and the net games won.

4. TEAM ROSTER LIMITATIONS

4.1 A WTT team shall consist of a minimum of three women and three men.

4.1.1 By March 1, each year, the maximum number of players signed or protected by a team shall be 15 (excluding amateurs drafted in special draft).

4.1.2 By the first regularly scheduled WTT match, the maximum number of players protected shall be 12 (excluding amateurs).

4.1.3 All trades and signings for the current WTT season must be consummated no later than July 15th.

5. FINES

5.1 Franchise

5.1.1 A team missing a regularly scheduled WTT match may be fined a minimum of $10,000 and fined up to the amount of the gate lost by the home team.

5.1.2 A home team, for delaying the starting of a match, may be fined $100 for the first offense and up to $500 for the second offense and every offense thereafter.

5.1.3 For using a player without a contract, a team may be fined up to $500 for the first offense, and for any offense thereafter, $1,000. If outcome of match is affected, match may be forfeited. (Contracts may be telecopied into the League Office prior to the match.)

5.1.4 Any member of a team or franchise staff interfering with decision of the referee or any official will be fined no less than $100 for the first offense; any offense thereafter, $500.

5.1.5 Any team fielding less than six players will be fined a minimum of $1,000 per player; if the outcome of the match is affected, a maximum fine of $6,000 per player will be levied.

5.1.6 Any team walking out on a match will be fined a minimum of $5,000.

5.1.7 A team which does not submit its Protected Listing on time will be fined a minimum of $100 per day for each day it is late.

5.1.8 A team which does not telecopy its match summary sheet to the League statistician the night of a match will be fined a minimum of $25 for the first

Exhibit 4 (continued)

offense; $50 for every offense thereafter.

5.1.9 A fine of $1,000 will be levied if a team arrives less than one hour before the match.

5.1.10 A fine of up to $5,000 may be levied if a team's arrival causes a delay in the start of a match.

5.2 Players

5.2.1 A home coach submitting an order of play, side or service choice and break period length to the referee at referee box at net after 60 minutes prior to the scheduled starting time of a match will be fined a minimum of $500. If home team has not set order of play within 25 minutes of scheduled time, or 35 minutes before the match, referee may award right of setting order to visiting team.

5.2.2 Any player out of uniform will be fined $50 for the first offense; $100 thereafter. If match is televised, fine is doubled.

5.2.3 A player leaving the bench will be fined $25 for the first offense.

5.2.4 Any player heard using abusive language or seen using obscene hand gestures will be fined a minimum of $100.

5.2.5 Any players fighting during a match will be fined $250.

5.2.6 Any player delaying the match for any reason will—after a warning—be fined $250.

5.2.7 Any fine which has been imposed upon a player and not paid within 14 days will result in that player being suspended.

5.3 Officials

5.3.1 At the completion of each match, referee must submit a "Match Evaluation Form" to the League Office within 72 hours. Failure to submit will result in a fine of $25.

5.3.2 For failure to report to the referee 90 minutes prior to a match, an official will be fined $5 for each 15 minutes he or she is late.

5.3.3 Each official must appear in the required WTT officials' uniform. For noncompliance: First offense $25; second offense, suspension. If match is televised, fine is doubled.

5.3.4 Officials may not drink alcoholic beverages prior to or during the match. First offense, $50; second offense, suspension.

5.3.5 Officials shall not fraternize with players, coaches, or franchise staff. First offense, $50; second offense, suspension.

5.3.6 Any official who has not payed a fine to the League Office within 14 days of notice will be suspended.

5.3.7 WTT officials will not wear their uniforms at non-WTT events.

6. PLAYER DRAFT

6.1 There shall be a player draft each year. It shall take place within one (1) week of November 15th.

6.2 All Teams must notify the League Office by October 15 of eight (8) protected players who will not be eligible for the draft. Protected players include those signed to a contract the preceding year, as well as those not signed.

7. PROTECTED LISTING

7.1 All changes made by a team to its Protected Listing shall be done in writing (telecopier or telegram). No telephone calls will be accepted.

8. DOCTORS AND TRAINERS

8.1 The home team shall provide a doctor in attendance at each match.

8.2 The home team's trainer must be available to the visiting team during its practice and warmup on the day of the match and at the match.

9. BEST EFFORTS

9.1 In good faith, all teams must field the best available tennis team, and best efforts possible must be given during the season and playoffs.

10. BALL BOYS AND GIRLS

10.1 A uniform of white shorts, white shoes and socks and a t-shirt provided by the team must be worn. The back or front of the t-shirt may have sponsor name; however, WTT logo must appear on shirt.

11. TELECOPIERS

11.1 A team must maintain a telecopier during the entire year.

> You cannot blame the staff. They are so busy—they've each got eight jobs. People in the critical positions come and go so fast we don't even know their names before they're gone. I really cannot complain because I'm getting a lot of money. I'll stay because I don't have much choice. I'll tell you something though. If there's one thing that's going to kill the league it'll be a handful of weak owners.

A player on a successful team echoed the same sentiments:

> The concept is great. You'll get all the players from America and Australia and maybe even some of the Europeans. The quality of ownership and management should improve in a few cities. By and large we think the owners are great but a few bad apples have to be weeded out.

A former general manager of a successful franchise cited three kinds of success in World Team Tennis:

> First is on-court success. There's not much I can do as general manager once the players are signed, other than hope they win. The players have told me, however, that they play better with the home crowd (assuming there is one) behind them. Second, you can have operational success. Such success includes good attendance, news coverage, excitement, happy players—all the trappings of fun and excitement. Third, you can have financial success. There is no mandatory relationship between operational and financial success. I had tremendous operational success but the owner wasn't prepared to sustain the losses resulting in the first year. I could have had great financial success but the operations would have suffered. The last place team might break even this (1976) season. But what have they created? They are a last place team with no names, they are the worst draw at home and on the road, and they obviously have no base from which to build.

When asked what he felt was the one critical consideration in the selection of ownership he replied:

> The owner has to have a complete understanding of his motives for getting involved. Does he want profits, appreciation, losses, ego, fun, or excitement? The owner must have a total understanding of what it will take to achieve his goals. The problem is that unlike a marriage where the two people have partners and friends asking probing questions, who is going to make the potential owner really examine his motives and their implications before getting involved?

Operating statistics for 1976 for two WTT franchises are shown in Exhibit 5.

Franchising. There was little action the league could take to insure that a group intended to sign a star player and promote WTT vigorously in a city. As Lennox explained:

> We've got to talk to the guys and see if they have an understanding of tennis and promotions. They must be willing to hire a staff and spend some money

Exhibit 5

WORLD TEAM TENNIS, INC.
Comparative Performances of Two
WTT Franchises, 1976 Season[j]
(in thousands of dollars)

	Franchise No. 1	Franchise No. 2
Income		
Season tickets	$231.0[a]	$ 32.5[b]
Gate ticket sales	225.0[c]	86.5[d]
Concessions[e]	—	—
Programs, banners, ads, etc.	18.0	26.0
League (net of assessments)[f]	12.5	12.5
Two non-city games[g]	—	18.5
Local TV	57.0	—
	$543.5	$176.0
Expenses		
Players' salaries and payroll taxes	$320.0	$262.0
Staff salaries and office rental	120.0	84.0
Promotion and advertising	80.0	78.0
Arena rental	200.0[h]	20.0[i]
Legal and accounting	12.0	6.0
Travel and entertainment (staff)	4.0	7.0
Insurance	6.0	4.0
Player travel and hotels	36.0	18.0
	$778.0	$479.0
Profit (loss)	($234.5)	($303.0)
Season Ticket Sales		
1974	282	363
1975	904	325
1976	1,400	250

[a] From 1,400 tickets for each of 22 games at $7.50 per game.

[b] From 250 tickets for each of 20 games at $6.50 per game.

[c] From an average of 2,395 tickets for each of 22 games at an average of $4.26 per ticket.

[d] From an average of 961 tickets for each of 20 games at an average of $4.50 per ticket.

[e] Concessions for both teams were operated by the arena.

[f] League assessments averaged approximately $40,000 for the year.

[g] Games which otherwise would have been played at home.

[h] For a private facility with a capacity of 14,062.

[i] For a public facility with a capacity of 22,048.

[j] All figures in this exhibit are disguised.

on players. We cannot do much more than work with the owners. Once a group is granted a franchise, the other owners have to hope they'll do the work. You cannot just hire good players, open the gates, and turn on the lights. You've got to do a lot of work—sell, sell, sell—and that's where it is difficult to judge the quality of the investor.

Franchise Valuation

The first step in the franchising process required that a value be placed on new franchises. Mr. Lennox felt that a new WTT franchise should be valued at $1 million. He explained:

> Sports is unlike my other business. A sports investor is buying losses for the first few years, and in WTT he is buying a future stream of positive earnings. From a financial standpoint, he is buying franchise appreciation. Unlike other pro sports teams, a club can make a profit in a few years.

When pressed to explain further why he arrived at the $1 million figure, Mr. Lennox indicated that was the amount at which the directors had decided to value a franchise. "I can see the time in the next few years when a franchise will be worth $5 million or $6 million. Someone buying now is getting in cheap."

Another owner put it more bluntly:

> A franchise is worth what you can get for it. If you can get $1 million, then it is worth $1 million. If all you can get is $1, then that's all it is worth. If we want to be sure to establish the price at $1 million, then we simply don't sell a team for less than that amount. Of course, we could be short-changing ourselves if we reject a solid group of investors because they are willing to pay only $750,000. Similarly, we'd be hurting ourselves if we took in a group willing to pay $2 million if we knew they would embarrass the league with a shoddy operation.

John Prince explained his reasoning for the $1 million valuation:

> An expansion group is buying part of an existing product. Each owner has invested at least $1 million in losses if they've been in operation for three years. The current owners have done the ground work. There is a certain value attached to the fact that Evert, Navratilova, Laver, Nastase and Billie Jean are involved in, and speak highly of, WTT. Second, we've had four games on national television. Our two All Star games outdrew any nationally televised tennis event including Forest Hills and Wimbledon (two famous tennis tournaments). Television brings the baseball leagues at least $500,000 per franchise annually on a national basis alone. We've contracted with a nationally known production company to handle our contract for next season. The potential for tennis television income and promotional tie-ins is unlimited because of the coed nature of the sport. (Exhibit 6 shows a WTT doubles match in progress.)

Exhibit 6

WORLD TEAM TENNIS, INC.
Scene From a Typical WTT Match

Pat Bostrom (Boston), Julie Anthony (Philadelphia), Kerry Melville (Boston), Billie Jean King (Philadelphia)—Walter Brown Arena, May 28, 1974.

Lennox said he had received an offer to buy his team for a deal amounting to $1.4 million. The owner of the Los Angeles team indicated he had received a $1.75 million offer to buy his club. The Pittsburgh franchise reported similar interests. These teams led the league in attendance and were three of the more successful teams on the court.

The league had witnessed a recent surge of interest among prospective franchises as a result of its growth in attendance and improved caliber of play. Most WTT committees were composed of owners who had shown a great deal of interest in a particular problem. Lennox's expansion committee was composed of the owners of the Phoenix (Western Division), Cleveland and Indiana (Eastern Division) teams. The committee had no formal means of either soliciting or approving franchise bids. The league, however, required that each applicant submit personal financial statements and character references.[2] The procedure for application was informal. Someone read an article about the league, saw a match, knew an

[2] This initial screen did not prove to be an effective means of eliminating potentially weak owners. Many past franchise owners had personal net worths of several million dollars but had folded their teams when they became discouraged.

owner, or had a friend who knew an owner. The original Boston franchise holder told of his experience:

> I read an article about the formation of the league and went to the organizational meeting in Chicago. I remember walking around the lobby asking whom to give my check to.

One individual trying to put a group together told how he got investors:

> It's really informal. I was at a cocktail party and met a bank vice-president. I was telling him about the league and the excitement of WTT. He was enthusiastic and asked why our city didn't have a team. That was a natural opening, so I told him what I was doing. He introduced me to some of his friends, and I took it from there.

After someone showed initial interest, he was usually invited to see a match and meet some of the other owners. The purpose of the match visit was to show him what he was buying into and to arouse his ego. Generally the applicant had dinner with an owner and a star player after the match. If the applicant was interested, he would make formal application, including the filing of personal, financial information, character reference, and whatever other information the league required. The other information could vary from a cursory verbal interview at a board meeting to detailed financial statements. A summer intern commented on the application process:

> One of the best ways to shake investors out of the woodwork is to hold a press conference, announce that you've got a group together with two more spots open and then wait for the telephone to ring. It's not like buying a McDonald's or getting a gas station. Those operations have a fixed set of procedures for handling new franchising. In the beginning they might have been informal and searching for formal methods but now they've got it to a system. We're not even trying to get from here to there yet. We're still trying to figure out where here is.

An additional issue regarding the expansion committee membership had not been resolved. It was expected to come to a head within six weeks, and concerned whether a member of the committee was entitled to a finder's fee (5% to 10% of the sale price) for bringing in a new franchise.

Three Applications

Lennox's committee had been approached by three groups, one in Atlanta and two in Chicago.

Atlanta

The Atlanta group was structured to be a limited partnership with the general partner and president a young insurance executive. The group agreed to pay $750,000 over three years. The general partner himself stressed the need to sign "the best player in the world." He said he not only understood the need to "pound the pavement" to sell tickets, but he felt his experience in building an insurance business gave him the necessary experience in putting together a good sales force.

The general partner indicated that the limited partners would have the following rights and obligations:

1. One percent interest in return for each $7,500 of loan plus $5,000 of investment.
2. No voting rights.
3. No liability for future assessments.
4. Equity interest would not be diluted in future issues (i.e., any future equity funding would have to result from the sale of the general partner's interest with the same covenants as other limited partners).

He said he wanted to make his team a city team and spread the interest throughout the community. "That's the best way I know to sell tickets. Make everyone a partner and everyone a season ticket holder. I can pay the loans back in five years, which gives me plenty of flexibility to get the operations together. Hey, I'm no Jack Kent Cooke (an owner of several professional sports teams on the West Coast). I can't afford to buy three teams and two stadiums, but I believe in WTT and it is within my price range. I know this will not be an easy sell and that's why I've allocated so much for promotion. The partnership arrangement will, in effect, give me dozens of field salespeople. My projections are very conservative with regard to league income. If properties generate $2 million, then my franchise makes a $150,000 profit. I put my insurance business together from nothing to a point where it is a very successful operation. I guess I'm lucky to be an entrepreneur with financial savvy."

A pro-forma operating statement which was presented to the franchising committee along with the Atlanta franchise application is shown in Exhibit 7.

Chicago I

The first group of Chicago investors had little previous knowledge or involvement in professional sports. Six investors would own equal shares of the team. The club would be structured under Subchapter S of the Internal Revenue Code to enable the investors to take the losses against personal income. The motive for their interest was presumed to be to keep WTT alive in Chicago. A franchise had operated there in 1974 but was one of the six which had ceased operations at the completion of the season. The investors said they wanted to "sign a star and run the club in a first-class way." They admitted they knew little about tennis but were willing to commit the time and money necessary to make the club successful. They were willing to pay $800,000 over four years for a franchise.

As one investor explained:

> This will be fun. If I'm involved in five deals, I'm involved in 50 deals. All of us can use the losses and this gives us a chance to have a good time.

Exhibit 7

WORLD TEAM TENNIS, INC.
Pro-Forma Statements Presented by
Atlanta Group
(in thousands of dollars)

	Year 1	Year 2	Year 3
Income			
Season tickets (@ $132 each)	$132	$264	$396
Gate and group tickets (@ $4 each for each of 22 games)	176	264	352
Banners, concessions, ads	35	45	55
League revenue	10	20	30
Local TV revenue	—	20	30
	$353	$613	$863
Expenses			
Players' salaries	$320	$330	$340
Office staff salaries	130	130	140
Promotion and advertising	100	80	90
Travel (team)	20	25	30
Travel and entertainment (staff)	5	5	5
Legal and accounting services	10	12	12
Arena rent	44	47	50
	$629	$629	$667
Profit (loss)	($276)	($ 16)	$196

Stadium: Public facility, capacity 14,408

Another investor who was to act as president of the corporation was more concerned with the business end of the operations:

> We're not going to make the same mistakes the other teams have. We're not going to overpay the players and waste all that money on ads and PR. Regarding my partners, if they can have their losses and some ego—they'll be happy. I'll keep them out of the operations. I've got my own business to run, but it will be only a 5-minute drive away from the team office. Besides, tennis is a seasonal business and my business runs by itself. I'd imagine we'll get a majority of our initial sales from the investors and their friends. We should get the newspapers to support us. Then we should be moving.

> This is a very well capitalized operation. We each have reconciled ourselves to projected losses and can live with no profits; just a breakeven. Frankly, I don't believe all the numbers, but it's nice to know there's a chance for profits. I think our sales should be no problem. After all, there are several major teams in town who all do well—the Virginia Slims tourney does much

better than my projections—and finally, we've got the right people involved with the right contacts.

Pro-forma financial statements for the first two Chicago groups are shown in Exhibit 8.

Chicago II

A second group was interested in a Chicago franchise. It consisted of three area businessmen organized by a former national tennis promoter, also under Subchapter S. The group was willing to pay $500,000 over four years for a franchise, but did not want to operate until 1978 when the northernmost of Chicago's three major areas would become available. (See Exhibit 9 for area locations and information regarding the Chicago metropolitan area.) It felt that the locations of the other two arenas would hurt the team's operations. (The first Chicago group had expressed a willingness to play in either McGaw Hall or Chicago Stadium, having given McCormick Place little consideration.)

The principal organizer of the second Chicago group made these comments:

Exhibit 8

WORLD TEAM TENNIS, INC.
First Chicago Group
(in thousands of dollars)

	Year 1		Year 2	
Income				
Season tickets	$220	(@ $110 each)	$462	(@ $154 each)
Gate and group tickets	44	(@ $2 each for each of 22 games)	99	(@ $3 each for each of 22 games)
Concessions	15		20	
Banners, advertising, etc.	15		20	
League revenue	15		20	
Local TV revenues	20		30	
	$329		$651	
Expenses				
Players' salaries	$250		$260	
Office staff salaries	70		80	
Promotion and advertising	70		80	
Travel (team)	15		20	
Travel and entertainment (staff)	5		8	
Legal and accounting services	10		7	
Arena rent	66		70	
	$486		$525	
Profit (loss)	($157)		$126	

Stadium: Public facility, capacity 17,095

I know my chances are limited in getting the franchise. First, we've offered less money, but that's because we think the thing is worth less. Second, we don't want to play until next season (1978) because I believe the arena problem is of major significance. Third, it's a limited partnership deal and these always take time. I'm looking at this from a business point of view. Not necessarily in the profit perspective, but certainly from what makes most sense to the operations: minimizing risk, maximizing loss advantages with least outflow —all that idea. Negotiating with the league is not easy since they're looking for people now with the money. I've got to decide if it's worth outbidding the other groups or not. I might be able to buy an existing team and pull an end

Exhibit 9

WORLD TEAM TENNIS, INC.
Major Tennis Arena Locations and Information

Arena 1

The first arena under consideration, McGaw Hall, was located on the campus of Northwestern University in Evanston, one of the largest suburbs on Chicago's prestigious North Shore. The arena could hold 9,800 for tennis and had parking for 4,000 cars. It could not be made available for professional tennis until 1978. Evanston was 30 minutes from O'Hare Air Field, 20 minutes north of Chicago and 20 minutes from Lake Forest, Illinois—the northernmost suburb considered part of the Chicago sports market. The outdoor football stadium adjacent to McGaw Hall was the home of the Northwestern University football team. The Chicago Bears (NFL pro football) had been negotiating to play several of their regular-season Sunday games in Dyche Stadium because of what management considered its ideal location and easy driving access to the wealthy northern suburbs. This was a private arena. As a result, it was considered easier to work a more favorable arrangement regarding rents, dates, concessions and parking. The rental was estimated at $2,000 plus expenses ($200 to $900 depending on attendance) per match. The group interested in McGaw felt the university would like a "quality" tenant such as a tennis team for 18 to 22 dates. University officials indicated they would share concession parking income.

Arena 2

The Chicago Stadium was the home of the Chicago Black Hawks (hockey) and the Chicago Bulls (basketball). The Stadium was located in a decaying neighborhood several blocks west of Chicago's Loop area. It could hold 17,095 for tennis. The stadium was privately owned, but it was doubtful that a favorable arena contract could be negotiated due to the demand for dates from the circus, concerts, conventions and other sports events. The Stadium rents were anticipated to fall between $5,000 and $9,000 per match, including expenses. While no specific offer had been made, stadium officials indicated they would take a guarantee against percentage of the gate.[1] The Stadium would get all concession and parking income.

Arena 3

McCormick Place was located on Lake Shore Drive. Its outdoor facility was the new home of the Chicago Bears. McCormick Place was well known to Chicagoans, was well maintained, and provided ample parking. Because it was a public facility, its managers had less negotiating room in giving contract concessions to renters. McCormick Place was ten minutes south of the Loop and 45 minutes driving distance from Evanston. McCormick Place rents and concession arrangements were estimated as roughly comparable to those of the Chicago Stadium.

[1] The arena contract called for a fixed percentage of all gate, advance and group sales but generally excluded season tickets unless purchased at the arena box office.

run and move to Chicago first. I'd have to operate in a third city for one year and that would cost the investors more while we were waiting for the arena to become available. Then again, I might be able to get the existing team cheaper if it was in trouble. I know what it takes to succeed, having promoted tennis events in the past. I've promised the investors certain losses and profits with appreciation "on the come." If they were in it to make a fast buck I would not be involved since I know WTT isn't that kind of a game. It's got a future but the loose money days of pro sports are over.

Pro-forma operating statements for the second Chicago group are shown in Exhibit 10.

Gerald Lennox wanted a franchise in Chicago because of the television possibilities. Thus far, only the two Chicago groups and one Atlanta group had sub-

Exhibit 10

WORLD TEAM TENNIS, INC.
Pro-Forma Statements Presented by
Second Chicago Group
(in thousands of dollars)

	Year 1	*Year 2*	*Year 3*
Income			
Season tickets (@ $100 for 20 games)	$100	$150	$250
Gate and group tickets (@ $5 each for each of 20 games)	75	100	150
Group tickets (@ $3 each for each of 20 games)	60	75	90
Revenue from two non-Chicago games	40[a]	50[b]	60[c]
Programs, ads, banners, concessions (net)	50	75	90
Income from league	20	30	50
Local TV	10	15	25
	$355	$495	$715
Expenses			
Players' salaries and payroll taxes	$300	$310	$320
Office rental and staff salaries	130	130	130
Team travel	30	35	40
Legal and accounting	15	10	12
Promotion and advertising	125	100	100
Travel and entertainment (staff)	15	10	10
Arena rental	35	30	33
	$650	$625	$645
Profit (loss)	($295)	($130)	$ 70

[a] Assuming combined attendance of 6,500.
[b] Assuming combined attendance of 8,200.
[c] Assuming combined attendance of 9,000.

mitted solid bids. In addition, interest was shown by groups in Dallas and New Orleans. WTT franchise owners wanted the New Orleans group to play in 1977 because the major investor was a well-known tennis promoter who had run many successful events in the past. He was also involved in two other pro sports leagues in addition to his large manufacturing business. Lennox did not know how long his committee should wait for a firm New Orleans bid. He did not want to take the initiative in soliciting any of the groups, because he felt this would hurt the league's negotiating position.

Lenox speculated about whether he should consider having the interested groups contact an existing franchise to combine with or buy one of the league's three weak teams. He wondered whether this approach might have negative repercussions if the investors got the impression that the league was not as solid as Lennox had described it. If they rejected the consolidation effort they could lower their offers on an expansion team in light of the weak financial position of some of the teams. Lennox felt he could possibly get more money from the second Chicago group if the league permitted them to hold off operating until the 1978 season. He felt that teams would be worth more in 1978 than in 1977. He wondered what additional requirements he should place on the groups.

Hartford Steam Boiler Inspection and Insurance Company[1]

"Inspection Is Our Middle Name"

The Hartford Steam Boiler Inspection and Insurance Company (HSB) had been the number one company in the $160 million boiler and machinery insurance industry since it was founded in 1866. Working through its nationwide network of 20 branches, HSB inspected and insured many types of industrial equipment ranging from small compressed air tanks and apartment building furnace boilers to 5,000 horsepower chemical plant compressors, electric utility steam turbines, and huge nuclear reactor pressure vessels.

During early 1974, HSB President Wilson Wilde and several other top-level HSB officers had begun to wonder whether increases in the quality of service being offered to the company's customers had been keeping pace with changing market demands.

One symptom of the problem was higher than desired turnover in several areas of the company; another symptom seemed to be an increasing amount of time needed to deliver policies. The time required to deliver a completed policy after an agreement to insure had been signed had been recently averaging between 50 and 70 days in some branches, and in a few instances delivery had taken as long as three years, the typical duration of an HSB policy. During this time period, the customer was insured under a loosely structured agreement known as a "binder" rather than under a specific and detailed policy. Firms that did not inspect could sometimes deliver policies in less than one week.

Company History

The Hartford Steam Boiler Inspection and Insurance Company had been the first insurance company of its kind when it was organized in 1866. After more than a century of operations, HSB in 1968 grossed $35.8 million in earned premiums and netted $1.94 a share in earnings; by 1973 the company had grown to $62 million in annual premiums and had earned $3.94 per share. Late in the summer of 1974, HSB stock had been trading over the counter for $25 a share (see Exhibit 1 for financial summary).

Exhibit 1

HARTFORD STEAM BOILER INSPECTION AND INSURANCE COMPANY
Comparative Income Statement
(dollar amounts in millions)

	6 Months 1974*	1973	1972	1971
Underwriting Income				
Premiums written	$33.2	$62.4	$61.0	$55.8
Change in unearned premiums	(2.9)	(.3)	(2.7)	(1.3)
Premium earned	30.3	62.1	58.3	54.5
Underwriting Expenses				
Losses and loss adjustment expenses	12.2	21.5	18.1	13.7
Taxes (excluding federal income)	1.4	2.5	2.2	2.1
Commissions	5.0	10.1	9.5	8.9
Inspection	6.4	12.4	11.2	10.7
General	6.5	12.4	11.0	10.5
Total Underwriting Expense	31.5	58.9	52.1	45.9
Underwriting gain (loss)	(1.2)	3.2	6.2	8.6
Net investment income	3.0	5.2	4.7	4.4
Net income—Canadian subsidiary	(.2)	.5	.7	.6
Income before federal income taxes	1.6	9.0	11.5	13.6
Federal income taxes				
Current	(.6)	1.8	2.6	4.6
Deferred	.2	.1	.9	—
Total federal income taxes	(.4)	1.9	3.5	4.6
Net Income	2.0	7.1	8.0	8.9
Net Income per Share ($) (1.8 million shares outstanding)	$1.13	$3.94	$4.47	$4.99

* Unaudited.

As of mid-1974, HSB insured more than one million separate objects in 200,000 different locations. The coverage normally provided by the company included provisions for actual dollar losses arising from accidental damage to and due to the equipment in question, various forms of liability coverage, and a provision for business interruption losses which indemnified the insured against the loss of profits due to machinery failure. HSB's accounts varied in terms of size of premiums, size of risk exposure to the company, number and location of objects and many other factors. A summary comparison of these characteristics is presented in Exhibit 2.

As of the end of 1973, five companies controlled approximately 80% of the

Exhibit 2

HARTFORD STEAM BOILER INSPECTION
AND INSURANCE COMPANY
Analysis of Premium System Policy Master File

Chart 1: Premium Size (by policy)

Premium Size ($000)	*Number of Policies*	*Percent of Total Policies*	*Percent of Total Premium*
0–.1	3,077	3.7%	0.3
.1–.5	56,477	67.5	22.6
.5–1	11,953	14.3	12.2
1–2	6,504	7.8	13.3
2–3	2,204	2.6	7.8
3–5	1,753	2.1	9.4
5–10	1,113	1.3	9.6
10–25	489	0.6	8.2
25–50	85	0.1	3.1
50–100	25	—	1.8
Over 100	29	—	11.6
Totals	83,709	100.0%	99.9

Chart 2: Location of Objects

Number of Object Locations for Policy	*Number of Policies*	*Percent of Policies*
1	71,486	85.4%
2	6,223	7.4
3	2,183	2.6
4	1,106	1.3
5	649	0.8
6–9	1,194	1.4
10–49	785	0.9
50–99	54	—
100–499	25	—
500–999	1	—
999+	3	—
Total	83,709	99.8%

Chart 3: Number of Objects

Number of Objects Insured	*Number of Policies*	*Percent of Policies*
1	20,687	24.7%
2	17,404	20.8
3	11,344	13.6
4	7,206	8.6
5	4,637	5.5
6–9	9,426	11.3
10–24	7,445	8.9
25–49	3,683	4.4
50–99	1,327	1.6
100–499	513	0.6
500–999	10	—
999+	27	—
Total	83,709	100.0%

business; the remainder was shared by nine other firms. For four out of the last five years, Hartford had experienced lower losses per dollar earned premium than any of the top four companies, and during that period the company had grown at a considerably faster rate than the industry average (see market share data, Exhibit 3). "We've been able to maintain our 35% of the market for the last ten years," said

Exhibit 3

HARTFORD STEAM BOILER INSPECTION AND INSURANCE COMPANY
BOILER AND MACHINERY INS. EARNED PREMIUMS AND LOSSES—MAJOR COMPANIES
(000's Omitted)

	Earned Premium					Incurred Losses					Loss Ratio				
	'69	'70	'71	'72	'73	'69	'70	'71	'72	'73	'69	'70	'71	'72	'73
HSB	40,193	45,487	53,620	56,931	60,167	10,384	13,900	12,341	16,463	19,044	26%	31%	23%	29%	31.7%
Factory Mutual Cos.	19,329	23,534	28,789	31,961	34,547	8,342	9,284	9,236	13,310	24,081	43%	39%	32%	42%	69.7%
Kemper Group	10,925	12,012	13,641	14,771	15,580	5,643	6,348	5,005	6,112	7,189	52%	53%	37%	43%	46.1%
Employer's Comm. Union	7,892	8,794	10,098	9,455	10,315	2,378	3,551	3,049	2,332	3,695	30%	40%	30%	25%	35.8%
Continental Ins. Co.	6,236	7,405	8,001	8,194	8,008	2,128	2,428	2,616	2,203	1,825	34%	33%	33%	27%	22.8%
Travelers Group	6,870	7,068	8,253	6,973	7,101	2,144	416	1,880	2,070	760	31%	6%	23%	36%	10.7%
Zurich American Grp.	3,905	4,392	5,266	5,566	5,908	2,119	977	2,096	1,537	3,452	54%	22%	40%	28%	58.4%
Royal-Globe Ins. Co. Grp.	5,176	5,693	5,025	3,137	4,698	3,874	3,137	2,017	2,060	1,334	75%	55%	40%	56%	28.4%
Home Group (Ins.)	2,833	3,298	3,488	3,361	3,689	1,098	1,313	1,706	1,089	1,296	39%	40%	49%	32%	35.1%
Maryland Casualty	6,678	8,232	3,856	3,605	3,166	1,959	4,112	1,837	1,130	717	29%	50%	48%	31%	22.6%
Chubb (Inc. P.I.)	1,456	1,721	2,231	2,295	2,236	379	360	340	1,366	629	26%	21%	15%	60%	28.1%
Crum & Forster Grp.	514	705	922	1,111	1,106	228	106	319	501	84	44%	15%	35%	45%	7.6%
Continental Nat'l. Am.	990	1,162	1,309	1,147	1,069	83	413	285	118	270	8%	36%	22%	9%	25.2%
New Hampshire Grp.	345	488	602	552	633	149	131	301	174	92	43%	27%	50%	32%	14.6%
TOTAL	113,445	129,991	145,101	149,059	158,223	40,908	46,476	43,028	50,465	64,468	36%	36%	30%	34%	40.7%

HSB as % of earned premium:	1969—35.4%; 1970—35.0%; 1971—37.0%; 1972—38.2%; 1973—38.0%.
HSB as % of all losses:	1969—25.4%; 1970—30.0%; 1971—28.7%; 1972—32.6%; 1973—29.5%.
Industry five-year growth:	28%.
HSB five-year growth:	33%.
Industry five-year growth excluding HSB:	25%.

Mr. Wilde. "We could get 50% of the market if we got geared up for it." HSB had planned to grow at a rate of 10%–11% annually in terms of earned premiums. Industry growth tended to be at a rate of 4% plus inflation.

In the past few years, the company had made several moves to modernize and streamline operations. In 1970, HSB installed an IBM 370/135 to ease its tremendous data handling task and to assist the company in developing management information systems and more efficient operational methods. In 1972 the company also initiated a formalized budgeting system, and by 1974 the system was being utilized in most areas of the company's operations.

HSB had also begun providing a Special Inspection Service (SIS) in 1971 to supplement its regular activities. SIS was offered to manufacturing firms on a fee basis and consisted of an HSB inspector inspecting a boiler or pressure vessel as it was being constructed. This service was often performed on a third-party basis (at the request of either an equipment purchaser or the government) to monitor a vendor. In addition, HSB was often consulted by manufacturers, industry associations and governmental authorities on the development and advancement of design and construction codes. In mid-1974, SIS involved approximately 80 full-time and 70 part-time HSB inspectors and was contributing to revenues at a $5 million annual rate.

As a result of offering its extensive and comprehensive inspection service combined with coverages tailored to individual insured clients, HSB was able to command a higher price in the market than most of its competitors while still maintaining market dominance. According to Mr. Wilde, HSB's prices averaged about 10% higher than those of its major rivals.

Industry Trends

There were several industry trends and characteristics that affected HSB's operations. The property and casualty industry, of which boiler and machinery was a small segment, had generally approached selling of insurance in two ways. One way was to deal directly with the insured customer through a salesman who was a full-time employee of the company; Allstate and State Farm used this method. The second way was to sell through independent agents. The agent was employed on a commission basis and the insurance companies using this method—called stock agency companies—employed few or no salesmen themselves. HSB had traditionally been a stock agency company and still used agents for all of its transactions. Even if HSB sold a policy on a direct basis, an agent was paid a commission, though often a reduced one since the agent performed little or no work to earn it. "The agent will always be a part of our distribution channel," explained Mr. Donald K. Wilson, Vice President for Agency, "even though we are moving towards more direct selling."

According to Mr. Wilde, there had been a trend over the last 10 to 15 years for direct writing companies to use agents more frequently, and conversely, a trend for stock agency companies to do more direct writing of policies.

It used to be that there was a spread of about 25% between the cost to a customer of direct-written policies and ones sold through agents. Most of that 20% was agents' commissions. Now there is a more competitive marketplace; the spread has been shrinking and over the next few years it will continue to shrink. Agents now average 10% commission on a stock agency policy and about 5% on a direct-written one. The agents are looking out for themselves now and that makes it tougher for us to sell.

Hartford Steam Boiler used both local and national agents, though it wrote much of its business with the larger insurance brokers such as Marsh & McLennan, Inc. and Johnson & Higgins, Inc. Mr. Wilde felt that there had been an increasing trend towards consolidation among agents; essentially the larger ones had been buying out smaller ones.

There had also been a move towards more "packaging" of insurance policies, that is, combining coverage on a wide range of risks. "If we don't deliver the policy in a reasonable period of time," noted Philadelphia branch manager William B. Mount, "then the agent can't wrap it up with his other coverages, so we're holding up his premium cash flow of, say, $100,000, even though we're taking only $5,000."

Additionally, there had been a trend towards self-insurance, especially in light of increasing insurance costs. "Sometimes a guy will gasp at the idea of $300,000 for boiler insurance in a big corporation," explained Mr. Zindel, "and will ask, 'What do we need that for?' Then the company might drop its insurance and effectively become self-insured." Mr. Wilson noted that "captive" insurance companies—firms nominally incorporated to provide parent companies only with insurance—had already affected the insurance industry: "The oil industry went captive a few years ago, and took millions of dollars out of the domestic insurance business."

Still, HSB was not as worried as some companies in its industry. "No matter what," noted Mr. Wilson, "we can always sell loss prevention service. Consumerism and OSHA (the 1971 Occupational Safety and Health Act) are both putting more pressure on a corporation's risk manager to do a better job. Our service is not always sold with an insurance policy."

Besides these trends, HSB along with other insurance companies, faced certain inherent characteristics of the business. One was the industry's historical cyclicality—after a few years of prosperity the companies start underselling each other and inevitably industry profits become leaner. "The last two years have been a disastrous period," noted Mr. Wilde. "Lots of price cutting in the fire and casualty industry—the industry as a whole lost money in 1973. That is, companies netted a profit by making money on their investments, but they lost on insurance."

Part of HSB's competitive problem was that for most insurance firms, boiler machinery insurance was but a tiny part of the parent company's business, whereas it was Hartford's only business. "Some of our competitors go in to a broker and look at our bid on a policy and simply undercut it 6%," explained Earl Kemmler, vice president for engineering. "Now that's a hell of a competitive situation, though they can get burned real bad. When losses get to a point where everyone notices, they will tell their salesmen to stop cutting prices willy-nilly." There can be a bright side to this competitive situation, however, Mr. Kemmler noted:

> We never used to insure many utilities. Then this price cutting happened and soon many insurance companies got out of the business—they couldn't make money insuring utilities. They were losing their shirts. One day we had as many as 15 utility company representatives in this building with their hats in their hands begging us to take on their insurance. We took the business on our terms. We didn't gouge or profiteer; we just said, "We'll take it if you will follow our inspection requirements." We took a lot of them on, and now we've got about 35% of the utilities in the country.

Inflation had recently proven a burden for HSB. Since the company operated normally with a three-year contract, the income HSB earned from a particular risk was fixed at the amount of the premium. However, the cost of repairing damage or compensating business losses increased as prices rose.

Organization and Personnel

The HSB organization consisted of five major functional areas reporting to President Wilde: agency (sales, marketing and branch office operations); engineering (inspection); underwriting; finance and legal (see organization chart, Exhibit 4). Underwriting, finance, and legal divisions operated from the home office, while the two other areas were primarily represented in branch offices. The company's 20 branch office managers (who were mainly responsible for sales and office administration) reported directly to Mr. Donald K. Wilson. The branch manager did not directly supervise the engineering functions; the chief inspector reported instead directly to Engineering Vice President Earl Kemmler. Branch managers, through office managers, supervised the branch underwriting operation, a generally routine clerical function. The home office underwriting staff, headed by Vice-President, Robert Wolf, provided the branch manager with (1) quality control evaluation for the clerical function and (2) active advice and participation on significant or specialized risks. Normally, if conflicts arose between the branch managers and the inspectors as to the advisability of taking on a risk, the problem was resolved at the branch office level. Unresolved disputes were sent to the home office for a decision; if the vice presidents could not agree, there was provision for the dispute to be placed before the Underwriting Committee, composed of five senior officers, for final resolution. This procedure was used only rarely in isolated cases and on very large accounts; indeed, disputes between branch managers and inspectors sent to the home office generally emanated only from a few branches. Despite these reporting relationships the branch managers retained profit and loss responsibility for all activities in the branch.

Inspection

Hartford Steam Boiler's distinctive competence was embodied in its inspection service. "We offer an inspection service like no one else," commented President Wilde.

Exhibit 4

HARTFORD STEAM BOILER INSPECTION AND INSURANCE COMPANY

Domestic Organization Chart *

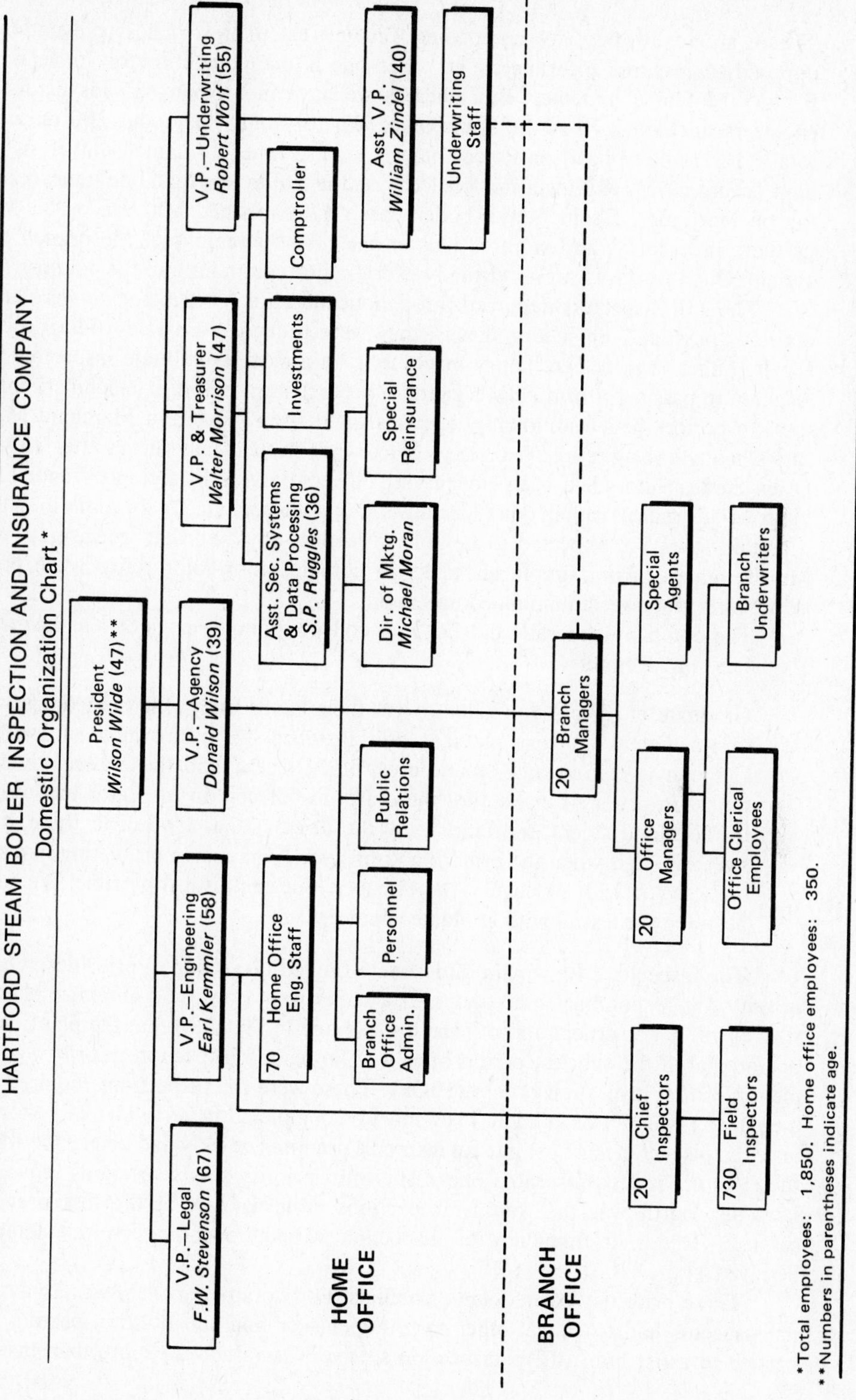

*Total employees: 1,850. Home office employees: 350.

**Numbers in parentheses indicate age.

"There are really only two companies with a great interest in loss prevention, as opposed to just loss insurance. The other one is our competitor of 75 years, the Factory Mutual Companies. But whereas we have more than 825 inspectors and engineers, including 70 at the home office, Factory only has about 200 inspectors total." HSB prided itself on its customer response time; it claimed that if an accident occurred, an HSB inspector could be on the site in less than one hour, depending on location. "If somebody's boiler goes off," explained Mr. Wilde, "he wants us there in a hurry, and we are. This is one of the strengths of the branch office system. Our inspectors are in virtually every major community in the country."

The 750 inspectors deployed throughout the branch office system were almost entirely "practical" engineers; that is, they were trained to be able to diagnose and repair, rather than design, heavy machinery. In almost every state inspectors were required to pass a uniform ASME exam to become licensed boiler machinery inspectors. Inspectors had traditionally been recruited from Navy and Merchant Marine ranks, many having retired from the service while in their late thirties after 20 years. Often the inspectors had been engineering officers on vessels, and most tended to be "jack-of-all-trades" rather than specialists. "Our inspectors, by the time they reach a certain level, are expected to be able to inspect anything that we insure," noted Mr. Kemmler, "from simple air tanks to complex four-color rotogravure presses or 5,000 horsepower ammonia compressors."

The company generally did not hire college graduate engineers as inspectors. Explained Mr. Kemmler:

> Graduate engineers don't like to get their hands dirty, and sometimes we do things that aren't very pleasant. For instance, we insure most of Swift and Company's equipment—storehouses, blood driers, and those awful rendering tanks. In order to make sure there are no defects, an inspector has to climb in the blood driers and chip away the dried blood. It's hot in there, you're sweating, and when the dried blood hits you, you come out looking like someone got you with a cleaver. And of course the smell is just horrible. We haven't been too successful with graduate engineers.

The inspector's four main duties were ranked according to priorities. The first priority was responding to accidents. If a boiler went down and an entire plant was shut down, it was crucial to both the insured and to Hartford that the plant become operational in the shortest period of time. The second inspection priority was completion of first inspection orders (FIOs). These were the inspections required when a company was put on binder. They must be completed prior to formal policy issuance; an inspector must get into an insured's premises quickly and determine whether the risks are indeed insurable ones. The third priority was inspections required by law; the fourth was the routine inspections done as part of the loss prevention service. (Required frequency of inspection varied depending on the equipment involved.)

These priorities created some conflicts. For example, if there was an accident, an inspector had to cancel other appointments or find substitute inspectors in the branch to assist him. HSB's inspection service was valued for more than insurance reasons; AT&T, for example, held a high-deductible policy partly because HSB's inspections eased AT&T's massive inventorying task.

An additional service that engineering performed was that of offering repair expediting capabilities to reduce downtime for a client who has experienced a serious accident. "Our people know who's who in the many big companies that supply heavy machinery and we can get those things moving in a hurry," explained Mr. Wilde. "Once when a 4,000 horsepower motor failed in a chemical plant, we knew where another firm had one sitting idle and we shipped it in about four days. It would have taken eight months for a new one."

Inspectors' salaries began at approximately $8,400 per year. The company provided a car of the inspector's choice and paid the operating costs of the vehicle. HSB estimated that these additions increased the "real" salary to close to $9,300 in total compensation, plus all normal fringes. HSB estimated that it required approximately one year and $8,000–$10,000 to train an inspector in HSB's methods. The company had consulted salary experts and had been assured that its salary scale was competitive within the industry. However, the company experienced a high turnover among its inspectors, averaging about 17% in 1973. Mr. Kemmler explained:

> HSB has a problem similar to that of IBM. It serves as a training ground. Inspectors are in demand by other companies—insurance, construction, architectural and such—and many of them are either working on a cost-plus basis or can simply afford to pay more for inspectors. They hire them away for $5,000 more than we can afford to pay. We've talked to several compensation experts, but no one seems to know how to reward inspectors or what incentives to provide them.

While HSB felt that its compensation schedule for inspectors was fair, moonlighting was an accepted fact of life for most inspectors. Various company employees estimated that between 50% and 75% of the company's inspectors held down some form of part-time job. Mr. Kemmler did not feel that this was detrimental to HSB operations.

> We have no objection to it as long as it does not interfere with his normal activities and does not provide a conflict of interest with the company. As long as an inspector is available for an emergency at 2 A.M. we don't care if he drives a taxi or raises chickens on the side.

Inspector Duties and Responsibilities

Each branch had one chief inspector who was in charge of the branch's inspection activities. Reporting to him were from two to nine supervising inspectors and to them, approximately eight field inspectors per supervisor. The chief inspector was responsible for all inspection activities, accident investigation and claim adjustments. Inspectors normally submitted all inspection reports to supervising inspectors for review. It was felt by the engineering department that this added an extra measure of experience and expertise to each inspection.

If a branch were required to inspect objects with which it had little inspection experience, the inspectors could contact the home office engineering staff for assistance. This staff of 70 engineers comprised a corps of specialists who assisted the branches with inspections, surveys, accident investigation and administrative functions.

Inspection territories varied depending primarily on the geographical location of the branch. An inspector in the New York branch, for instance, might have a territory a few square miles in size while his counterpart in the Denver branch might cover an area 300 by 400 miles, since that branch's total territory stretched from the Canadian border to the Mexican border. Travelling time ranged up to 30% of an inspector's total time, though a typical figure was 15%. In addition, Mr. Kemmler estimated that an inspector spent 15% of his day writing reports. According to Mr. Kemmler, an inspector was completely responsible for scheduling his workday, though he did have certain required inspections in a given time period. In most branches, inspectors rarely came into the branch, conducting most company business by mail and telephone from their homes. Mr. Kemmler felt that this certain degree of freedom to plan one's own time was an attractive fringe benefit for a prospective inspector, and helped compensate if an inspector felt the salary level was too low.

An inspector typically was responsible for about 1,400 objects in his territory. Time required for inspections ranged from three minutes for an air tank in good repair to more than several weeks for examination of a large complex turbine or compressor. A chief inspector familiar with the types and number of objects in his territory "works up what he feels is a proper workload for each of his inspectors," explained Mr. Kemmler. "This is done by hand, but by people who know the territory and who know what has to be done." Typically, an inspector averaged between 5 and 20 inspections per day for smaller equipment and between 1 and 20 per week on larger machinery. Approximately 10% of HSB's insured objects were considered to be "larger" objects requiring more inspection time, and these objects were generally distributed evenly throughout the branch system.

While the chief inspector was portrayed as slightly lower on the organization chart than the branch manager, the inspector maintained veto power over risks to be insured. If a risk did not meet the company standards, the inspector could prevent it from being insured, though if the client was large and the reason for rejection small or correctible, the risk could be insured for "agency reasons" at the discretion of the home office. Not all HSB employees felt that this veto power was an optimal situation. Said one HSB employee: "The *de facto* social system is that the chief inspector runs the branch manager's life. That creates an enormous problem. The engineers see themselves as the saviors of the company, the technicians who keep the lunatic salesmen and underwriters honest."

Underwriting

Underwriters at HSB appraised objects to be insured and determined what premiums, deductibles and other financial conditions—if any—would make the object an acceptable risk for HSB. The home office staff included a Vice-President, Mr. Robert Wolf, his Assistant Vice-President, Mr. William Zindel, and three regional underwriters who had overall responsibility for the underwriting activities of between six and seven branches each. Additionally an underwriting services staff of seven at the home office, which performed research and rating services for the regional managers, also collected and analyzed data on the performance of the branch underwriting departments.

Each branch employed between 5 and 30 underwriters (an average branch had 15) who performed the largely clerical function of "rating," that is, formally evaluating the data necessary to make an underwriting decision according to prescribed rules and procedures established by the home office. Since there was no true underwriting involved in the jobs, the branch office underwriters were generally referred to as "raters."

According to Mr. Zindel, an underwriter faced five alternative choices with regard to a policy. He or she could: (1) take the risk in question; (2) reject it; (3) adjust the premium and/or deductible amounts to compensate for unusual risk exposure; (4) adjust the coverages applicable to certain objects to be covered; or (5) have the objects physically modified with the help of the engineering department to ensure conformity with regulations. This last option was exercised more frequently at HSB than was the case in most other insurance companies.

Administratively, branch office underwriters reported to the branch managers and, ultimately, to the agency department. From a functional standpoint, the underwriters received guidance from the home office underwriting department. Mr. Zindel explained:

> The branch manager is administratively in charge of the operation but we give functional direction to our underwriters just as Earl Kemmler does to his engineers. Raters have an underwriting handbook similar to the one engineering uses to spell out what they can and cannot do as an underwriter.

Decision-making authority had been delegated to the branch level underwriters only for specific less hazardous risks, while larger risks were evaluated by the home office staff for a final decision. According to Mr. Zindel, however, some changes in this situation were likely:

> As we grow we discover that the problems get bigger and bigger, and the underwriting machinery gets more complex. Making all of these decisions in Hartford is getting more difficult. We can't respond to the customer quickly enough.

As much of the branch underwriting function required little decision making, the underwriters did not normally accompany the agents or the inspectors in the field. On larger accounts, the home office underwriters did go out into the field with the engineering staff to inspect risks. "You can gain a far better insight into just what it is you're insuring if you go out and see the damn thing instead of sitting here listening to someone else's description," explained Mr. Zindel. The underwriting department wanted special agents to become more "underwriting oriented" to reduce the number of underwriting rejections of salesmen quotes.

Mr. Zindel was especially concerned about the motivation and morale of the underwriters in the branches and the resulting high turnover (greater than 20% per year). He felt that not only was the job frustrating without decision-making responsibility, but that it was generally believed that there was no future in the job—no career path in underwriting.

Sales

The sales function was the branch manager's primary responsibility. Each branch employed "special agents" who were the company's salesmen and whose main task was to call on independent insurance agents and induce them to sell HSB coverage rather than that of its competitors. A typical branch employed seven or eight special agents, though the number varied depending on the number of accounts and the amount of premium volume the branch generated.

The special agent had several responsibilities. One was to attract new accounts; a second was to ensure renewal of policies in force. In addition, the special agents were usually conduits for any policy changes that the customer might initiate. The salesmen dealt with a wide range of risk and premium sizes, though the bulk of the special agents' business was in the small policies. On the small policies, according to Hartford branch manager James G. Miller, the independent insurance agents were the company's "salesman"; on these HSB often made no contact with the insured and special agents rarely visited the insured's place of business.

HSB employees disagreed as to who the HSB customer was. According to one branch manager, the independent agent was the only true customer. "On small policies, since we rarely send special agents out to the insured, the agent is the only real customer. On larger accounts, the boiler insurance may only be a small part of the total premium, so the insured isn't too concerned about who writes it. Either way, the agent controls the account." Mr. Wilson, the Agency Vice President, disagreed. "Some people say we have two customers, the agents and the ultimate purchaser of the policy," he explained. "I don't see it that way. The agents are just our marketing arm. We don't have direct solicitors or a high-powered salesforce because we are paying 16% or 17% out to our producers (independent agents); our customer is the insured."

The special agents spent a lot of time "beating the bushes" due to the relative unimportance of boiler insurance compared to other types of insurance and due to the fact that HSB's competitors often wrote other types of insurance. "The competitor is at the producer's much more often because he is probably selling auto and home insurance as well as boiler," explained Hartford branch manager Miller. Generally, a special agent was expected to see or telephone as few as three or four to as many as 35 agents in one day.

There had been an increased interest on the part of the home office in generating more "major" accounts, accounts which contributed large annual premiums.

Exhibit 5

HARTFORD STEAM BOILER INSPECTION AND INSURANCE COMPANY
Sales Commission, Inspection Costs, and Loss Ratio
(by size of annual earned premium per object)

	Annual Earned Premium per Object[1]					
	$25	*$50*	*$100*	*$500*	*$1000*	*$10,000*
Sales Commission	18%	16%	16%	13%	11%	7%
Inspection Costs	30%	22%	19%	16%	10%	4%
Loss Ratio	25%	33%	35%	35%	42%	52%
Total Dollars (000,000 of Annual Earned Premium) (Based on policies in force as of August 15, 1974.)	8.8	21.4	22.7	7.9	3.8	3.0

[1] The casewriter divided the 1 million objects insured into six categories by size of the annual earned premium for each object. The categories are identified by the estimated average earned premium per category. The simpler, more standard objects were, naturally, on the lower end of the scale; the more complex objects were on the higher end of the scale.

Historically, major accounts were handled by the branches in the same manner as small ones, though the branch manager often visited the insured with the selling agent. In general, the large purchaser received more attention than the typical small customers. Lately the home office had begun to handle some major accounts, and Mr. Wilson felt that the company was moving in the direction of home office control of all major account marketing activities. Recently Mr. Michael Moran was transferred from HSB's Canadian subsidiary to take charge of the home office major account marketing thrust. The Canadian subsidiary had traditionally done all major account marketing directly through its home office, not through branches, and Mr. Moran had been in charge of that effort.

There had been some concern about the major account marketing effort in certain quarters of the company. One branch manager was worried that, if an agent wrote the policy in Hartford directly from the home office, the agent would be the only person who could assist an insured who had a problem, even though a locally based branch manager might be much closer to the insured. Another questioned the economics of the decision: "We are probably making a heck of a lot more money on the $500 accounts than on the major ones if you look at the loss ratios. There's no reason to believe that we make more money on a large account." [2]

[2] Loss data by premium amount was not available, though the company expected to compile this data by early 1975. The casewriter developed estimates which are included in Exhibit 5. Also included are estimates of inspection and sales commission expense ratios.

Administration

Administration, along with sales and marketing responsibilities, fell under the jurisdiction of the agency vice president, his assistants, and the branch managers. Administrative responsibilities included branch accounting, physical production of the policies, accountability for all customer service relations, staffing, salary and other personnel-related issues (not including engineering personnel).

In 1970 HSB began using its computer to store policy data, calculate premiums and actually print completed policies. As of the end of 1973, approximately 65% of the company's policies had been produced by computer. It was generally believed that 85% or more of the company's policies would one day be produced by computer.

While the branch manager held overall responsibility for the branch, his primary concern was sales, and approximately 70% of his time was devoted to some aspect of that responsibility. Reporting to the branch manager was an office manager who was the person directly in charge of the branch's policy production process. Reporting to the office managers were all the typists, MTST (Magnetic Tape Selectric Typewriter) operators, receptionists, file clerks, and underwriters. In addition, the office manager was responsible for salary and staffing of the inspection records or "Slip Desk" Department (inspection data on objects was kept on "slips" of paper in large loose-leaf binders).

The twenty branch offices of HSB were divided into three major size categories according to amount of annual earned premiums. Ten small branches had earned premiums of less than \$2 million; premiums of eight medium sized branches ranged between \$2 million and \$5 million. Two branches, New York and Chicago, were classified as large, as their premiums exceeded \$10 million each.

Workflow of a New Policy

Typical workflow for the production of a new policy from request to delivery was as diagrammed in Exhibit 6. In general, this workflow was typical of all branches; however, the degree to which the computer was utilized for policy production and use of other production aids varied with size of earned premiums, types of risks, number of objects insured and other factors.

When a request for insurance was presented by or solicited from an independent agent (producer), the special agent assigned to that account performed a cursory inspection (survey), the insured filled out an application for insurance and the company issued a binder covering the insured until his completed policy was delivered and the insured could be billed. When a binder was issued, the special agent requested the inspection department in his branch to do the inspection required prior to policy issue by submitting a First Inspection Order (FIO) to the supervising inspector. When the FIO was completed by the field inspector and was approved by the supervising inspector, the company then proceeded to write the policy. If irregularities were discovered during the course of inspection, the special agent was notified as to the nature of and remedy for the fault.

Exhibit 6

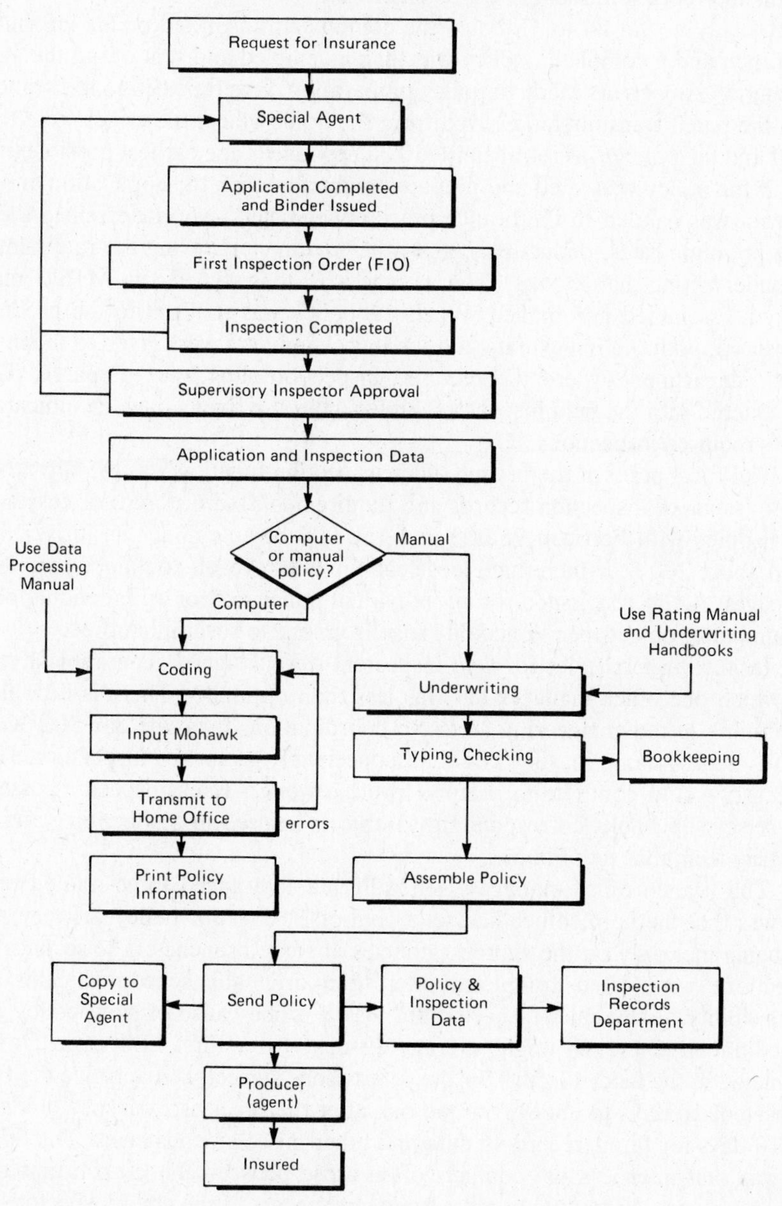
HARTFORD STEAM BOILER INSPECTION
AND INSURANCE COMPANY
Typical Branch Office Workflow
Request for Insurance
Special Agent
Application Completed and Binder Issued
First Inspection Order (FIO)
Inspection Completed
Supervisory Inspector Approval
Application and Inspection Data
Computer or manual policy?
Manual
Computer
Use Data Processing Manual
Coding
Input Mohawk
Transmit to Home Office
errors
Print Policy Information
Use Rating Manual and Underwriting Handbooks
Underwriting
Typing, Checking
Bookkeeping
Assemble Policy
Copy to Special Agent
Send Policy
Policy & Inspection Data
Inspection Records Department
Producer (agent)
Insured

With FIOs and approval completed, the branch office production machinery geared up. If the policy involved a fairly straightforward risk, the information on the application form was translated into machine language by "coders" using a data processing manual to guide their efforts. The data were then transferred to off-line terminals which connected with the home office computer twice daily for the transmission and reception of data on a batch basis.

Usually within 24 to 48 hours the computer transmitted policy information to the branch and a completed policy was then assembled and sent out to the agent and the insured. Any errors made in policy preparation were reported to the branch office when the batch transmission arrived from the home office; the errors were then corrected and the policy was retransmitted as a new one at the earliest possible time.

If the policy was rated and prepared manually, then the application and inspection data was handed to the branch office underwriters, who determined the appropriate premium rates, deductibles, and other parameters, using the rate manual and the underwriting handbooks. The policy was then typed on MTST machines, checked, assembled and mailed. When the policy was sent out to the producer and the insured, both the policy data and the inspection data were given to the inspection records department where the required inspection slips were prepared. The slips were entered into the field inspectors' bibles—the slip books—which indicated when objects required inspections.

The focal point of the branch office inspection function was the slip desk where the thousands of inspection records and requirements were stored for easy access. A typical office with between 75,000 and 150,000 objects under its jurisdiction possessed about 200 four-inch thick looseleaf slip books; each contained approximately 200 pages. A slip was issued for an individual policy not for an individual object, so the number of objects per slip could range from one to several hundred.

Inspection territories for field inspectors were assigned geographically, a situation which one office manager felt was less than optimal: "There is little flexibility or planning in the engineering area. No coordination. If in one day 50 FIOs—high priority items—came in, they could all conceivably go to two inspectors. The other inspectors would continue to perform routine work." Each inspector possessed his own set of slip books corresponding to objects insured in his territory and worked primarily from that set of books.

The branch office managers generally felt they faced three related problems. One was that the home office had set a goal of 21 days for policy delivery; this goal was being met only on the simplest policies at some branches. The second was that inspections were often completed later than originally scheduled. This was the responsibility of the chief inspector but was a prime cause of slow policy delivery. A medium-sized branch might average 29 days for a First Inspection Order to be completed in the field, 11 days for the supervisory inspector to approve the FIO once completed, 10 days to underwrite the risk after the supervisory inspector's approval, and 10 days for filing, recording data and other miscellaneous tasks. The third problem was that interpersonal conflicts often arose between the branch managers and chief inspectors. According to most branch managers, if the chief inspector "went by the book" on all risks big or small, the likelihood of conflict was great.

Development of Company Plans

As Wilson Wilde and other members of management had debated ways to cope with HSB's immediate problems of getting policies delivered more quickly and making sure those were profitable, several longer term issues had been raised. These focused largely on the implications of major trends for HSB's business in the future and the need to clearly define the firm's products, markets and operations to compete effectively. Mr. Wilde hoped that appropriate plans could be developed that would fit both the company and its environment.

CHAPTER 7: THE MULTISITE SERVICE FIRM LIFE CYCLE

The concept that products, companies, and even industries follow a life cycle pattern predictable in some aspects has been convincingly set forth by researchers.[1] This research, however, has been concerned primarily with *goods* and with the firms that manufacture goods; little research has been done to investigate the life cycle paradigm as it applies to *services* and the firms that deliver services; however, in this chapter the life cycle pattern of service firms is examined.

The multisite service firms, which are the focus of this chapter, have exhibited the capacity for spectacular growth in the last quarter century. Consider the spectacular growth records of firms like McDonald's, Holiday Inns, Hertz, and Manpower, Inc., as shown in Table 7-1. Multisite operators have become dominant forces in

Table 7-1

GROWTH OF SELECTED SERVICE FIRMS
(dollar figures in millions)

	1965	*1970*	*1975*
McDonald's			
Revenues	$170.8	$587.1	$2,400.0
Earnings	$ 3.4	$ 19.0	$ 86.9
Total Units	738	1,592	3,750
Holiday Inns			
Revenues	$ 71.2	$604.6	$ 916.9
Earnings	$ 4.0	$ 37.5	$ 41.9
Total Inns	587	11,191	1,750
Total Rooms	69,880	164,039	275,000
Hertz			
Revenues	$274.6	$563.2	$ 722.0
Earnings	$ 10.2	$ 15.6	$ 23.2
Manpower, Inc.			
Revenues	$ 47.3	$107.0	$ 161.2
Earnings	$ 2.0	$ 3.5	$ 2.9
Total Units	377	630	452

[1] For example, see Theodore Levitt, "Exploit the Product Life Cycle," *Harvard Business Review* (November–December 1965); Louis T. Wells, *The Product Life Cycle and International Trade,* Harvard Graduate School of Business, Division of Research, 1972; and Barrie G. James, "The Theory of the Corporate Life Cycle" *Long Range Planning* (June 1973).

many service industries. In the restaurant industry, which has long been dominated by individual restaurateurs, the top 400 chains accounted for 43% of all dining revenues in 1975, up from 33% in 1965. Even private garbage collection firms have witnessed a consolidation trend in their industry as many smaller firms with one location have been acquired by larger multisite firms. What happens to these service firms as they grow? What management functions are critical at different stages in the firm's life? What are the potential pitfalls that must be avoided? Obtaining answers to these questions can be greatly assisted by analyzing the life cycle of multisite service firms.

As the multisite service firm grows, it passes through several stages of a life cycle: entrepreneurial, multisite rationalization, growth, maturity, and decline/regeneration (Figure 7-1). A description of each stage is included below. For each stage, the five major functional areas of the firm (finance/control, operations, marketing, development, and administration) are examined in detail. At the end of the description of each stage, an example of a firm in that stage is given.

STAGE 1: ENTREPRENEURIAL

In the entrepreneurial stage, an individual recognizes a market need and offers a service at a limited number (usually one) of locations. Only a small number of entrepreneurs get beyond this initial step, but, of those few who produce profitable concepts, some begin thinking of additional facilities once their initial facility has been

Figure 7-1

The Multisite Service Firm Life Cycle and Functional Areas of Corporate Activity

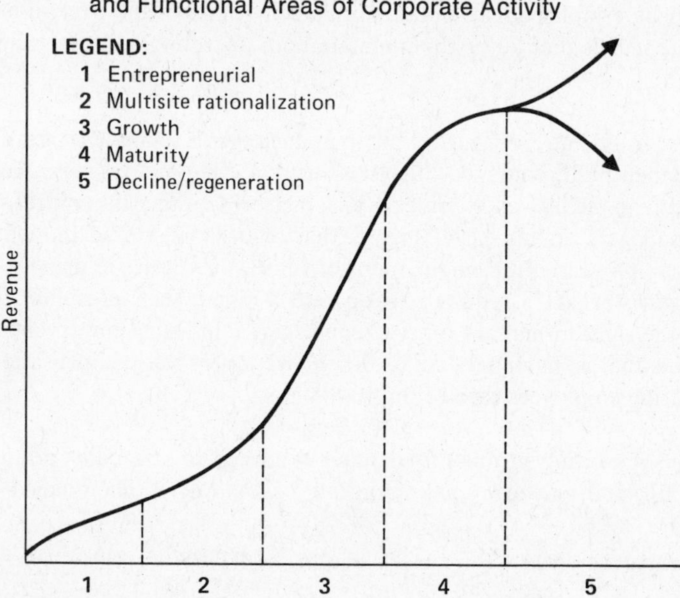

expanded either to its physical limit or market area limit. The physical limit arises from the lack of available space to expand. The market area limit arises from the characteristic that a service facility draws its customers from a limited geographic area. At the end of this first stage, these entrepreneurs have developed plans for new facilities in nearby market areas.

Finance/control. Because the delivery of most services is, as a rule, a labor intensive process not requiring elaborate and expensive equipment, financing the initial service facility can often be handled by a local banker who is accustomed to the real estate and working capital financing required in its early stage. Although the local banker can handle the financing, getting a banker to agree to back the start-up of a newly formed service is not simple. Many financial executives find it difficult to finance an idea, which is exactly what a service is before the service facility begins the delivery of the service. Lenders argue that a manufacturing firm in the start-up phase would at least have a prototype product to inspect. And, as a financial analyst noted:

> It's very difficult in the early stages to look at a hamburger operation or a motel operation or data processing operation and say, "My God, there's something unique, there's something that distinguishes them. They've carved out a niche for themselves." [2]

Lenders are also concerned by the lack of a finished goods inventory, assets that can be pledged as collateral for their loan. What's worse, they note, is that the same low barriers to entry that attract the prospective borrower to the business allows the same ease of entry to competitors if the concept proves successful. They point out that there are no patents on services; only service marks that protect trade names if they can be established. In obtaining financing, one of the overriding criteria for the entrepreneur is that he or she maintain both operating and ownership control of the firm.

Operations. If the entrepreneur is able to finance the development of the first facility, the unit is then built, equipped, furbished, and opened for business. Attention turns to operating the facility, and it quickly becomes evident that the critical skill required of most managers at this early stage is that of organizing and motivating a group of service employees. Past employment or military experience usually provides the manager with the skills required to operate a single service facility. However, in acquiring the right to manage others, many service industry entrepreneurs often pay a high price, that is, having to work 80-hour weeks for less compensation than many manufacturing employees receive for 40 hours.

Marketing. Marketing in this initial stage is limited to in-facility promotions, signs near the unit, and maybe a small ad in the *Yellow Pages*. The financal resources to

---

[2] These remarks were made by John Simmins in the *Wall Street Transcript,* April 26, 1976, pp. 43, 527.

develop newspaper, magazine, radio, and television advertising compaigns are usually not available to the single unit operator. In terms of marketing variables at this early stage, selection of the site for the unit and the atmosphere created by the facility's decor are extremely important. However, the most important marketing tool is the delivery of the service itself. If the consumer is satisfied with the service, then advertising by word of mouth will be generated. And word of mouth is not only the most effective means of marketing; it is the least expensive.

Development. The development function includes everything from site selection to starting up a new unit. In this initial stage, most of the activities under this function are contracted to outside architects and contractors. The entrepreneur selects the first site and communicates his or her ideas about facility design and equipment configuration to these outside vendors. The entrepreneur is intimately involved with the start-up of the initial units.

Administration. During the entrepreneurial period, the entrepreneur is primarily interested in survival. The planning horizon (the longest period for which the company makes plans) may be as short as a week or as long as several months at the most. The greatest concern may be: "Will we have enough to meet this week's payroll?" A number of service firms never make it through this first stage; those firms that do, survive mainly through the super effort exerted by the entrepreneur, the person who brought it all together.

An example. Lamar Perlis is a good example of someone in the entrepreneurial stage of the service firm life cycle. Perlis built a full-service truckstop on highway I-75 near his hometown of Cordele, Georgia. Perlis first had the idea for the site in late 1964. The truckstop, which opened in June 1971, had operating losses for 1971 and 1972. In the first year both Perlis and his wife Jackie worked 20 hours a day, 7 days a week.

The major marketing effort was in providing the truck drivers with the amenities they needed. Among the amenities offered were a restaurant, a motel, a message service, check cashing, and a store that stocked a broad range of items including western shirts, boots, and citizen band radios. However, the major key to the 1974 sales level of \$5 million and pretax earnings of \$600,000 was Perlis' ability to provide fuel to the truckers during the fuel shortage throughout the fall and winter of 1973–1974. The availability of fuel was transmitted rapidly throughout the trucking circles; truckers who stopped were also impressed with the facilities and many became regular customers.

Perlis served as general manager of the facility. Although he had made several attempts to hire a general manager to oversee all the activities of the truckstop, he had not found anyone who met his specifications. He kept a close tab on everyone in the organization. According to his accountant:

> If Lamar decides to leave here to go into other things we will have to develop a different management control system because a new general manager would not be controlling his own money and would, therefore, not stay quite on top of everything as Lamar does.

One of Perlis' largest problems was finding experienced workers and managers. In less than four years of operation the truckstop had hired more than 1,700 hourly employees for 150 positions. In that time there had been five different managers of the fuel department and a half dozen different managers of the restaurant.

As might be expected, Perlis had been considering for some time expansion to a second location. He noted:

> We now have a stable organization and each department is making money. I don't foresee any problems in controlling two truckstops. I could send in audit teams to each department of the truckstop on a regular basis to be sure all is in order. I would plan to make regular visits myself as long as I am in the Georgia-South Carolina region. I can hire a plane for $70 an hour to get me from one stop to the next.

STAGE 2: MULTISITE RATIONALIZATION

In this stage, the successful service firm entrepreneurs, after discovering the profitability of their service concept, begin adding to their limited number of facilities. If they can successfully reproduce the concept, they become multisite operators. During this stage, the distinctive skills of the multisite operator are developed. Additionally, the respective roles of managers of facilities in the field and of the staff at headquarters come into much sharper focus. A requirement for future success is that the individual facilities exhibit the profit potential to support both good management at the facility level and the overhead of a central organization. By the end of this stage, the company gains a certain degree of stability as a level of critical mass is reached. Management develops confidence that the service concept has national, or at least regional, potential. The organization is revving its engine and becoming ready to accelerate through the next stage.

Finance/control. In the multisite rationalization stage, the finance/control function begins to take shape. An accounting system is designed and implemented to handle multiple facilities and to provide some feedback to management on at least a weekly basis. During this stage the costs of opening a new facility become more known as the firm gains experience at this task. With capital cost, operating costs, and the revenues better known, financing through local banks becomes less difficult as the concept proves its profitability.

Yet, most service firms consider another financing vehicle at this phase in their lives—franchising. Franchising allows the firm to transfer its concept to other entrepreneurs for a front-end fee per unit franchised and a percentage of the ongoing revenues. The decision to franchise has its benefits. The concept can be spread quickly over many geographic areas, preempting competitors who might attempt to imitate a successful concept. The process is self-financing and can generate substantial cash flows. It also generates a system of owner/managers, managers who are strongly motivated to succeed out of self-interest. However, the decision to franchise must be balanced against the loss of control. Future profits are lost because the profits from a franchised facility are only a small percentage of the revenues. The company-owned facilities normally produce a much higher profit rate for the parent company. The loss of control results from the fact that franchisees are their own bosses tied to the franchise system by a legal contract, a contract that has gradually been reduced in its power through a series of court challenges instituted by discontented franchisees.

Operations. In this stage, the founding entrepreneur usually delegates the operations function to a trusted lieutenant. Decisions about sites, concept refinement, construction, and franchising consume increasingly more of the founder's time. For him or her, the real excitement is not in operating the existing facilities but rather in refining the concept and getting additional facilities underway.

A key constraint faced by the operations team is staffing the new facilities with both operating and managerial personnel. Each new facility opened in this stage requires a substantial increase in the total percentage of the workforce of the firm. The new facilities often drain talent away from the existing facilities. However, the esprit de corps is usually high; most workers are excited about working for a fledgling firm. The workers see it as a personal challenge to make the concept work. Some also recognize that they are getting in on the ground floor of a potentially large business.

Although the operations group is responsible for multiple facilities, the number of facilities is still reasonably small and most likely clustered in areas adjacent to the original facility. This usually allows operations personnel to be in any facility physically within a couple of hours if problems arise.

If the concept is franchised, the pressure on operations is to ensure that the franchisee learns the correct operating procedures and delivers the service according to prescribed standards. To assist in this task, operating procedures are written into manuals and company personnel visit the franchised facilities on both a scheduled and an unscheduled basis.

All training is done on the job in one of the existing facilities. Potential branch managers are recruited from a wider geographical area, trained (most likely as an assistant manager), and eventually given a facility to manage. Hourly personnel are normally recruited from a local area and trained on the job by the branch managers. During this phase, the operations group tries to determine the profiles of successful branch managers to assist in the recruiting of new managers.

Marketing. Site selection is still a key marketing decision. During this phase characteristics of a good site in terms of the demographics of the area, traffic patterns, extent of competition, and the like, are studied to develop a set of characteristics of the ideal site. Most sites, nevertheless, are selected using a very unscientific, but remarkably successful method, the intuition of the founder.

The existence of the facilities and their display signs in a particular geographic area also helps market the service as the recognition factor increases. If the facilities are clustered in a media area, it sometimes makes economic sense to use some form of media advertisement, usually newspaper and/or radio. However, since the dollars available at this point for such campaigns are generally small, the decision to advertise is more often made for noneconomic reasons such as the ego needs of the founder.

Just as in the initial stage, word of mouth will continue to work its magic if the service is delivered well. The ability to perform well, on a day-to-day basis, will develop a base of steady customers. Good performance also increases the probability that a consumer will stop at a branch of the firm other than the one near his or her home. When this point is reached, the customer's allegiance is not just to a single facility but to the concept.

Development. In this stage, many tasks of the development function are handled just as in the entrepreneurial stage. As mentioned above, the founding entrepreneur makes the site selection decision. The design function is awarded to an outside architectural firm and the construction is still handled by an outside contractor.

The size of the facility and its layout are continuously adjusted to maximize revenues and to make the delivery of the service as efficient as possible. The development activities, besides getting the new facilities underway, have another major purpose. They are all designed to create a reproducible concept, so that the "cookie cutter" can stamp out facilities during the anticipated growth phase to follow. For the cookie cutter to produce large volumes of new facilities (openings of one per week are not uncommon; some service systems have averaged more than one per day), the process must be standardized.

Administration. The entrepreneur must delegate some of his or her former duties to make the transition successfully into the second stage. Usually the operations function is one of the first functions to be delegated for reasons mentioned above. Next, the entrepreneur normally brings someone in from outside the organization to handle the finance/control function. The entrepreneur keeps a tight rein on the other functions. If the firm has decided to franchise its concept, the founding entrepreneur spends much of his or her time screening prospective franchisees for qualified prospects. If a firm has made a heavy commitment to franchise (there are some firms that have no company-owned or company-operated facilities), a franchise department may be created, even at this early stage, to handle the relationships with existing and potential franchisees.

An example. In developing a 12-site chain of budget motels from 1968 to 1973, Fred Roedel led Chalet Susse International through the multisite rationalization stage. During this period he developed standards of performance for operating the facilities.

The standard cost system included cost by item on a per-room-rented basis. The goal for direct cost per room rented was $1.86. Managers were expected to stay within such cost guidelines and were required to submit weekly reports on the number of rooms rented and costs incurred. Deviations could be spotted quickly and were the subject of quick action by Chalet's staff.

A standard design for a 60-room or 120-room property was developed. During this phase, Chalet tried numerous construction techniques in an attempt to minimize costs. Initial facilities were built of wood. However, severe weather, maintenance, and building code problems forced a change to a "block and planks" building—concrete blocks for vertical walls and precast concrete planks for floors and ceilings. Chalet used a few key subcontractors to construct the units and employed a staff of four construction superintendents to manage construction at each site; thus, Chalet saved about 20% of the construction cost of a new facility by eliminating the need for a general contractor.

The selection and training of managers were regarded as critical tasks. Originally, retired military couples were preferred, but as occupancy rates increased and more facilities were expanded to 120 rooms, Chalet management discovered that younger couples were required to handle the increased work load. Management looked for maturity, business sense, a helpful manner, and enthusiasm in prospective managers.

At first new managers were trained on the job at one of the motels. However, the number of couples requiring training forced the company to formalize its training program. As one executive explained:

> We just cannot continue using the current informal methods to train. The couple managing a motel cannot be trained and manage the property well at the same time. It's becoming too much of a strain as we move to more 120-room facilities which are always fully occupied.

Chalet Susse placed heavy emphasis on local promotion, primarily from personal selling by the manager. Billboards stressing the location of the nearest Chalet and its low price were used extensively. Ads were placed in local newspapers, travel guides, and the *Yellow Pages*. Public relations activities that resulted in a mention of Chalet Susse on talk shows and in magazines and newspaper articles were particularly effective in attracting new customers.

During this period, Fred Roedel tried franchising and did not like the results. He made a decision not to grant any more franchises beyond the five already granted. Roedel explained:

> We are not franchising because I started this company to have fun and build something. If I started a franchising program, I might as well have a legal staff next to me. I would also have to worry about providing services to the franchises. In addition, I would have to franchise six motels to make as much money as I do with one of my own. And remember, with franchises I lose most of the control, and control is the key to survival in this business.

STAGE 3: GROWTH

Once a service firm verifies that its concept is profitable and reproducible, a period of rapid expansion follows. The vehicles employed to achieve market penetration depend upon several factors, including how easily the service concept can be copied by competitors, the amount of capital required to finance new facilities, the ease of attracting and retaining capable managers, and the availability of operating authorities and licenses. Popular growth vehicles include: (1) the purchase of competitors; (2) franchise or license arrangements; and (3) construction of new company-operated facilities. Some service firms employ all three; many use two of the three.

While many firms decide to go public and fuel their revenue and earnings growth with additional facilities, the very success of the service firm during this "golden age" can lead to its eventual decline. Often the need to grow receives its impetus not only from the desires of the founders to grow but also from a need to satisfy the financial community. The firm often has trouble digesting the new business because the management team does not develop fast enough to handle the increasing complexity of the business. This factor is discussed in detail later in the chapter.

The firm normally grows by opening facilities in geographic areas contiguous to existing locations. By so doing, advertising economies are achieved and the management control problems are eased. Some firms, however, tackle several regions simultaneously; others even decide to expand beyond the borders. Often, these attempts at establishing new beachheads prove costly, if not in out-of-pocket dollars (which can be substantial), at least in terms of managerial time.

Finance/control. The growth phase generates the need for large amounts of cash to finance the construction and furnishing of new facilities and to finance the initial operating deficits. If the firm has elected to franchise its concept, some of the funds needed for development are provided by the franchisees, whose front-end fees can be used to support the growth in the number of company units and in the staff services needed to support both franchisee and company units. Large institutional lenders such as insurance firms and pension funds become interested in financing the development of a package of units. The sale and lease-back of currently owned properties is another popular vehicle for generating cash. Many service firms at this stage decide to have a public offering of their stock. The prospects of a fast growth stage make the stock an attractive investment in the eyes of the financial community. The entrepreneur will dilute his or her ownership unless effective operating control can be maintained. The entrepreneur normally uses the public offering as a way of realizing some capital gain and establishing a market value for the remainder of his or her holdings.

On the control side, most reports have been computerized to ease the tremendous clerical task of generating the reports needed to manage the firm. The control system must have the capability to assimilate a large number of new facilities in a short time with minimum trouble.

Operations. With the addition of a large number of facilities, the operations group develops a more formal structure, usually organized along geographic dimensions. A typical service firm organization chart would find five to ten branch managers reporting to a district manager, who, in turn, would be one of five district managers reporting to an area manager. About five area managers would report to a regional manager, who, with several other regional managers, report to the vice-president of operations. If the firm has chosen the franchising route, a similar organization might exist in parallel with a group of franchised facilities under the responsibility of a district manager.

The pressure on the operations group to develop a large number of competent branch managers during this phase is intense. A formal training program is created; often the program is housed in a separate training facility. As the growth rate increases, the tendency is to shorten the training program and the subsequent on-the-job experience to get managers into the new facilities as they are opened. The upward mobility in the organization seems almost without limit. Extremely competent personnel are often promoted several times a year; those who display any competence are promoted at least once a year. Morale is high.

Within operations, a separate purchasing department is usually created during this stage. The firm has now reached the size to qualify for purchasing discounts for most equipment and supplies needed to perform the service. Some firms generate such a high demand for certain products that they begin to manufacture them.

The operations group uses the organization to enforce the standards, systems, and procedures that have been developed. Furthermore, a staff group, reporting directly to the head operations person, is usually created to perform an independent auditing function by randomly inspecting the facilities of both the franchisees and the parent company.

Marketing. The positive effect of good sites and the delivery of a superior service are still important factors in marketing the service. However, a new set of marketing problems begins to emerge as a saturation point is reached in markets that were developed first. It is not only a saturation of the firm's facilities, but also those of competitors. As a result, some facilities begin to experience a decline in real volume. Marketing, which has now achieved departmental status within the firm, begins to develop programs to help raise the per facility volumes. The combined effect of a larger revenue base and clustering of facilities allows the firm to expand its advertising to regional editions of magazines and commercial television. The firm begins to perform some market research that is required to develop the media advertising. Most often the research is conducted and interpreted by the advertising agency selected to handle the development of the copy and the purchasing of space or time with the desired media.

Development. Development becomes a hotbed of activity as the cookie cutter goes to work stamping out new facilities. At this stage many of the development tasks are brought in-house. It is not uncommon to find an in-house architectural group designing buildings, and even an in-house construction crew erecting new facilities. If the construction process is not brought in-house it is usually done by one or two firms that have had prior experience with the firm's concept. The development group will also have a number of project managers who are given the responsibility for getting specific development projects completed on time and on budget.

As ideas are introduced into new facilities, there is pressure to incorporate those changes into the already existing facilities. In addition to the pressure to upgrade older locations, the need arises in many of the older facilities for a remodeling package or an expansion of capacity to meet excess demand. A portion of the development group may specialize in the remodeling and expansion process.

The first few weeks of operation of a new facility are often viewed as part of the development function. Often there is a special team of start-up specialists who help staff and train the branch employees, help promote the grand opening ceremonies, and in general, debug the new facility. The team may be organizationally a part of the development department or a part of the operations group.

Administration. In this stage, the scale of the business necessitates the division of tasks in such logical ways that one individual may become a specialist in handling finance, operations, or marketing. During this period formal procedures (some initiated in the prior stage) are finalized to handle day-to-day activities and questions that arise more routinely, because the chief executive need [can] not be consulted about every situation. The entrepreneur/founder often runs into problems in this stage because he or she is forced to delegate more and more of the power he or she once held. As leader of the organization, he or she is forced to manage more by the numbers than by personal observation. The pace within the organization is hectic during this stage: sites must be selected, plans approved, contracts let, construction supervised, facilities furnished with equipment and staffed with people, and new facilities opened. The organization chart is changed often to reflect new assignments and responsibilities.

An example. In the early fall of 1973, the three founders of Victoria Station, a chain of railroad theme restaurants, were in the midst of a growth phase. They had opened 17 restaurants since 1969 and had approximately 10 more on the drawing boards. In addition, the company had made a very successful initial public offering of its stock.

Members of the financial community described the Victoria Station growth record as "most impressive." The market price of the stock reflected a price earnings ratio of 59 times the prior year's earnings. Market analysts felt that such a price was justified based on past and anticipated growth. However, one market observer pointed out that such a favorable price-earnings ratio was dependent on a continued record of growth in the number of restaurants and their profitability.

The founders were preparing for the next phase of their growth by developing operating control and reporting procedures to maintain the profits from the existing facilities while continuing to open new ones. Dick Bradley, the president, felt that "if you can control the food quality, then your only remaining problem is one of execution." To achieve this, all beef was purchased nationally, cut to specification, and shipped directly to each location. Shrimp were also purchased nationally and shipped to all restaurants. Produce and most service items were purchased locally from an approved purveyor list.

Execution was primarily a matter of careful management supervision to ensure strict adherence to clearly defined standards as stated in the comprehensive operations manual. Appearance, food and beverage preparation, service, atmosphere, equipment maintenance, safety, inventory control, and other matters were set down in detail, together with complete job descriptions for all managers.

Financial control of restaurants was maintained through several detailed reports. Daily meal counts, sales receipts and expenditure reports, and sales breakdowns for food and beverages were tallied for each waiter at both lunch and dinner. Daily inventories were taken of ribs, steaks, and liquor, with other items inventoried no less often than monthly. While it was believed by top management that these control procedures enabled them to spot potential problems such as waste or pilferage before they got out of hand, they felt that the continued goodwill of a capable employee group could not be overemphasized.

The company used no advertising or paid promotion and therefore relied entirely on initial publicity before opening new facilities and word-of-mouth advertising for its marketing success. Simply being open for lunch, particularly in downtown areas, was considered by management as a form of advertising for couple or family dinner business.

Victoria Station management viewed its management activities as a series of delivery systems with restaurant operations in the center of the picture. The real estate, construction, and maintenance functions delivered to operations a complete restaurant; the human resources and training functions delivered trained management people and in-restaurant training services along with wage, salary, and benefit programs; the accounting and data processing functions delivered financial procedures, systems, and data; the operations analysis and quality control functions delivered interpretive feedback and analysis; and the operating restaurants delivered the product and service to the customer as well as sales and earnings to the corporation and its shareholders.

Dick Bradley commented on the growth stage and the preparation for it:

> We have built the foundations for a much larger company. The cost controls, quality controls, and organization we have installed are intended for the future. If we were planning to stay at our present size, these expenditures would not be necessary.

STAGE 4: MATURITY

In this stage, the growth rate of the prior stage is not sustained. The number of new facilities opened declines substantially and the per facility volumes in real terms level off or in some cases actually decline. The declines can normally be traced to a combination of four factors: changing demographics within the market area, changing needs and tastes of the consumers, increased competition from other service firms, and increased "cannibalization" by the service firm's new facilities of older ones. As a result, the firm's revenues level off from their rather steep ascent of the growth stage. Concentrated efforts are made to increase revenues by several means including increased advertising and promotion, addition of new services at existing facilities, and increased capacity at those locations where there are capacity bottlenecks.

By this time the service concept has lost much of the uniqueness it possessed in earlier stages. The battle in the marketplace is with well-entrenched competitors for each others' customers. Most primary demand has already been tapped. Marginal competitors fall by the wayside as intensive marketing campaigns are developed to differentiate the service that has assumed the characteristics of a commodity.

The firm scales down many of its development activities and adopts an operating posture. The focus is on getting more revenues and profits from each branch. Intensive price competition often accompanies this stage so that efforts are made to effect cost savings that will enable the firm to compete more favorably on price.

In this stage, the franchisor begins to experience problems with franchisees. Some franchises are profitable; others are not. The prescription for revival of the unprofitable franchises varies by location. The franchisee normally will not wait for the franchisor to find a solution for his or her branches. The franchisee undertakes a few "local" innovations such as offering new services not approved by the franchisor. With such local innovations being tried throughout the system, the system no longer maintains its integrity. The facilities in the field quickly lose their consistency in design, decor, and service offerings. It becomes much more difficult to get all the branches in the system to adopt approved service extensions and/or new concepts. Many franchisees will express more and more discontent about the amount of their royalty payments. They, too, will have experienced a life cycle of their own, and many of the services provided by the franchisor are no longer needed. If the franchisor has not expanded its services to fit the new needs of those franchisees, many of the franchisees will develop internally these skills within their own organizations.

Finance/control. In this stage the threat of saturation becomes a reality in many markets. The investment community, realizing that growth opportunities are now limited, discounts the price of the stock, but unless the volume per branch declines, the firm continues to generate a healthy cash flow. If the firm has adopted the franchise route, the front-end franchise fees evaporate, but royalty fees remain steady. However, the need for funds has also been diminished because growth has been stymied. At this stage the firm might use its cash flow to make an acquisition or increase its dividend payments to stockholders. It may even be an acquisition candidate if its stock gets too undervalued.

By now, there are usually few problems with the control system. The only negative factor is that the number of reports have a tendency to increase, especially when performance begins to level off. The paperwork burden may increase for the managers in the field, reducing the amount of time available for them to improve the performance of their facilities.

Operations. With few new facilities being opened, the operations function focuses on running the existing branches. The operations group gains increased status, because the growth in revenues and profits must come from efficient operation of those branches already in place.

The decline in number of new facilities, however, leads to a morale problem for the people in operations. The esprit de corps present in the earlier stages is diminished greatly as the myth of unlimited upward mobility is suddenly shattered when it is revealed that there is a real limit to growth. Managers who have recently joined the organization are especially vulnerable. They feel like the bottom rung of people in a "pyramid scheme" that has been exposed by a consumer or government watchdog. Many managers in the system leave because the opportunities no longer appear to be unlimited. Their departure creates the need for new managers, but the characteristics of the successful manager have changed. Management must look for a different profile. The hard-charger type who was so appropriate for the earlier stages of the business must be replaced by a manager who will not be frustrated by a slower rate of advancement. It becomes much more difficult to attract capable managers to a slow-growth or nongrowth situation. Although there is still a need to train replacement managers, the pressure to mass produce new managers has diminished greatly.

An important operations task now is to ensure that all branches adhere to the standards of the system. At this point there is a tendency for the individual branches to alter the concept without corporate approval to meet local competitive conditions and/or not to maintain the facility as well as in the past. This behavior is especially prevalent among franchisees over whom control is exercised by the threat of legal action rather than the threat of being fired such as it would be for managers of company facilities.

Maintenance is an important operations function as equipment in the facilities, especially the older facilities, requires increasingly more upkeep. Just as special teams are created to handle the start-up of a new facility, teams of specialists are often created to help turn a declining branch around. The team members possess the various marketing, operations, and administrative skills to set in motion a series of actions to improve the performance of a branch.

Marketing. This department, which was created in the prior stage, becomes an important function in the mature phase. All the available marketing tools are employed. As mentioned earlier, efforts are made to differentiate the service from the host of competitive services that now challenge it for a share of the market. Market research, which was begun in the prior stage, gains added importance as the firm recognizes that it must know with which consumer segments it has strengths and with which it has weaknesses. The density of unit locations is extensive enough in many instances to justify regional and national advertising campaigns.

Marketing research is also used to test the consumer's reaction to proposed changes in the concept. Such changes represent efforts to increase branch volumes; these changes take a variety of forms such as new services, new methods of service delivery, and expanded or contracted hours of operation.

Development. Just as many of the development functions are brought in-house and assimilated into the organization of the firm, the number of anticipated new facility openings diminishes drastically. As a result, some of the development functions are disbanded or reduced considerably in size. But because there are a number of older facilities in operation, the need for remodeling packages is great. There are also developmental efforts to alter the present concept and/or to design an entirely new one.

Administration. It would be surprising to find the original entrepreneur/founder in charge of the firm. Very few owners last beyond the growth stage. Just like the inventor/founder of manufacturing firms, he or she becomes overpowered by the administrative details and abdicates the managing of the business to a more professionally trained manager.

During the maturity phase, the company's management begins to develop doubts about the viability of the concept. They begin to question whether or not the firm should continue in the same business. However, the less hectic pace of the maturity phase as compared to the growth phase is very enticing. Those in management who are seduced and do not adapt to changing market conditions awaken to find themselves in the decline phase of their firm's life cycle. Those who do react and are successful will rejuvenate the tired original concept or generate a newer and more viable concept.

An example.[4] Kampgrounds of America (KOA) is a good example of a firm that had reached a mature stage after a decade of growth. At the end of 1974, there were 747 franchised campgrounds and 18 company-operated campgrounds in the KOA system. From a single private campground, built in Billings, Montana, in 1962 to serve Seattle World's Fair travelers, came an awareness of the impending growth in travel camping. Surveys among the families using that campground indicated a growing demand for similar facilities throughout North America. In 1963, plans were made to develop a system of campgrounds throughout the United States, similar to the Holiday Inn system of motels. In 1964, seven franchised Kampgrounds of America opened for business.

From the beginning, the company's strategy was to achieve rapidly a degree of market penetration and dominance that potential competitors could not hope to match. Rapid franchise sales and strong consumer marketing programs were the principal techniques used. These techniques were supplemented with support services for franchisees in the areas of construction and operation. As a result of this strategy, the KOA system became the leading campground system in the United States, with more campgrounds in the KOA system than in all its franchised competitors' systems combined.

The first campgrounds built were in keeping with the economics of the business at the time and the prevailing unsophisticated needs of campers. The early KOAs could be characterized as simple, plain, and built on faith in the future. The late sixties and early seventies were marked by changes in the market. As more families became aware of the fun and economy of camping, a new, more affluent type of customer entered the market and began buying more elaborate recreational vehicles. New, larger travel trailers and motor homes, equipped with such luxury features as bathrooms, double ovens, freezers, and air conditioners, began arriving at the campgrounds. To accommodate this changing market, campgrounds began to upgrade and add such amenities as utility hookups, recreational halls, and swimming pools.

The company was changing during this period, too. Experienced management personnel in the fields of sales, finance, marketing, construction, and retail store

---

[4] Adapted from the 1974 Kampgrounds of America Annual Report.

sales were brought into the company. Improved construction and operations manuals were prepared for the franchisees. New standards and a more stringent campground inspection program brought about an upgrading in the quality of facilities and services for campers. And a new training school, KOA University, opened in 1970, bringing a higher degree of sophistication to campground construction and operation.

During this period, new marketing efforts were directed at consumers to encourage more families to camp at KOA Kampgrounds. A national reservations service for campers began. New highway signs were introduced. And the KOA *Kampground Directory,* enlarged to magazine size, became the world's most widely circulated campground directory. New consumer advertising and promotion programs were being implemented. KOA's first venture into television advertising was scheduled to take place in 1975 when a new television commercial would be aired in several markets that had large numbers of camping families.

As the system grew, franchise sales began to decline because of the diminution of available territories to franchise, and the company began a transition from a franchise sales company to an operating company.

The early seventies also marked the expansion of the KOA system to Canada and Mexico and the signing of a licensing agreement for KOA Kampgrounds in Japan. In a program of diversification, the company went to the equity market for funds to build and operate company-owned campgrounds. Testing began in an effort to determine the potential market for overnight sleeping accommodations and restaurants on campgrounds. In addition, as part of a trailer rental program, the company acquired a manufacturer of recreational vehicles.

Significant gains were achieved during these years as camping grew in popularity and the KOA system spread across North America. Then came the 1973–74 international oil crisis. Like other companies in travel and energy-related industries, KOA was adversely affected. Franchise sales fell, new franchisees postponed plans to build campgrounds, sales of recreational vehicles dropped, and fewer families went camping in late 1973 and early 1974 than in the previous year.

Although the company lost money in the noncampground areas of its business in 1974, operations in the campground business were profitable. The principal sources of income that sustained the company in 1974 were the increasing royalties from franchise campgrounds and the increased revenue from company-owned campgrounds. In this atmosphere, emphasis within the company was being placed on programs and concepts that took advantage of the basic strengths of the KOA system and that would be somewhat less affected by fluctuation in the price and availability of gasoline. Both franchisees and managers of company-owned campgrounds were being encouraged to promote their grounds to local campers, to make them more esthetically appealing, and to add recreational activities and programs to encourage their guests to stay longer.

DECLINE/REGENERATION

If the multisite service firm discovers untapped markets for its present concept, executes a successful extension of its present concept, develops a new concept,

Table 7-2

THE MULTISITE SERVICE FIRM LIFE CYCLE:
OBJECTIVES, DECISIONS, PROBLEMS, AND ORGANIZATION

Stages	*Entrepreneurial*	*Multisite Rationalization*	*Growth*	*Maturity*
Major Objectives	1. Satisfy entrepreneurial drive of founder(s) 2. Generate positive cash flow 3. Maintain operating and ownership control	1. Making concept reproducible 2. Begin to delegate some responsibilities of founder 3. Developing controls to handle multisite system 4. Ensuring that individual units exhibit the profit potential to develop into a system and understanding the key success factors which contribute to the profitability	1. Putting up as many units as possible with "cookie cutter" 2. Preempt competition 3. Maintaining quality while growth occurs	1. Emphasis on profits, not revenue growth 2. Finding new markets for existing concept 3. Finding service extensions to create new demand 4. Differentiate service from that of competitors
Major Decisions	1. Which business to start? 2. How to finance the first unit? 3. Who to hire as employees?	1. What should the prototype unit contain? 2. Should the concept be franchised?	1. Which geographic areas should be attacked? 2. Whether to go public? 3. Whether to sell to larger firm? 4. Where to get managers needed to start new units?	1. What are best marketing tools to differentiate the existing concept from its competitors? 2. Which of new concepts should firm develop? 3. What to do with cash flow?

Table 7-2 (continued)

Stages	*Entrepreneurial*	*Multisite Rationalization*	*Growth*	*Maturity*
Major Problems	1. Communicating the concept to the consumers 2. Long hours required of entrepreneur/founder 3. Finding enough cash to keep concept afloat until unit reaches cash flow breakeven position	1. Founder not being able to delegate 2. Finding good sites 3. Control system is inadequate	1. Growing faster than internally generated funds can supply required equity 2. Growing faster than good managers can be developed 3. Losing control over the development function	1. Discontent among managers who see limited opportunities for advancement 2. Declining sales due to saturation of the concept and/or intense competition 3. Inability to attract capable managers to a mature concept
Organizational Transition	The entrepreneur handles almost all entrepreneurial tasks	The entrepreneur relinquishes some operational control to a trusted operations lieutenant and retains control over most other functions	The entrepreneur focuses on the development functions, especially finding new sites, developing and opening new units; outsiders are often brought in to handle the finance/control functions; many of the development activities are brought in-house	The entrepreneur, in most cases, loses control over the organization during the growth phase; outsider managers are usually in control by the time the mature phase is reached

and/or acquires a new concept, the firm regenerates itself and recycles through another growth phase. Until this happens (if, in fact, it does), the firm is trapped in a stage of decline and deterioration.

Once the service firm gets into a tailspin, it is very difficult to pull out of it. With literally hundreds of facilities and managers in the field, the system has developed a great deal of inertia that must be overcome to effect a turnaround. In the decline stage, a point is reached where management has serious doubts about making further investment in the concept. The only investments are of a defensive nature, accompanied by the following explanation: "If we don't spend this money, our market share will erode even faster." There is little confidence that real gains in volume can be made.

LIFE CYCLE SUMMARY

The life cycle paradigm as applied to multisite service firms is a useful concept for understanding the pattern of development of a service firm over time. There are some important lessons to be learned from the experiences of service firms that have passed through the various stages. By identifying a company's position in the life cycle, we can anticipate, by using Table 7-2 as a guideline, the major objectives, decisions, problems, and organizational transitions needed for the future. With these requirements known, firms can plan for the necessary changes rather than react to a set of conditions that could have been predicted in advance. Thus, as a predictor of certain problems and changing organizational requirements, the life cycle model is valuable; however, it does very little to explain the behavior of the firm's costs as it passes through each stage. To gain this understanding, we must examine more closely exactly how the typical service firm develops throughout the life cycle. The breadth of service/geographic market diagram is a good starting point.

THE BREADTH OF SERVICE AND GEOGRAPHIC MARKET DECISIONS

In Figure 7-2, we attempt, first, to represent diagrammatically the set of decisions made by the service firm regarding the range of services offered and the number of geographic markets served and then to relate the sequence of these decisions to the stages of the service firm life cycle and to the prior research of Abernathy and Utterback.[5]

At the beginning of the entrepreneurial stage, the service firm usually offers a narrow range of services at one geographic location (point *a* in Figure 7-2). This

[5] See William J. Abernathy and James M. Utterback's paper, "A Dynamic Model of Process and Product Innovation" in *Omega,* Vol. 3, No. 6, 1975. The essential aspects of their hypothesized model are that the characteristics of the innovative process systematically correspond with the stage of development exhibited by the firm's production process technology and with its strategy for competition and growth. Their dynamic model of process and product innovation suggests the sources, types, and rates of innovation a given firm might expect to undertake successfully at each stage of its development.

Figure 7-2

The Breadth of Service/Geographic Area Space

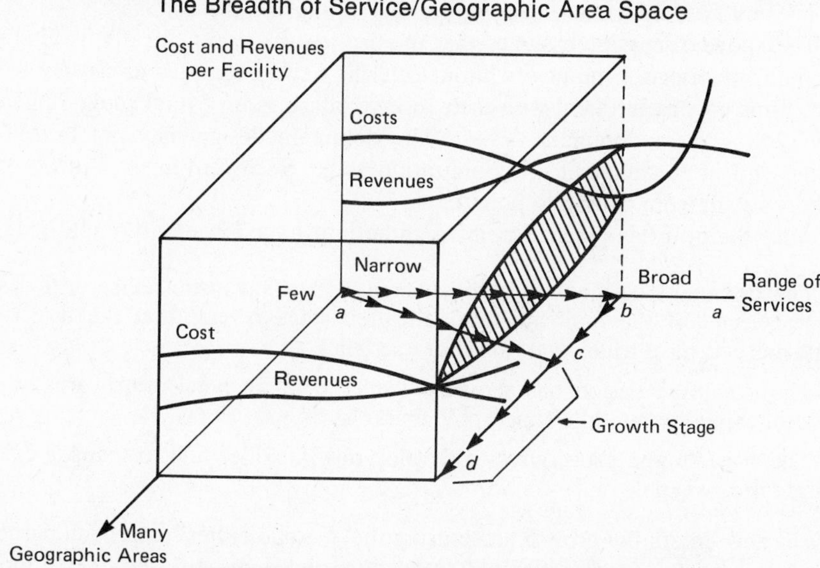

offering attracts certain market segments within the geographic market, yielding a stream of revenues. Associated with this level of revenues is a level of costs, fixed and variable. In Figure 7-2, total costs are depicted as higher than total revenues at point *a*; however, the service offering may be profitable at this point. Whether the service is profitable or not is not as important as the fact that the entrepreneur normally expands the number of services offered until a point is reached (point *b*) at which profits are maximized.

During this period of innovation and refinement, the entrepreneur attempts to develop a package of services that are not being offered by competitors in the market area. New services are added to the existing offerings as long as the incremental revenues attributed to the new services are higher than the incremental costs. In the entrepreneurial stage, the emphasis is not so much on cost reduction as on meeting market needs at a profit. The changes in service offerings are mainly stimulated by the market. In the Abernathy/Utterback model, this stage is the performance maximizing phase. At the end of the entrepreneurial stage, the firm has established the dominant design[6] for its service offering (point *b*).

During the multisite rationalization stage, the entrepreneur develops the systems and procedures to manage multiple sites. At the end of this stage (point *c*), the firm is ready to enter the growth stage.

The firm does not necessarily start at point *a*. It could begin by offering a wide range of services (point *a'*) and discover that, by narrowing the offerings, profitability increases. This is depicted by movement from *a'* to *b*. In addition, a

[6] The term "dominant design" has been suggested by William J. Abernathy to describe this prototypical design.

firm starting at point *a* might expand its services beyond *b* and be forced to reduce its offerings. The evolution of a dominant design is an iterative process with market feedback and cost information providing the stimuli for the changes.

The above discussion assumes that the firm moves systematically from point *a* to a dominant design at point *b* without entering new geographic areas. As a point of fact, firms may experiment with their reserve offerings in several geographic areas before settling on a dominant design. The dominant design may not be selected until the end of the multisite rationalization stage. Such movement can be represented by a path from point *a* to point *c*.

Once the firm has reached point *c,* three things have been accomplished:

1. The dominant design has been selected. (In some instances several designs may be selected if the multisite rationalization stage reveals that the target geographic markets have widely varying characteristics.)

2. The dominant design has shown evidence of a financial return greater than the cost of capital in multiple geographic markets.

3. The systems and procedures to develop new facilities and to manage existing ones are taking shape.

The firm now enters the growth stage using the "cookie cutter" approach described earlier by opening new facilities patterned after the dominant design. As long as the expected revenues from opening new facilities are greater than the expected costs (including the firm's cost of capital), the firm concentrates on two major tasks. The first task is to develop and open as many new facilities as site availability, financing, and management development constraints allow; the second is to operate the existing facilities. Abernathy and Utterback have labeled this phase the sales maximizing stage. Growth in the firm's revenues comes from the addition of new facilities and from increased revenues from existing sites. The growth stage ends and the maturity stage begins when the firm's planning horizon includes point *d,* the point at which the expected revenues from a new facility do not exceed the expected costs. In the maturity stage, the focus on new facility development rapidly fades and the emphasis quickly shifts to the cost minimizing behavior predicted by Abernathy and Utterback.

COSTS AND THEIR LIFE CYCLE DETERMINANTS

These insights about the behavior of the multisite service firm during its life cycle suggest that its cost structure depends on a number of factors as it moves from point *a* to point *d*. Before we examine those variables, we should describe the major cost categories and their components.

The costs fall into three categories: facility costs, operating costs, and general and administrative expenses.

1. *Facility costs* are the one-time costs required to develop and prepare the service facility to deliver the service. They might also be labeled "capital costs." They

include site costs, construction costs, equipment and fixture costs, and preopening costs.

2. *Operating costs* are the costs associated with the actual delivery of the service. They include the costs of supplies, labor, supervision, maintenance, and energy.

3. *General and administrative* expenses are most of the corporate and overhead accounts, which include the administration, control, and corporate marketing functions.

The actual items that fall into each cost category vary according to the service firm. Consider, for example, the costs of the following three firms: an overnight air-freight carrier, a motel chain, and a coffee house restaurant chain. Their costs can be placed into the three categories as illustrated in Table 7-3. These costs suggest that the typical service firm's costs can be broken down into components as shown in the bottom of Table 7-3.

Table 7-3

	Facility Costs	*General and Administrative*	*Operating Costs*
Air freight company	Airplanes Vans Branch offices Central package handling facility Start-up expenses	Management Computer services Advertising Licenses Insurance Interest	Pilots Van drivers Sorting employees Aviation fuel Branch office employees
Motel chain	Land Motel Furnishings and fixtures Start-up expenses	Management Computer services Advertising Licenses Insurance Interest	Motel employees Energy Linen Cleaning supplies Maintenance Uniforms
Restaurant chain	Land Restaurant Equipment Start-up expenses	Management Computer services Licenses Insurance Interest	Food Beverage Restaurant employees Energy Dishes, utensils Maintenance Uniforms
Typical service firm	Site Building Equipment Start-up	Management Control functions Support functions Advertising and promotion Interest Licenses Insurance	Facilitating goods Labor Supervision Maintenance

What variables have an impact on these costs? What is the nature of these impacts? The next section of this chapter is devoted to the presentation of a conceptual model to explain the pattern of these costs over time.

In addressing the question of what variables have an impact on each of the above cost categories, we can develop the following list:

1. Number of facilities
2. Rate of growth of facilities
3. Volume of transactions delivered by a facility
4. Volume of transactions delivered by facilities in a given market area.
5. Volume of transactions delivered by a firm
6. Number of consumers
7. Heterogeneity of consumers
8. Number of geographic markets served
9. Number of employees
10. Diversity of facility types
11. Density of facility locations
12. Heterogeneity of service offerings
13. Concentration of ownership of the firm
14. Form of ownership of the individual facilities
15. Degree of backward integration
16. Intensity of competition
17. External pressures (economic, government, social, labor)

This list of explanatory variables and the list of cost components for the typical service firm in Table 7-3 suggest a massive regression model to explain the behavior of costs over time. Fortunately, the effects of these 17 variables on the cost structure can be lumped into three major categories: (1) the economies of learning; (2) the economies of volume; and (3) the diseconomies of managerial complexity. Investigation of these three categories suggests a model to explain the behavior of a service firm's cost structure over time.

THE ECONOMIES OF LEARNING

The learning curve phenomenon, as a descriptive and analytical model of a company's cost structure, has received a great deal of attention in manufacturing firms,[7] but, to date, has attracted little attention in the service industries. However, opportunities for learning exist in both the function of developing new facilities and the function of running existing ones. Look at Figure 7-3a. In this figure the points *a* through *d* of Figure 7-2 are shown on the service firm life cycle diagram. In Figure

---

7 Fundamentally, the learning curve postulates that costs decline systematically by a common percentage each time volume doubles.

Figure 7-3

Product Process Innovation and Economics of Learning

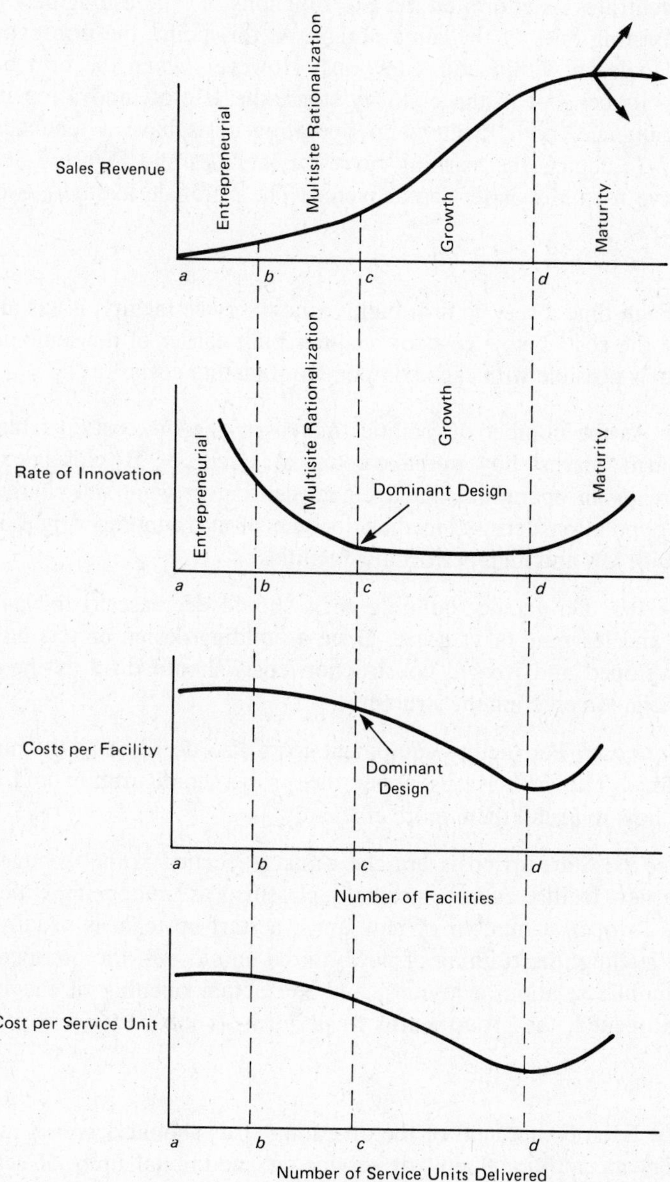

7-3b, the rate of innovation is plotted against time following the Abernathy and Utterback model. The entrepreneurial and multisite rationalization stages are periods in which the rate of innovation is high, as shown in Figure 7-3b, assuming the firm moves along the *a* to *c* line of Figure 7-2.

However, after the dominant design is selected, the rate of innovation drops as the firm concentrates its efforts on the two functions of establishing new facilities and operating existing ones of the same design. At this point, the firm experiences an opportunity to learn within both functions. However, when the firm begins to experiment with its concept in the maturity stage, the rate of innovation increases and, as a consequence, both facility and operating costs have a tendency to increase. Figure 7-3c depicts the learning curve for facilities and Figure 7-3d depicts the learning curve for units of service delivered. The rationale for these two curves is explained below.

Facility costs. Each time a service firm builds a new service facility, it has an opportunity to reduce the costs below costs of facilities built earlier of the same dominant design. Learning is possible with each component of facility costs.

1. *Site costs:* As the number of facilities increases, the site costs per facility are reduced as the firm "learns" how to make better site decisions. By closely examining the facilities already in operation, management can detect what site characteristics (for example, population density, median income of surrounding neighborhoods) are correlated with low and high performing facilities.

2. *Building costs:* Per facility building costs should decrease as the number of units increases and learning takes place. Once a building design or sets of building designs are developed and frozen, construction costs should drop as the firm becomes more efficient in erecting the structures.

3. *Equipment costs:* Per facility equipment costs also decrease as the number of facilities increases. The firm learns about the proper configuration and types of equipment and how to install them more efficiently.

4. *Start-up costs:* Start-up costs are the costs associated with "debugging" the operations of a new facility and are normally classified as preopening expenses. As the firm begins to open a number of new units, a start-up team is usually created to assist in the staffing, the training of newly hired employees, the preopening promotional and public relations activities, and the actual opening of the units. As more units are opened, the group learns to perform its job better and preopening costs decrease.

Operating costs. Each component of the operating costs should decrease every time the firm delivers an additional unit of service. As additional units of service are delivered, the individual service employees, maintenance employees, and their supervisors should learn to perform their jobs better.

ECONOMIES OF VOLUME

As both the number of facilities opened and the volume of service units delivered increase, the typical service firm can experience economies of volume at three levels: the facility level, the market area level, and the corporate level (see Figure 7-4).

1. *Facility level:* For a given service facility, there are some costs such as the cost of the manager, license fees, and taxes that are fixed and other costs such as labor, energy, and maintenance that have a fixed component. As per facility volume increases, these fixed costs on a per service unit delivered basis decline.

2. *Area level:* For a given market area that can contain a number of facilities, there are also economies of volume available. For example, supervisory and marketing expenses on both a per facility and a per service unit delivered in the area

Figure 7-4

The Economics of Volume

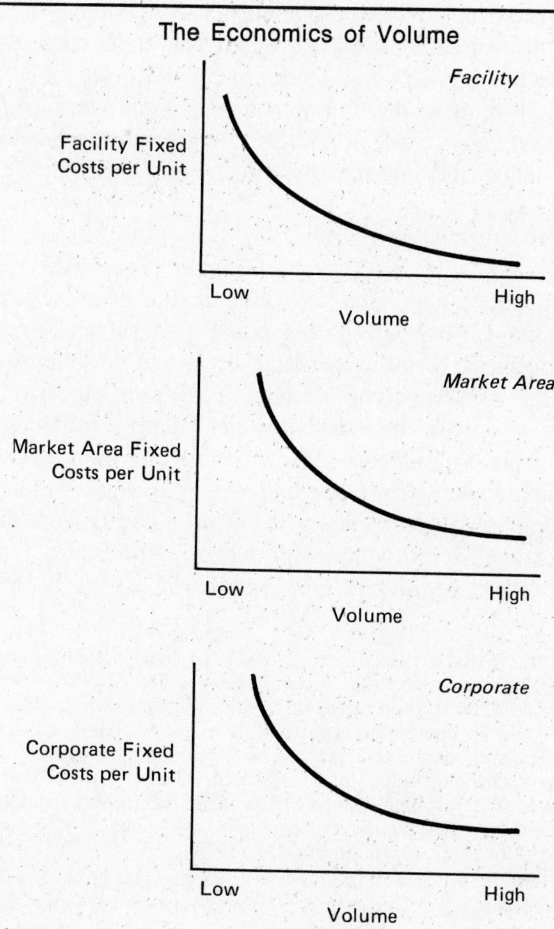

basis decrease as the number of facilities and the sales volume of these facilities increase.

3. *Corporate level:* At the corporate level, there are economies of volume in the administrative, purchasing, and financing areas. As more service units are delivered, the lower the administrative expenses per unit delivered. As the firm grows in both number of facilities in operation and number of service units delivered, it often achieves the bargaining power to negotiate lower prices for its equipment and supplies. If the demand for such items proves to be substantial, the firm may decide to integrate backwards into its supply channels to lower costs even more. In addition, as the firm grows larger, it is likely to attract outside capital at more attractive rates because many financial institutions equate size with stability.

DISECONOMIES OF MANAGERIAL COMPLEXITY

As the multisite service firm grows, the complexity of managing the firm increases and the associated diseconomies often outweigh the economies of learning and volume, especially in the growth stage of the firm's life cycle.[8] For any given executive team there is a limit to the amount of managerial complexity that can be assimilated within any given time period. Although managerial complexity is a difficult concept to define and measure, its effects are real. Managers understand when they have reached their capacity to absorb it, and the operating performance of the firm is negatively correlated with it.

In examining a number of firms in several service industries, we have noticed that many firms experience a difficult transition period as they grow beyond the capabilities of the management team. At this point, management is not able to focus on all facets of the business; certain key functions get out of control; costs rise; and the profitability of the firm begins to decline. If the firm survives this transition period, performance improves. In a recent study [9] of the fast-food industry, the presidents and chief operating officers of 13 fast-growing food service chains were interviewed to determine what was happening as they navigated their firms through the "Bermuda Triangle" [10] of multisite service firms. Insights from these interviews led to the concept of managerial complexity that we hypothesize as a major determinant of a service firm's cost structure (see Figure 7-5).

---

[8] Donald K. Clifford, Jr., in his article, "Growth Pains of the Threshhold Company," in the September–October, 1973, issue of *Harvard Business Review* describes the complexity faced by firms in the \$20 million to \$200 million range of annual revenues. His analysis pinpointed nine elements that tend to grow in complexity as a company grows. Clifford's article described a wide range of industries, both manufacturing and service. Our conceptual framework, which includes several of the factors included in the Clifford scheme, focuses on the behavior of multisite service firms. Similar problems were observed in the trucking industry by D. Daryl Wyckoff in *Organizational Formality and Performance in the Motor Carrier Industry* (Lexington, Mass.: Lexington Books, D. C. Heath and Co., 1974).

[9] W. Earl Sasser and Ivor P. Morgan, "The Bermuda Triangle of Food Service Chains," *The Cornell Hotel and Restaurant Administration Quarterly* (February 1977) pp. 56–61.

[10] The Bermuda Triangle is the zone of development of a company during which the managerial complexity facing the firm is greater than the firm's capacity to handle it.

Figure 7-5

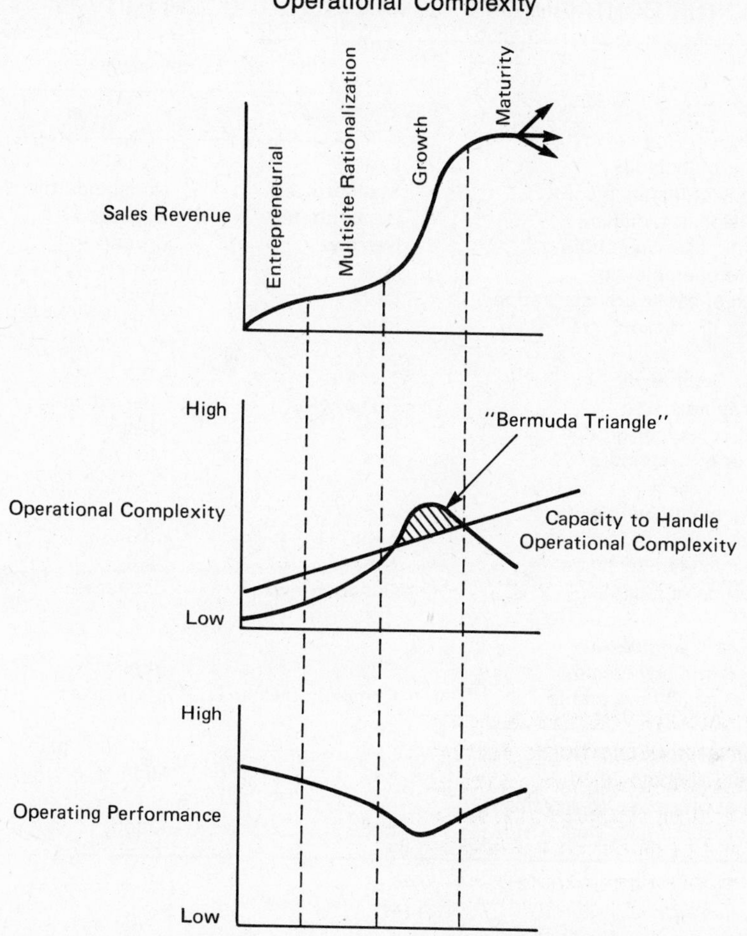

Managerial complexity is a function of the elements shown in Table 7-4. These 16 elements fall into five groups: operational complexity, marketing complexity, developmental complexity, ownership complexity, and environmental complexity.

Table 7-4 can be used in its present format to predict which firms are in danger of passing, or have already passed, their limits to handle managerial complexity. If a firm decides to operate at the high complexity end of the spectrum of many elements, it is in real danger. A firm that begins to experience the effects of managerial complexity can use Table 7-4 as a guideline to reduce this complexity. For example, if a firm that is growing by expanding into a number of new geographic areas with company-owned facilities begins to feel the overload of managerial complexity, it can reduce its complexity by narrowing its service offerings and standardizing its facilities. Certainly, it would not be judicious at this time to decide to franchise or to integrate backward into its supply channels.

Table 7-4

THE CONTRIBUTORS TO MANAGERIAL COMPLEXITY

	Managerial Complexity	
	Low	*High*
Operational Complexity		
Number of facilities	Few	Many
Diversity of facility types	Standardized	Nonstandardized
Dispersion of facilities	Concentrated	Scattered
Breadth of service offering	Narrow	Broad
Number of employees	Few	Many
Degree of backward integration	Little	Much
Volume of transactions	Few	Many
Market Complexity		
Geographic scope	Regional	International
Target consumer groups	Few	Many
Number of customers	Few	Many
Development Complexity		
Rate of growth of facilities	Slow	Fast
Diversity of facility types	Limited	Many
Dispersion of facilities	Concentrated	Scattered
Ownership Complexity		
Form of firm ownership	Private	Public
Form of facility ownership	Company-owned	Franchised
Environmental Complexity		
Intensity of competition	Low	High
External pressures (government, labor, economic, etc.)	Little	Much

AGGREGATING THE ECONOMIES AND DISECONOMIES

Combining the effects of learning and volume economies with managerial complexity diseconomies yields the cost model depicted in Figure 7-6. The model suggests cost per service unit delivered for a service firm drops until the diseconomies associated with increases in managerial complexity offset the learning and volume economies. When the firm increases its capacity to handle managerial complexity and/or reduces the managerial complexity it faces, the economies once again outweigh the diseconomies and total cost per service unit declines.

The model has a relevant message to providers of service at multiple locations. By taking advantage of the economies of learning and volume (neither occurs automatically) and by maintaining the level of managerial complexity below management's capacity to handle it, cost per service unit delivered can be lowered.

Figure 7-6

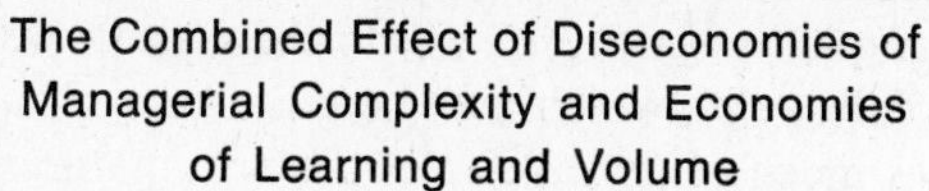

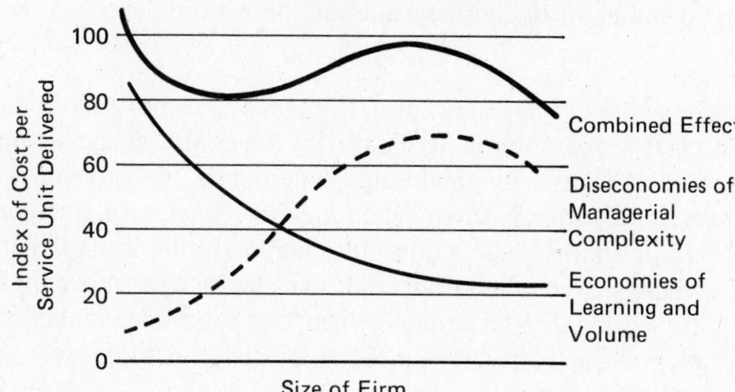

LESSONS FROM THE SERVICE FIRM LIFE CYCLE

What are the lessons that service managers can extract from the life cycle analysis? The major insight should be that the successful growth of a multisite service firm depends greatly on the ability of its executives to manage not only the present but also the future. As the firm advances through the different stages of its life cycle, there are a number of managerial actions as described below that should be undertaken.

1. *Management must understand that there are four basic, but quite different, functions to manage.*

New Unit Development: The first of these functions refers to all aspects of developing and starting up a new unit—site location, lease agreements, unit design, construction, equipment selection, selection and training of unit management and personnel, and opening the unit. There is a nonroutine nature to this part of the business, the management of which is ideally suited to people with a project management temperament. They are unlikely to enjoy the day-to-day pressures and details of the operating function. Proper management of this function will move the firm down its facility learning curve.

Operations: The management of operations concerns itself primarily with operating decisions of a recurring nature. Indeed, the establishment of a routine and the controls for maintaining the routine are mainstream responsibilities of this area of management. Proper management of this function will move the firm down its units of service delivered learning curve.

Marketing: The marketing function is concerned with understanding consumer needs, segmenting the different markets for the services, developing marketing plans, and creating advertising and promotion strategies. As one chief executive noted, "We devote our energies to finding excellent locations for our units, constructing quality facilities which are esthetically appealing but functional, and delivering a quality service. If we do these tasks well, our customers will find us." This philosophy, which may be quite appropriate in the infant stages of the firm, loses much of its validity as the firm matures. Coherent marketing strategies to maintain or increase market share becomes a matter of life and death.

Concept Development: By concept development we mean the important tasks whose successful execution is necessary for the health of the service firm over the long haul. Changes in unit design, equipment, decor, and service levels are all part of this management function. This function is comparable to the research and development function in a manufacturing firm. The coordination of these activities over time is essential, and the lack of such coordination can be extremely costly. For example, a firm can send out conflicting images to the consumer if the respective qualities of construction, decor, and service levels are not congruent.

In the early stages of a firm's life cycle, the emphasis is on new unit development and operations. By performing those functions well, firms thrive. However, as firms progress through later stages, they face strong competitors who are competent in handling both functions. Thus, the functions that differentiate the successful firm from the mediocre become marketing and concept development.

2. *The founder(s) must delegate responsibility.* As the firm leaves the entrepreneurial stage, the founder is faced with increasing demands on his or her time. The change from making all decisions to allowing others to make many of the decisions is a particularly difficult transition. "I'll never give up site decisions," said the chief executive of one concern with a current new location growth of over 20% per annum. The concept development, site selection, and marketing functions are usually the last functions to be delegated by the chief executive.

The inability of one founder to delegate responsibility to his subordinates led one subordinate to make the following remark after the founder's death: "Thank God he died. He was ruining the company." To a large extent, the managerial style and competence of the chief executive sets the tone for the entire company, which in turn affects the ability of the firm to attract or develop good managers.

3. *The management team must develop or acquire the competencies required to manage a larger firm.* The management team must grow as the firm grows. The skills of operations, marketing, and finance, if not present, must be acquired. Administrative skills are also necessary as the firm increases in size. Sometimes the members of the original management team are not capable of acquiring these skills; more often they are capable but not receptive to changing established patterns of behavior. If these competencies are not developed, the firm quickly experiences the diseconomies of managerial complexity.

4. *Management motivation must be maintained.* During the growth of a successful

firm, there is often the tendency for the management team to lose its enthusiasm and to become complacent. Important items that in earlier times would receive prompt action are now postponed. This behavior is even exhibited by some founders as they become bored. For them the operations function is usually the first to be delegated because of its dull repetitive nature. After a while, the new unit development function no longer presents a challenge as scores of new units are opened. Only new concepts or new activities can command their attention. Often, the founders sell a portion of their equity and/or declare dividends on their stock and use this liquidity to finance new ventures and interests, unfortunately scattering their attention in a variety of directions.

Managers of the four functions of the multisite service firms experience different motivational problems. Concept development represents a constant searching of the environment for new trends, testing new services, examining new unit designs, and experimenting with new concepts. Marketing is also a staff function that requires creative skills. Both functions, which are done in a fragmented way in the early stages, are consolidated as the firms grow in size. However, the staff size for these functions does not change dramatically with the growth of revenue and new units. Both functions take on added importance as the firm grows and matures, which makes motivation of its staff a relatively easy job.

Staffing for the operations function, however, increases roughly in proportion with the number of units operated. In the stages through the growth stage, there is a great deal of upward mobility in the operations group. Assistant managers advance quickly to become managers, managers become district managers, district managers become area managers, and area managers become regional managers. But the growth rate cannot be sustained forever, and when the rate declines, a motivation problem develops as employee morale drops when the path to advancement lengthens considerably.

The new unit development function ceases to grow as the expansion rate of the growth stage declines; in some extreme instances, no new units are planned. The function takes on less importance and the size of the staff is cut back considerably. Attention is channeled to remodel packages. Unless a new concept is developed to be exploited, the remaining members of the group face a very difficult motivation and status problem.

5. *Sloppy growth must be avoided.* Sloppy growth is haphazard growth, often done for the wrong reasons. It is growth that the firm cannot handle and that endangers the firm's health. Often, the offender is a public firm that, in haste to maintain a very high growth rate for the benefit of the financial community, adds a number of units to its system. Many of the new facilities turn out to be unprofitable because the sites are bad, the units are shabbily constructed, the competition is too well entrenched, the units are too scattered to be supervised well, or competent unit managers are not available to manage the units, just to mention a few reasons for failure. The firm then must write off the losers, which has an immediately adverse effect on revenues and earnings. If the firm is lucky, it is acquired; if it is unlucky, bankruptcy proceedings determine the distribution of the firm's remaining assets. The president of a public firm explained the pressure on his firm:

> The financial community has high expectations for our firm. They expect fast, steady, profitable growth. How fast a growth is necessary to satisfy the financial community and our investors? However, the real question is, what growth rate is necessary to satisfy ourselves? To what extent are we willing to sacrifice day-to-day operations to maintain growth just to please others?

6. *The firm must change a mature concept.* Many firms reach the mature phase of their life cycle with an out-of-date concept. Often, management does not recognize that its concept is dead. Others who recognize this fact are unable to organize a change in the concept. The remedy for such situations is tough to accept. New management and capital are often necessary to renovate the company both in its direction and in its facilities.

7. *The firm must not diversify too quickly.* Sometimes the source of the firm's problems is just the opposite of hanging onto a mature concept. The culprits are other ventures started by the founders. As described earlier, too often the entrepreneur is obsessed with finding new horizons to conquer after the company's initial direction is set and the many functional departments are well advanced in their development. The original principals of a successful business often use the net worth of the company as collateral for new businesses. The ease of their first fortune convinces them they have the Midas touch. Not uncommonly, the company that created the wealth is bled to support the losses of the other ventures.

8. *Communication channels must be kept open.* The establishment of clear functional areas produces communication gaps that must be bridged. "I can't understand why we need so many meetings now. We never used to have them and we got along fine. I used to be able to see the people at top whenever I wanted. Now, everything is so impersonal," is a typical comment. But more formalized channels of communication such as meetings and written reports are now necessary because there are more managers in the firm who are no longer familiar with all aspects of the business.

SUMMARY

Most service executives react to the effects of the service firm life cycle rather than plan for them in advance. Very few managers plan their internal changes or have time to maneuver and reflect before taking action. The often-heard lament, "We never knew it would be like this," can be avoided because, as we have demonstrated in this chapter, multisite service firms follow a fairly predictable life cycle pattern. Many of the critical problems have been experienced before by other firms; service managers can learn from these examples. They can ascertain what stage of the service firm life cycle they are in and anticipate the changes required in their organizational structures to pass safely into the next stage. They can manage their organizations to achieve the economies of learning and volume and minimize the diseconomies associated with managerial complexity. The ability to anticipate and plan for the problems described in this chapter are key skills of the service executive. Managers who have these skills are much more likely to succeed than reactive managers who do not.

Safecard Services, Inc.

> You may think it's simple to get into a service business. If so, you're right. But making a go of it is an entirely different matter.
>
> How do you package and market a service? How do you control quality? What level of service is appropriate to provide customer satisfaction, and, at the same time, generate company profitability? How do you really measure profitability? How do you package a service to appeal to the financial community? How do you inspect a service? How do you achieve growth—through direct marketing, acquisition, joint venture, or other means? What level of expertise is necessary to be successful?

These reflections by one of the principals of SafeCard Services, Incorporated (SSI), Steven Halmos, give an indication of the complexities encountered in the creation and operation of a small service business. Steven and his brother, Peter, were looking back on their first complete year of operations (after four years in business) in an effort to assess their present position and to develop a viable course of action for the future.

Start-Up

In 1969 Peter Halmos, a graduating MBA from the University of Florida, was faced with the unpleasant prospect of finding a job. At the same time, Steven was completing undergraduate study at Georgia Tech and therefore faced the same unpleasant dilemma. While commiserating one evening in May 1969, the Halmos' decided that they had to go into business for themselves in order to avoid a structured working environment and to realize the financial success they desired.

After reading at length about the increasing proliferation of credit cards in this country, the Halmos' felt that a service designed to provide the credit cardholder with protection and convenience in the event of credit card loss or theft would have universal appeal—and would generate meaningful profits. At that time, individuals were liable for all unauthorized charges made on their credit cards until such time as the various credit card issuers had received written notification of the loss or theft. But where were cardholders to send such notification? How would they know their lost card numbers? How would they notify—via letter (very slow) or telephone (no proof) or telegram (fast with documented proof)? In any event, the process could be costly and time consuming.

In June 1969 SSI was formed to provide a credit card registration and notification service to individual and corporate subscribers. An individual could register any number of credit cards with the company for an annual fee of $7.50. In the event of the subsequent loss or theft of his credit cards, the subscriber could call the company's nationwide toll-free telephone line at any time, around-the-clock, to report the loss. SSI computers would then automatically report the loss to the various credit card companies.

In addition, the subscriber would receive other credit card services, including the free addition of new cards at any time, notification of a subscriber's change of address to all the credit card companies, and several other auxilliary services.

The growth of the credit card industry had been phenomenal. Since the founding of the credit card concept in 1950 by the Diners Club, the number of cards being carried by individual and corporate cardholders had rapidly increased. By 1970, some 275 million credit cards issued by oil companies, retail stores, banks, and travel institutions were in the hands of American consumers. Exhibit 1 indicates the distribution. Well over one million retail establishments in the United States honored credit cards, making it possible to purchase an unlimited variety of products and services via "plastic credit." Unauthorized credit card use had grown at an equally alarming rate. In 1970, some $150 million in unauthorized charges resulted from credit card loss or theft. Some 1.5 million credit cards were lost, stolen, or counterfeited in the United States in 1970, making this medium a prime target for organized crime. With coast to coast acceptance of credit cards, immediate notification of credit card loss or theft appeared to be vital to thwarting fraudulent use. Therefore, the potential market for SSI's credit card registry services seemed to be vast in size.

On a more conceptual level, the Halmos' were intrigued by the thought of providing the individual—not just the corporation—with the many conveniences of using a computer. They coined the phrase "personal computer timesharing" to describe this concept, of which the credit card registry service was the forerunner.

SSI was formed on a shoestring. From their roughly-defined concept was developed a detailed business plan—complete with "rosy" projections—to be used to attract initial financing. With the sacrifice of 40% of the equity, $5,500 was raised from a former college professor and another friend. The Halmos' were ready to commence operations.

Repulsed by the idea of doing extensive initial "market research," the brothers decided to commission a printer to produce brochures describing the credit card registry service and to begin selling. The initial marketing plan called for the mass distribution of post-paid return brochures through the mails, hand distribution, or various other vehicles. Based on the assumption that ". . . if just one in ten people receiving a brochure decides to subscribe" to the service, it was projected that the company would be profitable on internally generated cash flow within four months.

The economics of the service seemed attractive. Based on their projected response rate, the company would be an immediate success. Furthermore, two additional factors seemed to provide the greatest potential for profitability. First, the service to subscribers was renewable annually. Therefore, since the major costs of computer input were absorbed in the initial year of subscription, renewals seemed to offer a substantial source of revenue in subsequent years at little incremental cost to the company. Secondly, the company would have a large mailing list which could

Exhibit 1

SAFECARD SERVICES, INC.
Number of Credit Cards Outstanding
in the United States in 1970

Institution	*Number of Cards (millions)*
Retail stores (department stores, etc.)	120
Oil Company	90
Banks (Bank Americard and Master Charge)	55
Auto Rentals	5
Travel and Entertainment (American Express, Diners Club, etc.)	5
Air Travel	1.8

Source: *Fortune Magazine*

ANNUAL VOLUME OF CREDIT CARD TRANSACTIONS:

1967	*1972*
$1 Billion	$10 Billion

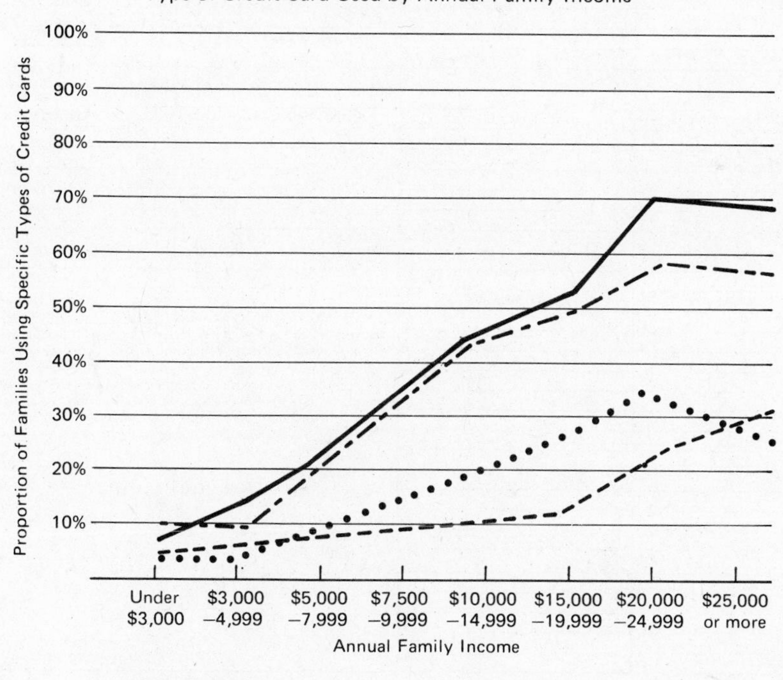

Exhibit 2

SAFECARD SERVICES INCORPORATED

OPERATIONS / CONTROL DATA BUILDING / 500 INTERSTATE NORTH / ATLANTA, GA. 30339

SAMPLE

Name Last First Middle

Address City State Zip

Home Phone Bus. Phone Occupation

SAFECARD

IMPORTANT: List all credit cards and charge accounts which are billed in your name even if used by other members of your family. List cards billed to other family members on the next page.

BANK CARDS	BANK NAME	CITY/STATE	CARD NUMBER
MASTER CHARGE			
BANKAMERICARD			

DEPARTMENT STORES	CITY/STATE	CARD NUMBER
SEARS		
PENNEY'S		

TRAVEL & ENTERTAINMENT	CARD NUMBER	RESTAURANT CARDS	CARD NUMBER
AMERICAN EXPRESS			
DINERS CLUB			
CARTE BLANCHE			
GETAWAY			

OIL COMPANY CARDS	CARD NUMBER	AIRLINE AND CAR RENTAL	CARD NUMBER
		HERTZ	
		AVIS	

OTHER CARDS	CARD NUMBER

MY SIGNATURE (sign here) ________ authorizes SafeCard Services, Inc. act on my behalf and that of my family for the purpose of notification concerning loss or theft of documents, charge accounts, and credit cards and any forms, letters or additional data that must be prepared to provide replacement. As a convenience to avoid lapse of registration, you may charge my designated credit card for each succeeding enrollment year.

———— FOR OFFICE USE ONLY ————

prove to be a valuable resource for mailing list rentals, merchandising of additional services, and the like.

Since the company was then headquartered in a linen closet in the Halmos' apartment in Atlanta, the entire $5,500 went into printing. Armed with thousands of brochures, the Halmos' set out to blanket the country with SafeCard. Being summertime, school teachers on vacation were hired at $1 per hour (plus all the beer they could drink) to place brochures on auto windshields in shopping center parking lots, to distribute them at office buildings, and to stuff envelopes for mailings. The response: a handful of returns, many with obscenities written inside.

Obviously, SSI was again without money. In the interim, Peter had taken a job with the Bank of New York and was living with his parents in New York City. Through the bank, Peter met Richard Smith, a Harvard MBA and for several years an executive with the advertising firm of Young & Rubicam. Mr. Smith, intrigued by the SSI concept, therefore provided an additional infusion of capital as well as valuable creative expertise for SSI mailings.

Again mailings were sent out, this time to a list of corporate presidents and college alumni. The brothers even hand signed the letters in the hopes of increasing response, and hand folded and stuffed envelopes. Again, minimal response.

By this time they were desperate. They couldn't understand why the response wasn't pouring in. Reflecting on this initial period, Peter remarked:

> The business was simple to enter—we just printed brochures and installed a phone. But, not only were we naive in our initial marketing efforts, we fell in love with our numbers. After repeatedly talking about the company's potential in our attempts to raise money, we actually came to believe our own projections. In fact, we did such a sales job, one of our stockholders predicted that SSI would become the largest user of computers in the U.S., second only to the Federal Government.

After an obviously discouraging beginning with intermittent small infusions of capital by investors (for more equity), the Halmos' again needed money. Still convinced of the viability of the SSI concept, they began scouring New York. Through a finder of questionable reputation, they secured a letter of intent from an underwriter[1] who promised to sell—on a best efforts basis—100,000 shares of SSI stock at $4. So, after convincing their attorney, Jack Fineberg, to handle the registration on an equity plus deferred payment basis, SSI filed the offering with the SEC on May 13, 1970.

The registration period, which was expected to take a matter of a few months, dragged into a year and a half of struggle for survival. During this period, the market changed dramatically with critical new legislation governing the credit card industry. The most striking legislation reduced an individual's liability on unauthorized credit card use to a maximum of $50 per card under certain conditions. The SEC, already disliking the SSI deal, took this opportunity to hold up the offering. Since the legis-

[1] This firm was subsequently expelled from the NASD and the principals indicted for a variety of felonies. Therefore, two additional firms, R. D. Viscount & Co. and Magnus Securities Corp., agreed to handle the offering.

lation was under the jurisdiction of two other governmental agencies, there were further delays.

The costs became enormous. In addition to legal and accounting fees, the printing expenses were substantial. The SEC required five amendments to the preliminary prospectus, each of which cost at least $5,000 in printing alone.

Steven reflected on the problems involved in packaging SSI to appeal to the financial community and to investors in a public offering:

> We had no cash to speak of, no fixed assets except a typewriter, no inventory—basically nothing. All we had was a room of leased space, a toll-free line which cost $400/month), a few filing cabinets containing our small list of customers, and a rather simple computer program. The only way to make this kind of service business appealing to the investor is to sell the concept. That's all you've really got.
>
> Even the "due diligence" requirements were a problem. Our lawyers, accountants, and underwriters were required to show due diligence in investigating our operations. But what can really be seen in a small service operation? Fortunately, Control Data Corporation leased us a small conference room in their data center for $100 per month. When Control Data subsequently partially abandoned the facility, we "expanded" our space to encompass a suite of furnished vacant offices. When underwriters came to inspect the company's service operations, they were astounded. After entering this huge computer complex and seeing the glass-enclosed computers in operation, they were favorably impressed and were more inclined to proceed.

After 18 months of registration, SSI became effective with the SEC. During the period, however, several things occurred. First, money was obviously scarce. Not only were payables "extended," but it was a difficult matter just to keep the telephones in operation. Also during this period, Steven Halmos completed his first year at Harvard Business School, spending a great deal of time away from the Boston area. Furthermore, the Halmos' constantly feared that the SEC might call the company's toll-free line at any time in an effort to claim that no services were actually being provided. In this way, they could stop the public offering. Therefore, the Halmos' had an extension of the toll-free line installed in their apartment and personally attended the line 24 hours a day, 7 days a week, holidays included. When not in the office, one of the brothers was "baby-sitting" at home with the line, since they felt that a service, being an intangible, was much more vulnerable to harassment by the SEC.

Looking back on the entire process of raising money, Peter stated:

> Everything that could go wrong went wrong. After five amendments and several trips to Washington, the SEC had enough and let us out. But not before requiring an unprecedented statement regarding risk on the cover of our prospectus (see Exhibit 3). The offering itself took two months. The underwriters had trouble with blue sky regulations in several states, thus causing additional problems in placing the stock. It was unbelievable.

Exhibit 3

150,000 Shares
SAFECARD SERVICES, INCORPORATED
COMMON STOCK ($.01 par value)

THESE SECURITIES ARE SPECULATIVE AND INVOLVE A HIGH DEGREE OF RISK. THE PURCHASE OF THE SECURITIES OFFERED HEREBY SHOULD BE CONSIDERED ONLY BY PERSONS WHO CAN AFFORD TO SUSTAIN A TOTAL LOSS.

Prior to this offering there has been no market for the common stock of the Company. The initial offering price has been determined by agreement between the Company and the Underwriters.

THESE SECURITIES HAVE NOT BEEN APPROVED OR DISAPPROVED BY THE SECURITIES AND EXCHANGE COMMISSION NOR HAS THE COMMISSION PASSED UPON THE ACCURACY OR ADEQUACY OF THIS PROSPECTUS. ANY REPRESENTATION TO THE CONTRARY IS A CRIMINAL OFFENSE.

	Price to Public (1)	*Underwriter's Discount, Commissions and Expenses (2) (3) (5)*	*Proceeds to Company (1) (4)*
Per Share	$3.00	Max. $.43	$2.57
		Min. $.43	$2.57
Total: Maximum of 150,000 shs.	$450,000	$64,000	$386,000
Minimum of 90,000 shs.	$270,000	$38,800	$231,200

(1) The Common Stock is being offered by the Underwriters on a best effort basis providing for the sale of a minimum of 90,000 shares and a maximum of 150,000 shares. All funds collected from subscribers will be held in a bank escrow account with American Bank and Trust Company, New York, N.Y. and will be promptly refunded, without interest or deduction, in the event that a minimum of 90,000 shares are not sold within sixty days of the date of this Prospectus, or within thirty additional days if so agreed between the Company and the Underwriters (see "Underwriting"). In the event of sale by the Underwriters of less than the maximum number of shares offered hereby, the amount of warrants to be sold to the Underwriters will be proportionately reduced.

(2) Includes $45,000 ($.30 per share) cash commission $18,000 ($.12 per share) cash for expenses for the Underwriters and their counsel, of which $1,500 has been advanced by the Company to counsel for the Underwriters for which they need not account, and a $1,000 ($.01 per share) cash finder's fee, paid in advance to the finder, Richmond Lisle-Cannon.

(3) Assuming the minimum number of shares is sold, the expense would include $27,000 ($.30 per share) cash commission and $10,800 ($.12 per share) cash for expenses of the Underwriters and their counsel, for which they need not account, and a finder's fee of $1,000 ($.01 per share).

(4) Does not include, additional filing, printing, legal, accounting and miscellaneous expenses of approximately $35,200 ($.23 per share if the maximum number of shares is sold and $.39 per share if the minimum number of shares is sold).

(5) Does not include substantial additional compensation to be received by the Underwriters (see below).

This offering involves:

(a) Special risks concerning the Company. For information concerning such risks see "Introductory Statement—Speculative Nature of This Offering," page 3.

Exhibit 3 (continued)

(b) Immediate substantial dilution of the book value of the stock from the public offering price. For information concerning such dilution see "Introductory Statement —Dilution," page 5.

(c) Significant additional underwriting compensation through the issuance to the Underwriters of warrants entitling them to purchase up to 15,000 shares of Common Stock (proportionately reduced if all the shares are sold and only in the event that the minimum offering of 90,000 shares are sold) for a period of four years commencing one year after the effective date of this offering at prices ranging from $3.30 per share to $4.20 per share; the right of first refusal on future offerings; and indemnification (see "Underwriting" page 18).

(d) Very substantial potential profit to the promoters of the Company who purchased 186,286 shares of the Common Stock of the Company at $.01 to $.075 per share; Company counsel who purchased 6,500 shares at $.01 per share; and other persons who purchased 33,214 shares at $.01 to $1.75 per share. For information concerning the potential profits to the promoters and such other persons, see "Introductory Statement—Speculative Nature of this Offering," page 3, "Organization and Business—Organization," page 6, and "Transactions with Management," page 17.

GRAYBAR SECURITIES, INC.
720 Fifth Avenue
New York, New York 10019

MAGNUS SECURITIES CORPORATION
1984 Chain Bridge Road
McLean, Virginia 22101

The date of this Prospectus is September 28, 1971

On September 28, 1971, SSI received some $300,000 from the proceeds of the public offering. Now the service had to be sold.

Marketing

During this period, the brothers began rethinking the marketing concept of the company. They realized that the key to profitability was volume. Therefore, their marketing efforts should be directed toward achieving high volume in a short period of time, given their existing financial constraints. After careful consideration, they decided that cooperative mailings with credit card issuers offered the most attractive means of mass distribution with the least cash requirement. Knowing that credit card issuers (i.e., department stores, bank cards, oil companies, travel cards, etc.) mailed regular monthly statements to their cardholders, the brothers felt that the insertion of an SSI brochure in these billings would be of no incremental cost to the credit card issuer. SSI would print the brochures at its expense, the credit card issuer would insert the brochure in its monthly statements, and the two parties would share the revenues. In addition to the cash savings in postage costs, the brothers felt that the implicit third party endorsement of the service obtained from enclosures in the credit card issuers' billings would certainly increase consumer response to SSI's service.

From the credit card issuer's standpoint, the concept would seem attractive. The credit card registry service seemed compatible with credit card issuer operations. Most importantly, the SSI mailings offered the credit card issuer a means of generating revenues, and perhaps customer good will, at no cost whatever.

The timing was right since credit card issuers throughout the country were losing a great deal of money. The issuers' 33% share of gross revenues from an SSI mailing would go straight to the bottom line. In addition, the service would provide the issuer with immediate notification of all lost or stolen credit cards. What could they lose?

From SSI's viewpoint, the concept of cooperative mailings with credit card issuers required a much smaller cash investment than initiating their own mailings. When SSI initiated its own mailings, the direct costs (minimum) would include the following, assuming reasonable volume:

Brochure	$ 15 per 1000 pieces
Cover Letter	15 per 1000 pieces
Reply	10 per 1000 pieces
Cost of Mailing List	30 per 1000 pieces
Envelope	10 per 1000 pieces
Postage (Bulk Rate)	50 per 1000 pieces
Inserting	15 per 1000 pieces
Creative Work	10 per 1000 pieces
	$155 per 1000 pieces of mail minimum

This figure represents the minimum material costs associated with a direct mail program. On the other hand, cooperative mailings with credit card issuers would require only the printing costs of the SSI brochures, although 33% of gross revenues must be sacrificed to the credit card issuer as compensation.

There appeared to be two additional benefits to cooperative mailings. First, the third party endorsement of the credit card issuer in whose billings the SSI brochure was inserted was seen to be an important factor in eliciting consumer response. Whether the brochure displayed the credit card issuer's name or not, the Halmos' felt that the endorsement would increase response. Secondly, by allowing the cardholder to charge the SSI service on his credit card, thus not requiring the enclosure of cash, the brothers felt that they could enhance the saleability of the service as an "impulse item."

To make the package more attractive to the credit card issuer, the Customer Good Will Program was developed. Under this arrangement, XYZ Department Store, for example, could tell its credit cardholders that their XYZ card had been registered free of charge with SSI. If a cardholder lost his XYZ card, he simply called SSI, which in turn notified XYZ. If the cardholder wished to register all additional credit cards in his wallet, he could so for $7.50 per year.

The Halmos' felt that this program would provide a valuable inducement for credit card issuers to do an SSI mailing. However, they were uncertain of the operational costs associated with providing this free service to a large proportion of a group of cardholders. It seemed impossible to estimate costs, since there was no means of estimating what proportion of individuals would actually make use of this free service in the event of credit card loss.

With their financing, the Halmos' initiated a marketing program designed to interest credit card issuers in a cooperative mailing program. Letters were mailed to credit card issuers throughout the country and were followed up with telephone calls and extended travel to major cities. Although several mailings with banks and retailers were negotiated, two critical problems were encountered.

First, the size of the company and its lack of a "track record" made it difficult to establish credibility. Even if a credit card issuer thought favorably of SSI's concept, it was usually skeptical about the size of the firm, its financial position, and its ability to perform. The fact that SSI sold services rather than tangible products severely compounded this problem. For instance, if a credit card issuer sells a cardholder a product, the quality of which is readily ascertainable, the transaction is complete upon delivery of the product. On the other hand, when a credit card issuer sells a cardholder SSI's service, the transaction is not complete until some time in the distant future, at least one year.

Credit cardholders are the credit card issuer's most vital asset. If SSI's were to go out of business, who would have liability for performance of the service? Even if SSI remained viable, would its level of service be satisfactory? Generally speaking, would there be any deterioration in cardholder goodwill? These questions consistently arose in discussions with credit card issuers.

Further compounding this credibility problem was the deteriorating reputation of the credit card registry service in the credit card industry. During the time of SSI's existence, many credit card registry firms entered the business throughout the country. Obviously, commencing operations was easy. Unfortunately, however, the marketing difficulties and operational complexities forced most of these firms to quickly close their doors, thus causing their subscribers a loss. These events became well known in the credit card industry. In fact, an article in *Time Magazine* regarding the credit card industry reported:

> . . . . credit card notification services, organizations that feed all of a holder's card numbers into a computer and notify the proper companies as soon as a loss is reported, are dying out. Just a year ago, there were at least 40; today the FTC knows of only four.
>
> *Time,* September 13, 1971

In conjunction with these credibility problems, it became apparent that additional inducement was needed to make an SSI mailing economically attractive enough to a credit card issuer to justify taking the risks. Assuming a mailing of 200,000 pieces, the response at 1% would be 2,000 subscribers. At $7.50 each, total revenues would equal $15,000. Considering a credit card issuer's 33% share in revenues, he could expect $5,000 from an SSI mailing. While this figure went straight to the bottom line, it became apparent that it was insufficient.

In order to make the SSI mailings more attractive financially, both to credit card issuers and to SSI itself, the Halmos' developed a package of five compatible services with a price of $19 per year (see Exhibit 4 for details on these services). In addition to making the mailings more financially sound, the new package served to expand the concept of "personal computer timesharing." Included in the new package were the original credit card registry service, a computerized reminder service, an important document registry, a medical data registry, and a luggage registry.

Exhibit 4

SAFECARD SERVICES, INC.

Credit Card Registry Package

The SafeCard credit card registry package serves as a valuable customer service, an effective card loss notification system, and a mechanism for generating meaningful revenues.

Using any telephone in the Continental United States, our subscribers have immediate toll-free access to our computer. We are at their service 24 hours a day, every day of the year.

Utilizing our toll-free WATS lines, a subscriber may report to us the loss of his credit cards. Immediately, we will notify via Western Union all credit card issuers he has registered with us.

And, in the event his credit cards are fraudulently used, the service includes a 100% Guarantee that he will not have to pay as much as one cent on these unauthorized charges.

It's as simple as that!

Included in the package are:

* Credit card registration and notification
* 100% Guarantee of non-responsibility
* Unlimited addition of new cards
* Change of address service
* Around-the-clock service
* Toll-free WATS line
* SafeCard Kit:
  Credit card stickers
  WATS telephone stickers
  Wallet card
  Personalized key tag
* Family coverage

MEDI-GARD

Personal Medical Data Registry

Medi-Gard is a personal medical records registry service, designed to place an individual's vital medical information as near as any telephone, at any time.

Any individual that travels—and most Americans do—should register his medical information with Medi-Gard..........blood type..........allergies..........diseases......... prescription medications............name of personal physician............past illnesses ....*all* medical information that would be of use to a doctor in case of an emergency involving the individual.

How It Works

A subscriber completes a comprehensive medical questionnaire. This information is fed into our computer for confidential around the clock storage. He then receives a personalized plastic ID card and "dog tag" imprinted with his name, our toll-free WATS number, and that medical information which is most vital in emergencies (blood type, diseases, etc.). If a subscriber is not able to tell his medical story after an accident or sudden illness, this card and tag could save his life.

In the event of an accident or illness no matter where he is—and, unfortunately these things happen—a subscriber's vital medical information is available to the attending physician via our nationwide WATS line at any time of the day or night. Accessing our computer, we will provide whatever medical information is necessary. And, we will contact the sub-

Exhibit 4 (continued)

scriber's personal home-town physician and put him in touch with the attending physician, wherever he may be.

Medi-Gard cannot guarantee that accidents and illnesses will not happen—unfortunately, that's impossible. But, Medi-Gard *does* guarantee that treatment for accidents will not be delayed or improperly given due to the lack of vital medical information.

It's as simple—and as essential—as that!

COMPU-MINDER

Personal Memory/Reminder Service

Compu-Minder is a computerized personal memory/reminder service, designed to remind individuals of important days and events.

.... birthdays .... anniversary .... dental appointments .... social engagements .... jury duty .... board meetings .... *any* important day or event that might be forgotten.

How it Works

All dates and events of any importance to a subscriber are fed into our computer. Then, approximately one week prior to each date, he is reminded via our computer-generated REMO forms.

It is as simple as that!

The Compu-Minder package serves as a unique and popular customer service. Any important events of which *you* wish to remind your customers may be automatically included. And, the package will generate meaningful revenues.

DOCU-GARD

Important Document Registry

Docu-Gard puts all vital information regarding a subscriber's important documents and personal property as near as any telephone.

Any document of value to an individual or family—stock certificates, bonds, insurance policies, etc.—may be registered by number with Docu-Gard. Personal property—automobiles, cameras, watches, etc.—may also be registered. Special stickers are then provided for attachment to these items as a warning to potential thieves that they have been registered.

Then, at any time of the day or night, this information is available to a subscriber via any telephone in the Continental United States. One toll-free call on our WATS line sets our computer to work. The vital information is available immediately.

Docu-Gard .... for peace of mind. It is designed as protection against the aggravation and potential cost of trying to replace lost, stolen, or destroyed vital information .... and fast. In case of emergency, Docu-Gard's computer is available ONLY TO A SUBSCRIBER .... as near as any telephone, any day or night.

LUGGAGE-GARD

Worldwide Luggage Registry

Every year, thousands of dollars in luggage containing valuables of every description are lost or stolen from airports, hotels, and terminals across the country.

Luggage-Gard is designed for both businessmen and vacationers as protection against the potential cost, aggravation, and inconvenience of losing luggage.

Exhibit 4 (continued)

Our special Luggage Protection Kit provides a means of positive identification of a subscriber's luggage, and includes:

* Special permanent labels for attachment to all bags
* WATS number telephone stickers
* Emergency wallet card
* Personalized key tag

In the event of the loss of a subscriber's luggage, our tracing system is ready to swing into action .... 24 hours a day, every day of the year. The subscriber simply calls us toll-free from any telephone, and tells us what happened. He gives us his name, special number, and departure date or itinerary if he is continuing on a trip. And, if he wishes, a reward for the finder. We'll take it from there. When found, we will route his valuables to him by whatever means are necessary.

And, a crook will have a hard time explaining what he is doing with specially marked luggage!

The new package rounded out the product line. The concept of five services in a single package was unique. It offered the credit card issuer more attractive financial compensation in a mailing. It provided the ultimate consumer with a greater variety of services. And, most importantly, it offered to provide SSI with greater revenues without greater mailing costs.

The new package, described by the company as "five new friends to help you simplify the business of living," was met with great interest. However, the credibility problem still existed. In addition, the competition for the limited space available in credit card issuer mailings had grown to be intense. Competition came from mail order concerns, manufacturers, retailers, and a host of other marketing organizations who had come to appreciate the effectiveness of these cooperative credit card issuer mailings. What's more, the competition proved to be very sophisticated in the mail order field—an industry of seasoned professionals.

Growth During First Year as a Public Company

At the time of the company's public offering in November 1971, SSI had approximately 5,000 subscribers to its credit card registry service. One year later, this number had grown to a total of approximately 50,000 subscribers. This growth was attributable both to successful mailing programs and to acquisition.

Most of the company's mailing programs had been a success. Exhibit 5 represents a partial list of firms with which SSI has had cooperative mailings. Of these, Trans World Airlines and E. J. Korvettes were among the most vital on-going relationships of the company.

To meet fixed costs and operate at a profitable level, the Halmos' determined that a sizeable customer base was a necessity. They knew that none of the firms in the business had such a base and that SSI was the only firm in the business with any cash. Therefore, the brothers contacted every known competitor regarding the possibility of consolidation. Although many letters were returned "addressee un-

Exhibit 5

SAFECARD SERVICES, INC.
A Partial Listing of Credit Card Issuers with
Whom the Company Has Had Cooperative Mailings

Several Master Charge banks
Several Bank Americard mailings
Trans World Airlines
Pan American World Airways
E. J. Korvettes
Peck and Peck Stores
Tenneco Oil Company
May Department Stores
K-Mart Stores
GEX Stores
NAC Charge Plan
Hecht Company—Baltimore
Bullock's Department Stores
May—Cohens
Bellex Super Stores
Hecht Company—Washington
Renberg's Department Stores
TraveLodge International Hotels
Eastern Airlines

known" due to the bankruptcy of many firms, this effort ultimately resulted in the acquisition of two of the major firms in the business. Important Data Registry Corporation (IDR) of Philadelphia was a subsidiary of a firm active in other areas of the credit card industry. The other firm, Hot Line Charge Card Services, Inc. of New York, had been a leader in the field and had achieved a certain level of prominence throughout the U.S. The acquisitions had proven to be quite successful, but not without difficulties. In fact, certain material omissions regarding Hot Lines resulted in an $8 million legal action.

Peter regards the acquisition of a service business as a particularly difficult matter:

> When considering the acquisition of a service business, what are you really buying? In our case, we only wanted the assets—their rosters of subscribers to the credit card registry service. But evaluating these lists is extremely difficult. If they claim to have 10,000 subscribers, how do you know they really aren't just names out of a telephone directory? In placing a value on the list, it was difficult to estimate what percentage of the subscribers would renew their service next year since we had no feel for the level of service to which those subscribers were accustomed. In general, it was impossible to place a cash value on this kind of service business.
>
> The key to our acquisitions was structuring. We structured payment in such a way as to pay a negotiated amount for each subscriber who subsequently re-

news his service, plus a small cash consideration in advance. The result: a risk-free deal for us. In essence, however, you must structure the acquisition in this way since you really don't know what you are buying. Unfortunately, the original Hot Line owners took a $500,000 loss.

Operations

The Halmos' expressed a vital concern for operations and considered this a crucial factor to profitability. For example, prior to acquiring Important Data Registry and Hot Line, these firms had in excess of 35 operational employees. The Halmos' now serviced these two operations plus SSI's own subscriber list with fewer than ten operational employees, most on a part-time basis.

A major question that had to be constantly evaluated was: What level of service must be provided in order to foster customer satisfaction and, at the same time, yield company profitability? With the average SSI account being less than $10 per year, this service level question had great significance. For instance, the cost of fulfilling a single customer request of some kind could easily constitute 5% of the annual revenues generated by that customer. That is, when considering labor, postage, materials, etc., these costs in relation to only $10 in annual fees would be substantial. But, if customer requests were ignored, the renewal rate would suffer. This trade-off was one that had to be reckoned with on a continual basis.

Ms. Madelaine Cloutier, head of SSI's operation, commented on this situation:

Our customers drive us crazy. Since we have a nationwide toll-free line for subscriber use, they use it for every imaginable purpose. In addition, we receive thousands of pieces of mail from subscribers requesting materials, adding new information to their files, questioning our billing, etc. The more personally we handle this correspondence, the better is our renewal rate, at least to a degree. But, just how far can we go and still make money?

This service level question was of even greater significance to SSI due to its dependence on cooperative mailings with credit card issuers. For instance, if for any reason a subscriber became upset with his SSI service, his complaints would not only be directed toward SSI, but probably also to the credit card issuer through whom he originally subscribed. A series of complaints from customers to a particular credit card issuer could jeopardize SSI's on-going relationship with this credit card issuer.

Steven discussed the problem of service level:

When dealing with thousands of individuals, mistakes are bound to happen. It's inevitable. But the unhappiness of a single subscriber can have greater significance than simply the loss of a subscriber. You don't like this to happen, but you can afford to lose a customer occasionally. In our situation, however, the unhappiness of a subscriber can get back to a credit card issuer. If this happens too often, our relationship with the issuer is jeopardized. It's a delicate situation.

The degree of computerization also represented a serious question. The Halmos' felt initially that as much as possible should be handled by computer. However, there appeared to be many functions which were best handled manually. For this reason, the entire billing and renewal system was computerized while the major portion of the day-to-day servicing was handled manually.

The acquisitions made by the company also caused operational problems. One of the acquired companies made no use of a computer, but maintained information on microfilm. The other utilized a highly sophisticated computer system which was totally unreliable. Therefore, the operations had to be consolidated into a single operation compatible to all.

A major question arose as to which name should be continued. The Halmos' felt that the renewal rates must be maintained at all costs. They further felt that subscribers to a service build a certain degree of loyalty to that service. Therefore, despite the higher costs associated with running parallel operations, they decided to maintain the operations under the three different names. This presented operational problems.

The operations at SSI seemed to run from crisis to crisis. Dealing with a multitude of small transactions made the measurement of labor productivity very difficult. The measurement of quality was even more difficult. As a matter of fact, even after four years in business, the Halmos' had no handle on the actual cost per subscriber per year. They were painfully aware of their problem, but were unsure of any effective means of monitoring the productivity and quality of operations and of establishing costs. Peter commented on this issue:

> You have to constantly keep the economics of the business in mind. If you try to build in too much sophistication, you can quickly let things get out of hand. But, we seem to be on the right track, since we are operating profitably now, and our renewal rate is in excess of 80% per year.

The Future

Steven was optimistic regarding the viability of their services:

> The economics are there. On a mailing with a credit card issuer, we just hope to break even on first year costs, though we usually do better than that. The costs are front-loaded, in that we incur heavy costs at the time of initial subscription due to computer input, materials, mailing, and labor costs. Since the services generate a high renewal rate at little additional cost, the profitability in subsequent years is very attractive. In fact, profits of 50% on revenues from renewals are certainly possible.

At the end of 1972, SSI had some 50,000 subscribers to its various services. Since many subscribed only to the credit card registry service, the average annual fee per subscriber was $8. However, while the company had grown substantially since the public offering in 1971, the future posed several questions.

The credit card issuer mailings had become more difficult. While the company enjoyed a good reputation, the market required more credibility. The credit card is-

Exhibit 6

SAFECARD SERVICES, INCORPORATED
Balance Sheet, October 31, 1972

ASSETS	
Current assets:	
Cash—includes certificate of deposit; $25,000—1972	$33,264
Accounts receivable	10,353
Miscellaneous receivables	400
Prepaid expenses	11,385
Total current assets	55,402
Property and equipment—at cost:	4,074
Less: Accumulated depreciation	328
	3,746
Deferred costs—net of accumulated amortization	
Program development costs	8,624
Start-up costs	18,085
Marketing costs	19,177
Cost of customer lists acquired	110,069
Covenant not to compete	4,292
Organization costs	513
	160,760
Investment in Valcometrix Corporation	40,179
Security deposits	1,309
	$261,396
LIABILITIES	
Current liabilities:	
Accounts payable	$ 36,346
Accrued expenses and taxes	13,822
Notes payable—stockholders	—
Loan payable—stockholders	1,200
Total current liabilities	51,368
Accrued officers' salaries	14,800
SHAREHOLDERS' EQUITY	
Common stock, $.01 par value, authorized 1,000,000 shares; issued and outstanding 317,400	3,174
Additional paid-in capital	209,646
Deficit	(17,592)
	195,228
	$261,396

Exhibit 7

SAFECARD SERVICES, INC.
Statement of Operations and Deficit for the Year
Ended October 31, 1972

Revenues:	
Subscription income	$130,557
Interest income	2,414
Total revenues	132,971
Cost and expenses:	
Cost of services	59,173
Selling, general and administrative expenses	77,324
Amortization and depreciation (not included above)	17,970
	154,467
Loss before extraordinary item and provision for state and local income taxes	(21,496)
State and local income taxes	(650)
Loss before extraordinary item	(22,146)
Extraordinary item—gain on sale of investment	4,554
Net loss and deficit	$(17,592)
Per share:	
Net loss per share before extraordinary gain	(.07)
Extraordinary gain	.01
Net loss per share	(.06)

suers had grown to realize the great value of their cardholder lists and their monthly billing mailings. Therefore, the competition for space in these mailings had become intense. The competition furthermore consisted of seasoned professionals with established working relationships. In addition, the problems of establishing the credibility of a service company existed.

However, SSI had developed working relationships with Trans World Airlines, E. J. Korvettes, and contracts had been negotiated with TraveLodge Hotels and Eastern Airlines for large mailings. The economics of these mailings were attractive, although the volume was certainly limited. It was estimated that the response required to break even on mailing costs was approximately .25%. Since actual mailing response ranged from .4% to 1.2%, these mailings appeared to be profitable.

As a means of directly controlling the volume of SSI mailings, the Halmos' wondered whether they should consider the alternative of circumventing credit card issuer mailings and initiating direct mail campaigns of their own. This form of marketing appeared to be viable, but would certainly require a great deal more financing. Considering the costs of between $150 and $200 per 1,000 pieces of mail (indicated earlier), substantial volume would require the commitment of a great deal of cash. In addition, direct mail programs would require extensive testing, mailing list selection, and design work while lacking the third part endorsement considered so valuable. The Halmos' were unsure as to whether they should take such a high risk course of action, considering the company's present position. However, initiating direct mail programs of its own would allow SSI to grow as rapidly as its financing would tolerate.

A third alternative would involve the introduction of an experienced partner to handle the marketing function. Negotiations had recently been initiated with a large insurance company interested in promoting the SSI concept as "aggravation insurance." This firm had the financial, creative, and marketing expertise to sell the SSI services in large volume.

But this alternative would not be without its costs. The insurance company had indicated its willingness to take on the marketing responsibility, but required the option to purchase 51% control of SSI. This relationship would be based on volume. If the insurance company succeeded in securing 100,000 new SSI sub-

Exhibit 8

SAFECARD SERVICES, INC.
Excerpt from Prospectus

PRINCIPAL STOCKHOLDERS

The following table sets forth as of August 31, 1971, the Common Stock owned by each person whose ownership of record and beneficially is more than 10% of the Common Stock of the Company, and the holdings of the officers and directors as a group. Each of the following named stockholders may be deemed promoters of the Company.

Name and Address	*Title of Class*	*Type of Ownership*	*Amount Owned*	*Percent of Class*	*Percent of Class after Offering (1)(2)*
Peter A. Halmos 520 E. 72nd Street New York, N.Y. President, Treasurer and Director	Common	Record and Beneficially	93,286	42.1	25.1
Steven J. Halmos Harvard Business School, Chase Hall C-41 Boston, Mass. Vice-President, Secretary and Director	Common	Record and Beneficially	45,000	20.3	12.1
All officers and directors as a group	Common	Record and Beneficially	172,286	77.7	46.3

(1) Assuming sale of 150,000 shares of Common Stock.
(2) Does not include Common Stock issued on exercise of warrants.

scribers during the ensuing two years, it would then be issued warrants to purchase new shares representing 51% ownership of SSI at $1 per share.

A fourth alternative existed. During this period, the company had formed a joint venture (owned 50/50 by the parties) with the United States Banknote Corporation in New York which added another possible dimension to SSI operations. The new company, Valcometrix Corp., was established to complete development and begin marketing of a family of technologies for the credit card industry. These technologies, valued by U.S. Banknote at $300,000, included a point-of-sale terminal for credit card authorization, a device for capturing an individual's "voiceprint," a counterfeit-proof credit card, and other related products. Of greatest apparent significance, however, was the unique development of FM radio data transmission for communication with the point-of-sale terminals. Realizing that major firms including IBM and National Cash Register had entered the credit authorization field, the Halmos' were reluctant to make a major commitment to this area.

The Halmos' were uncertain as to which course of action should be taken. While the first year as a public company resulted in a small loss (see Exhibits 6, 7, and 8 for financial information), SSI was now operating profitably. But marketing still presented a problem. They had recently developed two new services, one of which had proven to be very successful in an initial direct mail test. With some $50,000 in cash and a positive cash flow, they felt the company was financially sound for the foreseeable future. However, they felt that a decision as to the long-term growth of the firm should be made soon.

Premier Cinema Company

In January 1975, Mr. Marvin Foley, President of Financial Services, Inc. (FSI), was faced with making a final decision on a new venture which could materially change his future. He was evaluating a business plan to form a partnership with Mr. James Brown for the purpose of opening a new theater complex in the Newport County area of Rhode Island. The new venture would operate as a separate company and FSI would continue to specialize in finance and real estate consulting to major theaters. Although both Foley and Brown had been in the theater business for nearly eight years, their experience had been limited to staff management and consulting. The opening of their own theater would require considerable capital, and would put them into head-on competition with a major movie chain which controlled the Rhode Island area. Foley described some of the problems he and his partners would face:

> The biggest problem is breaking into the region. Rhode Island Cinema has successfully controlled the region for over 20 years. They have 15 theaters in 9 towns and have been successful at preventing other theaters from getting a foothold through site preemption and control of distribution. This competitive situation compounds the problem of acquiring capital. Obviously it is more difficult for us as newcomers to be convincing about our future success than it is for an established chain. This affects not only capital but it will mean a higher debt service charge. Finally, this theater venture is presently a sideline to my main consulting business and I'm not sure what impact it will have overall.

Motion Picture Industry

During the 1930s, at the height of Hollywood's "Golden Age," the motion picture industry was dominated by the major studios from the production through to the exhibition of films. The studios owned the cameras, the sets, the stars, the theaters, and anything else worth owning. Antitrust action in the mid-1930s forced the major studios to sell their theater chains, beginning the end of concentration.

Exhibit 1 shows the U.S. attendance trends from 1957 to 1973. Domestic gross receipts were in excess of $1.9 billion in 1974, the highest in the history of the business (1946 was the previous record at $1.7 billion). During the period covered by the exhibit, movie admission prices rose some 300–500%. Exhibit 2 shows the count of U.S. motion picture theaters for census years. These data are

Exhibit 1

PREMIER CINEMA COMPANY
U.S. Motion Picture Industry Statistics

	Admissions (millions $)	*Percent of U.S. Personal Consumption Expenditure*	*Percent of Recreation Expenditures*	*Percent of Spectator Amusement Expenditures*
1957	1,126	.40	7.3	68.0
1958	992	.34	6.3	64.5
1958	958	.31	5.5	61.0
1960	951	.29	5.2	59.2
1961	921	.27	4.7	56.6
1962	903	.24	4.4	54.9
1963	904	.24	4.1	53.4
1964	913	.23	3.7	51.8
1965	927	.21	3.5	51.2
1966	964	.20	3.3	50.1
1967	989	.20	3.2	48.7
1968	1,045	.20	3.1	49.1
1969	1,099	.19	3.0	48.6
1970	1,162	.19	2.9	48.0
1971	1,198	.18	2.8	47.3
1972	1,203	.16	2.5	45.1
1973	1,292	.16	2.5	44.6

Source: U.S. Department of Commerce.

Exhibit 2

PREMIER CINEMA COMPANY
U.S. Motion Picture Theaters

Investment in New Theaters Opened, 1966 Through 1973

	Number of Theaters	*Investment $ Millions (estimated)*	*Investment Per Theater $ Thousands (estimated)*
1966	223	75.8	339.9
1967	212	70.8	334.0
1968	191	61.3	320.9
1969	287	94.8	330.3
1970	275	108.5	394.5
1971	321	115.8	360.7
1972	299	104.7	350.2
1973	291	116.4	400.0
Total (8 Years)	2,099	748.1	356.4
Annual Average	262	93.5	

Exhibit 2 (continued)

(End of Year) Theaters in Operation

	1939 (Census)	*1948 (Census)*	*1954 (Census)*	*1958 (Census)*	*1963 (Census)*
Indoor	N.A.	17,811	14,716	12,291	9,150
Drive-in	N.A.	820	3,775	4,063	3,502
Total	15,115	18,631	18,491	16,354	12,652

	1964 (est.)	*1965 (est.)*	*1966 (est.)*	*1967 (est.)*	*1968 (est.)*
Indoor	9,200	9,240	9,290	9,330	9,500
Drive-in	3,540	3,585	3,640	3,670	3,690
Total	12,740	12,825	12,930	13,000	13,190

	1969 (est.)	*1970 (est.)*	*1971 (est.)*	*1972 (est.)*	*1973 (est.)*
Indoor	9,750	10,000	10,300	10,580	10,850
Drive-in	3,730	3,750	3,770	3,790	3,800
Total	13,480	13,750	14,070	14,370	14,650

NOTES: Alaska and Hawaii are included from 1963 on. For 1958, U.S. Census reported Alaska and Hawaii separately (106 theaters, comprised of 98 indoor and 8 drive-in).

Estimated total capacities, based on average per theater of 743 seats (indoor) and 520 cars (drive-in), were 8,062,000 seats and 1,976,000 cars at end of 1973.

SOURCE: *Boxoffice* magazine.

complemented by figures showing the pattern of investments in new theaters from 1966 through 1973. Of the 275 theaters shown for 1970, 251 were indoor theaters and nearly 50% of these were multiauditorium complexes.

In 1975 the motion picture industry contained elements of both concentration and fragmentation. Exhibit 3 presents a simplified view. The industry process begins with the production of the product. The first segment consisted of two subsegments, the major production companies and the independent production companies. Both of these subsegments were highly fragmented; the fragmentation was a direct result of the risk involved in picture making. When television destroyed the safe market for films in theatrical release, the probability of failure for film projects increased dramatically. The major studios began to lose money and the new high risk situation resulted in an increase of independent production companies which attempted to sell directly to the distributors.

However, distributors were in most cases the major studios which had established sales networks domestically and internationally. This segment of the industry had the greatest degree of ownership concentration. Distributors bought from the majors and independents and sold to the exhibitors (theater owners). Each deal be-

Exhibit 3

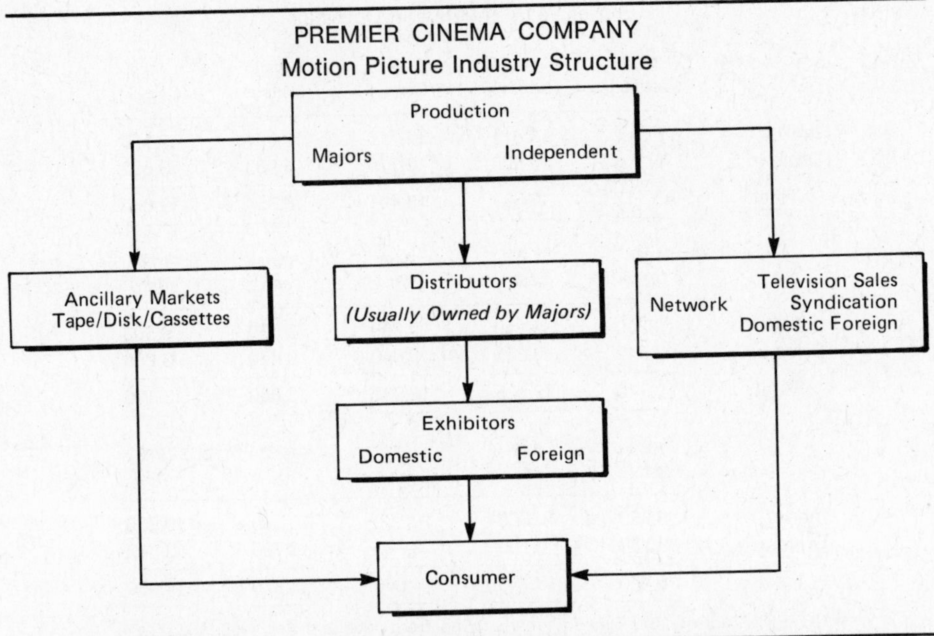

tween these parties was unique and the transactions conducted were quite complex. The disadvantaged position which had resulted in the loss for film producers changed abruptly in the 1970s. A 1975 headline from the industry newspaper *Variety* read "Theatre Crisis Over Film Famine." It was this famine which had caused the change by transferring negotiating power to the distributors from the hands of the exhibitors.

The exhibitor segment was also a combination of concentration and fragmentation. The vertical fragmentation achieved by antitrust movements caused a break between the distribution and exhibition levels. This break also opened an opportunity for some companies to concentrate in the exhibition area. For example, General Cinema, the largest U.S. movie theater chain, went from being a company with \$8 million sales to one with \$160 million sales over a period of 15 years. By law, each theater had the right to bid for a picture, and the distributor had to consider the cinemas submitting bids as being on equal terms. In practice, older or poorly sited theaters did not generate sufficient volume to warrant bidding for first-run films and choose not to bid. In addition, concentration in the exhibitor segment was an important factor in the dealings between distributors and exhibitors. The major metropolitan areas were naturally the largest film markets, and within these markets were preferred locations, suburban or "shopping center" theaters versus the inner-city sites. Owners of a large number of key national sites were in a strong position to arrange special deals with a distributor. For example, a major theater chain might be able to negotiate a lower percentage take for the distributor because the distributor had a strong desire to show the picture in the key sites owned by the chain. The number of screens owned in a geographical area was also a factor in the "bidding" process.

Historically a system of bidding areas developed through the United States with the necessary theater in each area entering into a contract for the first run of a particular film. For example, downtown Boston would have first-run "availability," and the next center or area would be 30 miles away. Thus two towns, side by side, could have first- and second-run availability, respectively. However, a strong newcomer to a second-run market could outbid the existing first-run theaters and change the distribution patterns. In essence, the exhibitor was selling his ability to sell seats when he bids for a picture. Bids would state the amount of front money the exhibitor would stand and whether or not this constituted an advance or a guarantee. Exhibitors would further specify the screen on which the film would be shown and the length of the "run" control. Mr. Foley commented:

> Let's say I owned theaters in 30 major cities and wanted a big film like "The Godfather." Even if only 24 of my theaters would normally get first-run rating, my chain size could make it possible for me to run the film in almost all of my theaters. However, if then along comes a bomb, say "Jonathan Livingston Seagull," I'd probably have to play that too. Theater chains which are big regionally have similar bargaining positions.
>
> Agreements are not restricted to those between distributor and exhibitor. Some theater chains have agreements not to bid against a competing chain within a certain area, though there would, of course, be other bidders. Such an agreement would be reciprocated elsewhere.
>
> In short, though all bidders are equal under the law, the equality is subject to some not-so-subtle differences.

Distributor-Exhibitor Contract

The distributor-exhibitor contract generally revolved around percentages of gross receipts. Within the bidding process, the usual contract contained a base level which was raised when the base level point was exceeded. Mr. Foley commented again:

> The way pictures are bought today is incredible. And it all started with the original "Godfather" in November 1971. I may be wrong with my date and numbers but they'll give a rough idea of how things are done. There were expected to be about 146 first-run showings of "The Godfather." The producer, Paramount, went to the exhibitors, and asked for \$50 thousand down per theater plus 90% of the box office for the first four weeks with a 70% floor, 80% for the next four weeks with a 60% floor, and 70% for the next four weeks with a 50% floor. In addition, there was a holdover condition. At this time the picture did not have a cast or director and was not expected to be ready for 12 months.

The "box office" referred to by Mr. Foley was net box office takings after deducting "overhead," but the "floor" referred to was a minimum of the theater's gross takings. The "holdover" condition was a clause which would force the theater owner to extend the run of a film for a net period if takings were above a specified level on a specified date. A simpler contract structure would be a choice between a percentage of gross box office receipts or a larger percentage of gross box office receipts net of operating expenses (including overhead); the distributor receiving the larger amount resulting from the two formulas. Mr. Foley continued:

> The producer removed all risk from his scene. He was fully financed by the exhibitors before the picture was made. Exhibitors were, in fact, making blind bids. "The Godfather" was a great success but others like "The Great Gatsby" made money only for the studios. Holdover clauses and contract terms can be particularly punishing when films have a weak staying power such as "The Exorcist." Present contracts can put a severe squeeze on the exhibitor and only if a given film does extremely well does the exhibitor show a profit on a particular run.

Advertising and promotion expenses were an integral part of the contract and costs were usually split in a similar fashion to the split of box-office receipts. Should the film require greater promotion and advertising than planned, additional expenses would be subject to a new negotiation between the distributor and exhibitor.

Marketing

The trends in the number of films produced in the United States declined from over 400 a year in the 1940s to just over half that number by the early 1970s. In conjunction with this, inventories of older films were being used for television, reducing further the variety available for the distributors and exhibitors. Since some chains had a declared policy of avoiding X-rated or pornographic films, the effective number available was only about 120 films in 1974, and this was an improvement from the 90 or so available in 1972. The relative scarcity of new films meant careful handling of them in the marketplace.

First-run films played in strong theaters which had obtained the film through the bidding process. This "limited-run" distribution was by far the most widely used technique for first-run films. Even narrower distribution was through "showcasing."

"Showcasing" a film by limiting its first run to a very few major metropolitan areas attempts to capitalize on good reviews, creating lines at the theaters and good word-of-mouth advertising by film goers. "Showcasing" was used in cities like New York but no longer counted among the frequently used marketing strategies.

Lesser films must be given "wide distribution," which meant they were played at many theaters in an area with the support of a heavy radio and television campaign, plus advertisements in newspapers. The effect was to create a short-term demand for the film and most "wide distribution" films have short runs.

"Fourwalling" was another technique employed by distributors. This effectively meant the purchase of a theater's operation or "fourwalls" by the distribution for the duration of a particular feature, so that the distributor would pay the exhibitor a fixed fee for a fixed time. Potential reasons for fourwalling were many but generally rested on the theater owner's unwillingness to show the film otherwise. An instance might be where contract terms were too stiff; United Artists was faced with fourwalling "Fiddler on the Roof" for this reason. Another reason for fourwalling could be the use of the theater by a local church group for a film which otherwise would not be shown.

Pricing of performances was a complex affair. Special low rates might be given to "early bird" theater goers (those attending the 1 P.M. performances), and other special rates might be available for senior citizens or students. Weekend prices (typically around $2.50 per adult) were usually higher than during the week (typically $2 per adult), and this was not surprising since 42% of the total U.S. movie theater was taken on Saturdays, 22% on Sundays, and 19% on Fridays. Distributors, also, may set price minimums for certain films as part of the contract.

At that time the recent success of the $1 theaters underlined the great elasticity of demand in the cinema business. These cinemas relied on low overhead and high attendance figures to generate their profits. High sales of concessionary items such as candy and popcorn often compensated relatively lower box office revenues.

Company Background

FSI, the consulting company operated by Marvin Foley, provided a wide range of services including real estate selection, negotiations for sites, sale and leaseback financing, and assisting in the sale of major assets. Though a relatively new undertaking, the company's services had been in demand and by mid-1974 the company was engaged in nationwide expansion activities for several companies.

The main portion of their business, however, was to provide site selection reports for one of the major New York theater chains. It was at this time that Foley and Brown decided to form Premier Cinema with the understanding that the venture would be dropped should the assessment of the business plan prove unfavorable after initial fact finding. If favorable, the Premier Cinema Company would stand as a separate company and Marvin Foley would act as president.

Prior to his experience with FSI, Foley had been a vice-president of a major regional shopping center development company where he had been responsible for tenant leasing, preparation of financial projections for new projects, and structuring of equity participation in shopping center ventures. Foley's other experience included over four years as assistant to the president of National Cinema, Inc., where he was responsible for theater real estate and assisting in theater acquisitions and disposals. He had also spent a number of years with a major Boston-based consulting group as a staff consultant.

Brown had been branch manager of Warner Bros. Boston office, serving New England for five years. Prior to this he had worked in New England and Washington, D.C., as Warner's salesman.

The Premier Cinema Company had evolved from the experience of the Foley and Brown families at their summer houses in Newport, Rhode Island. And though

Foley and Brown knew of the downward trend in cinema attendances, they felt there were considerable opportunities in the film industry. The purpose of Premier Cinema was to enter into a long-term leasehold interest in a three-screen cinema to be built within a vacant building in a recently completed shopping center in Newport.

The Theater and Site

Newport, Rhode Island, was a coastal town with a population of over 40,000. During the summer months its population, and that of the surrounding countryside, increased more than fivefold. The shopping center site proposed for Premier Cinema was located on the western side of the town on the way to Jamestown (population 25,000). Jamestown and Middletown (population 30,000) were Newport's closest neighbors and were both about five miles distance from Newport. As its principal tenant, the shopping center had a K-Mart store of 99,000 square feet and an additional 68,000 square feet of smaller specialty shops.

The entire three-screen theater would be contained within approximately 9,200 square feet and would have a seating capacity of approximately 850 seats. The multiple auditorium concept would allow for reduced operating costs while providing for broader market appeal and greater film flexibility.

The common automated projection booth required a single operator, while the common box office required one cashier. The remaining staff consisted of a manager, ticket taker, ushers, and concession employees. Experience indicated that the second and third screen would add a total of only 35% to operating costs when compared to a single screen theater. The three screens would offer the opportunity to attract three distinctly different audiences. For example, one screen could be used to provide entertainment for children with a Walt Disney attraction, while the second and third screens could be used to provide teenage- or adult-oriented pictures.

Foley mentioned foreign films, few of which were shown in Newport or festivals. "We have this luxury with three screens," he commented. No X-rated films would be shown as a matter of policy though Mr. Foley qualified this by allowing that some major releases which were valuable artistic productions (such as, "Midnight Cowboy" or "Clockwork Orange") would be shown. The company "no X" policy referred to so-called "skin flicks" or hard- and soft-core pornography.

The success of the multiple screen theater was well established with almost every major regional and national theater circuit in the United States.

Competition

Competition in Newport was from the Crown Mall Cinema and the downtown theater. The Crown Mall Cinema was a freestanding single screen theater located behind the Crown Mall Shopping Center, directly across from Premier Cinema's prospective site. The Crown Mall Cinema, with box office revenues of $350,000 in 1974, played first-run pictures as did the downtown theater. Both of these theaters were among the 15 owned and operated by Rhode Island Cinemas, Inc., the dominant theater chain in the nine-town area. Premier Cinema intended to

Exhibit 4

PREMIER CINEMA COMPANY
Theater Equipment Requirements

1. *PROJECTION BOOTH/AUDIO/SCREEN*	
Three projector automated systems including spare parts @ $17,700 per auditorium	$ 53,100
Screens	1,200
2. *CHAIRS*	
Delivered and installed chairs @ $40.70 per chair	34,600
3. *BOX OFFICE*	
Six-ticket unit, cash drawers, and chair	2,500
4. *CONCESSION EQUIPMENT*	
Ice machine, drink machine, popcorn warmer, jet spray, butter dispenser, and candy display stand	8,500
5. *CARPETING*	
Woven nylon or nylon wool blend, 200 yards delivered, installed with padding	3,000
6. *DRAPES*	
Soundpleat, three walls, floor to ceiling @ $1,500 per auditorium	4,500
7. *READER BOARD SIGN*	
10′ x 10′ reader board on building face with 300 8″ snap lock letters	5,100
Total	$112,500

pursue vigorously a first-run policy in its theaters but believed it could provide film distributors with an alternative method of distribution in the market for both first- and second-run products. During the heavy release dates of June–July and December–January, many pictures were not shown or were played short of their potential. The additional screens would offer the distributor a flexibility not previously available.

The position of Rhode Island Cinemas in the area had put them in a strong position when bidding for films. Because of their dominance of the area, the normal bidding process was not adhered to, and negotiation was directly with the distributors. Normally the bidding process restricted the showing of first-run film to the theater named in the bid. Rhode Island Cinemas were not normally restricted this way and could move their films amongst their theaters at will. Premier Cinema's entrance in the market could change this substantially.

Exhibit 5

PREMIER CINEMA COMPANY
Capital Balance at Start-up

Initial Capital		
Equity	$ 20,000	
Loans to PCC	130,000	$150,000
Capital Requirements		
Architectural and engineering services	5,000	
Deposits and preopening expenses and inventory	4,500	
Legal fees	2,000	
Theater equipment	112,500	
Sales tax	3,300	
Incidental expenses and contingency	2,700	130,000
Capital Balance		$ 20,000

Lease

The leasehold interest to be taken by Premier Cinemas was of great value. In order to prepare the theater space, the landlord would spend an additional $160,000 for remodeling. The lease itself would provide very favorable terms for the tenant. Nominally for 20 years, the lease had two 10-year options with the 9,200 square foot area at $5 per square foot. Premier Cinema would pay its pro rata share of real estate taxes and common area maintenance costs, and for 1975 these had been calculated at $2,760 and $1,380, respectively. It was expected that the value of Premier Cinema's investment in the lease would increase significantly because of

Exhibit 6

PREMIER CINEMA COMPANY
Pro-Forma Balance Sheet Start-up

Current Assets		*Long-term Liabilities*	
Cash	$ 20,000	7-year, $10\frac{1}{4}\%$ theater equipment mortgage	$100,000
		8-year demand note	30,000
Fixed Assets			
Theater equipment	112,500	*Stockholders' Equity*	
Other Assets		Common stock	20,000
Incorporation expense	17,500		
Total assets	$150,000	Total liabilities and stockholders' equity	$150,000

Exhibit 7

PREMIER CINEMA COMPANY
Pro-Forma Profit and Loss Statement
First Year of Operation

		Break-even		*Target*
		$5,575/week		$7,000/week
		129,000 patrons		162,000 patrons
Average admissions @ $2.25 per person (approx.)		$290,000		$364,000
Less: film cost @ 44% (approx.)		127,000		160,000
Gross profit before operating expenses		$163,000		$204,000
Operating Expenses (excluding rent)				
Advertising	$ 12,000			
Payroll (including payroll tax)	65,000			
Booking and management fee	15,000			
Repairs	1,000			
Insurance	3,000			
Utilities	10,000			
Real estate taxes	2,760			
Professional fees	3,000			
Architectural plans (24 mos. @ 187.50/ month @ 6%)	2,400			
Operating supplies and expenses	5,000			
Common area maintenance @ 15¢/sf	1,380			
Miscellaneous expenses	960			
Total Operating Expenses (excluding rent)		$121,500		$121,500
Gross Profit		41,500		82,500
Concession sales @ 35¢ per person	$ 44,000		$57,000	
Estimated concession profit @ 60%		26,000		35,000
Net profit before depreciation, rent, interest		67,500		117,500
Rent @ 5.00/square foot @ 9,200 square feet		46,000		46,000
Net profit before interest and depreciation		$ 21,500		$ 71,500
Equipment loan	$100,000			
Equipment loan interest and depreciation[1]		$ 21,500		$ 21,500
Net Profit before tax		$ 0		$ 50,000

[1] Assumes $112,500 of theater equipment, payment of principal and interest @ $20,000 per year over a seven-year term to amortize $100,000 equipment loan. Assumes straight-line depreciation over a ten-year period on $112,500.

Exhibit 8

PREMIER CINEMA COMPANY
Pro-Forma Cash Flow, First Year of Operation

		Break-even	*Target*
Net profit before taxes and investment credit		$ 0	$50,000
Less: State tax @ 8.55%	4,275		
Amortization	9,750	(9,750)	(14,025)
		$(9,750)	$35,975
Add depreciation		11,250	11,250
Cash available for distribution		$ 1,500	$47,225
Investment tax credit available for distribution		$11,250	$11,250

the general increasing real estate values for commercial space in shopping centers. However, the lease terms called for strict adherence to certain standards of performance. These were particularly important from a financing standpoint.

The Decision to Invest

The solid background in the film industry of both Foley and Brown left them little doubt that they could count on several of their many acquaintances to help with the buying and marketing side of Premier Cinema.

On the financial side, Brown had put together an estimate of theater equipment requirements (see Exhibit 4) and estimated capital needs (Exhibit 5). He had gone further by generating start-up balance sheet (Exhibit 6), and pro-forma-statements for the first year's operation (Exhibits 7 and 8). In putting his figures together, James Brown had assumed a 365-day operation with daily operation from 1 P.M. through 11 P.M. from the end of May to September. Operation for the remaining period would be 7 P.M. to 11 P.M. Monday through Friday and 1 P.M. to 11 P.M. on Saturdays and Sundays. Prices were assumed to be set at a level to meet those of the competition.

In spite of the favorable figures, Marvin Foley was concerned. "The lease and permit to create the three movie theaters will not be a problem," he said, "but Rhode Island Cinemas has acquired a special exception permit to build two extra auditoriums in Crown Mall Theater. My present reading of the situation is that they will not be built." James Brown felt little discomfort on this point but was more concerned about Premier Cinema's bidding power and strategy. Rhode Island Cinemas Newport theaters were after all only a small fraction of the chain's total number of screens.

Perlis Truckstop

In August 1974, Perlis Truckstop located on Interstate Highway 75, 150 miles south of Atlanta in Cordele, Georgia, had been in operation for three years, providing fuel, food, and other services to truck drivers. The previous year had been a particularly successful one, with pretax profits in excess of $600,000 from revenues of over $5 million. Lamar Perlis was considering a number of growth alternatives for his company, including opening another truckstop and expanding the amenities available at the Cordele truckstop.

The Truckstop Industry

According to the National Association of Truck Stop Operators (NATSO), there were approximately 4,000 truckstops in the United States in 1974, of which some 1,200 were "full-facility" truckstops, the remainder being "fuel stops." The distinction between the two forms of truckstop was one of degree, the former category offering a wider range of services to the long-distance truck driver (see Exhibit 1). However, most truckstops offered the basic 24-hour services of diesel fuel, tire repair, restaurant facilities, and sleeping facilities.

The industry had grown rapidly since the late 1950s, when there were approximately 800 truckstops, as a result of the construction of the U.S. interstate highway system. As the "super highways" were completed there was a rapid increase in the volume of intercity freight moved by truck and concomitant increase in those industries serving the motor carrier. In addition, the average size of trucks grew as did the average length of the haul. These developments created a demand for new truckstops offering an increased range of services. By the late 1960s, the industry was annually generating over $1 billion in revenues, and according to a 1971 *Fleet Owner* article, a new facility was opening every 6.5 days. Since many motor carrier industry observers projected a continued rapid rise in truck traffic through the 1970s (a rise of up to 50% in tonnage and 25% in number of trucks by 1980), the future outlook for the truckstop industry was considered bright.

Although half of the truckstop operators owned their own facility, many truckstops were owned or franchised by major oil companies. Union Oil Co. was the industry leader with a chain of over 600 truckstops, approximately 150 of which were on the interstate system. Under the brand name of Union 76, Union Oil had entered the truckstop industry in 1965 with its acquisition of the Pure Oil Co., which had previously developed a chain of truckstops. Union 76, in the early 1970s, was opening full-facility truckstops at the rate of 15 per year. A major source of Union 76's strength in the truckstop industry was their controlled credit

Exhibit 1

PERLIS TRUCKSTOP
Qualifications for Membership of National Association of Truck Stop Operators (NATSO)

Minimum Facilities

(I) 24-hour service
(II) Diesel fuel
(III) Adequate parking facilities
(IV) Tire repair facilities
(V) Overall cleanliness
(VI) Restaurant*
(VII) Sleeping facilities*
(VIII) Showers*

*Optional Facilities***

1. Ticket printer pumps***
2. Truck washing
3. Scales***
4. Propane gas***
5. Laundry service***
6. Steam cleaning
7. Truck lubrication***
8. Wet ice
9. Dry ice
10. Blast chilling
11. Barber/beauty salons***
12. Garage or mechanic***
13. Wrecker service***
14. Western Union
15. Teletype***
16. Drivers lounge***
17. Brokerage service
18. Warehouse facilities
19. Tire bank***
20. Merchandise for sale (Safety equipment, accessories, clothing, etc.)***

* Membership requirements allow these facilities to be offered at an adjoining building to the truck stop.
** Membership requirements included at least five of the services.
*** Facilities offered by Perlis Truckstop.

card system, which recorded expenses by vehicle and combined them into a single monthly billing to fleet owners.

The second largest oil company participating in the truckstop industry was the Skelly Oil Company, with over 200 truckstops. Like most other oil companies, Skelly truckstops were operated in three basic ways: (1) Skelly owned and operated the truckstop; (2) Skelly owned the outlet and leased it to the operator; or (3) Skelly was the supplier and offered financial assistance to the operator to build a stop. In the South, Union 76 supplied 50% of the diesel fuel to truckstops, but Skelly at 6% came in the third behind Texaco, who supplied 13%. In a national survey conducted by NATSO, it was revealed that 60% of the truckstops were bound by contract to a single oil company for their supplies of gasoline and diesel fuel.

While the oil companies were the main owners and sponsors of truckstop chains, the early 1970s saw other organizations entering the industry. Ryder Truck Rentals, Inc., based in Miami, had launched an extensive truckstop acquisition program, commencing with the purchase in 1972 of Truckstops of America, a chain of 20 truckstops. Industry observers believed that Ryder was aiming at a network of 100 truckstops, with the company's own trucks providing the "core business." Other recent entrants into the truckstop business included B.T.R. Corp. (a North Carolina company owned by Holiday Inn) and the Greyhound Corporation who both operated a number of Union 76 franchises.

With the increased range of services offered, the average cost of a full-facility truckstop had increased from approximately $800,000 in 1968 to over $2 million by 1972. Average yearly gross revenues had jumped in the same period from $700,000 to $2 million. At the same time, average yearly gallonage had almost doubled from 2.4 million to 4.2 million.

In the NATSO survey of truckstops, the following averages were discovered. Fuel accounted for 62% of the revenues of the typical truckstop, which had 9.5 pumps. Owner operators accounted for 30% of customers, with the remainder being fleets. Of the 1 million truck tractors employed in the United States in 1970, approximately 700,000 were operated by 65,000 fleet owners; the remainder were operated by individual "owner operators." Fifty-three percent of truckstops operated "printer pumps," which automatically printed sales tickets for fuel sales. These pumps were considered to be an important sales tool, since they provided a guarantee to fleet owners of the accuracy and honesty of transactions between the truck driver and the truckstop operator.

The average truckstop restaurant seated 116 people, 83% with waitress service. Sixty-five percent of truckstops operated their own restaurant, the remainder licensed others to do so. Average revenues per restaurant were over $400,000 with a pretax profit as a percentage of sales of 10.4%.

Sleeping facilities, with an average of 14.6 rooms, provided 3.3% of revenues, with average charges being $7.25 a night for a room with a bath. Garage facilities yielded an average of 11% of revenues, and sale of merchandise in the truckstop provided 8.3% of revenues. Typical inventory turn for the stores was 5. The typical operator had been in business for 9.5 years, although this average fell to less than 6 years for the South.

Perlis Truckstop

Lamar Perlis, who was 50 years old in September 1974, had been raised in Cordele, Georgia (pop. 13,000), and trained as an industrial engineer at Georgia Tech. In 1949, after military service and college, he had entered his father's retail clothing store in Cordele, I. Perlis & Sons. In 1954, Lamar and his two brothers, Louis and Marvin, bought out shares of I. Perlis & Sons, so that the father and each of the brothers owned one-fourth of the company. In 1959 the father and brothers formed Perlis Realty, owned equally between them, to handle the realty transactions involved in opening new stores, as well as other independent realty deals. In 1962, Lamar Perlis, acting for Perlis Realty, built a shopping center, leasing sites to other retail stores. In 1965, another shopping center was established in Tifton, Georgia, 45 miles from Cordele, which was leased and built by Lamar Perlis, and later supervised by Marvin Perlis.

In 1964, Perlis Realty purchased 175 acres of land adjoining the I-75 highway, for $125,000. At the time, the brothers did not have a definite purpose for the land. However the location of the site on the highway suggested some facility related to either the traveling public or the motor carrier industry. Dissuaded from single-purpose facilities such as a motel, restaurant, or service station by the seasonality of those businesses, Lamar Perlis began to investigate the potential of the site as a truckstop.

> In late 1964 my wife, Jackie, and I passed the Union 76 truckstop in Wildwood, Florida, and we stopped to take a look. It was the first time I had seen a truckstop, and I was impressed by it, especially when I learned that one could serve both the tourist and truck trade, since these two businesses have

Exhibit 2

PERLIS TRUCKSTOP
Map of Georgia and South Carolina[1]

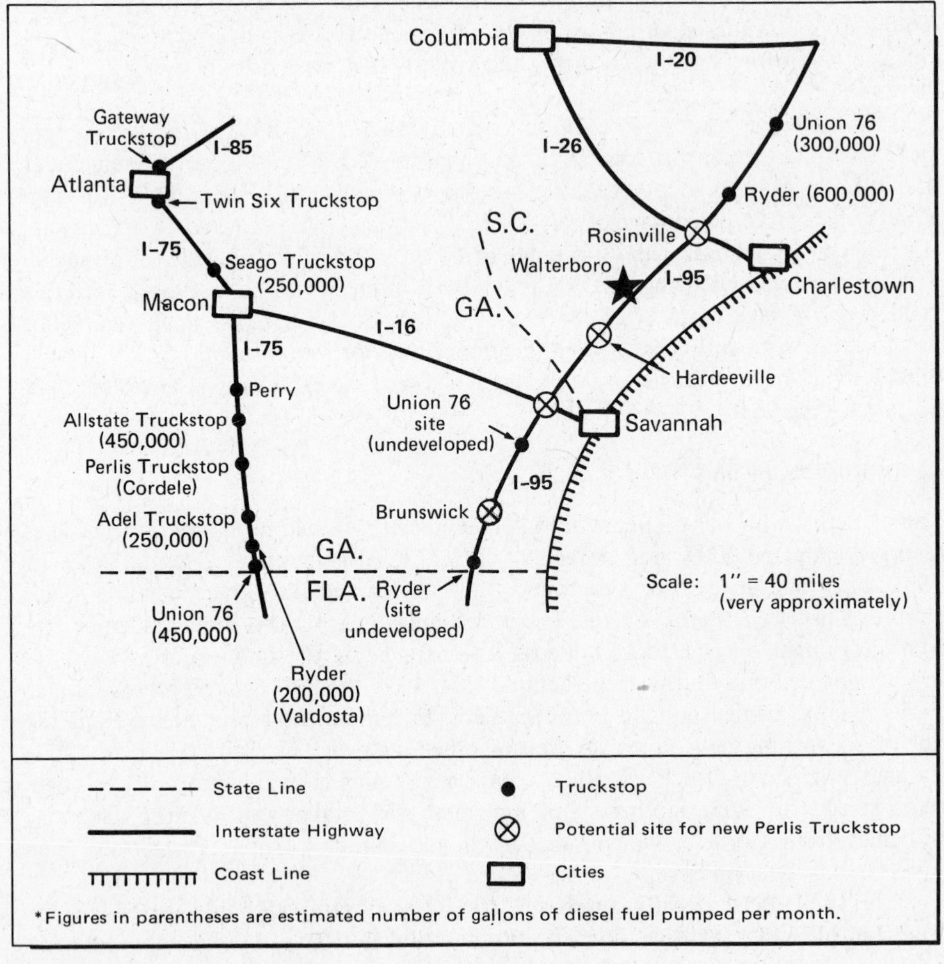

complementary seasonality. The idea germinated in my mind that our site would be perfect for a truckstop since Interstate 75 was the only completed interstate highway going into Florida (see Exhibit 2). Early in 1966 I approached the Gulf Oil Co., since I had grown up with their local distributor. Gulf sponsored a trip for him and me to visit several of their truckstops. I was disappointed with them because they were small operations and did not match with my vision of a truckstop. We continued our trip until we finally discovered a truckstop close to what I had in mind, near Richmond, Virginia. It was a Texaco stop, so I contacted Texaco and began negotiations.

Mr. Perlis had proposed to develop the real estate and lease it to Texaco. However, Texaco had turned down this proposal and persuaded Mr. Perlis to operate the truckstop. The final contract arrangements involved the leasing of the site of 18.5 acres by I. Perlis & Sons to Texaco for a 15-year term. A new company was formed by the three Perlis brothers, called Perlis Truck Terminal, Inc., which leased back the site for 15 years. The purpose of the lease and leaseback arrangement was to enable the brothers to use Texaco's lease as a basis for obtaining an $850,000 loan at 7¼% from the Continental Assurance Co. Perlis Truck Terminal, Inc., also entered into a fuel purchasing contract with Texaco. The contracts were all signed in March 1968. Mr. Perlis recalled his feelings at that time:

> However, even after all this, I was a little wary of proceeding. A truckstop was something very new for our family, because we were taking a big risk. We had left our father out of participation in the truckstop, because we didn't want to risk possible bankruptcy for him. Union 76 had just built a truckstop 27 miles north of our site, and I didn't know how to assess traffic potential. I thought the traffic count was very low relative to its potential (traffic counts for I-75 are given in Exhibit 3).

Because of his uncertainty about the current levels of the traffic count, and also because of a family cash constraint caused by the opening of the family discount shopping center in Cordele, Mr. Perlis delayed commencing the construction of the truckstop by over a year. He was forced to renegotiate the loan arrangement with Continental Assurance Co., paying a penalty of $33,000 to keep the option open. However, during this period Mr. Perlis held discussions with the owner of the Richmond, Virginia, truckstop that had impressed him. He was encouraged by the high sales of nonfuel items, such as store merchandise and meals, and so when family finances permitted construction of his truckstop, Mr. Perlis decided to go ahead. He entered negotiations with Texaco about the building, which Mr. Perlis wished to alter from the Texaco prototype since he wished to have a building that could be put to another purpose if the truckstop venture should fail. The original construction contract was for $550,000 and another $250,000 was spent on site improvement (detailed asset costs are given in Exhibit 4). Mr. Perlis recalled the financial condition of his company at its beginning.

> We projected a loss in our first year and expected to break even in our second year. We were in a "cash bind" in the first year, because one of my

Exhibit 3

PERLIS TRUCKSTOP
Traffic Count on I-75 *, 1970 and 1973

	Seasonal Factors	
January	.860	
February	.927	
March	1.141	
April	1.161	
May	.903	
June	1.196	
July	1.242	
August	1.215	
September	.814	
October	.816	
November	.895	
December	.837	
	1970	*1973*
Annual Average Daily Traffic	16,182	22,966
% Passenger cars	74.8%	73.0%
% Light trucks (gasoline)	6.0%	7.4%
% Heavy trucks (diesel)	19.1%	19.2%
% Buses	0.1%	0.2%

* Data are measurements taken by the State Highway Department of Georgia (Division of Highway Planning; Statistical 449–70), at station no 107, on I-75 just S.W. of the town of Perry (see Exhibit 2).

brothers had developed a new shopping center during our planning stages that was drawing heavily on the family's funds. We were very much undercapitalized, and the truckstop was expected to be $300,000 short in needed cash in the first year.

We opened in June 1971 and pumped 88,000 gallons of diesel in our first month. Our restaurant had no ceiling or refrigeration, but we opened it anyway, serving soft drinks and donuts.

We started with an employment of 50 people. Both my wife and I put in 20 hours a day in the first year. We had a very amateur organization. I had made earlier efforts to recruit people I knew for the managerial positions. I made it a rule not to recruit from my competitors, because I thought I would need to get along with them.

I had a great deal of trouble finding people with experience, and we didn't have the funds to train a cadre of workers before we opened. Cordele is a small town, and the quality of workers was not high, so we had a lot of problems. Our turnover rate in workers and management has been extremely

Exhibit 4

PERLIS TRUCKSTOP
Balance Sheet Data ($000)

Assets	Sept. 30 1971[1]	June 30 1974
Cash	(58)	2
Accounts Receivable	23	204
Inventory	64	345
Other current	4	115
Total Current	33	666
Fixed Assets		
Land	259	259
Building and improvements[5]	806	861[5]
Fuel service equipment	68	90
Autos and trucks[5]	10	121
Restaurant and equipment	111	120
Store equipment	9	13
Motel furniture	9	25
Office furniture[5]	9	46
Signs, lights, etc.[5]	306	325
Shop and parts department	12	30
Total fixed assets	1599	1890
Accounting depreciation	51	433
Net fixed assets	1548	1457
Other assets	43	37
Total Assets	1624	2160

Liabilities	Sept. 30 1971[1]	June 30 1974
Accounts Payable	154	181
Notes and mortgages	0	162
Other current	19	98
Total Current	173	441
Long-Term Debt		
Mortgage-Continental Assurance Co.[2]	817	714
Notes Payable-USC[3]	16	9
Mortgage—1st State Bank[4]	239	136
Loan—Perlis Rlty.	93	0
Loan—I. Perlis & Son	101	98
Loan—I. R. Perlis	73	50
Note payable	0	86
Less current portion	(73)	(162)
Total Long-Term Debt	1,266	931
Equity		
Capital stock	150	151
Paid-in capital	130	130
Retained earnings	(9)	47
Net income	(86)	555
Total equity	185	789
Total Liabilities and Equity	1624	2160

1. September 30, 1971 represented the end of the first quarter of operation.
2. Matures October 1985, guaranteed by stockholders, secured by land.
3. Matures January 1976, secured by phone system.
4. Matures May 1976, guaranteed by stockholders, secured by equipment.
5. The allocation of these assets by department was as follows:

	Buildings and Improvements	*Autos and Trucks*	*Signs, Lights, etc.*	*Office Furniture*
Fueling	19.94%	40%	63%	0
Parts	26.30%	20%	7%	0
Restaurant	15.58%	0	21%	0
Store	9.76%	0	7%	0
Motel	25.57%	0	2%	0
G & A	2.85%	40%	0	100%
	100%	100%	100%	100%

high. We hired whatever workers were available at the time, hoping to improve as we went along.

Operating History

Although the truckstop operated at a deficit every quarter until June 1972, break-even was reached at that time, and operations had become increasingly profitable (see Exhibit 5). The net operating loss carry-forward from the fiscal years ending September 30, 1971 and 1972 totaled $94,598 and was used to reduce taxable income in the fiscal year ended September 30, 1973. A statement of income by department is given in Exhibit 6.

Discussing the success of his operation, Mr. Perlis commented:

To do well in this business, you have to do a few simple tasks well. You have to provide fuel, food, and rest to the drivers, consistently and dependably. Other services are secondary but are important as marketing tools. These secondary services include message services, check cashing, store merchandise, newspapers, etc. Some truckstops even provide chapels and banks, both of which I am seriously considering for this location.

I am also thinking of additional amenities such as a swimming pool or running track, where the drivers can exercise. Exercise is one of the most easily over-looked needs of the driver because a driver can get very stiff driving all day.

Exhibit 5

PERLIS TRUCKSTOP
Quarterly Income Data
($000)

Period Ending	*Total Sales*	*Gross Profit**	*Expenses***	*Income Before Taxes*	*Depreciation*
December 31, 1971	387	146	170	(24)	35
March 31, 1972	465	177	187	(10)	36
June 30, 1972	543	208	206	2	36
September 30, 1972	512	240	228	12	35
December 31, 1972	535	195	189	6	36
March 31, 1973	718	262	207	54	28
June 30, 1973	1017	354	238	116	32
September 30, 1973	1063	397	307	91	32
December 31, 1973	1264	423	280	142	33
March 31, 1974	1727	549	343	207	36
June 30, 1974	1920	573	367	206	35

* Gross profit = total sales − cost of goods sold.

** Total expenses shown here includes labor, depreciation, overhead, incidental supplies, and all other expenses.

Exhibit 6

PERLIS TRUCKSTOP
Quarterly Income Data, by Department *
($000)

	FUELING		*PARTS AND SERVICE*		*RESTAURANT*		*STORE*		*MOTEL*	
	Sales	*Income***	*Sales*	*Income***	*Sales*	*Income***	*Sales*	*Income***	*Sales*	*Income***
December 31, 1971	224	23	34	(7.7)	84	1.8	36	17	4.5	(3.9)
March 31, 1972	268	38	60	6.6	95	(7.8)	43	7	5.0	(3.9)
June 30, 1972	282	32	67	7.8	107	(1.1)	53	20	5.6	(3.5)
September 30, 1972	265	25	73	(17.1)	108	7.7	51	3.5	8.6	(.6)
December 31, 1972	294	36	72	(1.5)	105	20.0	55	13.8	7.1	(2.0)
March 31, 1973	460	55	68	6.6	125	32.9	54	13.8	7.7	0
June 30, 1973	695	114	97	2.5	126	37.7	70	23.5	7.4	(.7)
September 30, 1973	715	107	107	7.4	157	42.5	67	23.9	8.4	(.5)
December 31, 1973	907	154	78	(4.2)	152	35.8	74	24.8	6.8	(.7)
March 31, 1974	1273	215	104	18.2	161	39.0	76	19.7	6.4	(.9)
June 30, 1974	1421	193	136	22	193	42.5	98	42.0	6.8	(1.9)

* In the period October 1, 1973–December 31, 1973, the Transportation department was established. The relevant data in $000 are

December 31, 1973:	Sales $39	Income: 12.5
March 31, 1974:	Sales $88	Income: 20.8
June 30, 1974:	Sales $136	Income: 30.6

** All income data includes attributable cost of depreciation but no allocated general and administrative expense.

> However, one must never forget the driver's priorities. First comes fuel, then getting clean, then food, then merchandise, then sleep.
>
> The real keys to success are honesty and cleanliness. This used to be a very rough business. Truckstops were associated with prostitutes and "bennies" (benzedrine tablets used by drivers to keep alert). Those days are gone; both drivers and fleet owners are looking for people they can trust.
>
> Cleanliness is extremely important. The one-stop operator usually keeps a cleaner place than the larger truckstop chains.
>
> These factors have helped us grow and will continue to keep us competitive. Of course, our success was certainly speeded up by the fuel crisis.

The Fuel Crisis

During 1972 the demand for petroleum products began to outstrip its supply, and shortages developed in many industries. The gasoline and diesel oil markets felt the pinch later than some other petroleum-based industries, but by early 1973, Perlis was hearing from other truckstop operators that they were encountering difficulty in obtaining oil supplies. However, Texaco continued to supply Perlis Truckstop because it was a new business and a cutback in supplies would have led to severe financial difficulties for Perlis .

In May 1973, a voluntary allocation scheme was urged upon the oil companies by the government. It was recommended that oil companies supply their wholesaling customers the same amount of fuel as in the corresponding month of the base period (October 1971–September 1972). Then, in September 1973, the Arab oil-producing countries placed an embargo on oil shipments to the United States, and in October 1973, President Nixon signed the Emergency Petroleum Act of 1973, which established the Office of Petroleum Allocation in the Department of Labor. The voluntary allocation scheme outlined above became mandatory. At one point, oil companies were supplying only 90% of base-period allocations.

Because a reduced allocation of fuel would have meant financial disaster to him, Perlis prepared a petition to Texaco and the Federal Energy Office, which argued that since 65% of Perlis' customers were engaged in the movement of food products, his service was essential and should be exempted in some part from reduced allocations, Perlis explained:

> It was obvious that I had Texaco on my side and that they wanted to supply me. They told me that the Perlis Truckstop was the largest single outlet in an eight-state region. I called upon Sam Nunn, our Senator, and he was very helpful in ensuring that we received sufficient fuel. Our allocation was 1 million gallons of diesel oil a month, which meant that I often had fuel when others didn't. Trucks were often backed up for hundreds of yards. By purchasing outside fuel and obtaining additional state allocations, we were able to sell 1.2 million gallons of diesel fuel in March 1974.
>
> The fuel shortage did us no harm. We received and sold more fuel than I would have sold if the fuel shortage hadn't hit. We could have made excess

profit by charging more at the height of the shortage. But we were happy to make a legitimate profit on a large amount of fuel. Even before price controls were established, I had invited the IRS to audit my books to prove I was charging a fair price. When price controls came in, I did not charge the maximum allowable price and even today I am below my allowable maximum. Between July 1973 and February 1974, Texaco's prices for fuel rose by 51% (the selling price of diesel oil at the Perlis Truckstop is shown in Exhibit 7).

The Shutdown

As the fuel crisis deepened in late 1973, the owner operators called a national shutdown of operations and persuaded many fleet drivers to join them. Although the owner operators, being independent entrepreneurs, were not extensively coordinated, most drivers read *Overdrive* magazine, which played a central role in communications of mutual grievances between drivers.

The owner operators were frustrated by the lack of fuel. They also argued that rising fuel prices hit them particularly hard since, unlike fleet owners, they could not easily pass on their cost increases to their customers. They also were particularly aggravated by the reduction in speed limit, which reduced their productivity and threatened their profitability.

Exhibit 7

PERLIS TRUCKSTOP
Sales Price of Diesel Fuel, June 1971–July 1974 *
(cents per gallon)

Year	Date	Price
1971	June	30.9
1973	May 15	31.9
	24	32.9
	June 1	33.9
	September 7	32.9
	29	34.9
	October 21	35.9
	November 5	36.9
	December 8	38.9
1974	January 1	40.9
	March 5	43.9
	20	44.5
	April 20	44.9
	May 8	46.9
	June 6	45.9
	25	46.9
	July 30	48.9
	31	47.9

* The data given are all the changes in diesel price at the Perlis Truckstop. Hence, each price was maintained until the next indicated change.

In December 1974, Lamar Perlis was awakened from his sleep at 3 A.M. (his home was located directly behind the truckstop) and was told that the truckers had asked the fuel supervisor to shut down the pumps.

> I came down to the truckstop immediately not knowing quite what to expect. I had seen the warnings in *Overdrive* but had never felt that the shutdown would occur. There had been one or two incidents of truckers blocking highways in Ohio in the previous week, and even though there had been some violence there, I didn't think it would really occur here. When I arrived at the truckstop, I was introduced to three leaders of the action and asked them to come to my office to discuss it. As we were ascending the stairs, I was aware that I had never dealt with an organized group and was wondering how I could "cool down" the situation. So I turned to the leader and asked, "Do you believe in God?" When he said "Yes," I replied, "Good. Then we'll have something to talk about." We talked until dawn, and I convinced them that I was in sympathy with their objective to obtain a government fuel priority for trucks, since they were spending half their time on the road looking for fuel. After all, a healthy trucking industry is essential to our success. So, I shut down the pumps for a promise that there would be no violence between either striking and nonstriking truckers, or between truckers and law enforcement officers. I was among the first truckstops to be hit in a nationwide shutdown, and the next day all the television networks flew their news teams down to interview me, and I appeared on nationwide television. I repeated my sympathy with the truckers' objective of a higher fuel priority for trucks and stated that I could understand their predicament.
>
> My comments also appeared in many newspapers across the country, and I received a great deal of mail from other truckstops and fleet owners. There was only one fleet owner who openly criticized me, but I believe my action was right, especially as deaths had occurred elsewhere during the shutdown. The shutdown ended in four days, when most drivers had left, and I reopened the pumps. Of course, today my truckstop is well known, and when during the February 1974 shutdown, I refused to shut down the pumps, I encountered no trouble. It was a token action on my part because the shutdown was so effective elsewhere that our business was zero for a week.
>
> In retrospect, I am glad that I did not have a general manager involved and was able to handle the situation myself. A man on the scene is very important in this business.

Organization

Upon its formation, Lamar Perlis became president of Perlis Truck Terminals, Inc. He had made several attempts to hire a general manager to oversee all the activities at the truckstop but had not found anyone who performed to his satisfaction.

> I wanted someone who could do it better than I could. After all, I'm entitled to someone who's capable for the $35–45,000 that I must pay a general

manager. None of the people I have tried in the last three years have been satisfactory. When we opened I hired an assistant general manager for $175 a week, and he was here for a year. But he did not develop into a man I could trust and had certain health problems, so I let him go.

It's a difficult position for me to fill. Even an experienced truckstop operator might not be qualified to take over all my duties. For example, he would not be likely to have the merchandising background that has helped me in making our truckstop successful. And he would be unlikely to be able to make investment decisions, as well as perform the duties of sales promotion and public relations with the fleets and drivers.

Although no formal organization chart or structure existed, activities at the truckstop were divided into four operating departments, each with its own department head (see Exhibit 8). These were fueling, restaurant, store, and parts and service (the motel was under the control of the fueling manager). A description of each department follows.

Fueling

The fueling operation, which generated revenues of nearly $1½ million in the second quarter of 1974 (see Exhibit 6), was the backbone of the truckstop, providing

Exhibit 8

PERLIS TRUCKSTOP
Organization, August 1974 *

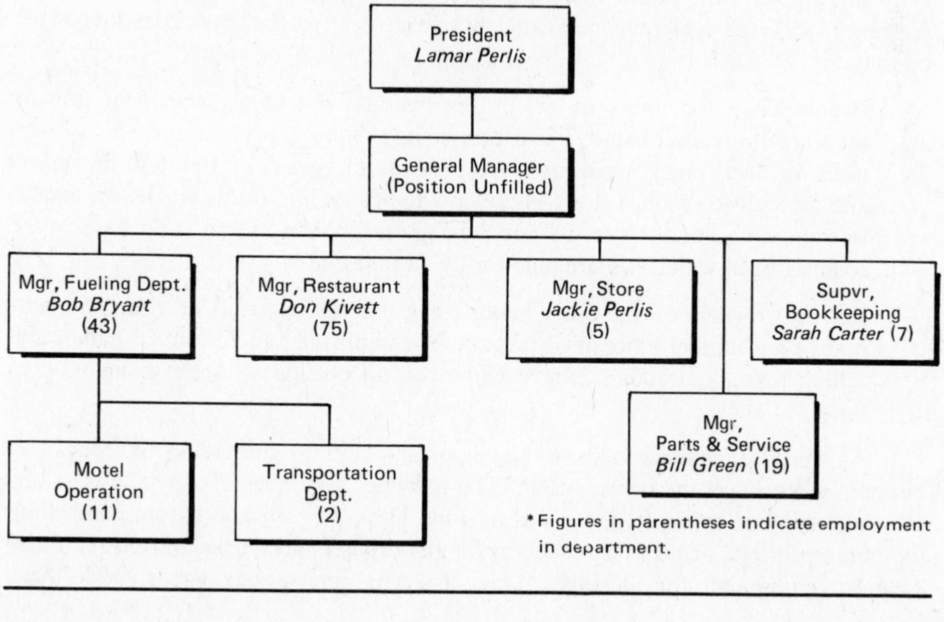

President
Lamar Perlis

General Manager
(Position Unfilled)

Mgr, Fueling Dept.
Bob Bryant
(43)

Mgr, Restaurant
Don Kivett
(75)

Mgr, Store
Jackie Perlis
(5)

Supvr, Bookkeeping
Sarah Carter (7)

Mgr, Parts & Service
Bill Green (19)

Motel Operation
(11)

Transportation Dept.
(2)

*Figures in parentheses indicate employment in department.

nearly 50% of the contribution to overhead. Open 24 hours a day, approximately 35,000 gallons of diesel fuel were pumped per day. An average "fill" was 65 gallons.

In 1971, Perlis had installed an automatic printer pump, controlled by computer. As he explained:

> Without this, you would always get the occasional driver who would question how much fuel had been pumped. Or else he would ask for a receipt for more fuel than he received so that he could bill his company more. With this device there can be no argument. It's a simple method of ensuring honesty on both sides. With the reputation this business has had in past years, this is an important consideration. With the printer pump, a trust can be built up between ourselves, the driver, and the fleet owner, since sales are accurately validated.

As well as fueling the trucks, Perlis insisted that his employees always clean the trucks' windshield and "bump the tires" (i.e., hit the tires with a billy club to check their pressure).

Customers at the truckstop could pay in a number of ways: cash, Texaco credit card, Master Charge, National Truckers Service card (NTS), Mid Continent card, or charge to the fleet owner's account. The NTS card was a nationwide trucking credit that charged its user 2% of the value of the transaction, and the truckstop operator the same amount. The Mid Continent card cost the truckstop operator 4% of the value of the transaction with no charge to the customer. Payment to Perlis in both cases was 60 days.

Perlis preferred that the fleet owner maintain an account at the truckstop. "In this way the drivers are dedicated to you, since Perlis Truckstop becomes the scheduled stop and they have to stop here. Otherwise the choice of stop is up to the driver and you must fight harder for his business."

In August 1974, Perlis Truckstop had 900 accounts with operators and fleets. However, 65% of fuel revenues came not from fleet trucks, but from the owner operators.

> Even though the majority of our revenues do not come from fleet drivers, they are more accessible. I can design marketing programs and special services for fleets much more easily than for owner operators. Being so numerous and difficult to reach, I don't know how to attract him to the truckstop, except by running a good operation and relying on word of mouth. I do have seven road signs, of which two are paid for by Texaco.
>
> For fleet owners on the other hand, I can make a few calls or visits and generate a substantial amount of revenue by establishing an account. I handle the selling myself, although I have employed an outside salesman from time to time.

As Perlis explained, one of the important keys to success in the truckstop business was to "get the driver inside." To this end, a number of special attractions were offered. For example, there was a "Fuel Desk," which apart from controlling the pump printers, acted as a reception for the drivers and offered various communications equipment for messages. One of Perlis' innovations was a Wide Area

Telephone Service (WATS) line that he had installed, which allowed drivers to call anywhere in the United States free of charge. It was in almost constant usage. This facility cost $1,600 a month, but because it was unique, Perlis felt that the expense was justified. Other services offered were free showers to drivers who fueled, a barber shop, and a "drivers' lounge" with two pool tables and a color television.

In charge of the fueling department was Bob Bryant, who had joined Perlis Truckstop in April 1974, being the fifth man in three years to hold that position.

> Mr. Perlis brought me in because of my six years of experience as operations manager supervising 100 employees. He wanted someone to train and supervise people, not to change things.
>
> My biggest problem is motivation. Pump attendants, who are mainly high school kids, get $2.25–$2.50 an hour for a continuous 8-hour shift. We have three island attendants to man the 12 pumps in each 8-hour shift and expect them to pump 3,500–4,500 gallons each per shift. This means putting through a truck every 10–12 minutes. Since they have to clean the windshield, check the oil, headlights, and tires, it can be a very strenuous job. Mr. Perlis can be very demanding and has been known to call down from his office overlooking the pumps to get a resting attendant back to work. I have been told that the truckstop as a whole has gone through 3,000 people in 3 years.[1]

Bryant controlled the fueling operation by keeping a close watch on the pumping cost per gallon, a figure that he recorded and charted every day. He was also responsible for the motel, the janitors, and the transportation department. In his judgment, the motel had experienced a reasonable occupancy rate since his appointment. He noted that it was often possible to rent the same room twice in the same day since drivers took their rests at different times of the day. The motel charge was $7 a night for any of the 17 rooms. The transportation department was composed of four tanker trucks which hauled in the fuel from Texaco's storage tanks. Two of the drivers had recently quit, and Bryant stated that they had left for higher pay. (Perlis discovered that Bryant had hired one of the drivers away from the truckstop to operate his own trucks.)

Restaurant

The 160-seat restaurant, the second largest source of revenue to the truckstop operation, had an atmosphere described by Perlis as "convivial."

> It is a pragmatic place—no place mats or fancy trimmings. Atmosphere and good food are much more important. Running a restaurant is a very specialized task, however, and I have been through half a dozen managers in the past, none of whom really provided the service I required. However, each time we changed we got better, and we are now working towards a really efficient operation.

---

[1] This fact was not proven by the records. 1,700 U.S. Government W-2 forms were on file in August 1974, covering all classes of regular and part-time workers since opening.

The current manager of the restaurant was Don Kivett who had joined Perlis Truckstop in December 1973 after a career in catering. He commented:

> I think we now have a good operation, since morale is very high and the customers seem satisfied. We have almost doubled our revenues since I took over, but unfortunately profits are about the same. The man in this post before me was good at getting profit, but he did it by gouging the staff and gouging the customers. I have changed all that. I added labor to raise volume.
>
> We serve all fresh food, never freezing our chicken and using fresh vegetables. Our prices are competitive, about 25¢ cheaper than our main competition, the Ryder stop in Valdosta, Georgia. We charge $2.25 for a main course with three vegetables. However, with our costs skyrocketing, we will have to raise our prices.

In August 1974 the restaurant had 70 employees, but Kivett indicated that he was in the process of reducing the staff to 50, both for seasonal reasons and to increase profits. Kivett's bonus was based upon the profitability of the restaurant, under a scheme jointly devised by him and Perlis prior to Kivett's appointment. However, he had become dissatisfied with his total remuneration of $20,000 for the year and was negotiating with Perlis for a change of contract.

> There are really only three things I would like to see changed around here. At the moment there is a carpet in the tourist section of the restaurant, and none in the truckers'. I think this is a mistake, as the truckers must be our first priority. In any event, the carpet needs cleaning so often it is more trouble than it's worth. It should be removed.
>
> The second change I would like to see is the construction of a special room to serve the bus traffic. At the moment the restaurant can seat 160 people and this make it difficult for me if a bus driver comes to me and asks if I can seat a whole busload. We could build a room to seat 50 people for $35,000.
>
> A final change I would like is an office, which I do not have at the moment. When I want to speak to an employee, I have to go into the stockroom or some other place.

Store

The store operation was under the general direction of Jackie Perlis. Like her husband, Lamar, Jackie had come from a merchandising family.

> Although none of us knew anything about truckers when we started, we did not find it difficult to discover what they need, and we now have a stable product line. The store is a big success. Some other truckstops may sell more than we do, but few make as much money. The secret is to avoid the conventional truckstop suppliers and rack jobbers, and to trade direct with the manufacturers.

The biggest selling items were "cool cushions" (used by the drivers in their cabs), western shirts and boots, and citizen band radios. Mrs. Perlis noted that the truckers like to see well-known brand names, and she had stocked the store with Levi jeans and Thom McAn shoes obtained through the downtown Perlis store. The store employed one salesclerk on each eight-hour shift, as well as a general supervisor to whom Mrs. Perlis had delegated the day-to-day operating decisions.

Parts and Service

The parts and service department at the Perlis Truckstop had three drive-in bays, one for general repairs, one for lubrication, and one for tire repair. No major repair service was offered since Perlis considered that the key maxim for a shop at a truckstop was "can we do it while the driver waits?" He also noted that since Cordele was not near any major truck destination, it was likely that a driver would come there mostly for minor and emergency repairs. It was for this reason, among others, that a brief experiment in performing engine overhauls was abandoned.

As with other departments, Perlis had encountered difficulty in finding a competent manager. The current manager, Bill Green, had originally been hired as a fueling supervisor. Perlis described him as "not a real professional, but he has stabilized and organized the operation."

Perlis was considering an expansion of the parts and service operation. Noting that inventory was excessive in relation to sales (Exhibit 9), he was seeking ways to increase sales. Among these was an attempt to purchase such items as tires at lower prices by being classified as a warehouse distributor. In order to qualify for this classification, Perlis had taken over one of his family's downtown warehouses and was planning to build a 10,000 square foot warehouse at the truckstop at a cost of approximately $75,000. He projected that with an inventory of $400,000 he would be in a position to supply fleets, truck-leasing companies, and other truckstops with their parts and supplies. He was also investigating the possibility of constructing three more bays at a cost of $73,000 to handle the current overflow of work. Labor charges in the parts and service department were $15 per hour and labor costs $5 per hour.

Administration and Control

Perlis received three types of reports. Each day he received a computer printout of the previous day's sales, by department. Each week he received a handwritten "Labor Report" which gave total labor costs by department. Each month he received a computer printout of the complete monthly income statement by department.

> I sometimes have some difficulties in assessing these reports. From what I have recently learned at school [2] I know I should be calculating a number of ratios, but except for cost per gallon, I don't know what these should be. So, I just keep a close watch for trends.

[2] Perlis had been attending a small company management program at Harvard Business School.

Exhibit 9

PERLIS TRUCKSTOP
Inventories, by Department, June 30, 1974

Fueling		
Gasoline	7,530	
Diesel fuel	35,268	
Motor oil	6,580	
Total		49,378
Parts and Service		
Batteries, accessories, and parts	73,996	
Tires	100,168	
Supplies and parts	859	
Total		175,023
Restaurant		
Food	9,640	
China, glassware, and silver	3,151	
Total		12,791
Store		
Store merchandise	106,896	
Vending machine	1,159	
Total		108,055
Total Inventories		345,246

Will Kidd, accountant for Perlis Truckstop, agreed that it would be difficult to establish productivity standards because of the rapid change in volume and the inability in some departments, such as parts and service, to decide upon a valid measure of output. He considered that the most significant improvement in control of the truckstop had been the development of meaningful departmental operating statements. However, he did see the need for future development of productivity measures.

> When Lamar decides to leave here to go into other things, we will have to develop a different management control scheme, if only because a new general manager would not be controlling his own money and would therefore not stay quite on top of everything as Lamar does. Lamar thinks everyone is stealing from him and keeps a very close tab on everyone. Of course, you must remember that for 20 years he was in a retailing store where, if anything was wrong, you went straight over and pointed it out to an employee. He hasn't yet learned that you shouldn't do that here.

Perlis later commented:

> I do know that I shouldn't skip my channels of management. After all that is one of the first rules of management. But I find it difficult not to when I look

> out onto the concrete and see something being done wrong. By the time I went through the supervisor, the damage would have been done. I am very aware that my biggest problems are organizational. People management is my weakness. But I don't want to live with a department head that I do not trust. On advice from other operators, I tried general polygraphing of my employees. It was moderately successful, but I am not very proud of having done it. I know it is better to cultivate trust and understanding. I want a man whose character I can build on. So my objective is not to identify an area of improvement, but to find ways of solving problems we already know exist.

Perlis had contacted a consultant who specialized in organizational diagnosis and executive search. The consultant had proposed a $20,000 project to design motivation and incentive schemes, written policies, procedures and objectives, and search for a general manager. Perlis was unsure whether he should accept the proposal.

The Future

Perlis was determined to cease his day-to-day involvement in the truckstop within six months. He felt that with a cash flow of $60–70,000 a month, the truckstop was now "on its feet," and that his first priority was to recruit a general manager. He noted that the prime consideration in appointing a general manager was that he would be responsible for a 24 hours a day, 7 days a week, operation and consequently had to be someone that could be trusted with such a large responsibility.

> The big chains do not have these problems. They have the advantages of scale and can train general managers as assistants before giving them control of their own truckstop. But I don't think they would be a good source for me. It goes against my morality to steal staff from a competitor, and I am not sure they will be good enough, because they will be too used to strong guidance and set company procedures.

Perlis had been considering for some time an expansion to a second truckstop. With a cash flow of approximately $1 million per year, the Perlis family did not expect a problem with the availability of loan capital, but Perlis could not commit any of his family's funds to a new truckstop venture, primarily because of the prevailing high interest rate (10% in August 1974) and current construction of a shopping center in Dublin, Georgia. He also saw many benefits from a possible joint venture with a company such as Hertz, which leased trucks, because such a company could provide advertising, personnel, and other professional assistance not possessed by the Perlis family. Such a company would also provide a base of guaranteed business and would have an existing fuel allocation. Government allocation regulations were still in effect until October 1974, and Perlis considered the availability of fuel crucial to any truckstop venture, since the oil companies in August 1974 were not entering into supply contracts with new truckstops.

Perlis had approached Texaco about another fuel supply contract and Hertz about a joint venture on a new truckstop, but he had not received a positive response from either. However, he was still investigating this approach, because he believed that "one successful venture in this form would carry us further and faster than any other method."

> In presenting my plans to Hertz (see Exhibit 10) I was prepared to accept any share of the business between 40% and 60%. I would have preferred to provide none of the funds and take 40%, but I would also accept providing an equal share of the funds and not less than 51% of the equity. I wouldn't be concerned about whether the name Perlis was used, but I think it has value now.
>
> In any new truckstop that I did alone, I would begin by "overstaffing," getting a really top-notch manager who could help limit the start-up costs and do a good job in recruiting and training. I would pay $40–50,000 for such a person and if need be would include a share of equity, which I would not do for the present truckstop.

In assessing the site of a new truckstop, Perlis believed there were a large number of factors to take into account, including the physical properties of the land, the proximity to utilities, and the extent of local business. In addition, a site that was at the junction of two interstate highways which provided a good "cross traffic" would obviously be preferable. Perlis believed that the type of labor available was important and that any decision would be influenced by the level and existence of fuel taxes. He considered that, other things being equal, he would prefer to locate in Georgia, because he had already establishd contacts with the people he had to deal with on a political level. However, he also saw the advantages of a site on I-95 which did not have a lengthy portion in Georgia. I-95, which was not due to be completed for two to four years, was expected to become the main artery from Florida to the Northeast, with a projected "truck count" of 5–6,000 trucks per day.

> There are really three sites that I am now seriously considering. My top priority is Pooler, Georgia, just outside Savannah (see Exhibit 2). It is at the junction I-16 and I-95 and has the advantage of being near the major port of Savannah. The development of container ships has greatly increased the volume of truck traffic out of this and other ports. Being close to a destination would give you personnel advantages and allow tie-ins with fleets, whereby one could act as a substitute garage and terminal for them. The opportunity to go in for wholesaling of truck supplies would be great. It does have the disadvantage of being the last portion of I-95 to be complete and would have a much higher cost of acquisition than other sites I am considering. I have already tendered an offer of $300,000 for the land, which was turned down.
>
> A second site I am considering is Brunswick, Georgia. Like the Savannah site it would develop from scratch, but I can get the land for $250,000. It has good

Exhibit 10

PERLIS TRUCKSTOP
Proposed Full-service Truckstop Venture*
(all figures in $000)

	(A) High Capital Proposal		(B)** Low Capital Proposal	
Current assets	450		450	
Fixed assets				
Land	450		275	
Buildings and improvements	1,500		1,030	
Equipment	925		900	
Loan costs	42		42	
Total assets	3,367		2,697	
Current liabilities	450		450	
LTD				
Mortgage	2,100		1,430	
Venturer's loan	317		317	
Venturer's equity	500		500	
	3,367		2,697	
	Most Likely	%	*Most Likely*	%
Sales***	10,000	(100)	10,000	(100)
CGS	7,700	(77)	7,700	(77)
Gross profit	2,300	(23)	2,300	(23)
Operating expenses	950	(10)	1,080	(11)
Operating profit	1,350	(13)	1,220	(12)
Interest and depreciation	468	(5)	340	(3.4)
Pretax income	882	(8.8)	880	(8.8)
Tax @ 50%	441	(4.4)	440	(4.4)
	441	(4.4)	440	(4.4)
Cash flow	675		673	

* The data given in this exhibit are taken from Mr. Perlis' proposal to Hertz.
** Low cost construction with reduced facilities. Reaches maturity in four years.
*** All income data are projections for fourth year of operation.

access to the highway and the utilities are good. It would not have the advantage of being near a major city, but it would also avoid the disadvantages of loitering and congestion from retail (local) trade that such a site would have. One big problem is that Ryder will be opening a stop just south of there (see Exhibit 2).

The final site is the Cater's Truckstop in Rosinville, South Carolina. It is a going concern (see Exhibits 11 and 12 for Balance Sheet and Income Data) but could do with a great deal of improvement. It has no store, and the restaurant, which is only halfway decent, seats only 67 people. He leases out his shop work and is pumping about 375,000 gallons of diesel a month.

I took my architect to have a look at it, and he threw up his arms in horror, saying there was little he could do with it. Another problem is that most of the business comes from one fleet that is using the stop as a terminal. I would be fighting a very poor reputation and would have to clean up the place, unless I decided to "milk" the facility. But that is not really my style.

I have a big problem in deciding on the site's value. The figures I have seen (Exhibits 11 and 12) are all unaudited, and I have a feeling that the cash flow should be more. He wants $1.4 million for the place, but my CPA says I should not pay more than four to six times earnings for it. The question is, what could the real earnings become?

I don't foresee any problems in controlling two truckstops. I could send in audit teams to each department of each truckstop on a regular basis to be sure all was in order and would plan to make regular visits myself as long as I am in the Georgia–South Carolina region. I can hire a plane for $70 an hour to get me from one stop to the next.

Of course, I could sell the existing stop and would be tempted by a $4½ million offer, but it is not something I really want to do. We now have a stable organization, and each and every department is making money. I don't want to

Exhibit 11

PERLIS TRUCKSTOP
Balance Sheet, April 30 1974, Cater's Truckstop

ASSETS		*LIABILITIES*	
Cash	$(34,103)	A/P	$40,542
A/R	56,273	Notes payable	
Inventories	50,228	and taxes payable	131,104
Total current	72,458	Total current	171,646
Fixed assets	640,536	L.T.D.	296,327
Depreciation	172,843		
Net fixed assets	467,693	Equity	101,023
Land (net)	22,000	Total	$568,996
Prepaid expenses	6,425		
Other assets	418		
Total	$568,996		

Exhibit 12

PERLIS TRUCKSTOP
Income Statement, January 1–April 31, 1974, Cater's Truckstop

Sales	
Gas	$112,977
Diesel	629,724
Service	13,393
Oil	18,575
Rooms	8,340
Restaurant	60,129
Other	
	879,334
Cost of sales	645,923
Gross profit	233,411
Expenses	139,722
Net operating profit	93,689
Other income	5,480
Interest	11,952
Net profit	$ 88,216

get out of the truckstop business, although if I do, I will return to the real estate work that I enjoy. The key thing is that, at 50, I am at a turning point in my life and must decide what I am going to do next.

Victoria Station, Inc. (A)

In early fall of 1973, the three founders of Victoria Station, a chain of railroad theme restaurants, had completed the initial phases of their development strategy. They had opened 17 restaurants with an additional 5 under construction, and approximately 10 more on the drawing boards, as shown in Exhibit 1. Sales in the year ending March 31, 1973, were $11,350,089, as shown in Exhibit 2. In addition, the company had made a very successful initial public offering of its stock. The founders were preparing for the next phase of their growth by developing operating controls and reporting procedures to maintain the profits from the existing units, while continuing to open new units. Observers in the restaurant industry were watching to see if these "youngsters would clear the next hurdle."

Company Background

Victoria Station was founded by three classmates of the Cornell University School of Hotel and Restaurant Administration. After graduation in 1963, Richard Bradley was a registered representative for a large brokerage firm; Robert Freeman was an in-flight service supervisor for Pan American World Airways; and Peter Lee was manager of budgets and cost analysis for Sky Chefs, Inc. Victoria Station was formed in San Francisco in 1969, after continued discussions and development of a business concept.

Richard Bradley, president, said that the original intention of the venture was to create "a top-notch operating company." The three were prepared to undertake nearly any business if operations were critical to success; however, "the restaurant opportunity presented itself first": Bradley, Lee, and Freeman felt that they had the ability to operate nearly any type of business. The question was where did they feel they could gain the maximum leverage. Finally they decided on entering the limited menu, theme restaurant, medium-priced market. See Appendix for a description of this market, made by Connors Investor Services, Inc.

The concept of Victoria Station was based on "a carefully thought-out program involving the elements crucial for success in the restaurant business: concept and uniqueness, quality control, and financial control."

Uniqueness of Concept

The basic concept at Victoria Station was to serve the rapidly growing number of singles, couples, and families who enjoyed well-prepared food but who could not

Exhibit 1

VICTORIA STATION, INC. (A)
Record of Restaurant Openings

Location	Seats	Site Selected	Leases Signed	Ground Broken	Open	Site Selection to Opening (Months)	Construction Cost ($)	Monthly Rental Minimum[b]	% Sales[e]
San Francisco	210[a]	1/69	4/69	9/69	12/69	11	344,099	4,015[c]	5
Thomas Lords (SF)	70	3/70	7/70	8/70	11/70	8	Remodeled existing structure	2,250	5
Atlanta	156	3/70	5/70	7/70	12/70	9	188,354	2,100	8
Oakland	140	3/70	7/70	12/70	4/71	13	170,468	653[c]	5¼
New Orleans	180	2/71	6/71	5/71	9/71	7	226,945	2,158	10
Denver	170	9/70	12/70	5/71	9/71	12	313,383	2,917	9¼
Quinns (Oakland)	100	6/71	8/71	12/71	4/72	10	Remodeled existing structure	653[c]	5¼
Sunnyvale	205	7/71	9/71	3/72	7/72	12	350,655	2,917	8
Royal Exchange (SF)	150	4/71	7/71	5/72	8/72	16	Remodeled existing structure	2,000	6
Los Angeles	205	8/71	11/71	4/72	8/72	12	317,354	2,917	8
Phoenix	205	8/71	11/71	5/72	9/72	13	383,128	2,917	8
Dallas	205	8/71	11/71	4/72	9/72	13	362,795	2,175[c]	—
Houston I	205	12/71	4/72	9/72	1/73	13	371,826	5,310	8
Cincinnati	218	4/72	7/72	11/72	6/73	14	380,000	2,500[e]	—
Portland	218	4/72	7/72	11/72	3/73	11	328,000	1,250[d]	—
Boston	300	3/72	3/73	?	?	?	No final estimate	3,000	—
Indianapolis	218	7/72	11/72	12/72	5/73	10	363,000	1,250	
Kansas City	218	7/72	10/72	2/73	6/73 (est.)	11 (est.)	378,000 (est)	1,350	—
Miami	218	6/72	8/72	12/72	5/73	11	392,000	2,762	
Columbus	218	4/72	11/72	2/73	?	?	395,000 (est.)	2,000	—
Philadelphia	218	5/72	11/72	5/73	?	?	420,000 (est.)	1,833	
Darien	245	6/72	8/72	5/73	?	?	459,000 (est.)	3,333	—
Minneapolis	218	?	?	?	?	?	No final estimate	?	—

Exhibit 1 (continued)

VICTORIA STATION, INC. (A)
Record of Restaurant Openings

Location	*Seats*	*Site Selected*	*Leases Signed*	*Ground Broken*	*Open*	*Site Selection to Opening (Months)*	*Construction Cost ($)*	*Monthly Rental Minimum*[b]	*% Sales*[e]
Sacramento	218	?	?	?	?	?	No final estimate	?	—
St. Louis	218	12/72	2/73	?	?	?	No final estimate	?	—
Houston II	218	10/72	12/72	5/73	?	?	330,000 (est.)	2,325	—
Seattle	218	10/72	1/73	?	?	?	No final estimate	7,550	—
Louisville	218	12/72	2/73	?	?	?	No final estimate	1,950	—
Woodland Hills, California	218	11/72	2/73	?	?	?	No final estimate	2,833	3
Vancouver	218	12/72	2/73	?	?	?	No final estimate	2,500	—
Newport Beach, California	218	11/72	4/73	?	?	?	No final estimate	6,333	6
Northbrook	218	2/73	4/73	?	?	?	No final estimate	2,500	—

[a] Increased to 210 seats from 158 seats, July 14, 1972; construction costs include expansion.

[b] Minimum—some leases provide for preestablished rent increases during the lease term or for additional rent based on changes in consumer price index or property taxes.

[c] Rental for land only. Building to be owned or leased by company.

[d] Plus 1 % of construction costs.

[e] The company pays the stated rental, or the percentage stated, whichever is greater; all percentages based on gross sales.

Exhibit 2

VICTORIA STATION, INC. (A)
Financial Summary
Fiscal Years Ending March 31, 1970–1973
($000)

	1970	*1971*	*1972*	*1973*	*1974 (Est.)*
Sales	$229.3	$1,548.1	$5,471.2	$11,350.1	$23,000
Cost of sales	147.7	965.3	3,256.9	6,619.6	x
Operating expenses	46.5	405.6	1,375.8	3,220.6	x
Depreciation	3.7	25.6	104.4	291.3	x
Interest expenses	2.2	10.5	24.5	105.3	x
Earnings before taxes	29.2	141.1	709.6	1,113.3	x
Taxes (current and deferred)	10.0	62.2	330.5	478.0	x
Other	—	—	—	57.9	x
Minority interest in earnings	—	6.8	30.2	10.6	
Net earnings	19.2	72.1	340.9	566.8	1,700
Earnings per common share	$ .02	$ .06	$ .24	$ .32	$ .74
Stock price range	—	—	15–29	17–29	—
Restaurants operated at year end	1	3	6	13	x
Current assets	x	x	622.0	3,034.1	x
Other assets	x	x	87.4	199.3	x
Equipment and improvements Less depreciation	x	x	1,235.6	4,308.0	x
Deferred costs	x	x	150.0	374.8	x
			2,095.0	7,916.2	
Current liabilities	x	x	899.8	1,749.7	x
Long-term debt	x	x	183.4	0	x
Deferred taxes	x	x	43.3	131.9	x
Minority interests	x	x	36.5	32.9	x
Paid-in capital	x	x	500.0	5,002.7	x
Retained earnings	x	x	432.0	999.0	x
			2,095.0	7,916.2	

afford high prices. Victoria Station featured prime rib of beef served in a unique railroad atmosphere utilizing actual rolling stock (i.e., boxcars) converted into restaurants. Authentic artifacts and memorabilia from the British Railways further enhanced the decor of the restaurants. The layout of a typical Victoria Station is shown in Exhibit 3, and photographs of several of the restaurants are shown in Exhibit 4.

The interiors of the boxcars were refurbished and decorated with wall-to-wall carpeting. There was heavy use of natural sandblasted woods and heavy redwood timbers. Cocktail lounges were designed to give the feeling of a stand-up cocktail

Exhibit 3

VICTORIA STATION, INC. (A)
Layout of Typical 205-Seat Restaurant

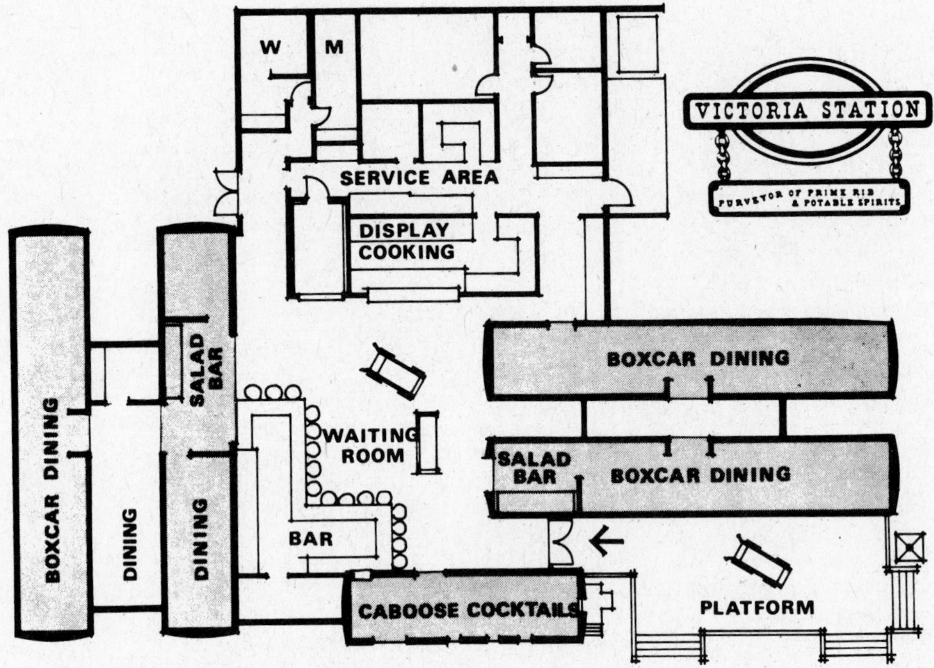

party with a bar, and old baggage carts were used as room dividers and tables. Prime rib was attractively displayed in large glass-front refrigerators in the central bar area. Seating in the restaurant was designed so that every table had a view of an authentic piece of railroad equipment or memorabilia. The decor was described as "real," and anything that suggested "plastic culture" was avoided.

In front of the restaurants, there usually were operating gas lights, a red English telephone booth, and a London taxi. While Victoria Station signs were tastefully displayed, the restaurants depended largely on the unique exteriors (railroad cars) to draw customers to the restaurants.

Management believed that most customers resented tipping parking lot attendants and hatcheck girls, so all restaurants featured adequate free parking and coat racks near tables.

The original Victoria Station had facilities to seat approximately 156 persons. However, through additions this was later expanded to 205 places.

Tables were waited on and bussed by male college students, with young women providing cocktail service at the tables and in the waiting areas. Each waiter started as a busboy, progressed to lunch waiter, then advanced to dinner waiter; each step provided a significant increase in earning capacity. All tips were pooled

Exhibit 4

VICTORIA STATION, INC. (A)
Interior and Exterior Views of Typical Restaurants

Exhibit 5

VICTORIA STATION, INC. (A)
Lunch and Dinner Menus

NOTICE

Platform #1

	$	3
Baggage cart salad bar	Included with dinner	

Platform #2

Roast Prime Rib of Beef		
Track #1 — Julia C. Bulette Cut	41/3	4.95
Track #2 — Enginemen's Cut	49/7	5.95
Side Track — Owner's & Friends' Cut	66/3	7.95
Filet	49/7	5.95
Top Sirloin	41/3	4.95
Shrimp Victoria — Giant shrimp sauteéd in wine & garlic sauce	43/9	5.25

Platform #3

Sauteed mushrooms served in a skillet	7/11	.95
Baked Idaho potato	4/3	.50

Platform #4

Sta Station Master's dessert	6/3	.75

Dinners include salad, rolls, butter and coffee

CHIEF GENERAL SUPERINTENDENT

Sales Tax will be added to all food and beverages

Platform #1

	£	$
Baggage cart salad bar	Included with lunch	

Platform #2

English Dip	18/9	2.25
Roast Prime Rib of Beef	24/7	2.95
One half pound choice Chuckburger	15/10	1.90
One half pound choice Cheeseburger	16/3	1.95
Top Sirloin Steak	24/7	2.95
London Broiled Flank Steak	22/11	2.75
Shrimp Victoria— Giant shrimp sauteéd in wine and garlic sauce	24/7	2.95
Beef Kebob	22/11	2.75
Bar-B-Que Prime Ribs — limited	18/9	2.25

Platform #3

Sauteéd mushrooms served in a skillet	7/11	.95

Platform #4

Station Master's dessert	6/3	.75

Luncheon includes salad, rolls, butter and coffee

California House Wines

	½ Carafe	Full Carafe
Red: Burgundy	1.75	3.00
White: Chablis	1.75	3.00
Rosé:	1.75	3.00
by the glass	.75	
Sangria: Red or White—by the jug	2.00	3.75

CHIEF GENERAL SUPERINTENDENT

Sales Tax will be added to all food and beverages.

and divided on a prearranged formula among waiters, busboys, cocktail waitresses, and cooks. As a result, service was a self-policing, team affair, rather than a divisive competition. For a restaurant that thrives on volume and turnover, the atmosphere at Victoria Station was considered to be unusually relaxed.

The menu was relatively limited (i.e., six entrees, as shown in Exhibit 5). Entree prices ranged up to $7.50, but 80–90% of the main courses were purchased for $4.75 or $5.75 ($4.95 or $5.95 in some locations). While beverages and a la carte items such as baked potato and sauteed mushrooms increased the average dinner check substantially, it was possible for a couple to enjoy prime-rib dinner with salad and wine for approximately $15.00, including tip. The average lunch check (not including tip) was $4.00.

Approximately 70% of meals ordered were roast beef. Display carving and cooking were done in full view of the cocktail area. However, because of the limited menu and specialization in roast beef, most of the display area was devoted to carving meat. Steaks were prepared on a broiler, while mushrooms and shrimp were prepared on a stove next to the broiler. Potatoes and beef were cooked in a back kitchen in large ovens.

Salads were offered from a do-it-yourself salad bar frequently located on an old baggage cart. Plates were stacked in a cooling chest near a large display of salad greens, condiments, dressings, and San Francisco sourdough bread and dark rye bread. A wide selection of excellent California wines was also offered.

The company employed no advertising or paid promotion and therefore relied entirely on initial publicity before opening and word-of-mouth advertising for its marketing success. Simply being open for lunch, particularly in downtown areas, was considered by management as a form of advertising for couple or family dinner business.

Quality Control

Richard Bradley felt that, "If you can control the (food) specs, then your only remaining problem is one of execution." He believed that the first job of management was to ensure that the supply of raw materials at all locations was of uniformly high quality.

To achieve this, all beef was purchased nationally, cut to specification and shipped directly to each location. Besides prime-rib roasts, Victoria Station used controlled portion filets and top sirloin butts. The latter item appeared on both the lunch and dinner menus, providing a minimum of waste. Luncheon ribs (a noontime specialty) were derived as a by-product of the least expensive prime-rib dinner, which was served without the bone.

Shrimp were purchased nationally and shipped to all restaurants. Produce and most service items and accessories were purchased locally from an approved purveyor list. All invoices were paid from the San Francisco headquarters. A computerized checking system assured that the names of vendors not on the approved list would be brought to the attention of operations management.

Execution was primarily a matter of careful management supervision to ensure

Exhibit 6

VICTORIA STATION, INC. (A)
Organization, Spring 1973

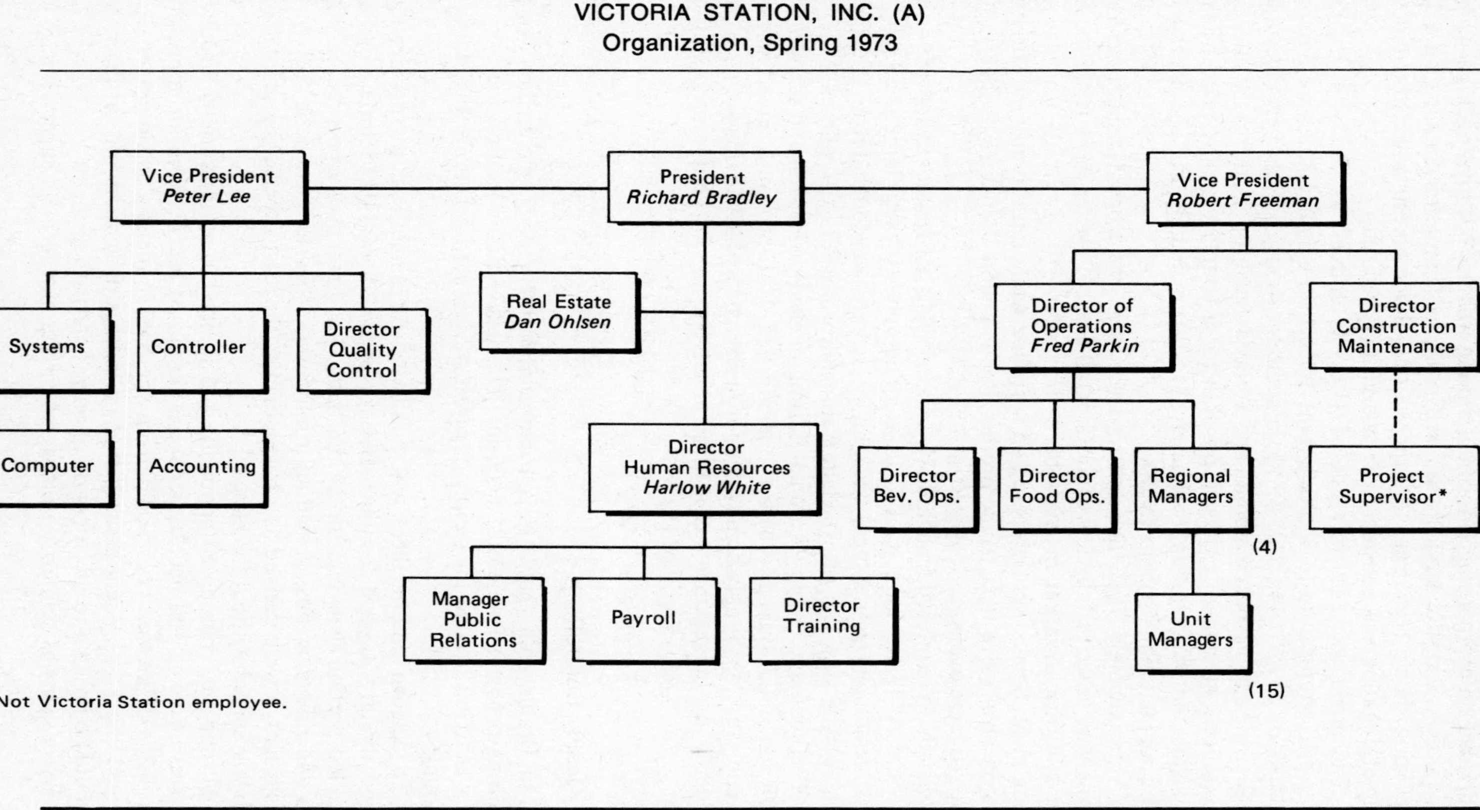

*Not Victoria Station employee.

Exhibit 7

VICTORIA STATION, INC. (A)
Description of Regional Manager Position

Job Description

Because the restaurants of Victoria Station are located in distant geographical areas of the country, the Director of Operations delegates to the Regional Manager the overall day-to-day supervision of all the units assigned to his field of operations.

Victoria Station contemplates using this position to promote to a higher supervisory level any manager who has proven in the operation of his restaurant to be a fully dedicated, hard-working, honest administrator and leader of people. He is expected to be capable of maintaining in an outstanding manner the supervision, coordination, and flow of information essential for the smooth operation of the restaurants entrusted to him.

Responsibilities

Develop and coordinate existing and future operations within the geographical area to include continuing in-house inspection to guarantee exact adherence to all Operations Manual policies, requirements, and specifications.

Day-to-day supervision of the quality of food, beverage, and service through unannounced visits to all restaurants.

Overall food, beverage, payroll, and direct expense cost supervision of all area operations.

With the approval of the Director of Operations, the selection of future management personnel and, in coordination with the Director of Training, the responsibility for their training if accomplished within his area.

Performance evaluation of all management personnel as directed by the Director of Operations.

Supervision of tests to be given to all employees on a regular basis to check quality of training and awareness of restaurant operations.

Develop criteria for regular group meetings with the managers in the same city or nearby, in order to convey instructions, correct deficiencies, and to study the value of the information obtained from them on the daily problems encountered at the restaurant level.

Develop a complete control of the operations in his area to make sure that every one of the restaurants complies to the smallest detail with the standard operational procedures outlined in the manual and any unapproved deviations from the policies originated by the owners of Victoria Station and the Directors appointed by them are quickly and totally discouraged.

Develop, within the limits specified in the Operations Manual, a good relationship with the information media, local authorities, and civic groups directed to a better dissemination of the Victoria Station image.

Above all, the Regional Manager is responsible for keeping open at all times the channels of communication and information between the Victoria Station office in San Francisco and the managers of the restaurants, so that the efficiency of the operations is not curtailed for lack of proper information.

The Regional Manager supervises all management personnel and hourly employees in the geographical area assigned to him by the Director of Operations.

The Regional Manager reports to the Director of Operations and is directly responsible to him. Any decisions affecting variance from existing policies and requirements as outlined in the Operations Manual must be approved by him prior to initiation.

strict adherence to clearly defined standards. Each prospective restaurant manager was put through three months of on-the-job training, followed by a ten-day seminar at headquarters and nine months as assistant manager.

Standards were defined in a comprehensive operations manual. Appearance, food preparation and service, beverage preparation and service, atmosphere, equipment maintenance, safety, inventory control, and other matters were set down in detail, together with complete job descriptions for all managers.

For example, there was a checklist which was used by each regional manager in evaluating restaurants and managers in his area. Included on the list were such details as the level of lighting and whether the beans at the salad bar were properly drained. In addition to providing the regional manager with a useful vehicle for correcting deficiencies (which might otherwise be picked up by his superiors in one of their periodic visits), the checklist formed the basis for determining whether the manager and his two assistants would be eligible for the semiannual performance bonus. Failure to qualify for the performance bonus eliminated an individual from participation in the profitability bonus.

Financial Control

Financial control of restaurant operations was maintained through several detailed reports. Daily meal counts; sales receipt and expenditure reports; and sales breakdowns for food, house and bottle wine, and other beverages were tallied for each waiter at both lunch and dinner. Sales and collections were reconciled on the same report. Daily inventories were taken of ribs, steaks, and liquor, with other items inventoried no less often than monthly. Lunch and dinner meal counts for a typical restaurant (Portland, Oregon) are included as Exhibits 8 and 9.

Bar stock was replenished on the basis of one full for one empty. A profit and loss statement (Exhibit 10) was prepared monthly for each restaurant. Computer operations to be introduced shortly would soon provide financial analysis of similar-sized restaurants by region, budget/actual variance, man-hours, revenues per seat, and revenues per square foot. Daily revenue figures for a typical restaurant (Portland) are included in Exhibit 11.

While it was believed by top management that the control procedures enabled them to spot potential problems such as waste or pilferage before they got out of hand, they felt that the continued goodwill of a capable employee group could not be overemphasized. In this regard, management had set up a stock-purchase plan to augment its bonus system and tip-pooling program. It was the feeling of management that the stockholder-employee was a vigilant employee, because the broken stack of dishes or the purloined loin was potentially money out of his pocket.

Because meat costs represented 70% of food costs, management constantly monitored meat prices. There were some debates among observers as to the general trend in meat prices. While all felt that prices were on an upward trend, some felt that there might be a slight short-term down trend due to imports. However, most felt that there was an increase of as much as 12–18% due over the next 12 months. It was felt that this would magnify the need for a very well-executed cost control program.

Exhibit 8

VICTORIA STATION, INC. (A)
Daily Synopsis
Lunch

VICTORIA STATION
PURVEYOR OF PRIME RIB & POTABLE SPIRITS

Day	P.R.	Dip	Burger	Cheese	Top	BBQ	Flank	Shrimp	Kebob	Salad	TOTAL MEALS	Mush.	Dessert
1 S	21	11	17	20	12	11	11	19	5	3	130	7	9
2 S	—	—	—	—	—	—	—	—	—	—	—	—	—
3 M	—	—	—	—	—	—	—	—	—	—	—	—	—
4 T	62	17	25	19	13	23	16	35	17	3	220	16	15
5 W	49	32	17	17	26	20	28	35	17	6	247	17	8
6 Th	75	50	14	31	30	29	27	40	20	3	319	15	18
7 F	70	43	36	36	25	23	20	37	43	13	346	20	21
8 S	15	13	17	10	6	15	4	22	10	8	120	6	9
9 S	—	—	—	—	—	—	—	—	—	—	—	—	—
10 M	47	29	23	23	21	22	7	41	26	8	247	9	10
11 T	60	26	39	31	24	24	19	32	31	3	289	16	17
12 W	74	37	27	33	11	16	27	50	21	2	298	20	11
13 Th	48	36	19	26	9	22	23	34	17	5	239	12	15
14 F	78	51	28	30	18	12	15	55	32	9	328	19	30
15 S	14	17	11	13	6	11	5	15	4	—	96	5	4
16 S	—	—	—	—	—	—	—	—	—	—	—	—	—
17 M	40	42	19	46	15	29	17	32	21	2	263	10	6
18 T	44	38	27	52	19	25	12	29	19	3	268	10	10
19 W	85	54	36	39	29	14	12	35	23	3	325	18	12
20 Th	89	43	33	38	27	18	24	40	26	4	342	23	27
21 F	60	30	32	46	14	22	34	40	11	4	295	16	17
22 S	21	14	9	10	9	9	4	12	4	3	95	7	3
23 S	—	—	—	—	—	—	—	—	—	—	—	—	—
24 M	46	21	21	36	20	27	21	33	21	4	250	—	9
25 T	66	28	33	42	14	27	28	30	6	6	280	13	8
26 W	63	49	22	30	17	28	15	35	26	4	289	3	17
27 Th	39	71	34	30	32	19	19	41	20	2	307	20	16
28 F	97	37	26	31	24	16	23	55	27	2	338	19	23
29 S	24	10	15	19	12	18	10	18	10	1	137	14	20
30 S	—	—	—	—	—	—	—	—	—	—	—	—	—
31													
Total #	1277	799	580	703	433	480	423	815	457	101	6068	315	335
Total %	21.0	13.2	9.6	11.6	7.1	7.9	7.0	13.4	7.5	1.7			

Exhibit 9

VICTORIA STATION
PURVEYOR OF PRIME RIB & POTABLE SPIRITS

VICTORIA STATION, INC. (A)
Daily Synopsis
Dinner

Day	Track 1	Track 2	Track 3	Top	Filet	Shrimp	Ch. Top	Ch. P.R.	Ch. Shrimp	Salad	TOTAL MEALS	Mush.	Potato	Dessert
1 S	225	93	5	164	56	102	1	3	–	2	651	114	325	43
2 S	143	43	–	92	33	63	–	6	3	3	386	49	175	26
3 M	156	49	5	74	25	58	–	2	1	4	374	61	167	42
4 T	117	50	3	79	26	42	–	1	1	10	329	78	150	30
5 W	142	51	9	74	22	56	–	–	2	5	361	62	180	39
6 Th	149	49	3	61	32	32	1	5	1	2	335	81	142	18
7 F	169	80	9	144	68	89	1	4	2	3	569	118	272	38
8 S	245	119	5	200	54	106	2	3	–	2	736	134	358	41
9 S	126	27	–	69	20	41	4	2	–	1	290	37	135	2
10 M	103	29	4	72	39	37	4	–	–	8	296	61	139	28
11 T	131	42	5	64	30	36	1	1	3	3	316	63	149	51
12 W	170	55	–	98	32	47	1	2	2	1	408	80	185	35
13 Th	142	70	7	73	41	52	6	3	1	0	395	91	89	33
14 F	210	65	5	136	91	84	2	1	–	5	599	95	286	39
15 S	254	81	9	167	106	89	–	2	1	3	712	120	390	42
16 S	126	41	3	103	36	53	7	2	2	2	375	61	200	41
17 M	134	35	3	54	43	52	1	3	–	1	326	34	195	46
18 T	126	45	3	73	24	52	1	–	–	5	329	71	141	32
19 W	139	52	5	96	53	59	1	3	1	3	412	84	170	36
20 Th	119	41	3	53	54	37	1	1	1	2	312	50	170	21
21 F	210	75	4	124	80	47	2	2	–	3	547	89	278	31
22 S	239	88	8	192	120	102	3	1	1	3	757	130	381	55
23 S	123	26	2	39	28	17	3	3	–	1	242	30	130	22
24 M	107	36	–	83	29	26	–	1	–	5	287	62	142	12
25 T	128	43	7	85	47	38	1	1	–	7	357	75	166	20
26 W	137	48	–	81	41	51	–	–	–	–	358	68	142	14
27 Th	146	50	5	80	59	43	–	–	–	2	385	85	140	35
28 F	201	81	5	166	89	81	2	2	1	2	630	119	304	37
29 S	263	91	1	212	126	93	6	–	5	4	801	159	388	63
30 S	127	42	4	43	38	29	–	4	4	10	301	46	132	33
31 –														
Total	4807	1697	122	3051	1542	1714	51	58	32	102	13176	2407	6271	1005
%	36.5	12.9	.8	23.2	11.7	13.0	.4	.4	.3	.8				

Exhibit 10

VICTORIA STATION, INC. (A)
Portland Income Statement
September 30, 1973

			Current Period		Six Months Year to Date	
			$	%	$	%
Income						
Sales						
Food			95,457	72.2	638,691	72.3
Beverage			36,510	27.6	243,299	27.6
Total Sales			131,967	99.9	881,990	99.9
Other income						
Telephone			11	.0	75	.0
Music			0	.0	0	.0
Cigarettes			154	.1	906	.1
Miscellaneous			2	.0	9	.0
Total Other Income			167	.1	990	.1
Total Income			132,134	100.0	882,980	100.0
Expenses						
Cost of Sales						
Food	45.4	45.8	43.368	32.8	292,818	33.2
Beverage	32.3	32.7	11,787	8.9	79,470	9.0
Bar supplies	4.0	3.9	1,466	1.1	9,545	1.1
Mirrors			0	.0	0	.0
Total Cost of Sales			56,621	42.9	381,833	43.2
Payroll and Related Expenses						
Salaries and wages						
Operating						
Waiter			2,117	1.6	15,411	1.7
Busboy			2,809	2.1	21,170	2.4
Cook			2,686	2.0	18,954	2.1
Dishwasher			1,085	.8	7,563	.9
Bartender			1,993	1.5	14,366	1.6
Cocktail waitress			985	.7	8,023	.9
Hostess			704	.5	4,790	.5
Total Operating			12,378	9.4	90,276	10.2
Management						
Management			3,755	2.8	21,665	2.5
Administrative assistant			224	.2	1,849	.2
Trainee			0	.0	0	.0
Bonuses			0	.0	2,500	.3
Total Management			3,979	3.0	26,014	2.9

Exhibit 10 (continued)

VICTORIA STATION, INC. (A)
Portland Income Statement
September 30, 1973

	Current Period		Six Months Year to Date	
	$	%	$	%
Other				
Vacation—Hourly	769	.6	1,191	.1
Sick pay	0	.0	0	.0
Severance pay	0	.0	0	.0
Training—Hourly	0	.0	0	.0
Total Other	769	.6	1,191	.1
Total Salaries and Wages	17,126	13.0	117,481	13.3
Related Payroll Costs				
Payroll taxes	1,511	1.1	11,065	1.3
Workmen's compensation	329—	.2—	4,095	.5
Employee benefit—insurance	833	.6	4,022	.5
Employee benefit—meals	1,198	.9	8,826	1.0
Casual labor	46	.0	694	.1
Management training costs	0	.0	0	.0
Employee benefits	99	.1	323	.0
Stock purchase plan	162	.1	827	.1
Total Related Payroll Costs	3,520	2.7	29,851	3.4
Total Payroll and Related Expenses	20,646	15.6	147,332	16.7
Total Gross Profit Loss	54,868	41.5	353,815	40.1
Controllable Expenses				
Maintenance & repairs				
Cleaning supplies	535	.4	3,978	.5
Repairs	134	.1	873	.1
Maintenance	326	.2	1,579	.2
Janitorial service	630	.5	3,780	.4
Replacements	0	.0	0	.0
Total Maintenance & Repairs	1,624	1.2	10,209	1.2
Laundry				
Linens & laundry	1,366	1.0	9,419	1.1
Uniforms	3	.0	215	.0
Total Laundry	1,369	1.0	9,634	1.1
Serviceware				
China	1,176	.9	5,243	.6
Glassware	378	.3	3,529	.4
Utensils	36	.0	285	.0
Small equipment	0	.0	742	.1

Exhibit 10 (continued)

	Current Period		Six Months Year to Date	
	$	%	$	%
Silverware	138	.1	1,048	.1
Serviceware depletion	188	.1	1,129	.1
Total Serviceware	1,915	1.4	11,976	1.4
Guest supplies	833	.6	5,027	.6
Equipment Rental				
Office furn & equip	0	.0	0	.0
Bar & restaurant equipment	595	.5	2,782	.3
Furn, fixt, & equipment	0	.0	0	.0
Artifacts	0	.0	0	.0
Total Equipment Rental	595	.5	2,782	.3
Administrative				
Bad debt	79	.1	219	.0
Decorating	0	.0	193	.0
Telephone	239	.2	1,231	.1
Office	162	.1	872	.1
Automobile	0	.0	0	.0
Dues and subscriptions	0	.0	104	.0
Travel-managers	0	.0	0	.0
Contributions	0	.0	0	.0
Total Administrative	480	.4	2,618	.3
Advertising & Promotion				
Promotion and entertainment	102	.1	935	.1
In house promotion	239	.2	2,153	.2
Small signs	0	.0	109	.0
Advertising	16	.0	16	.0
Total Advertising & Promotion	357	.3	3,214	.4
Utilities				
Utilities	904	.7	5,474	.6
Waste removal	156	.1	936	.1
Total Utilities	1,060	.8	6,410	.7
Miscellaneous				
Restaurant supplies	83	.1	706	.1
Cash over/short	8–	.0	242	.0
Menus	0	.0	746	.1
Music	88	.1	525	.1
Other	5	.0	62	.0
Total Miscellaneous	167	.1	2,281	.3
Total Controllable Expenses	8,401	6.4	54,151	6.1
Total Operating Expense	85,667	64.8	583,316	66.1
Total Operating Profit Loss	46,467	35.2	299,664	33.9

Exhibit 10 (continued)

VICTORIA STATION, INC. (A)
Portland Income Statement
September 30, 1973

	Current Period		Six Months Year to Date	
	$	%	$	%
Non-Controllable Expense				
Rent				
Land	7,918	6.0	53,747	6.1
Building	0	.0	0	.0
Artifacts	0	.0	0	.0
Other	0	.0	0	.0
Total Rent	7,918	6.0	53,747	6.1
Insurance	208	.2	1,248	.1
Depreciation & amortization	1,594	1.2	9,589	1.1
Interest	0	.0	0	.0
Professional fees				
Legal	0	.0	110	.0
Accounting	0	.0	0	.0
Other	0	.0	0	.0
Total Professional Fees	0	.0	110	.0
Management services*	15,627	11.8	58,584	6.6
Licenses	305	.2	923	.1
Taxes	0	.0	74	.0
Staff Training & Evaluation				
Transportation	138	.1	856	.1
Lodging & meals	123	.1	542	.1
Salary	0	.0	0	.0
Recruiting	0	.0	0	.0
Moving expense	0	.0	0	.0
Miscellaneous	0	.0	0	.0
Total Staff Training & Evaluation	261	.2	1,397	.2
Miscellaneous				
Credit card commissions	781	.6	6,019	.7
Corporate organization cost	0	.0	755	.1
Pre-opening expense	783	.6	4,697	.5
Miscellaneous	105	.1	119	.0
Total Miscellaneous	1,669	1.3	11,590	1.3
Total Non-controllable Expense	27,582	20.9	137,261	15.5
Net Profit Loss Before Inc Tax	18,886	14.3	162,403	18.4
Federal and State Inc Tax Est	9,065	6.9	77,953	8.8
Net Profit Loss After Inc Tax	9,821	7.4	84,450	9.6

* The management services charge for the month of September is high to adjust for previous months; the year-to-date is consistent.

Organization

The Victoria Station organization as of spring 1973 is charted in Exhibit 6, as constructed by Harlow White, director of human resources for the company. The three officers, Richard Bradley, Peter Lee, and Robert Freeman were described as a "management team" in which each member had special responsibilities. Lee was oriented toward the controller function and the development of management information systems. He was also responsible for quality control. Robert Freeman was primarily responsible for operations. Under Freeman was a director of operations and four regional managers. It was believed by the top management team that the overall success of Victoria Station operations depended heavily on the performance of the regional managers. These managers were selected from highly experienced Victoria Station unit managers, as were nearly all of the members of middle management. The purpose of the regional-manager organization was to provide localized management and relieve Fred Parkin from heavy involvement in day-to-day operating decisions as the number of units grew. The description from the personnel manual of the unit manager position is shown in Exhibit 7.

Restaurant Expansion Activities

"New activity is the primary challenge—new restaurants, businesses, and locations. People have a pride of working with a well-respected growth company," was said by Peter Lee. Victoria Stations numbered 17, with an additional 5 under construction, and 10 more committed to or being designed.

Members of the financial community described the Victoria Station growth record as "most impressive." The market price of the stock was running about $18/share, which reflected a price-earnings ratio of approximately 59 times previous year's earnings. Market analysts felt that such a price was justified based on past and anticipated growth. However, one market observer pointed out that such a favorable price-earnings ratio was dependent on a continued record of growth in the number of units and profitability.

Peter Lee described the process of new site selection, construction, and opening in the following general terms:

> Bob Freeman, Dick Bradley, and I are all actively involved in nearly all aspects of a new location. However, we each have different time commitments. I would say that Bob Freeman might spend the most time—approximately 80% of his available time—on new location work. He is really the one responsible for implementing our expansion strategy. Dick Bradley spends closer to 50% of his time in expansion activities. His role tends to be more typically associated with establishing the locations and securing the real estate. My own role is relatively small—only about 20% of my time. This consists of final site approval, some aspects of project control, and helping establish the control system in the new operating unit.
>
> We have tended to depend on outside architectural firms to provide a design and a certain degree of project management during construction. Fairly early in the game, we established a basic standard design for our stores. However,

Exhibit 11

VICTORIA STATION, INC. (A)
Portland Daily Revenues, September

September	*Food*	*House Wine*	*Bottled Wine*	*Liquor*	*Total Beverage*	*Total Sales*
1 Saturday	$ 4260	$ 143	$ 190	$ 1230	$ 1563	$ 5823
2 Sunday	2273	90	77	505	672	2945
3 Monday	2252	79	81	455	615	2867
4 Tuesday	2542	83	127	825	1035	3577
5 Wednesday	2839	92	128	795	1015	3854
6 Thursday	2889	79	114	944	1137	4026
7 Friday	4486	177	191	1589	1957	6443
8 Saturday	4862	185	201	1458	1844	6706
9 Sunday	1702	71	61	328	460	2162
10 Monday	2433	72	107	729	908	3341
11 Tuesday	2684	122	103	922	1147	3831
12 Wednesday	3272	105	167	1195	1467	4739
13 Thursday	3097	123	144	790	1057	4154
14 Friday	4518	124	168	1514	1806	6324
15 Saturday	4602	151	211	1374	1736	6338
16 Sunday	2235	85	76	541	702	2937
17 Monday	2609	94	110	776	980	3589
18 Tuesday	2672	99	105	871	1075	3747
19 Wednesday	3353	132	163	1244	1539	4892
20 Thursday	2801	103	118	851	1072	3873
21 Friday	4124	132	205	1625	1962	6086
22 Saturday	4921	162	183	1653	1998	6919
23 Sunday	1425	41	38	413	492	1917
24 Monday	2349	75	130	710	915	3264
25 Tuesday	2859	102	107	907	1116	3975
26 Wednesday	2883	100	83	888	1071	3954
27 Thursday	3138	91	160	958	1209	4347
28 Friday	4751	134	138	1720	1992	6743
29 Saturday	5223	154	214	1706	2074	7297
30 Sunday	1766	75	73	470	618	2384
	$95,820	$3,275	$3,973	$29,986	$37,234	$133,054

we have had to make some modest modifications of the design for each location. These architects that we have worked with have tended to be captives. The first firm we worked with did some very good work with us and was instrumental in helping us develop some of our basic concepts. When we really started to grow about two years ago, our business outgrew his capacity. He simply did not care to expand, so we changed architects. The present firm is keeping up, but there is a real question in the minds of some around here why we don't have our own in-house capability on this.

We have handled construction in a number of ways. Originally, we tried to use the same contractor at all locations. We were more comfortable doing it that way. That was all right as long as we were building new stores locally. As we expanded geographically, it has become necessary to use local contractors in each area. We still tend to minimize the number of companies we work with to reduce the hassle.

The local legal work can be very tedious. Boston is a good example of this. We thought that building permits, liquor licenses, and other necessary legal details would progress much more quickly than it has. As of right now, we are about one year behind schedule on that project. We are still not sure why the delays have been so great. We use our own law firm in such matters but often rely on their associates or correspondents in each area to help us. Now and then you simply get stalled—that really has hurt us in Boston. We are finding good locations more difficult to secure, and we have at least one location that has been a disappointment. While it will be profitable, it certainly will not provide the volume that we had anticipated. We are also finding that construction time is creeping up, after a period when we were actually shortening it. Building costs are also drifting up—probably partially due to the inflation in building materials.

Dan Ohlsen, who handled real estate activities for Victoria Station, described the new unit location and construction process as follows:

A site might be selected in a number of ways. In some cases, one of us may know something about the particular city we are interested in. Dick Bradley in particular has very good knowledge of a number of cities, and I feel that he has a real flair for this type of work, and he has a great personal interest in this. Also, Dick Bradley has something like a photographic mind—this is really helpful. The selection of the Boston location was an example of another situation. I had moved to Boston as a base of my real estate operations during the construction of several eastern stores. I actually lived in Boston for about eight months. During the first two to three weeks, January 1972, I spent a considerable amount of time driving in the suburbs and downtown. I felt that Boston was an unbelievably good market, and that it might support as many as four restaurants without jeopardizing any one of them. We thought that downtown Boston was a great market, clean, and the Boston Redevelopment Authority would keep it a stable and healthy location. The spot that we picked (near Boston's Pier 4) was near the financial center and convenient to many offices for luncheon traffic. It also had good visibility and you had to drive by it to the highest volume restaurant in the United States, which was located within a block of our site. It was an area that most Boston residents knew fairly well.

As you may know, we have experienced some delays in getting building approval. However, they may have been as much the result of our own making as anything. We thought that we knew how to handle things in Boston. We took some poor advice, and found that it was ill-founded.

We have a practice of having all three of the founders approve the site before we go ahead with a lease. We have found that actually settling the lease is relatively straightforward now.

About this point, I would also begin intense local research on liquor license requirements.

After the site was chosen, I gathered all building requirements and zoning information and presented it, together with land survey information, to the outside architect. From that point, I coordinated the flow of information between the architects and the city planning group. I would act as the representative for the company in any decisions that had to be made. In the meantime, the architect was checking out local building codes and began adapting the standard prototype design to the unique situation of the particular location. This was done by marking up standard drawings. By the time we have a building permit, we have a completed set of drawings.

Typically, we tried to find the most qualified contractor in a particular city and to negotiate a price for the construction. In some cases, like on the West Coast, we used one contractor we were very familiar with. He has built about seven jobs for us. Now we have a similar relationship developing on the East Coast. We feel that specialized restaurant experience is important. Also, we like a middle-sized firm which is large enough to be financially responsible and small enough that we can deal directly with the principal of the company.

At the time of construction, project responsibility would pass from me to Bob Freeman, and he works directly with the project supervisor in the architects' office. This project coordinator would do the bulk of the construction supervision but be subject to supervision by Bob Freeman. This would continue up to about three weeks prior to the opening. In the final three weeks, Bob Freeman takes on a very active role. This is when the building is really developed into a restaurant. Here is where he really makes it happen. He has a crash crew who bring it on-stream. Bob Freeman was able to really pour it on because he was well supported on the daily activities by Fred Parkin. This allowed him to be relatively free of day-to-day operating problems. I guess we all think of Bob as the resident genius in restaurant design, construction, and opening, and I would estimate that about 95% of his time was devoted to these activities.

We have considered the idea of trying to bring most of the research for adaption of the prototype design to the actual site into our own organization. As a matter of fact, we might try to build an in-house architect capability. This should probably be done as soon as possible, but I doubt that it could really be accomplished in less than a year.

Review of Objectives and Strategy

The following summarizes several quotations from the letter to the shareholders in the annual report for the year ended March 31, 1973.

It is gratifying to report that Fiscal Year 1973 which ended March 31, 1973, was unquestionably the most successful in the history of Victoria Station. In many ways, 1973 was truly a spectacular year, particularly for so young a corporation. Challenges, often severe and frequently beyond our control or that of any lone corporation, also abounded during fiscal 1973. Sharply rising costs in virtually all areas, frequent frustrating construction delays, and significantly increased competition, often from vastly larger organizations, were major problems we faced most of the year. Nevertheless, we closed out 1973 by all standards a far stronger company than we were 12 months ago. Perhaps then, the true measure of 1973 is the height of our achievements, given our rapid rate of growth and the challenges created by it and a host of other factors. . . .

We are tending increasingly to view our management activities as a series of delivery systems with, of course, restaurant operations in the center of the picture. For example, the real estate, construction and maintenance functions deliver to operations a completed restaurant; the human resources and training functions deliver trained management people and in-restaurant training services along with wage, salary, and benefits programs, payroll and other administrative services; the accounting and data processing functions deliver financial procedures, systems and data; the operations analysis and quality control functions deliver interpretive feedback and analysis; and the operating restaurants deliver our product and service to the customer as well as sales and earnings to the corporation and its shareholders. Additionally, specialists on the operations staff are able to provide help and guidance in such areas as food operations, beverage operations, and internal control. The advantages of this approach include streamlining the flow of information, pinpointing responsibility for various activities, and providing a basis for measurement of results.

At a meeting with Richard Bradley, Peter Lee, and several other members of the Victoria Station organization in San Francisco, the following remarks were made.

We have built the foundations for a much larger company. The cost controls, quality controls, and organization we have installed are intended for the future. If we were planning to stay at our present size, these expenditures would not be necessary.

The financial community has high expectations for Victoria Station. They expect fast, steady, profitable growth. How fast a growth is necessary to satisfy the financial community and our investors? However, the real question is, what growth rate is necessary to satisfy ourselves? To what extent are we willing to sacrifice day-to-day operations to maintain growth just to please others? We are concerned that we are losing our objective.

Appendix

What distinguishes medium-price, limited menu restaurants from the approximately 350,000 others in the United States?

First, they must offer table service, with waiters or waitresses in attendance. A number of steak houses which are operated as fast-food outlets—such as Ponderosa Systems—are excluded by this element of our definition.

Another distinguishing feature: limited menu. Steak and Ale, Reubens, and others in the field list six to ten entrees on the bill of fare. Similar limited selections mark the hors d'oeuvres, vegetable and dessert lists. Most of these restaurants feature a specialty of the house, usually steak, and most offer a self-service salad bar. An advertised special of several: "As much beer as you can drink" at no added cost.

All of these outlets offer meals at various prices. Entrees generally range from \$4.00 to \$6.00. Finally, all of these restaurants are chain operations, and most are chain-owned and operated rather than franchised. Most outlets have uniform layouts, standardized controls and central purchasing of the most important food items.

While these are the characteristics that distinguish all outlets in the medium-price, limited menu restaurant business, a number of other features are characteristic of many. Restaurant atmosphere is usually given high priority. Whether it be the sunken fireplace area in a Charley Brown Restaurant, or the old English pub of a Steak and Ale, the decor is impressive and very professional. The chains have a great opportunity in this way to go one up on the restaurants run by local entrepreneurs, where the wallpaper doesn't quite match the carpet or the prints on the wall are tired hunt scenes. In these new outlets, the waiters and waitresses are usually young and clean-cut, often students at the local college or university. They are pleasant, courteous and attentive. All in all, this is an atmosphere that's hard to beat. On top of this, the food is good and prices reasonable.

Almost all of these outlets serve liquor. Many feature evening entertainment as well. Two, Emersons, Ltd. and Ireland's, have set their sights on the college student trade, locating outlets in academic communities to attract their business.

All in all, these are formidable newcomers to the restaurant business. We believe that most are here to stay.

Our featured industry was not even in existence before the 1960's. Valle's Steak House was in operation before that time, but with only one restaurant. Steak and Ale Restaurants of America was one of the pioneers in the field, starting a chain of extremely successful steak houses in 1965. There have been many entrants since, including a handful of companies devoted exclusively to this type of operation. Some major corporations, including W. R. Grace and Ralston Purina, are also in the business, although their restaurants represent a small portion of total corporate sales.

MEDIUM-PRICE, LIMITED MENU
Restaurant Chains

Company	Name of Restaurant	Calendar Year 1972 Restaurant Sales ($ millions)	Total Company Sales ($ millions)	Restaurant Sales as % of Total	Est. Number of Restaurants in Operation, End of 1972
Steak and Ale Restaurants of America, Inc.	Steak and Ale	33	33	100	48
Valle's Steak House	Valle's	31	31	100	16
Grace (W.R.) & Co.	Reubens	30	2,330	1	40
Steak 'n Brew, Inc.	Steak 'n Brew	22	22	100	33
Saga Administration Corp.	Velvet Turtle; Black Angus	15	97	15	21
Ralston Purina Co.	Boar's Head	12	1,898	1	16
Victoria Station Incorporated	Victoria Station	9	9	100	13
Emersons, Ltd.	Emersons	8	8	100	16
Ireland's Restaurants, Inc.	Ireland's	5	5	100	15
Host International, Inc.	Charley Brown	4	140	3	7
		20			30
Total		$189			255

SELECTED MEDIUM-PRICE, LIMITED MENU
Restaurant Chains

	Fiscal 1972						
	Sales ($ millions)	Pre-tax Margin	Return on Average Equity	Increase in Sales Over 1971	Latest 12-month Earnings Per Share	Price 3/2/73	Price/ Earnings Ratio
Valle's Steak House[1]	$28.7	10.9%	14.9%	26%	$.96	$ 9 3/4	10
Steak and Ale Restaurants		18.1	38.4	92	.77	32 1/2	42
of America, Inc.[1]	23.6						
Steak 'n Brew, Inc.[2]	20.0	12.0	20.8	77	.78	15 1/4	20
Emersons, Ltd.[2]	6.3	9.5	17.2	80	.49	19	39
Victoria Station Incorporated[1]	5.5	13.0	46.9	253	.33	17	52
Ireland's Restaurants, Inc.[3]	4.0	14.4	41.1	61	.44	8 3/8	19
Mean		13.0	29.9	98			30

[1] Fiscal year ended March, 1972

[2] Fiscal year ended October, 1972

[3] Fiscal year ended May, 1972

At the end of 1972, about 20 firms were operating almost 260 units which in 1972 provided sales of $190 million. By the end of 1973, we expect 375 outlets to be in operation, generating a total 1973 volume of $275 million.

To analyze the growth and profitability of medium-price, limited menu restaurant chains, we examined the record of six publicly-held companies with all revenue coming from this type of business. These six represent about 60% of the volume of the industry. Their records have been impressive.

These achievements have not gone unnoticed in the stock market. On March 2, the mean price/earnings ratio of the six companies was 30 times latest twelve-month results. This is well below an earlier peak—but still a lofty multiple. If future growth and profitability come anywhere near matching past results, however, we think a portfolio of these stocks will do quite well.

Victoria Station, Inc. (B)

The Site Selection Process

In July 1974, the management of Victoria Station, Inc., was wrestling with the question of whether or not to enter the Washington, D.C., area market with one or more of its theme restaurants. The firm had carefully scrutinized a large number of sites over a period of several months and had narrowed the choices down to five sites in Montgomery County, Maryland, and nearby Fairfax County, Virginia. One site in the Georgetown area near downtown Washington had been considered but had been rejected because local authorities had threatened possible condemnation of the property for use as a highway exit ramp a few years out. The remaining sites included one near a freeway interchange in Tyson's Corner, Virginia, two in Springfield, Virginia, near Interstate 95, a fourth near Gaithersburg, Maryland, northwest of Bethesda and a fifth in Alexandria, Virginia, overlooking the Potomac river.

The Washington area sites presented Victoria Station (VSI) management with a difficult dilemma. The firm was eager to enter the market as it felt strongly that Washington offered a number of large affluent, and growing markets, and eventually would be capable of supporting three or four company restaurants. However, the sites under consideration raised a myriad of complex questions which had to be resolved before the firm could make a final decision on which—if any—site might provide the company's best beachhead.

Company Background

Victoria Station was founded in 1969 by three classmates from the Cornell University School of Hotel and Restaurant Administration to develop a chain of railroad-theme roast beef restaurants. During the six years between graduation in 1963 and the establishment of the company, the three founders had worked in different areas, each developing skills which complemented those of the others. Richard J. Bradley, President and a director, had been a registered representative for a large brokerage firm; Robert A. Freeman, Vice-President and a director, had been an in-flight service supervisor for Pan American World Airways, Inc., and Peter E. Lee, Vice-President, Treasurer, and a director, had been manager of budgets and cost analysis for Sky Chefs, Inc.

Victoria Station had grown rapidly and steadily during the first five years of its existence. By March 31, 1974, the end of VSI's fiscal year, sales had topped $24.7

million, a 120% increase over FY 1973, and the company earned $.82 per share, a 156% jump (see Exhibit 1 for FY 1974 financial summary). Twelve new restaurants had been opened during FY 1974 and four came onstream shortly thereafter, raising the company total to 30. Thirteen more were scheduled to open during the remainder of FY 1975 (see Exhibit 2). The typical restaurant in operation more than a year averaged $1.4 million in sales per year, and the company as a whole sold more than 1500 tons of roast beef in FY 1974.

To keep pace with this growth, Victoria Station had nearly doubled its employment to about 2,000 in FY 1974. At the close of fiscal 1974, 65 management

Exhibit 1

VICTORIA STATION, INC. (B)
Financial Summary
Fiscal Years ending March 31, 1972, 1973, 1974
($000)

	1974	*1973*	*1972*
Sales	$24,741	$11,315	$5,471
Interest income	18	135	—
Cost of sales	14,196	6,619	3,256
Operating expenses	6,667	3,220	1,375
Depreciation	868	291	104
Interest expense	274	105	24
Earnings before taxes	2,754	1,113	709
Taxes (current and deferred)	1,888	478	331
Extraordinary item	—	(58)	—
Minority interest in earnings	12	11	38
Net earnings	1,553	567	341
Earnings per common share ($)	.82	.32	.24
Stock price range	8–15	7–28	15–29
Restaurants operated at year end	26	14	6
Current assets	$ 4,686	$ 3,034	$ 622
Other assets	367	199	87
Equipment and improvements	14,386	4,552	1,326
Less: depreciation	(686)	(245)	(90)
Deferred costs	846	375	150
	$19,599	$ 7,916	$2,095
Current liabilities	3,985	$ 1,749	$ 900
Long-term debt	6,186	—	183
Deferred taxes	362	132	43
Minority interests	46	33	37
Paid-in capital	6,468	5,003	500
Retained earnings	2,552	999	432
	$19,599	$ 7,916	$2,095

Note: Numbers may not add due to rounding.

Exhibit 2

VICTORIA STATION, INC. (B)
Record of Restaurant Openings (7/74)

Location	Seats	Site Selected	Leases Signed	Ground Broken	Open	Site Selection to Opening (Months)	Construction Cost ($)	Monthly Rental Minimum[b]	% Sales[e]
San Francisco	210[a]	1/69	4/69	9/69	12/69	11	344,099	4,015[c]	5
San Fran. (Thomas Lord's)	70	3/70	7/70	8/70	11/70	8	Remodeled existing structure	2,250	5
Atlanta	156	3/70	5/70	7/70	12/70	9	188,354	2,100	8
Oakland	140	3/70	7/70	12/70	4/71	13	170,468	653[c]	5¼
New Orleans	180	2/71	6/71	5/71	9/71	7	226,945	2,158	10
Denver	170	9/70	12/70	5/71	9/71	12	313,383	2,917	9¼
Oakland (Quinn's)	100	6/71	8/71	12/71	4/72	10	Remodeled existing structure	653[c]	5¼
Sunnyvale	205	7/71	9/71	3/72	7/72	12	350,655	2,917	8
San Fran. (Royal Exchg.)	150	4/71	7/71	5/72	8/72	16	Remodeled existing structure	2,000	6
Los Angeles	205	8/71	11/71	4/72	8/72	12	317,354	2,917	8
Phoenix	205	8/71	11/71	5/72	9/72	13	383,128	2,917	8
Dallas	205	8/71	11/71	4/72	9/72	13	362,795	2,175[c]	—
Houston I	205	12/71	4/72	9/72	1/73	13	371,826	5,310	8
Cincinnati	218	4/72	7/72	11/72	6/73	14	380,000	2,500[c]	—
Portland	218	4/72	7/72	11/72	3/73	11	328,000	1,250[d]	—
Boston	300	3/72	3/73	6/73	1/74	22	524,000	3,000	—
Indianapolis	218	7/72	11/72	12/72	5/73	10	363,000	1,250	
Kansas City	218	7/72	10/72	2/73	7/73	12	390,000	750	—
Miami I	218	6/72	8/72	12/72	5/73	11	392,000	2,762	
Columbus	218	4/72	11/72	2/73	10/73	18	410,000	2,000	—
Philadelphia	218	5/72	11/72	5/73	12/73	19	418,000	1,833	
Darien	245	6/72	8/72	5/73	12/73	18	442,000	3,333	—
Minneapolis	?			Still no site chosen					
Sacramento	218	4/73	7/73	1/74	6/74	14	456,000	5,250	5½
St. Louis I	218	12/73	5/74	—	—	—	—	purchase	—
Houston II	218	10/72	12/72	5/73	9/73	11	427,000	2,325	—
Seattle	218	10/72	1/73	7/73	11/73	13	433,000	7,550	—
Louisville	218	12/72	2/73	2/73	12/73	12	451,000	1,950	—
Woodland Hills, Calif.	218	11/72	2/73	9/73	3/74	16	503,000	2,833	3

Location	Seats	Site Selected	Leases Signed	Ground Broken	Open	Site Selection to Opening (Months)	Construction Cost ($)	Monthly Rental Minimum[b]	% Sales[e]
Vancouver	218	12/72	2/73	11/73	9/74 (est.)	21 (est.)	518,000	2,500	—
Newport Beach, Calif.	218	11/72	4/73	11/73	6/74	19	517,000	6,333	6
Northbrook	218	2/73	4/73	10/73	6/74	16	428,000	2,500	—
Tahoe City, Calif.	250	4/74	4/74	4/74	6/74	2	272,000	1,500	1/2
Torrance, Calif.	218	5/73	8/73	1/74	7/74	14	535,000	2,250	—
Memphis	218	4/73	8/73	1/74	9/74 (est.)	17 (est.)	492,000	6,781	—
Rocky River, O.	218	7/73	10/73	4/74	9/74 (est.)	14 (est.)	509,000	1,250	—
Arlington, Texas	218	10/73	12/73	4/74	8/74 (est.)	10 (est.)	505,000	2,100	—
Honolulu	190	4/73	4/74	4/74	12/74 (est.)	20 (est.)	640,000 (est.)	10,115	—
Birmingham, Ala.	300	6/73	10/73	5/74	12/74 (est.)	18 (est.)	428,000 (est.)	1,040	1 1/4
Schaumberg, Ill.	218	5/73	11/73	6/74	12/74 (est.)	19 (est.)	406,000 (est.)	2,500	2
Jacksonville, Fla.	218	11/73	3/74	7/74	12/74 (est.)	13 (est.)	463,000 (est.)	purchase	—
Tampa, Fla.	218	11/73	3/74	7/74	1/75 (est.)	14 (est.)	455,000 (est.)	2,000	1 1/2
Southfield	218	6/73	7/74	9/74	3/75 (est.)	21 (est.)	553,000 (est.)	purchase	—
Villa Park, Ill.	218	7/73	2/74	8/74	2/75 (est.)	19 (est.)	446,000 (est.)	1,916	2
Toledo, O.	218	2/74	3/74	8/74	2/75 (est.)	12 (est.)	525,000 (est.)	purchase	—
Atlanta II (Quinn's)	292	5/73	4/74	?	?	?	900,000 (est.)	1,875	2 1/2
Larkspur, Calif.	300	10/73	5/74	8/74	2/75 (est.)	16 (est.)	623,000 (est.)	purchase	—
Montreal	218	8/73	?	?	?	?	No final estimate	?	
St. Louis II	218	?	?	?	?	?	No final estimate	?	
Pittsburgh	218	4/74	10/74 (est.)	?	?	?	No final estimate	purchase	—
Toronto	300	5/74	?	?	?	?	No final estimate	1,500 (est.)	
Atlanta III	—[f]	12/73	?	?	?	?	No final estimate	?	
Miami II	?	3/74	?	?	?	?	No final estimate	?	
San Antonio, Texas	?	3/74	?	?	?	?	No final estimate	?	
Whippany, N.J.	?	?	?	?	?	?	No final estimate	?	
Universal City, Calif.	600+[2]	6/74	?	?	?	?	No final estimate	?	
West Palm Beach, Fla.	?	12/73	10/74 (est.)	?	?	?	No final estimate	?	

[Eleven additional cities under consideration but no sites chosen as of 7/74].

[a] Increased to 210 seats from 158, July 14, 1972; construction costs include expansion.

[b] Minimum—some leases provide for preestablished rent increases during the lease term or for additional rent based on changes in consumer price index or property taxes.

[c] Rental for land only. Building to be owned or leased by company.

[d] Plus 1% of construction costs.

[e] The company pays the stated monthly rental, or the percentage stated, whichever is greater; all percentages are based on gross sales.

[f] Nonprototype Victoria Station.

[g] Nonprototype—to be designed.

trainees had completed the company's three month classroom and on-the-job management training program, and 20 more had been enrolled. More than half of these 85 trainees had come from the company's employee ranks (mostly waiters). With new restaurants opening at a rate of about one per month, the company had acquired 77 boxcars and 39 cabooses during the year (VSI employed one person full time to track down available rolling stock).

Growth Strategy

Victoria Station planned to maintain a rapid rate of growth over the next five years. The company projected sales growth of 50% per year during that period and a 40% increase in the number of restaurants, subject to current economic conditions and the ability to finance its growth. The founders had decided early that the company would penetrate markets anywhere in the world that they felt were capable of supporting a Victoria Station or a similar medium-price, limited-menu establishment.

The company's basic expansion strategy had been to grow city by city on a national basis rather than to develop regional strength. "We didn't see any real economies in building first in San Francisco, then in Los Angeles and then Fresno, concentrating just on one geographic area," Mr. Bradley explained.

> Because Atlanta had a better potential market than Fresno, we went to Atlanta. It was a few dollars more airfare, but we'd really rather hit the best markets first. If we find two potentially good markets in one metropolitan area, we will not locate halfway between the two. We locate in the best area and build in the other later if conditions warrant..

By the summer of 1974, VSI built or had under construction restaurants in 26 different cities, with as many as four each in two large metropolitan areas. The company operated three other types of eating establishments in addition to Victoria Stations, all in the San Francisco Bay area within a few miles of the company's headquarters. One was Thomas Lord's, a "British sporting pub named for the father of cricket," which specialized in "uncommon dishes like shepard's pie, lamb curry, and potted vegetable salad." A second was the Royal Exchange, molded after the London Stock Exchange, which served "enormous sandwiches, shrimp salad, and a full beverage" selection. The last was Quinn's Lighthouse, a seafood-theme restaurant housed in and named after the 70-year-old Coast Guard lighthouse that had been decommissioned and floated to its present site on Oakland's Embarcadero Cove.

The actual rate of future growth, Mr. Bradley noted, "depends largely on the economy, the availability of capital, and the company's ability to 'digest' a large number of stores in terms of personnel requirements and operating capability. The company plans, if all factors prove favorable, to open 17 new restaurants in FY 1975, 12–15 in FY 1971, and 15–20 in FY 1977."

Of the 100+ restaurants VSI plans to have opened by 1979, 15–20 were expected to be non-Victoria Station types, most likely similar to Quinn's Lighthouse. Quinn's had originally been configured with 95 seats, but the company was considering increasing this number to 220 or 230 in order to develop a unit capable of the $1.4 million average annual sales a Victoria Station typically grossed. With a 95-seat design, Quinn's averaged a higher per-seat volume than did Victoria Stations, a fact which encouraged management to consider the larger version. The plan of the company was to develop a different theme restaurant similar enough in size, configuration, equipment, pricing, controls, and other aspects of operation so that the company could switch managers with a minimum of difficulty from one type to another. There were no plans to enter any business other than food service.

In addition to domestic expansion, Victoria Station expected that approximately 10–20 of the 100+ restaurants planned through 1979 would be constructed internationally. At the end of FY 1974, the company had one store under consideration in Vancouver, British Columbia (now open), and was negotiating for sites in Montreal and Toronto. During the next three or four years, Mr. Bradley explained the company plans to open restaurants in Europe as well, though they would likely be operated under a name other than Victoria Station and, due to the high cost of land, would likely be built in existing buildings rather than freestanding as were typical Victoria Stations. Mr. Bradley felt that VSI would eventually enter the real estate development business, though not in the near future.

> We think that at some point we will end up doing what Sears does, though on a much smaller scale. Sears puts in its own store and then develops the rest of the shopping center and in effect gets its own store for virtually nothing. Downstream when a landowner says, "here's a five acre parcel," there's no reason why we shouldn't finance out our restaurant by developing the rest of the property.

At the end of 1973, the company had arranged a $16 million financing package with which to repay a prior loan and to "help fuel future progress." Of the $16 million, $5 million had come from the placement of 12-year subordinated notes and 120,000 common shares with a pension fund, and the remaining $11 million came from a three-year revolving credit agreement (convertible to a term loan for an additional four years) with the First National Bank of Chicago.

Site Strategy

In selecting cities in which to build, Victoria Station generally followed one self-imposed rule: build only in metropolitan areas with a population of one million or more (see Exhibit 3). "There are about 50 such markets in the United States," Mr. Bradley explained. "We decided to go into those areas first so we could be pretty certain of establishing a consistently high volume all during the week. There are a number of smaller markets of, say, a half-million people in which we would probably do quite well. But why should we take the risk until we've gone through all of the larger markets?"

There had, of course, been a few exceptions to this rule. For example, in Columbus, Ohio, VSI had chosen a location although Columbus' population was only 900,000. However, the city had exhibited a high rate of population growth

Exhibit 3

VICTORIA STATION, INC. (B)
RANK OF STANDARD METROPOLITAN AREAS IN THE UNITED STATES BY POPULATION: 1970

[Figures relate to areas as defined for 1970. For meaning of symbols, see text]

	1970 SMSA's	1970 Population
1	New York, N.Y.	11,571,899
2	Los Angeles–Long Beach, Calif.	7,032,075
3	Chicago, Ill.	6,978,947
4	Philadelphia, Pa.–N.J.	4,817,914
5	Detroit, Mich.	4,199,931
6	San Francisco–Oakland, Calif.	3,109,519
7	Washington, D.C.–Md.–Va.	2,861,123
8	Boston, Mass.	2,753,700
9	Pittsburgh, Pa.	2,401,245
10	St. Louis, Mo.–Ill.	2,363,017
11	Baltimore, Md.	2,070,670
12	Cleveland, Ohio.	2,064,194
13	Houston, Tex.	1,985,031
14	Newark, N.J.	1,856,556
15	Minneapolis–St. Paul, Minn.	1,813,647
16	Dallas, Tex.	1,555,950
17	Seattle–Everett, Wash.	1,421,869
18	Anaheim–Santa Ana–Garden Grove, Calif.	1,420,386
19	Milwaukee, Wis.	1,403,688
20	Atlanta, Ga.	1,390,164
21	Cincinnati, Ohio–Ky.–Ind.	1,384,851
22	Paterson–Clifton–Passaic, N.J.	1,358,794
23	San Diego, Calif.	1,357,854
24	Buffalo, N.Y.	1,349,211
25	Miami, Fla.	1,267,792
26	Kansas City, Mo.–Kans.	1,253,916
27	Denver, Colo.	1,227,529
28	San Bernardino–Riverside–Ontario, Calif.	1,143,146
29	Indianapolis, Ind.	1,109,882
30	San Jose, Calif.	1,064,714
31	New Orleans, La.	1,045,809
32	Tampa–St. Petersburg, Fla.	1,012,594
33	Portland, Oreg.–Wash.	1,009,129
34	Phoenix, Ariz.	967,522
35	Columbus, Ohio	916,228
36	Providence–Pawtucket–Warwick, R.I.–Mass.	910,781
37	Rochester, N.Y.	882,667
38	San Antonio, Tex.	864,014
39	Dayton, Ohio	850,266
40	Louisville, Ky.–Ind.	826,553
41	Sacramento, Calif.	800,592
42	Memphis, Tenn.–Ark.	770,120
43	Fort Worth, Tex.	762,086
44	Birmingham, Ala.	739,274
45	Albany–Schenectady–Troy, N.Y.	721,910
46	Toledo, Ohio–Mich.	692,571
47	Norfolk–Portsmouth, Va.	680,600
48	Akron, Ohio	679,239
49	Hartford, Conn.	663,891
50	Oklahoma City, Okla.	640,889
51	Syracuse, N.Y.	636,507
52	Gary–Hammond–East Chicago, Ind.	633,367
53	Honolulu, Hawaii	629,176
54	Fort Lauderdale–Hollywood, Fla.	620,100
55	Jersey City, N.J.	609,266
56	Greensboro–Winston-Salem–High Point, N.C.	603,895
57	Salt Lake City, Utah	557,635

Exhibit 3 (cont.)

VICTORIA STATION, INC. (B)

Rank	Area	Population
58	Allentown–Bethlehem–Easton, Pa.–N.J.	543,551
59	Nashville–Davidson, Tenn.	541,108
60	Omaha, Nebr.–Iowa	540,142
61	Grand Rapids, Mich.	539,225
62	Youngstown–Warren, Ohio	536,003
63	Springfield–Chicopee–Holyoke, Mass.–Conn.	529,922
64	Jacksonville, Fla.	528,865
65	Richmond, Va.	518,318
66	Wilmington, Del.–N.J.–Md.	499,493
67	Flint, Mich.	496,658
68	Tulsa, Okla.	476,945
69	Orlando, Fla.	428,003
70	Fresno, Calif.	413,053
71	Tacoma, Wash.	411,027
72	Harrisburg, Pa.	410,626
73	Charlotte, N.C.	409,370
74	Knoxville, Tenn.	400,337
75	Wichita, Kans.	389,352
76	Bridgeport, Conn.	389,153
77	Lansing, Mich.	378,423
78	Mobile, Ala.	376,690
79	Oxnard–Ventura, Calif.	376,430
80	Canton, Ohio	372,210
81	Davenport–Rock Island–Moline, Iowa–Ill.	362,638
82	El Paso, Tex.	359,291
83	New Haven, Conn.	355,538
84	Tucson, Ariz.	351,667
85	West Palm Beach, Fla.	348,753
86	Worcester, Mass.	344,320
87	Wilkes-Barre–Hazleton, Pa.	342,301
88	Peoria, Ill.	341,979
89	Utica–Rome, N.Y.	340,670
90	York, Pa.	329,540
91	Bakersfield, Calif.	329,162
92	Little Rock–North Little Rock, Ark.	323,296
93	Columbia, S.C.	322,880
94	Lancaster, Pa.	319,693
95	Beaumont–Port Arthur, Tex.	315,943
96	Albuquerque, N. Mex.	315,774
97	Chattanooga, Tenn.–Ga.	304,927
98	Trenton, N.J.	303,968
99	Charleston, S.C.	303,849
100	Binghamton, N.Y.–Pa.	302,672
101	Greenville, S.C.	299,502
102	Reading, Pa.	296,382
103	Austin, Tex.	295,516
104	Shreveport, La.	294,703
105	Newport News–Hampton, Va.	292,159
106	Madison, Wis.	290,272
107	Stockton, Calif.	290,208
108	Spokane, Wash.	287,487
109	Des Moines, Iowa	286,101
110	Baton Rouge, La.	285,167
111	Corpus Christi, Tex.	284,832
112	Fort Wayne, Ind.	280,455
113	South Bend, Ind.	280,031
114	Appleton–Oshkosh, Wis.	276,891
115	Las Vegas, Nev.	273,288
116	Rockford, Ill.	272,063
117	Duluth–Superior, Minn.–Wis.	265,350
118	Santa Barbara, Calif.	264,324
119	Erie, Pa.	263,654
120	Johnstown, Pa.	262,822
121	Jackson, Miss.	258,906
122	Lorain–Elyria, Ohio	256,843
123	Huntington–Ashland, W. Va.–Ky.–Ohio	253,743
124	Augusta, Ga.–S.C.	253,460
125	Salinas–Monterey, Calif.	250,071
126	Vallejo–Napa, Calif.	249,081
127	Pensacola, Fla.	243,075
128	Columbus, Ga.–Ala.	238,584
129	Colorado Springs, Colo.	235,972
130	Scranton, Pa.	234,107
131	Ann Arbor, Mich.	234,103
132	Evansville, Ind.–Ky.	232,775
133	Lawrence–Haverhill, Mass.–N.H.	232,415
134	Charleston, W. Va.	229,515
135	Raleigh, N.C.	228,453
136	Huntsville, Ala.	228,239
137	Hamilton–Middletown, Ohio	226,207
138	Saginaw, Mich.	219,743

Source: 1970 U.S. Census.

and also met several other requirements, such as generally high income levels. Likewise, some areas of more than one million population were excluded from consideration for a variety of reasons. For example, the company preferred not to build in New York City due to construction difficulties there.

A major criterion in VSI's site selection strategy was the high probability of a steady trade all week long, day and night. In order to achieve the typical sales goal of $1.4 million, a restaurant had to be able to attract a heavy lunch business and a reasonable early-in-the-week dinner trade. "The key to doing $1.4 million is doing your business on Monday, Tuesday, and Wednesday nights," Mr. Bradley explained. He added:

> If you are reasonably well located you can always do a good lunch trade, but to do well early in the week at dinner you need a fairly large population base nearby. You just have to have more people around who will continually eat out.
>
> We always attempt to determine the overall size of the market when we enter a city. We will look at all of the figures we have and then go and look at the competition—how many lunches are they doing, how many early-in-the-week dinners, Friday and Saturday trade, and so on. We find we can interpret the figures we come up with pretty well and know how big the market is for a particular area. If there are, say, five popular restaurants in a town and the best one does about $1.5 million, it would stand to reason that that city might not be as strong as Boston, where you've got two or three restaurants doing $5 million to $7 million each, and one, Anthony's, which grosses more than $10 million.
>
> We also try to determine why the successful restaurants are successful. We have found that many high-volume restaurants are family owned, offer a good value for the price, and are formidable competition. Anthony's and the Hilltop Steak House in Boston are good examples. We also carefully examine the business of the chains like Emerson's, Steak & Brew, and Steak & Ale. They compete for our market, though we think their product is inferior to ours. If they are doing a brisk business, that's always encouraging because we know we can do far better.

One problem that occasionally arises is that of having to predict success in an area in which there is no comparable competition. "In New Orleans, for example, where most restaurants specialize in Creole cooking, seafoods, and sauces, we were the first prime rib or steakhouse to come into the area," Mr. Bradley pointed out. "We were pioneers and we surely didn't know if a limited menu prime rib and salad bar store would be accepted." Mr. Bradley felt that it was a positive factor to be near competition since in many metropolitan areas the population has designated certain restaurant areas. "If there were four restaurants together and one a mile away, I would rather be one of the four rather than a mile away."

Data Collection

In its site selection process, VSI did not usually analyze demographic data "as scientifically as one might expect," according to Mr. Bradley. "We don't buy marketing studies or the like. The game plan has been pretty much to take the top 50 markets in the country and pick them off one by one. From a census data standpoint they are all pretty similar, though if we had limited funds and wanted to choose between two similar markets, say Tucson and Spokane, we might use census data just to point us at the larger of the two."

The primary source of "hard data" which VSI utilized in determining which cities to enter came from *Sales Management Magazine*. This publication compiled data on buying power, population growth, income and other factors (see Exhibit 4 for the data on the Washington, D.C. SMSA).

Once the strategic decision to investigate a metropolitan area was made, a member of the firm went to the city to meet with brokers and to obtain other information such as local "Chamber of Commerce type data," real estate price data from tax stamps and other official records, and the locations of "high-quality" apartment growth, the "better" suburban office parks, new civic developments, and the highway system. Noted Mr. Bradley:

> One of the key things that has happened to most cities in the last five years is the growth of the perimeter highways that are part of the interstate system with connections to major north-south or east-west interstates. In most cities these perimeter systems have been completed in the last five years, and a lot of growth happens at the major intersections. Also, the real estate is often cheaper out there—virgin land. Still, we will not build out there if we don't think the population density is or will be there soon. We aren't going to build there and hope that the population grows in ten years.

One desirable location is near new large, higher quality, shopping centers due to both high visibility and the fact that sophisticated shopping center developers usually study planned site areas extensively. "We find that with major regional shopping centers," Mr. Bradley said, "somebody's done an awful lot of research to determine that there's where the center should be. It's probably in the path of growth. Though we don't follow the centers in every case, it is always a major consideration in my mind."

A secondary consideration is the location of hotel and motel development. "We feel that if we locate near them it is a plus, though we don't build at a spot just because of the presence of motels or hotels," Mr. Bradley explained.

The company usually establishes contact with one or more brokers in the area or investigated known sites and contacts the brokers involved in each. However, VSI's strategy is to do much of the early site research in-house. "If you go to a commercial real estate broker in any town, he'll drive you around the city to a number of sites," Mr. Bradley explained. "The trouble is, you tend to see only the sites on which he has a listing." Further, brokers sometimes try harder than they should to make a sale. "We found over time that there are very few experts in the

Exhibit 4

VICTORIA STATION, INC. (B)
1974 Survey of Buying Power
Washington D.C. Area

District of Columbia

D.C. — EFFECTIVE BUYING INCOME[1]—1973

METRO AREA

County	EBI ($000)	% of U.S.	Per Capita EBI	Median Hsld. EBI	Avg. Hsld. EBI	% of Hslds. by EBI Groups: $0–$2,999 Hslds.	$3,000–$4,999 Hslds.	$5,000–$7,999 Hslds.	$8,000–$9,999 Hslds.	$10,000–$14,999 Hslds.	$15,000–$24,999 Hslds.	$25,000 & Over Hslds.	Buying Power Index[2]	Graduated Buying Power Indexes: EPP (Economy-Priced Products)	MPP (Moderate-Priced Products)	PPP (Premium-Priced Products)
WASHINGTON	17,278,071	1.9616	5,627	12,341	17,107	5.8	5.5	14.6	12.6	24.5	24.0	13.0	1.7613	1.2470	1.5490	2.1060
District of Columbia, D.C.	4,300,939	.4883	5,792	11,373	15,754	8.8	7.2	16.0	12.0	21.8	21.4	12.8	.4345	.3343	.3681	.5626
Charles, Md.	200,198	.0227	3,633	10,001	13,527	10.9	9.0	17.1	13.0	23.1	18.1	8.8	.0250	.0229	.0234	.0177
Montgomery, Md.	3,578,805	.4063	6,207	13,257	19,556	4.2	4.1	12.7	12.3	25.7	25.5	15.5	.3518	.2020	.2900	.4648
Prince Georges, Md.	3,350,800	.3805	4,738	10,901	15,259	4.5	5.5	18.7	16.5	26.8	20.8	7.2	.3710	.3088	.3873	.3590
Alexandria, Va.	665,678	.0756	6,113	11,521	15,027	6.3	6.7	16.1	13.2	25.0	22.4	10.3	.0715	.0550	.0692	.0799
Arlington, Va.	1,232,904	.1400	7,326	13,211	17,365	5.5	4.8	12.7	10.9	25.1	26.8	14.2	.1145	.0707	.0984	.1439
Fairfax, Va.	2,997,378	.3403	5,920	14,942	20,130	3.0	3.1	9.0	9.3	25.9	31.3	18.4	.2802	.1623	.2186	.3600
Fairfax City, Va.	128,140	.0145	5,905	15,024	20,022	2.7	1.7	7.6	10.1	27.8	32.9	17.2	.0200	.0132	.0178	.0201
Falls Church, Va.	70,014	.0079	6,732	13,733	17,952	4.3	3.5	10.1	10.8	28.5	28.5	14.3	.0096	.0068	.0090	.0117
Loudoun, Va.	179,966	.0204	4,234	9,024	14,060	14.2	11.4	18.5	11.5	16.9	15.1	12.4	.0199	.0212	.0163	.0191
Prince William, Va.	573,249	.0651	4,383	12,614	17,748	5.4	6.0	15.3	11.9	21.9	23.3	16.2	.0633	.0498	.0509	.0672
TOTAL ABOVE AREAS	17,278,071	1.9616	5,627	12,341	17,107	2.7	1.7	7.6	10.1	27.8	32.9	17.2	1.7613	1.2470	1.5490	2.1060
STATE TOTALS	4,300,939	.4883	5,792	11,373	15,754	8.8	7.2	16.0	12.0	21.8	21.4	12.8	.4345	.3343	.3681	.5626

Exhibit 4 (continued)

D.C. — RETAIL SALES BY STORE GROUP—1973

METRO AREA			Food		Eating & Drinking Places	General Merchandise		Apparel	Furn.-House.-Appl.		Auto-motive	Gas Station	Lumber-Bldg.-Hdwre.	Drug
County	Total Retail Sales ($000)	% of U.S.	Total ($000)	Super-markets ($000)	Total ($000)	Total ($000)	Dept. Stores ($000)	Total ($000)	Total ($000)	Furn.-Home Furnishings ($000)	Total ($000)	Total ($000)	Total ($000)	Total ($000)
WASHINGTON	8,383,280	1.6309	1,828,020	1,660,218	731,196	1,299,316	1,092,595	494,322	391,953	265,536	1,547,959	637,341	267,804	412,860
District of Columbia, D.C.	2,055,562	.3999	351,656	301,009	312,578	283,813	254,915	175,027	110,630	69,337	196,150	121,800	37,800	120,039
Charles, Md.	144,061	.0280	32,904	26,186	26,617	3,779		1,215	1,049	670	29,101	21,336	11,309	6,195
Montgomery, Md.	1,609,897	.3132	334,124	301,383	86,006	302,620	258,615	99,058	95,078	65,204	338,340	110,865	56,859	57,157
Prince Georges, Md.	1,947,604	.3789	480,276	435,932	136,250	308,081	244,143	102,682	60,733	39,824	416,953	160,198	51,263	92,298
Alexandria, Va.	399,923	.0778	62,968	59,820	19,249	104,392	96,820	26,313	13,611	9,120	105,406	21,513	8,455	15,016
Arlington, Va.	488,556	.0950	77,076	73,222	51,246	74,342	63,855	18,747	25,106	19,214	150,053	29,166	11,224	22,340
Fairfax, Va.	1,062,976	.2068	315,606	299,826	73,168	199,461	164,081	51,690	54,259	40,136	94,795	103,307	50,582	63,011
Fairfax City, Va.	182,633	.0355	38,670	36,737	6,698	1,899		2,955	10,057	7,036	85,065	14,327	4,840	8,738
Falls Church, Va.	80,465	.0157	16,999	16,149	1,762	893		2,623	5,669	3,968	39,501	4,623	3,356	2,614
Loudoun, Va.	96,541	.0188	28,517	26,631	3,955	2,077		2,597	2,425	1,697	17,075	11,303	12,785	6,208
Prince William, Va.	315,062	.0613	89,224	83,323	13,667	17,959	10,166	11,415	13,336	9,330	75,520	38,903	19,331	19,244
TOTAL ABOVE AREAS	8,383,280	1.6309	1,828,020	1,660,218	731,196	1,299,316	1,092,595	494,322	391,953	265,536	1,547,959	637,341	267,804	412,860
STATE TOTALS	2,055,562	.3999	351,656	301,009	312,578	283,813	254,915	175,027	110,630	69,337	196,150	121,800	37,800	120,039

D.C. — RETAIL SALES BY MERCHANDISE LINE—1973

	Groceries, Other Foods		Cosmetics, Etc.		Women's, Girls' Clothing		Men's, Boys' Clothing		All Footwear		Major Appliances		Furn., Sleep, Etc.	
METRO AREA	Mdse. Lines	In Food Stores	Mdse. Lines	In Drug-stores	Mdse. Lines	In Dept. Stores	Mdse. Lines	In Apparel Stores	Mdse. Lines	In Apparel Stores	Mdse. Lines	In Appliance Stores	Mdse. Lines	In FHF Stores
WASHINGTON	1,727,939	1,586,721	310,181	196,109	603,596	286,260	285,032	129,512	176,049	120,120	268,265	95,951	318,565	140,469
TOTAL ABOVE AREAS	1,727,939	1,586,721	310,181	196,109	603,596	286,260	285,032	129,512	176,049	120,120	268,265	95,951	318,565	140,469

[1] Effective Buying Income (EBI) is roughly equivalent to personal disposable income.
[2] Buying Power Index is a weighted index that combines EBI, retail sales and population factors.
Source: *1974 Sales Management Survey of Buying Power*, July 8, 1974, Vol. 113, No. 1, Page C-28. © 1974 Sales Management Survey of Buying Power; further reproduction is forbidden.

real estate field and we have to confirm just about everything a broker says. It seems that every shopping center they point out is always the world's largest and the department stores in the mall have the highest income per square foot in the world, and so on."

There frequently were debates at VSI about the price the company should pay for its land. "A site is worth pretty much what you pay for it," Mr. Bradley noted. "The cheaper sites are usually cheaper for a reason. If we choose a secondary site to save $10,000 a year, our competition may build on the more expensive site. On a long-term basis, when everyone is serving a comparable product, the better sites will prevail."

Physical Property

Victoria Station preferred to construct its own buildings on bare land rather than renovate an existing structure. While it may cost slightly less to renovate, the company believed that it was easier to start from scratch than to attempt to adapt a standing building to VSI's unique design. "You never know what you are going to find inside an old building until you get behind the walls. And then it's too late," Mr. Bradley pointed out.

VSI also prefers to stick with its "prototype" restaurant; that is, a standard design with four boxcars and a caboose joined together in a specific pattern (see Exhibit 5 for a sketch of a typical site plan.) This allows economies in development of architectural plans and helps project a consistent image between Victoria Stations in different locations.

> We don't have much hard data on it, but we think that we are now getting more and more cross-traffic between cities. When a salesman from Atlanta travels to Houston or Dallas, he knows Victoria Station, he knows our price, and our product and he feels comfortable when he brings his clients into our restaurant.

Whenever possible, the company selects sites which offers room to expand both the size of the building and the parking area. The typical Victoria Station has 220 seats; this number could be increased to 295 by the addition of one boxcar and the space between cars.

The minimum site size was roughly 70,000 square feet if the company had to provide adequate parking. The optimal dimensions were 200′ x 350′; however, it was not always possible to find this optimal shape. As a result, VSI generally sought sites in the 75,000–80,000 square foot range. In some cases the required square footage could be reduced markedly if a site was extremely close to someone else's parking, such as a shopping center. VSI had determined that 125 spaces could adequately service a 220-seat unit; this figure assumed approximately 16 spaces for employees during the week and about 30 on the weekends.

One important factor in sizing up a property was the specific access to the site. "If a customer can't turn left into the parking lot and has to go down the street two blocks out of his way, he might just keep on going. That scares us," Mr. Bradley noted. However, the use of traffic counts and similar data were minimized.

Exhibit 5

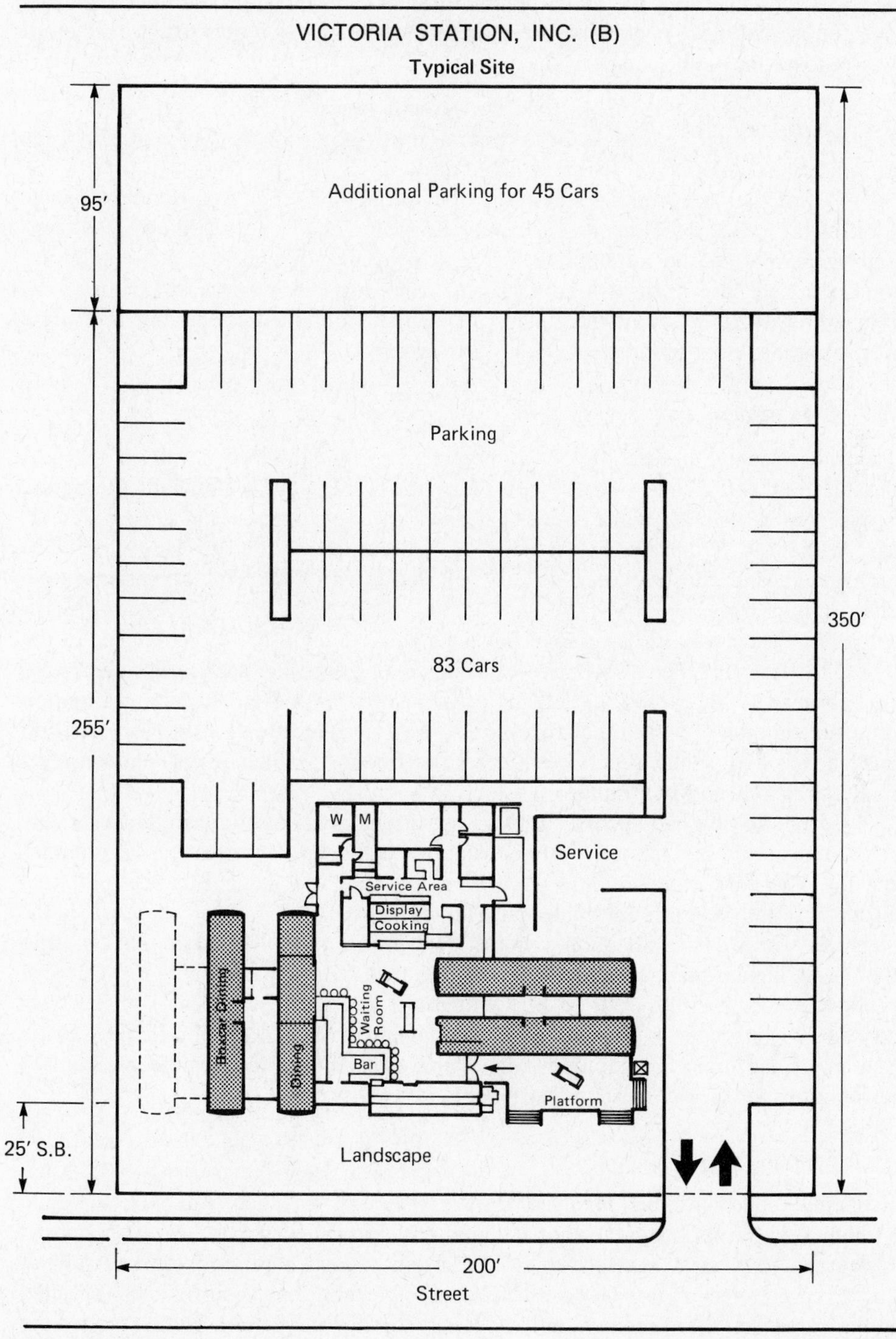
VICTORIA STATION, INC. (B)
Typical Site
Additional Parking for 45 Cars
95′
Parking
83 Cars
350′
255′
W
M
Service Area
Display
Cooking
Service
Boxcar Dining
Dining
Waiting Room
Bar
Platform
25′ S.B.
Landscape
200′
Street

> We don't need high traffic counts. We think that a person chooses Victoria Station ahead of time, not when he or she drives by; a person doesn't pull in on an impulse. What's important is that when a person gets to the restaurant chosen, he or she can park easily.

A location near a railroad siding was not necessary. The company laid the needed tracks itself and trucked the cars in on low-boy trailers. "We don't need the railroad environment," Mr. Bradley noted dryly.

It was the company's policy not to pay money or other considerations in the form of bribes to obtain licenses, permits, or zoning changes. In addition, the company generally did not attempt to rezone a property, though it had from time to time obtained "use" permits and variances from municipal agencies. For example, if an area was zoned for an office park, the company obtained use permits to operate a restaurant and bar in the area.

Organization

The site selection process involved several people at different levels in the VSI organization. Mr. Bradley had responsibility for real estate development. Reporting to him was Wayne H. White, age 36, head of the development and legal divisions. Mr. William T. Wamsley, 28, manager of real estate, reported to Mr. White. The architecture and construction divisions reported to Mr. Freeman (see organization chart Exhibit 6).

Mr. White was VSI's original outside corporate counsel and a member of the board of directors. He also had held the title of corporate secretary since 1969. In February 1974, Mr. White left his private law firm and joined Victoria Station on a full-time basis with the dual responsibility for the real estate development and legal areas. Mr. White supervised an assistant counsel, Glen Jones, and on legal matters reported to Mr. Bradley.

Mr. Wamsley had spent 2½ years in various areas of commercial real estate development and had managed VSI's restaurant in Phoenix for one year before joining the VSI corporate staff in early 1974. He held a B.A. in Finance and Real Estate and an M.A. in International Management. His job involved most of the "legwork" in the site selection process. His predecessor, Mr. Dan Ohlson, who had been higher placed in the VSI organization, left the company for personal reasons several months prior to Mr. Wamsley's joining. It was Mr. Wamsley's responsibility to locate, investigate, and recommend sites to Mr. White and Victoria Station management. In addition, Mr. Wamsley handled much of the preliminary negotiations for the purchase or leasing of land.

Economics

Economic considerations involved in site selection included value of the land (whether leased or bought), annual rental cost, projected volume of the proposed restaurant, renovation costs (if any), construction costs, and VSI's cost of capital.

VSI preferred to lease land whenever possible, and some sites had been rejected in the past when the company could not lease. However, Victoria Station owned the

Exhibit 6

VICTORIA STATION, INC. (B)
Organization—July, 1974

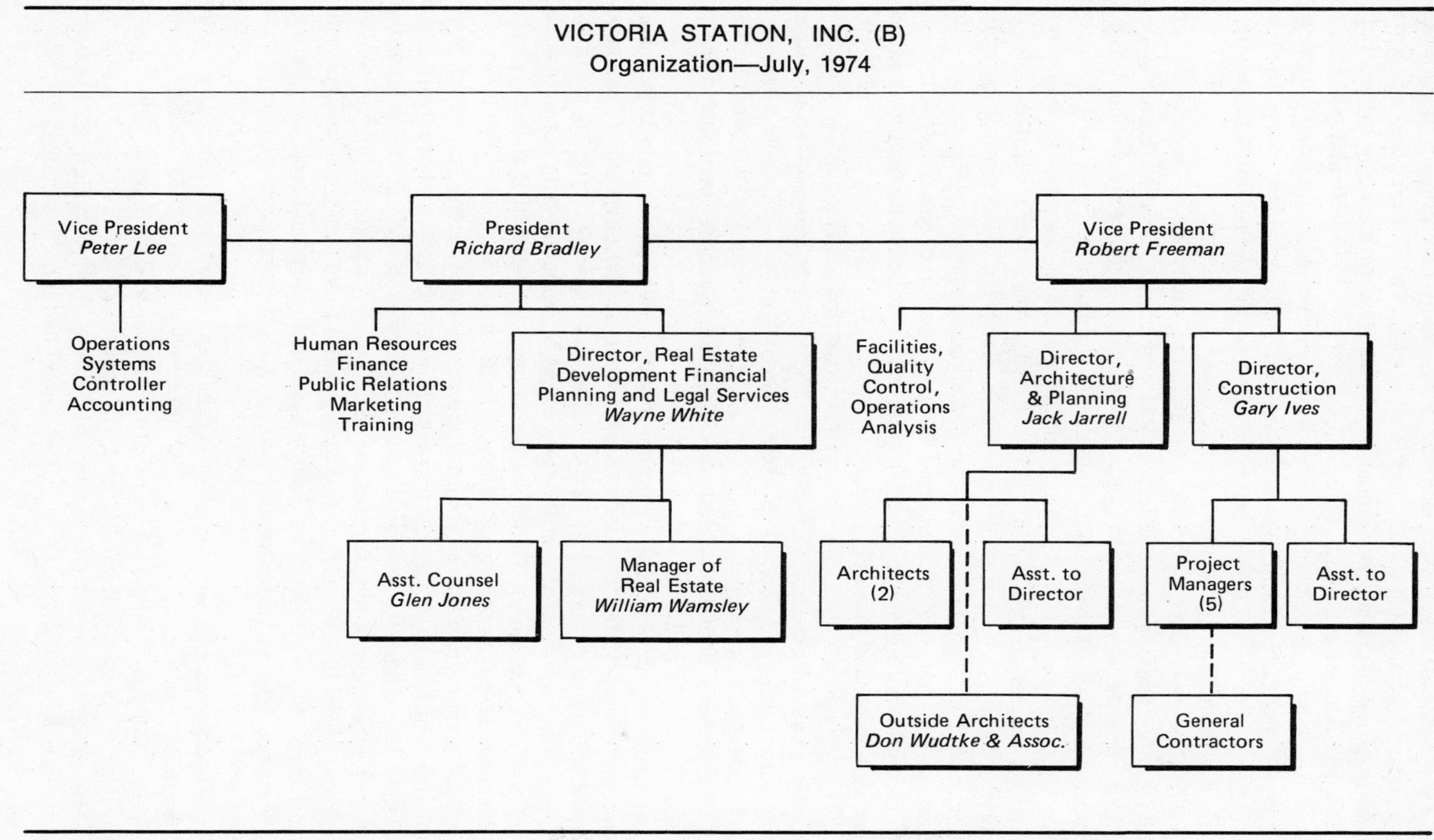

land on which four units were located. Occasionally the company negotiated sale and leaseback arrangements with third parties. The value of property was generally quoted in terms of dollars per square foot and this cost typically ranged between $3 and $5. Annual minimum rents ranged between $15,000 and $35,000 for a normal freestanding site, though some ran higher and in one unusual situation VSI was paying more than $100,000 per year for a building alone. Lease costs varied considerably due to local real estate conditions, the desirability of the land, the length of time the previous owner held title, and other factors.

With the emergence of double-digit inflation, many landlords were demanding some form of escalator clause in leases. VSI preferred a "straight" lease or one with flat dollar rent increase every five or more years, but had executed some leases with a percentage "cost of living" adjustment. The company had executed a number of leases with a minimum rent and an additional rental based on a percentage of annual gross sales (e.g., $25,000 or 2% of sales, whichever is greater). Mr. White explained, "you get cooperation from the landlord. He looks upon it as partly his business, and he's going to do all he can to maximize sales, talk it up with his friends, give us help with the city and he won't interfere with construction. It may cost us a little more in the long run, but the fact that he is on our team and helping us is a very important factor."

By the summer of 1974, construction cost for a prototype Victoria Station generally averaged between $600,000 and $650,000. If VSI decided to add a fifth car, the cost of the addition would average about $60,000. If the site were occupied by a building to be modified and renovated to resemble a Victoria Station, the cost could range from $150,000–$200,000 to as high as 10% more than the cost of constructing a new building.

Estimating the projected volume of a planned Victoria Station involved a subjective evaluation of the proposed market area. A thorough study was normally undertaken by one or more VSI executives to determine as closely as possible both the total eating-out market and the sales levels of competitors in the area (see Site Selection Process, below). Generally the company preferred that the typical $1.4 million volume be apparently available. The minimal acceptable projected volume of a new restaurant was one million dollars. Breakeven was projected at about $700,000; VSI had units whose sales ranged from $900,000 to more than $2 million annually. The company generated rough proformas based on the sales estimate; however, since the firm felt that the cost structure of Victoria Station was well established and varied little from restaurant to restaurant, the proformas were not utilized extensively in site determination. Sales volume and occupancy costs were seen as the key variables (see Victoria Station, Inc. [A]) for a breakdown of restaurant operating costs).

All projected expenses were factored into an overall "occupancy cost" estimate to determine whether or not the deal appeared attractive. VSI normally set the allowable occupancy cost at 6% of projected sales. This figure included ground rent (if any), cost of capital for land (if applicable) and for the building, taxes, etc. For example, a store with an annual volume of $1.4 million, $25,000 annual rent, $5,000 in taxes, and a 10% cost of capital had a 6.4% occupancy cost. "We'd be willing to pay a little more ground rent," Mr. Bradley had noted, "if we really felt that the site was good for \$1.6 million or \$1.7 million a year."

Other Considerations

When signing leases, Victoria Station always included the stipulation that the finalization of the lease was subject to obtaining regulatory and other approvals needed to commence operations. The reason for this was that there were many potential difficulties that could prevent operation once a building is in place. A large number of these potential difficulties were surmountable; however, some precluded consideration of a site.

Liquor licensing. A license to serve distilled spirits was a prerequisite for any site. However, laws and regulations governing alcohol varied from state to state, county to county, and municipality to municipality. The company always attempted to obtain a locally based lawyer experienced in liquor licensing. "This is usually a specialized breed," Mr. Bradley explained. (VSI also employed a local attorney for real estate matters). Local counsel was necessary since conditions such as zoning restrictions and license moratoriums varied widely depending on locale. For example, Utah was a "club state"; that is, a small "state store" was required in every establishment and a customer had to buy his or her liquor from it. Virginia and Maryland prohibited stand-up bars, so patrons had to sit while they drank. Maryland required that dinner be available at cocktail tables. In Birmingham, Alabama (where VSI was constructing a new Station), a bar was required to serve liquor in "miniatures" —the little bottles commonly served on airlines.

The cost of liquor licenses varied from area to area. Some licenses could be obtained for virtually nothing; some cost as much as \$150,000 in certain fast growing areas. The average cost in the Washington, D.C., metropolitan area in 1974, however, was only about \$2,000. VSI had paid as much as \$70,000.

Building restrictions. As liquor licensing requirements varied, so too did building requirements. For example, in addition to the myriad of building codes there were fire zones, with the maximum fire zone usually in the center of downtown with lesser ones spreading out radially. Different types of construction were required for different zones; for example, cement block was often needed in maximum zones while wood frame was acceptable in others. Setback requirements posed other problems: A site with perfect dimensions might be troublesome if local codes required a 30-foot setback.

Building code interpretations were a problem for VSI. "We have found that with the environmental considerations and pollution control regulations, interpretation of the codes becomes a serious hassle," Mr. Bradley said. Working through municipal government agencies posed a major time problem if not planned correctly. In Boston, for example, VSI experienced almost a year delay because the waterfront property required a use permit—which was normally granted—but there was a seven month waiting list to go before the appeals board and argue the company's case.

Before VSI signed a lease for a piece of property, it had a title search conducted to ascertain the status of the land. This was customary on most real estate transactions, though VSI had once been roasted when a person leased VSI some land on the assumption that a third party—unknown to VSI—would lease it to him. After the lease was signed, VSI's lessor's end of the deal fell through. VSI was suing its "lessor" and the real estate broker involved for damages.

Architectural considerations. Often plans were submitted to an architectural review board, and there were a few communities which would not allow a Victoria Station-type building to be built. Any restaurant that VSI wanted to build in these areas would necessitate either extensive design changes or the construction of the restaurant within an existing structure.

Building and sewer moratoriums. Due to overbuilding and local political factors, a growing number of municipalities had placed a temporary moratorium on both new building construction and new sewer hookups. This was a particular problem in the Washington area market, for both Maryland and Virginia had sewer bans in force so the company had to be careful to pick a site with either a sewer hookup in place or one for which the owner had been granted a permit to install a hookup before the moratorium. (Several suits had been filed by others challenging both bans; rulings were expected in the next few months.)

One possible alternative open to Victoria Station in the face of sewer bans in the Washington area was the use of septic tanks, though this action had had both plusses and minuses in the past for VSI. Some installations had performed admirably; some had not. In other instances the company was precluded by local regulations from utilizing septic tanks. For example, in Montgomery County, Maryland, an unpaved leach field of more than 130,000 square feet would be required to handle the effluent of a typical Victoria Station.

Site Selection Process

Once VSI determined that a particular city suitably fit its site and growth objectives, Mr. Wamsley usually went to the city in search of a specific site. The company received approximately 50 site proposals a week from all over the country, most of which "don't bear a second look." However, the submissions occasionally produced sites worth examining, and VSI kept on file all site proposals of adequate size in areas of 200,000 population and over. When a new city was to be examined the files were checked for any worthwhile sites.

Normally three trips to an area were taken before a final decision was made on a site: one during the middle of a week, one early in a week, and one on a weekend, to gauge business at those different times. On his first trip Mr. Wamsley generally visited 10 to 20 sites; he scheduled a second trip about one month after the first unless there was unusual pressure for a quick decision. On the second trip Mr. Wamsley or another staff member returned to look at the most promising sites and to examine more specific site characteristics. On the third trip, a top management person made an independent evaluation of the leading sites.

On his first trip to a city, Mr. Wamsley normally spent at least one day driving the area by himself to "try to get a feeling for the town." Next Mr. Wamsley called on VSI contacts (often from the VSI files), including brokers, developers, or owners, and arranged to spend time with four or five of them examining potential sites. "If private individuals rather than brokers have a site, I always try to contact them" Mr. Wamsley noted.

> A private individual offers a different viewpoint on the marketplace than a broker—a layman's viewpoint. He can offer a much better idea of what I'm after. After all, we sell a hell of a lot more prime rib to laymen than to brokers. In any case, if you ask about eight different people around town about high-income areas, schools, offices, and such, you get a pretty good feeling for the town.

Mr. Wamsley was usually able to obtain from brokers data which allowed him to check his more subjective findings, such as census studies of the area, number of high-rise buildings, number of office workers, and commuting patterns. During his three or four days in an area, Mr. Wamsley spent lunch time and evenings scouting the local competition. It was not unusual for Mr. Wamsley (and Mr. White on occasion) to visit 15 restaurants and bars in one evening. By talking to waiters, bartenders, waitresses, and owners, quite reliable data on competitors was obtained, including sales estimates, meal counts, capacity, peak and slack periods, and nature of the clientele. Mr. Wamsley explained:

> We're always looking for a site that will do more than $1.4 million. You drive yourself crazy trying to think of reasons why a site is going to do better than $1.4 million, and a large part of it is just gut feel—but educated gut feel. In Tyson's Corner, for example, Marriott's 250-seat Joshua Tree opened at 5 P.M., and at 5:10 there was a wait. When we left, the girl was quoting two to two-and-a-half hour wait, and in Maryland it's against the law to have a stand-up bar. If people will wait for 2½ hours without a drink, that really tells you a lot about the market. The cars in the parking lot included many new Porsches and Mercedes, which tells you a lot more than you learn poring over the census statistics measuring median income and white collar population.
>
> Still, this volume consideration is very uncertain. I think we could put in a five-car store in Gaithersburg, just on the sheer numbers of people, the lack of good restaurants and such, but not everyone here agrees. We have a five-car store in Boston and are adding a fifth car in Kansas City.

One site criterion was the proximity to the "dinner market"—a large population base that can afford to and does go out to dinner fairly regularly. "Our success is an appeal to a casual, upper-middle income crowd," Mr. Wamsley explained.

> They are the type of people where one spouse will come home and say, "Gee, honey, I had a tough day at the office. Let's go out to dinner," and the other

will say, "so did I. Let's get a sitter." It's a snap decision like that they don't want to get all dressed up and go back downtown for formal dining at the Rive Gauche. They're just going to dress casually, hit Victoria Station for a little prime rib and head home. That's it. That's one secret to our success.

Because this dinner trade has to be available during the early part of the week, both income level and actual size of the population are important; this was the reason VSI generally stuck to markets of over 1 million people.

Lunch Potential

In addition to dinner business, VSI looked for substantial nearby lunch potential. "It is a common tale," Mr. Wamsley explains, "for someone to come to a Victoria Station, discover a 30-minute wait and think, 'I only have an hour and a half for lunch, I have to spend 30 minutes getting here and driving back with a wait of 30 minutes that leaves a half hour for lunch. Sorry, I don't want to be rushed so I'll go somewhere else.' "

The lunch potential, Mr. Wamsley stressed, came primarily from white-collar office workers. Mr. Bradley added:

> Lunch business is important to us for a couple of reasons. First, once you build a restaurant it's like an airplane—you might as well use it. Lunch helps pay the heat, light, and power. Second, we view lunch as a marketing tool. If we get 300 people a day in for lunch during the week, that's 1,500 people who might come back for dinner. Still, we don't sacrifice our dinner business in order to improve lunch. In certain cities, people don't do back downtown for dinner. We won't locate downtown in those cities to maximize lunch at the expense of cutting off our dinner business.

One measure of lunch potential was the square footage of office space in office parks or in downtown commercial centers within a ten minute drive (a radius of about five miles from a site). This data was normally obtainable from real estate organizations such as the Society of Industrial Realtors (*SIR*). Within five miles of the Gaithersburg, Md. site, for example, Mr. Wamsley determined approximately 6 million square feet of office space existed.

Mr. Wamsley explained the next step in the process:

> After you've looked at all these factors for a few days, that's when the gut feel really starts to take effect. I've worked in a lot of restaurants and I have a pretty good idea what makes a good site. Victoria Station, with its strong product, unique physical plant, good value for the money, accessible location, and availability of parking will attract its share of the existing eating-out customers.

Detail Evaluation

After Mr. Wamsley's "gut feel" argued eloquently that a particular area was the right one for a Victoria Station, the evaluation of sites was focused on more specific criteria. For example, the ease of access was often critical, Mr. Wamsley explained.

> We have a problem in Phoenix. We are located just off a major artery, with three lanes going down to two just after a light. Right where the jamming starts to take place is where the entrance to the Station is. The older people there are a bit fearful of getting rear-ended. It's a negative factor when they are deciding to go out to dinner and they subconsciously think, "I was really scared the last time I tried to turn into Victoria Station's parking lot because a pickup truck almost ran over me."

Prior to a second visit, Mr. Wamsley usually called the brokers having sites in which he had an interest and asked them to consult all regulatory agencies with whom a potential lessee or buyer might have to deal. VSI gave the broker an agency form to complete and mail back to VSI so VSI could do its own checking as well. (The broker was originally responsible for checking items such as sewer capacity, utility availability, planning commission attitudes about a boxcar restaurant, general topography, etc., but after a number of difficulties, VSI felt it best to do its own checking on these matters.) In addition to this form, Mr. Wamsley filled out an information sheet of his own (see Exhibit 7).

Whenever Mr. Wamsley returned from a trip, he met with Mr. White or sometimes with Mr. White and Mr. Bradley to discuss sites under consideration. These meetings often lasted several hours. Before any offer was extended, one of the three founders tried to visit the site to add another informed opinion. In addition to these meetings the firm held weekly real estate meetings to discuss all factors pertaining to VSI's real estate situation. Excerpts from the minutes of one of these meetings is reproduced in Exhibit 8.

Once a site was selected, Mr. Wamsley usually wrote to the broker or owner involved initiating a nonbinding solicitation to buy or lease and inquiring whether the party was interested. Following a series of letters and phone calls, the broker (or owner) and Mr. Wamsley usually agreed on general terms. Then, Mr. Wamsley normally sent out a lease or purchase contract for review. At this point in the process Mr. White usually commissioned the architecture department to solicit bids for soil testing and surveying from local engineers. When it appeared fairly certain that a deal would be made, VSI gave the go-ahead for the survey and soil tests. "This is probably betting $1,500 to $2,000 on the site in advance," Mr. White noted, "but we pick it up tenfold on the other end because of the time factor. If we wait until the deal is closed, we will probably lose a month's to six weeks' profit."

Design and Construction

As soon as the surveys were completed (or close to completion) a title search was initiated and an investigation of easements, encumbrances and other factors was undertaken. When the deal was finalized, VSI's director of Architecture and Planning, John H. (Jack) Jarrell, assigned VSI's outside architectural firm, Don Wudtke & Associates, to begin code research—the investigation of building and municipal codes—and to prepare the detailed site plan. "By this time the deal is signed," Mr.

Exhibit 7

VICTORIA STATION, INC. (B)
Site Information Sheet

City: GAITHERSBURG

County: MONTGOMERY Date: 4-20-74

State: MARYLAND

Location: Street Md 355 Cross Street N. WESTLAND

Broker: JON SWINDLE Address 4400 JENIFER ST NW
LAND LTD. OF AMERICA WASHINGTON DC

Owner: JOE BERLIN Address ______

Recorded: Yes ___ No ___ Where ______

Number of Parcels: ONE Area 89,911 Sq. Ft.

Dimensions: 184 × 484 - IRREGULAR

Asking Price: Sale 446,000 Lease 45,000

Adjoining Property: SHELL SERVICE STATION TO SOUTH
CHURCH TO WEST ACROSS STREET
OFFICE BUILDING UNDER CONST. TO NORTH

Access: DIRECT FROM Md 355

Zoning: Current Zoning: C-2

Governing Agency CITY OF GAITHERSBURG PLANNING COMMISSION

Building Code Used: BOCA X UBC ___ So. B.C. ___ NBC ___ Other ___

Set Backs: Front NONE Rear NONE Side NONE Other ___

Zoning Ordinance: Requested YES Map NO

Fire Zone: NO

Parking Requirements: 1 SP/150 SQ. FT. OF BUILDING

Boundary Survey Available YES Topo YES

Topography: Flat (X) Low ( ) Rolling ( ) Wooded ( )

Exhibit 7 (continued)

Victoria Station, Incorporated – Site Information Page 2

City Water: Available? Yes (X) No ( ) Size of pipe 16"

Location FRONT OF SITE

Distance from site ON SITE

Storm Sewer: Available? Yes (X) No ( ) Size ______

Location FRONT OF SITE

Gas: Available? Yes (X) No ( ) Propane/LPG ( ) Natural (X)

Location FRONT OF SITE

Size of line 8" Distance from site ______

Fire Hydrants: Yes ( ) No (X) Distance from site ______

Key Contacts: ______

______

Information Gathered by: ______

General Comments WIDENING OF Md 355 TO OCCUR IN 1975; CROSSOVER PARKING WITH OFFICE BLDG. TBB TO NORTH MEANS NO PARKING PROBLEM – BERLIN TO OBTAIN SEWER HOOKUP AS CONDITION OF PURCHASE – OWNER WILL GO $420,000 ON 79,911 SQ. FT.

Attachments:

Survey: ______

Plat: ✓

Photographs: ✓

Exhibit 8

VICTORIA STATION, INC. (B)
Excerpts From Departmental Report, June 12, 1974

On Tuesday, June 11, 1974, the combined Architectural Legal and Real Estate meeting was held by and among Jack Jarrell, Brian Smith, Glen Jones, Bill Wamsley and Wayne White. The results of the meeting are as follows:

A. *Architectural*

1. The architectural status sheet sent weekly by Don Wudtke & Associates to Jack has been revised to more fully explain problem areas with respect to each site for which drawings are being prepared. This project status report shows the activities of the architects and ourselves from the time the project is delivered to them until the drawings are completed.
7. Villa Park, Illinois—Plans are progressing. The holdup in part has been due to a dispute between the Fire Marshall and the Building Commissioner concerning the use of natural gas and LPG. We are also awaiting word concerning the availability of the liquor license.
8. The plans are dragging with respect to Montreal, allegedly because of a code interpretation the Building Commissioner has as to the classification of our building and also the fact that the Montreal building code is being rewritten.
11. With respect to Pittsburgh, Pennsylvania, we are awaiting the survey and soils report. A preliminary site plan has been forwarded to Planning Directors and we are awaiting comment. There is a local requirement for brick on all commercial buildings and it will probably be necessary to obtain a variance in connection therewith.

B. *Legal*

The transfer of the liquor license in New Orleans in the name of Mark Covert should now be completed. The shareholders of the subsidiary corporation had to consent to the transfer which held it up for some period of time.

C. *Real Estate*

Various sites were discussed and the following decisions made subject to final review by Bob Freeman:

4. All of the problems with respect to the Cumberland site in Atlanta, Georgia have been resolved with the exception of revising the agreement concerning the utility sizing and storm drains. WHW will contact the developer concerning the storm drain requirements.
9. Long Island, New York—The site proposed has been rejected. Continued investigation of this area will be made.
14. Hartford, Connecticut—Neither BW or WHW feels that there is an adequate market in Hartford except possibly a downtown location. Downtown property is not readily available at the right price and a further market survey and study of this entire area must be made before any action is taken.

D. *General*

The following general decisions were made concerning future site selection:

1. Additional time will be spent by Bill W. in each city or area to obtain more in-depth market information; particularly with respect to real estate value and business being done by other restaurants. Bill W is coordinating with Tom Blake to develop reasons

Exhibit 8 (continued)

why certain of our units are successful in some areas and not in others even though the demographics seem to be the same in each instance.

2. The Architectural/Construction departments will endeavor to develop a historical problem list for the benefit of Bill W. so that additional information can be obtained at the front end concerning the site which may cut down on the surprises once the site has been developed.
3. A revised priority list of cities will be developed within the next few weeks, particularly as it relates to second site locations, winter-building problems and property values.

White explained, "We're not going to start the expensive meters ticking until we know we have a firm deal."

Architectural costs for code research and drawings averaged $15,000 for a typical Victoria Station. The work usually took six weeks, a time span which Mr. White hoped to shorten.

On occasion, VSI faced zoning or variance problems which held up architectural work until the matter was settled. In some cases, the company had gone ahead with the architectural work despite a potential problem. "We went ahead in Southfield, Michigan, because it looked so good. We took a chance, asked for a hearing, and won," Mr. White explained.

VSI employed its own staff of two architects, but still contracted much of the work to Wudtke. The company maintained "prototype" sets of drawings—right and left versions of both a large and a small-sized unit—which helped hold down architectural costs.

After the plans for the restaurant were submitted to the appropriate municipal authorities for approval and any necessary corrections were performed, the Director of Construction, Gary R. Ives, solicited bids from contractors for construction. Mr. Ives was kept advised on site status through the weekly staff meetings. When a contractor was picked to build the building, a VSI project manager was assigned to see the unit through to completion.

VSI historically worked with a small number of contractors. A Florida contractor, the First Florida Corporation, had built ten units for VSI, and also had built units for Burger King, Holiday Inns, and other service firms. Two or three contractors had also built units for VSI, including a San Francisco-based company which had done all of the Northern California units and most of the West Coast units. The use of a previously-utilized contractor as opposed to soliciting bids from local contractors depended on several factors including the familiarity of the contractor with local building conditions, distance from the contractor's home base, local political considerations, and others. A local contractor was used in Boston and in Darien, Connecticut. "I'd like to broaden our contractor base," Mr. White mentioned. "But, unfortunately, whenever contractors look at boxcars and what has to be done they think it is the Taj Mahal and they highball a bid. We've had a whole pattern of bids coming in at $150,000 over those submitted by the firms we normally work with."

If it was expected that VSI would be working with a known contractor at a given site, the contractor was periodically advised of the site status. When the deal appeared firm the contractor was to line up subcontractors to cut down on lead time.

VSI assumed a 12-month time frame from the initial investigation to the site opening. Mr. White noted that the company was attempting to reduce this period to nine or ten months. VSI had shortened the actual construction period since it first began in 1969 to around 120 working days, or about 4½ to 5 months including weekends and holidays. The major delays usually occurred on the "front end"—obtaining approvals through city or town agencies, environmental impact problems, zoning and variance questions, and so forth.

Negotiation Strategy

Mr. White handled approximately 95% of lease and purchase negotiations, though Mr. Wamsley played a key role in preliminary negotiations and VSI's assistant counsel, Glen Jones, assisted Mr. White. Victoria Station always negotiated a six–nine month rent-free period that began the date the lease was signed. This allowed the company to pursue liquor requirements, perform code research, and check other problems to insure that a prototype Victoria Station could be built on the property in question. The lease was always conditional upon Victoria Station's ability to open and operate the restaurant. Sometimes terms called for rent to begin accruing as construction commenced, but to be deferred until actual operations began.

Generally the time between preliminary agreements to final signing was four to six weeks. As Mr. White (himself an attorney) explained:

> We know that when the lawyers get involved, it can drag on for weeks. I do not try to write a one-sided lease. I go down the middle on those items I don't consider terribly important because I don't want to get bogged down negotiating those things. Why should I waste the time? Nothing is more infuriating than to have an attorney negotiating those points which are irrelevant and immaterial. Ninety percent of the changes made by attorneys are cosmetic changes—ego builders, if you will—attorneys trying to earn their fees. Often all they do is hold up a good deal for both parties.

Mr. White did not advertise the fact that he was an attorney when dealing with brokers or owners. "My title is Director of Development," he explained, "for two reasons. One, many people simply don't like dealing with an attorney. Two, if they don't know my background, so much the better—I have a leg up on them."

As did many involved in the real estate business, Victoria Station utilized several negotiating tactics to improve its position. One was the "good guy/bad guy" approach. Mr. Wamsley did most of the site research, checked economics, and submitted a recommendation to Mr. White on how he felt on certain points and noted the points that he had suggested to the broker or owner. Mr. White explained:

> Bill can be the good guy in the field and hold the hand of the sellers and brokers, but the ultimate responsibility for the site recommendation is mine. I have spent many years looking at the economics of real estate and I look

> at what I have and make my recommendation to the directors or the staff. We had a situation recently where a fellow called up and said, "Bill Wamsley said such and such." I said, "Well, you have to remember that Bill works for me and I say no, so if you want to make a deal, you come on our basis or don't come at all."

Added to this had sometimes been an attempt to develop some auction action between prospective sites. "I'll get on the phone with a couple of brokers," Mr. Wamsley explained, "and tell them something has altered our thoughts on a site and say 'How much will your guy go for?' "

> He'll say $20,000 and I'll say "my guy will go for $16,000; do you think you can get your guy down a bit? We really like your site better than the other ones we're looking at, but site B is going for $16,000 and site A for $17,000." You've got to be willing to squeeze these guys a little bit—and they expect it. It's a little tough for me because often the brokers are about my age and after a while we are friends. That's when I have to say, "It's not me, it's Wayne." You've got to have somebody to put the blame on even if you are the one making the decision. But in any case, whenever you are negotiating, you have to have done your homework—it pays off. In Pittsburgh we once got a quote of $5.75 a square foot. That was the best the broker could do; that's what it was going to be. After a few phone calls, we found that that just wasn't true. We went down the road a mile and found a site for $3.75 a foot. On an 80,000 square foot property, that's a big difference.
>
> Also, I always think it's a good negotiating tactic not to slobber all over a certain site right in the guy's arms. You just know that he's going to go back and say, "I've got these pigeons on the hook and we can throw $30,000 at them and they'll take it." All the time we could have thrown $20,000 at the broker and he would have jumped at the privilege. So I usually make our initial offer from San Francisco after I have done some checking around on prices.

Washington Sites

The five sites under consideration in the Washington, D.C., area posed a difficult decision for Victoria Station management because none possessed clearcut advantages over the others. A brief description of each site and its attendant positive and negative points is presented below. (Refer to Exhibit 9 for demographic data on the areas and to Exhibit 10 for individual site characteristics.)

Springfield, Virginia

There were two sites in Springfield under consideration, one almost directly across the street from the other. The location of Springfield Number 1 was directly adjacent to a new large (1 million square feet) shopping mall with Sears and two larger department stores as tenants. Visibility and general access to the site were

Exhibit 9

VICTORIA STATION, INC. (B)
Demographic Data (1970) [1]

Site	Population	Population Change 1960–1970	Density—Persons Per Square Mile	Medium Family Income	Percent of Families Over $15,000	Percent of Persons 25 Years & Older Who Completed 4 Yrs. High School or More	Percent of Total Persons 16 Yrs. & Older Employed[3] Who Are: Male				Housing: Percent Owner-Occupied Housing Units	Percent Vacancy Factor: Owner-Occupied	
							Male	Female	In Professional, Technical or Managerial Jobs	Percent Civilian Labor Force Unemployed		Owner-Occupied	Rental
Washington, D.C. Md., Va. SMSA[2]	2,861,102	37.8%	1,216	$12,933	39.6%	68.5%	57.4%	42.6%	35.2%	2.7%	46.0%	1.4%	4.4%
Washington, D.C.	756,510	−1.0	12,321	9,583	25.1	55.2	51.2	48.8	25.7	3.8	28.2	1.2	5.3
Gaithersburg, Md.	8,344	116.9	1,227	12,378	34.2	69.5	62.2	37.8	37.7	0.9	27.0	2.3	11.4
Rockville, Md.	41,564	59.3	3,711	14,252	45.5	73.1	61.6	38.4	37.9	2.2	59.5	1.0	2.4
Alexandria, Va.	110,938	21.9	7,396	11,474	33.0	69.2	53.3	46.7	34.9	2.0	26.0	1.4	4.2
Arlington, Va.	174,284	N.A.	6,703	13,743	44.1	77.6	51.4	48.6	40.5	2.3	33.5	0.5	2.4
Fairfax, Va.	21,970	61.7	3,662	14,537	47.4	76.6	60.5	39.5	37.7	3.0	59.3	1.1	2.6
Springfield, Va.	11,613	7.7	3,056	15,701	52.9	81.4	62.5	37.5	43.5	2.4	72.1	0.3	1.8
Vienna, Va.	17,152	49.9	3,898	16,048	54.2	80.0	63.1	36.9	59.6	1.5	81.4	0.6	1.9

[1] Population Data Source: 1970 Census of the Population: Characteristics of the Population, Vol. 1, Part 1: United States Summary; Part 10: District of Columbia; Part 22: Maryland; Part 48: Virginia.

Housing Data Source: 1970 Census of Housing; Part 10: District of Columbia; Part 22: Maryland; Part 48: Virginia.

[2] SMSA = Standard Metropolitan Statistical Area includes: Montgomery Cty, Md.; Prince Georges Cty., Md.; Washington, D.C.; Fairfax Cty, Va.; Loudoun Cty, Va.; Prince William Cty, Va.

[3] Total employed—16 Yrs. and older varies between 40% and 50% of the total population.

Exhibit 10

VICTORIA STATION, INC. (B)
Washington Site Characteristics

Characteristic	*Springfield #1*	*Springfield #2*	*Tyson's Corner*	*Alexandria*	*Gaithersburg*
Size—Sq. Ft.	36,000	60,000	49,310	8,000[a]	89,111 (79,111)[b]
Approx. Dimensions	90′ x 400′/ 180′ x 200′	Irregular[c] 200′ x 350′	205′ x 240′	—	Irregular[c] 184′ x 484′
Sale Price	N.A.	$300,000	N.A.	N.A.	$420,000
Annual Lease Cost	$27,000	$30,000	$25,000	$42,000–$52,000	50 (45)
Sq. Ft. of Office Space Within 5 Mile Radius	1 million ±	1 million ±	3 million ±	4 million ±	6 million ±
Number of Shopping Centers Within 5 Mile Radius/Sq. Ft. of Space	One/1 Million	One/1 Million	Two/1.7 Million	One/.7 Million	One (Under Const.)/ 1.6 Million
Cost of Liquor License	2,000	2,000	2,000	2,000	1,000
Sewer or Plumbing Permit?	Not Currently Available	Not Currently Available	Not Currently Available	Yes	Yes
New Building Permits?	Uncertain—Suits Pending	Uncertain—Suits Pending	Uncertain–Suits Pending	Not Needed	Yes
Parking	Unlimited	80–85	65	130	120
Specific Problems	Requires Pipe Relocation & Paving—$15,000 Long Narrow Parcel—will Landlord trade?	Requires Leveling $15,000. Specific access restricted.	Must wait until sewer ban lifted to build. Not enough parking to satisfy normally, but City is satisfied.	Renovation cost $150–$200,000.	Odd shape—narrow lot.

[a] Building only (one of three floors).
[b] Numbers in parentheses indicate characteristics of alternative proposal by owner.
[c] Odd shape; dimensions approximate only.

considered good due to its proximity to Interstate Route 95 (at the Virginia Route 644 exit). It was less than one mile from the interchange of I-95 and I-495 (the Capitol Beltway) and was within approximately 25 minutes of downtown Washington and 5–10 minutes of Alexandria. Specific access to the site was considered excellent as the site could utilize the mall's entrance roads, which had been well laid out. The mall provided virtually unlimited parking for customers and, therefore, did not require that VSI plan for parking spaces on its property.

The dimensions of the site caused some concern, as the available parcel had been 90′ x 400′, a rather long, narrow piece of land that could not accommodate a prototype restaurant. However, since the land was an end strip of the parking area, it was felt that the mall owner would be willing to trade sections so Victoria Station could purchase a site with dimensions of approximately 180′ x 200′, thereby leaving the mall with the same amount of parking spaces it would have if the long narrow parcel were sold. The annual lease cost for the 90 x 400 plot had been $27,000, but it was thought that a higher price would be required if a land swap were to take place.

In addition to this problem, office park density in the area was relatively low, suggesting the possibility of a lower-than-desired lunch volume despite the shopping crowd at the mall. Dinner volume was projected at close to the desired amount, though lower than some of the other sites under consideration, due to a slightly lower population density. Initial building costs were anticipated as slightly higher than normal (by about $15,000), due to the fact that some pipes would have to be rerouted and the parking lot paved if the site dimensions were altered.

Springfield Number 2 was located in the same vicinity as Springfield Number 1 but behind some buildings. It boasted the same adequate general accessibility as did 1, though specific access was more limited. Because of the surrounding buildings the visibility factor had not been considered quite as high as that of 1. The parcel in question also suffered some topography problems, as it sloped sharply at the rear and would require about "$15,000 in bulldozer time" to level it. Though luncheon business was expected to be low for the same reasons as 1, dinner volume was expected to be as good. The site was 60,000 square feet in area and the asking price was $5/square foot; the annual lease cost was $30,000.

Tyson's Corner, Virginia

The Tyson's Corner site was located near the interchange of I-495 and Virginia Route 7 near Vienna, roughly equidistant from Fairfax, Arlington, and McLean. The proximity to a number of major arteries afforded excellent general access and visibility. Specific access had been considered good as the site was located on Route 7, a six-lane divided highway with turn-throughs every eighth of a mile. The site was 49,000 square feet in size and its annual lease cost was $25,000. Mr. Wamsley's predecessor, Mr. Ohlson, had done all the original site evaluation work at Tyson's Corner, and based on his favorable recommendation, Victoria Station had actually signed a lease with the owner in October 1973. Subsequent to the signing, however, Fairfax County had proclaimed its moratorium on all new construction. Since VSI had not been obliged to either pay rent for a specified period nor to honor the lease if construction or operation had been frustrated, no payments to the owner had been made for the first nine months. However, on June 1, 1974, a token $600 payment had been made—not considered rent—to help the owner defray costs of holding the property.

In mid-June 1974, Fairfax County had partially lifted the building ban. According to VSI, it had been felt that the County had reacted to increased pressure from developers who had held sewer permits. The restriction that remained had been that no building could be erected within one mile of a freeway interchange, thereby stymieing VSI.

Mr. White noted that the new restrictions would only be in effect until June 1975 due to local laws and the ban could not be extended after that. Moreover, Mr. White felt quite strongly about the legality of the building moratoriums in the first place.

> I can almost guarantee that the state's whole zoning process is illegal. It is without rhyme or reason the way it is now, and is tantamount to condemnation without compensation. There is a court suit coming up soon (to which we are not a party) in which the judge should decide against the ban on the basis of unequal protection, the fourteenth amendment, and so forth. This suit is trying to kill the whole zoning process in Virginia. It questions (a) whether a building moratorium can be imposed at all and (b) whether it is being imposed in a discriminatory fashion. The alleged reason that our site wasn't released was that it was within one mile of a freeway interchange and the county wanted to reserve their options for future development. If that is really the reason, then we might as well can the site because we are never going to be any further away. If they want to have it for a freeway, take it and do it. They have effectively condemned the owner's property as it stands now; it's commercial property that no one can build on, yet they haven't paid him for it. But in any case, with the ban scheduled to go off in June 1975, we could build then if we want to wait.

In addition to the suit filed with regard to the building moratorium, Mr. White had noted that there had been one or more suits filed in Maryland and the District of Columbia challenging the sewer ban.

There had been one bright spot with regards to Tyson's Corner. The owner of the Tyson's property had some property in Alexandria in which he had been trying to get VSI interested. The property consisted of a large three-story building near the Potomac River on what was considered by VSI management to be a particularly good site. According to Mr. Wamsley, VSI was seriously considering "putting Tyson's Corner into hibernation for a year and moving into Alexandria in the meantime."

Alexandria, Virginia

The Alexandria building, owned by the principal of the Tyson's Corner site, posed both an opportunity and a dilemma for VSI. It was a dilemma because the firm under no circumstances could build a prototype Victoria Station on the site; architectural regulations would have required that VSI remodel only the interior of the building. The company had an option of (a) making the interior resemble other Victoria Stations by cutting up boxcars or constructing replicas or (b) building a different theme store such as a Quinn's lighthouse or similar operation on the site. The site provided an opportunity because (a) the site was considered to be excellent on an overall basis and (b) the company had stated a desire to examine other restaurant concepts more thoroughly, to gain more expertise with remodeling of existing structures (especially if it were to build in Europe eventually in existing structures), and to further develop its in-house architectural capabilities.

The site overlooked the Potomac River with a city parking lot of 130 spaces directly across the street and usually empty at night. Since it was an existing building, it already had its own sewer connections. The size and style, according to Mr. Wamsley, resembled that of a building in which a Chart House restaurant or a Rusty Scupper might conceivably be located. The annual rental cost of the 8,000 square foot building was anticipated to be between \$5/square foot and \$6.50/square foot depending on the amount of work required to remodel and renovate. Mr. Wamsley had estimated that VSI would have to spend between \$150,000 and \$200,000 in renovation costs, though the owner had agreed to bear some of the expense. If a nonprototype restaurant were to be constructed, the cost for new architectural drawings might increase this amount by \$15,000. "It is the kind of building and character that we could really do something with," Mr. White mentioned. In addition, Mr. Wamsley noted, due to the Tyson's Corner delay, the owner had been willing to "bend over backwards to get us into the building. For someone else and with another landlord, a building like this might cost \$10 a foot and we would have to do all the work ourselves."

Mr. White, while intrigued with the site, cautioned that "We don't want to start running in the direction of other ideas too quickly."

> I think we should expand our themes—we've all agreed on that. But the expansion of a theme has to be done in an orderly process. Bill and I are currently developing a "white paper" on the orderly progression of our growth, just as the three founders once did. We're not precluding the idea of additional theme restaurants, but we don't want to run in too many directions at once. We only have two guys—three counting Glen Jones—doing real estate, and only five in architecture. Still, if the structural report on Alexandria comes back satisfactorily, either I or someone else can go back for a second look, and we can send Bill back for an additional market look.

Gaithersburg, Maryland

The site in Gaithersburg, Maryland, was an attractive one. It was located on Maryland Route 355, approximately two minutes from I-70 via the Shady Grove Road exit, just northwest of Rockville. This was a 30-minute drive from downtown Washington and, according to Mr. Wamsley, was an area of rapid high-income population growth. "Everywhere you drive in the area you see new \$80,000 town homes going up, big high-class government office buildings—the ones the people making $30,000–$35,000 a year work in. Right now this site is on the outer edge of the growth belt; within three years this will be the center of suburban Montgomery County."

One indicator of the growth potential, according to Mr. Wamsley, was the plan of a large Detroit-based shopping center developer, The Alfred Taubman Company, to put in a large center just northwest of Gaithersburg.

> They are putting in 1.6 million square feet, which is a big center. The fact that a company like Taubman is putting in that much area is a sign that they have done some pretty good research on the area. A big company like Taubman has 40 guys like me who just run around with statistics and computer programs. Lots of heavy analysis. That's an ability that we don't really have, but we can kind of follow along on the coattails of it.

However, a number of negative factors existed in connection with this site. The site itself was 89,111 square feet, a slightly larger plot than VSI desired. In addition, part of the site was steep, which might preclude parking in certain areas. A further problem was that the property was not for lease but for sale, and at the relatively steep price (for a Victoria Station site) of $500,000. It was located on a two-lane road (Route 355) that was expected to be widened to four lanes in the near future. The property had two minor cross-easements that precluded use of a small portion of the land. The shape of the parcel was not optimal, as it was fairly long and narrow. Mr. Wamsley explained:

> A row of parking takes 60 feet of width, so on any site, you end up with some wasted space that you can't use. This one is bad with regard to wasted space.

There were also several positive factors in favor of the site. Importantly, this site had been one of two sites in Montgomery County that VSI had uncovered with a sewer hookup. Sewer permits—called plumbing permits—had been issued to some owners before the sewer ban had gone into effect. In addition, the owner had been extremely friendly and interested in getting Victoria onto the site. He had agreed to assist in getting all of the necessary approvals from the various municipal agencies. He had further offered to compromise on the purchase price: if VSI had agreed to give him 10,000 square feet of the parcel on which to erect a storage warehouse, he had agreed to sell the property for $420,000 or $5.30 a square foot. Comparable prices in the area, Mr. Wamsley had noted, were often $6.50 and $7 per foot.

The site had excellent general and specific accessibility, according to Mr. Wamsley. There were two ways commuters from Gaithersburg traveled to Washington—one via I-495 and I-70 and the other via Route 355. "The market is there," Mr. Wamsley continued, "and there is literally no decent place to eat in the area as a result of the sewer bans. No one is building restaurants there." There was a Phineas Rib and a Steak and Ale located southeast of Rockville on Route 355, but few others were to be found.

The major problems, as far as VSI was concerned, were the high price (compared to what the company was used to paying for ground rent) and the method of financing. "Taking a $420,000 chunk out of your line of credit doesn't really feel good," Mr. Wamsley had noted. As it happened, about the time the site came up for consideration, VSI's lessor in St. Louis called to ask if there were other properties the company would like to lease, or have him buy and lease back. "His banker is an old Cornell buddy of Bradley's and has been giving him the hard sell on us," Mr. Wamsley explained. "His banker apparently is willing to loan him a fair amount of money, so when he called up I told him about the plot in Gaithersburg and told him that it was $420,000 and we wouldn't pay more than $42,000 ground rent. He sounded interested and said he would get back to me on it." Mr. White felt $42,000 a year a bit steep and favored a lower price or a percent-of-sales rental arrangement, but Mr. Wamsley disagreed. "Forty-two thousand is a lot of money to pay for a ground lease. But I know the market is there. I am certain, in fact, that we should put in a five-car unit. It would gross $2.5 million for sure. If it didn't do $2.5 million, I'd quit."

This was the situation that Victoria Station management faced in the summer of 1974. Since the company's rapid growth created a need for personnel and capital resources in other parts of the country, all concerned felt it in the company's best interests to arrive at a final decision on the Washington market as soon as possible.

Peek 'n Peak Recreation, Inc.

In early June of 1975, Mr. Philip T. Gravink, Chairman of the Board and General Manager of Peek'n Peak Recreation, Inc., looked out across the expansive golf course from his office on the second floor of the main ski lodge. "Our biggest problem," he responded to his visitor, is reducing the debt service burden on our operations by renegotiating the terms of our mortgage. After that problem is solved there are many options for growth facing us." The high debt service had resulted from a $3.5 million building program to convert Peek'n Peak from a day ski area to a year-round resort with the construction of an inn, golf course, and indoor tennis and swimming facilities during the 1971 to 1974 period. During the three years of expansion many things occurred to create the present debt situation. First, the bottom dropped out of the money market and in spite of five years of substantial growth in revenues, profitability and net worth (see ten-year summary in Exhibit 1), a public offering of $1.3 million in March 1972 proved to be inadequate. Internal generation of funds were also restricted by a three-year snow drought. Double digit inflation in construction costs and rising interest costs inflated the $4.0 million building program to over $5 million; and a shortfall of $1 million during this period raised capital needs to $6 million. As a result total debt grew from $860,000 to $5.5 million. In spite of all these problems, Philip Gravink felt sure that he would be able to renegotiate the existing $4.3 million mortgage loans and turn a profit by 1976.

> All indicators now available to us, including reservations for skiing, golfing, lodging, and business meetings make it clear that our concept is sound and that we can expect to become a profitable operation in the near future.

Origins of the Company

Peek'n Peak Recreation, Inc., started as a day ski area in French Creek. The idea of a ski area in the Clymer, New York, area was born in the mind of Philip Gravink during the winter of 1961–1962. A 1957 graduate of Cornell's School of Agriculture, Mr. Gravink was an avid skier. In 1962 his primary occupation was farming in partnership with his father in Clymer, New York. Mr. Gravink believed that a ski area in Clymer was a viable enterprise. This belief rested on two facts which he discerned on his ski junkets to Ellicottville in the Allegheny region of New York some 60 miles east of Clymer. First, a high percentage of skiers in the Allegheny region came by Clymer from Ohio. Second, the Chautauqua County area around Clymer

Exhibit 1

PEEK'N PEAK RECREATION, INC.
Ten-Year Financial Summary

Year Ending June 30	*1965*	*1966*	*1967*	*1968*	*1969*	*1970*	*1971*	*1972*	*1973*	*1974*
Gross Revenues	$ 36,699	$ 66,317	$106,319	$188,076	$337,986	$531,417	$ 897,157	$ 951,475	$ 953,239	$2,021,800
Operating Expenses	43,696	70,422	81,625	137,035	230,207	363,281	739,787	878,075	930,378	2,145,655
Interest Expenses	4,219	8,664	9,226	9,067	14,261	15,593	32,976	61,109	78,971	254,496
Taxes*	—	—	—	3,437	39,309	71,942	59,390	(13,867)	(34,552)	(10,700)
Extraordinary Credit	—	—	—	—	—	—	—	—	—	354,279
Net Income (Loss)	(11,216)	(12,769)	15,468	38,535	54,209	80,601	65,004	26,158	(21,558)	(13,372)
Number Shares Outstanding	1,054	1,277	1,277	1,272	1,270	1,218	1,218	665,280	665,280	666,135
Income (Loss) Per Share	(10.64)	(10.00)	12.11	30.29	42.68	66.17	53.37	.04	(.03)	(.02)
Cash and Securities	15,111	7,897	11,143	18,260	60,211	17,095	18,043	829,760	28,532	95,205
Accounts Receivable	145	—	1,016	3,482	3,194	3,163	853	56,811	48,583	84,551
Inventory and Other	7,896	8,056	8,853	8,581	13,811	13,253	41,858	80,344	100,978	208,566
Total Current Assets	23,152	15,953	21,012	30,323	77,216	33,511	60,754	966,915	178,093	388,322
Land, Building and Equipment	251,079	324,170	348,519	419,093	612,531	758,063	1,420,051	2,399,711	4,914,149	7,522,604
Accumulated Depreciation	8,015	23,813	42,823	72,476	119,069	188,447	306,035	423,642	564,899	800,225
Other Assets	6,269	4,702	3,135	2,364	—	5,000	28,890	21,958	25,839	131,826
Total Assets	$272,485	$321,012	$329,915	$379,304	$570,678	$608,127	$1,203,660	$2,964,942	$4,553,182	$7,242,527
Notes Payable	—	—	5,000	28,000	28,500	10,000	300,000	249,000	116,100	96,500
Current Portion Long-Term Debt	—	6,070	7,633	14,681	33,600	33,600	59,178	91,669	149,773	247,724
Accounts Payable	10,815	10,924	5,626	1,698	23,836	23,499	79,771	62,568	51,452	396,820
Accrued Liabilities	1,012	939	1,081	5,616	38,831	58,753	43,451	14,328	29,018	85,364
Total Current Liabilities	11,827	17,933	19,340	49,995	128,167	125,832	482,400	417,565	346,343	826,408
Long-Term Debt	120,000	148,430	140,458	114,200	181,668	160,514	364,448	754,736	2,425,648	4,540,988
Land Sale Deposits and Deferred Taxes	—	—	—	8,000	5,000	4,000	13,503	24,723	34,831	134,831
Capital Stock and Paid-In Surplus	151,242	176,739	175,476	173,933	171,858	149,795	106,481	1,520,862	1,520,862	1,528,174
Retained Earnings	(10,584)	(22,090)	(5,359)	33,176	87,385	167,986	236,828	247,056	225,498	212,126
Total Liabilities and Equity	$272,485	$321,012	$329,915	$379,304	$570,678	$608,127	$1,203,660	$2,964,942	$4,553,182	$7,242,527

Exhibit 2

PEEK'N PEAK RECREATION, INC.
Financial Data for Nine Months Ending March 31, 1975

	Nine Months Ending March 31 1975	1974
Gross Revenues	$2,825,646	$1,597,070
Operating Expenses		
Cost of Services,	274,646	171,056
Depreciation & Amortization	2,293,603	1,407,815
Interest Expenses	321,437	151,825
Total Expenses	2,889,686	1,730,696
Operating Loss	(64,063)	(133,626)
Provision for Income Taxes	(3,700)	(3,800)
Net Loss from Operations	(60,363)	(129,826)
Assets		
Cash	26,058	(29,076)
Accounts Receivable	73,413	77,396
Inventories	153,133	137,968
Prepaid Expenses & Operational Supplies	49,447	26,102
Total Current Assets	302,051	212,390
Land, Buildings & Equipment	7,655,861	7,001,147
Accumulated Depreciation	1,056,658	741,393
Other Assets	116,186	104,847
Total Assets	7,017,440	6,576,991
Liabilities		
Notes Payable	68,500	460,000
Current Portion Long Term Debt	368,961	177,966
Accounts Payable	241,302	217,220
Accrued Liabilities	95,023	21,847
Accrued Interest	41,856	28,790
Total Current Liabilities	815,642	905,823
Long Term Debt	4,390,730	3,564,199
Land Sale Deposits	107,000	107,000
Deferred Income Taxes	24,131	24,031
Total Long Term Liabilities	4,521,861	3,695,230
Stockholders' Equity		
Common Stock $.40 par value; 1,000,000 shares authorized issued and outstanding 667,358 shares	266,943	266,943
Capital in Excess of Par Value	1,261,231	1,261,231
Retained Earnings	151,763	447,764
Total Stockholders' Equity	1,679,937	1,975,938
Total Equity and Liabilities	$7,017,440	$6,576,991

was a much better snow belt, that is, the average annual snowfall was higher than the Allegheny region.

During the summer of 1962, Mr. Gravink worked with two local businessmen —Mr. Myrl D. Babcock, a Clymer dairy farmer and retail feed distributor, and Mr. Ernest W. Caflisch, a Clymer lumber distributor and builder—to test the feasibility of the idea of a local ski area and identify a possible site. By November 1963, a tax deed on a 250-acre site had been acquired in French Creek, five miles northwest of Clymer, which was to become the core of the Peek'n Peak Ski Center. In early 1964 a committee of five was established, Messrs. Babcock, Boozel, Caflisch, Gravink, and Dean, to put together a viable tract of land. Eleven parcels, including the 250-acre tax deed, comprising 400 acres were identified with the aid of a professional day ski area architect.

At a meeting in February 1964, the committee identified four tasks which had to be completed before proceeding to organize the ski resort.

1. Obtain clear title to the 11 parcels of land.
2. Establish satisfactory division of ownership among the founders.
3. Convince the town to relocate a recently upgraded road.
4. Obtain commitment from Niagara Mohawk Power Company to transmit enough electrical power for two 70HP lifts.

Mr. Gravink described the problems the committee faced in accomplishing these tasks:

> Getting clear title was a problem which greatly added to the cost of the land. The land itself was second growth timber land of little value. The acquisition cost was about $56 per acre, but clearing title increased the cost threefold.
>
> Establishing the equity relationship was not difficult. The original five would maintain over 50% of equity in the form of voting stock with the balance in the form of nonvoting stock, being sold to friends, neighbors, skiers, and local businessmen.
>
> Moving the road was the tough one. The existing way went through the middle of the proposed slopes and had to be moved to the base of the mountain. We could not afford to do it. Getting the town to move it was made more difficult because a substantial effort had just been expended to upgrade the existing road. We had some sympathy on the town board and finally convinced them that it would be of substantial economic interest to the town to have the ski area. It was an emotional period.
>
> The power problem was never really solved until after we started operation. It's said that during the first season of operation that when the lifts started up they dropped the milkers from the cows all the way to Clymer.

In June 1964, the group incorporated under the name Western Chautauqua Recreation, with Philip Gravink as Chairman and Chief Operating Officer. The Peek'n Peak Ski Center opened on December 8, 1964, for its first ski season with four slopes, a T-bar and J-bar lift, and a small base lodge. Total investment for the land and improvements, lifts and lodge were $68,346, $43,120, and $139,613, respectively. The first season closed on April 4, 1965, after serving 10,362 skiers at an operating cost (before depreciation and interest expense) of $34,379 to produce revenues of $36,699.

Western Chautauqua Recreation continued to operate Peek'n Peak Ski Center as their exclusive business through 1967, turning their first profit in that year (see

Exhibit 3

PEEK'N PEAK RECREATION, INC.
Layout of Central Facilities

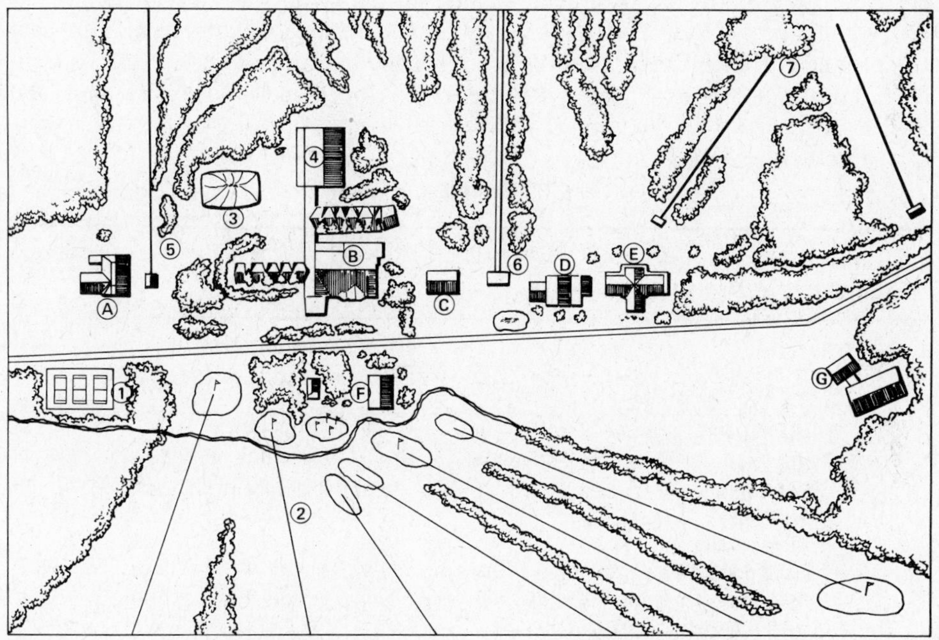

A. Sugar'n Ouse (Ski Lodge)	1. Outside Tennis Courts
B. Inn at the Peak	2. 18-Hole Golf Course
C. Laundry	3. Indoor Tennis Courts
D. Tickets-Ski School-Patrol-Rental	4. Indoor Swimming Pool
E. Main Ski Lodge	5. No. 2 Chair Lift
F. Golf Pro-Shop	6. Two T-Bars
G. Service Center/Maint. Bldg.	7 Two J-Bars

Peek'n Peak Recreation, Inc.

Exhibit 1). During 1968 the company expanded its activities into the development and sale of vacation homesites. Although the original 400 acres were still devoted to skiing the company had acquired an additional 225 acres, 125 of which it planned to devote to vacation homesites. In 1968 four homesites were sold.

On September 30, 1970, the company acquired Hill Enterprises, Inc., which operated a day ski area in Youngsville, Pennsylvania, and changed the name to Peek'n Mountain. This facility was acquired for $210 purchase of all outstanding capital stock and the assumption of Hill Enterprises' outstanding liabilities of approximately $100,000.

Facilities and Services

In 1975, Peek'n Peak Recreation, Inc., operated three recreation areas in the Western New York State area. The main facility, Peek'n Peak, was a destination resort area located in the New York "snow belt" in Chautauqua County on a 1,000-acre complex near French Creek, New York. Originally known as Peek'n Peak Ski Center this operation had expanded to 53 acres of ski slopes, an 18-hole golf course, and

Exhibit 4

PEEK'N PEAK RECREATION, INC.
Breakdown of Revenues (in thousands of dollars)

	Year Ending March 31			
Facility	*1972*	*1973*	*1974*	*1975*
Ski Lift Tickets[1]	482,6	433.8	423.0	733.9
Ski Shop	103.7	123.2	149.1	180.8
Ski Rentals	71.1	57.9	67.4	134.0
Ski Repair & Service	6.0	7.6	10.8	12.2
Sugar'n House	9.5	6.9	15.8	48.9
Ski Lodge Restaurant	99.2	97.9	103.3	120.9
Auto Service	9.9	12.8	30.8	32.6
Number of Ski Days	93	80	91	121
Peek'n Mountain				
Ski Lift Tickets	29.2	30.2	27.6	39.1
Ski Shop	10.5	10.9	11.6	14.2
Ski Rental & Service	10.7	12.6	12.3	17.9
Restaurant	11.6	11.8	10.9	15.2
Number of Ski Days	62	57	55	72
Inn at the Peak[2]	—	—	724.4	1456.3
Other Income[3]	109.2	147.6	110	20

[1] This includes season tickets of approximately $90K in 1972, $110K in 1973, $110K in 1974, and $130K in 1975.

[2] All inn-related activities including golf and tennis.

[3] Includes vacation homes and homesites, concessions, and other uncategorized income.

a 60-suite inn with indoor swimming and tennis facilities, conference rooms, dining room, cocktail lounge, and coffee shop by 1975. In addition, the facility hosted a large ski lodge which was used for banquets in off season, the Sugar'n House (a separate ski lodge), and a service station. Both ski lodges contained cafeteria-style restaurants.

Thirty-five miles southeast of Peek'n Peak, the company owned and operated Peek'n Mountain, a day ski area with its own ski shop, restaurant, and ski school facilities. The third facility was Peek'n-on-the-Lake, a swimming, boating, and fishing complex located three miles north of Peek'n Peak on the shore of 320-acre Findley Lake.

Peek'n Mountain and Peek'n-on-the-Lake represented a very small portion of the company's resources and revenues. The major portion of the company's resources and efforts were concentrated in the Peek'n Peak central facilities in French Creek. These facilities are shown in Exhibit 3. Until the opening of the Inn in 1973, skiing accounted for 70–80% of the company's gross revenues with ancillary services and sales (restaurant, service station, and homesite sales) accounting for the remainder. The Inn opened in October 1973, and for the year ended March 1974 Inn at the Peak accounted for 50% of revenues. Exhibit 4 gives detailed annual revenues for the various Peek'n Peak operations from 1972 through 1975. Exhibit 5 shows a breakdown of revenue and direct expenses for the year ending June 30, 1974.

The French Creek ski area consisted of 12 slopes ranging in length from 500 to 3,000 feet and vertical drop from 60 to 370 feet. Seven lifts (three double chairs, two T-bars, and two J-bars) provided a total lift capacity of 7,200 skiers per hour. The slopes provided terrain for all levels of skiers with 20% in the beginner skier category, 60% in intermediate, and 20% in expert. Peek'n Peak competed in the ski market primarily on the basis of its proximity to market and its superior snow conditions. The two primary markets for Peek'n Peak were the Erie, Pennsylvania, area and the Cleveland, Ohio, area as shown in Exhibit 6. Peek'n Peak's proximity to these areas coupled with a long snowfall season (mid-November through the end of March) was their competitive advantage over ski areas to the east and south of Clymer. Exhibit 7 highlights the ski conditions at Peek'n Peak and Peek'n Mountain. In 1973 an investment of $108,000 was made in snow-making equipment, and as a result, 50% of all skiing in the 1973 season was on man-made snow.

The year 1971 was a year of change for Peek'n Peak. The addition of Peak'n Mountain had brought the first major diversification for the company. However, it was an unplanned geographical diversification, and according to Phil Gravink something more was needed.

> We had reached the point of diminished growth when we became a 100,000 skier ski area. We had been a very successful ski area, but the increased size of operation demanded specialty people—engineers, mechanics, financial managers—which the ski area alone could not support. We tried to hedge this problem at first by using part-time people and by incremental growth. In addition, we could get away with all part-time direct labor people while we were

Exhibit 5

	Ski Lift	*Ski[1] School*	*Cafeteria*	*Ski Shop*	*Rental Shop*	*Accommodations*	*Real Estate*	*Inn*
Revenue	$423,000	$31,000	$116,000	$151,000	$90,000	$171,000	$10,000	$952,000[2]
Direct Labor	63,000		36,000	21,000	8,000	25,000		481,000
Other Direct Expense	58,000		65,000	105,000	3,000	5,000		354,000
Total Direct Expense	121,000		101,000	126,000	11,000	30,000		835,000
Gross Margin	$302,000	$31,000	$ 15,000	$ 25,000	$79,000	$141,000	$10,000	$117,000
Average Number Employees—Peak Day[3]	59		32	6	10	7		206
Average Number Employees—Average Day	21		7	3	3	5		160

[1] The ski school was a concession and the $31,000 was Peek'n Peak Recreation's share of lesson revenues.

[2] Includes $850,000 generated from operations of the hotel facility including restaurant, lounge, gift shop, golf, tennis, swimming, etc. Also includes $56,000 generated from beach front facility and restaurant which operates March thru September.

[3] A peak day occurred when excellent snow conditions coincided with a weekend or holiday. In 1974 Peek'n Peak had eight peak days. A peak day would bring as many as 4,000 skiers to the ski center.

Exhibit 6

PEEK'N PEAK RECREATION, INC.
Map of Ski Market Area

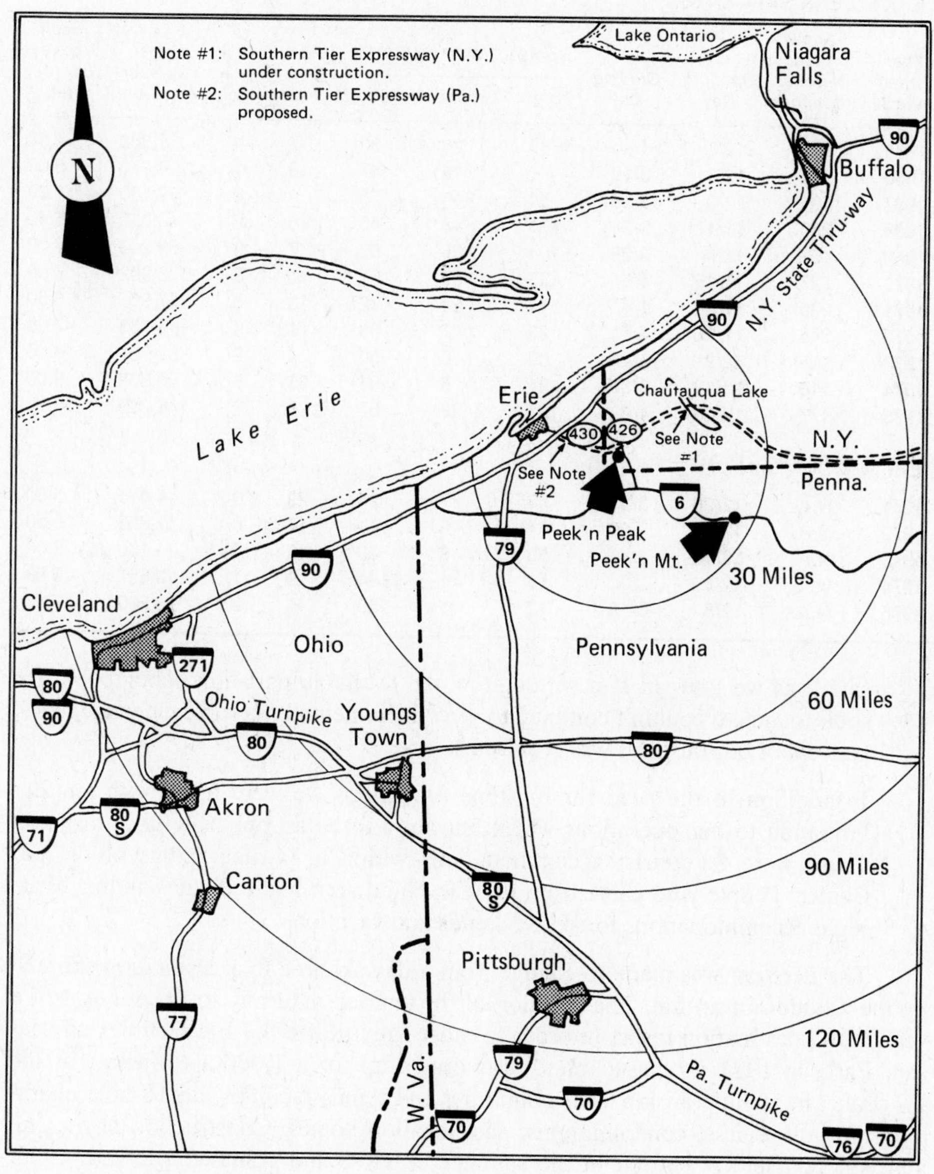

Exhibit 7

PEEK'N PEAK RECREATION, INC.
Statistical Highlights of Ski Operations

PEEK'N PEAK SKI CENTER

Year Ended June 30	*Snow Total Number of Inches*	*Opening Day*	*Closing Day*	*NUMBER AND QUALITY OF SKI DAYS*					*Total Number of Skiers*	*Basic Weekend (per day) fee*
				Total	*Excellent*	*Good*	*Fair*	*Poor*		
1965	N.A.	12/8	4/4	66	25	30	7	4	10,362	$4.50
1966	231	12/3	3/19	72	14	47	10	1	16,973	5.00
1967	191	12/3	3/25	84	15	58	9	2	29,130	5.00
1968	250	11/17	3/24	101	43	40	16	2	46,859	5.50
1969	193	12/6	3/23	104	36	59	7	2	69,203	6.00
1970	227	11/16	4/5	125	57	61	4	3	103,992	6.50
1971	276	11/26	4/4	114	24	72	13	5	117,955	6.50
1972	244	11/26	4/1	93	7	63	14	9	110,763	7.00
1973	138	12/2	3/24	80	6	50	22	2	88,951	8.00
1974	118	12/12	3/30	91	8	61	13	9	98,338	8.00
1975	177	12/29	4/9	121	28	67	19	7	146,862	9.00
PEEK'N MOUNTAIN										
1971	N.A.	12/26	3/14	63	7	24	29	3	4,415	5.50
1972	N.A.	12/2	3/26	64	6	41	17	0	12,283	5.50
1973	N.A.	12/10	3/4	58	8	38	12	0	14,160	6.00
1974	N.A.	12/12	3/3	55	1	44	9	1	10,657	6.00
1975	N.A.	12/5	3/16	72	5	50	15	2	13,200	7.00

small; as we grew in size we outgrew the available part-time labor pool. We soon found we couldn't continue to grow incrementally; a radical change in the concept of our business was required.

In addition to the need for full-time operations we were faced with another limitation to our operations which appeared to be an opportunity in disguise. There were no tourist accommodations within a 14-mile radius of the Ski Center. People who came from the Cleveland area had difficulty finding overnight accommodations for ski weekends and vacations.

The decision was made to change from a day ski area to a destination ski area by the addition of an inn. The addition of the Inn led naturally to the concept of a year-round destination resort in order to more fully utilize the Inn facilities off season. Early in 1971 a "master plan" was drawn up for a 1,000-acre facility at the ski center to include an inn with swimming and tennis facilities, an 18-hole championship golf course, condominiums, and vacation homes. Construction of the Inn and golf course was started in the summer of 1972 and completed in late 1973. The first round of golf on the course occurred in 1974.

Inn at the Peak was a beautifully appointed 60-suite inn (room accommodations and prices are summarized in Exhibit 8). Built on an English Tudor motif (see Exhibit 9), the Inn contained an indoor heated swimming pool, saunas, game room,

Exhibit 8

PEEK'N PEAK RECREATION, INC.
Year-Round Room Rates, Inn at the Peak

60 Suites—Total

16 1st floor suites—2 queen size beds & 1 day bed in each suite
$45.00 double occupancy.

4 1st floor fireplace suites—1 queen size bed & 1 day bed in each suite
$50.00 double occupancy.

35 Balcony suites—2 queen sizes beds & 1 day bed in each suite
$40.00 double occupancy.

1 Balcony suite with connecting dorm room—2 queen size beds & 1 day bed
$40.00 double occupancy.
Connecting dorm room with 10 bunks
$10.00 per bunk additional charge.

4 Balcony fireplace suites—1 queen size bed in each suite
$50.00 double occupancy

Exhibit 9

PEEK'N PEAK RECREATION, INC.
Inn at the Peak

Exhibit 10

PEEK'N PEAK RECREATION, INC.
1975
Summer Rates
Peek'n Peak Golf Course

Green Fees:	Weekends & Holidays	$7.00
	Weekdays	$5.00
Cart Rental:	18 Holes	$9.00
	9 Holes	$5.50
	Pull Carts	$1.00

(tax included)

Tennis

Members: No court fee daytime—indoor or outdoor
With lights–$3.00 per hour per court
Registration & fee to be paid at Inn front desk

Guests of Inn:

Indoor*—	Non-lighted	$5.00
	Lighted	$7.00

(May 1st thru August 31)

Outdoor—	Non-lighted	$3.00
	Lighted	$5.00

(Any playable time)

General Public:

Indoor*—	Non-lighted	$7.00
	Lighted	$9.00
Outdoor—	Non-lighted	$3.00

Bike Rental

2-Wheel, Tandems & 5-Speeds	$3.50/hr.
Each Additional Hour	$1.00
Max. for day	$8.00
Standard	$2.00/hr.
Each Additional Hour	$ .75
Max. for day	$5.00

Swimming Memberships

A combined Peek'n Peak swimming membership program provides you with your choice of indoor pool at the Inn and lake swimming at Peek'n-on-the-Lake. Memberships include use of both facilities with rates as follows:

Individual Membership	$40.00
2nd Individual Membership	$35.00
Family Max. Membership	$100.00

One Time Rates At Inn Pool

Swim after tennis	$1.00 per person
Swim after golf	$1.00 per person
General Public swim	$1.50 per person

Recreation department reserves the privilege to close the pool at any time to the general public at their discretion.

* Indoor fee to return to regular & prime rates after August 31, 1975, for members, guests and general public.

boutique shop, several conference rooms, a coffee shop, lounge, and a restaurant which had developed a reputation for quality dining in the Erie, Pennsylvania, area. The interior of the Inn's lobby and dining room contained furniture, paneling, and fixtures which had been rescued from the Reed Mansion in Erie, Pennsylvania. The mahogany paneling, crystal, and stained glass fixtures traced their origin to craftsmen of the Rhine area of Germany who had handcrafted them in the nineteenth century for the Reeds. When Peek'n Peak purchased the interior of the Reed Mansion for the interior of the Inn, they acquired a great deal of local publicity for saving the interior of this fine old mansion which had been slated for demolition to make way for a parking lot. To encourage the use of the dining facilities and lounge by skiers and golfers there were no dress regulations for either the dining room or the lounge. More recently, a buffet dinner had been introduced in the lounge.

The swimming pool and saunas were available free to overnight guests, and nonguests could avail themselves of these facilities for a fee of $1 a person, and group rates were available for local groups of all ages. The indoor tennis facilities consisted of four courts in a heated bubble building, a short walk from the Inn. These courts were available to both guests and nonguests. In addition eight outdoor courts had recently been constructed across from the Sugar'n House. The 18-hole golf course had been built in a flat wetlands area across the road from the base lodge and the Inn. Exhibit 10 lists the facilities and their fees.

Exhibit 11

PEEK'N PEAK RECREATION, INC.
High & Low Revenues for Inn at the Peak

1/20/75—1/26/75 Typical Week During Peak Period (Ski Season)

	Total	*Room*	*Restaurant*	*Bar*	*Recreation*	*Boutique*
S	$ 6,520	$ 2,116	$ 2,584	$1,299	$ 168	$ 353
M	3,933	2,041	1,159	521	127	85
T	3,186	925	1,234	717	171	139
W	4,008	955	1,893	963	122	75
Th	5,279	2,066	2,068	872	135	138
F	6,443	2,306	2,541	1,322	119	155
S	9,805	2,438	4,616	1,912	253	586
	$39,174	$12,847	$16,095	$7,606	$1,095	$1,531

4/6/75—4/12/75 Typical During Low Week (Between Ski and Summer Season)

	Total	*Room*	*Restaurant*	*Bar*	*Recreation*	*Boutique*
S	$ 2,075	$ 110	$1,209	$ 423	$152	$181
M	927	104	365	212	176	70
T	1,810	331	938	423	47	71
W	2,207	308	1,121	609	50	120
Th	1,016	115	583	200	61	57
F	2,154	400	1,224	410	62	57
S	5,726	785	3,235	1,248	236	222
	$15,915	$2,153	$8,675	$3,525	$784	$779

Exhibit 11 shows revenues from recreation, dining, and other amenities. Room occupancy at the Inn averaged 40% over the first 1½ years of operation as shown in Exhibit 12. Much of the planning for the Inn was based upon advanced registration. Advanced registrations as of June 17, 1975, for July through October are shown in Exhibit 13. All occupancy figures, both historical and projected, were on a room basis rather than a per person basis. It was estimated that room occupancy averaged 3½ persons per occupied room during ski season and 1½ persons per room during the off season.

Management of Facilities

Overall operational responsibility for Peek'n Peak rested with Phil Gravink. The management organization chart is shown in Exhibit 14. The two main operating managers were Mr. Donald Rothenberger, who was mountain superintendent and was responsible for all outside operations; and Mr. Doug Geiger, who was manager of the Inn. Mr. Rothenberger had been with Peek'n Peak since its inception and was a jack-of-all-trades who believed in working with his people to get the job done. Doug Geiger had been hired as manager of the Inn when the plans were first drawn up. He had no previous experience as an innkeeper, but had a large number

Exhibit 12

PEEK'N PEAK RECREATION, INC.
Room Occupancy

Month	*Rm. Avail.*	*Rm. Occupancy*	*Occupancy % Month*	*Cumulative % Occupancy*
October '73	720	199	27.64	27.64
November '73	900	168	18.67	22.65
December '73	1001	483	48.25	32.43
January '74	1336	672	50.30	38.46
February '74	1528	903	59.10	44.21
March '74	1860	422	22.69	38.76
April '74	1800	454	25.22	34.86
May '74	1860	787	42.31	34.95
June '74	1800	666	37.00	35.65
July '74	1860	630	33.87	36.71
August '74	1860	915	49.19	38.12
September '74	1800	869	48.28	39.12
October '74	1800	654	36.33	39.28
November '74	1800	519	28.83	38.42
December '74	1860	1052	56.56	39.84
January '75	1860	1297	69.73	42.01
February '75	1680	1247	74.23	43.69
March '75	1860	724	38.92	43.38
April '75	1800	553	30.72	42.65
May '75	1860	954	51.29	43.14

Exhibit 13

PEEK'N PEAK RECREATION, INC.
Advanced Reservations as of 6/17/75
(Number of Rooms Reserved)

July	*August*	*September*	*October*
1—48	1—26	1—0	1—0
2—3	2—20	2—2	2—0
3—1	3—9	3—31	3—2
4—38	4—14	4—30	4—34
5—60	5—56	5—20	5—0
6—14	6—57	6—22	6—1
7—30	7—5	7—9	7—1
8—29	8—2	8—60	8—1
9—30	9—0	9—60	9—0
10—19	10—13	10—60	10—6
11—33	11—25	11—60	11—23
12—38	12—25	12—36	12—5
13—10	13—7	13—37	13—0
14—14	14—2	14—14	14—0
15—14	15—38	15—4	15—0
16—13	16—48	16—11	16—2
17—4	17—0	17—60	17—60
18—39	18—6	18—60	18—60
19—34	19—12	19—20	19—7
20—34	20—20	20—30	20—7
21—38	21—20	21—0	21—7
22—42	22—60	22—0	22—0
23—35	23—41	23—0	23—0
24—4	24—1	24—40	24—0
25—17	25—1	25—10	25—0
26—27	26—1	26—0	26—0
27—15	27—60	27—2	27—0
28—32	28—60	28—0	28—0
29—43	29—4	29—0	29—0
30—47	30—12	30—0	30—0
31—19	31—5		31—0
Total 794 (406)	Total 650 (206)	Total 678 (571)	Total 220 (347)

Reservations as of 6/22/74 for similar months in 1974.

of years experience in retail store management. Mr. Gravink explained how Mr. Geiger had come to be hired as innkeeper.

> We interviewed a lot of experienced innkeepers in 1971 but were not really happy with any of them. Don Geiger who is on our board and had done a lot of promotion work for us through his sports equipment shop in Cleveland, mentioned his twin brother Doug. At the time Doug was store manager for one of Halle Brother's large Cleveland department stores. We felt that his experience here was similar to that of a manager of a large resort since a large de-

Exhibit 14

PEEK'N PEAK RECREATION, INC.
Management Organization Chart

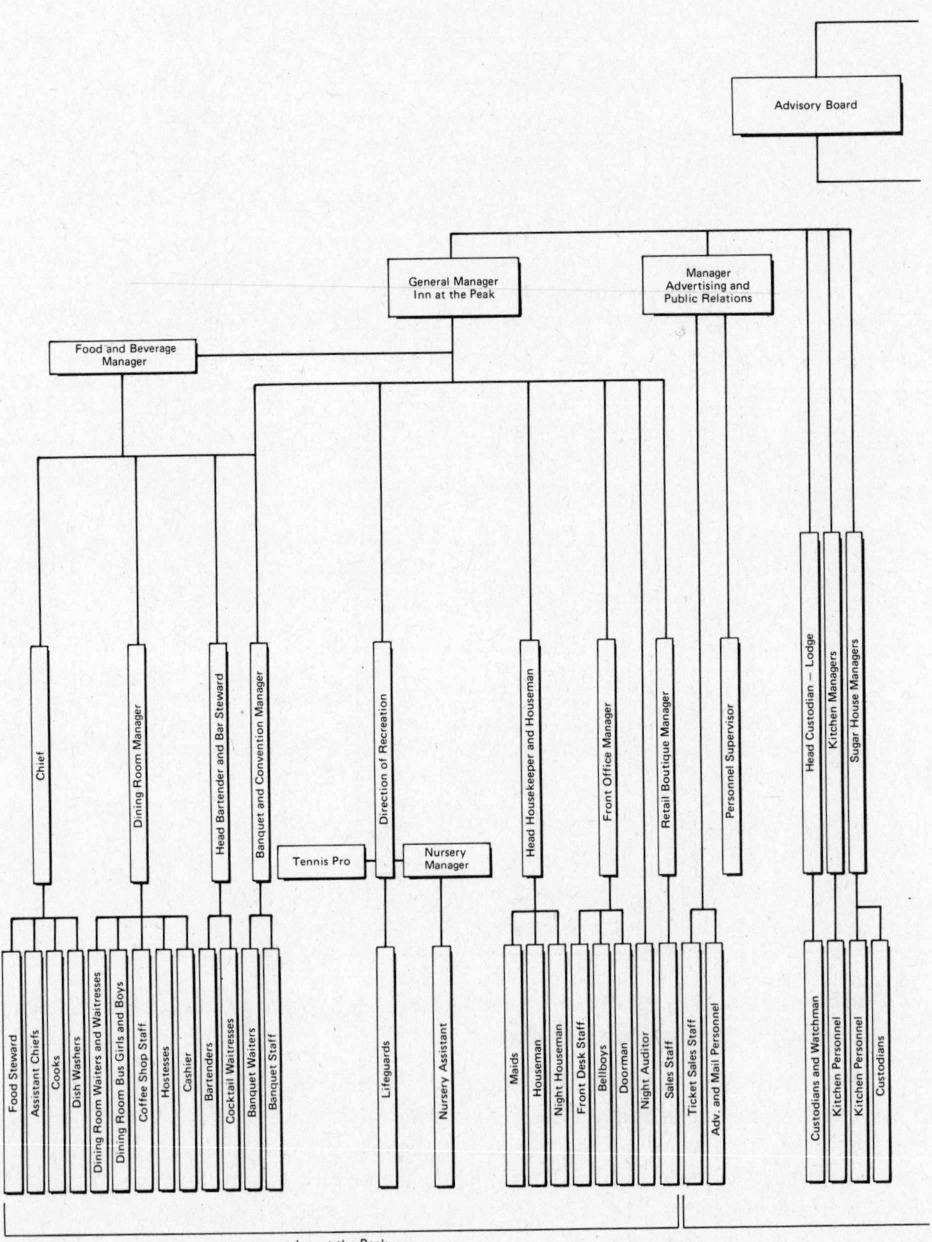

Exhibit 14 (continued)

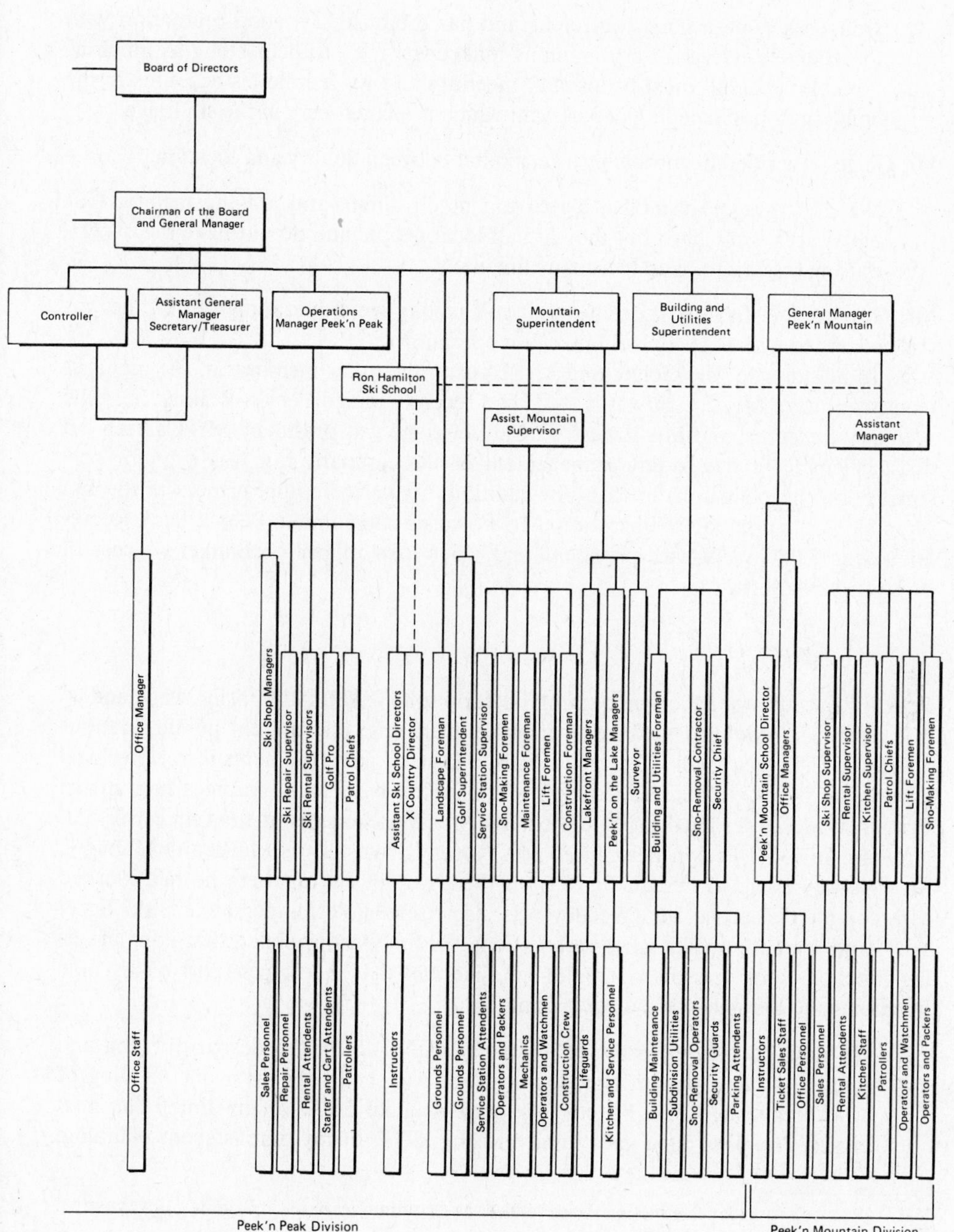

partment store requires the management of large numbers of people in diverse activities. We intended to hire a new graduate from Cornell's Hotel Management School to assist Doug. However, we did not; we hired an experienced food and beverage manager instead.

Doug has done a good job for us and has established a good reputation with the clientele. He is a very gracious innkeeper. I try to help Doug as much as possible. I attend most of his staff meetings and we handle his accounts in the company's bookkeeping department which is located here in the ski lodge.

Mr. Geiger described his problems as a conflict between quality and location.

We are trying to establish a real top notch dining and lodging facility. Our employees work hard but they are all local people and do not have the experience necessary to operate a really fine inn.

Mr. Gravink felt that the ski center and golf facility were operating well but he was still concerned with cost control in the Inn operation.

In addition to Mr. Geiger and Mr. Houser, the other members of the management team were Mr. Joe Edwards, who had recently joined Peek'n Peak as full-time secretary-treasurer, and Mr. Ernest W. Caflisch, who was president. Mr. Caflisch did not participate in day-to-day management of the company but was a major personality on the board of directors. In addition, his periodic appearances at the Inn often led to changes in the operation. Mr. Edwards had come to Peek'n Peak Recreation from his job of vice-president and chief loan officer of Banker's Trust of Western New York.

Marketing

Peek'n Peak did not have a marketing function until 1973. Advertising was handled informally and confined to word-of-mouth advertising, intermittent public relations articles in Erie area media, four road signs, and small advertisements in various local advertising flyers. All the advertising was handled by a local graphics firm in the Erie area which designed print and road sign advertisements at the request of Mr. Gravink. In 1970 Peek'n Peak hired Mr. Roger L. Westley as Marketing Manager. Mr. Westley came to Peek'n Peak from their graphics firm where he had worked as a commercial artist. Mr. Westley was also responsible for personnel,[2] ski ticket sales, and recreation (ski/golf) reservations. Roger Westley stated that nonmarketing functions took less than 10% of his time and that the biggest part of his time was doing the graphics for the advertising.

We now do all our graphics internally and I do all the design drawing and setup. I have a person two days a week who helps me with our printing of brochures and flyers. I'd say the graphics take 50% of my time. The next biggest chunk of time goes to advertising; 20% of my time is spent planning,

[2] Mr. Westley's personnel function was defined as "communications and policy development with three other staff members."

placing, and following up on printed advertising and 15% on TV and radio communications. This latter includes insuring our ski conditions are broadcast. The remaining 5% is involved with what I call image and promotion; this involves promoting local publicity for the company such as special events at the Inn, community and professional activities of personnel, and various other public relations.

My biggest need right now is someone who could back me up by handling the writing tasks for news releases, brochures, etc.

Recently Mr. Westley had increased media advertising with ads in *Training Magazine, Cleveland Magazine,* and *Buffalo Fan Magazine* and planned to develop advertising plans for national trade magazines and travel industry trade journals.

With the development of the Inn we backed into the conference business for small meetings such as board of directors meetings, planning committees, etc. Our problem is how to expand this business. I believe that selective advertising in industry trade journals can reach this market.

Another recent change made by Mr. Westley was the development of a detailed advertising and promotion budget. The 1975–76 advertising and promotion budget is shown in Exhibit 15. The major marketing foci of Peek'n Peak were the "Ski and Stay" and "Golf and Stay" packages which promoted the use of the Inn in conjunction with the ski and golf facilities by providing a single fee for a two to five day package, which included lift tickets or green fees with lodging and meals. Fees for golf packages and advanced golf reservations are shown in Exhibit 16.

Financial Structure

Mr. Gravink's concern for the company's debt position stemmed from the company's current debt service obligations. As shown in Exhibit 2, the recent nine-month period gross operating profit before interest, depreciation, and taxes was $532,000; interest expense was $321,000, and debt amortization was $217,000. The long-term debt and maturity dates are summarized in Exhibit 17. Approximately $170,000 of the long-term notes were due to directors, $36,500 directly and $133,000 to E. W. Caflisch Lumber Company. The $36,500 notes bear interest of 8½% and the $133,000 bears average interest of 9¾%. The $4.2 million mortgage loans were held by Banker's Trust of Western New York and two other commercial banks which bought participation in the mortgage. In addition, Pennsylvania Bank & Trust held the mortgage on Peek'n Mountain.

The Future

With the completion of the Inn and the golf course, Peek'n Peak was well on the way to the full implementation of its master plan; the development of condominiums and resort homes were the next major growth area. However, Phil Gravink did not see any changes around the corner but saw his problems as focusing on operational issues.

Exhibit 15

PEEK'N PEAK RECREATION, INC.
1975–76 Advertising & Promotion Budget

Advertising #581	*P'N PK*	*P'N MT.*	*Ski Shops*	*Inn*	*Golf*	*P'N-ON-LK.*	*Corp.*	*Off Seas. Promo.*	*Conv. & Ban.*	*Totals*
1. Newspaper	500	500	500	3,000	500	500	—	500	—	6,000
2. Radio/T.V.	2,900	500	500	1,000	500	—	—	—	—	5,400
3. Yellow Pages	1,200	200	—	500	—	—	—	—	—	1,900
4. National Survey	400	100	—	—	—	—	—	—	—	500
5. National & Trade Pub.	1,000	—	—	3,000	1,000	—	—	—	1,000	6,000
6. Club Mag. & Annuals	1,000	350	—	—	—	—	—	—	—	1,350
7. Direct Mail	250	—	—	250	250	—	—	—	—	750
8. Goodwill Adv.	—	100	—	—	—	—	500	—	—	600
9. Shows & Displays	—	—	—	—	—	—	3,000	—	—	3,000
10. Special Promotions	—	—	—	—	—	—	1,000	—	—	1,000
11. Coop. Adv.	6,000	—	—	—	—	—	—	—	—	6,000
12. Road & Gen. Signs	15,000	4,500	—	—	—	—	—	—	—	19,500
13. 3M-Travel Aide	500	—	—	500	—	—	—	—	—	1,000
14. Msc. Adv. & Prep. Costs	—	—	—	—	—	—	500	—	—	500
Totals for 581	28,750	6,250	1,000	8,250	2,250	500	5,000	500	1,000	53,500
Graphics & Sales Units #582										
1. Brochures (3)	5,000	3,000	—	2,500	—	—	—	—	2,500	13,000
2. Rate Shts. (3)	1,200	750	—	750	—	—	—	—	—	2,700
3. Golf'n Stay (brochure and rate card)	—	—	—	—	1,200	—	—	—	—	1,200
4. Ski 'n Stay (brochure) and rate card)	1,200	—	—	—	—	—	—	—	—	1,200
5. Envelope Stuffers (series of 6)							2,750			2,750
6. Post cards							2,000			2,000
7. Photography & Movies							2,000			2,000

Exhibit 15 (continued)

	P'N PK	P'N MT.	Ski Shops	Inn	Golf	P'N-ON-LK.	Corp.	Off Seas. Promo.	Conv. & Ban.	Totals
8. Misc. Print. & Prep. Costs							900			900
Totals for 582	7,400	3,750	—	3,250	1,200	—	7,650	—	2,500	25,750
Communications #583										
Public										
1. Peek'n Country News (3/yr.)	—	—	—	—	—	—	3,500	—	—	3,500
2. Snow Reporting	2,500	1,000	—	—	—	—	—	—	—	3,500
Employee										
3. Manual	—	—	—	—	—	—	1,500	—	—	1,500
Financial										
4. Annual Report	—	—	—	—	—	—	5,900	—	—	5,900
5. Interim Reports (3)	—	—	—	—	—	—	600	—	—	600
Total for 583	2,500	1,000	—	—	—	—	11,500	—	—	15,000
Sales Promotion Expense #584							3,000			3,000
Image & Promo. Give-Aways #585										
1. Matches	500	—	—	750	—	—	—	—	—	1,250
2. Pens	250	—	—	400	—	—	—	—	—	650
3. Pencils	100	—	—	—	—	—	—	—	—	100
4. Scratch (adr.) Pads	—	—	—	—	—	—	—	—	250	250
Unassigned	—	—	—	—	—	—	500	—	—	500
Total for 585	850	—	—	1,150	—	—	500	—	250	2,750
Grand Total	39,500	11,000	1,000	12,650	3,450	500	27,650	500	3,750	100,000

Exhibit 16

PEEK'N PEAK RECREATION, INC.
Golf Packages Report as of June 17, 1975

Golf Package[1] Actual Count 1974		*Golf Package Reservations for 1975*	
May	8	May[2]	63
June	33	June	149
July	48	July	245
August	91	August	157
September	51	September	76
October	57	October	6
November	10		
Total	208	Total	696[3]

Package	*Prices Per Person[4] Double Occupancy*	*Additional Persons w/Golf*	*No Golf*
5 Day Weekday	$142	$104	$77
4 Day Weekday	115	79	58
3 Day Weekday	83	55	39
2 Day Weekday	45	30	19
Weekender	49	34	—
Weekender Plus One	88	58	—

[1] Package = One Person for 2 to 5 day package
[2] Actual number of golf guests.
[3] 106 of the above packages are results of mail campaigns to previous golf package customers and season ski ticket customers.
[4] Prices include room, green fees, breakfasts and dinners.

We are a service company supplying sports services and hotel services. Our main job now is marketing this concept. Growth in the area of condominiums and homes is really incremental land sales; the utilities are already in and under control.

There is no big corporate expansion on the horizon. What we have to do now is a thousand little things mainly in the area of marketing. I expect our revenues will reach $3.6 million this next year. However our break-even under present financing conditions is somewhat higher. My goal is for revenues in the $4 million plus range within two years.

Our biggest problem is the capacity of the Inn. What we saw as an opportunity before building—the lack of local facilities—has turned out to be a real problem. Room number 61 is 14 miles away and Inn revenues are very dependent upon the number of guests. In addition, we have found what appears to be a lucrative market—the conference convention market. However, this market usually requires single occupancy rooms, and we are designed for the three to

Exhibit 17

PEEK'N PEAK RECREATION, INC.
Summary of Outstanding Debt

Notes Payable

The notes payable at June 30, 1974 and March 31,

	Year Ended June 30, 1974	*Nine Months Ended March 31, 1975*
Interest rate at balance sheet date	8%	10½%
Maximum amount of short-term borrowings at any month and during the period	$ 460,000	$ 60,000
Average aggregate of such debt outstanding during the period	329,394	50,000
Weighted average interest rate, based on monthly outstanding principal amounts	7.79%	8.00%

Long-Term Debt

The Company's long-term debt is comprised of:

	June 30, 1974	*March 31, 1975*
7½%—10½% Mortgage loans	$4,301,850	$4,237,067
6%—7% Land purchase contracts	186,500	181,500
5½%—11½% Notes	300,362	319,498
Capitalized lease obligations	—	21,626
	$4,788,712	$4,759,691
Less: Current portion	247,724	368,961
	$4,540,988	$4,390,730

The mortgage loans are due at various dates from August 20, 1982 to May 30, 1991 in monthly installments of approximately $41,200, including interest, and are secured by substantially all of the real property of the Company.

The land purchase contracts are due at various dates from October 1, 1975 to April 1, 1981 in annual installments of approximately $30,000, plus interest.

The 5½%—11½% notes consist of construction and equipment demand notes due at various dates from April 8, 1975 to November 1, 1977 of which approximately $168,000 are due within one year. Approximately twenty-two percent (22%) of these notes are secured by certain assets of the Company.

The capitalized lease obligations represent two long-term lease transactions, relating to the financing of equipment, which are being accounted for as installment purchases. The terms of the leases are for five year periods ending August 25, 1978 and February 1, 1979, respectively, with monthly installments of $400 and $300, including interest. At the end of the leases, title for the equipment passes to the Company upon payment of a premium equal to ten percent of the cost of the equipment, aggregating approximately $2,900.

The aggregate maturities of all long-term debt for the five years ending March 31, 1976 through March 31, 1980 are $368,961, $322,098, $223,068, $231,576 and $262,380, respectively.

five people per room requirements of ski parties. The Inn was originally for 120 rooms in four wings, but with the rising costs it was reduced to two wings and 60 units.

One of the alternatives we are looking at is to add two condominium wings to the Inn. This would add another 50–60 units at a cost of $30,000–$35,000, each of which could be financed by preselling the units before construction of each wing. By managing the rental of the condominium units for the owners we would be able to add substantially to the capacity of the Inn for our ski season and conferences.

The other opportunity we have to exploit is utilizing the capacity of the Inn during off season by marketing golf packages. Here we are at a disadvantage with our location. While we are the nearest ski resort to the Cleveland area, we are competing with the 30 golf courses in that area.

The opportunities are there, it is just going to take time and work to take advantage of them.

Dobbs House (A)

As Jerry McKenzie returned to New York in January 1971, he was still struggling with the decision he had been asked to make one month earlier by the president of the Squibb Corporation, the parent of Dobbs House. Consistent with Jerry's personal philosophy that every problem can be reduced to three alternatives, he saw his options as: (1) take a position with Dobbs House as Director of Corporate Planning with the first task of helping the General Manager of the Fast Foods Division; (2) become the General Manager of Fast Foods himself; or (3) continue in his present job on the corporate staff of Squibb in New York. Besides the personal problems involved in a move to Memphis (his wife did not relish the thought of moving south from her home in New York), Jerry, who had never been in a restaurant except to eat before this month, was unsure if he even understood the business well enough to make a well-reasoned decision or present a viable plan of action to Squibb management.

Squibb Corporation

Squibb Beech-Nut was formed on January 15, 1968, when E. R. Squibb & Sons, Inc. was spun off from the Olin Corporation and simultaneously merged with Beech-Nut, Inc. The merger brought together a leading pharmaceutical company and a well-known manufacturer and marketer of specialty foods, beverages, and confections. Previously, in 1966, Beech-Nut had acquired Dobbs Houses, Inc., a Memphis-based company engaged in airline catering, airport restaurants, coffee shops, and related services. Each of these activities was organized as a separate operating division of the parent corporation.

History of Dobbs House

Dobbs House was variously described by the trade press as the "second largest airline caterer in the world" and as the "sleepy giant of the food industry out in Tennessee." The company was founded during the Depression by James K. Dobbs, Sr., who was described as "running it with an iron fist." Dobbs began his business career as an ambitious car salesman and became, among other things, the largest Ford dealer in the world.

He first became involved in the food business as an investor in the Toddle House chain that began as a 12-unit chain of 11-seat mobile food houses that could be relocated by truck. On moving, they were said to "toddle" from side to side, from which they received their name. At one point Toddle Houses were considered by many as the leader in the fast-food and hamburger business. Dobbs became dissatisfied with his partners and set out to build his own restaurant chain,

Exhibit 1

DOBBS HOUSE (A)

called Dobbs Houses. He often located his Dobbs Houses across the street from Toddle Houses just as a challenge. In 1961, after years of competition, Dobbs bought out the Toddle House chain.

The "Dobbs concept" of the 1930s was to build small "mom-and-pop" snack bar units. His overall philosophy was "if you have good food, people will find you." A large sign and attractive site were considered by Dobbs as secondary (see Exhibit 1). Toddle and Dobbs Houses, open 24 hours a day, featured real cream in their coffee, homemade pies, vegetable soup, and their own daily-ground hamburger meat (see Exhibit 2).

When James Dobbs, Sr., died in 1961, his two sons alternated as president, but because of other interests, they elected to sell the company to Beech-Nut Life Savers in 1966. At the time of the sale, Dobbs Houses, Inc., was traded on the New York Stock Exchange.

Background of Jerry McKenzie

Jerry McKenzie, born in 1941, attended an eastern prep school. After a spotty undergraduate career of two years at an Ivy League school, he terminated his education and worked for a period as a lumberjack in Maine and then joined the Coast Guard. After a two-year stint with the Coast Guard, he moved to New York and obtained a job as a salesman with a chemical company. During this period he married and acquired a new degree of motivation. While holding a full-time job during the day, he finished four years of college in three years at night. After this, he received a master's degree in business administration with honors from Harvard Business School.

Upon graduation, he joined Beech-Nut in 1967 on the recommendation of one of his professors, who was a director of the company. Up until his assignment to investigate Dobbs House, he had worked in various staff functions in New York establishing profit centers, information systems, accounting systems, strategic planning, and acquisition analysis.

He described his personal career strategy up to this point as an attempt at an end run to the top through energetic and high-profile activities in a corporate staff position.

Dobbs House as of 1970

Although Dobbs Houses was sold in 1966, the Dobbs brothers continued to be involved in management until they left active management in August 1971. It was at that time that Squibb management decided to change Dobbs into what they described as a professionally run company (bottom up management and control).

Dobbs House consisted of three separately managed divisions:

	Sales
Airline Catering and Restaurants (two divisions)	$ 77 million
Fast Foods	29 million
Total	$106 million

Exhibit 2

DOBBS HOUSE (A)

Exhibit 2 (continued)

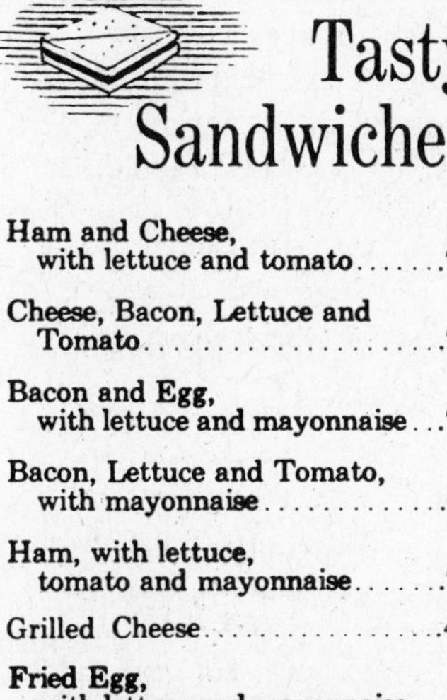

Tasty Sandwiches

Ham and Cheese,
with lettuce and tomato .... .75

Cheese, Bacon, Lettuce and Tomato .... .75

Bacon and Egg,
with lettuce and mayonnaise ... .75

Bacon, Lettuce and Tomato,
with mayonnaise .... .65

Ham, with lettuce,
tomato and mayonnaise .... .70

Grilled Cheese .... .40

Fried Egg,
with lettuce and mayonnaise ... .45

Lettuce and Tomato, mayonnaise .40

Soups/Salads

Vegetable Soup
prepared daily – piping hot ... .40

Lettuce and Tomato Salad ...... .35

Head Lettuce Salad .... .35

Tossed Vegetable Salad .... .35

All salads chilled and served with your choice of Mayonnaise, Honey French or 1000 Isle Dressing

From our Grill and Broiler

TENDERLOIN STEAK PLATE 2.15
Tender and juicy, grilled to your taste. Served with individual Hashed Brown Potatoes, Chilled Salad, Choice of our famous Dressings

CHOPPED STEAK 1.95
Choice cuts blended together by experienced cooks. Served with Individual Hashed Brown Potatoes, Chilled Salad, Choice of our famous Dressings

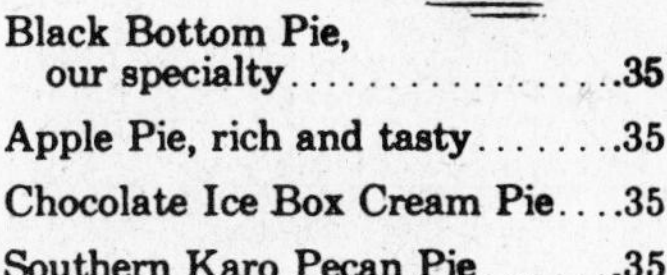

Desserts

Black Bottom Pie,
our specialty .... .35

Apple Pie, rich and tasty .... .35

Chocolate Ice Box Cream Pie ... .35

Southern Karo Pecan Pie .... .35

We have special containers for carrying out any of the food on this menu

---

The Airline Catering Division was traditionally profitable, but the 1969 and 1970 slump in airline traffic had seriously eroded the company's profit margins.

The Airline Restaurant Division was also severely affected by the airline traffic slump. To further aggravate the situation, the Fast Foods Division was showing declining sales and profits since a record year in 1968 (see Exhibit 3). As a result, it appeared that the Dobbs House as a whole would show flat earnings, and the Fast Foods Division would show a loss for the first time in over 35 years.

While the problems experienced in the airline-oriented divisions were expected to be short-term and probably outside the control of management, Squibb did not feel that the same was true of the traditionally stable and profitable Fast Foods Division. The anxiety in Squibb's New York offices was further increased by reports of failures of several fast-food chains. The nervousness of the investment community was reflected by a tumble in the food service-lodging stock price index in 1970, shown in Exhibit 4. The fast-foods industry was described as "shark-infested waters," from which there would be few survivors.

Real Estate Commitments

One of the reasons for several notable failures being experienced by other companies in the fast-food industry was associated with long-term real estate commitments. The success of a restaurant was often very dependent on site locations. To secure

Exhibit 3

DOBBS HOUSE (A)
Fast Foods Division Income Statements
January 1970, 1971

Item	*January 1970* $	%	*January 1971* $	%
Net Sales	2109731	100.0	2094114	100.0
Cost of Sales	1878974	89.1	1963053	93.7
Materials Cost	642771	30.5	628460	30.0
Direct Labor	668644	31.7	754942	36.1
Controllable Operating Expenses	284105	13.5	272955	13.0
Semi-Fixed Oper. Expenses	192338	9.1	196354	9.4
Managers' Compensation	91116	4.3	110342	5.3
Gross Margin	230757	10.9	131061	6.3
Division Management	71925	3.4	119230	5.7
Earnings from Operations	158832	7.5	11831	.6
General and Administrative	59108	2.8	65353	3.1
Operating Income	99724	4.7	(53522)	(2.5)
Other Income, Net of Other Deductions	47730	2.3	55000	2.6
Earnings Before Taxes	147454	7.0	1478	.1
Federal Income Taxes	70776	3.4	741	nil
Net Earnings After Taxes	76678	3.6	737	nil

Exhibit 4

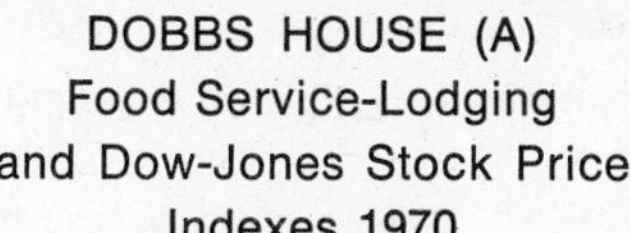

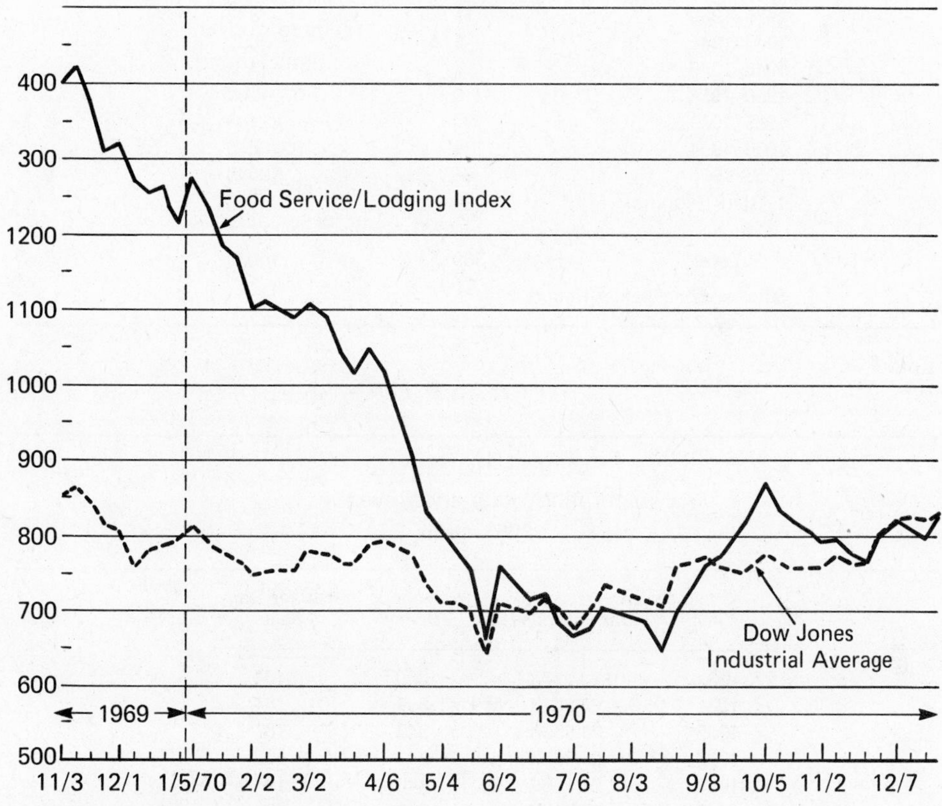

SOURCE: *Wall Street Journal*
Service World Report

attractive sites, it was generally necessary (and desirable) to make relatively long-term commitments in leases or purchases of real estate. Such leases represented substantial contingent liabilities, not represented on the balance sheets, if it became necessary to discontinue a location. While Squibb had only approximately $14 million invested in the Fast Foods Division, the possible loss due to unexpired lease write-offs could potentially have been several times book investment.

Company Operating Statistics

As of September 1970, there were 369 Snack Bars in operation in the Fast Foods Division. Exhibit 5 shows the approximate opening dates of these units. Exhibit 6

Exhibit 5

DOBBS HOUSE (A)
Units in Operation by Year of Opening

Opening Year	*Number of Units*	*Percent of Total*
1935–1939	11	(3.0)
1940–1944	1	(0.3)
1945–1949	4	(1.1)
1950–1954	9	(2.4)
1955–1959	90	(24.4)
1960–1964	134	(36.2)
1965–1969	94	(25.5)
1970 (9 months)	26	(7.1)
Total	369	(100.0)

Source: Consultant's Report.

Exhibit 6

DOBBS HOUSE (A)
Operating Units and Revenues
1963–1969

Year	*Annual Snack Bar Revenues*	*Number of Units*	*Average Daily Sales*
1963	$22,417K	360	$184
1964	23,281K	357	184
1965	23,856K	343	187
1966	25,305K	347	202
1967	24,106K	340	197
1968	25,443K	351	204
1969	27,092K	354	215

Average Daily Sales of Competitors, 1969

Competitor	*Average Daily Sales*
Howard Johnson's	$ 950
International House of Pancakes	734
Denny's	967
Original House of Pancakes	819
Dutch Pantry	1,341
Waffle House	349

Source: Consultant's Report, various annual reports, and *Institutions Magazine*.

shows the Annual Snack Bar revenue, the number of units in operation at the end of the year, and the average daily sales. Original plans to build over 50 new units in 1970 were abandoned when the Division's operating results softened. Interestingly, not until 1970 was the total number of units as large as it was in 1963. Monthly figures are shown in Exhibit 7, and the sales revenue rankings by opening year are shown in Exhibit 8. Aside from the expected general pattern of newer (and frequently larger) units doing better than older units, the units opened in 1965–66 stand out as being unusually successful, though design of the units had not varied appreciably over the years. The only conclusion that management could draw was that in 1964–65 site selection was especially good. As seen in Exhibit 9, Dobbs House units were appreciably smaller than those of other fast-food operators.

The revenue of the Fast Foods Division was generated almost entirely from food sales (95.4% in 1968 and 97.7% in 1969). Liquor and sundry sales amounted to only 0.1% in 1968 and 1969. Vending and other revenues amounted to 1.5% in 1968 and 2.2% in 1969.

Consultant's Conclusions

In preparation for the management transition from the Dobbs brothers to Squibb management, a consulting study of the situation at Dobbs House was initiated, which was completed by the end of 1970.

Exhibit 7

DOBBS HOUSE (A)
Operating Units and Revenues
Monthly
1968–1970

	1968		*1969*		*1970*	
	# of Units	*Daily Avg.*	*# of Units*	*Daily Avg.*	*# of Units*	*Daily Avg.*
Jan.	340	$187	349	$222	354	$208
Feb.	345	197	351	205	353	208
Mar.	345	200	353	204	356	209
Apr.	345	199	353	203	359	209
May	343	201	355	208	361	216
June	343	209	353	216	362	217
July	344	210	352	220	367	222
Aug.	349	218	355	227	370	223
Sept.	348	206	353	212	369	210
Oct.	349	202	356	214	—	—
Nov.	351	206	357	216	—	—
Dec.	351	214	354	228	—	—

Source: Consultant's Report.

Exhibit 8

DOBBS HOUSE (A)

1969 Sales Revenue, Ranked by Year of Opening

Year of Unit Opening	Over $100M #	Over $100M (%)	$75M–100M #	$75M–100M (%)	$50M–75M #	$50M–75M (%)	Under $50M #	Under $50M (%)	Total #	Total (%)
1968–69	11	(25)	11	(25)	13	(30)	9		44	(100)
1966–67	7	(19)	16	(44)	11	(31)	2	(6)	36	(100)
1964–65	14	(46)	6	(20)	8	(27)	2	(7)	30	(100)
1962–63	12	(27)	14	(31)	14	(31)	5	(11)	45	(100)
1960–61	10	(14)	16	(23)	29	(42)	15	(21)	70	(100)
1958–59	6	(11)	16	(30)	26	(48)	6	(11)	54	(100)
1956–57	4	(14)	7	(24)	10	(34)	8	(28)	29	(100)
1954–55	3	(18)	1	(6)	7	(41)	6		17	(100)
Before 1954	8	(27)	4	(13)	13	(43)	5	(17)	30	(100)
Total	75	(21%)	91	(26%)	131	(37%)	58	(16%)	355	(100)

Source: Consultant's Report.

The consultant's report presented three major conclusions, together with several recommendations.

I. Over the coming decade success in the fast-food business will be increasingly hard to come by. The traditional requirements of cleanliness, high-quality food, good value, and good service will continue to be the prime prerequisites, but no longer will success in these basic operating areas be entirely sufficient. Three additional elements which will come increasingly into play:

Exhibit 9

DOBBS HOUSE (A)

Fast Foods Division

Average Unit Size and Seating Capacity

Year	Dobbs House Average: Revenue/Year/Unit	Dobbs House Average: Seats/Unit	Dobbs House Average: Area/Unit, Sq. feet	Fast Food Industry Average: Revenue/Year/Unit	Fast Food Industry Average: Seats/Unit	Fast Food Industry Average: Area/Unit, Sq. feet
1968*	72,500	25	1,145	140,000	36	1,700
1969**	76,500	28	1,004	165,000	49	1,850

Source: Consultant's Report and *Nation's Restaurant News*.

* Units stated in 1968 and before.

** Units stated in 1969.

1. Marketing
The first element will be marketing clout and expertise. The advertising and sales promotion abilities of the market leaders will continue to put strong competitive pressure on less capable smaller operators as the big chains attract greater numbers of their former customers. Long-term viability in the retail food business will require continuing and increasing advertising and sales promotion inputs.

2. Research and Development
A second requirement for long-term success will be for food operators to invest a portion of their earnings in a formal research and development effort aimed at introducing new food items into existing types of restaurants and at creating and testing new restaurant concepts. The rate of change in the retail food business has increased, and those operators who hope to share importantly in the growth of the market will have to be among the leaders in developing innovations in menus and restaurant styles that are merchandisable to consumers.

3. Format
Lastly, the retail food business will gradually evolve into one whereby the late 1970s, "style" (decor, pizazz on food selection and service, etc.) will be as important as "content" (cleanliness, food quality, etc.). The successful operators of the late 1970s will be the ones which "romance" the consumer, making a meal in their restaurants more than just a meal and, instead, somewhat of an experience.

II. Continued long-term success of the Snack Bar Division is by no means assured. The current Snack Bars will become increasingly outdated over the coming decade as competition continues its expansion with bigger, more appealing units. While refurbishment of the old Dobbs units will help hold off the decline of consumer acceptance, it is nonetheless inevitable.

The long-term ability of the current Snack Bars to compete effectively against other major fast-food operations is in doubt, simply because the Snack Bars do not have the potential of generating the funds required to spend competitively on advertising and sales promotion. The upside sales potential of the current group of Snack Bars is probably limited to an average of $300 per day.

III. Signage is probably the weakest link in the entire Snack Bar Divisions' operation. There are at least four different signs currently in use in the Snack Bar Division, two for Toddle Houses (the old neon sign and the newer backlighted one) and two for Dobbs Houses (the older oval one and the newer blue and white rectangular one).

All of the current signs are typically smaller, placed lower to the ground, and carry less noticeable graphics than the signs of major competitors such as Waffle House, Pickwick House, or Denny's. Furthermore, Dobbs Houses is the only chain using two different names and such divergent styles of signs on shops in the same market. Furthermore, only a few Dobbs units have signs in front of the building.

Consultant's Recommendations

• *Emphasis should be placed on the development of novel restaurant concepts which will afford consumer positions which are strongly differentiated from those of current competitors.* Most of the new restaurant chains of the 1970s will depend importantly on "style" for their success. For many of them, decor, new and different food items, and unusual service will all be key elements in attracting customers.

• *The Division should proceed with a longer-term project of developing and testing the self-service/disposable ware coffee shop concept, which Division Management has begun.* The Company will have to initiate a long-term development program (in addition to the short-term one discussed in the previous section) if it is going to have competitive operation in ten or fifteen years. Increasing numbers of major food manufacturers and retailers are looking for a way into the retail restaurant business and are investing money in the development and testing of new restaurants. General Mills is currently testing three restaurant concepts: Betty Crocker's Pie Shop and Ice Cream Parlor (pies, ice cream specialties, and sandwiches), Red Lobster Inns of America, and Betty Crocker Restaurants and Bake Shops. The American consumer has been trained in the self-service ethic by the franchised-type of fast-food outlets. As labor and food costs continue to rise, there is no reason to believe that a large body of consumers will not prefer self-service to higher prices in a coffee shop.

• *The Snack Bar operations should undertake a limited program of newspaper advertising and sales promotion in its large markets.* The objectives of the program would be to increase consumer awareness of Dobbs Houses, to build overall customer traffic, and to promote added sales volume in current slack periods. Dobbs Houses could run two newspaper advertisements per week, on Monday and Wednesday. Both weekly insertions would advertise a "special" where Dobbs Houses would offer a food item at a reduced price or a free food item on a combination purchase (e.g., a free Coke with a steakburger). Total costs for this program in 30 of Dobbs biggest markets would cost about $600,000 per year. Since the advertising effort would cover 230 units accounting for about 60% of sales, an increase in sales of about 5.7% would payout the cost of the program on an on-going basis.

• *The Division should convert all units to the Dobbs name and adopt new signage.* The recommended sign package would cost about $4,000 per unit converted. It includes a large oval road sign (9 feet x 12 feet) and a large rectangular sign (4 feet x 20 feet) for the roofs of existing units. Properly developed new signs would have the potential to materially increase sales volume in many units by increasing "impulse" traffic. The old oval Dobbs House signs are unattractive, small and typically so low to the ground as to be all but unnoticeable to passersby. The old neon Toddle House sign is an anachronism. The cost of the new signage will easily pay for itself. If one assumes that incremental sales volume generates a 65% contribution to profit and overhead (by taking out only the variable cost of food and minor supporting expenses), the signage costs would pay out with a $6,150 per year increase in sales per unit. On this basis an increase of only about 4% in average annual sales per unit would pay out the signage cost in two years.

• *The Division should retain its policy of having all units open 24 hours a day.* Twenty-four hour operation is an important element in the success of a Snack Bar. Many customers first become acquainted with a Snack Bar during those hours when it is the only open restaurant in town. If they like it, they become good potential customers for other hours as well. A customer check survey disclosed a strong sales volume in the "typical" unit through 2 A.M. with a strong resurgence at 6 A.M. If all Snack Bars were to close between 2 A.M. and 6 A.M., the lost sales would cut $27 off the daily average (lowering it from $215 to $188). Assuming that about 40% of the sales dollars in that period are contributed to fixed overheads and profits, the profit loss is $11/day or about 55% of the current daily profit of an average unit. To close between 2 A.M. and 5 A.M. would cut $18 off the daily average and about $7 (or 35%) off of daily contribution to profit and overheads.

Jerry McKenzie's 30 Days at Dobbs House

During his month at Dobbs House in Memphis, Jerry McKenzie took a relatively "low profile." He stated that he had been sent from New York to act as a consultant to "help" the organization in any way possible. To attempt to gauge the operations, he spent the majority of his time reading reports, attending meetings, and asking questions. He found that obtaining data was no problem. In fact, if anything, there was too much of it. The controller's report which he carried with him was humorously referred to as the "hernia book." It even had its own oversized, custom-made carrying case. Selected material from the hernia book is summarized in Exhibit 10. Food and labor percentages for competing chains are included in Exhibit 11.

By attending meetings and performance reviews of area managers, he felt he was able to gain a sense of the situation. He found, however, that most meetings were simply presentations of the "25 things" that were wrong; rarely was a plan of action for solving the problems discussed (see Appendix A).

By taking the results from the consultants' report plus the data available in Memphis, he constructed breakeven cost-revenue charts. He was unable, however, to determine in his mind which variables were most relevant and critical to the success of the business.

His initial reaction in examining the data was a sense of frustration. Clearly there were a number of units that were below breakeven volume. He was unsure, however, whether to stop operating the loss units or try to convert them to profitable operations.

Upon examining individual units he found they were profitable only because of unique situations. The high volume in one inner-city snack bar in Detroit was directly related to the number of prostitutes that used it as a base of operations. In another case, he found that a unit appeared to be successful because it was considered as the "clubhouse" of a motorcycle gang.

Complaints about the difficulties of hiring people to work in snack bars had been filed with the Memphis headquarters. It was almost impossible to find employees who were willing to work by themselves on late shifts.

During his third week at Memphis, Jerry had an interesting experience. Howard Berkowitz, a regional operations manager, had guessed Jerry McKenzie's pur-

Exhibit 10

DOBBS HOUSE (A)
Operating Data of Sample Units, 1969

Operating statistics for 36 units in 1969 were randomly selected from the total 360 odd units in the Dobbs House chain. The sample was stratified to include four units of each ownership type [wholly-owned (1), owned building on leased land (2), and wholly-leased (3)] in combination with each location type [city (c), suburban (s), and rural (r)]. The size of each unit as measured by the number of seats was also noted [1 = 15 and under, 2 = 16–25, and 3 = 26 and over].

						Expenses, % Revenue[1]					
Unit	*Ownership*	*Location*	*Size*	*Annual Revenue ($000)*	*Annual Expenses ($000)*	*Food*	*Labor*	*Other[2] Var. Cost*	*Unit[3] O.H.*	*Total Unit Cost*	*Total[4] Expenses (Inc. Corp. O.H.)*
1	1	r	2	75	65	29	28	8	14	79	87
2	1	r	2	46	47	27	29	10	28	94	102
3	1	r	3	87	73	29	28	12	7	76	84
4	1	r	3	109	89	28	27	9	10	74	82
5	1	s	3	160	123	29	29	5	5	68	76
6	1	s	2	50	55	28	28	14	32	102	110
7	1	s	3	113	103	30	29	11	13	83	91
8	1	s	3	97	90	29	28	14	14	85	93
9	1	c	2	45	50	29	29	17	27	102	110
10	1	c	3	170	150	33	30	13	4	80	88
11	1	c	3	50	60	31	29	14	38	112	120
12	1	c	3	83	88	30	29	16	23	98	106
13	2	r	2	82	63	27	28	10	2	68	76
14	2	r	3	92	72	29	29	8	4	70	78
15	2	r	3	102	78	28	28	9	3	68	76
16	2	r	2	61	52	31	29	12	5	77	85

Exhibit 10 (continued)

Unit	Ownership	Location	Size	Annual Revenue ($000)	Annual Expenses ($000)	Expenses, % Revenue[1] Food	Labor	Other[2] Var. Cost	Unit[3] O.H.	Total Unit Cost	Total[4] Expenses (Inc. Corp. O.H.)
17	2	s	3	139	109	30	28	10	2	70	78
18	2	s	2	89	79	27	32	11	11	81	89
19	2	s	3	112	94	30	30	14	2	76	84
20	2	s	3	122	100	29	30	12	3	74	82
21	2	c	3	90	87	31	31	16	11	89	97
22	2	c	3	100	94	32	30	15	9	86	94
23	2	c	2	67	67	33	30	12	17	92	100
24	2	c	2	142	135	29	32	17	9	87	95
25	3	r	2	56	51	29	30	10	14	83	91
26	3	r	2	77	67	28	29	9	13	79	87
27	3	r	2	90	78	29	30	9	10	78	86
28	3	r	3	110	83	29	27	8	3	67	75
29	3	s	1	60	59	30	30	11	19	90	98
30	3	s	3	160	130	27	32	12	2	73	81
31	3	s	3	102	93	30	32	11	10	83	91
32	3	s	3	140	105	29	28	8	2	67	75
33	3	c	2	70	78	30	29	14	34	107	115
34	3	c	2	90	90	34	28	12	18	92	100
35	3	c	3	115	110	31	30	17	10	88	96
36	3	c	3	125	115	30	30	16	8	84	92

[1] These figures were obtained from similar data as shown in Exhibit 3 for individual units.
[2] Controllable Operating Expenses.
[3] Semi-Fixed Operating Expense and Managers' Compensation.
[4] Division Management and General and Administrative.

Exhibit 11

DOBBS HOUSE (A)
Food and Labor Costs as Per Cent of Revenue for Selected Fast-Food Chains, 1969

Operator	*Food Cost %o of Revenue*	*Labor Cost %o of Revenue*
Taco Bell	30	18
Arby's Roast Beef	40	16
Kentucky Fried Chicken	42	18
Hardee's Food Systems	40	22
A & W Root Beer	33	30
Dobbs House	31	32

pose for being in Memphis. Howard, who had come from a restaurant family, held a bachelor's degree in hotel and restaurant management, and had approximately seven years of chain-restaurant experience, had been slightly dismayed by Jerry's graphs and numbers. Finally he said, "Jerry, I think I know why you are here. I like you, and I'd like to work with you. But you really don't know anything about this business. Maybe those charts will help, but if you sincerely want to learn, I'll show you what I know about how this business has to be run."

They drove to a local Dobbs House in Howard's region, and Howard showed Jerry around the unit. After a brief tour, Howard went into the kitchen and dumped the garbage pails on the floor. He rolled up his sleeves and began to rummage through the unappetizing and noxious heap of garbage. From this he pulled out unused containers of cream, dishes, dishrags, silverware, a salt shaker, and partially eaten food. He noted that the discarded dishes and silver were the result of carelessness by waitresses and busboys. Part of the food wastage was carelessness of the cooks and waitresses. When a partially eaten steak was dissected, it was found to contain gristle. An inspection of other steaks in the refrigerator showed similar problems, though Dobbs House had paid for top quality meat.

Howard estimated the value of the contents of this garbage, annualized for this unit, was approximately $10,000.

Return to New York

Now as Jerry returned to New York to make his report, he was trying to reconcile the findings of the consultants, the cost data, the interviews and meetings, and the vivid experience with the garbage pails.

His experiences with Howard Berkowitz left him with the gnawing feeling that there might be many key facets to running the business that he still did not know about or understand. He was also unsure that even if he had identified the true problems of the business that he would be able to effect any change. He had seen Dobbs management try to introduce several new ideas during the month, but most had been abandoned. For example, Dobbs headquarters staff had determined that reducing the size of the free matches with Dobbs advertising at the check-out counter could save over $100,000 per year in the 369 units. Trying to get each unit manager to make the switch had proven an almost impossible task; therefore the idea was discarded.

While the situation at Dobbs House could represent a personal opportunity, it held some risks. He now felt that the strategy of an "end run to the top" through brilliant staff work was not as likely to succeed as he once thought. Here was a chance to be an operating executive in a line position. However, if the situation proved to be hopeless, and he was unable to turn the Fast Foods Division around, his reputation would be tarnished for several years, with the possible loss of his job, and setback. The thought of being responsible for 3,500 Dobbs House cooks, waitresses, and other employees was rather chilling.

Appendix A
Dobbs House (A)

Minutes of Dobbs House Management Progress Review Meeting of January 29, 1971

Those attending were:

Phil Barksdale, General Manager
Lamar Bell, Controller
Howard Berkowitz, Regional Operations
John Emerson, Training
Sam Jones, Regional Operations
Jack Larson, Regional Operations
Bill Lynch, Personnel

In the morning, we discussed money and inventory losses. Mr. Barksdale asked Steve Crain, our legal counsel, to discuss this matter. Mr. Barksdale stated that our policy concerning and regarding theft has been too lenient. In the couple of instances where we have tried to prosecute in the courts, we really haven't accomplished anything. Mr. Barksdale stated that we now are going to take a "hard nose" approach and will prosecute all offenders in the future.

Steve Crain was quick to point out that we have to be extremely careful in accusing anyone of stealing money or inventory. We must be sure we have all facts, figures, information, and witnesses. Our count must be right, and our procedure in conducting a cash audit must be exactly correct before we accuse anyone of any type of money theft or inventory shortage. Steve Crain pointed out that inventory losses are most difficult to prove and we have to be extremely careful in this matter. Mr. Barksdale asked Steve to develop written guidelines for our handling money and inventory losses. Steve Crain said he would do so as rapidly as possible. Upon completion of these written guidelines, he is to submit them to Mr. Barksdale, and Mr. Barksdale will submit them to corporate headquarters for approval.

During the discussion of inventory losses there was a general discussion of inventory being inflated over the past to make us look good for one particular month. Perhaps a lot of our people are carrying these inflated inventories forward. Each regional manager was advised to inform his area managers to conduct inventories as soon as possible in each of their commissary locations to determine whether or not the inventories are inflated or are accurate.

There then was a discussion of the money losses at the unit employee level. Mr. Barksdale said that we are more interested in the losses of large sums of money. However, he did explain that we are looking at a computer-type cash register, which would give us control that we do not now have. It would also determine sales mix for us. Mr. Barksdale assigned John Emerson, Lamar Bell, and Pat Maher to develop procedures for handling money at different levels in the operation.

In the afternoon we returned to our original agenda of talking about what we have accomplished in the last quarter, and what we hope to accomplish in the forthcoming quarter.

The first subject discussed was personnel. Bill Lynch gave us a summation of our Train the Trainer program.

One of the important things that Mr. Barksdale was concerned about that we had discussed back in October was that we had hoped to develop a "back-up procedure," so that all the city managers and unit managers would get a day off. Apparently, this is being done in a few areas. Mr. Barksdale set a deadline of March 1 to review progress on this procedure. He asked Bill Lynch to develop a flow chart similar to the one that Bob Ryan has submitted for his schedule of what is coming up in regards to personnel and what we can look forward to in the Fast Food Division.

We had a lengthy discussion as to what progress we have made with our training program in Houston, Miami, and Atlanta. Mr. Barksdale suggested that since personnel and training are so closely related, John Emerson and Bill Lynch should get together and get organized and establish objectives to get the program committed to writing. Mr. Barksdale also asked John Emerson to establish a flow chart similar to the one that Bill Lynch will establish, and perhaps they can get together and establish one together to show how the program is going to be implemented and show what John Emerson has implemented up to now. In essence, Mr. Barksdale wants a plan of action—What are we going to do for the next year?

There was also a lengthy discussion between Mr. Barksdale and Bill Lynch. Mr. Barksdale feels that each area should have a designated person for training of personnel. For example, when we have information to go into the field in regards to personnel or training, the information would go to one particular individual rather than the way it is now being disseminated. Our communications must be improved. It was again brought up that not all of our people are aware of our fringe benefits, and we must get the information to the people. Bill Lynch and John Emerson are going to work on this.

The next area that was covered was that of the weekly and end-of-the-month reports. Lamar Bell explained that beginning in February the new weekly form will show the true gross margin; that is, it will include the semi-fixed costs and manager's compensation. Also, Lamar is developing a new form, which should make the area secretary's job much easier. John Simank and Peter Gonzales are to go over the form with each area secretary. The new form will be mailed out to the area office, and the area secretary will be told not to open the package until John and Peter arrive to go over it with them thoroughly.

The third area that Mr. Barksdale discussed was that of end-of-month inventory. Two people are required to sign the inventory form. The three regional managers agreed that it was being done. Not all were certain that it was being done in each and every instance. They are to follow up on this to be sure that it does get done, especially in the light of the inflated inventories that have been discovered recently. The regional managers thought that cost control in general has been greatly improved during the last quarter, especially in the payroll area.

There was a lengthy discussion in regards to part-time help receiving 50¢ an hour more than regular employees are receiving. It was pointed out that Norman Sidner is trying this in the Tampa Area. Mr. Barksdale asked Jack Larson to give him complete follow-up information on its effect on the payroll; its effect on the employees; and their reaction to part-time help receiving this additional pay over regular full-time employees.

The next area that was discussed on the agenda was that of purchasing. Mr. Barksdale informed us that he has a master purchasing manual, and we will be working on distributing the parts that relate to the Fast Food Division as soon as possible. We know that the people in the field are asking for the Approved Products List and the new purchasing procedures that we told them about earlier.

The physical appearance of the units was discussed next. It was the general opinion of the regional managers that the unit physical appearance has improved in general. There seems to be some problems with air conditioners, especially in the southern part of the country and in Texas. However, it was felt that this is normal and is under control. All the regional managers felt that their units are in acceptable condition, and the general consensus was that we hold the line wherever possible as far as maintenance, painting, and roofing.

Mr. Barksdale asked the question, "What will make it difficult to make budget in future months?" The answers were: we would not be able to make the sales that we would make; the budget is not realistic. Mr. Barksdale reviewed rather quickly that our goals are (1) to meet the budget; (2) to upgrade people; (3) to train properly was to produce profit and sales.

Sam Jones was concerned about the ability of the company to manage labor, food costs, and other controllable expenses because we have so many new people. Jack Larson feels that we are on top of the situation, and in general was in agreement with Sam and Howard that people are improving in their proficiency. Because of the introduction of performance reviews, people are becoming more knowledgeable about their business. It is expected that the morale of the employees will be much better during the second quarter.

Mr. Barksdale asked, "Should we expand the present Fast Foods business concept?" There was a unanimous answer of "No." Mr. Barksdale explained that we are definitely looking for new concepts in the future. It is important now to get the people, the controls, and the training procedures right before entering into any new concepts or ventures. Most important, we must build creditability within our division and New York.

Mr. Barksdale said that in any cases where we have losing units to let Lamar know. Lamar and John Simank will investigate all possibilities to see whether or not it would be practical to keep the unit open or close it. Lamar also said that price increases are still being studied. Lamar reviewed the projects and responsibilities of several different people in the room, and everyone was of the general opinion that we were all slightly behind what we had hoped to accomplish. He felt that we had all done what we could in the last quarter, and would maintain the same pace in the second quarter.

Mr. Barksdale asked each individual what he thought had been accomplished during the last quarter. It was the general consensus that we had made tremendous progress, though it was not easy to see the evidence. We are making an investment in the future. We all felt it was frustrating. We were trying to accomplish so many things so rapidly.

All in the room gave Mr. Barksdale a unanimous vote of confidence.

INDEX FOR TEXTUAL MATERIAL

INDEX FOR TOPICS BY CASE